Contents for Your Teacher's Edition

UNIT 1

Get the Message!

Contents for Your Teacher's Edition, continued

UNIT 2

A Sense of Place

UNIT 3

Follow Your Dreams

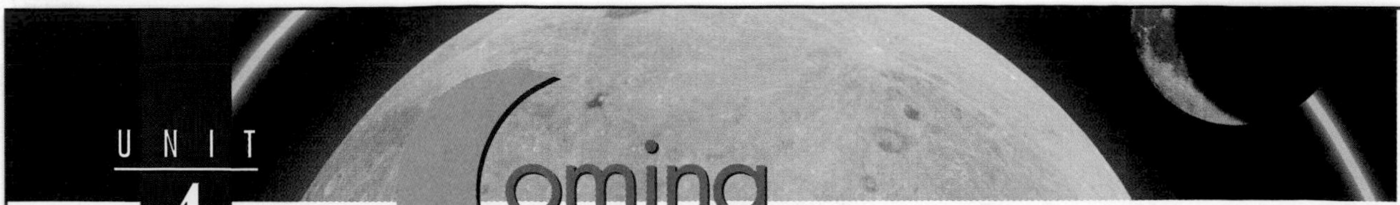

UNIT 4

Coming Full Circle

UNIT 5

Overcoming Obstacles

Resources

For Success in Language, Literature, and Content

Student Book pages 8–69

For Skills Practice

Practice Book
pages 1–29

For Planning and Instruction

Teacher's Edition
pages T8a–T69

For Vocabulary and Language Development

Language Tape Side A
Language CD Track 1

For Selection Readings

Selection Tape 1
Selection CD 1

For Technology Support

Inspiration
Visual Learning Software
with Graphic Organizers

For Classroom Activities

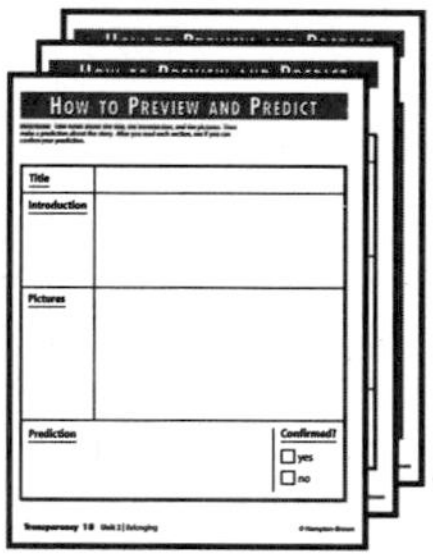

Transparencies or Masters 1–16

For Home-School Connections

High Point Newsletters 1 and 2

For Comprehensive Assessment

Language Acquisition Assessment, Selection Tests, Unit Test, Writing Assessment, Self-Assessment

In the Theme Library

Zora Hurston and the Chinaberry Tree
by William Miller

Aesop's Fox
by Aki Sogabe

From *The Basics Bookshelf*

- ***Good News***
- ***I Make Pictures Move***
- ***A Year Without Rain***

Theme-related books with simple text for including newcomers

Get the Message!

Joy, Ed Young, mixed media. Copyright © 1997.

THROUGH IMAGE AND WORD, FROM LONG AGO TO MODERN TIMES, HUMANS COMMUNICATE TO CONVEY INFORMATION, FEELINGS, AND CONCERNS. IN THIS UNIT, STUDENTS, WHO INTERPRET A VARIETY OF MESSAGES DAILY, EXPLORE VERBAL AND NONVERBAL WAYS TO COMMUNICATE.

THEME 1 Messages That Matter

Students discover how messages that express our feelings, preserve history, or honor heroes are all messages that matter.

THEME 2 Messages Across Time and Space

Students read messages from long ago and from far away that connect them to places they may have never seen.

Activity Planner

THEME 1: Messages That Matter

LESSONS

1 — THEME 1 OPENER ▶ pages T10–T11

- **Function**: Engage in Discussion
- **Learning Strategy**: Make a Chart
- **Vocabulary**: Words About Communication
- **Critical Thinking**: Make Judgments

2 — BUILD LANGUAGE AND VOCABULARY ▶ pages T12–T13

- **Function**: (T) Express Opinions
- **Learning Strategy**: Take Notes in a Chart
- **Vocabulary**: Words About Communication
- **Patterns and Structures**: (T) Complete Sentences

PACING SUGGESTIONS

LESSONS	45–55 MINUTE PERIODS	BLOCK SCHEDULE SESSIONS
1	1 period	1 session (lessons 1–2)
2	1 period	
3–7	6 periods	3 sessions
8–14	6 periods	3 sessions

3–7 — *The Power of Poetry* by Gary Soto — POEMS AND INTERVIEW ▶ pages T14–T23

PREPARE TO READ page T14

- **Activate Prior Knowledge**: Idea Exchange
- **Vocabulary** (T): Relate Words
- **Reading Strategy**: Visualize

READ THE SELECTION pages T15–T21

- **Pre-Reading Strategies**: Identify Genre: Poetry; Set Purpose
- **Strategy Focus**: Visualize
- **Vocabulary**: Use New Words in Context; (T) Use Context Clues
- **Comprehension**: Before you Move On: Think and Discuss
- **Grammar Minilessons**: (T) Common and Proper Nouns; Singular and Plural Nouns
- **Literary Analysis Minilesson**: Free Verse

RESPOND pages T22–T23

CHECK YOUR UNDERSTANDING

- **Critical Thinking and Comprehension**: Sum It Up: Visualize; (T) Summarize; Determine the Author's Message; Think it Over: Discuss and Write
- **Function**: Express Yourself: Express Feelings and Ideas

LANGUAGE ARTS AND LITERATURE

- **Literary Analysis and Speaking/Listening**: Recognize Mood
- **Technology/Media and Literary Analysis**: Compare Poets

8–14 — *Talking Walls* by Margy Burns Knight — ESSAY ▶ pages T24–T35

PREPARE TO READ page T24

- **Activate Prior Knowledge**: Study Walls in Your School
- **Vocabulary** (T): Relate Words
- **Reading Strategy**: (T) Relate Main Idea and Details

READ THE SELECTION pages T25–T31

- **Pre-Reading Strategies**: Preview and Predict; Identify Genre: Essay; Set Purpose
- **Strategy Focus**: (T) Relate Main Idea and Details
- **Vocabulary**: (T) Use Context Clues; Use New Words in Context
- **Comprehension**: Before You Move On: Think and Discuss
- **Grammar Minilessons**: Singular and Plural Nouns; Possessive Nouns

RESPOND pages T32–T35

CHECK YOUR UNDERSTANDING

- **Critical Thinking and Comprehension**: Sum It Up: (T) Relate Main Ideas and Details; Write a Paragraph; Think It Over: Discuss and Write
- **Function**: Express Yourself: Express Opinions

LANGUAGE ARTS AND LITERATURE

- **Grammar in Context**: (T) Use Subjects and Predicates
- **Vocabulary**: (T) Use Context Clues

CONTENT AREA CONNECTIONS

- **Fine Arts and Mathematics**: Create Classroom Wall Art
- **Mathematics and Social Studies**: Create a Miniature Monument
- **Technology/Media and Social Studies**: Make a Presentation About Famous Walls

(T) = Assessed on **Unit 1 Test** (T) = Assessed on **Unit 1 Language Acquisition Assessment**

THEME 2: Messages Across Time and Space

LESSONS

1

THEME 2 OPENER
▶ pages T36–T37

- **Function**: Engage in Discussion
- **Learning Strategy**: Make a Chart
- **Vocabulary**: Words About Communication
- **Critical Thinking**: (T) Make Comparisons

2

BUILD LANGUAGE AND VOCABULARY
▶ pages T38–T39

- **Function**: (T) Make Comparisons
- **Learning Strategy**: Make a Communication Chart
- **Vocabulary**: Words About Communication
- **Patterns and Structures**: (T) Compound Sentences

PACING SUGGESTIONS

LESSONS	45–55 MINUTE PERIODS	BLOCK SCHEDULE SESSIONS
1	1 period	1 session (lessons 1–2)
2	1 period	
3–8	6 periods	3 sessions
9–15	7 periods	4 sessions

3–8

Tales Across Time by Dawn Lippert and Margaret H. Lippert
FOLK TALES ▶ pages T40–T49

PREPARE TO READ
page T40

- **Activate Prior Knowledge**: Share Folk Tales
- **Vocabulary** (T): Relate Words
- **Reading Strategy**: (T) Make Comparisons

READ THE SELECTION
pages T41–T46

- **Pre-Reading Strategies**: Preview and Predict; Identify Genre: Folk Tale; Set Purpose
- **Strategy Focus**: (T) Make Comparisons
- **Vocabulary**: Use New Words in Context
- **Comprehension**: Before You Move On: Think and Discuss
- **Grammar Minilessons**: Articles; (T) Present Tense Verbs/Subject-Verb Agreement

RESPOND
pages T47–T49

CHECK YOUR UNDERSTANDING

- **Critical Thinking and Comprehension**: Sum It Up: (T) Make Comparisons; (T) Summarize; Think It Over: Discuss and Write
- **Function**: Express Yourself: Retell and Listen to a Story

LANGUAGE ARTS AND LITERATURE

- **Grammar in Context**: (T) Use Nouns
- **Literary Analysis and Speaking/Listening**: Tell a Never-Ending Story

CONTENT AREA CONNECTIONS

- **Social Studies**: Compare Political Leaders
- **Speaking/Listening and Health**: Learn About Grains and Diet

9–15

Fat Men from Space by Daniel Manus Pinkwater
SCIENCE FICTION ▶ pages T50–T61

PREPARE TO READ
page T50

- **Activate Prior Knowledge**: Share Experiences
- **Vocabulary** (T): Relate Words
- **Reading Strategy**: (T) Analyze Story Elements (plot)

READ THE SELECTION
pages T51–T58

- **Pre-Reading Strategies**: Preview and Predict; Identify Genre: Science Fiction; Set Purpose
- **Strategy Focus**: (T) Analyze Story Elements (plot)
- **Vocabulary**: Use New Words in Context
- **Self-Monitoring and Comprehension**: Use Visuals; Visualize; Before You Move On: Think and Discuss
- **Grammar Minilessons**: (T) Compound Sentences; (T) Present Tense Verbs/Subject-Verb Agreement
- **Literary Analysis Minilesson**: Fantasy and Reality

RESPOND
pages T59–T61

CHECK YOUR UNDERSTANDING

- **Critical Thinking and Comprehension**: Sum It Up: (T) Analyze Story Elements (plot); (T) Summarize; Think It Over: Discuss and Write
- **Function**: Express Yourself: Ask for and Give Advice

LANGUAGE ARTS AND LITERATURE

- **Grammar in Context**: (T) Use Verbs
- **Writing and Speaking/Listening**: Write a Science Fiction Story

CONTENT AREA CONNECTIONS

- **Health**: Analyze Your Diet
- **Science and Mathematics**: Explore the Solar System

BUILD WRITING SKILLS

WRITING THAT TELLS A STORY
NARRATIVE: FANTASY ▶ Pages T62–T68

- **Writing Mode/Form**: (T) Narrative; Fantasy
- **Writing Process** (T): Prewrite; Draft; Revise; Edit and Proofread; Publish
- **Writer's Craft**: Introductions; (T) Show, Don't Tell
- **Grammar in Context**: (T) Complete Sentences
- **Reflect and Evaluate**: Self-Assessment

(T) = Assessed on **Unit 1 Test** (T) = Assessed on **Unit 1 Language Acquisition Assessment**

Theme-Related Resources

THEME 1: Messages That Matter

MORE RESOURCES

THEME LIBRARY

Zora Hurston and the Chinaberry Tree
by William MIller
B Zora's mother teaches her that dreams, like each branch of the chinaberry tree, are always within reach. (Available from Hampton-Brown)

The Unbreakable Code
by Sara Hoagland Hunter
I John, a Navajo boy, learns from his grandfather how a code based on the Navajo language helped to win World War II. (Northland)

Toliver's Secret
by Esther Wood Brady
A Ellen takes a message hidden in a loaf of bread to George Washington during the Revolutionary War. (Random House)

The Great Kapok Tree: A Tale of the Amazon Rain Forest
by Lynne Cherry
B In this best-selling book, the animals of the Amazon rain forest deliver an important message about caring for the earth. (Harcourt Brace)

Talking Walls; Talking Walls: The Stories Continue
B I A These extensions of the award-winning books by Margy Burns Knight include videos and links to selected Web sites. (Edmark) **Multimedia CD-ROM**

In My Own Voice: Multicultural Poets on Identity
I A Multicultural poets read their own poetry and discuss their sources of information. Includes examples of fine art and musical selections. (Sunburst) **Multimedia CD-ROM**

THEME 2: Messages Across Time and Space

MORE RESOURCES

THEME LIBRARY

Aesop's Fox
retold by Aki Sogabe
I Several of Aesop's timeless fables are combined into a single tale about a day in the life of Aesop's Fox. (Available from Hampton-Brown)

Radio Man
by Arthur Dorros
B The radio keeps Diego connected to the world while he's on the move. In English and Spanish. (HarperCollins)

The Adventures of Sojourner
by Susi Trautmann Wunsch
A The story of the spacecraft *Sojourner*: its historic trip to Mars and the images it sent back to Earth. (Firefly Books)

Quennu and the Cave Bear
by Mary Day
A In this prehistoric adventure, Quennu must face her biggest fear in order to find her way when she becomes separated from her family. (Greey de Pencier Books)

I Am the Mummy Heb-Nefert
by Eve Bunting
B This award-winning author tells the tale of Heb-Nefert, a mummy who reflects on her life and realizes that all things change over time. (Harcourt Brace)

Cocoon
directed by Ron Howard
B I A In this humanist fantasy directed by Ron Howard, a group of elderly friends experience renewed youth as they befriend visitors from another planet, who have come to Earth on a rescue mission. **Film/Video**

B Beginning I Intermediate A Advanced

UNIT 1 Assessment Options

ONGOING, INFORMAL ASSESSMENT

Check for understanding and achieve closure for every lesson with the targeted questions and activities in the **Close and Assess** boxes in your Teacher's Edition.

INDIVIDUAL AND GROUP-ADMINISTERED TESTS

The **Assessment Handbook** includes these comprehensive assessment tools for Unit 1:

- **Selection Tests**
  Test students' mastery of reading strategies and the vocabulary, comprehension, and language arts skills taught with each main selection of Unit 1.
- **Unit Test in Standardized Test Format**
  The multiple-choice sections of this test measure students' cumulative understanding of the skills and language developed in Unit 1. A Writing Prompt measures progress in writing skills and fluency. The Read, Think, and Explain section offers open-ended items to measure strategies and comprehension.
- **Language Acquisition Assessment**
  To verify students' ability to use the vocabulary and grammar structures taught in Unit 1, conduct these performance assessments.

UNIT 1 ASSESSMENT OPPORTUNITIES

	Assessment Handbook Pages
Unit 1 Language Acquisition Assessment	1–2
Selection Tests	
The Power of Poetry	3–4
Talking Walls	5–6
Tales Across Time	7–8
Fat Men from Space	9–10
Unit 1 Writing Assessment	11
Unit 1 Self-Assessment Form	12
Unit 1 Test	13–20
Peer-Assessment Form	101
Portfolio Evaluation Form	103

SELF- AND PEER-ASSESSMENT

Students use the Unit 1 Self-Assessment Form in the **Assessment Handbook** to evaluate their own work and develop learning strategies appropriate to their needs. Students offer feedback to their classmates with the Peer-Assessment Form.

WRITING ASSESSMENT / PORTFOLIO OPPORTUNITIES

You can evaluate students' writing using the rubrics and scoring guidelines provided in the **Assessment Handbook**. Then collaborate with students to choose work for their portfolios.

INTRODUCE UNIT 1

OBJECTIVES

Function: Engage in Discussion
Concepts and Vocabulary: Communication—*express, messages, verbal, nonverbal, lasting, preserve*
Viewing: Interpret a Visual Image
Critical Thinking and Learning Strategies: Predict; Build Background; Classify; Preview; Use Graphic Organizers (mind map)

INTRODUCE UNIT CONCEPT

1 **Read the Title and Make a Prediction** Ask: *When have you heard someone say "get the message"? What kinds of messages do you think you will learn about in this unit?*

2 **Create an Image** Invite students to identify the figures in the visual image and the ideas they symbolize. Then have students work in pairs to create symbolic images. Reconvene to complete the activity. Ask: *Are words or images more effective in communicating a feeling? Why?*

3 **Discuss Communication** Write *verbal* and *nonverbal* and define (with/without language). Give an example of verbal communication by saying or writing: *Stop!* Then illustrate nonverbal communication by holding your hand up in front of you. Point out that both the gesture and the word communicated the same meaning. Invite students to discuss:

- other ways to communicate without words
- why communication is so important
- what kinds of communication last over time.

Use the Discussion Prompts in the **Multi-Level Strategies** to create a class mind map.

UNIT 1 Communication

Joy

A happy heart.

words

mouth

two legs

The mouth and legs together represent an older person. Wise words from a respected person bring good fortune and joy to the heart.

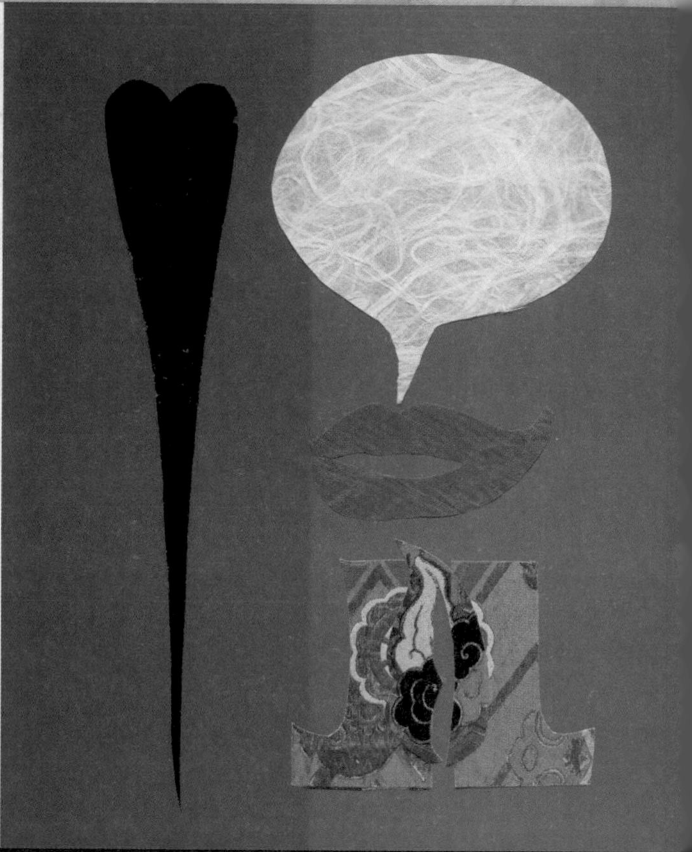

Joy, Ed Young, mixed media. Copyright © 19

8

REACHING ALL STUDENTS

Multi-Level Strategies

DISCUSSION PROMPTS

BEGINNING Ask questions that elicit short answers, such as: *Is talking verbal or nonverbal? Is dancing verbal or nonverbal?* Note students' replies on the group mind map. Elicit more examples. Then ask: *Which lasts longer, a painting or a conversation?* Elicit more examples of lasting communication.

INTERMEDIATE Elicit examples of verbal and nonverbal communication. Then have students work in pairs to brainstorm more examples for the group mind map. Guide pairs to identify examples of lasting communication and add them to the mind map.

ADVANCED Write *A picture is worth a thousand words.* Ask students to agree or disagree. Challenge students to discuss the powers and limitations of nonverbal communication as they enter ideas on the mind map.

Get the Message!

Look at the symbols this artist uses to portray a joyful heart. With a partner, create your own set of symbols that portray a feeling. Have other students guess what feeling you are trying to express through your art. What did you learn about how messages can be communicated? Can communication occur without words?

THEME 1

Messages That Matter

Messages that express our feelings, preserve history, or honor heroes are all messages that matter.

THEME 2

Messages Across Time and Space

Messages from long ago or far away connect us to people and places we may never know or see.

UNIT 3 Mind Map

Communication

Verbal	Nonverbal
spoken words	pictures
e-mail	music
newspaper	sign language

Temporary	Lasting
spoken words	newspaper
sign language	e-mail
	music
	pictures

Technology Support
See **Inspiration** Visual Learning software for support in creating the mind map.

PREVIEW UNIT THEMES

4 **Preview Theme 1: Messages That Matter** Read aloud the theme statement. Define *message* as "a way to give information," and *preserve* as "to keep alive."

Invite students to leaf through pages 10–31 to preview the kinds of messages they will find in this unit.

5 **Preview Theme 2: Messages Across Time and Space** Read aloud the theme title. Ask: *How do messages travel across time and space?* Develop the idea that some messages are a key to the past. Invite students to look over pages 36–58 to look for messages that may link us to the past.

6 **Set up Student Mind Maps** Have students draw the mind map in their notebooks or start the map in the **Practice Book**. Point out that every entry should appear twice in the chart, once in either the verbal or nonverbal column and again in either the temporary or lasting column. Encourage students to add to the map as they move through the unit.

▶ **Practice Book** page 1

CLOSE AND ASSESS

Ask:

- *What will this unit be about?* (communication)
- *What are some examples of verbal communication?* (speech, letters) *Nonverbal?* (gestures, pictures)
- *What are some examples of communication that lasts?* (quilts, paintings)

INTRODUCE THEME 1

OBJECTIVES

Function: Engage in Discussion
Concepts and Vocabulary: Communication—*message, meaning*
Viewing: Interpret a Visual Image
Learning Strategies: Relate to Personal Experience; Use Graphic Organizers (chart)
Critical Thinking: Generate Ideas; Make Judgments

TAP PRIOR KNOWLEDGE

1 **Discuss Messages** Invite students to consider the theme title. Ask: *If you were handed two sealed messages, one from your best friend and one from your principal, which would you open first? Why?* Invite students to share their opinions about what makes a message matter.

VIEW AND DISCUSS

2 **Make Judgments** Invite students to study the picture. Then have them make a chart to show the messages the postage stamp sends and the potential recipients.

Messages the stamp sends	• We hope for peace. • We speak many languages. • We are moving ahead.
People who might receive the messages	• People who get mail from Israel. • Drivers along the road.

Use the Discussion Prompts in the **Multi-Level Strategies** to involve all students in making the chart.

REACHING ALL STUDENTS

Multi-Level Strategies

DISCUSSION PROMPTS

BEGINNING Have students point to the name of the country from which the stamp comes. Ask: *How many languages are used on the sign?* Explain that the stamp communicates messages to everyone who sees it. Ask: *What messages does the stamp send? Who might see the messages?*

INTERMEDIATE Have students work in small groups to complete the chart. Challenge groups to compete to see which group can think of the most situations in which the messages might be seen. Invite students to write sentences explaining their choices of important messages.

ADVANCED Have students work in groups to complete the chart. They can then write an imaginary tale about the most important message. Stories should include: what the message is, how someone happened to see the message, and how the message affected that person's life.

ɪotations offer strategies for
ʒeginning students

THEME 1

Messages That Matter

- Why do people send messages? **B** **Define *messages*:** ways people share their thoughts. They can be sent many ways—through notes, telephone, stories, poems.
- How do people add to—or take away from—the meaning of other people's thoughts?
- Why do some messages affect us more deeply than others? **B** **Encourage elaboration:** What are some examples of messages that affect us deeply?

B **Restate:** How does your own experience affect your understanding of messages you receive?

HEME-RELATED BOOKS

ora Hurston and the hinaberry Tree
ɣ William Miller

ora's mother teaches her that ·eams, like each branch of the ɪinaberry tree, are always ·ithin reach.

EGINNING

The Unbreakable Code
by Sara Hoagland Hunter

John, a Navajo boy, learns from his grandfather how a code based on the Navajo language helped to win World War II.

INTERMEDIATE

NOVEL

Toliver's Secret
by Esther Wood Brady

Ellen takes a message hidden in a loaf of bread to George Washington during the Revolutionary War.

ADVANCED

DISCUSS THE GUIDING QUESTIONS

3 **Set the Theme** Some key points to develop during the discussion are:

- People send messages to communicate. Sometimes people communicate out of necessity. Other times people communicate to share thoughts and ideas.
- People can write letters, make phone calls, or send e-mails to express opinions. They can respond to newspaper articles by writing a letter to the editor. They can restate a message in their own words.
- Some messages affect us deeply because of personal interests and feelings. For example, one person may be deeply affected by a message written by a child. Someone else may find poetry very moving.

Form groups and use the **Multi-Level Strategies** so that all students can participate.

CLOSE AND ASSESS

Write *Your brother has a cold* and *Call me about the homework.* Have students choose the more important message and explain their choices.

Multi-Level Strategies

GROUPING GUIDELINES

BEGINNING Group students so you can define words and pose choices for response. See the red annotations on the facsimile for page 11 for suggestions.

INTERMEDIATE Guide students to work in small groups, using a dictionary or thesaurus to clarify unfamiliar words and phrases. Have them select one student to record group responses. Have two groups discuss their thoughts.

ADVANCED Have students share examples of messages that have affected them deeply and explain why. Then have the groups compose several sentences about why messages affect people.

THEME LIBRARY

■ ***Zora Hurston and the Chinaberry Tree*** by William Miller

Invite students to read this book and compare the messages Zora got from her two parents. Ask: *How were the messages different? How were they alike? How did the setting influence her father's message? What is the importance of the chinaberry tree? How did Zora Hurston's life reflect the messages of her parents?*

BUILD LANGUAGE AND VOCABULARY

OBJECTIVES

Function: Ⓣ Express Opinions
Concepts and Vocabulary: Words About Communication
Patterns and Structures: Ⓣ Complete Sentences
Viewing: Interpret a Visual Image
Learning Strategy: Use Graphic Organizers (chart)
Critical Thinking: Form Opinions
Writing: Opinion Sentences

START WITH A COMMON EXPERIENCE

1 **View and Describe** Encourage students to describe the painting and to give their overall impression of it. Model use of specific vocabulary: *I see eleven rectangles. This line points toward the center.* Point out the title and elicit how it helps the viewer understand what the painting communicates.

2 **Model How to Express an Opinion** Explain that an opinion tells how a person feels about something. Give two sentences to show the difference between fact and opinion.

Fact: The painting is called "The Studio."

Opinion: I think the painting is creative.

Then model how to express an opinion effectively.

How to Express an Opinion
- Tell what you think:
  I like this painting.
  I think this painting is creative.
  In my opinion, this is a great painting.
- Give reasons for your opinion:
  The colors are used in an interesting way.

3 **Prompt the Opinion Exchange** Form small groups and invite students to tell what they think about the painting.

Use the Discussion Prompts in the **Multi-Level Strategies** to involve students at all proficiency levels.

Build Language and Vocabulary

EXPRESS OPINIONS

Study the painting. Tell what you think about it.

The Studio, Pablo Picasso, oil on canvas. Copyright © 1928.

REACHING ALL STUDENTS

Multi-Level Strategies

DISCUSSION PROMPTS

BEGINNING As a group, create a T-chart to trap students' opinions about the painting. Use the headings Things I Like and Things I Don't Like. Students take ideas from the T-chart to produce oral sentences, using these sentence frames: *I like this painting because* _____. *I don't like this painting because* _____. Encourage use of opinion words.

INTERMEDIATE Ask students to discuss likes and dislikes about the painting in small groups. Ask: *Which colors do you like? What do you like about the lines?* Have the groups summarize their feelings. Encourage use of opinion words.

ADVANCED Have students speculate about the painting style: *Is this a style of painting that appeals to you? What do you feel makes this painting interesting or uninteresting to look at? Why?* Encourage use of opinion words.

KE NOTES IN A CHART

Listen to what one group of students had to say about the painting. ke a chart to note their opinions. Then add your own opinions.

Student	Opinions About the Painting
Kim	thinks it's great; likes the colors
Felicia	thinks it's odd; thinks the eyes are weird
Roberto	thinks it's neat; thinks grey is a dull color

ILD YOUR VOCABULARY

rds About Communication Painting is just one way to communicate. lect other words about ways to communicate. Add words to the web you read this unit.

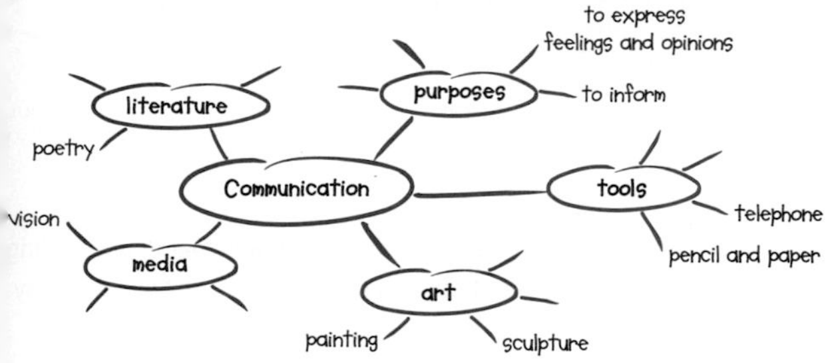

E LANGUAGE STRUCTURES ▶COMPLETE SENTENCES

iting: Express Opinions Write one or two complete sentences that tell at you think about the painting.

Example:

I like all the triangles.

I think the colors are great, too.

CONDUCT THE ACTIVITIES

4 Take Notes in a Chart Tape 1A CD 1 Track 1 Play the recording or read aloud the conversation on page T413. Have the class create a blank opinion chart for note-taking as they listen to the conversation on the **Language Tape/CD**.

5 Build Your Vocabulary: Words About Communication Have students begin by brainstorming words about different ways to communicate (art, writing, speech, etc.).

6 Use Language Structures: Complete Sentences Present the skill, using the definitions and examples on **Transparency 1**. Then have students use the subjects and predicates in Try It! to write complete sentences.

Writing: Express Opinions Conduct the activity at the bottom of page 13. Have students look at their opinion charts for ideas.

Use the Writing Activity Options in the **Multi-Level Strategies** to adjust instruction.

▶ **Practice Book** page 2

CLOSE AND ASSESS

Have partners create a test item for recognizing a complete sentence. Have one student in each pair write a phrase and the other write a sentence. Include all the test items in a review.

Multi-Level Strategies

WRITING ACTIVITY OPTIONS

BEGINNING Help students pick one of the opinions from their charts to expand into a complete sentence. Provide a frame: *I _____ the _____ in the painting.* They may want to dictate a sentence they produced orally during the earlier discussion.

INTERMEDIATE Have students write one or two complete sentences that give their opinions and at least one additional sentence to tell why they like or dislike the painting. Then have them use all their sentences to present their opinions to each other.

ADVANCED Have students write their opinions and pick the most relevant reasons from all the sentences in their group. Then they can review their classmates' opinion sentences to be sure they are complete sentences.

Transparency 1 / Master 1

LEARN ABOUT COMPLETE SENTENCES

Every complete sentence has two main parts—the subject and the predicate.

The artist (subject) paints a picture (predicate).

1. The subject tells whom or what the sentence is about. The **complete subject** includes all the words that tell about the subject.

   The beautiful painting shows a flower garden.

2. The predicate tells what the subject is, has, or does. The **complete predicate** includes all the words in the predicate part of the sentence.

   The garden **is full of daisies.**

Try It!

Add a subject or a predicate to make a complete sentence.

1. _________ painted a picture of a little house.
2. The straight black lines _________.
3. The windows _________.
4. _________ has bright colors in it.

Transparency 1 Level B, Unit 1 | Communication © Hampton-Brown

PREPARE TO READ

OBJECTIVES

THINK ABOUT WHAT YOU KNOW
Reading Strategy: Activate Prior Knowledge

LEARN KEY VOCABULARY
Vocabulary Strategy: Relate Words

LEARN TO VISUALIZE
Reading Strategy: Visualize

THINK ABOUT WHAT YOU KNOW

1 **Idea Exchange** Make a T-chart, with a plus sign heading for one column and a minus sign heading for the other. Record students' ideas about how poems communicate effectively in the plus column and about how poems do not communicate effectively in the minus column.

LEARN KEY VOCABULARY

2 **Relate Words** Read each vocabulary word and its definition aloud. Clarify meanings. Then conduct the web activity.

Use Vocabulary Options in the **Multi-Level Strategies** to tailor the activity to proficiency levels.

▶ **Practice Book** page 3

LEARN TO VISUALIZE

3 **Model How to Visualize** Define *visualize.* Demonstrate how to visualize with **Transparency 2**:

- Read the lines from the poem.
- List the words and phrases that create images.
- Draw a picture that shows what you saw in your mind.

Have students close their eyes and listen to the poem again.

CLOSE AND ASSESS

Ask students to agree on why it is important to visualize as you read. (to help you enjoy and understand poetry)

The **POWER** *of* **POETRY**

poems
by Gary Soto
and interview
with the poet

Prepare to Read

THINK ABOUT WHAT YOU KNOW

Idea Exchange Is a poem a good way to communicate? Why or why not?

attention care and thoughtfulness

concentrate focus on or think about only one thing

creativity ability to think of new ideas and to express them

experience something that happens to a person

inspired filled with ideas, encouraged to create

inventive able to think of new ideas, creative

memory the ability to remember, something remembered from the past

motive reason for doing something

routine something that is done the same way all of the time

LEARN KEY VOCABULARY

Relate Words Study the new words and their definitions. Use the wo[rds] to fill in the webs. Some words can be used in both webs. Then write a sentence about each web.

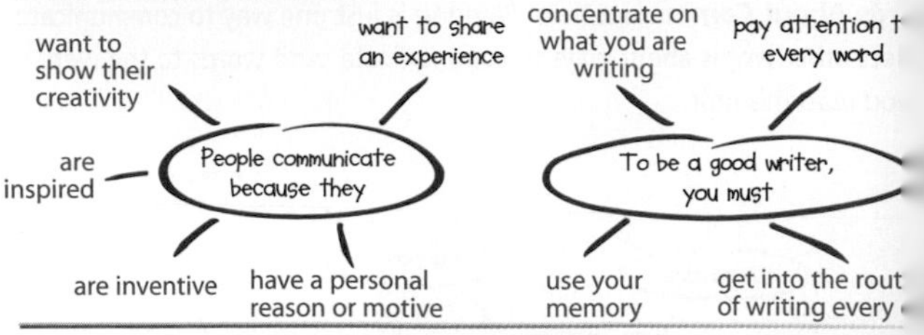

LEARN TO VISUALIZE

Poetry uses powerful words and phrases that create images and feeling[s]. When you **visualize**, you see these images in your mind. You will enjoy and understand poetry more if you visualize while you read.

READING STRATEGY
How to Visualize

1. Read the poem once to get the general feeling of it.
2. Look back through the poem for words that create images.
3. Use those words to make a picture in your mind of the images.
4. Reread the poem.

Now listen to "The Power of Poetry." As you listen, visualize the images the poet creates in each poem.

REACHING ALL STUDENTS

Multi-Level Strategies

VOCABULARY OPTIONS

BEGINNING Group students to read ***Good News***. Work with the vocabulary in that selection.

INTERMEDIATE Work with students to restate the definition for each vocabulary word. Then have students work as a group to complete the webs and write the sentences.

ADVANCED Have students complete the webs individually and then share them with a partner.

Transparency 2 / Master 2

HOW TO VISUALIZE

Directions: Read the first five lines of the poem. In a chart, list the words and phrases that create images. Use those words to make a picture in your mind. Draw a picture that shows what you visualized. Write a caption for your picture.

from **Big Eaters**
by Gary Soto

I stepped into the cold rush
Of a river until I was waist deep.
I screamed, "Check out this 20-foot trout,"
But the people on the shore
Kept eating their hotdogs and hamburgers.

Words	Pictures
waist deep	
20-foot trout	
hotdogs and hamburgers	

Transparency 2 Level B, Unit 1 | Communication © Hampton-Brown

READ THE SELECTION

OBJECTIVES

Reading Strategies: Preview; Visualize
Literary Analysis: Poetry

INTRODUCE THE POEMS

4 **Identify Genre: Poetry** Elicit students' impressions about poetry. Point out that poetry can be about common, everyday things and can have many forms. Explain that what makes a piece of writing poetry is that it expresses strong emotions in a powerful or colorful way.

5 **Introduce Poems** Point out the picture of Gary Soto and read the introduction on page 15. Explain that students will first listen to and then read three poems by this author. Remind students to focus on visualizing the scenes inspired by the poet's colorful language.

The Power of Poetry
by Gary Soto

Theme Connection This selection illustrates that poetry is one way to deliver a powerful message. It also examines a poet's process for communicating messages that matter to him.

Selection Summary The introduction on page 15 of the student book offers a summary of the selection.

Author Awards Gary Soto was awarded the Academy of American Poets Prize (1975) and was a finalist for both the National Book Award and the *L.A. Times* Book Award (1995). He was one of the youngest poets ever to appear in *The Norton Anthology of Modern Poetry.*

THE BASICS BOOKSHELF

■ ***Good News*** by Suzy Blackaby

The power of communication comes through in this story about a family who, via phone, fax and e-mail, spreads the good news about a family visit. Patterned text supported by realistic visuals introduces basic vocabulary related to communication.

For Lesson Plans: See the Teacher's Guide for ***The Basics Bookshelf***.

READ PAGES 16–17

OBJECTIVES

Function: Read a Poem
Vocabulary Strategy:
Use New Words in Context
Grammar:
Ⓣ Common and Proper Nouns
Listening: Listen to a Poem
Reading and Learning Strategies:
Set a Purpose for Reading;
Visualize; Paraphrase
Comprehension: Identify Details; Identify Character's Motive; Draw Conclusions; Make an Inference

SET PURPOSE

1 Say: *Listen for details that create pictures in your mind.*

LISTEN AND READ

Tape 1A
CD 1
Track 1

2 **Strategy Focus: Visualize**
Instruct students to listen with books closed as you read or play the **Selection Tape/CD**. Repeat, stopping after every two or three lines so students can write words and/or draw images inspired by the poems.

Invite students to open their books and compare their images to the illustrations. Then involve them in reading and reciting activities.

Choose Reading and Reciting Options in the **Multi-Level Strategies** to involve all students.

Red annotations offer opportunities to clarify meaning and check for understanding.

Big Eaters

I stepped into the cold rush
Of a river until I was waist deep.
I screamed, "Check out this 20-foot trout,"
But the people on the shore
Kept eating their hotdogs and hamburgers.
I called, "There's a mermaid down here!"
But they only pushed their hands into bags
Of potato chips and sucked on ice.
I shouted, "Hey, a shark almost bit my toes!"
They lapped their ice creams
And bit into cookies.
No one seemed excited.
When I stepped out of the water
And looked at the sandy shore,
I called, "Hey, the steaks are almost done!"
Everyone came running with their forks.

—*Gary Soto*

Define *check out*: look at.

Use visuals: What details in the picture help you understand the poem?

BEFORE YOU MOVE ON...

1. **Details/Character's Motive** How does th boy try to communicate? Why does he say things that aren't true?
2. **Conclusions** Which message matters most to the people on the shore? Why?

rush fast-moving water
waist deep in the water up to my waist
Check out Look at
mermaid creature that is half fish, half woman
lapped licked, ate with their tongues

16 Unit 1 | Communication

REACHING ALL STUDENTS

Language Development

ADJUST COMMUNICATION TO THE OCCASION

Guide students to understand that the speaker in "Big Eaters" is trying to get people's attention. Invite students to brainstorm ways to begin a conversation or get someone's attention. Have students decide when "Hey!" would be all right or when "Excuse me, I'd like to speak to you" would be better. Start a T-chart to record formal and informal language, pointing out that appropriate language depends on the audience and occasion.

Multi-Level Strategies

READING AND RECITING OPTIONS FOR LESSON 4

BEGINNING Use the illustrations and red annotations to help students read the poems. Have students add details and labels to their drawings.

INTERMEDIATE / **ADVANCED** Use a paired reading technique and invite students to plan choral readings of the poems for two voices:

- "Big Eaters": One group reads the narration parts of the poem; others call out the dialogue portions.
- "Letter to a Father Working in Tulare, California": Groups alternate sentences. Point out that sentences may be more than one line in length.
- "What They Don't Tell You About Cereal": Both groups read the first verse. Then one group reads the sections printed in all capitals; the other group reads the rest of the poem.

The POWER of POETRY CONTINUED

Letter to a Father Working in Tulare, California

Father, I spent my first hours of school
Lifting a pencil. Pencils
Can be heavy if you have a lot to say.
I wrote, The giraffe is my favorite animal.
I wrote, My best friend Marta broke her arm.
I wrote and wrote.
And then played soccer while eating an orange.

Restate: Are you picking grapes now?

Father, I know you're working in the fields.
Is it grapes right now? I know it's not cotton or beets.
You chop those in March and April.
Now it's August. Maybe you're pouring sand
From your boots
And your hands are sticky from the blood of grapes.
Maybe you're sitting under a tree, peeling an apple
With a small tiny knife.

Encourage elaboration: What do these details show about the writer's feelings for the father?

Father, I miss you.
I've grown tall in four months.
Mama must raise her eyes up when she speaks to me.

—*Gary Soto*

Use visuals: From the picture of the father, what can you tell about his work?

fields farmlands
chop cut
sticky gummy
blood juice
raise her eyes up look up

BEFORE YOU MOVE ON...

1. **Paraphrase** What does the boy tell his father in the letter?
2. **Inference** How does the boy feel about his father? Explain your answer.

The Power of Poetry 17

REVIEW KEY VOCABULARY

3 Use New Words in Context Have pairs create a sentence or drawing to illustrate the meaning of each key vocabulary word. The pairs then join to form groups of four. Have groups compare their work and revise it to improve the expression of the word's meaning. Invite the class to vote on the picture that best illustrates each word. To facilitate proficiency, post these pictures on a classroom word wall.

CHECK COMPREHENSION

4 Answers to "Before You Move On"

page 16

1. **Details/Character's Motive** He tries to communicate by yelling outrageous statements to get people's attention.
2. **Conclusions** The message about the steaks matters the most because the people like to eat.

page 17

1. **Paraphrase** He tells his father about his life over the last four months.
2. **Inference** The boy loves his father and wants him to know about his life. He says, "Father, I miss you."

INTERNET

SCIENCE CONNECTION

Tell students that the boy in the poem has a father who is a migrant worker. Define *migrant worker* as a person who moves to different locations to obtain work. Clarify that migrant crop work is based on seasonal crops. Using the Internet, have students research the types of crops grown in various parts of the country. Web sites often change, but here is one you might suggest.

Web Site
http://seasonalchef.com

Grammar Minilesson

▶ COMMON AND PROPER NOUNS

TEACH Draw students' attention to the words *shore, trout,* and *people* on page 16. Point out that all three words are nouns. Define a noun as a word that names a person, place, thing, or idea. Give an example of each.

Compare *river* with *Colorado River* to explain that a common noun names any person, place, thing, or idea while a proper noun names one particular person, place, or thing. Point out correct capitalization. Refer students to page 432 in the Handbook for more examples.

PRACTICE Have students fill in the chart with related nouns.

Common	Proper
	Aunt Sonia
friend	
city	
	Guatemala
restaurant	

▶ **Practice Book** page 4

READ PAGE 18

OBJECTIVES

Function: Read a Poem
Grammar: Singular and Plural Nouns
Listening: Listen to a Poem
Reading and Learning Strategies: Visualize; Make Predictions
Comprehension: Ⓣ Identify Character's Motive

CHECK COMPREHENSION

5 Answers to "Before You Move On"

1. **Character's Motive** He is in love with her. He believes that the cereal is giving him energy to write a letter telling her so.
2. **Prediction** Answers will vary. Some students will be optimistic, others may not be.

CLOSE AND ASSESS

Have students share the comparisons between their mental images and the illustrations in the book.

WHAT THEY DON'T TELL YOU ABOUT CEREAL

Restate: The cereal gave me so much energy I felt as if I could take off like a rocket.

In love, I ate three bowls of cereal,
The flakes so full of energy.
I put down my spoon and raced around the house.
There was rocket fuel in my heart.

Then I sat down to write a love note to Marta,
A girl in the second row, you know, by the window.
Marta, I wrote, I have a secret:
I LOVE YOU! I LOVE YOU! I LOVE YOU!

When my rocket fuel burned off,
I poured another bowl so that I could finish my note.
Again, I raced around the house,
Then sat down to write: I DO! I DO! I DO! I DO!

By the end of this note, all the cereal was gone.
My fingers were blistered from holding the pencil,
Sharpened so many times it was a nub
When I finally signed my name: JOSÉ, JOSÉ, JOSÉ.

—Gary Soto

Pose choices: What details are the funniest? How much he ate, what he wrote, how he ran?

flakes flat, thin pieces of cereal
rocket fuel high energy, excitement
burned off was used up, was gone
blistered red and hot
nub small, pointed object

BEFORE YOU MOVE ON...

1. **Character's Motive** Why is the boy writing a letter to Marta?
2. **Prediction** What would Marta say in a letter back to José?

18 **Unit 1** | Communication

REACHING ALL STUDENTS

Vocabulary
SENSORY WORDS

Tell students that words create a picture in the mind by appealing to the five senses. These kinds of words are called *sensory words.* Play environmental music, such as the sounds of a rainstorm or the ocean, or show a picture. Have students write the words that come to mind around the outside of the web, and the overall feeling or event in the middle.

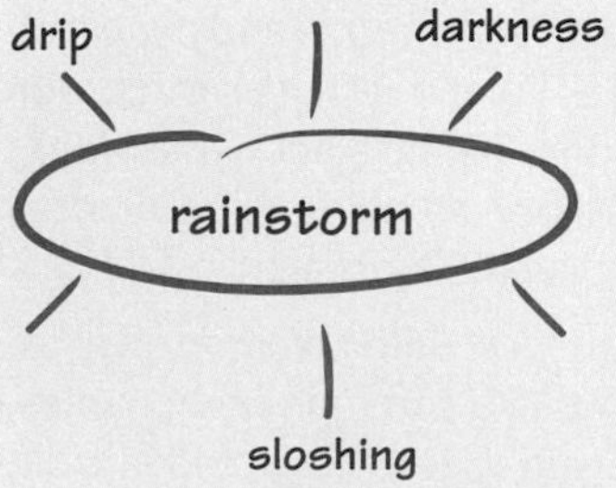

Health Connection
NUTRITION

Ask: *Is there good reason for the poet to compare cereal to rocket fuel?* Have students look into the nutritional value of cereal by examining a variety of cereal boxes. Groups can study the information on the side panels. They can research how sugar and other ingredients found in cereal affect the body. Groups report findings to the class.

ₙn Interview with Poet Gary Soto

poem is a personal message from the poet to readers. Where do poets their ideas? What is the best way to read poetry? Find out the swers to these questions and much more about communication in s interview with Gary Soto.

e text features: Point out that "**Q**" indicates an interviewer's estion and "**A**" indicates Soto's answer.

Where do your poems come from?

They come from my **memory** or from a story someone told me; they come from feelings and the **inventive** side of the mind. Most of my poems come from real **experiences**. But, like other artists, I treat the experiences with **a measure** of **creativity**.

Clarify: He bases his poems on real experiences, but he adds to them from his imagination.

Do you have to get **inspired** to write?

When I began writing fifteen years ago, I waited to be "inspired," which for me was a **physical sensation**—my body **tingled**. Now I get this feeling less frequently. I **doodle** a few phrases or lines, and **a nice feeling settles on my shoulders**. This is a sign that I'm ready to write.

Q When do you write?

A Each poet has a **routine**. I write in the morning because **my mind is clear** and I can **concentrate**. After breakfast, I go out to my garage, which I've turned into a **study**, and write for two or three hours; then I have lunch, and do something else in the afternoon.

neasure a certain amount
ysical sensation feeling in my body
ıgled felt like it was full of electricity
odle write without thinking very much
a nice feeling settles on my shoulders I feel good, I start to get comfortable
my mind is clear I can think clearly
study room for reading and writing

READ PAGE 19

OBJECTIVES

Function: Read a Selection
Listening: Listen to a Selection
Reading and Learning Strategies: Set a Purpose for Reading; Visualize

SET PURPOSE

1 Read aloud the title and introduction and give students a moment to page through this part of the selection. Set the purpose for reading: *Look for information about the poet's life and creative process. Make a list of techniques that he uses.*

READ AND THINK

Tape 1A
CD 1 Track 1

2 **Strategy Focus: Visualize** Involve students in reading pages 19–21. After each question and answer set, ask students to share the mental images they formed from the set.

The recording of "An Interview with Poet Gary Soto" on the **Selection Tape/CD** offers an oral language model and the opportunity to build reading fluency.

Language Development

GIVE INFORMATION

Gary Soto shares information about his daily routine. Write common daily routine phrases: *take a shower, do homework, eat dinner.*

Invite students to work in pairs to describe their routines. Remind them to borrow from the posted ideas and generate some of their own. Ask students to tell the class what they learned about their partners' daily routines. Encourage them to use complete sentences in describing their routines.

Grammar Minilesson

▶ SINGULAR AND PLURAL NOUNS

TEACH Remind students that a noun names a person, place, thing, or idea. Use words in the poem on page 18 to discuss singular and plural nouns. Explain that some nouns, like *spoon* in line 3, name things you can count. Almost all of these nouns add an ending when they tell about more than one thing. Use Handbook page 433 to review rules for forming plurals of count nouns.

Then point out the words *cereal* and *energy.* Explain that these nouns name things you cannot count. They have only one form to show "one" and "more than one." For more examples, refer students to Handbook page 434.

Show students how to use a count noun with a noncount noun to show "more than one." Write:

Give me a bowl of cereal.
Give me two bowls of cereal.

PRACTICE Have students use these nouns to write sentences:

Count Nouns: flake, spoon, window
Noncount nouns: cereal, energy, fuel

▶ **Practice book** page 5

READ PAGES 20–21

OBJECTIVES

Vocabulary Strategy: Context Clues
Reading Strategy: Relate to Personal Experience
Comprehension: Identify Details; Form Opinions; Make Decisions
Literary Analysis: Free Verse; Respond to Literature

EXPAND VOCABULARY

3 Use Context Clues Point out how the context of a word can explain its meaning. Direct students' attention to the line on page 21: "they write 'free verse'—poetry that has no regular rhyme or rhythm". Explain how the phrase "poetry that has no regular rhyme or rhythm" defines *free verse.*

For practice, have students discover the definition of *lonely* found in the context "It's about a lonely man who feels sad that no one wants him" on page 21.

Encourage students to apply this strategy to other unfamiliar words as they read.

Q Do you have to change any of your words?

A Since most poems are short, compared to other kinds of literature, every line needs **a great deal** of **attention**. I once worked on a single fourteen-line poem for a week, changing verbs, **reworking line breaks**, cutting out unnecessary words.

Q Do you write the titles of your poems first?

A I usually come up with a title when I'[m] about halfway through a poem. A title often **hints** to the reader what the po[em] is about. At times, however, poets will use wild titles that they may not whol[ly] understand but may like for the way t[hey] sound or the way they look on the pa[ge].

Q Should I read a poem more than once?

A Yes, by all means. Read it again and again. One poet **remarked** that "poetr[y] is **an act of** attention"—you have to concentrate when you read a poem.

I also like to think of a poem as a new person. Just because you say hell[o] once doesn't mean that you never wan[t] to see this person again. Of course, yo[u] do. A poem also needs to be seen agai[n] and again.

Ask: How is a po[em] like a new perso[n]

BEFORE YOU MOVE ON...

1. **Details** Where does the poet say his ideas come from?
2. **Opinion** Do you agree that a poem is like a new person? Explain.

a great deal a lot
reworking line breaks changing where the lines end
hints gives a clue
remarked said, made the comment
an act of an effort or action involving

REACHING ALL STUDENTS

A WORLD OF LANGUAGES

Multicultural Proverbs Proverbs are a frequent part of conversations in many languages and countries. Invite students to discuss the meanings of the following proverbs related to poetry and other forms of communication. Ask: *Is there a similar proverb in your native language? How does understanding proverbs help you understand people from other cultures?*

PROVERB	ORIGIN
Poetry moves heaven and earth.	Japan
Words have no wings, but they can fly a thousand miles.	Korea
The palest ink is better than the best memory.	China
The mouth tastes food; the heart tastes words.	Laos (Hmong)

Why don't your poems rhyme?

Most poets today don't use rhyme; they write "free verse"—poetry that has **no regular rhyme or rhythm**. Poetry has changed over the years, but poets' **motives** for writing poetry haven't changed. Most poets write because they feel something and want to share it with others.

Clarify: Poets write to communicate their feelings.

When did you decide to become a poet?

I decided to become a poet after I read a funny/sad poem by Edward Field called "Unwanted." It's about a lonely man who feels sad that no one wants him. He hangs a picture of himself at the post office next to **posters** of dangerous criminals. He wants people to **recognize** him and love him. I was inspired by this poem and **identified with** it because it seemed to speak about my own life. I read the poem over and over, and even **typed it out** to see what it looked like. I read this poet's book and began to read other poets. After a while, I decided to write my own poems, and have been doing it ever since.

regular rhyme or rhythm no …tterns for the sounds at the end of …e lines or the beat of the lines

…sters pictures placed for people to …e or read

…cognize see or know

…entified with understood or …ared in

…ped it out used a machine or a …mputer to print the words

BEFORE YOU MOVE ON...

1. **Personal Experience** Think of a poem that impressed you. Describe the poem and how it made you feel.
2. **Making Decisions** Think of a question you would ask Gary Soto if you were the interviewer.

ABOUT THE POET

Gary Soto started writing poetry when he was twenty years old. One of his very first poems was a love poem he wrote for a girl he knew at school. Unfortunately, the girl rejected him and his poems, but Gary Soto continued writing poetry anyway. Since then, he has written eleven books of poetry and many plays, novels, and short stories.

CHECK COMPREHENSION

4 Answers to "Before You Move On"

page 20

1. **Details** He says that his ideas come from real experiences.
2. **Opinion** Answers will vary.

page 21

1. **Personal Experience** Answers will vary. Suggest poems from this selection. Prompt with feeling words, such as: *inspired, sympathetic, cheered.*
2. **Making Decisions** Answers will vary, but may include: *How old were you when. . . ? Do you ever feel. . . ?*

ABOUT THE POET

5 Respond to Literature Read About the Poet. Say: *The three poems in "The Power of Poetry" represent very different voices.* Ask: *Did you like one poem more than another? Can you explain why?* Point out that one person may find that a poem "speaks" to his or her own experiences. Another may feel differently, but all the responses are equally valid.

CLOSE AND ASSESS

Have students review the unit mind map on page 9 and add to the chart.

HOME CONNECTION

Interview a Family Member Send home a copy of *High Point Newsletter 1* in the **Teacher's Resource Book**. In this home activity, students interview family members, asking them to share a favorite poem or song lyric and explain their reasons for liking or remembering it. Ask students to record or write down the poems or songs and share them with the class.

Literary Analysis Minilesson

▶ POETRY: FREE VERSE

TEACH Draw attention to Soto's definition of free verse poetry on page 21. Explain that a poem does not need to rhyme or have a specific rhythm to convey its message. Discuss how poetry, including free verse, often relies on visual images and sensory words.

PRACTICE Have students create a free verse poem by following these steps:

- Select a magazine or newspaper story.
- Find and mark powerful words and phrases.
- Put the marked words together into lines.
- Arrange the line order and length until it looks right to you.
- Read the poem aloud and listen to how it sounds. Adjust as necessary.
- Give the poem a title.

Students can illustrate and share their poems with the class.

▶ **Practice Book** page 6

RESPOND

OBJECTIVES

SUM IT UP

Function: Give Information

Reading and Learning Strategies: Visualize; Ⓣ Summarize; Identify Author's Message; Use Graphic Organizers (word web, chart)

THINK IT OVER

Function: Engage in Discussion

Comprehension and Critical Thinking: Draw Conclusions; Identify Author's Purpose; Form Opinions

Literary Analysis: Style

EXPRESS YOURSELF

Function: Express Feelings and Ideas

Speaking and Listening: Role-play

CHECK YOUR UNDERSTANDING

1 Sum It Up Annotations to the webs and the chart show possible answers.

▶ **Practice Book** page 7

2 Think It Over Possible answers are:

1. **Conclusions** Poetry is often about personal subjects that interest the poet. Poems should be read more than once to get the most meaning from them.
2. **Author's Style** A young boy is the narrator of each poem. The poems do not rhyme. All the poems are written in first person and in free verse.
3. **Author's Purpose** He chose the topics because they are important to him. The topics show he has a sense of humor and cares about people.
4. **Opinion** Answers will vary. Ask students to provide reasons for their choices.

3 Express Yourself Prompt the use of sensory words in the role-plays.

CLOSE AND ASSESS

Ask: *What do poetry and visual images have to do with communication?*

Respond to the Poems and Interview

Check Your Understanding

SUM IT UP

Visualize and Summarize Make a web of the words that helped you see what happened in each of the poems.

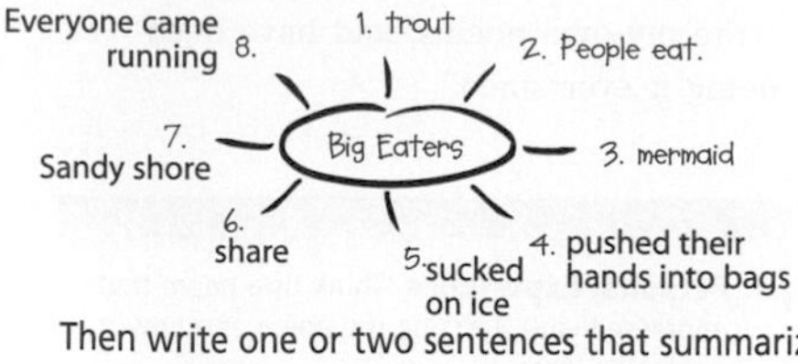

Then write one or two sentences that summarize the poem.

Example:

No one paid attention to the boy because everyone was busy eating. Then the boy said the steaks were almost ready, and all the people came over.

Determine the Author's Message Review your summaries. Make a chart to show what the poet has to say about communication.

Poem	Poet's Message About Communication
Big Eaters	People listen to the things they want to hear.
Letter to a Father...	Sometimes it's hard to express yourself when you have a lot to say.
What They Don't Tell You About Cereal	Messages from the heart have to be expressed.

THINK IT OVER

Discuss and Write Talk about these questions with a partner. Write the answers.

1. **Conclusions** What did you learn about poetry and communication from the interview with Gary Soto?
2. **Author's Style** Who is the narrator of each poem? What else can you say about the author's style?
3. **Author's Purpose** Why do you think Gary Soto chose these topics for his poems? What do the topics say about him?
4. **Opinion** Which is your favorite poem? Why?

EXPRESS YOURSELF

▶ Express Feelings and Ideas

Work with a partner. Role-play an imaginary conversation between characters in the poems. Choose one of the following:

- a conversation between the boy and one of the people eating steak in "Big Eaters"
- a telephone conversation between the boy and his father in "Letter to a Father Working in Tulare, California"
- a conversation between the boy and Marta in "What They Don't Tell You About Cereal"

REACHING ALL STUDENTS

Multi-Level Strategies

SUM IT UP OPTIONS

BEGINNING Encourage students to copy words from the poem or show pictures in their webs. Provide a sentence frame for the summary: *This poem is about a boy who* _____. Have students dictate ideas for the message chart. Restate the ideas and vocalize as you write on the chart.

INTERMEDIATE / **ADVANCED** Have students complete their webs individually, then share them with a group and agree on a summary to write for each poem. Have the group collect several possible messages for the chart, vote for the best one, and write it in the chart.

ASSESSMENT
Selection Test 1 on page 3 of the Assessment Handbook tests students' mastery of the reading strategies and the vocabulary, comprehension, and language arts skills taught with this selection.

nguage Arts and Literature

ITERARY ANALYSIS
PEAKING/LISTENING

COGNIZE MOOD

arn About Mood The feeling of a poem story is its **mood**. Mood can be happy, sad, cited, angry, or any other feeling.

ry Soto chose words and phrases to create nood for each of the three poems. For ample, he creates a playful mood in "Big ters" by using words like these:

20-foot trout
shark almost bit my toes

actice Reread "Letter to a Father Working Tulare, California" and "What They Don't ll You About Cereal." Pay attention to ood as you read. Make a list of key words at create the mood. Share your words with ur classmates.

xpress Mood Work with a group. Tape cord yourselves reading the poems. Express e mood of each poem with your voice. Listen the tape and talk about ways to improve e reading. Record the poems again.

TECHNOLOGY/MEDIA
LITERARY ANALYSIS

COMPARE POETS

Choose another poet you like. Compare that poet to Gary Soto. Write a paragraph to compare each poet's subject matter, style, and way of working.

1. **Locate Information** Use poetry anthologies to find several poems by the poet you chose. Start with this Web site and use key words to find biographical information.

INTERNET
INFORMATION ON-LINE
Key Word:
poets
Web Site:
➤ **Poets**
• www.poets.org/index.cfm

Take notes and download useful information.

2. **Write a Paragraph** Write a paragraph that compares Gary Soto with the other poet. Then read your paragraph to your class and share the poetry that you found.

For more information on using the **Internet**, see Handbook pages 392–393.

Multi-Level Strategies
ACTIVITY OPTIONS FOR RECOGNIZING MOOD

BEGINNING Have students review their Sum It Up webs. Help them identify the mood expressed in each poem. Then have them write the word describing the mood on a self-stick note and use it to mark the page. Move from this warmup into listing key words.

INTERMEDIATE Have students work in pairs, using their Sum It Up webs to make their lists. Then have pairs compose a brief statement that labels the mood of each poem and explains why that label was chosen.

ADVANCED Encourage students to complete the activity individually. Then have students compare their lists. Invite them to compose a group statement for each poem, identifying its mood and supporting their identification.

RESPOND

OBJECTIVES

RECOGNIZE MOOD
Concepts and Vocabulary: Mood Words
Listening and Speaking: Poetry Readings
Literary Analysis: Mood

COMPARE POETS
Function: Give Information; Write
Critical Thinking and Research Skills: Gather Information; Ⓣ Make Comparisons; Use Graphic Organizers (Venn diagram)
Literary Analysis: Compare Literature
Technology/Media: Use the Internet
Writing: Paragraph

LANGUAGE ARTS AND LITERATURE

1 **Recognize Mood** Guide students to find words that create a thoughtful mood in "Letter to a Father. . . " (Pencils can be heavy; blood of grapes) or an excited mood in "What They Don't Tell You. . . ." (raced around; fingers were blistered)

▶ **Practice Book** page 8

2 **Compare Poets** Provide samples of poetry by Robert Louis Stevenson, Maya Angelou, Shel Silverstein, and Naomi Shikab Nye. Support students in locating print and electronic resources.

To provide prewriting support, model how to set up a Venn diagram for comparing poets:

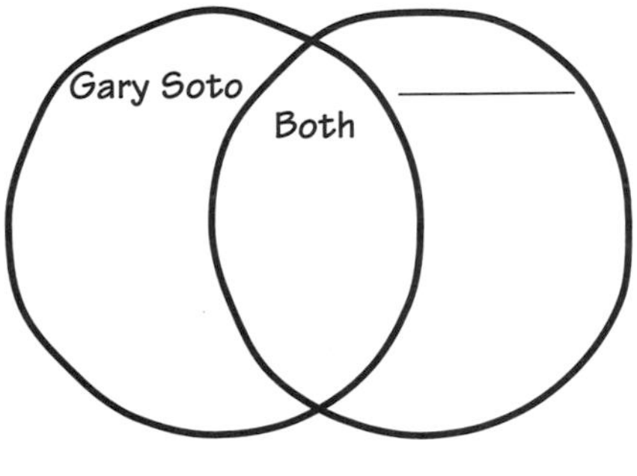

CLOSE AND ASSESS

Ask students to write two sentences telling what they learned about poetry and poets from this lesson.

PREPARE TO READ

OBJECTIVES

THINK ABOUT WHAT YOU KNOW

Reading Strategy:
Relate to Personal Experience

LEARN KEY VOCABULARY Ⓣ

Vocabulary Strategy: Relate Words

LEARN TO RELATE MAIN IDEA AND DETAILS

Reading Strategy:
Ⓣ Relate Main Idea and Details

THINK ABOUT WHAT YOU KNOW

1 **Study Walls in Your School** Direct students to look at walls in and around the school. Ask students to take notes describing what the walls tell about the school, as well as what the walls communicate to them.

LEARN KEY VOCABULARY

2 **Relate Words** Have students read each vocabulary word and its definition. Conduct the chart activity.

Use the Vocabulary Options in the **Multi-Level Strategies** to tailor the activity to proficiency levels.

▶ **Practice Book** page 9

LEARN TO RELATE MAIN IDEA AND DETAILS

3 **Model How to Relate Main Idea and Details** Define *topic, main idea,* and *details.* Demonstrate the steps in the box with **Transparency 3**:

- Read the title and write the topic.
- Model how to take notes as you read the article. As you write notes, say: *One important idea is. . . ; I don't want to forget that. . . ; "lonely" is an important word here.*
- Survey your notes to identify the main idea. Write it in the diagram.
- List details that support the main idea.

CLOSE AND ASSESS

Ask students to agree on why it is helpful to identify the main idea and details. (It gives an overview of what a selection is about.)

TALKING WALLS

essay
by Margy Burns Knight

Prepare to Read

THINK ABOUT WHAT YOU KNOW

Study Walls in Your School What do the walls in your school say to you? What do they say about your school?

history story of a country and its people

legacy thing or idea handed down from the past

memento reminder of the past, souvenir

memorial something that keeps alive the memory of a person or event

monument something built to last a long time that honors a person or an event

mural large picture painted on a wall or other large surface

portray make a picture of

represent be an example or model of something

tribute something given to show thanks or respect

For the vocabulary activity, help students supply an example of each type of message. Then they can check off the applicable boxes.

LEARN KEY VOCABULARY

Relate Words Study the new words and their definitions. In a chart, give an example of each kind of message. Check the boxes that apply.

Messages:	Mural	Monument	Memento
Examples:	workers' mural		
Does it portray people and places?	✓		
Does it provide a legacy?			
Is it a memorial?			
Does it represent an event in history?			
Does it honor a living person or people?	✓		

LEARN TO RELATE MAIN IDEA AND DETAILS

A **topic** is what a writer writes about. It is the writer's subject. A **main idea** is the most important idea about the topic. **Details** are pieces of information that tell more about the main idea.

READING STRATEGY

How to Relate Main Idea and Details

1. Read the title to see what the topic is.
2. Take notes as you read.
3. Review your notes. Ask yourself: What is the most important idea about the topic? This is the main idea. Then find the details that go with the main idea.

Read "Talking Walls." Find the main idea and details about each wall.

REACHING ALL STUDENTS

Multi-Level Strategies

VOCABULARY OPTIONS

BEGINNING Group students to read ***I Make Pictures Move*** or the Key Points Reading on **Master 4**. (See page T27.) Work with the vocabulary in those selections.

INTERMEDIATE / **ADVANCED** Ask students to suggest an example in their community of a mural, a monument, and a memento to write on the chart. Or use the photographs on pages 27 and 29. Compare the messages by answering the questions in the chart.

Transparency 3 / Master 3

RELATE MAIN IDEAS AND DETAILS

Directions: Read the title. Write the topic. Take notes. Then make a diagram to show the main idea and details.

The Walls at Angel Island

The poems on the walls of the barracks at Angel Island preserve the history of many Chinese immigrants. Angel Island was an immigration center in California's San Francisco Bay. From 1910–1940, thousands of Chinese immigrants were held against their will at the center. Many were lonely because they missed their families in China. They were angry because they were being treated unfairly. Some of them communicated their loneliness and anger by carving poems into the walls of the barracks.

Topic: Walls at Angel Island

Notes:
preserve history of Chinese in U.S.
immigrants held there
lonely, angry
carved poems into the walls

Main Idea: The Walls at Angel Island preserve the history of Chinese immigrants to the United States.

Detail: They wrote poems and carved them into the walls.

Detail: The poems tell about their loneliness and anger.

Transparency 3 Level B, Unit 1 | Communication

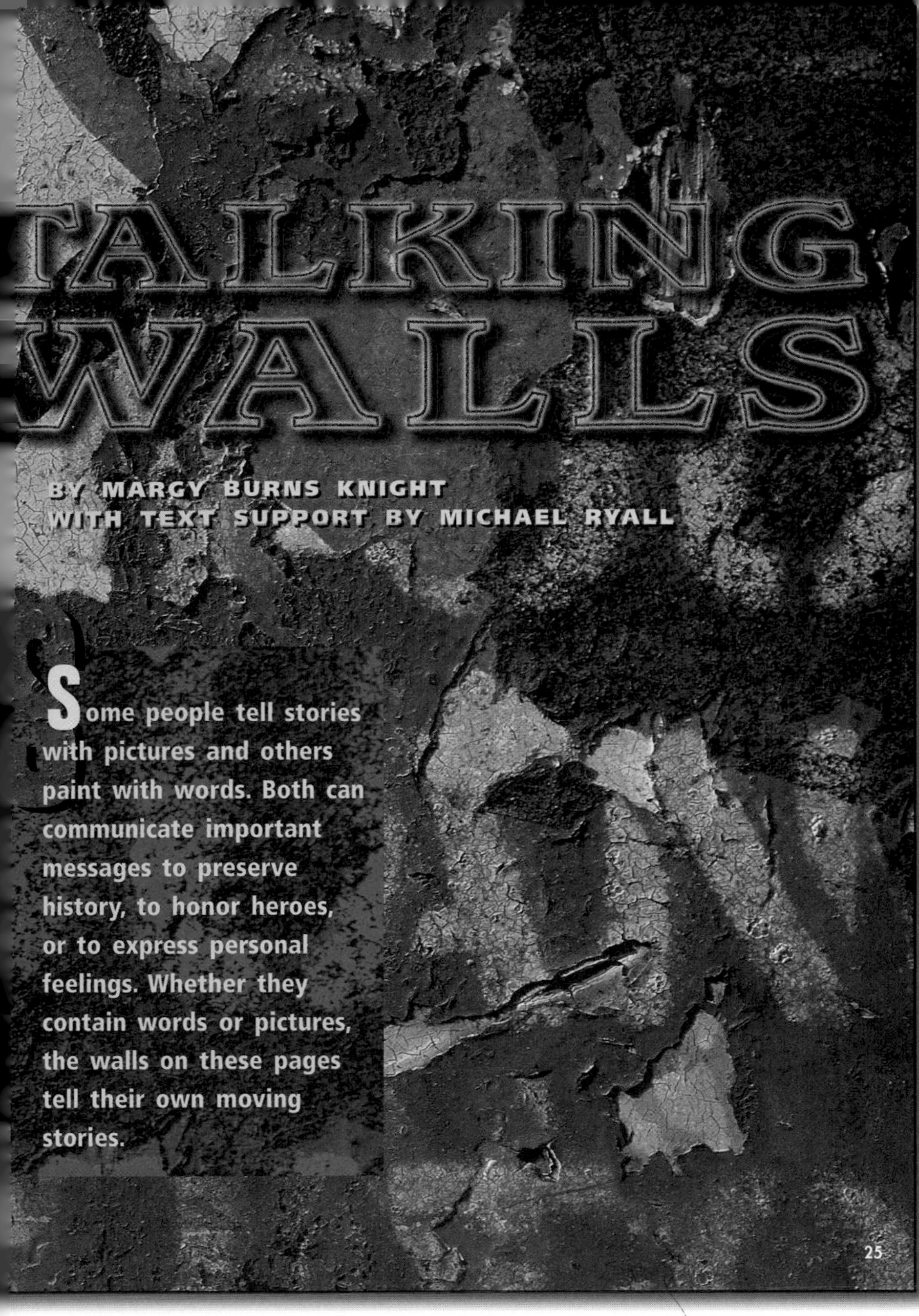

TALKING WALLS

BY MARGY BURNS KNIGHT
WITH TEXT SUPPORT BY MICHAEL RYALL

Some people tell stories with pictures and others paint with words. Both can communicate important messages to preserve history, to honor heroes, or to express personal feelings. Whether they contain words or pictures, the walls on these pages tell their own moving stories.

25

READ THE SELECTION

OBJECTIVES

Reading Strategies: Preview; Predict
Literary Analysis: Essay

INTRODUCE THE SELECTION

4 **Preview and Predict** Read the title, author's name, and the introduction to the essay on page 25. Ask: *In what ways can walls tell stories?* Have students page through the selection, looking at the pictures and reading the captions for ideas.

5 **Identify Genre: Essay** Point out that this selection gives factual information about how walls can communicate messages. Tell students that a piece of nonfiction writing that examines a single topic is called an essay.

Talking Walls
by Margy Burns Knight

Theme Connection This selection examines how walls can communicate messages that matter by honoring and remembering people and events.

Selection Summary and Awards The introduction on page 25 of the student book offers a summary of the selection. The essay presents the murals of Diego Rivera, the Vietnam Veterans Memorial, and a simple wooden fence surrounding the house of poet Pablo Neruda. The book containing this selection was among the top twenty-five nonfiction children's books cited by the *Boston Globe* in 1992.

THE BASICS BOOKSHELF

■ ***I Make Pictures Move*** by Daphne Liu

Some pictures tell a story, but moving pictures always do. In this book, an animator creates a story about a unique dining experience. The patterned text provides basic vocabulary for food, colors and shapes. Students will also enjoy flipping the pages to animate the artist's final illustration.

For Lesson Plans: See the Teacher's Guide for ***The Basics Bookshelf***.

READ PAGES 26–27

OBJECTIVES

Function: Read a Selection
Vocabulary Strategy: Ⓣ Context Clues
Listening: Listen to a Selection
Viewing: Respond to Murals
Reading and Learning Strategies: Set a Purpose for Reading; Ⓣ Relate Main Idea and Details; Use Graphic Organizers (chart)
Comprehension: Ⓣ Make Comparisons

SET PURPOSE

1 Read aloud the information about the mural. Set the purpose for reading: *Look for details about the people Rivera included in his murals.*

READ AND THINK

Tape 1A
CD 1 Track 2

2 **Strategy Focus: Relate Main Idea and Details** Have students identify the topic of each section. Involve them in note-taking with **Transparency 5**. See page T32 where students use notes to relate main ideas and details.

Choose Reading Options in the **Multi-Level Strategies** to tailor the reading to proficiency levels.

The recording of "Talking Walls" on the **Selection Tape/CD** offers an oral language model and the opportunity to build reading fluency.

Red annotations offer opportunities to clarify meaning and check for understanding.

DIEGO RIVERA'S MURALS

Build background: If you've ever seen a billboard or a poster, you've seen a talking wall. People throughout history have used walls to communicate thoughts, feelings, and ideas.

This mural is called *The Mechanization of the Country*. It was painted in 1926 on a wall in the **stairwell** of the Ministry of Education in Mexico City. In it, Rivera shows that Mexico's economy was changing from one based on farming to one based on industry and technology.

The Mechanization of the Country, Diego Rivera, mural. Copyright © 19

Use visuals: What details in the paintings show that farming is giving way to industry and technology?

The walls that Diego Rivera painted are like the pages of a large picture book. Many of the huge **murals** that he painted on walls throughout Mexico show the **glorious** and painful **history** of his country. Women **hard at work** with babies on their backs, farmers bending over in the fields, and people fighting for their **rights** are just some of the characters that Rivera **portrayed** i his murals.

Ask: What story did Diego Rivera t in many of his murals?

An artist of tremendous energy and passion, Rivera worked for ten, twelve, sometimes fourteen hours a day. He painte to share **his vision of** Mexico's history wi his people.

Ask: Why did Diego Rivera wor many hours every day?

stairwell part of a building where stairs are located
glorious proud, beautiful, impressive
hard at work working very hard
rights fair and equal treatment, legal and moral justice
his vision of what he thought was important in

REACHING ALL STUDENTS

Vocabulary
SYNONYMS AND ANTONYMS

Have students locate the words *huge* and *tremendous* on page 26 and explain what they mean. Point out that *huge* and *tremendous* are synonyms, words that have the same meaning. Explain that an antonym is a word that means the opposite of another. *Tiny* is the antonym of *huge*. Write words such as *big, small, happy, sad, quiet, noisy* on individual index cards. Groups can brainstorm and use a thesaurus to identify as many synonyms and antonyms for the words as they can.

Multi-Level Strategies
READING OPTIONS FOR LESSONS 9–11

BEGINNING Students should work with ***I Make Pictures Move*** while the class reads "Talking Walls." Or, distribute copies of **Master 4** to conduct a Key Points Reading. Model how to take notes on **Transparency 5**.

INTERMEDIATE Read the essay aloud or play the recording of "Talking Walls" on the **Selection Tape/CD**. Ask students to dictate notes and record them on **Transparency 5**.

ADVANCED Have students take notes on copies of **Master 5** as they read short sections silently. They can then work with a partner to compare their notes and confirm what they have read.

POINT-BY-POINT

Walls Around the World

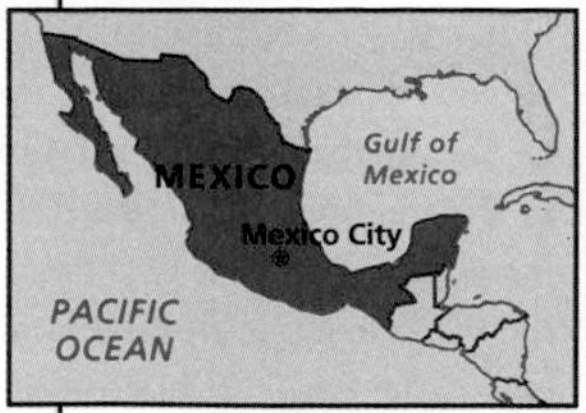

What Murals by Diego Rivera

Where Mexico City

Message Celebrate the people and history of Mexico.

Pause to locate Mexico City on the map.

ego Rivera

Wall paintings, like the one above, were common in the ancient city of Teotihuacán in Mexico. Diego Rivera helped to revive this art form in the 1930s. His murals show what daily life was like in Mexico then. Rivera believed that working people represented the real Mexico.

Ask: What does Diego Rivera think of working people? How does he show this in his art?

BEFORE YOU MOVE ON...

1. **Context Clues** What special meaning does the word *characters* have here? What characters are in Rivera's mural?
2. **Viewing/Comparison** How is the mural in Teotihuacán like Rivera's mural? How is it different?

cient very old
vive bring back to life
form kind of art

CHECK COMPREHENSION

3 Answers to "Before You Move On"

1. **Context Clues** Here, *characters* means *people.* The characters that Rivera painted include women with babies on their backs, farmers, and people fighting for their rights.
2. **Viewing/Comparison** Both murals are done on walls, have similar colors, and were painted in Mexico. The mural in Teotihuacán is ancient; Rivera's mural is modern.

CLOSE AND ASSESS

Have students share the notes they took for pages 26–27. Check for examples of how Rivera portrayed the daily lives of workers.

Transparency 4 / Master 4

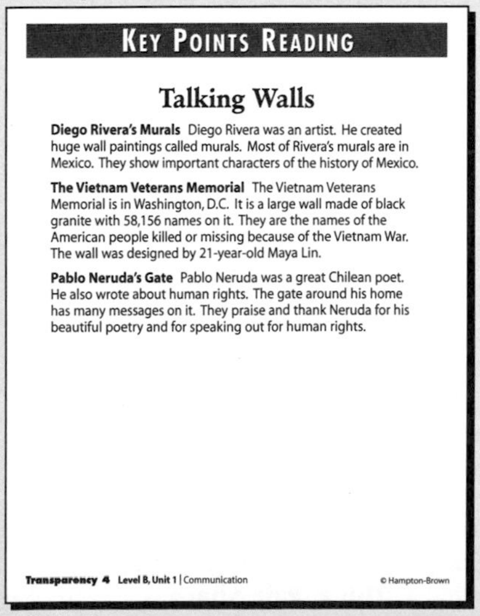

KEY POINTS READING

Talking Walls

Diego Rivera's Murals Diego Rivera was an artist. He created huge wall paintings called murals. Most of Rivera's murals are in Mexico. They show important characters of the history of Mexico.

The Vietnam Veterans Memorial The Vietnam Veterans Memorial is in Washington, D.C. It is a large wall made of black granite with 58,156 names on it. They are the names of the American people killed or missing because of the Vietnam War. The wall was designed by 21-year-old Maya Lin.

Pablo Neruda's Gate Pablo Neruda was a great Chilean poet. He also wrote about human rights. The gate around his home has many messages on it. They praise and thank Neruda for his beautiful poetry and for speaking out for human rights.

Transparency 4 Level B, Unit 1 | Communication © Hampton-Brown

Transparency 5 / Master 5

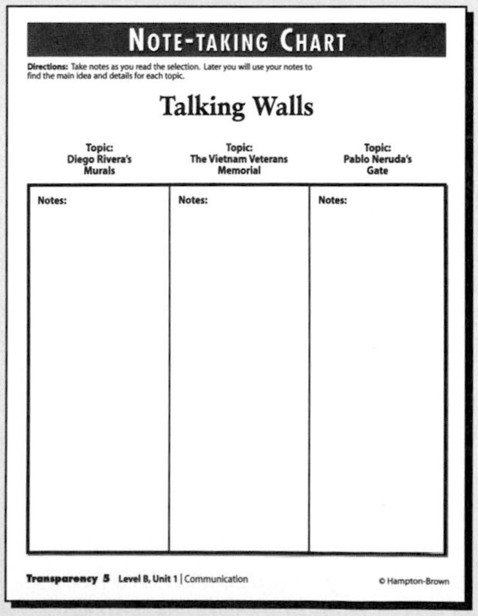

NOTE-TAKING CHART

Directions: Take notes as you read the selection. Later you will use your notes to find the main idea and details for each topic.

Talking Walls

Topic: Diego Rivera's Murals	Topic: The Vietnam Veterans Memorial	Topic: Pablo Neruda's Gate
Notes:	Notes:	Notes:

Transparency 5 Level B, Unit 1 | Communication © Hampton-Brown

READ PAGES 28–29

OBJECTIVES

Function: Read a Selection
Vocabulary Strategy: Use New Words in Context
Grammar: Singular and Plural Nouns
Listening: Listen to a Selection
Reading and Learning Strategies: Set a Purpose for Reading; Ⓣ Relate Main Idea and Details; Use Graphic Organizers (chart)
Comprehension: Identify Cause and Effect; Form Opinions

SET PURPOSE

1 Set the purpose for reading: *Look for details about how people react to the Vietnam Veterans Memorial.*

READ AND THINK

Tape 1A
CD 1 Track 2

2 **Strategy Focus: Relate Main Idea and Details** Involve students in reading pages 28 and 29.

See the **Multi-Level Strategies** on page T26 to tailor the reading experience to all proficiency levels.

THE VIETNAM VETERANS MEMORIAL

Pause to show the location on the Point-by-Point map, page

Flowers, letters, candles, and boots are lovingly placed under the names written on the Vietnam Veterans **Memorial**, in Washington, D.C. Each day these **mementos** and many others are left at the long, black **reflective wall** that rises out of the earth. The **monument** is about **one hundred sixty-five giant steps** long and was designed by Maya Lin, a twenty-one-year-old **architecture student**. She chose black **granite** for her design because she felt you could **gaze** into it forever. Every day people come to visit the wall, and many cry as they look at, touch, and remember the names of American men and women who were killed or are still missing as a result of the war in Vietnam.

Many more men, women, and children died during this war. If the names of these Vietnamese, Cambodian, and Laotian dead were **chiseled** into the wall, it would **extend** for at least another seven thousand giant steps.

Have a student pace off the length of the classroom. Ask: How many classrooms would equal the length of the monument?

In 1954, Vietnam gained independence from France. Two separate governments formed and fought a civil war that kept the country divided. In the late 1950s the United States began supporting South Vietnam in its fight against North Vietnam. In 1975, North Vietnam won the war. When it was over, more than 58,000 Americans had been killed. At least 2,000,000 Vietnamese, 200,000 Cambodians, and 100,000 Laotians were also killed during the fighting.

Restate: The war in Vietnam began as a civil war between two parts of the same country—North Vietnam and South Vietna

reflective wall wall that shines like a mirror
one hundred sixty-five giant steps 493.5 feet (One giant step is about three feet long.)
architecture student student who studies how buildings and other structures are made
granite stone that is very hard
gaze look deeply
chiseled carved
extend go on, continue
gained independence became free
civil war war between two groups of people in the country

REACHING ALL STUDENTS

Cooperative Learning

FOR A RESEARCH PROJECT: Political Systems

Think Ask students to work independently, writing down three questions to research for a report about the present-day political systems of the countries mentioned in the essay.

Pair Students pair up and discuss the questions they wrote. They choose the two best questions to research. Together they decide where they might begin looking for information to answer the questions. They then conduct their research.

Share The students in each pair take turns reporting to the class about their research.

Debrief the Content Ask: *What did you learn about the country and its political system from your research?*

Debrief the Cooperative Process Have students think about how their ideas for researching political systems changed when they discussed them with a partner. Ask: *When planning research, do you agree that two heads are better than one? Why or why not?*

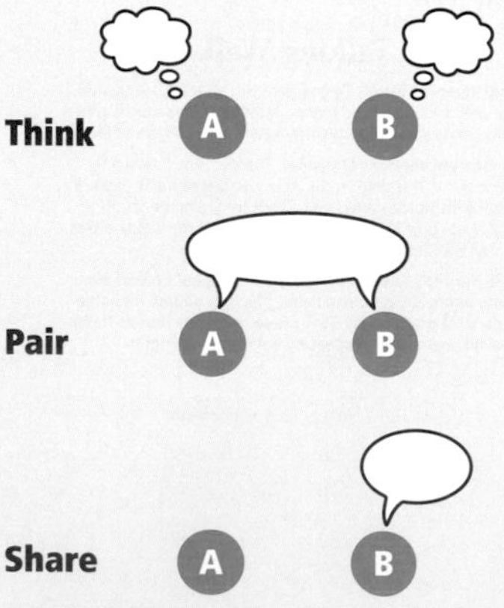

Cooperative Learning Structure: Think, Pair, Share

POINT-BY-POINT

Walls Around the World

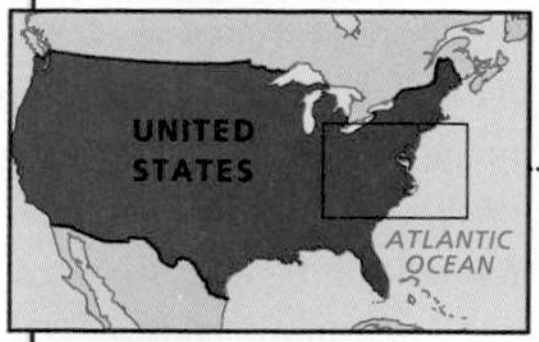

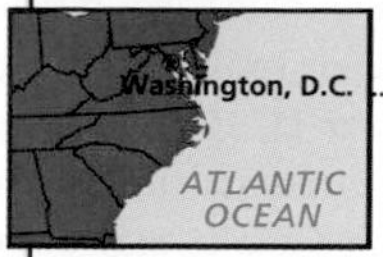

What The Vietnam Veterans Memorial by Maya Lin

Where Washington, D.C.

Message Honor the Americans who died in the Vietnam War.

text features: Read the caption.
: Who designed the Vietnam Veterans
morial? What else has she done?

ya Lin is an American architect well known her public works. Her design for the Vietnam erans Memorial shows the names of 58,156 erican men and women chiseled into black nite. It was chosen over 1,400 other entries. also designed the Civil Rights Monument in ntgomery, Alabama.

BEFORE YOU MOVE ON...

1. **Cause and Effect** How did the Vietnam War start?
2. **Opinion** Do you think the Vietnam Veterans Memorial sends a message that matters? Explain your answer.

REVIEW KEY VOCABULARY

3 **Use New Words in Context** Invite students to write sentences with blanks for key vocabulary words. Encourage them to include all words listed on page 24. Then have them exchange papers with a partner. Partners fill the blanks with key vocabulary words and discuss their answers with the writer.

CHECK COMPREHENSION

4 **Answers to "Before You Move On"**

1. **Cause and Effect** After Vietnam gained independence from France, two separate governments formed and fought a civil war.
2. **Opinion** Students' responses will vary and should be supported by details.

CLOSE AND ASSESS

Ask students what they would tell someone from another country about the importance of the Vietnam Veterans Memorial to the people of the United States.

Mathematics Connection

MEASUREMENT

Have students compare the length of the Vietnam Veterans Memorial with a known length, such as that of a paper clip. They can measure how many paper clips, laid end to end, equals a foot. Then, using information included in the text, they figure out how many paper clips would be needed to stretch a chain of paper clips along the length of the memorial. Extend the activity by having them determine how many boxes of clips they would need, given the number per box.

Grammar Minilesson

▶ SINGULAR AND PLURAL NOUNS

TEACH Draw students' attention to the first sentence on page 28. *Flowers, letters, candles, and boots are lovingly placed under the names written on the Vietnam Veterans Memorial, in Washington, D.C.*

Remind students that most nouns can be counted. They have a singular form that means "one" and a plural form that means "more than one." Ask students to identify six nouns in the sentence that are in the plural form.

Refer students to page 433 in the Handbook to review the rules for forming plurals.

PRACTICE Write these words. Have students change the singular nouns to plural nouns.

1. wall
2. tooth
3. fox
4. lunch
5. puppy
6. person

Then have students write the plural nouns on page 28 and their singular forms.

READ PAGES 30–31

OBJECTIVES

Function: Read a Selection
Grammar: Possessive Nouns
Listening: Listen to a Selection
Reading and Learning Strategies: Set a Purpose for Reading; Ⓣ Relate Main Idea and Details; Use Graphic Organizers (chart)
Comprehension: Ⓣ Identify Main Idea and Details; Make an Inference
Literary Analysis: Evaluate Impact of Author's Background on Meaning

SET PURPOSE

1 Set the purpose for reading: *As you read this part of the selection, compare the creation of this wall with the creation of the other two walls.*

READ AND THINK

Tape 1A
CD 1 Track 2

2 **Strategy Focus: Relate Main Idea and Details** Involve students in reading pages 30 and 31.

See the **Multi-Level Strategies** on page T26 to tailor the reading experience to proficiency levels.

PABLO NERUDA'S GATE

Pause to show the location on the Point-by-Point map, page 31.

Thousands of messages have been written on the fence that **surrounds** the Isla Negra home of Chilean poet Pablo Neruda. Many of the messages **praise** and thank Neruda for writing beautiful poetry and for speaking out for **human rights**.

Neruda didn't like it when a military government **took over** his country on September 11, 1973. A few weeks later he died, and the new military leader of Chile **warned** people to stay away from Neruda's home. However, for seventeen years people came **secretly** to write on the fence of the poet who as a child was known to say he was "hunting for poems."

When he was ten, Neruda showed one of his poems to his father. The father was so surprised by the beautiful words that he asked his son who really wrote the poem. Neruda's father thought that his son spent too much time writing poetry, and Pablo's schoolmates often made fun of him. But Pablo couldn't stop writing, and at thirtee his first poems were **published**. Three ye later, he **took the pen name** Pablo Neru He chose Neruda after one of his favorite Czechoslovakian poets.

Ask: How did Pablo's father and his schoolmates feel about his writing poetry?

Ask: Why do you think people were told to stay away from Neruda's home? Why did they come?

Today, the government of Chile is free elected and is proud of Neruda's **legacy**. Neruda's admirers continue to visit his home to write **tributes** to the boy who grew up to become one of the greatest poets in the world.

Restate: Today, people can freely wr notes on Neruda's gate, and they sti honor his memory.

Pablo Neruda won the Nobel Prize for Literature in 1971. This prize is awarded each year to the writer or poet who has given "the greatest benefit to mankind" through his or her work.

surrounds goes around
praise say nice things about, give many compliments to
human rights equality, justice, and fair treatment for all people
took over took control of
warned said in a way that caused fear in
secretly without anybody seeing or knowing about it
published printed in a book
took the pen name changed his name as a poet to
benefit to mankind gift to all people in the world

30 Unit 1 | Communication

REACHING ALL STUDENTS

COMMUNITY CONNECTION

Walls in Your Neighborhood Have students take a walking tour of their neighborhood in small groups. Ask them to note, sketch, or photograph walls that are painted, decorated or have messages written on them. For each wall, students should note the wall's location, how the wall is decorated, and what message the wall sends. Have students use the information they gathered to create a guided tour of their neighborhood, including a map and a suggested route.

Vocabulary
ARTISTS AND WORKS OF ART

Materials: dictionaries

Make a two-column chart. Label the first column "Works of Art" and the second "Artists." Help students fill in the terms for the works of art and the artists in the three sections of this selection. (mural/muralist, monument/architect, poem/poet) Then ask students to work in small groups. Have each group think of other types of art and fill in more pairs of examples on the chart. Invite them to use dictionaries if they wish.

POINT-BY-POINT

Walls Around the World

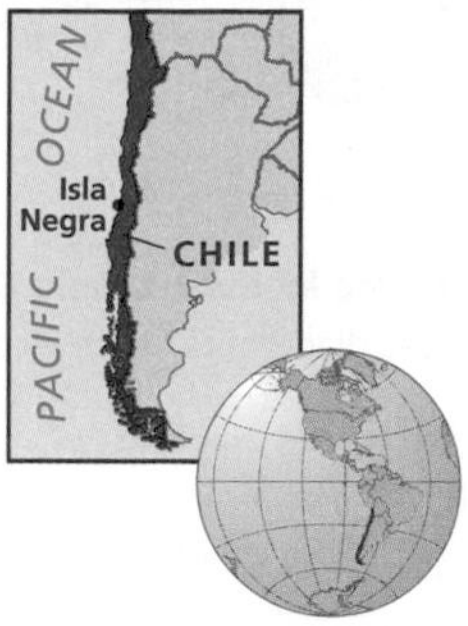

What The gate to Pablo Neruda's House

Where Isla Negra, Chile

Message Honor and respect one of the world's great poets.

BEFORE YOU MOVE ON...

1. **Main Idea and Details** Find three details to support this main idea: Neruda began to write at an early age.
2. **Inference** Why do you think the people of Chile still love and admire Neruda?

ABOUT THE AUTHOR

Margy Burns Knight is from Winthrop, Maine, where she teaches English as a Second Language. She served as a Peace Corps Volunteer in Nigeria and as a teacher in Switzerland. Her concern for her students' need for geographical knowledge and understanding of other cultures led her to write the book *Talking Walls.*

CHECK COMPREHENSION

3 Answers to "Before You Move On"

1. **Main Idea and Details** As a child, Neruda was always hunting for poems. Even at ten years of age, Neruda wrote beautiful poetry. At thirteen, his first book of poems was published.
2. **Inference** Answers should include the idea that people admire Neruda's courage for speaking out for human rights and against a military government.

ABOUT THE AUTHOR

4 Evaluate Literature: Author's Background Read aloud About the Author. Ask: *Why do you think the author wrote a book about walls in different parts of the world? How could her book help young people learn about other cultures? About geography?*

CLOSE AND ASSESS

Have students return to the unit mind map they began on page T9 and add more examples of verbal and nonverbal communication to the T-chart.

CULTURAL PERSPECTIVES

U.S. Culture: Murals Collect photos or obtain books that include works of American muralists, such as Aaron Douglas or Thomas Hart Benton. Display the murals and have students identify what is happening in each. Provide information about the muralists and their murals. Work together to identify the main idea of each mural and conclude what message it sends about U.S. culture.

Grammar Minilesson

▶ POSSESSIVE NOUNS

TEACH Draw attention to the possessive nouns in the sentence on page 30 that begins *Neruda's father. . . .* Explain that a possessive noun always has an apostrophe. The placement of the apostrophe depends on whether there is one or more than one owner.

One Owner	More Than One Owner
the poet's words	the poets' words
the boy's pictures	the boys' pictures

Use Handbook page 436 to review the rules for forming possessives. Model forming possessives for different owners:

The blue car belongs to my parents.

My parents' car is blue.

PRACTICE Have students use the information below to form possessives and then use each phrase in a sentence.

1. the poems belong to one boy
2. the happiness of all the students
3. the success belongs to one poet

RESPOND

OBJECTIVES

SUM IT UP
Function: Write
Reading and Learning Strategies: Ⓣ Relate Main Idea and Details; Use Graphic Organizers (main idea diagram)
Writing: Paragraph

THINK IT OVER
Function: Engage in Discussion
Critical Thinking and Comprehension: Identify Cause and Effect; Ⓣ Make Comparisons; Draw Conclusions; Make Judgments

EXPRESS YOURSELF
Function: Ⓣ Express Opinions
Speaking and Listening: Oral Presentation

CHECK YOUR UNDERSTANDING

1 **Sum It Up** Students can use the notes taken during reading to complete the main idea diagrams. Sample entries on page 32 show possible answers for the Rivera diagram.

▶ **Practice Book** page 10

2 **Think It Over** Possible answers are:

1. **Cause and Effect** Talking walls record history, honor people, and communicate important messages.
2. **Comparison** Answers will vary. All of the walls honor the work, sacrifices, and ideas of those for whom they were made.
3. **Conclusions** Answers will vary. Encourage students to think of images that reflect their perspective.
4. **Judgments** Answers will vary. Use prompts: *What leaders do you admire? Who are your heroes?*

3 **Express Yourself** Prompt the use of new vocabulary in students' responses.

CLOSE AND ASSESS

Ask students to write in their notebooks one thing they learned about communication from this lesson.

Respond to the Essay

Check Your Understanding

SUM IT UP

Relate Main Ideas and Details Make a main idea diagram for each section of the essay.

Main Idea Diagram

Write a Paragraph Use the main idea diagram to write a paragraph. A paragraph is a group of sentences that all tell about the same idea. One sentence gives the **main idea** of the paragraph. The other sentences give details that support the main idea.

Example:

Diego Rivera's Murals

Diego Rivera painted walls to celebrate Mexico's history. He painted people hard at work. He also painted people fighting for their rights. Rivera got some of his inspiration from ancient murals of Teotihuacán.

THINK IT OVER

Discuss and Write Talk about these questio with a partner. Write the answers.

1. **Cause and Effect** Why have people in the and in the present created talking walls? W are they important?
2. **Comparison** How do you think viewers fee about each of the talking walls in the essay How are each of their messages similar?
3. **Conclusions** If you were a painter or archit how would you represent the people of th U.S. in a mural? Why?
4. **Judgments** Imagine that you could leave a message on the fence of someone whom y admire. Whose fence would it be? Explain what tribute you would write and why.

EXPRESS YOURSELF ▶EXPRESS OPINION

Tell a group about your favorite wall from the essay. Give three reasons that tell why you like that wall. Think about the way it looks, how i makes you feel, and the message it gives.

✔ **LANGUAGE ACQUISITION ASSESSMENT**
See page 1 of the Assessment Handbook.

32 **Unit 1** | Communication

REACHING ALL STUDENTS

Multi-Level Strategies

SUM IT UP OPTIONS

BEGINNING Review the notes on **Transparency 5** (see page T27) and have students point to the most important idea. Work together to turn it into a main idea sentence or provide a sentence frame: *The wall created by Maya Lin honors* _____. Also provide frames for adding details: *The wall shows* _____.

INTERMEDIATE Display **Transparency 5** (see page T27) with students' notes. Have them work with a partner to complete their diagrams. Ask each pair to choose one wall and write a short summary paragraph about it. Have partners share their paragraphs in small groups.

ADVANCED Students use their notes on copies of **Master 5** (see page T27) to complete their diagrams. They then write a paragraph about each wall and share their paragraphs with the class.

ASSESSMENT
Selection Test 2 on page 5 of the Assessment Handbook tests students' mastery of the reading strategies and the vocabulary, comprehension, and language arts skills taught with this selection.

nguage Arts and Literature

GRAMMAR IN CONTEXT

E SUBJECTS AND PREDICATES

arn About Simple Subject and Simple edicate Every sentence has two main parts— e subject and the predicate.

The **subject** tells whom or what the sentence is about. The **complete subject** includes all the words that tell about the subject. The **simple subject** is the most important word in the complete subject.

Some painters create murals.

The **predicate** tells what the subject is, has, or does. The **complete predicate** includes all the words in the predicate. The **simple predicate** is the verb.

A mural **is a painting on a wall.**
It **has a lot of room for big scenes.**
Diego Rivera **painted many murals.**

actice Write each sentence. Add a subject for ch black line and a verb for each red line.

Maya Lin ________ the Vietnam Veterans Memorial.

The long, black ________ rises out of the earth.

Every day, many people ________ the wall.

Some ________ leave mementos at the foot of the wall.

VOCABULARY

USE CONTEXT CLUES

Learn About Context Clues Sometimes you can use **context clues** to understand new words. One type of context clue gives an example of the word:

Farmers are some of the **characters** that Rivera portrayed in his murals.

The word *farmers* is an example of a character. *Characters* must mean "people in a painting."

Another type of context clue contrasts one word with another. Signal words such as *but, however,* and *instead* can introduce a contrast:

Rivera showed the people's **fortitude** instead of their weak side.

Fortitude is in contrast with the word *weak*. It must mean "strength."

Practice Use context clues to figure out the meanings of the underlined words. Then tell which kind of clue you used for each word.

1. The farmers planted, weeded, and watered the crops. They labored all day long.
2. In Rivera's time, many people lived in the countryside. Today, however, the majority of people live in urban areas.
3. Life in Mexico City is very mechanized, but people still do some chores by hand.

Research Skills

▶ USING THE DICTIONARY

TEACH Display a dictionary page and explain that dictionaries contain an alphabetical listing of words and their meanings. Walk students through a dictionary entry, pointing out guide words; entry words; pronunciations; information about plurals, verb tenses, and parts of speech; definitions; and related forms. Then model using the dictionary to find word meanings.

PRACTICE After students complete the Vocabulary Practice on page 33, ask them to use a dictionary to find information about the underlined words. For each word, they identify:

- the base word
- the part of speech for its use
- the definition

▶ **Practice Book** page 13

RESPOND

OBJECTIVES

SUBJECTS AND PREDICATES
Grammar: Ⓣ Subjects and Predicates
CONTEXT CLUES
Vocabulary Strategy: Ⓣ Context Clues
Research Skills: Use the Dictionary

LANGUAGE ARTS AND LITERATURE

1 Use Subjects and Predicates Suggested answers to Practice items are:

1. designed
2. wall
3. visit
4. visitors

▶ **Practice Book** page 11

2 Use Context Clues Work through the examples with students. Remind them to look for examples or contrasts for the unfamiliar words. Answers are:

1. labored = worked (example clues: *planted, weeded, watered*)
2. urban = crowded, city (contrast clue: *countryside*)
3. mechanized = run by machines (contrast clue: *by hand*)

▶ **Practice Book** page 12

CLOSE AND ASSESS

Ask students to choose one of the underlined words from the Vocabulary Practice and use it in a new sentence. Then have them underline the simple subject of the sentence and circle the simple predicate.

RESPOND

OBJECTIVES

CLASSROOM WALL ART

Learning Strategies and Critical Thinking: Generate Ideas; Interact with Peers; Plan; Make Decisions

Representing: Mural

MINIATURE MONUMENT

Function: Demonstrate Non-Verbal Communication

Learning Strategies and Critical Thinking: Generate Ideas; Interact with Peers; Plan

Representing: Model

CONTENT AREA CONNECTIONS

1 **Create Classroom Wall Art** Before creating the mural, students should discuss the overall design and make a scale drawing of each part. Remind students that they may use original art, photographs, or pictures from magazines in their mural. Have students think of an appropriate title for their wall.

2 **Create a Miniature Monument** Guide students through the steps provided. When the monuments are completed, groups make a presentation to the class. Presentations should include whom or what the monument honors and the message the monument communicates.

Respond to the Essay, continued

Content Area Connections

FINE ARTS

MATHEMATICS

CREATE CLASSROOM WALL ART

Follow these steps to create a "talking wall" in your classroom.

1. **Plan Your Wall Project** Answer these questions:
   - What topic do we want to explore?
   - What message do we want to communicate?
   - Will we communicate with pictures or words or both?

   Have a volunteer record decisions.
2. **Prepare the Space** Measure the area of your talking wall. Cover the area with paper. Divide it into equal spaces for each group. Then draw light pencil lines on the paper to show each group's space.
3. **Design and Create** With your group, draw a sketch of your part of the mural. Work with other groups to plan how the different parts will go together. Each group should take turns creating its part of the talking wall.
4. **Present Your Mural** Invite visitors to view the wall. Explain what each part means.

MATHEMATICS

SOCIAL STUDIES

CREATE A MINIATURE MONUMENT

Make a monument to honor a person or event

1. **Choose a Subject** Work with a group. Choose a person or event that you would li to honor. It should be an event or person th you feel strongly about.
2. **Think About Form** Think about the effect that the form of your monument will have viewers. For example, the designer of the Vietnam Veterans Memorial chose polished black stone to create a sense of peace and provide a quiet space to think about the los of lives.
3. **Design the Monument** Draw a sketch of the monument. Give measurements for all it sides. If you want an inscription (short text) appear on your monument, be sure to write the text and to show where it goes.
4. **Make and Display a Model** Use your sketch to build a model of the monument. Each group can display its model in a "gallery." Invite visitors to take a guided tour of the gallery.

The Washington Monument

REACHING ALL STUDENTS

Multi-Level Strategies

OPTIONS FOR CREATING CLASSROOM WALL ART

BEGINNING Brainstorm ideas for the wall art. Make notes, restating the students' ideas in simple phrases. Help students choose an idea and decide how to illustrate it. Ask yes/no or short-answer questions about the next steps: *Who will draw the tree? Do you want more than one tree? What words will you write under the tree?*

INTERMEDIATE Ask students to list several ideas for the wall art and then vote to pick one or two to work on. Prompt students to choose roles for themselves, such as Project Leaders, Writers, and Artists.

ADVANCED Have students work as a group to decide on a topic and message for the wall art. Then invite them to describe the purpose they had in mind and outline the steps they went through in creating their work of art.

NOLOGY/MEDIA

AL STUDIES

:E A PRESENTATION ABOUT OUS WALLS

he Internet or other resources to learn t more walls around the world. Then make sentation to share what you learned. Follow steps.

cate Information These Web sites might e good places to start, but remember that ew sites appear every day! Use key words in ur search and look for links.

INTERNET

INFORMATION ON-LINE

Key Words:
murals
monuments
memorials

Web Sites:

- **Murals**
  - www.diegorivera.com
  - www.lamurals.org
- **Information about Monuments and Memorials**
  - www.britannica.com
  - www.yahooligans.com

ownload information, take notes, and draw ‹etches to prepare your presentation.

2 Organize Your Information Make a chart that gives information about each wall:

Walls Around the World

Name	Location	Date	Purpose
Great Wall	China	about 214 BCE	to protect China from invaders
Berlin Wall	Berlin, Germany	1961	to separate West Berlin from East Berlin

3 Present Your Findings Evaluate the information in your chart and make comparisons. Find pictures or make sketches of each wall. Add captions. Then display the pictures and point to them as you talk about the walls.

For more information on the **research process**, see Handbook pages 394–399.

OBJECTIVES

FAMOUS WALLS

Function: Give Information

Learning Strategies, Critical Thinking, and Research Skills: Use the Library; Locate Resources; Gather Information; Take Notes; Use Graphic Organizer (chart); T Make Comparisons

Speaking: Oral Report

Technology/Media: Use the Internet

Representing: Chart; Pictures; Oral Report

Writing: Captions

3 Make a Presentation About Famous Walls Student reports should include the following information:

- the names and locations of the walls
- descriptions of the walls
- when the walls were created and why

Encourage the class to ask any questions they have about the walls and to provide positive feedback.

CLOSE AND ASSESS

Ask students to write on an exit slip two things they've learned from each activity.

Research Skills

USING THE LIBRARY AND LOCATING RESOURCES

TEACH Remind students that the library has books and other resources that are organized so they can be found easily. Explain what resources are found in each of these sections of the library:

- nonfiction
- periodicals
- reference materials: dictionaries, encyclopedia, atlases, almanacs

Tell students that every book is listed in the library's catalog with information that will help them locate it.

PRACTICE Have students name the resource(s) they could use to find:

- a map showing the location of the Great Wall of China
- pictures of Diego Rivera's murals
- tomorrow's weather forecast

Have students go to the library and locate resources for the research project on walls.

INTRODUCE THEME 2

OBJECTIVES

Function: Engage in Discussion
Concepts and Vocabulary: Communication—*messages, connect*
Viewing: Interpret a Visual Image
Learning Strategies: Relate to Personal Experience; Use Graphic Organizers (chart)
Critical Thinking: Ⓣ Make Comparisons; Generate Ideas

TAP PRIOR KNOWLEDGE

1 Compare Messages Make a class list of messages students know about and messages they have read about so far in the unit. (letter to a father, love letter, notes on Neruda's gate, Rivera's murals, etc.)

Divide the class into four heterogeneous teams. Assign a category to each team: long ago messages, recent messages, far away messages, nearby messages. Ask each group to record examples from the class list in its category. Then, combine the four categories into a time and space chart. Point out how each example can appear in more than one space in the chart.

Long ago messages	Recent messages
• Cave drawings	• Neruda's gate
Far away messages	**Nearby messages**
• Neruda's gate	•

VIEW AND DISCUSS

2 Discuss Communication Devices Invite students to view the collage. Have them identify the communication devices and explain their uses.

See the annotation on page T37 for a list of devices and their uses portrayed on page 36.

Use the Activity Options in the **Multi-Level Strategies** to involve all students.

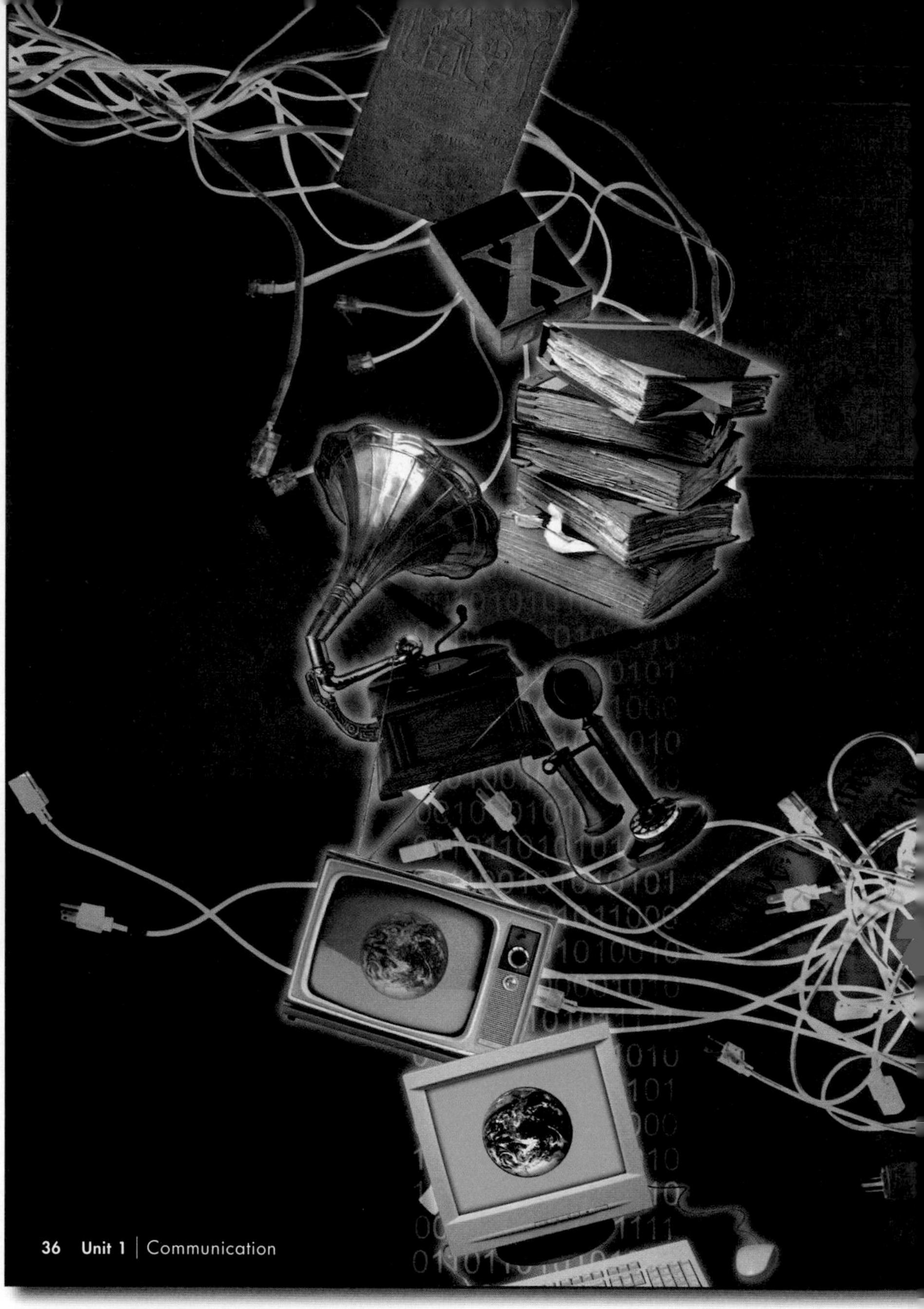

REACHING ALL STUDENTS

Multi-Level Strategies

ACTIVITY OPTIONS

BEGINNING Discuss the objects pictured. Prompt students to point to and name each device they recognize. Then write the names of unfamiliar devices and have students copy them. Explain uses of unfamiliar devices.

INTERMEDIATE / **ADVANCED** Suggest that students work in pairs, identifying familiar objects in the picture and explaining their uses. Then students should speculate on the names and uses of unfamiliar items. Finally, write the names of unfamiliar objects and have students look them up in a dictionary or an encyclopedia to determine their uses. Confirm or correct their findings.

rify: From top to
tom, the devices
l their uses are:
ephone connector
le, to connect
ephones devices;
yptian slate
wing, to record
torical information;
nting block, to
nt letters on
per; ledgers, to
re bookkeeping
ormation;
mophone, to play
unds recorded on
stic disks; early
ephone; computer
d electrical cords,
connect electronic
vices to power
urces and to each
ner; television set;
mputer monitor;
use and keyboard.
the background,
ckwise from upper
: analog clock,
yptian calendar,
ly English page of
nt, binary code
ntout.

Annotations offer strategies for
B Beginning students

THEME 2

Messages Across Time and Space

- What kinds of messages have been left behind from other times and other places?
- What forms do messages take today? How do they connect us to other people? **B Pose choices:** Which forms of messages didn't exist in the past—e-mail, movies, television, and radio, for example.
- Why do you think some messages remain important for many years while others are forgotten?
  B Clarify: What ideas do people want to remember a long time?

B Explain: We have all learned a great deal about the world and its history from messages, for example: books, newspapers, letters, paintings, photographs.

HEME-RELATED BOOKS

adio Man
y Arthur Dorros

e radio keeps Diego connected to e world while he's on the move. In glish and Spanish.

BEGINNING

Aesop's Fox
retold by Aki Sogabe

Several of Aesop's timeless fables are combined into a single tale about a day in the life of Aesop's fox.

INTERMEDIATE

The Adventures of Sojourner
by Susi Trautmann Wunsch

The story of the spacecraft *Sojourner*: its historic trip to Mars and the images it sent back to Earth.

ADVANCED

37

DISCUSS THE GUIDING QUESTIONS

3 Set the Theme Some key points to develop during the discussion are:

- Messages from other times and places have been left behind in the form of letters, books, paintings, and photographs. Buildings also say something about the people who built and used them; songs and stories tell us about the cultures that created them.
- Today we use telephones, fax machines, and the Internet to deliver many of our messages. We are often connected to other people through technology.
- Some messages are remembered for their delivery: thrilling speeches, moving letters, and beautiful works of art. Other messages are remembered because of their context: Paul Revere's call to arms; Edison's first telephone connection; Neil Armstrong's first message from the moon.

Form groups and use the **Multi-Level Strategies** so all students can participate.

CLOSE AND ASSESS

Ask students to give an example of a memorable message that was sent from far away or created long ago.

Multi-Level Strategies

GROUPING GUIDELINES

BEGINNING Group students so you can define words and pose choices for responses. See suggestions in red on the facsimile for page 37.

INTERMEDIATE Organize students into three groups. Ask each group to discuss the answer to one question and make notes on their discussion. Then have the groups present their results to the class.

ADVANCED Ask students to give specific examples to support their answers. Then they share answers, listing as many examples for each question as they can.

THEME LIBRARY

■ ***Aesop's Fox*** by Aki Sogabe

Invite students to read *Aesop's Fox* and, with a partner, identify the timeless messages Fox learns in the course of his day. Partners can discuss how these messages could be applied to their lives today. Invite students to "grade" the book, based on class-developed criteria (importance of the message, appeal of characters, interest in plot, etc.). Encourage them to grade each selection in the theme and other books they read.

BUILD LANGUAGE AND VOCABULARY

OBJECTIVES

Function: Ⓣ Make Comparisons
Concepts and Vocabulary: Words About Communication
Patterns and Structures: Ⓣ Compound Sentences
Viewing: Interpret Visual Information
Learning Strategy: Use Graphic Organizers (chart)
Critical Thinking: Make Comparisons
Writing: Compound Sentences

START WITH A COMMON EXPERIENCE

Tape 1A
CD 1 Track 2

1 **Listen, Imagine, and Recite** Play the recording of the poem or read it aloud and ask students to talk about its message. Read the poem again while students close their eyes and visualize what it would be like to stand in the canyon, listening to the echo of the voices from long ago. Have students recite the poem as a group.

Use the Reciting Options in the **Multi-Level Strategies** to include students at all proficiency levels.

2 **View and Make Comparisons** Have students view the petroglyph and describe what they see. Then model how to make an effective comparison.

How to Make a Comparison

- Choose two subjects: *The page shows a petroglyph and a poem.*
- Tell how the two subjects are alike: *Both have messages that express thoughts and feelings.*
- Tell how the two subjects are different: *The poem has words on paper. The petroglyph has drawings on rock walls.*
- Use words that help compare: *both, either, neither, too.*

Build Language and Vocabulary

MAKE COMPARISONS

View the photo and read the poem. Hundreds of years ago, Native Americans drew images on rocks and on the walls of caves. What message do you get from this poem?

from
Before You Came This Way

Did they ever
wonder
who
in some far later time
would stand
in their
canyon
and think of them
and ALMOST hear
the echo of those voices
still in the wind?

—*Byrd Baylor*

REACHING ALL STUDENTS

Multi-Level Strategies

RECITING OPTIONS

BEGINNING Divide the poem into small segments. Lead beginners to echo each line of the poem after you say it: *Did they ever* (Did they ever); *wonder who* (wonder who). . . . After reciting the poem in segments several times, invite students to recite the entire poem as a group.

INTERMEDIATE Invite students to read with expression, for example, speaking more loudly for the word written in capital letters. Conduct alternate recitation with the teacher reciting one line and students the next. Trade roles and recite again.

ADVANCED Have students learn the poem by heart and take turns reciting it for the class.

AKE A COMMUNICATION CHART

ink about the ways people send and leave messages for others. Work with a
oup to make a chart. List both old and new forms of communication.

Forms of Communication

Written	Spoken	Other
e-mail	tape recording	time capsule
letter	storytelling	cave painting

JILD YOUR VOCABULARY

ords About Communication Collect words to compare two different rms of communication. You may want to compare written and spoken forms communication. Or you may choose to compare a form used in the past th one used today.

Form of Communication	Tools Used	Where Message Is Found	How Sent
cave paintings	sticks, plants	cave walls	can't be sent
e-mail	computer	computer, printer	Internet

SE LANGUAGE STRUCTURES ▸ COMPOUND SENTENCES

Word Bank

and
but
or
nor
yet

riting: Compare Forms of Communication Write compound sentences tell how two forms of communication are alike and different. Use onjunctions from the **Word Bank**.

Examples:

Drawings are often used to communicate. Cave paintings were made up of drawings, **and** even today's e-mail can include them.

Messages on the walls of caves could not be sent to anyone, **but** e-mail messages can be sent to many people in the world.

CONDUCT THE ACTIVITIES

3 Make a Communication Chart Have students work in groups and then share their lists to create a class communication chart.

4 Build Your Vocabulary: Words About Communication Have students use their communication charts to help them choose forms of communication to compare.

5 Use Language Structures: Compound Sentences Present the skill, using the definitions and examples on **Transparency 6**. Remind students to use a comma before a conjunction in a compound sentence. Then have students turn the sentence pairs into compound sentences in Try It!

Writing: Compare Forms of Communication Conduct the activity at the bottom of page 39. Suggest that students use ideas from their comparison charts.

Use the Writing Activity Options in the **Multi-Level Strategies** to adjust instruction.

▶ **Practice Book** page 14

CLOSE AND ASSESS

Have students tell what a compound sentence is. Then ask them to finish one of these sentences: *I love receiving e-mail, but I _____. I love receiving e-mail, and I _____.*

Multi-Level Strategies

BRAINSTORM PROMPTS

BEGINNING Have students combine two simple sentences to create one compound sentence: *Poets tell stories with words. Artists use drawings to tell stories.* Provide this sentence frame and have students add a conjunction: *Poets tell stories with words, _____ artists use drawings.*

INTERMEDIATE Have students work in pairs to ask each other questions based on their communication charts. Encourage students to write their answers as compound sentences. *What are forms of written communication? Writing letters is one form, and sending e-mail is another.*

ADVANCED Encourage students to write three or more compound sentences about communication, each one using a different conjunction.

Transparency 6 / Master 6

LEARN ABOUT COMPOUND SENTENCES

1. A **clause** has a subject and a verb. An **independent clause** can stand alone as a sentence.

   Juan writes poetry.   Pam paints portraits.

2. A compound sentence is made up of two independent clauses. The clauses are joined by a **conjunction**.

   Juan writes poetry, (independent clause) **and** Pam paints portraits. (independent clause)

3. When you put two ideas that are alike together, use **and**.

   I wrote an e-mail to my parents, **and** my sister did, too.

   When you want to show a difference between two ideas, use **but**.

   I love television, **but** my sister prefers books.

   When you want to show a choice between two ideas, use **or**.

   You can send me an e-mail, **or** you can send me a letter.

Try It!

Choose *and, but,* or *or* to join each pair of sentences. Write the compound sentence.

1. We can make sand sculptures. We can make fish prints.
2. Ernie likes video games. I prefer crossword puzzles.
3. Sarah can write poetry. She can play the saxophone.

Transparency 6 **Level B, Unit 1** | Communication

PREPARE TO READ

OBJECTIVES

THINK ABOUT WHAT YOU KNOW
Reading Strategy: Activate Prior Knowledge
LEARN KEY VOCABULARY Ⓣ
Vocabulary Strategy: Relate Words
LEARN TO MAKE COMPARISONS
Reading Strategy: Ⓣ Make Comparisons

THINK ABOUT WHAT YOU KNOW

1 **Share Folk Tales** Ask students to share folk tales they've heard on similar topics, such as animals or weather.

LEARN KEY VOCABULARY

2 **Relate Words** Have students read each vocabulary word and its definition. Then conduct the activity.

Use Vocabulary Options in the **Multi-Level Strategies** to tailor the activity to all proficiency levels.

▶ **Practice Book** page 15

LEARN TO MAKE COMPARISONS

3 **Model How to Make Comparisons** Compare the Rivera mural and the Vietnam Veterans Memorial from "Talking Walls" to model the steps in the box. Record information on **Transparency 7**:

- Show students how to survey a list of details about the mural and the memorial to find what they have in common. List those details in the overlap.
- Then list the differences in the spaces at the left and right.
- Show students how to incorporate information about similarities and differences in the summary.

CLOSE AND ASSESS

Ask students how making comparisons helps them understand what they read. (It helps organize information.)

Tales Across Time

Prepare to Read

folk tales retold
by Dawn Lippert and
Margaret H. Lippert

THINK ABOUT WHAT YOU KNOW

Share Folk Tales Work with a group. Each person tells a folk tale. How are the folk tales alike? How are they different?

grain seed of wheat or other cereal grasses
granary place where grain is stored
harvest gather crops when they are ripe
kernel seed of corn or wheat
kingdom country controlled by a king or queen
palace home of a king or queen
plantation large farm with many workers
storyteller person who tells stories
village community that is smaller than a town
villager person who lives in a village

Answers to the vocabulary activity:
People: storyteller, villager
Places: granary, palace, kingdom, plantation, village
Things: grain, kernel
Actions: harvest

LEARN KEY VOCABULARY

Relate Words Study the new words and their definitions. Make a chart. Write each vocabulary word in the correct column.

People	Places	Things	Actions
storyteller	palace		

LEARN TO MAKE COMPARISONS

When you **make comparisons**, you look to see how things are alike and how they are different. This strategy will help you organize information.

READING STRATEGY
How to Make Comparisons

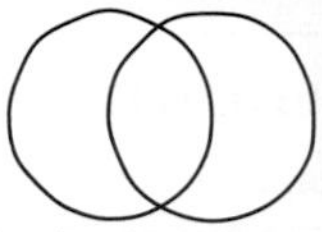

1. A Venn diagram is one way to show how two things compare.
2. In the space where the circles overlap, list the ways the two things are alike.
3. List the differences in the two outer spaces.
4. Write a summary statement that explains how the two things are alike and different.

As you read, think about how the two folk tales in "Tales Across Time" are alike and different.

REACHING ALL STUDENTS

Multi-Level Strategies

VOCABULARY OPTIONS

BEGINNING Group students to read ***A Year Without Rain*** or the Key Points Reading on **Master 8**. (See page T43.) Work with the vocabulary in those selections.

INTERMEDIATE Ask students to work in pairs to decide where to place each vocabulary word in the chart.

ADVANCED Ask students to complete the activity on their own. They should then compare charts with a partner.

Transparency 7 / Master 7

HOW TO MAKE COMPARISONS

Directions: Fill in the names of the two items being compared. In the middle, list how the items are alike. List the differences in the two outer spaces. Write a summary at the bottom.

Item 1	Both	Item 2
Diego Rivera's Mural		Vietnam Veterans Memorial
made by an artist in Mexico	honor people	made by an architecture student in Washington, D.C.
a series of pictures inside a building	bring out strong feelings	a list of names outdoors

Summary: Both walls were created to honor people. Both bring out strong feelings. The mural is a series of pictures inside a building in Mexico. The memorial is a list of names on an outdoor monument in the United States.

Transparency 7 Level B, Unit 1 | Communication © Hampton-Brown

Tales Across Time

by Dawn Lippert and Margaret H. Lippert

Stories and storytellers are as old as time. Though they may travel across many cultures, some stories can be surprisingly similar. The folk tales that follow have been retold by a modern mother-and-daughter storytelling team, yet they carry ideas and values from the past that are still important today.

41

READ THE SELECTION

OBJECTIVES

Reading Strategies: Preview; Predict
Literary Analysis: Folk Tale

INTRODUCE THE SELECTION

4 Preview and Predict Read aloud the title, authors' names, and introduction to the folk tales. Ask students to look at and describe the illustration. Ask: *What do you think these stories will be about?* Then have students page through the selection, reading the introduction for each folk tale.

5 Identify Genre: Folk Tale Explain that the stories in this selection are folk tales. Identify their key elements: folk tales are based on the traditional myths or stories of a culture; they teach a lesson or illustrate a belief; they have been passed on from one generation to the next.

Tales Across Time
by Dawn Lippert and
Margaret H. Lippert

Theme Connection These modern versions of two ancient folk tales provide a connection across time with the ancient cultures of Ethiopia and Spain.

Selection Summary The introduction on page 41 of the student book offers a summary of this selection.

Background and Awards Whereas early folk tales in Ethiopia focused on religious themes and the lore of origins of the country, present-day folk tales tell fictitious stories with a moral. The authors of the book from which these folk tales were taken have won the Best Book for Older Readers Award from the African Studies Association, and the Aesop Award from the American Folklore Society.

THE BASICS BOOKSHELF

- ***A Year Without Rain*** by Shirleyann Costigan

This story, set in ancient China, tells a timeless tale about generosity and sharing in a time of drought. Beautiful art supports the patterned text, which includes number words and ordinals to build basic vocabulary for beginning English learners.

For Lesson Plans: See the Teacher's Guide for ***The Basics Bookshelf***.

READ PAGES 42–43

OBJECTIVES

Function: Read a Selection
Grammar: Articles
Listening: Listen to a Selection
Reading and Learning Strategies: Set a Purpose for Reading; Ⓣ Make Comparisons; Paraphrase
Comprehension: Ⓣ Analyze Story Elements (character, plot)
Literary Analysis: Ⓣ Plot

SET PURPOSE

1 Read aloud the introduction to "The Storyteller." Set the purpose for reading: *Read to find out how the farmer wins half the kingdom.*

READ AND THINK

Tape 1B
CD 1 Track 3

2 **Strategy Focus: Make Comparisons** Have students take notes about the characters and events in each folk tale. See page T47 where students will use their notes to make a Venn diagram.

Choose Reading Options in the **Multi-Level Strategies** to tailor the reading to proficiency levels.

The recording of "Tales Across Time" on the **Selection Tape/CD** offers an oral language model and the opportunity to build reading fluency.

Red annotations offer opportunities to clarify meaning and check for understanding.

1

THE FARMER'S TALE

When an Ethiopian king holds a storytelling contest, a farmer uses her skill to tell a never-ending story. She then wins half the kingdom.

Build background: Around the world, a favorite theme in traditional tales is that of the clever problem-solver.

The Storyteller

a folk tale from Ethiopia retold by Dawn Lippert

Long ago in Ethiopia, there lived a king who loved nothing more than listening to stories. Eventually, the **storytellers** in the **kingdom** ran out of stories. So, the king sent out **a proclamation**. It said that if anyone could tell him a story until he cried "Enough, no more!" she or he would receive half the kingdom. Many storytellers came, but none could make the king shout "Enough!"

Then one day, a farmer came to the **palace** gates. The guards tried to send her away, but she **insisted on telling** the king her story. She walked up to the king's throne and began: "Once, long ago, it was harvest time on a huge wheat **plantation**. The whole **village** helped the farmer **harvest** his wheat. On the farm was a **granary** so tall you could hardly see the top. The **villagers** began to fill the granary with wheat. They were all so busy that nobody noticed a small hole at the bottom of the granary. An ant came through it and took a

Ask: Why didn't anyone notice the hole in the granary?

a proclamation an important message
insisted on telling said again and again that she must tell

REACHING ALL STUDENTS

Language Development
EXPLAIN

Present several common English proverbs or sayings like the one at the end of this tale and interpret their meanings. For example, *Haste makes waste* means "Work done too quickly usually isn't done right." Then ask students to work in groups and explain these proverbs:

A stitch in time saves nine.
The early bird catches the worm.
A penny saved is a penny earned.
Don't judge a book by its cover.

Multi-Level Strategies
READING OPTIONS FOR LESSONS 4–5

BEGINNING Students should work with ***A Year Without Rain*** while the class reads "Tales Across Time." Or distribute copies of **Master 8** (see page T43) to conduct a Key Points Reading. Students can then work as a group to list details about the characters and events in each story.

INTERMEDIATE After students listen to the stories on the **Selection Tape/CD**, ask them to make notes about the characters and the events of each story. Also encourage the use of describing words such as *clever* or *little.*

ADVANCED Have students do a paired reading of the folk tales. Both students read a few paragraphs silently. Then one student retells the section to the other. The partner listens for accuracy. Both students then agree on notes to record about the characters and events.

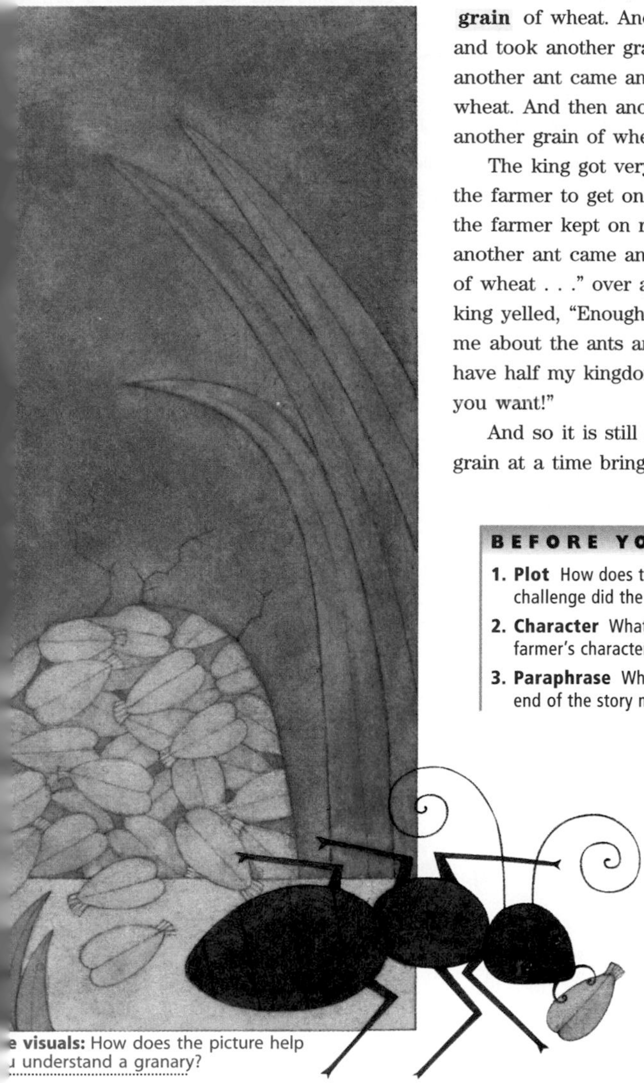

...e visuals: How does the picture help ...u understand a granary?

...noyed upset, bothered

Define *get on with*: finish quickly.

grain of wheat. And then another ant came and took another grain of wheat. And then another ant came and took another grain of wheat. And then another ant came and took another grain of wheat. . . ."

The king got very **annoyed** and asked the farmer to get on with the story but the farmer kept on repeating, "And then another ant came and took another grain of wheat . . ." over and over. Finally, the king yelled, "Enough, no more! Stop telling me about the ants and the wheat! You can have half my kingdom and whatever else you want!"

And so it is still said in Ethiopia: "One grain at a time brings good fortune."

BEFORE YOU MOVE ON...

1. **Plot** How does the story start? What challenge did the king put before his people?
2. **Character** What did you learn about the farmer's character?
3. **Paraphrase** What does the saying at the end of the story mean?

CHECK COMPREHENSION

3 Answers to "Before You Move On"

1. **Plot** The people ran out of stories to tell the king. The king offered half his kingdom to anyone who could tell a story that would make him say, "Enough, no more!"
2. **Character** Answers will vary but should include the idea that the farmer is clever and persistent.
3. **Paraphrase** Possible answers include: Slow, steady progress is the best way to accomplish something; success is achieved by thinking about one thing at a time.

CLOSE AND ASSESS

Ask students to describe a story they might tell to get the king to say "Enough, no more!"

Transparency 8 / Master 8

KEY POINTS READING

Tales Across Time

The Storyteller This is a story about a king who lives in Ethiopia. The king wants to hear a story so long that he will say, "Enough, no more!" He offers half of his money for such a story.

A farmer tells the king a story about ants. The ants take wheat, one grain at a time. It is a long, long story. Finally the king says, "Stop!" and gives the farmer the money. Today people in Ethiopia still say, "One grain at a time brings good fortune."

The Clever Goatherd This is a story about a goatherd who lives in Spain. One day he hears two women talking. One says, "The king has a daughter. She wants to marry a storyteller. He must tell a story that lasts for a year and a day."

The goatherd tells the princess a story about birds. The birds take corn from a barn, one grain at a time. It is a very long story. The princess says, "You can tell a story that lasts for a year and a day! I will marry you."

Transparency 8 Level B, Unit 1 | Communication © Hampton-Brown

Grammar Minilesson

▶ ARTICLES

TEACH Write the words *a, an,* and *the* and tell students these words often come before a noun. Give examples:

<u>An</u> ant came and took <u>a</u> grain of wheat.

<u>The</u> king got annoyed with <u>the</u> story.

Use Handbook page 435 to teach the use of *the* when referring to something specific and *a* or *an* when referring to something that is not specific.

Also use the examples on Handbook page 435 to teach the use of *an* before nouns beginning with vowel sounds and to model usage where *the* is omitted before nouns.

PRACTICE Have students complete these sentences, using *a, an,* or *the.*

1. I read _____ book of African folk tales.
2. I saw photos of _____ elephant.
3. I read about _____ tallest tree in Africa.

▶ **Practice Book** page 16

READ PAGES 44–45

OBJECTIVES

Function: Read a Selection

Vocabulary Strategy: Use New Words in Context

Listening: Listen to a Selection

Reading and Learning Strategies: Set a Purpose for Reading; Ⓣ Make Comparisons

Comprehension: Ⓣ Analyze Story Elements (character, setting)

Literary Analysis: Ⓣ Setting

SET PURPOSE

1 Read aloud the introduction to "The Clever Goatherd." Set the purpose for reading: *Find out how the goatherd manages to marry the princess.*

READ AND THINK

Tape 1B

CD 1 Track 3

2 **Strategy Focus: Make Comparisons** Involve students in reading pages 44–46 of the selection.

See the **Multi-Level Strategies** on page T42 to tailor the reading experience to proficiency levels.

2

THE GOATHERD'S TALE

A lonely goatherd learns of a contest for a story that lasts for a year and a day. The goatherd tells his tale, wins the contest, and marries the king's daughter.

The Clever Goatherd

a folk tale from Spain retold by Margaret H. Lippert

Long ago there lived a village **goatherd** named Manuel. Every morning he led his goats to a **meadow** outside the village. Although Manuel loved his goats, he was often lonely. So sometimes he invented stories **to fill the time**. **Define *invented*:** made up.

One evening he **overheard two women talking** at the village **well**. "The king has a daughter. She will agree to marry the m[an] who can tell her a story that lasts for a ye[ar] and a day."

"I can tell such a story," Manuel thoug[ht]. "Then I will never be lonely again."

The next morning he walked to the palace. **Ask:** Why does Man[uel] want to tell a long s[tory]

goatherd person who takes care of goats
meadow flat grassy area, field
to fill the time so that he would not get bored
overheard two women talking heard two women talking to each other
well water supply

REACHING ALL STUDENTS

Vocabulary
GRAIN WORDS

Help students expand their food vocabulary. Divide the class into several teams and assign the name of a different grain to each. On poster paper, have each team make a web showing foods made from that grain. Set a time limit. When the time is up, display the webs and prompt the class to suggest additional words to add. Then invite the teams to draw a sketch of each food next to its name. Display the posters in the classroom.

HOME CONNECTION

Values Send home a copy of *High Point Newsletter 2* in the **Teacher's Resource Book**. In this activity, students ask a family member to tell them a favorite folk tale from their home culture. Students take notes and retell the story in class. Create a chart showing the values exemplified by each story. These might include the importance of hard work, the sacredness of family, or the benefits of frugality. Discuss similarities in values across cultures.

"I can tell a story that lasts for a year d a day," he **announced**. The guards took n into the palace.

Manuel bowed low before the princess, en he began:

"Last year in my village, the people rvested so much corn that their **corncribs** uldn't hold it all. So they stacked the corn a huge barn. But there was a hole under e **eaves**. One day a **dove** flew through the le and ate a **kernel** of corn."

The princess smiled. She had not heard s story, and she liked the young man ling it.

Manuel continued, "The next day another ve came and ate another kernel. And e next day another dove came and ate other kernel. . . ."

"Go on," said the princess. "What next?"

"Well, the next day another dove came d ate another kernel. . . ."

The princess laughed, "I understand. You uld go on for a year and a day! You have oved yourself **worthy of my hand**."

state: The princess agrees to marry the goatherd.

BEFORE YOU MOVE ON...

1. **Setting** Where and when does this tale take place?
2. **Character's Motive** Why does Manuel decide to tell the princess a story?

nounced said in an important way
rncribs small buildings for storing corn
ves part of the barn where the roof joins e wall
dove small white or light-colored bird
worthy of my hand good enough to marry me

REVIEW KEY VOCABULARY

3 Use New Words in Context Invite a group of more advanced students to write a short, original story incorporating the ten key vocabulary words. Underline these words and number them from 1–10. Below the story, add a column of numbers 1–10 with a blank line after each. Distribute copies of the story to pairs of students and ask them to write their own definitions for the underscored words in the numbered blanks.

CHECK COMPREHENSION

4 Answers to "Before You Move On"

1. **Setting** The story takes place long ago at a palace in Spain.
2. **Character's Motive** Manuel wants to marry the princess so he will never be lonely again.

CLOSE AND ASSESS

Refer to the unit mind map (see page T9) and ask students which types of messages on their mind maps are illustrated by these two stories.

Social Studies Connection

RESOURCES

Ask students to explain why grains were so important to the people in the stories. Ask: *What other resources are important to the survival of human beings?* (fish, fruits, vegetables, water, air) Discuss how to conserve and protect such resources. For example, there are quotas on how many fish can be caught and laws governing what chemicals can be sprayed on the fruit we eat. Have students research how resources are safeguarded in different countries and record the results.

Countries	U.S.	Japan
Resource	fish	
Importance	food source	
Protection	laws to keep other countries from fishing in U.S. waters	

INTERNET

SOCIAL STUDIES CONNECTION

Guide students to research grain production worldwide. Have them report their findings using charts, graphs, and diagrams. Help them narrow their topics.

Web Sites

Web sites undergo frequent modifications, but here are some you may want to suggest to students:

www.ag.iastate.edu
www.wheatworld.org
www.apps.fao.org

READ PAGE 46

OBJECTIVES

Grammar: Present Tense Verbs;
Ⓣ Subject-Verb Agreement

MORE TO EXPLORE

Multicultural Folk Tales Read "A Note from the Storytellers" aloud and discuss how the tales reflect the cultures they came from. Point out that "The Storyteller" and "The Clever Goatherd" are just two examples of messages across time and space. Invite students to share the folk tales they gathered from their families for *High Point Newsletter 2* and discuss ways that these tales reflect distinct cultures and connect to other cultures. Encourage students to state values expressed in each and identify other characteristics of the tales.

A Note from the Storytellers

Stories connect us to the past. Every culture has its own **distinct** stories, but sometimes the stories are based on a similar **plot** or idea. Look at these two tales, for example. The basic plot is the same: the **main character** uses his or her intelligence and skill at storytelling to meet a challenge. However, some differences in the tales **reflect** the cultures they come from. In "The Storyteller," the granary is filled with wheat, which is an important crop of Ethiopia. In "The Clever Goatherd," the barn contains corn, which Spaniards use in their cooking. These stories illustrate the **similarities** between cultures while also celebrating the differences between them.

—Margaret H. Lippert

Ask: What challenge did each storyteller have?

ABOUT T
STORYTELLE

Dawn and **Margaret Lippert** live with their family in Mercer Island, Washington. They have been telling stories together, and with Dawn's sister Jocelyn, since the two girls were first able to talk. They tell stories at schools and libraries near Mercer Island and around the country. Both Dawn and Margaret also enjoy reading in their spare time. Margaret usually curls up with historical novels and biographies. Dawn's favorite genres include adventure and mystery novels.

distinct special, different
plot chain of events in the story
main character most important person in the story
reflect tell us about, show us about
similarities things that are almost the same

REACHING ALL STUDENTS

Grammar Minilesson

▶ PRESENT TENSE VERBS/SUBJECT-VERB AGREEMENT

TEACH Write these sentences:

Stories connect us to the past.

The barn contains corn.

Point out the verbs and say: *The verb* connect *tells about something that happens all the time. The verb* contains *tells about what the barn has now. Both verbs are in the present tense.*

Then explain that present tense verbs must agree with the subject of the sentence. Say: *When you are talking about one thing, like the barn, the verb ends in* s.

For more on subject-verb agreement, refer students to Handbook page 427–428.

PRACTICE Have students choose the correct present tense verb for each sentence.

1. The storyteller (speak, speaks) softly.
2. We all (listen, listens) carefully.
3. The storyteller (ask, asks) a question.
4. All the people (answer, answers).

▶ **Practice Book** page 17

Respond to the Folk Tales

Check Your Understanding

IT UP

Comparisons Make a Venn diagram to are "The Storyteller" and "The Clever erd." Then share it with a group.

Diagram

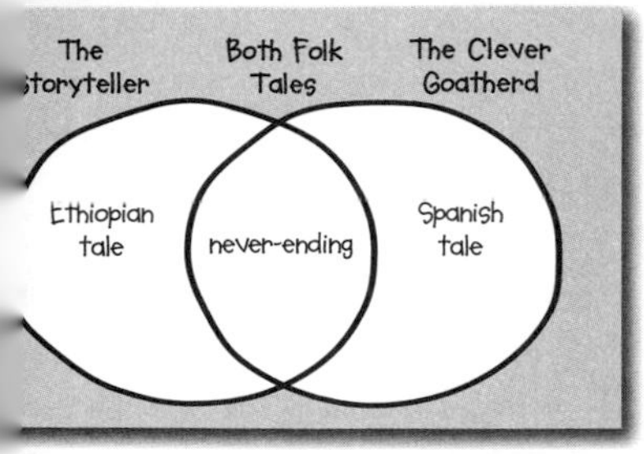

a Summary Tell how the two folk tales ike and how they are different. Here are ways that you might start your sentences:

th folk tales...

one tale...

owever, in the other tale...

ANGUAGE ACQUISITION ASSESSMENT
ee page 1 of the Assessment Handbook.

THINK IT OVER

Discuss and Write Talk about these questions with a partner. Write the answers.

1. **Judgments** Which folk tale did you like best? Why?
2. **Conclusions** How are folk tales like messages across time?
3. **Comparison** How are some of the characters and plot elements similar to the folk tales you know?
4. **Opinion** Some people say storytelling is not important now because of television, books, and movies. What do you think?

EXPRESS YOURSELF

▶ RETELL AND LISTEN TO A STORY

Retell one of the folk tales in "Tales Across Time" to a partner. Then switch roles and listen as your partner retells the other folk tale.

Multi-Level Strategies

SUM IT UP OPTIONS

BEGINNING Have students reread the Key Points Reading of the two stories and check their notes. Ask guiding questions to help students compare the stories. For example: *What actions were the same in the two stories? How were the characters different? How were the endings alike?* Record answers on a group Venn diagram.

INTERMEDIATE Form groups. Ask students to use their notes to complete the Venn diagram comparing the two tales. Point out the sentence starters on page 47 and have each group write a summary.

ADVANCED Invite students to review the two folk tales and their notes before adding information to their Venn diagrams. Then have them write the summary and share it with a partner.

RESPOND

OBJECTIVES

SUM IT UP
Function: Write
Reading and Learning Strategies: Ⓣ Make Comparisons; Use Graphic Organizers (Venn diagram); Ⓣ Summarize
Writing: Summary

THINK IT OVER
Function: Engage in Discussion
Comprehension and Critical Thinking: Make Judgments; Ⓣ Make Comparisons; Draw Conclusions; Form Opinions

EXPRESS YOURSELF
Functions: Retell and Listen to a Story

CHECK YOUR UNDERSTANDING

1. **Sum It Up** Students' diagrams may include these ideas:
   - Left circle: "The Storyteller"—*Ethiopian tale, farmer, wheat, ants, storyteller gets half the kingdom*
   - Overlapping area—*never-ending, storytelling contest, grain, storyteller wins contest*
   - Right circle: "The Clever Goatherd"—*Spanish tale, goatherd, corn, doves, storyteller marries princess*

▶ **Practice Book** page 18

2. **Think It Over** Possible answers are:
   1. **Judgments** Answers will vary. Elicit reasons.
   2. **Conclusions** The original message is brought to life again every time the story is told.
   3. **Comparison** Students may mention royalty and challenges.
   4. **Opinion** Answers will vary. Encourage elaboration.

3. **Express Yourself** Encourage students to retell the folk tales with the books closed.

CLOSE AND ASSESS

Have students write on an exit slip two things they learned about folk tales.

RESPOND

OBJECTIVES

NOUNS

Grammar: Ⓣ Common and Proper Nouns

NEVER-ENDING STORY

Speaking and Listening: Story

Literary Analysis: Ⓣ Characters; Ⓣ Setting; Ⓣ Plot

LANGUAGE ARTS AND LITERATURE

1 **Use Nouns** Answers to the Practice items will vary. Sample nouns to complete the paragraph are: *sun, night, problem, heavens, stars.*

The proper nouns in the paragraph are: *Arizona, Eagle, Great Spirit.*

▶ **Practice Book** page 19

2 **Tell a Never-Ending Story** Provide support:

- Ask students to explain in their own words the meaning of the terms "character" and "setting."
- Brainstorm with students a variety of ways they can create endings that are "never-ending." (a repeated journey that always starts and ends in the same place, a conversation that always consists of the same exchanges, a character who always makes the same wrong choice)

▶ **Practice Book** page 20

CLOSE AND ASSESS

Ask groups to discuss what they learned in this lesson. Then ask the groups to share their ideas with the class.

ASSESSMENT
Selection Test 3 on page 7 of the Assessment Handbook tests students' mastery of the r
strategies and the vocabulary, comprehension, and language arts skills taught with this

Respond to the Stories, continued

Language Arts and Literature

GRAMMAR IN CONTEXT

USE NOUNS

Learn About Nouns A **noun** is a word that names a person, place, thing, or idea. A **common noun** names any person, place, thing or idea. A **proper noun** is the name of one particular person, place, thing, or idea.

	Common Noun	Proper Noun
Person	storyteller	Margaret Lippert
Place	country	Spain
Thing	story	The Clever Goatherd

Use Specific Nouns You can use nouns to give a clear picture of what you mean.

NO: **Things** flutter on the **building**.
YES: **Flags** flutter on the **castle**.

Replace each **noun** in these sentences with a more specific noun.

The huge **thing** was full of **stuff**.

Two **birds** flew around the **place**.

Practice Write this paragraph. Add a noun in each blank. Circle the three proper nouns.

Long ago the night sky in Arizona was very dark. The ________ shone in the daytime, but at ________ there were no stars. Eagle wanted to solve the ________. He flew up to the ________ and asked the Great Spirit for ________ to shine at night.

LITERARY ANALYSIS
SPEAKING/LISTENING

TELL A NEVER-ENDING STORY

Learn About Fiction Folk tales, like other stories, are **fiction**. They are made up from a person's imagination. They include **characters** and a **setting**. The characters are the people c things that speak in the story. The setting is th time and place in which the story happens. For example:

- The characters in "The Storyteller" are a ki a farmer, and some guards.
- The setting is in Ethiopia a long time ago.

Most stories end when a problem gets solved, but in "The Storyteller" and "The Clever Goatherd," the farmer and the goatherd tell never-ending tales. The last line of each story repeated over and over again.

Tell Your Story Plan your own story. Think about the setting, characters, and events. Thir of a way to make your story go on "forever."

Then take turns telling your new story to a partner. Stop your partner when you think yo hear "the ending that never ends."

For tips on how to **tell a story**, see Handbook page 402.

REACHING ALL STUDENTS

Multi-Level Strategies

BRAINSTORM PROMPTS

BEGINNING Provide examples of nouns that relate to students and what they are doing in the classroom. *A **boy** reads a book. **Jairo** reads a book.* Ask volunteers to create more sentence pairs of this type; chart the common and proper nouns they use. As a group, create several versions of the specific noun sentences. Complete the Practice paragraph together.

INTERMEDIATE Have students work with a partner to complete the Practice activity. Compare students' answers as a group.

ADVANCED Have students complete the Practice independently and then trade papers with a partner. Suggest that partners discuss their answer choices and decide whether they want to make revisions. Then have them add new sentences and identify the common and proper nouns in them.

RESPOND

ontent Area Connections

LANGUAGE ACQUISITION ASSESSMENT
See page 1 of the Assessment Handbook.

OCIAL STUDIES

)MPARE POLITICAL LEADERS

king is the leader of the country in both of e folk tales. Today, there are many other ıds of leaders. Find out how the roles and nsibilities of today's leaders are different m country to country.

Research World Leaders Choose several countries. Look them up in an encyclopedia, almanac, or other reference sources. Find the title for each country's leader and tell what roles the leader takes. Scan the text for words like these: *emperor, king, president, prime minister, prince, premier,* and *queen.*

Make a Chart Record your information.

Country	Leader's Title	Roles
United States	President	1. enforces laws 2. gives orders to the military 3. appoints judges to the Supreme Court
Japan	Emperor	1. symbol of national unity 2. preserves traditions 3. welcomes foreign leaders

Share Information Review your chart. Discuss how the leaders' roles are alike and different.

SPEAKING/LISTENING

HEALTH

LEARN ABOUT GRAINS AND DIET

Grains are the seeds of plants such as rice, corn, quinoa, and wheat. Most countries produce one or more grains that are an important part of the food supply. Find out about a grain and give an oral report.

1. **List Research Questions** Choose a grain to research. Brainstorm questions such as:
   - Where is this grain grown?
   - How is it prepared in different countries?
   - What important nutrients—vitamins, minerals, or carbohydrates—does it provide?
2. **Gather Information** Look at encyclopedias, science books, health magazines, and the Internet. Take notes to answer your questions.
3. **Give an Oral Report** If possible, show a sample of the grain. Use your notes to tell about it.

Example:
"Corn grows in many places, including the U.S., Canada, and Brazil. It contains vitamins A and B...."

Learn how to give an **oral report**. See Handbook pages 401–402.

Tales Across Time 49

OBJECTIVES

POLITICAL LEADERS

Concepts and Vocabulary: Political Leaders—*emperor, king, queen, prince, president, prime minister, premier*

Learning Strategies, Critical Thinking, and Research Skills: Scan; Gather Information; **T** Make Comparisons; Use Graphic Organizers (chart)

Representing: Chart

GRAINS AND DIET

Function: Give Information

Speaking: Oral Report

Critical Thinking and Research Skills: Formulate Research Questions; Gather, Organize, and Synthesize Information; Take Notes

Technology/Media: Use Computerized Card Catalogue

CONTENT AREA CONNECTIONS

1. **Compare Political Leaders** Prepare students to engage in the research activity by explaining how to scan. Say: *Allow your eyes to move quickly through the sentences. Don't try to read every word. When you find a key word, slow down and read the information carefully.* Then introduce these terms:
   - ***emperor, king, queen, prince, president, prime minister, premier*:** Ask students to work in groups to define each type of leader and to name a country each type leads today. Point out that some countries have two leaders. One is political (prime minister) and another a traditional figure (queen). Have groups share their answers with the class.
2. **Learn About Grains and Diet** Start the brainstorming by asking students to name all the grains they have eaten in the past week.

▶ **Practice Book** page 22

CLOSE AND ASSESS

Have each student ask a question about one of the topics covered in this lesson. Other students should volunteer answers.

Research Skills

▶ USING THE COMPUTERIZED CARD CATALOGUE AND KEY WORDS

TEACH Show students an on-line catalogue. Explain the meanings of title, author, and subject searches, and tell students they will use a subject search for their research.

Remind them that information about a single topic may be in more than one place. To find out about grains, for example, they could look up the key word *grain* or a specific grain *(rice)*.

Pose a question and guide students in identifying the key word. Then demonstrate using the catalogue to find information.

PRACTICE Have pairs of students conduct a catalogue search on a topic of interest related to grains. Tell them to outline the procedure they used, list key words that led them to important information, and note the number of references they found.

▶ **Practice Book** page 21

PREPARE TO READ

OBJECTIVES

THINK ABOUT WHAT YOU KNOW

Reading Strategy: Relate to Personal Experience

LEARN KEY VOCABULARY Ⓣ

Vocabulary Strategy: Relate Words

LEARN ABOUT PLOT

Reading and Learning Strategies: Ⓣ Analyze Story Elements (plot); Use Graphic Organizers (story staircase map)

THINK ABOUT WHAT YOU KNOW

1 **Share Experiences** Encourage students to elaborate with details, such as sounds, tastes, temperature, and the numbness they may have felt during or after dental work.

LEARN KEY VOCABULARY

2 **Relate Words** Have students read each word and its definition. Clarify meanings, then conduct the activity. Ask students to explain the relationships they see between the words they identify as going together.

Use the Vocabulary Options in the **Multi-Level Strategies** to help all students complete the activity.

▶ **Practice Book** page 23

LEARN ABOUT PLOT

3 **Model How to Identify Events in the Plot** Define *plot.* Demonstrate the steps in the box with **Transparency 9**:

- Read the story. Have students identify the main character and her problem.
- Have the class identify the events that move the plot along and write them on the steps of the Story Staircase Map.
- Identify the story's conclusion and write it on the top step.

CLOSE AND ASSESS

Ask students why it is helpful to identify the events in the story. (It helps you understand the beginning, middle, and end of a story.)

Fat Men from Space

science fiction
by Daniel Manus Pinkwater

Prepare to Read

THINK ABOUT WHAT YOU KNOW

Share Experiences Have you ever visited a dentist? In a group, talk about what happens in a dentist's office.

cavity hole in a tooth

dentist doctor who cleans and repairs teeth

filling metal or other material used to fill a cavity

invader person who enters a country by force to attack it or to steal

invasion act of entering a country by force

launch send into the air by force

receive get

spaceman man who comes from another planet

station place that sends out radio signals

stay tuned stay on the same radio station

Answers to the vocabulary activity will vary. Sample sentences are:

A **dentist** filled my cavity with a silver **filling**.

The **invasion** started with one **spaceman**.

Stay tuned to this radio **station** for more news.

LEARN KEY VOCABULARY

Relate Words Study the new words and their definitions. Then look at each group of words. Two words in each group go together. Write one sentence using the two words that go together.

dentist filling launch	invasion cavity spaceman	invader stay tuned station

LEARN ABOUT PLOT

The order of events in a story is its **plot**. In many stories, the first event begins with a problem that the main character has. Each following event in the story carries the plot to its conclusion, or end. If you understand the plot, you know the beginning, middle, and end of a story.

READING STRATEGY

How to Identify Events in the Plot

As you read, ask yourself:

1. Who is the main character?
2. What is the character's problem?
3. What events lead to the conclusion of the story?

As you read "Fat Men from Space," look for the events in the plot.

REACHING ALL STUDENTS

Multi-Level Strategies

VOCABULARY OPTIONS

BEGINNING Group students to read ***I Make Pictures Move*** or the Key Points Reading on **Transparency 10**. (See page T52.) Work with the vocabulary in those selections.

INTERMEDIATE Have students work in groups to complete the chart and explain why one word per group does not belong.

ADVANCED Have students complete the chart and then form additional word groupings to include every key vocabulary word in at least one group.

Transparency 9 / Master 9

IDENTIFY EVENTS IN THE PLOT

Directions: As you read the story, identify events in the plot and record them on the story staircase map.

Zaxton and Meepar

The people on the planet Zaxton are lonely and want to meet some new people. One day Loomie, the Queen of Zaxton, looks through a telescope and sees people on the planet Meepar. She wants them to come and live on Zaxton.

Loomie flies to the planet Meepar and meets the king. He says t Meepars are lonely, just like the people of Zaxton, and he puts Loom in a big cage to keep her there.

Many Meepars come to see Loomie and hear about her problem Finally, they suggest a solution. For six months, some Meepars will g to Zaxton to visit. Then some people from Zaxton will visit Meepar f the next six months. That way, everyone will always have company. Everyone likes the solution, and Loomie flies back to Zaxton in a spaceship full of new Meepar friends.

Story Staircase Map for "Zaxton and Meepar"

Transparency 9 Level B, Unit 1 | Communication © Hampt

READ THE SELECTION

OBJECTIVES

Reading Strategies: Preview; Predict
Literary Analysis: Science Fiction

INTRODUCE THE SELECTION

4 Preview and Predict Read aloud the title, author's name, and introduction to the story. Ask: *Do you think this story will be about messages across time or space? Why? What do you think the messages will be about?*

5 Identify Genre: Science Fiction Explain that science fiction is literature in which science-related information is included in a make-believe story. For example, "Fat Men from Space" is a fantasy story that features space travel and beings from other parts of the universe. Ask students to share other examples of science fiction they have read or viewed and explain why they qualify as examples of this genre.

Fat Men from Space
by Daniel Manus Pinkwater

Theme Connection This is an imaginative story about a filling in a boy's tooth that receives radio messages from outer space.

Selection Summary The introduction on page 51 of the student book offers a summary of the selection.

Author Awards Daniel Pinkwater won the Parents' Choice Award for literature (1982) and the Children's Choice Award from the Internationl Reading Association and Children's Book Council (1981). He also wrote an ALA Notable Children's Book (1976).

THE BASICS BOOKSHELF

■ ***I Make Pictures Move*** by Daphne Liu
Here's a book even fat men from space could enjoy. It tells how an animator artist can create a unique dining experience through moving pictures. The patterned text includes basic vocabulary for food, colors, and shapes. Students will also enjoy flipping the pages to animate the artist's final illustration.

For Lesson Plans: See the Teacher's Guide for ***The Basics Bookshelf***.

READ PAGES 52–53

OBJECTIVES

Function: Read a Selection
Concepts and Vocabulary: Sensory Words
Grammar: T Compound Sentences
Listening: Listen to a Selection
Reading and Learning Strategies: Set a Purpose for Reading; T Analyze Story Elements (plot); Use Graphic Organizers (story staircase map)
Comprehension: Identify Details; Analyze Information (fantasy and reality)

SET PURPOSE

1 Read aloud the introduction to pages 52–53. Set the purpose for reading: *Read to find out what William hears.*

READ AND THINK

Tape 1B
CD 1 Track 4

2 **Strategy Focus: Identify Events in the Plot** Have students track the problem and story events as they read.

Choose Reading Options in the **Multi-Level Strategies** to tailor the reading to proficiency levels.

The recording of "Fat Men from Space" on the **Selection Tape/CD** offers an oral language model and the opportunity to build reading fluency.

Red annotations offer opportunities to clarify meaning and check for understanding.

1

THE FIRST SIGNAL

William goes to the dentist to get his tooth filled.
That night, he hears a radio program coming from his new filling.

Build background: If space visitors arrived on Earth, what do you think they would talk about? In this story, William gets to listen in.

William went to the **dentist**. It wasn't so bad—just a **filling**. The dentist said it wouldn't hurt a bit, and it was almost true. William went home **feeling a little bit numb**. There was a funny sour taste in his mouth. It made him think of electricity. When he sucked in his breath, the tooth with the new filling felt cold. He was able to eat his supper without any trouble. After watching television with his mother and father, he went to bed.

Clarify: The dentist gave William a shot to numb his gums so he wouldn't feel any pain.

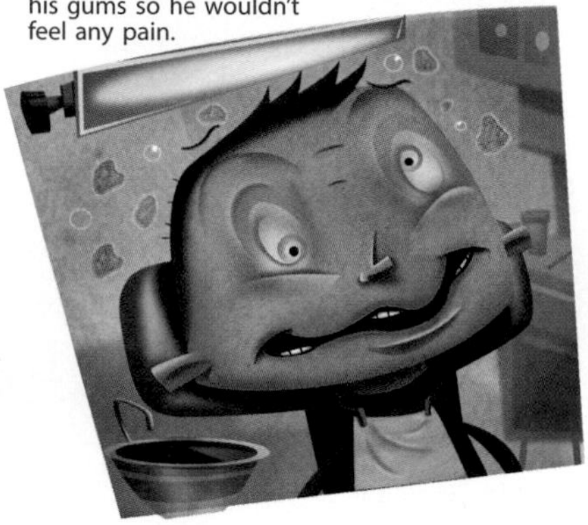

This particular night, William was lying in bed listening to the radio. He was listening to a talk show. A man said he had taken a ride in a flying saucer. He was telling how the people from outer space were crazy about **potato pancakes**. They had come to Earth **in search of** millions of them, which they planned to freeze and ta[ke] back to their own **galaxy**. It was a good show, and William was enjoying it. He was ready to **drift off** to sleep. Then he realize[d] that he had never turned the radio on.

William lay very quietly, trying to figure out where the radio program was coming from. It seemed to be coming from inside his head. "Maybe I'm imagining the whole thing," he thought. "Maybe I'm going crazy." He rubbed the tip of his tongue against the new filling. The **volume dropped** very low. Wait a second! He did it again. The volume dropped. He pressed his tongue against the tooth. No radio program at all! It was the tooth! The one with the new filling was **receiving** radio programs!

Ask: How did William hear the sho[w]

feeling a little bit numb without much feeling in his mouth
potato pancakes thin round cakes made with potatoes
in search of looking for
galaxy very large group of stars and planets
drift off slowly go
volume dropped level of sound went down

REACHING ALL STUDENTS

Transparency 10 / Master 10

KEY POINTS READING

Fat Men from Space

William goes to the dentist to get his tooth filled. That night he hears the radio but it is not turned on! The sound is coming from William's mouth. He touches his tooth with his tongue, and the radio sound gets softer. Then he hears a sound almost like a language.

The noises are spacemen talking to each other. There are many conversations going on at once. Most of them are about a plan to invade Earth to steal potato pancakes. Then millions of fat men dressed in funny jackets land on Earth.

The fat men eat all the junk food on Earth. People begin to panic. All that is left is healthy food. Then a giant potato pancake is sent into space. The fat men chase after it and go to another solar system. William's tooth radio plays less. But on some nights William hears a sound that is almost like a language.

Transparency 10 Level B, Unit 1 | Communication © Hampton-Brown

Multi-Level Strategies

READING OPTIONS FOR LESSONS 10–12

BEGINNING Group students to read ***I Make Pictures Move*** or distribute copies of **Master 10** to conduct a Key Points reading of "Fat Men from Space." As a group, have students identify events in the plot and record them on the Story Staircase Map.

INTERMEDIATE Read the story aloud, or play the recording on the **Selection Tape/CD**, pausing to clarify meaning. Also use the red annotations on the facsimile pages with this group. At the end of each section, have students discuss the story events and complete **Transparency 11** as a group.

ADVANCED Have students read the story independently. At the end of each section, have students identify plot events on copies of **Master 11**. Then have them write sentences predicting the eventual conclusion.

After a while, William **noticed** that his
oth was not receiving. At first, he thought
e tooth **had gone completely dead**. Then
was able to hear **some faint static**. The
atic was kind of rhythmical, like music.
was interesting. William thought it was
most like a language.

Define *rhythmical*: sounds with a regular beat.

BEFORE YOU MOVE ON...

1. **Vocabulary** List all of the words in the first paragraph on page 52 that describe a feeling or a taste.
2. **Details** What did William hear as he was lying in bed? What happened when he touched his tooth with his tongue?
3. **Fact and Fantasy** Which parts of the story so far could happen in real life? Which parts could not really happen?

ticed knew for the first time
d gone completely dead was no longer getting
y radio signals at all
me faint static a low sound of crackling and
sing on the radio

CHECK COMPREHENSION

3 Answers to "Before You Move On"

1. **Vocabulary** Answers should include *hurt, numb, sour,* and *cold.*
2. **Details** William heard radio programs and faint static. The volume became much lower when he touched his tooth with his tongue.
3. **Fact and Fantasy** The trip to the dentist could happen in real life. Receiving radio programs and hearing unknown languages through a filling in a tooth is fantasy.

CLOSE AND ASSESS

Have students submit an exit slip on which they have written the name of the main character and the main character's problem. (William; his problem is that a tooth is receiving radio signals)

Transparency 11 / Master 11

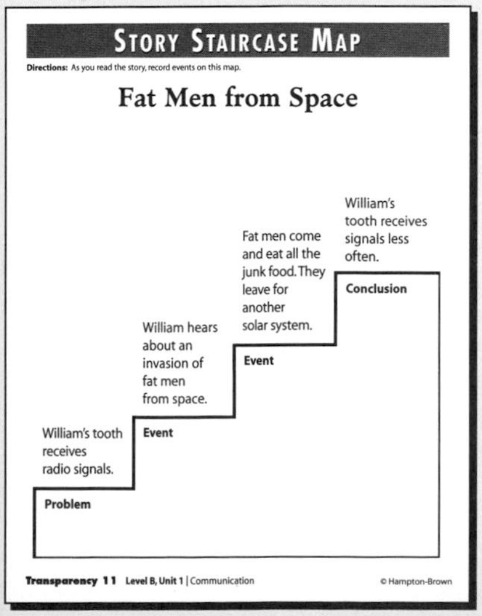

Grammar Minilesson

▶ COMPOUND SENTENCES

TEACH Write these sentences:

William rubbed his tongue against the filling.

The volume dropped.

Have students circle each simple subject and underline the verb. Then demonstrate how to combine the sentences into a compound sentence:

William rubbed his tongue against the filling, and the volume dropped.

Have students circle the subjects and verbs again. Say: *An independent clause has a subject and a verb. It can stand alone as a sentence. When you join two independent clauses, you make a compound sentence.*

Use Handbook page 430 to review the conjunctions used in compound sentences *(and, but, or, for, nor, yet).*

PRACTICE Distribute index cards, each with a different coordinating conjunction, to small groups. On the back of each card, have students write a compound sentence about the story, using the conjunction on the card.

▶ **Practice Book** page 24

READ PAGES 54–55

OBJECTIVES

Function: Read a Selection
Vocabulary Strategy: Use New Words in Context
Listening: Listen to a Selection
Reading and Learning Strategies: Set a Purpose for Reading; Ⓣ Analyze Story Elements (plot); Use Graphic Organizers (story staircase map)
Comprehension: Make an Inference; Summarize; Analyze Information (fantasy and reality)
Literary Analysis: Mood; Science Fiction

SET PURPOSE

1 Read aloud the introduction to pages 54–55. Set the purpose for reading: *Find out what kinds of messages William heard.*

READ AND THINK

Tape 1B
CD 1 Track 4

2 **Strategy Focus: Identify Events in the Plot** Involve students in reading pages 54–55.

Use the **Multi-Level Strategies** on page T52 to tailor the reading to proficiency levels.

2

THE INVASION

Radio messages from William's tooth tell about spacemen coming to take potato pancakes from Earth. And they know that William can hear their plans!

The more William listened to the strange static, the more he felt that he could almost understand it. The static was starting to make sense. It wasn't like anything William had ever heard. He knew what the noises meant. He could tell the directions they came from. The noises were **spacemen** talking to one another.

William was listening to twenty or thirty conversations at once. Some of the conversations were about potato pancakes. Some spacemen were **assembling** huge piles of potato pancakes in **remote places** on Earth. Spaceships would come and collect the potato pancakes and speed away with them. Other conversations were about **navigation**, and spaceships keeping in touch with one another. Some of the conversations were about a boy, an Earth boy who was listening in. The spacemen knew that William was listening! It made him shiver.

Encourage elaboration: What else might William hear?

Spaceships would come and collect the potato pancakes and speed away with them.

Clarify: Now William is hear the radio station again.

"Flash—the millions of round objects falling slowly through space are not meteorites as previously thought. They have now been identified as fat men, wearing ***plaid sport jackets****, falling slowly into our atmosphere.* ***Stay tuned*** *to this* ***station*** *for further reports on the amazing story."*

The **invasion** had started. William hoped hi mother and father weren't too scared.

Pose choices: Who was scared William or his parents?

BEFORE YOU MOVE ON...

1. **Inference** Why do you think that William could hear the spacemen's messages from his filling?
2. **Summary** What were the conversations abou
3. **Mood** Do you think this story is serious or funny? Explain your answer.

assembling putting together, gathering
remote places places that were hard to get to
navigation ways of finding directions
plaid sport jackets jackets with a large, bold pattern of lines and squares

REACHING ALL STUDENTS

Vocabulary
COMPOUND WORDS

Explain that compound words are words made up of two smaller words. Give common examples, such as *homework, classroom,* and *weekday.* Then ask students to identify some compound words on page 54. (spacemen, spaceship, pancakes) Ask students to define the words they find. Have students begin a chart of compound words. Encourage them to add to their charts as they encounter more examples. Set up a challenge to see who can find the most compound words in the story.

Art Connection
FASHION

Explain that, although the plaid jackets worn by the fat men were considered funny and unfashionable by the author, in another era they might have been considered very stylish. Ask groups of students to research clothing that has been popular at different times in the past. Groups can create costumes, collages, or sketches to present their research to the class.

REVIEW KEY VOCABULARY

3 Use New Words in Context In pairs, have students categorize the vocabulary words in two groups—the dentist and space. Then have them write a story for each category, using as many of those vocabulary words as they can. As an extension, suggest that students erase the vocabulary words, switch stories with another pair, and fill in the blanks in each other's stories.

CHECK COMPREHENSION

4 Answers to "Before You Move On"

1. **Inference** A possible answer is that the metal in William's filling worked like a radio and allowed him to receive radio messages.
2. **Summary** The conversations were about the spacemen's plans to invade Earth.
3. **Mood** Students will probably say that this selection is funny. They may refer to the images of fat men wearing plaid jackets.

CLOSE AND ASSESS

Have students add ideas about radio communication to their unit mind maps from page T9.

Vocabulary

SLANG AND COLLOQUIALISMS

Explain that *slang* and *colloquialisms* are informal language used by people in informal situations. Point out examples from page 54: *make sense, speed away*. Model formal ways of saying the same things. Have students find other examples of slang words and phrases as they continue to read.

Literary Analysis Minilesson

▶ FANTASY AND REALITY IN SCIENCE FICTION

TEACH Define *fantasy* and *reality*. Explain that many science fiction stories have elements of both fantasy and reality. For example, the boy in this story seems real. He goes to the dentist, and he listens to the radio like anyone else. Elicit from students details in the rest of the story that are not so realistic. Explain that it is this combination of fantasy and reality that makes the story so enjoyable for the reader.

PRACTICE Have students work with a partner to complete a Reality and Fantasy Chart.

Reality	Fantasy
William goes to the dentist.	William receives radio signals through his filling.

READ PAGES 56–57

OBJECTIVES

Function: Read a Selection
Grammar: Present Tense Verbs; Ⓣ Subject-Verb Agreement
Listening: Listen to a Selection
Reading and Learning Strategies: Set a Purpose for Reading; Ⓣ Analyze Story Elements (plot); Use Graphic Organizers (story staircase map); Use Visuals; Visualize

SET PURPOSE

1 Read aloud the introduction to pages 56–57. Set the purpose for reading: *Read to understand what happens when the spacemen invade.*

READ AND THINK

2 **Strategy Focus: Identify Events in the Plot** Involve students in reading pages 56–58.

See the **Multi-Level Strategies** on Page T52 to tailor the reading experience to all proficiency levels.

3

BACK TO NORMAL

The spacemen land on Earth. Luckily, the invasion ends quickly, and life returns to normal. But on certain nights William can still hear the spacemen.

*Reports from our **affiliated stations** seem to **indicate** that the fat men have started to land. **It is estimated** that there are hundreds of millions of them still in the sky. The fat men are landing in all parts of the world, but the **greatest concentrations** appear to be in California and New Jersey.*

Ask: Who is speaking now?

*"What do these fat men from space want? Is this the beginning of a war? Do they want to conquer the people of Earth? . . . It appears that, for the moment, they want hamburgers. . . . Crowds of fat men have surrounded roadside hamburger stands throughout the civilized world. . . . They are also **consuming great quantities** of pizza, and cupcakes wrapped in cellophane . . . and hot dogs . . . and ice cream bars . . . and jelly doughnuts . . . halvah . . . chocolate-covered marshmallows. . . . It*

Encourage elaboration: What other kin of junk food can you name?

*seems that the **invaders** from space are after every sort of **junk food**. . . . Stand by for further bulletins."*

Do they want to conquer the people of the Earth?

William was starting to get the picture now. The news bulletins were coming faster and faster.

Define *get the picture*: understanc

*"**Conditions of panic exist** in many parts of th United States. **Residents of most areas** cannot get anything to eat but lean meat, fish, fruit, and vegetables."*

William could see that the **situation** was very serious. The fat men from space were eating up all the junl food on Earth **at a fantastic rate.** William thought there would be nothing left for the next day's snacks. Then he heard tha a giant potato pancake had been **launched** into space near the planet Ziegler. The spacemen were off for another solar system.

Encourage elaboration: Invite students add other healthy items to the list.

affiliated stations radio offices with which we share information
indicate show, suggest
It is estimated Experts think
greatest concentrations largest numbers
consuming great quantities eating a lot
junk food food that is full of fat and sugar
Conditions of panic exist A lot of people are afraid
Residents of most areas People living in most cities and neighborhoods
situation problem
at a fantastic rate very quickly

56 **Unit 1** | Communication

REACHING ALL STUDENTS

Social Studies Connection

GEOGRAPHY AND CULTURE

On a U.S. map, have students locate the states mentioned on page 56. Ask: *What do these states have in common?* (Each is located on a coast.) Explain that major population centers are often found on coastlines or along rivers. Ask students to hypothesize about reasons for this. Have students research major population centers of the world to verify or refute their hypotheses.

Vocabulary

PREFIXES

Elicit prior knowledge of prefixes. Point out *return* on page 56. Present other words with the same prefix: *review, reread, rediscover.* Elicit meaning of *re-* (again or back). Present, and have students chart, these and other common prefixes and words in which they are found, along with their meanings: *pre-* (before), *preview, prefix; un-* (not), *unhappy, unfair.* Encourage students to add to their lists more examples they encounter.

MONITOR YOUR READING

3 Use Visuals Tell students they can use illustrations to check their comprehension. Have students work with partners to examine the picture on page 57. Challenge students to match details in the picture to the story text. Then have partners share their findings with the class.

4 Visualize Tell students they can monitor their reading by making a picture in their minds of the action in the story.

Encourage them to imagine what their neighborhood would be like if all the junk food began disappearing. Have them draw pictures to show the images that form in their minds. Encourage them to include as many details as possible in their drawings.

Finally, have the class compare specific details in the students' drawings with the text.

Learning Styles

STRATEGIES FOR CONSTRUCTING MEANING

- **Visual Learners** Have students create large murals with details from the story to be the backdrop for a skit.
- **Auditory Learners** Have students make the sound effects to go along with the events in the skit.
- **Kinesthetic Learners** Ask students to act out the major events in the story.

Grammar Minilesson

▶ PRESENT TENSE VERBS/SUBJECT-VERB AGREEMENT

TEACH Display this chart and say: *The verb in a sentence must agree with its subject.* Singular *means "one." A singular subject names one person or thing and needs a singular verb.* Make up sentences using the singular subjects and verbs in the chart. Repeat to teach *plural.*

Singular		Plural	
The girl	is	The girls	are
The story	is	The stories	are
He	is	They	are

For more on subject-verb agreement with irregular verbs, have students use page 427 of the Handbook.

PRACTICE Have students choose the verb that agrees with the subject.

1. He (is/are) interested in science fiction.
2. These novels (is/are) full of details about outer space.
3. The writer (is/are) also a scientist.
4. Often his characters (is/are) comical.

▶ **Practice Book** page 25

READ PAGE 58

OBJECTIVES

Function: Read a Selection
Reading Strategy: Paraphrase
Comprehension:
Identify Details; Identify Cause and Effect
Literary Analysis: Evaluate Literature

CHECK COMPREHENSION

5 Answers to "Before You Move On"

1. **Details** They wanted junk food, such as hamburgers, pizza, and cupcakes.
2. **Cause and Effect** The fat men ate the junk food.
3. **Paraphrase** Sample answer: After the fat men left Earth, William's tooth still received radio signals, but not as frequently.

ABOUT THE AUTHOR

6 Evaluate Literature Read aloud or have students read About the Author. Ask: *How amusing is the message in "Fat Men from Space"?* Have students rate the message on a scale of 1 to 10, with 10 being very amusing.

CLOSE AND ASSESS

Ask students to take turns, round-robin style, retelling the story. Encourage students to include plot details.

In the morning, William's radio tooth still worked, although not as well as it had the night before. Sometimes the tooth would be **silent** for days at a time. Sometimes it would play fairly well. When William went to the dentist a year later, the tooth hadn't played for almost a month. Dr. Horwitz thought it would probably stop playing altogether after a while. He also told William that he had no new cavities—**a common occurrence** worldwide, since sugar was still scarce.

But the radio tooth **was not entirely dead**. Some nights it would play quite well. And on special nights—ones that were clear and cold—William could hear a kind of rhythmic static that was almost like a language.

Clarify: Sometimes William could hear the radio program clearly.

silent completely quiet
a common occurrence an everyday happening
was not entirely dead still worked a little bit

BEFORE YOU MOVE ON...

1. **Details** What were some of the things the fat men from space wanted?
2. **Cause and Effect** Why couldn't most people on Earth get anything to eat but lean meat, fish, fruit, and vegetables?
3. **Paraphrase** In your own words, tell how the story ends.

ABOUT THE AUTHOR

Daniel Manus Pinkwater communicates with an old friend as he writes. That "old friend" is the younger Daniel who still lives inside his head and heart. He says, "I can vividly remember portions of my own childhood. I can see, taste, smell, feel, and hear them." Perhaps that's why the amusing "messages" in Pinkwater's books come through to young people so clearly. He has written many weird and wonderful books, including the ALA Notable *Lizard Music*.

REACHING ALL STUDENTS

Vocabulary
DENTAL HEALTH WORDS

Write *enamel, floss, filling, drill, brush, plaque, root, decay, diet.* Invite small groups to look up the meaning of each word. Then students can classify the words in a chart.

Categories	Words
Parts of teeth	enamel, root
Tooth care	brush, floss, diet
Tooth problems	plaque, decay
Tooth repair	filling, drill

Language Development
EXPRESS OPINIONS

Assign students a position: "The people of Earth were happier before the invasion because. . ." or "The people of Earth were happier after the invasion because. . . ." Remind students that there were only healthy foods left on Earth after the invasion. Also remind students about the harmful effects of sugar on teeth. Then encourage a friendly debate between the two groups. Encourage students to support their positions with facts and logic.

Respond to the Story

Check Your Understanding

UM IT UP

lentify Events in the Plot Think about the vents in the story and complete a Story Staircase lap. Begin at the bottom "step" and move up the top to show when events happened.

tory Staircase Map

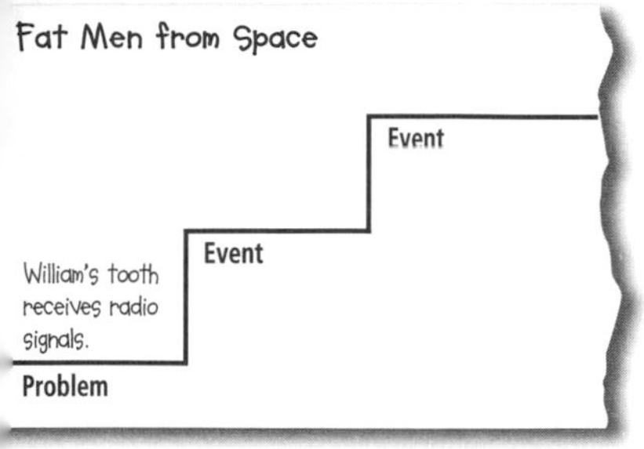

Vrite a Summary Use the information om the map to complete this summary.

William's problem was that ________. The first thing that happened was that ________. Then, ________. After that, ________. The story ended when ________.

THINK IT OVER

Discuss and Write Talk about these questions with a partner. Write the answers.

1. **Judgments** What would you do if you heard about an invasion from space?
2. **Prediction** William can still hear the rhythmic static through his filling. Do you think William will hear the spacemen again? What might they say?
3. **Author's Purpose** Why do you think Daniel Manus Pinkwater wrote this story?
4. **Comparison** What other stories do you know about visitors from space? Compare one other science fiction story with "Fat Men from Space."

EXPRESS YOURSELF

▶ Ask for and Give Advice

Work with a partner. One of you is William, and the other is the dentist. William tells the problem and asks for advice on how to solve it. The dentist suggests a solution for the problem. Use words like these:

William:
"Hello, doctor. This is William. I have a problem . . ."

Dentist:
"Oh, my. That's quite a problem. I think you should . . ."

Multi-Level Strategies

SUM IT UP OPTIONS

BEGINNING Using the Key Points Reading of "Fat Men from Space" on **Master 10** (see page T52), complete the Story Staircase Map with students. Then have them work with a partner to complete a summary, using the sentence starters.

INTERMEDIATE Have students work with partners to complete the Story Staircase Map. Encourage them to support their map entries with details from the story. Then they should create a summary of the story, using the sentence starters.

ADVANCED Students should complete the Story Staircase Map and summary statements independently. Then they share their maps and write new endings for the story that give different solutions to William's problem.

OBJECTIVES

SUM IT UP
Function: Write
Reading and Learning Strategies: Ⓣ Analyze Story Elements (plot); Use Graphic Organizers (story staircase map); Ⓣ Summarize
Writing: Summary

THINK IT OVER
Function: Engage in Discussion
Critical Thinking and Comprehension: Make Predictions; Identify Author's Purpose; Ⓣ Make Comparisons; Make Judgments

EXPRESS YOURSELF
Function: Ask for and Give Advice
Speaking and Listening: Role-play

CHECK YOUR UNDERSTANDING

1 **Sum It Up** See the annotations to **Transparency 11** on page T53 for a sample of the completed Story Staircase Map. Encourage students to add details to improve their summary statements.

▶ **Practice Book** page 26

2 **Think It Over** Possible answers are:

1. **Judgments** Answers will vary. Elicit a variety of responses.
2. **Prediction** Answers will vary. Elicit elaboration.
3. **Author's Purpose** Pinkwater probably likes to make people laugh.
4. **Comparison** Answers will vary. Ask students to think about science fiction stories in books, films, and comic strips.

3 **Express Yourself** Ask students to use words from the problem when formulating a solution.

CLOSE AND ASSESS

Have students write three sentences telling what they know about events in the plot.

RESPOND

OBJECTIVES

VERBS

Grammar: Verbs; Ⓣ Subject-Verb Agreement

SCIENCE FICTION STORY

Function: Tell an Original Story; Write

Speaking and Listening: Story

Learning Strategy: Use Graphic Organizers (story staircase map)

Literary Analysis: Ⓣ Plot

Writing: Science Fiction Story

LANGUAGE ARTS AND LITERATURE

1 **Use Verbs** Answers to Practice items will vary. Each sentence should include a subject and verb that agree.

▶ **Practice Book** page 27

2 **Write a Science Fiction Story** Help students brainstorm:

- a list of things that might happen to William when he gets his next filling
- some reactions he might have to one of these situations.

CLOSE AND ASSESS

Ask students: *What did you learn in this lesson?*

ASSESSMENT
Selection Test 4 on page 9 of the Assessment Handbook tests students' mastery of the readin strategies and the vocabulary, comprehension, and language arts skills taught with this select

Respond to the Story, continued

Language Arts and Literature

GRAMMAR IN CONTEXT

USE VERBS

Learn About Verbs An **action verb** tells what the subject does.

The dentist **fills** William's tooth.

A **linking verb** connects, or links, the subject of a sentence to a word in the predicate. The word in the predicate can describe the subject.

The noises **are** strange.

Or, the word in the predicate can be another way to name the subject.

Now William's tooth **is** a radio.

Learn About Subject-Verb Agreement The **verb** must agree with the subject of the sentence. A singular subject and verb tell about one thing. A plural subject and verb tell about more than one thing.

Singular: William **listens**. He **is** surprised.
Plural: The spacemen **listen**. They **are** hungry.

Practice Choose words from each column to make as many sentences as you can.

Subject	Verb	Rest of Sentence
The invaders	are	on Earth.
The filling	collect	potato pancakes.
The situation	is	serious.
The spacemen	receives	signals from space.

WRITING

SPEAKING/LISTENING

WRITE A SCIENCE FICTION STORY

Use your imagination to write a science fiction story about William's next filling.

1. **Plan and Write Your Draft** Make a Story Staircase Map to plan your story. Use the events to write a rough draft of your story.
2. **Edit Your Work** Does your story have even that create excitement? Check your sentence for correct spelling and punctuation.
3. **Share Your Work in a Group** Take turns reading your stories aloud in a group. Talk about the events in each story.

Sample Story

William's New Filling

William got a new filling in the back of his mouth. Now the tooth was like a radio, and beautiful music from outer space came out of it. So many people wanted to listen to the music that William decided to ask them for food in exchange for listening. One day, the spacemen found out about the large quantities of food William had received.

Develop your skill in the **writer's craft**. See Handbook pages 414–423.

REACHING ALL STUDENTS

Multi-Level Strategies

OPTIONS FOR WRITING A SCIENCE FICTION STORY

BEGINNING Students draw or write to fill out a Story Staircase Map for a science fiction story. Then they can make a storyboard with more detailed pictures and captions to tell the story. Have students share their storyboards and ask the class to identify events in the plot.

INTERMEDIATE Students should work with partners to write a science fiction story. Have them collaborate to develop a Story Staircase Map and a rough draft. After writing, they join with other partners forming groups of four to share their stories, discuss events in the plot, and suggest changes.

ADVANCED Have students plan and write rough drafts independently. Prompt them to share their drafts with a partner to get feedback about events, problems, and solutions and to discuss revisions. Then students revise their stories and share the finished products with new partners.

ontent Area Connections

HEALTH

NALYZE YOUR DIET

earn About the Food Pyramid Do you eat a ealthier diet than the spacemen? The food ramid shows how much you should eat from ach food group every day.

e Food Pyramid

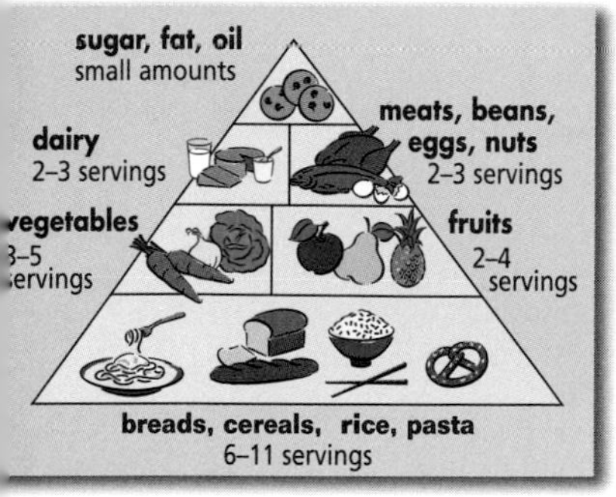

nduct a Study Keep track of the foods you t for a day. Compare the number of your rvings to those in the pyramid. What did you arn about your eating habits?

SCIENCE

MATHEMATICS

EXPLORE THE SOLAR SYSTEM

Prepare a research report on space travel.

1. **Brainstorm Questions** Work with a group. Think of at least three questions about space travel. Here are some ideas:
   - What is the distance between each of the planets in our solar system?
   - How long would it take to reach one of the planets in our solar system? At what speed?
   - Have we sent spacecraft to other planets? What did we learn from those missions?
2. **Gather Information and Take Notes** Use an encyclopedia, the Internet, and other sources to find answers. The NASA Web site **www.nasa.gov** is one good source. Write an outline to organize your information.
3. **Prepare a Report** Use your outline to write a report. Present your findings to the class.

The surface of Mars

Research Skills

▶ USING AN ENCYCLOPEDIA

TEACH Have a full set of print and/or electronic encyclopedias available for student use. Ask a volunteer to state a research goal: *I want to find out what kind of sugar bananas have.* Then model how to use alphabetical order in both the index and regular volumes to locate information about this topic.

PRACTICE Have pairs of students select a topic of interest and work together to find an appropriate article.

On 3 x 5 cards, they should write:
- the title of the volume used
- the title of the article and its page number(s)
- two interesting facts they learned from reading the article

Explain cross references and encourage students to use those cited in the original article to continue their research in other volumes.

▶ **Practice Book** page 28

RESPOND

OBJECTIVES

ANALYZE DIET
Function: Give Information
Concepts and Vocabulary: Words About Diet
Learning Strategies, Critical Thinking, and Research Skills: Gather Information; Draw Conclusions; Use an Encyclopedia

SOLAR SYSTEM
Function: Give Information; Write
Learning Strategies, Critical Thinking, and Research Skills: Formulate Research Questions; Gather Information; Take Notes; Use Graphic Organizers (outline); Organize and Synthesize Information
Writing: Report

CONTENT AREA CONNECTIONS

1 **Analyze Your Diet** Prepare students by explaining the food pyramid and previewing content area vocabulary:

- ***protein, carbohydrates, fat*:** Explain that *protein* is a key element in the growth and repair of tissue. *Carbohydrates,* found in breads, cereals, sugar, and fruits, supply energy to the body. *Fat* stores energy in the body. Ask students for examples of each.

▶ **Practice Book** page 29

2 **Explore the Solar System** Present a brief description of the solar system. Encourage students to think up more questions that interest them.

CLOSE AND ASSESS

Have students state at least two new facts they learned from their research.

BUILD WRITING SKILLS

OBJECTIVES

Function: Engage in Discussion; Listen Actively

Reading Strategy and Critical Thinking: Use Text Structures (story elements); Analyze and Evaluate Information

Listening: Listen Critically

Literary Analysis and Writing: Ⓣ Narrative (fiction); Fantasy

INTRODUCE WRITING THAT TELLS A STORY

1 **Discuss Narrative Writing** Read the introduction and ask students to name stories about real people and events, and stories about people and events that are made up.

2 **Study the Professional Model** Read the excerpt and ask students how they know it is a fantasy. (Students should identify the unbelievable event: the radio program is coming from inside William's head.)

3 **Explore Text Structure** Explain that all stories have the same elements: characters, setting, and plot. Use the Story Chart to teach one way to structure a fantasy story.

Use the Options for Studying Text Structure in the **Multi-Level Strategies** to adjust instruction.

Writing That Tells a Story

Narrative writing tells a story. Some stories are about real places and real people. Others tell about people, places, or events that are made up.

PROFESSIONAL WRITING MODELS

"Fat Men from Space" is a science fiction **fantasy**—a story that could never happen in real life. It begins with an everyday character in a real-life setting, but events soon become unbelievable!

from **Fat Men from Space**

> This particular night, William was lying in bed listening to the radio. . . . Then he realized that he had never turned the radio on.
>
> William lay very quietly, trying to figure out where the radio program was coming from. It seemed to be coming from inside his head. "Maybe I'm imagining the whole thing," he thought. "Maybe I'm going crazy."

ELEMENTS OF A STORY

Stories are usually set in a specific time and place. In the beginning of a story, you get to know the setting and the characters. Often, one of the characters has a problem. The story tells the events that happen next. The events lead to a conclusion. Discuss the story elements in "Fat Men from Space." Which characters and events are real? Which are unbelievable?

Story Chart

CHARACTERS	SETTING	BEGINNING	EVENTS IN THE MIDDLE	CONCLUSION
William fat men from space	**Time:** Now **Place:** William's hometown in the U.S.	**The Problem:** William gets a filling at the dentist's. William's filling receives radio messages from spacemen about to invade Earth. 	Hundreds of millions of spacemen fall from space to Earth, eat up all the junk food, and leave for another solar system. 	William's filling rarely receives messages. He has more cavities to fill becau the fat men have eaten n of all the world's sugar.

REACHING ALL STUDENTS

Transparency 12 / Master 12

STORY CHART

Characters	
Setting	Time: Place:
Beginning	The Problem:
Events in the Middle	
Conclusion	

Transparency 12 Level B, Unit 1 | Communication ©Hampton-Brown

Multi-Level Strategies

OPTIONS FOR STUDYING TEXT STRUCTURE

BEGINNING Display **Transparency 12** and lead students through a simple shared experience involving a familiar story such as Cinderella. Use prompts to help students identify story elements: *What are the names of the characters (people/animals)? Where does the story happen? What is the problem in the story?* Record the elements on the transparency. Then use the art on page 62 to present the story elements in "Fat Men from Space."

INTERMEDIATE / **ADVANCED** Work through the Story Chart for "Fat Men from Space." Say: *In a story, the author often starts by describing the characters, setting, and the main character's problem. The rest of the story tells what happens as the character solves the problem.* Then have students work in pairs to fill out **Master 12** with elements from another familiar story.

)ENT WRITING MODEL

sy

Textbook Adventure

' Darya Litvinchuk

Sheila's World Studies class was studying ancient Egypt, but she
.d been sick and missed school. Now she had to catch up. The test
as the next day, and she hadn't learned anything about Egypt.
The teacher said Sheila could catch up by taking the textbook
me. She read the chapters on ancient Egypt twice. Then the
ost amazing thing happened to her.
She was sitting at the kitchen table looking at a picture of an
cient Egyptian woman. The woman's lips moved! Then she
oke to Sheila, and Sheila jumped out of her chair!
"I will take you to ancient Egypt," said the woman as she
ted herself off the page. She pointed to a machine in the kitchen.
e and Sheila stepped into it, and the woman pressed the button
r ancient Egypt. A couple of seconds later, they stepped out.
eila knew she was in Egypt because she saw pyramids.
The woman gave Sheila ancient Egyptian clothes to wear: a
.ort-sleeved linen dress, an elaborate necklace, and sandals of
aided reeds.
Sheila learned everything about ancient Egypt—how the people
rmed, what the pyramids were for, and how to read hieroglyphics.
The visit was exciting, but Sheila began to wonder how she
uld get home. The woman seemed to read Sheila's mind, "We
.ve to go back now."
Sheila packed up the Egyptian clothes to take home. They went
.ck into the machine, the woman pressed U.S.A. 21st Century,
.d the next thing Sheila knew she was sitting at her kitchen
.ble again.
"You won't believe what happened," she said to her mother.
eila told her about the trip. She wanted to show her mom the
cient clothes, but for some reason, she couldn't find them.
Sheila did bring back a lot of information on ancient Egypt,
wever. By the way, she got an A on her World Studies test!

BEGINNING
The first paragraph introduces Sheila, the **main character.** We also learn about her **problem.**

MIDDLE
The **events** in the middle move the story along. Many of the events **could not really happen.**

The characters are **realistic but do unbelievable things.**

The **setting** changes from Sheila's kitchen in the present time to ancient Egypt and back again.

CONCLUSION
The ending tells how Sheila's problem got resolved.

STUDY A STUDENT WRITING MODEL

4 Listen for Story Elements Have students take notes on copies of **Master 12** as you read the Student Model aloud. Go over their notes together to identify the story elements.

5 Analyze and Evaluate Fantasies Display **Transparency 13** and lead students in studying the features of a fantasy. Students should then evaluate the Student Model against the rubric on the transparency.

Use the Roles for Cooperative Groups in the **Multi-Level Strategies** to involve all students.

CLOSE AND ASSESS

Call on a different **Manager** to report the group conclusions for each feature on **Master 13.** Encourage students to add relevant information and opinions each time, either verbally or by drawing quick sketches to represent their ideas.

Multi-Level Strategies

ROLES FOR COOPERATIVE GROUPS

BEGINNING / **INTERMEDIATE** / **ADVANCED** Distribute **Master 13** to groups of three students with varying proficiencies and have them compare the model to the rubric. Assign these roles:

- ▶ **Manager**
- ▶ **Reader**
- ▶ **Artist**

Before groups begin, work through the title and the first feature, pointing out the sample answer. The **Manager** should start by writing the title of the Student Model above the right column. Groups should then discuss each feature of a fantasy. The **Manager** can restate the feature so that the group understands it. The **Reader** should read the part(s) of the model relevant to the feature. The **Artist** then represents the feature by drawing an illustration to go with each section of the Master. The **Manager** checks the box and adds phrases to be read later.

Transparency 13 / Master 13

FEATURES OF NARRATIVE WRITING

Directions: Read "A Textbook Adventure" and compare it to the features of a fantasy story. Check the box if "A Textbook Adventure" shows the feature. Then give an example.

A Fantasy Story. . . A Textbook Adventure

must have unbelievable characters and settings or events that could not happen	☑ **unbelievable characters:** ancient Egyptian woman **events that could not happen:** A machine takes Sheila to ancient Egypt.
may have some real-life characters and settings or events that could happen	☑ **real-life characters:** Sheila, teacher, mother **an event that could happen:** Sheila has to take a test.
tells where and when events take place	☑ **where:** in Sheila's kitchen and in Egypt **when:** now and in ancient times
describes a problem	☑ Sheila hasn't studied for the test on ancient Egypt.
has events that lead, in order, to a conclusion	☑ **events:** describes the unbelievable trip to ancient Egypt **conclusion:** brings Sheila back to her world; tells how she did on the test

Transparency 13 Level B, Unit 1 | Communication

BUILD WRITING SKILLS

OBJECTIVES

PREWRITE

Function: Write

Learning Strategies and Critical Thinking: Plan; Generate Ideas; Interact with Peers; Identify Story Elements; Organize Ideas; Self-Assess

Representing: Web

Writing: Ⓣ Writing Process

PRESENT THE WRITING PROCESS AND PROMPT

Read the prompt together. Check understanding. Then leaf through pages 64–68 to preview the stages in the Writing Process.

For more about the **Writing Process**, refer students to pages 408–413 in the Handbook.

PREWRITE

Before students begin their prewriting, preview the steps with the group. Discuss the sample FATP chart.

Use the Prewriting Support in the **Multi-Level Strategies** to tailor this stage to proficiency levels.

CLOSE AND ASSESS

Have students work with a partner to answer the questions in Reflect and Evaluate.

The Writing Process

WRITING PROMPT

Now you will write a fantasy story for your classmates and friends. In your story, tell about an adventure that cannot really happen.

PREWRITE

❶ **Collect Ideas** What settings, characters, and story ideas could you write about? Brainstorm with a partner. Write your ideas in a web.

Choose the characters, setting, and story idea you like the best.

❷ **Unlock the Writing Prompt** Before you begin, fill out an **FATP** chart to help guide your writing.

- Name the **form**, or what type of story you are writing.
- Name the **audience**, or who will read your writing.
- Name the **topic**, or what you are writing about.
- Tell the **purpose**, or why you are writing.

❸ **Plan and Organize Your Writing** What problem will get your story started? What will happen next? Make a list of events. Plan some that are realistic and some that could never happen. You may want to draw the events in sequence on a storyboard.

FATP Chart

HOW TO UNLOCK A PRO

Form: *fantasy*

Audience: *classmates and friends*

Topic: *boy gets caught inside a video game*

Purpose: *to tell an entertaining story*

Reflect and Evalu

- Why do you think your story idea is a good cho
- How will you introduce the problem your chara faces?
- How can you make you writing interesting for your audience?

REACHING ALL STUDENTS

Multi-Level Strategies

PREWRITING SUPPORT

BEGINNING Students can draw their ideas for characters, settings, and story ideas. Remind them to include events that couldn't be real. Ask them to choose their characters, setting, and story idea from their web. Have them dictate their FATP charts. Then they can plan the story on a storyboard with pictures.

INTERMEDIATE Students can work together to collect ideas and fill out FATP charts. Guide them in determining a problem and in developing unbelievable events. Check their FATP charts and have them organize their ideas on copies of **Master 12**. (See page T62.)

ADVANCED Students can expand their ideas by listing many possible events, characters, and settings and then putting the least likely ones together. To organize ideas, they can use **Master 12** or draw their own story map.

T

›ur **FATP** chart to focus on what you are writing, whom you are g for, and why. Write quickly to get yourself involved in the action.

'rite the Beginning Grab your reader's interest with a good troduction. Describe the characters and setting. Begin the plot by troducing the problem.

Writer's Craft: Introductions

Grab your reader's interest.

I had just become a high level Desert Destroyer when Mom walked in. "If you don't stop playing video games, you're going to turn into a video game."

I ignored her and kept playing. Suddenly, it seemed like I really was in the game. At first, I thought it was a really neat effect, but then I realized I was IN THE GAME!

'rite the Middle Tell what happens next. Include some events that ›nnot really happen. Use descriptive words and phrases that show ›ther than tell.

Writer's Craft: Show, Don't Tell

Use dialogue.

This tells:

It was amazing how well I could jump in the video game!

This shows:

"Whee, it's like a trampoline!" I shouted as I jumped and spun around in the air.

Use descriptions to show action and how the characters feel.

This tells:

Suddenly, I saw danger ahead. I had never been so scared!

This shows:

All at once, the sweet smells and rainbow colors vanished, and I was staring into the yellow eyes of the evil tortoise! My heart beat so loudly I could hear it.

'rite an Ending Tell how the problem gets resolved.

Reflect and Evaluate

- Did you introduce the characters and a problem in the beginning?
- Did you show most of the details, rather than tell about them?
- Does your fantasy include unbelievable characters, settings, or events?

OBJECTIVES

DRAFT

Function: Ⓣ Decribe; Write

Learning Strategies and Critical Thinking: Generate Ideas; Self-Assess

Writer's Craft: Ⓣ Introductions; Show, Don't Tell

Writing: Ⓣ Writing Process

DRAFT

Before students begin their drafts, discuss the Writer's Craft models:

- In **Step 1**, ask a volunteer to describe how the introduction gets the reader interested in the story.
- In **Step 2**, ask volunteers to explain how the second model in each set "shows" rather than "tells."

Use the Drafting Support in the **Multi-Level Strategies** to tailor this stage to proficiency levels.

For more about the Writer's Craft, refer students to pages 414–423 in the Handbook.

CLOSE AND ASSESS

Have small groups discuss the questions in Reflect and Evaluate while you work with those who may need more support in assessing their drafts.

Multi-Level Strategies

DRAFTING SUPPORT

BEGINNING To draft their fantasy stories, students can write one or more sentences for each drawing they included in their storyboard. Prompt them to cover all story elements: *Your first sentences can name the characters and describe the setting. Then tell the problem. . . .* For additional support, ask students questions about their drawings, and then guide them in forming simple sentences as captions.

INTERMEDIATE / **ADVANCED** Have partners apply the Writer's Craft skill as they create examples that "show" rather than "tell" on **Master 14**. Partners can then discuss ways to "show" and not "tell" in their own stories as they prepare to write their drafts.

Transparency 14 / Master 14

WRITING: SHOW, DON'T TELL

Directions: Read each writing tip and each example that "tells." Change the example to make it "show."

Writing Tips	This tells	This shows
Use dialogue.	Sheila and the woman went to ancient Egypt.	"I will take you to ancient Egypt," said the woman.
	Sheila told her mother that the trip was unbelievable.	"You won't believe what happened to me," Sheila said to her mother.
Use descriptions to show action and how the characters feel.	When the woman spoke, it really surprised Sheila.	Then the woman spoke to Sheila, and Sheila jumped out of her chair!
	Then Sheila was back at home.	The next thing Sheila knew she was sitting at her kitchen table again.

Transparency 14 Level B, Unit 1 | Communication

BUILD WRITING SKILLS

OBJECTIVES

REVISE

Function: Write; Engage in Discussion

Learning Strategies and Critical Thinking: Generate Ideas; Review; Clarify; Interact with Peers; Self-Assess

Listening and Speaking: Peer-Conferencing

Technology and Media: Use Word-Processing Software

Writing: T Writing Process

REVISE

First have students reread their drafts. They should turn the entries on their FATP charts into questions to answer as they assess their work. For example: *Is my fantasy story entertaining?*

Next model how to evaluate someone else's writing in a peer conference by asking questions about the content and clarity of the draft. Also model how a writer makes revisions. Students can then conduct the peer conferences and revise their drafts.

Use the Peer Conference Support in the **Multi-Level Strategies** to model how to evaluate and revise writing.

CLOSE AND ASSESS

Have peers discuss the questions in Reflect and Evaluate.

Writing That Tells a Story, continued

REVISE

1. **Reread Your Draft** Review your **FATP**. Are your form, audience, topic, and purpose clear? Does your story include enough events that cannot really happen?

2. **Conduct a Peer Conference** Talk to a partner or group about your writing.

Here is part of the conference that a writer, Luca, had with his reviewers, Yoshi and Sarita.

Sarita and Yoshi tell what they like about Luca's story.

Yoshi: I liked the part about how you realized you were inside the video game. You made me feel like I was right there!

Sarita: When you dropped into the dark tunnel, you used clear, descriptive words. I liked the sentence about how it smelled like rotten eggs.

Luca: Is there any part that confused you?

Sarita: Well, I wasn't sure about how you got from the top of the brick wall into the cave.

Yoshi: That happened a little too fast.

Luca: OK. I can add a sentence there to explain more.

3. **Mark Your Changes** Decide on the changes to make. Revising Marks appear on Handbook page 411. For how to make changes on the computer, see Handbook pages 386–387.

Key In TO Technology

On the computer, you can save different versions of your writi[ng.] Use the **Save As** command fro[m] the File menu and add a numb[er to] the document name. Then you [can] look back and choose the versi[on] you like best.

Reflect and Evalua[te]

- Were your peer reviewer[s] confused by anything in your story? What change[s] did they suggest?
- Are there parts of the st[ory] that you can drop?
- Are there details you car[n] add to make your fantas[y] even more lively?

REACHING ALL STUDENTS

Transparency 15 / Master 15

REVISING

Red annotations show changes related to the sample questions. Revisions should vary to reflect questions students propose.

"I will take you to ancient Egypt," said the woman as she lifted herself off the page. [She pointed to a machine in the kitchen.] She and Sheila [stepped] into it, and the woman pressed the button for ancient Egypt. A couple of seconds later, they stepped out. Sheila knew she was in Egypt [because she saw pyramids].

Revising Marks	
^	Add.
(loop arrow)	Move to here.
(caret with line)	Replace with this.
(arrow)	Take out.

Ask Questions in a Peer Conference

1. Ask about anything that isn't clear to you.
   - What did Sheila and the woman step into?
   - Students' questions will vary.
2. Think about the writing. Ask a question to make a suggestion.
   - Doesn't this sentence about the woman and Sheila need a verb to make it complete?
   - Students' questions will vary.
3. Ask about what else you want to know.
   - How did Sheila know she was in Egypt?
   - Students' questions will vary.

Transparency 15 Level B, Unit 1 | Communication © Hampton-Brown

Multi-Level Strategies

PEER CONFERENCE SUPPORT

BEGINNING Display **Transparency 15**. Read the paragraph on **Transparency 15**, in the box and support students' comprehension by role-playing coming out of a page of a book, getting into a time machine, etc. Then model how to evaluate the writing and formulate questions to express suggestions. Provide sample questions and have volunteers dictate other questions. Then model how to revise the writing, based on the questions.

INTERMEDIATE / ADVANCED Read the paragraph on **Transparency 15**, and have students identify parts that are not clear or that need more detail. Model with the sample questions and then have students suggest more of each type of question. Have volunteers suggest revisions to the writing, based on the questions.

AMMAR IN CONTEXT

MPLETE SENTENCES

mplete sentence has two main parts: the subject and the predicate. verb in the predicate must agree with the subject.

ne subject tells whom or what the sentence is about. The **complete ubject** includes all the words that tell about the subject. The **imple subject** is the most important word in the complete subject.

Examples: **Some people** love video games.

They play for hours.

The mall in our neighborhood has a great video arcade.

ne predicate tells what the subject is, does, or has. The **complete redicate** includes all the words in the predicate. The **simple predicate** the most important word in the predicate. It is the verb.

Examples: Some people **have fun with the adventure games.**

Others **prefer athletic games.**

My brother's favorite **is a snow-boarding game.**

Irregular Verbs	
Singular	**Plural**
is	are
has	have
does	do

ne **verb** must agree in number with the **simple subject.**

Examples: His **board glides** down the video mountains.

The mountains are under a blanket of snow.

ne **simple subject** and **verb** must agree even if other words come etween them.

Examples: **Conditions** during the game **change** often.

A **mudslide** in the mountains **is** around the next curve.

:tice Make up predicates to add to the subjects in column 1. Make up ects to add to the predicates in column 2.

ects	Predicates
ly favorite game	5. like the Jungle Adventure.
he object of the game	6. isn't a fun game.
ly friends	7. costs a lot.
he most popular games the arcade	8. has a good time at the mall.

OBJECTIVES

GRAMMAR IN CONTEXT

Grammar: Ⓣ Complete Sentences

GRAMMAR IN CONTEXT

1 Teach Complete Sentences Read the definitions and study the examples together. Then conduct the cooperative learning activity below.

2 Answers to Practice Items Student answers will vary. These are samples:

1. My favorite game is called Space Station 3.
2. The object of the game is to build a space station quickly.
3. My friends also like the game.
4. The most popular games in the arcade are the adventure games.
5. My sisters like the Jungle Adventure.
6. Deep Sea Fishing isn't a fun game.
7. A new video game costs a lot.
8. Ruth has a good time at the mall.

CLOSE AND ASSESS

Have partners each write a subject or a predicate, trade papers, and then complete each other's sentence.

REACHING ALL STUDENTS

Cooperative Learning

FOR LANGUAGE DEVELOPMENT: Complete Sentences

Materials: several index cards per student

Create Complete Sentences Groups of four choose a topic. One student creates a complete sentence about it. Another student writes the subject of the sentence on one card and the predicate on another. The remaining two students each take one card and create a new sentence from it. Repeat the activity until everyone has performed each task. Encourage group members to assist one another.

Debrief the Skill Ask students to share some of the sentences they created. List the subjects and predicates. Ask: *Was it easier to think of subjects or predicates? Which predicates have irregular verbs?*

Debrief the Cooperative Process Have students reflect on the activity: *How did working with a group make it easier to create sentences? How were you able to help someone else?*

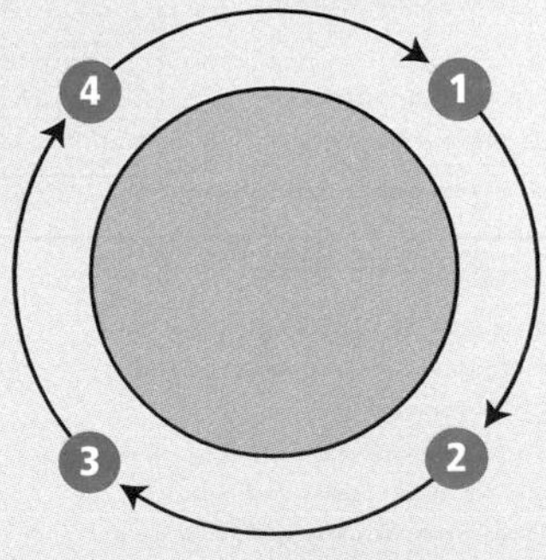

Cooperative Learning Structure: Roundtable

BUILD WRITING SKILLS

OBJECTIVES

EDIT AND PROOFREAD

Learning Strategies and Critical Thinking: Review; Clarify; Self-Assess

Technology and Media: Use Word-Processing Software

Writing: Ⓣ Writing Process

PUBLISH

Learning Strategies and Critical Thinking: Interact with Peers; Self-Assess; Make Decisions

Speaking: Read Aloud

Technology and Media: Use the Internet

Writing: Ⓣ Writing Process

EDIT AND PROOFREAD

Before students edit and proof their own writing, use **Transparency 16** to model the process.

PUBLISH

Ask volunteers to share publishing ideas or choose from those suggested on page 68.

Use the Editing and Publishing Support in the **Multi-Level Strategies** to meet the varying needs of students.

CLOSE AND ASSESS

Have groups discuss the questions in Reflect and Evaluate. Monitor how students complete the checklist.

WRITING ASSESSMENT
Use the Writing Rubric on page 11 of the Assessment Handbook to evaluate this writing assignment.

Writing That Tells a Story, continued

EDIT AND PROOFREAD

1. **Check for Mistakes** Look through your writing to correct any mistakes in capitalization, punctuation, and spelling. If you need help, see Handbook pages 459–469.
2. **Check Your Sentences** Make sure every sentence has a subject and a predicate. Check that every verb agrees in number with its subject.
3. **Make a Final Copy** If you are working on a computer, print out the final, correct version of your story. If you are writing, carefully copy a final version.

PUBLISH

Use these ideas for publishing your writing or come up with your own.

- Collect everyone's stories to make a class anthology. Add a cover and a table of contents. Include a short author biography and author photograph at the end of each story.

"I NEED TO GET OUT!" I screamed. I shut my eyes tight as an echo bounced around the dark cave: *GET OUT, GET OUT, GET OUT.* When I opened my eyes, I was back in my living room. I stared at the video screen. "I think I'll go outside to play after all," I said to myself. And that's just what I did.

THE END

ABOUT THE AUTHOR

Luca Benini is in the seventh grade. In addition to writing stories, he likes playing soccer, listening to music, and playing video games. The idea for this story came to him because his mother says he plays video games too much!

- Illustrate your story and display it on a bulletin board.
- Submit your story to a teen magazine.

Key In TO Technology

After you've checked your spelling, double-check by usin[g] the spell-check feature of you[r] word-processing program.

Reflect and Evalua[te]

- Are you pleased with yo[ur] fantasy? Does it
  - ☑ introduce the charact[ers] and a problem in the beginning?
  - ☑ include unbelievable characters, settings, o[r] events?
  - ☑ have events that lead in sequence to a conclusion?
- What do you like best about your story? What you like least?
- Will this work go in your portfolio? Why or why n[ot]?

REACHING ALL STUDENTS

Transparency 16 / Master 16

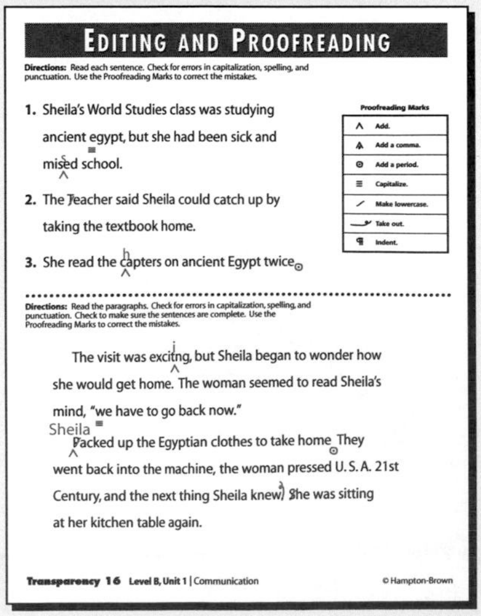

EDITING AND PROOFREADING

Directions: Read each sentence. Check for errors in capitalization, spelling, and punctuation. Use the Proofreading Marks to correct the mistakes.

1. Sheila's World Studies class was studying ancient egypt, but she had been sick and mised school.
2. The Teacher said Sheila could catch up by taking the textbook home.
3. She read the capters on ancient Egypt twice

Proofreading Marks

^	Add.
^,	Add a comma.
⊙	Add a period.
≡	Capitalize.
/	Make lowercase.
⌒	Take out.
¶	Indent.

Directions: Read the paragraphs. Check for errors in capitalization, spelling, and punctuation. Check to make sure the sentences are complete. Use the Proofreading Marks to correct the mistakes.

The visit was excitng, but Sheila began to wonder how she would get home. The woman seemed to read Sheila's mind, "we have to go back now."

Sheila
Packed up the Egyptian clothes to take home They went back into the machine, the woman pressed U. S. A. 21st Century, and the next thing Sheila knew, She was sitting at her kitchen table again.

Transparency 16 Level B, Unit 1 | Communication © Hampton-Brown

Multi-Level Strategies

EDITING AND PUBLISHING SUPPORT

BEGINNING Model finding and correcting errors in the top section of **Transparency 16**. After marking the edits, have students write out the corrected sentences. For publishing, help students who made storyboards scan and import their art into a word-processing document and then choose a special font for their final sentences.

INTERMEDIATE Guide students in finding and correcting the errors in the paragraph at the bottom of **Transparency 16**. For publishing, encourage students to illustrate their stories and read them aloud to younger students.

ADVANCED Distribute copies of **Master 16** and have students work on the activities individually or with partners. Students may wish to create their own web site to publish these stories and their future writing.

Debrief

Get the Message!

UNIT 1

ASSESSMENT
The Unit 1 Test on page 13 of the Assessment Handbook measures students' progress in reading, language arts, literary study, and writing. Additional forms in the Assessment Handbook allow for:
- **Self Assessment on page 12**
- **Peer Assessment on page 101**
- **Portfolio Evaluation on page 103**

Look Back at the Unit

Rank Messages In this unit, you read about many different messages. Talk with a partner about the messages in each selection. What ideas and information did each one communicate?

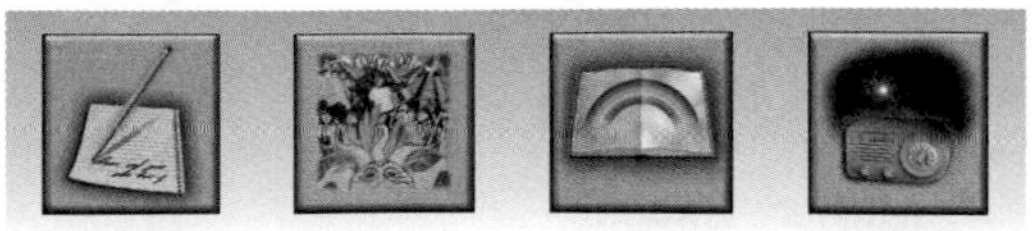

The Power of Poetry | Talking Walls | Tales Across Time | Fat Men from Space

Write the titles and a brief summary of the messages on index cards. Put the cards in order from most important to least important message. Tell why some messages are more important than others.

Show What You Know

Sum It All Up Expand and organize your ideas on this chart. Share your ideas about communication with a partner.

Communication

Verbal	Nonverbal	Temporary	Lasting

Reflect and Evaluate Make a list of things you discovered about communication from this unit. Add this list to your portfolio, along with work that shows what you learned.

Make Connections

To Your Community Explore your community. Try to find a place that has some historical importance. Tell your class about the message that has been preserved by that historical landmark.

DEBRIEF UNIT 1

OBJECTIVES

Function: Engage in Discussion; Express Opinions

Learning Strategies and Critical Thinking: Interact with Peers; Generate Ideas; Make Judgments; Summarize; Self-Assess; Form Opinions; Use Graphic Organizers (mind map)

Literary Analysis: Respond to Literature; Compare and Evaluate Literature

EXPLORE "GET THE MESSAGE!"

1. **Look Back at the Unit** Help students develop criteria to use when ranking the messages. For example: *Will the message stand the test of time?* Then begin the Cooperative Learning Activity.

2. **Show What You Know** Suggest that students include in their portfolios work that shows the impact of effective communication.

3. **Make Connections** Help students identify historical sites and the messages they convey about your community.

CLOSE AND ASSESS

Have students tell you the most important thing they learned in the unit.

Cooperative Learning

FOR CRITICAL THINKING: Summarize

Discuss Messages Develop criteria, then place students in inside-outside circles, as shown. Pairs facing each other discuss and summarize the message in the first selection, then discuss the second selection with the next partner. Continue until students have talked about all four selections.

Rank Messages Students complete an index card after each discussion, then rank the messages after all have been discussed.

Debrief the Content Have students share what they learned about communication from the unit, for example: *I learned that many different kinds of messages matter.*

Debrief the Cooperative Process Have students evaluate how working with a partner helped them summarize. Ask: *What ideas did your partners provide that gave you new ideas?*

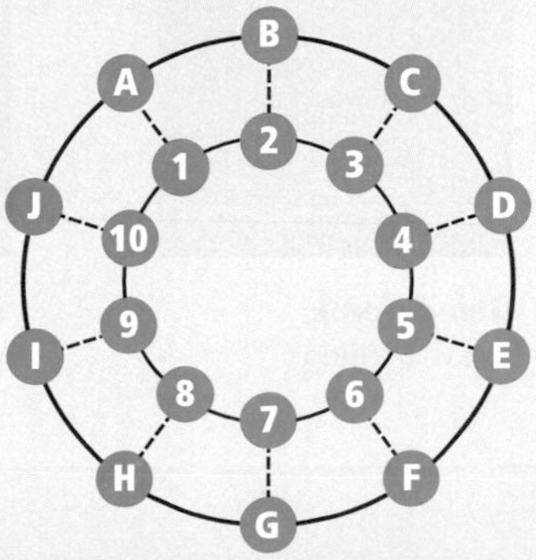

Cooperative Learning Structure: Inside-Outside Circle

Resources

For Success in Language, Literature, and Content

Student Book pages 70–139

For Skills Practice

Practice Book
pages 30–62

For Planning and Instruction

Teacher's Edition
pages T70a–T139

For Vocabulary and Language Development

Language Tape Side A
Language CD Tracks 2 and 3

For Selection Readings

Selection Tape 2
Selection CD 2

For Technology Support

Inspiration
Visual Learning Software
with Graphic Organizers

For Classroom Activities

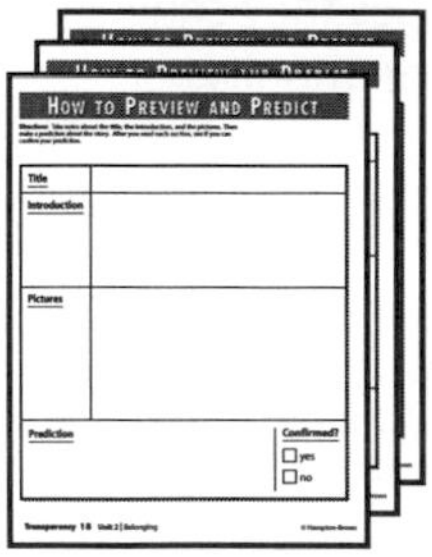

Transparencies or Masters 17–33

For Home-School Connections

High Point Newsletters 3 and 4

For Comprehensive Assessment

Language Acquisition Assessment, Selection Tests, Unit Test, Writing Assessment, Self-Assessment

In the Theme Library

Going Home
by Eve Bunting

Seedfolks
by Paul Fleischman

From *The Basics Bookshelf*

- ***Families***
- ***Let's Dance!***
- ***More Than a Meal***

Theme-related books with simple text for including newcomers

A Sense of Place

Rhythm, Joie de Vivre, Robert Delaunay, oil on canvas. Copyright © 1930.

THE LONGING TO BE A PART OF SOMETHING—TO BELONG—IS A POWERFUL FORCE. IT IS THE FIRST STEP TOWARD UNDERSTANDING AND CELEBRATING OUR DIFFERENCES. THIS UNIT CHALLENGES STUDENTS, WORKING TO FIND THEIR OWN PLACE IN THE WORLD, TO LOOK AT WHAT IT MEANS TO BELONG.

THEME 1 Fitting In

Students learn that finding the place where they belong can help them connect to other times and other places.

THEME 2 Bridging the Gap

Students explore how cultural differences can be overcome by looking beyond the surface and finding common interests.

Activity Planner

THEME 1: Fitting In

LESSONS

1 **THEME 1 OPENER** ▶ pages T72–T73

Function	Learning Strategy	Vocabulary	Critical Thinking
Engage in Discussion	Make a T-chart	Words About Belonging	Draw Conclusions

2 **BUILD LANGUAGE AND VOCABULARY** ▶ pages T74–T75

Function	Learning Strategy	Vocabulary	Patterns and Structures
Ⓣ Ask and Answer Questions	Make a Personal Data Chart	Words About People and Places	Ⓣ Questions: Present and Past Tense Verbs

PACING SUGGESTIONS

LESSONS	45–55 MINUTE PERIODS	BLOCK SCHEDULE SESSIONS
1	1 period	→ 1 session
2	1 period	
3–9	6 periods	3 sessions
10–11	2 periods	1 session
12–17	6 periods	3 sessions

3–9 ***The Keeping Quilt*** by Patricia Polacco — FAMILY HISTORY ▶ pages T76–T86

PREPARE TO READ
page T76

Activate Prior Knowledge
Brainstorm Traditions

Vocabulary Ⓣ
Locate and Use Definitons

Reading Strategy
Ⓣ Preview and Make Predictions

READ THE SELECTION
pages T77–T83

Pre-Reading Strategies
Identify Genre: Personal Narrative
Set Purpose

Strategy Focus
Ⓣ Make and Confirm Predictions

Vocabulary
Use New Words in Context

Comprehension
Before you Move On: Think and Discuss

Grammar Minilessons:
Ⓣ Past Tense Verbs
Ⓣ Irregular Past Tense Verbs
Ⓣ Future Tense Verbs

RESPOND
pages T84–T86

CHECK YOUR UNDERSTANDING

Critical Thinking and Comprehension
Sum It Up:
Ⓣ Confirm Predictions; Review and Retell a Story
Think It Over: Discuss and Write

Function
Express Yourself: Ask and Answer Questions

LANGUAGE ARTS AND LITERATURE

Grammar in Context
Ⓣ Use Verb Tense

Literary Analysis and Speaking/Listening
Learn About Symbolism

CONTENT AREA CONNECTIONS

Fine Arts and Technology/Media
Make a Keeping Quilt

Social Studies and Technology/Media
Compare Wedding Traditions

10–11 **from *Human Family*** by Maya Angelou — POEM ▶ pages T87–T89

PREPARE TO READ
page T87

Activate Prior Knowledge
Make a Venn Diagram

Vocabulary
Relate Words

Reading Strategy
Use Text Structures (stanzas)

READ THE POEM
pages T88–T89

Pre-Reading Strategies
Set Purpose

Strategy Focus
Use Text Structures (stanzas)

RESPOND
pages T89

Critical Thinking and Comprehension
Think It Over: Discuss

Literary Analysis
Alliteration
Assonance

Function
Express Yourself: Recite a Poem

12–17 ***Beyond the Color Lines*** by Janell, Jenny, and Christian — SELF-PORTRAITS ▶ pages T90–T99

PREPARE TO READ
page T90

Activate Prior Knowledge
Idea Exchange

Vocabulary Ⓣ
Locate and Use Definitions

Reading Strategy
Ⓣ Distinguish Between Facts and Opinions

READ THE SELECTION
pages T91–T97

Pre-Reading Strategies
Preview and Predict
Set Purpose

Strategy Focus
Ⓣ Distinguish Between Facts and Opinions

Vocabulary
Use New Words in Context

Comprehension
Before You Move On: Think and Discuss

Grammar Minilessons:
Questions
Transitive and Intransitive Verbs

RESPOND
pages T98–T99

CHECK YOUR UNDERSTANDING

Critical Thinking and Comprehension
Sum It Up:
Ⓣ Distinguish Between Facts and Opinions; Write an Opinion
Think It Over: Discuss and Write

Function
Express Yourself: Dramatize

LANGUAGE ARTS AND LITERATURE

Grammar in Context
Use Helping Verbs

Writing and Technology/Media
Write a Self-Portrait

Ⓣ = Assessed on **Unit 2 Test** Ⓣ = Assessed on **Unit 2 Language Acquisition Assessment**

THEME 2: Bridging the Gap

LESSONS

1

THEME 2 OPENER
▶ pages T100–T101

Function	Learning Strategy	Vocabulary	Critical Thinking
Engage in Discussion	Make a List	Connection Words	Generate Ideas

2

BUILD LANGUAGE AND VOCABULARY
▶ pages T102–T103

Function	Learning Strategy	Vocabulary	Patterns and Structures
(T) Express Likes and Dislikes	Make Class Graphs	Words About Likes and Dislikes	(T) Pronouns

PACING SUGGESTIONS

LESSONS	45–55 MINUTE PERIODS	BLOCK SCHEDULE SESSIONS
1	1 period	1 session (lessons 1–2)
2	1 period	
3–9	6 periods	3 sessions
10–16	6 periods	3 sessions
17–20	3 periods	1 sessions

3–9

Teammates by Peter Golenbock
BIOGRAPHY ▶ pages T104–T115

PREPARE TO READ page T104

Activate Prior Knowledge
Quickwrite

Vocabulary (T)
Use Context Clues

Reading Strategy
Connect New Information to Known

READ THE SELECTION pages T105–T112

Pre-Reading Strategies
Build Background
Identify Genre: Biography
Set Purpose

Strategy Focus
Connect New Information to Known

Vocabulary
Relate Words

Self-Monitoring and Comprehension
Paraphrase
Before You Move On: Think and Discuss

Grammar Minilesson:
(T) Pronouns

Literary Analysis Minilesson:
(T) Narrator's Point of View

RESPOND pages T113–T115

CHECK YOUR UNDERSTANDING

Critical Thinking and Comprehension
Sum It Up: Connect New Information to Known
Think It Over: Discuss and Write

Function
Express Yourself: Describe

LANGUAGE ARTS AND LITERATURE

Grammar in Context
(T) Use Pronouns

Writing and Literary Analysis
Evaluate Literature

CONTENT AREA CONNECTIONS

Social Studies and Representing/Speaking
Make an Historical Events Chart

Technology/Media and Speaking/Listening
Investigate Media

10–16

Amir by Paul Fleischman
REALISTIC FICTION ▶ pages T116–T126

PREPARE TO READ page T116

Activate Prior Knowledge
Create a Chart

Vocabulary (T)
Use New Words in Context

Reading Strategy
(T) Relate Sequence of Events

READ THE SELECTION pages T117–T123

Pre-Reading Strategies
Preview and Predict
Identify Genre: Realistic Fiction
Set Purpose

Strategy Focus
(T) Relate Sequence of Events

Vocabulary
Use New Words in Context

Comprehension
Before You Move On: Think and Discuss

Grammar Minilessons:
Possessive Nouns
(T) Possessive Pronouns
Negative Sentences

Literary Analysis Minilesson:
Flashback

RESPOND pages T124–T126

CHECK YOUR UNDERSTANDING

Critical Thinking and Comprehension
Sum It Up:
(T) Relate Sequence of Events; Analyze Characters; Make a Generalization
Think It Over: Discuss and Write

Function
Express Yourself: Express Likes and Dislikes

LANGUAGE ARTS AND LITERATURE

Grammar in Context
(T) Use Indefinite Pronouns

Literary Analysis and Writing/Speaking
Write a Story

CONTENT AREA CONNECTIONS

Technology/Media and Science
Research Food Chains

17–20

Starting a Community Garden by DyAnne DiSalvo-Ryan
HOW-TO ARTICLE ▶ pages T127–T131

PREPARE TO READ page T127

Activate Prior Knowledge
Idea Exchange

Vocabulary (T)
Use Words in Context

Reading Strategy
Set a Purpose and Reading Rate

READ THE SELECTION pages T128–T129

Pre-Reading Strategies
Set Purpose

Strategy Focus
Set a Purpose and Reading Rate

Comprehension
Before You Move On: Think and Discuss

Grammar Minilesson:
Progressive Forms of Verbs

RESPOND pages T130–T131

CHECK YOUR UNDERSTANDING

Critical Thinking and Comprehension
Sum It Up: Analyze Information
Think It Over: Discuss and Write

Function
Express Yourself: Describe

LANGUAGE ARTS AND CONTENT AREA CONNECTIONS

Representing/Speaking and Social Studies
Food Banks Speech

Science and Social Studies
Compare Gardens

BUILD WRITING SKILLS

WRITING FOR PERSONAL EXPRESSION
EXPRESSIVE: PERSONAL HISTORY ▶ Pages T132–T138

Writing Mode/Form	Writing Process (T)	Writer's Craft	Grammar in Context	Reflect and Evaluate
(T) Expressive Personal History	Prewrite; Draft; Revise; Edit and Proofread; Publish	(T) Paragraph Structure	(T) Verb Tenses	Self-Assessment

(T) = Assessed on **Unit 2 Test** (T) = Assessed on **Unit 2 Language Acquisition Assessment**

Theme-Related Resources

THEME 1: Fitting In

MORE RESOURCES

THEME LIBRARY

Going Home
by Eve Bunting
B Mexico doesn't seem like home to Carlos until he realizes home can be anywhere you are loved. (Available from Hampton-Brown)

Journey to Ellis Island: How My Father Came to America
by Carol Bierman
I Ellis Island authorities want to send Yehuda back to Russia, but Yehuda proves his strength and stays. (Hyperion)

Yang the Third and Her Impossible Family
by Lensey Namioka
A Yingmei Yang adapts to life in America while keeping her Chinese customs. (Yearling Books)

Home to Medicine Mountain
by Chiori Santiago
I Based on a true story, this book is about two Native American children who are forced to fit into a culture that is not their own. (Children's Book Press)

New Kids in Town: Oral Histories of Immigrant Teens
by Janet Bode
A A collection of the true stories by teen immigrants who left their home countries to come and start new lives in America. (Scholastic)

Fiddler on the Roof
B I A This musical drama is a loving portrayal of family traditions in the Russian Jewish community before political tensions forced many to seek new homes in other lands. **Film/Video**

THEME 2: Bridging the Gap

MORE RESOURCES

THEME LIBRARY

Seedfolks
by Paul Fleischman
I People of different backgrounds get together and change an ugly city lot into a beautiful garden. (Available from Hampton-Brown)

The Bicycle Man
by Allen Say
B Not long after World War II, two American soldiers make friends with a group of children at a school in Japan. (Parnassus Press)

Oh, Freedom!
by Casey King and Linda Barrett Osborne
A Young people interview adults about their involvement in the Civil Rights movement. (Knopf)

The Foxman
by Gary Paulsen
A A teenage city boy has to go live with his relatives in a farm in the wilderness. There he meets an old, disfigured man who teaches him many things. (Penguin)

In My Own Voice: Multicultural Poets on Identity
I A Multicultural poets read their own poetry and discuss how their writing expresses a sense of identity and belonging. (Sunburst) **Multimedia CD-ROM**

The Jackie Robinson Story
B I A Starring Jackie Robinson himself, this 1950 film stirringly relates the events and emotions of Robinson's entry into Major League baseball. **Film/Video**

B Beginning I Intermediate A Advanced

Assessment Options

ONGOING, INFORMAL ASSESSMENT

Check for understanding and achieve closure for every lesson with the targeted questions and activities in the **Close and Assess** boxes in your Teacher's Edition.

INDIVIDUAL AND GROUP-ADMINISTERED TESTS

The **Assessment Handbook** includes these comprehensive assessment tools for Unit 2:

- **Selection Tests**
  Test students' mastery of reading strategies and the vocabulary, comprehension, and language arts skills taught with each main selection of Unit 2.
- **Unit Test in Standardized Test Format**
  The multiple-choice sections of this test measure students' cumulative understanding of the skills and language developed in Unit 2. A Writing Prompt measures progress in writing skills and fluency. The Read, Think, and Explain section offers open-ended items to measure strategies and comprehension.
- **Language Acquisition Assessment**
  To verify students' ability to use the vocabulary and grammar structures taught in Unit 2, conduct these performance assessments.

UNIT 2 ASSESSMENT OPPORTUNITIES

	Assessment Handbook Pages
Unit 2 Language Acquisition Assessment	21–22
Selection Tests	
The Keeping Quilt	23–24
Beyond the Color Lines	25–26
Teammates	27–28
Amir	29–30
Unit 2 Writing Assessment	31
Unit 2 Self-Assessment Form	32
Unit 2 Test	33–40
Peer-Assessment Form	101
Portfolio Evaluation Form	103

SELF- AND PEER-ASSESSMENT

Students use the Unit 2 Self-Assessment Form in the **Assessment Handbook** to evaluate their own work and develop learning strategies appropriate to their needs. Students offer feedback to their classmates with the Peer-Assessment Form.

WRITING ASSESSMENT / PORTFOLIO OPPORTUNITIES

You can evaluate students' writing using the rubrics and scoring guidelines provided in the **Assessment Handbook**. Then collaborate with students to choose work for their portfolios.

INTRODUCE UNIT 2

OBJECTIVES

Function: Engage in Discussion

Concepts and Vocabulary: Belonging—*belong, fitting in, sense of place, connections, bridging the gap*

Viewing: Interpret a Visual Image

Critical Thinking and Learning Strategies: Build Background; Make Comparisons; Use Graphic Organizers (mind map); Preview

INTRODUCE UNIT CONCEPT

1 **Read the Title and Contribute Ideas** Refer students to the titles and art on pages 70 and 71. Ask: *What does it mean to belong? In what situations do you feel you belong? In what situations do you feel you don't? What does it mean to have a sense of place? Can you have more than one sense of place?*

2 **Create and Compare Circles** Conduct the activity. After students write their names in various circles, discuss where they fit in and where they don't. Then have students work in pairs to compare the circles. Ask them to think of ways the various circles are the same and ways they are different.

3 **Discuss Belonging** Invite students to discuss:

- what groups they automatically belong to without having to join
- how they choose what groups they would like to be part of
- how it feels to belong or not to belong to a certain group.

Use the Questioning Techniques in the **Multi-Level Strategies** to create a class mind map.

UNIT 2 Belonging

Rhythm, Joie de Vivre, Robert Delaunay, oil on canvas. Copyright © 1930.

70

REACHING ALL STUDENTS

Multi-Level Strategies

QUESTIONING TECHNIQUES

BEGINNING Encourage students to verbalize their connections by completing sentence starters: *I am (a girl, Chinese, a student)... I can....* Ask yes/no questions to help students contribute ideas to the mind map: *Do you belong to more than one group? Do you and your friends all belong to the same groups?*

INTERMEDIATE Ask students open-ended questions to prompt ideas for the mind map: *How does it feel to belong? To what groups do you belong now? To what groups might you belong in the future?*

ADVANCED Ask students questions requiring more complex answers about their feelings and experiences with groups: *To which group do you most enjoy belonging? Why?*

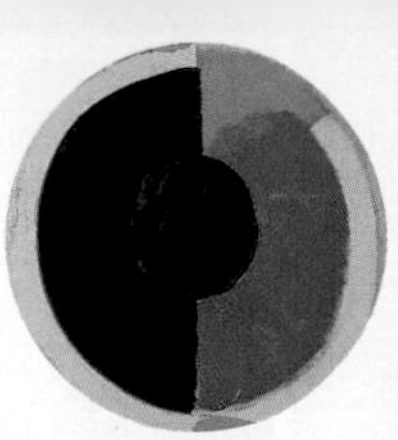

A Sense of Place

Draw some large circles and put them on your classroom wall. Name them with words like brother, sister, American, good at sports, teenager, over five feet tall, speak Spanish and English, and so on. Write your name in each circle you fit in. How many groups do you belong to? Are there groups that everyone belongs to? In five years, could you add your name to more groups?

THEME **1**

Fitting In

When you find a place to belong in the world, you can connect with people from other times and other places.

THEME **2**

Bridging the Gap

You can overcome cultural differences by looking beyond the surface and finding your common interests.

UNIT 2 Mind Map

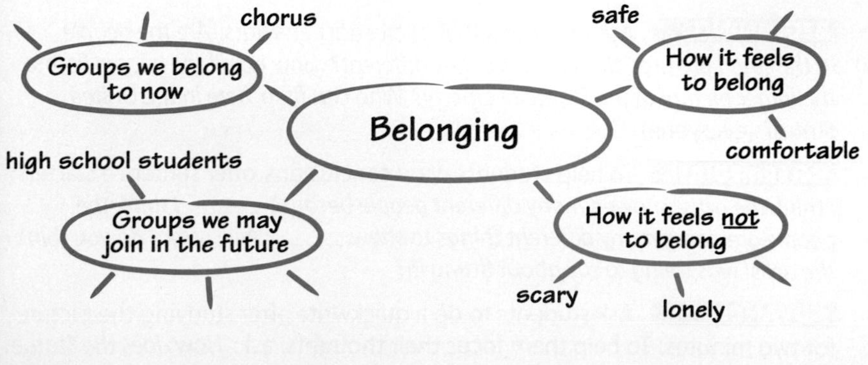

Technology Support

See **Inspiration** Visual Learning software for support in creating mind maps.

PREVIEW UNIT THEMES

4 **Preview Theme 1: Fitting In** Read aloud the theme title and statement. Talk about what it means to *fit in.* Ask: *Does everyone have to look and act the same in order to fit in?* Ask students to suggest ways in which people can make connections with each other.

Then relate the theme to students' lives. Ask: *What connections have you made since becoming a member of this class? Who was the first person you connected with? Why did you connect with that person?*

Invite students to leaf through the pages 72–97 and tell you the kinds of connections they will be reading about.

5 **Preview Theme 2: Bridging the Gap** Read aloud the theme title and statement. Ask students to discuss differences (such as gender, culture, and background) represented by students in the class.

Relate the theme to students' lives by asking: *With whom have you connected, despite your differences?* Explain that this is sometimes called "bridging the gap."

Invite students to leaf through pages 100–129 and find examples of people who have bridged the gap between themselves and someone different from themselves.

6 **Set up Student Mind Maps** Have students draw the mind map in their notebooks or start the map in the **Practice Book**. Encourage them to add to the map as they move through the unit.

▶ **Practice Book** page 30

CLOSE AND ASSESS

Ask:

- *What will this unit be about?* (belonging)
- *To which groups do you automatically belong? Which groups do you join by choice?*
- *How can people bridge gaps and connect with each other?*

INTRODUCE THEME 1

OBJECTIVES

Function: Engage in Discussion
Concepts and Vocabulary: Belonging—*fitting in*
Viewing: Interpret a Visual Image
Learning Strategies: Relate to Personal Experience; Use Graphic Organizers (T-chart)
Critical Thinking: Generate Ideas; Draw Conclusions

TAP PRIOR KNOWLEDGE

1 Think, Pair, Share on Fitting In Write these questions: *What makes you feel that you fit in with people in your family and in your class? What does it take to fit in with new people?* Tell students to exchange ideas with a partner and then share with the class.

VIEW AND DISCUSS

2 View a Photo Collage Have students work in triads for three minutes to jot down what they see in the small photos. After each group shares, ask: *What image is made when all the small pictures are put together?* (They form the Statue of Liberty.)

3 Draw Conclusions Explain the significance of the statue. Ask:

- *Why did the photographer use pictures of many different people?*
- *Why did he choose to represent the Statue of Liberty?*
- *Who can fit in, here in the United States?*

Use the Discussion Prompts in the **Multi-Level Strategies** to involve all students in drawing conclusions.

Observations	Conclusions
Many different kinds of people are doing many different things.	Different kinds of people can fit together.
The collage shows the Statue of Liberty.	There are many kinds of people in this country.

Liberty, Robert Silvers, photomosaic. Copyright © 1997.

REACHING ALL STUDENTS

Multi-Level Strategies

DISCUSSION PROMPTS

BEGINNING Ask questions that elicit short answers: *Are the people in the small pictures all alike or are they different? How do all the people fit into the larger picture of the Statue of Liberty? Who can fit in, here in the United States?* (everyone)

INTERMEDIATE To help students draw conclusions, offer sentence starters: *I think the artist showed many different people because ______. I think the people are doing many different things to show ______.* Ask: *What do you think the artist was trying to say about fitting in?*

ADVANCED Ask students to do a quickwrite after studying the picture for two minutes. To help them focus their thoughts, ask: *How does the Statue of Liberty symbolize fitting in?* When they have finished, have them add more ideas to the chart.

otations offer strategies for
eginning students

THEME 1

Fitting In

B Encourage elaboration: Include groups that relate to your interests or hobbies.

- What groups do you belong to? Think about your family, friends, and cultural background.
- How do people learn to fit in and become members of a new cultural group?

Restate: What are some
d ways to learn about a
rent cultural group?
can you make friends
at cultural group?

- What do they keep from the old culture? What do they add from the new one?

B Have students list and categorize elements of old and new cultures such as language, holidays, and customs. Then have them pick one element as most important and explain their choices.

B Pose choices: Do people keep their language, holidays, food, customs, and music? Which of these from the new culture are easiest to add?

EME-RELATED BOOKS

ng Home
Eve Bunting
cico doesn't seem like home to
os until he realizes home can
anywhere you are loved.

INNING

Journey to Ellis Island
by Carol Bierman
Ellis Island authorities want to send Yehuda back to Russia, but Yehuda proves that he is strong enough to be an American.

INTERMEDIATE

NOVEL

Yang the Third and Her Impossible Family
by Lensey Namioka
Yingmei Yang adapts to life in America while keeping her Chinese customs.

ADVANCED

73

DISCUSS THE GUIDING QUESTIONS

4 Set the Theme Some key points to develop during the discussion are:

- We all belong to many different groups. We automatically belong to some groups because of where we were born. We become members of other groups by deciding to join.
- People who live in a new cultural setting begin to adapt to some of the ways of the new culture. We may choose to dress a certain way, listen to certain music, participate in certain activities. All these choices can help us to fit into new groups.
- People generally hold onto old beliefs and attitudes that continue to provide guidance in their lives. Most people also adopt new ideas that make sense to them and that make it easier to fit in with the new culture.

Form groups and use the **Multi-Level Strategies** to allow all students to participate.

CLOSE AND ASSESS

On a head-and-shoulders-shaped paper ask students to write one sentence summarizing what they learned in this lesson. Display a large circle and post students' sentences inside it.

Multi-Level Strategies

GROUPING GUIDELINES

BEGINNING Group these students so you can define words and pose choices for responses. See suggestions in red on the facsimile of page 73.

INTERMEDIATE Ask students to work in groups to read the questions on page 73 and to look up the meanings of any words or phrases they don't understand. Then have them discuss their answers and be prepared to report to the class on their discussion.

ADVANCED Invite students to read and discuss the questions with a partner. Have each pair respond to the last question by brainstorming lists of things people might keep from their old culture and things they might adopt from their new one.

THEME LIBRARY

■ ***Going Home*** by Eve Bunting

Invite students to read *Going Home*. After they read, ask them to report about the book. Reports should include a short summary that compares how this story and one of the text selections communicate the theme of fitting in. Provide questions to help students begin: *Which story shows best how people feel about fitting in? Which character's experience is similar to yours?*

BUILD LANGUAGE AND VOCABULARY

OBJECTIVES

Function: Listen Actively; Recite; Ⓣ Ask and Answer Questions
Concepts and Vocabulary: Words About People and Places
Patterns and Structures: Ⓣ Questions; Ⓣ Present and Past Tense Verbs
Speaking: Interview
Learning Strategy: Use Graphic Organizers (chart)
Critical Thinking: Formulate Questions

START WITH A COMMON EXPERIENCE

1 Listen to and Recite a Poem Play "We're All in the Telephone Book" on the **Language Tape/CD** or read aloud the poem on page 74. Have students recite the poem several times.

Tape 1A
CD 1 Track 2

Use the Reciting Options in the **Multi-Level Strategies** so that all students can participate.

2 Ask and Answer Questions Model how to ask and answer questions.

How to Ask and Answer Questions

Yes/No Questions

- Start with a word like *Is, Do, Can* or *Will*: *Is your family's number in the telephone book?*
- Answer like this: *Yes, it is./No, it isn't.*

Short-Answer Questions

- Start with a word like *Who, What, Where, When, Why, Which,* or *How*: *Why is the telephone book alphabetical?* Give the information in your answer: *The telephone book is alphabetical so you can find a name easily.*

Tag Questions

- Put the question at the end of the sentence: *You can find my name, can't you?* Answer like this: *Yes, I can./No, I can't.*

Build Language and Vocabulary

ASK AND ANSWER QUESTIONS

Listen to the following poem, then recite it with your classmates.

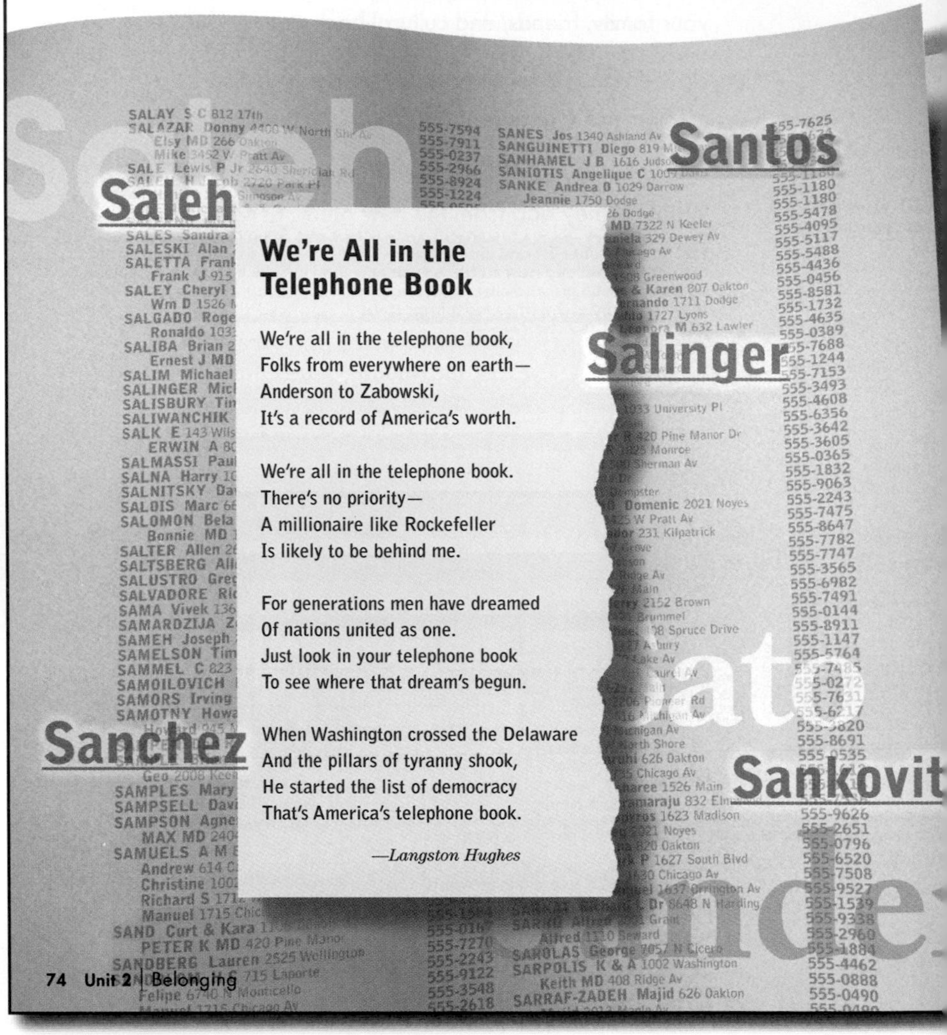

We're All in the Telephone Book

We're all in the telephone book,
Folks from everywhere on earth—
Anderson to Zabowski,
It's a record of America's worth.

We're all in the telephone book.
There's no priority—
A millionaire like Rockefeller
Is likely to be behind me.

For generations men have dreamed
Of nations united as one.
Just look in your telephone book
To see where that dream's begun.

When Washington crossed the Delaware
And the pillars of tyranny shook,
He started the list of democracy
That's America's telephone book.

—*Langston Hughes*

REACHING ALL STUDENTS

Multi-Level Strategies

RECITING OPTIONS

BEGINNING Have Beginning students chime in as they can. Invite students to say the line, "We're all in the telephone book," whenever it appears. Then have them use the same line to answer the question "Who's in the telephone book?" in a call-and-response group reading.

INTERMEDIATE / ADVANCED Have students work with heterogeneous partners. Assign each pair one of the stanzas. Invite pairs to practice reading their stanza aloud. Then have the pairs recite the stanzas in order. Explain that one way to bring expression to the reading of a poem is to have a good understanding of the meaning. Point out that the first and last lines of the poem summarize its meaning. Ask students to paraphrase the meaning of the poem. Then have the groups recite the poem again. Ask: *Do you notice an improvement?*

AKE A TELEPHONE BOOK

ake a telephone book for your class. List your names in alphabetical order, d write your last name first. Then make up a telephone number for yourself:

Think of a short word that describes you.

Use the code to turn the word into numbers.

Put a dash between each number.

Example:
Gonzales, Hector............1-20-8-12-5-20-9-3
Lee, Ming........................13-21-19-9-3-1-12

CODE	
A 1	N 14
B 2	O 15
C 3	P 16
D 4	Q 17
E 5	R 18
F 6	S 19
G 7	T 20
H 8	U 21
I 9	V 22
J 10	W 23
K 11	X 24
L 12	Y 25
M 13	Z 26

JILD YOUR VOCABULARY

ords About People and aces Copy the Personal ata Chart. Complete it with formation about yourself.

PERSONAL DATA CHART

Name: Manuel (first) S. (middle initial) Márquez (last)

Address: 324 Pine St. (street and no.) Otay (city) CA (state) 92010 (zip)

Places I Have Lived Before: (List in order; give city and state or country.)
1. Sabinas, Mexico
2. Del Rio, Texas
3. San Antonio, Texas
4.

Words That Tell Who I Am:		Places I Like to Go:	
brother	baby-sitter	Mexico	museums
soccer player	student	Seaport Village	movies
band member		the beach	

SE LANGUAGE STRUCTURES

QUESTIONS: PRESENT AND PAST TENSE VERBS

peaking: Interview a Classmate Work with a partner. Exchange charts. eview your partner's chart. Then come up with questions to ask your partner an interview. Ask about the past and the present. Use words like *when*, *hat*, *how*, *who*, *where*, *can*, and *is*.

Examples:
How old were you when you left Mexico?
What is your favorite movie?

CONDUCT THE ACTIVITIES

3 Make a Telephone Book Have students begin by working together to arrange their last names alphabetically.

4 Build Your Vocabulary: Words About People and Places Make a word wall with all the words from the students' charts.

5 Use Language Structures: Questions; Present and Past Tense Verbs Present the skill, using the definitions and examples on **Transparency 17**. Refer students to the Handbook (pages 450–451) to see more examples of irregular verbs. Then have students write answers and questions in Try It!

Speaking: Interview a Classmate Conduct the activity at the bottom of page 75. Suggest that students begin by asking when their classmates started school in the United States.

Use the Speaking Activity Options in the **Multi-Level Strategies** to adjust instruction.

▶ **Practice Book** page 31

CLOSE AND ASSESS

Call out a verb from this list.

give	talk	laugh
go	think	make

Have students tell the past tense form of the verb and then use it in a sentence.

Multi-Level Strategies

SPEAKING ACTIVITY OPTIONS

BEGINNING Work with partners to help them formulate questions. Provide a question and answer frame: *What was your favorite place to live? My favorite place was* _____.

INTERMEDIATE Have students ask their questions to their partners, taking notes about each other's answers. Then have them exchange papers and look for questions about the present and questions about the past.

ADVANCED After students have interviewed their partners, have them present a short biography of their partner to the class.

Transparency 17 / Master 17

PRESENT AND PAST TENSE VERBS

Present:	**is**	**are**	**do/does**	**has/have**
Past:	**was**	**were**	**did**	**had**

1. The tense of a verb shows when an action happens. Use a **present tense verb** if the action is happening now or if it happens all the time.
   My mom **calls** Grandma every week.
2. Use a **past tense verb** to show action that happened earlier, or in the past. Regular past tense verbs end in **-ed**.
   My mom **called** Grandma yesterday.
   Irregular verbs do not add **-ed**.
   Last year my grandparents **had** a pretty garden.
3. You can use present and past tense verbs to ask a question.
   Do your grandparents live in Mexico? **Was** their garden pretty?

Try It!

Write an answer for the question and a question for the answer.

1. Where do your grandparents live now?
2. Jason moved to New York two weeks ago.

Transparency 17 Level B, Unit 2 | Belonging

PREPARE TO READ

OBJECTIVES

THINK ABOUT WHAT YOU KNOW
Reading and Learning Strategies:
Relate to Personal Experience;
Use Graphic Organizers (word web)

LEARN KEY VOCABULARY Ⓣ
Vocabulary Strategy:
Locate and Use Definitions

LEARN TO PREVIEW AND MAKE PREDICTIONS
Reading Strategies:
Preview; Ⓣ Make Predictions

THINK ABOUT WHAT YOU KNOW

1. **Brainstorm Traditions** Have students work in pairs, then merge ideas in a class word web.

LEARN KEY VOCABULARY

2. **Locate and Use Definitions** Use each vocabulary word in a sentence. Then conduct the activity.

   Use the Vocabulary Options in the **Multi-Level Strategies** to help all students complete the activity.

▶ **Practice Book** page 32

LEARN TO PREVIEW AND MAKE PREDICTIONS

3. **Model How to Preview and Make Predictions** Define *preview* and *prediction.* Demonstrate the steps in the box with **Transparency 18**:

   - Distribute **Master 18**. Have students write the title. Read aloud the introduction and record notes. Model taking notes about the picture on page 77. Have students repeat for other pictures.
   - Then model how to review the notes and predict what the story will be about. Students can then make a prediction from their notes.

CLOSE AND ASSESS

Ask: *Why should you preview a reading and make predictions?* (It can help you focus and prepare for the reading.)

The Keeping Quilt
family history
by Patricia Polacco

Prepare to Read

THINK ABOUT WHAT YOU KNOW

Brainstorm Traditions What traditions does your family have? Think about births, weddings, and holidays. Make a web naming traditional objects and activities.

traditions

apron piece of clothing that protects other clothes
babushka scarf worn over the head and tied under the chin
bouquet bunch of flowers

bride woman about to be married or just married
celebrate have special activities in honor of an event
engaged promised in marriage
husband man who is married

nightdress loose garment worn in bed
quilt bed cover made of piecesof cloth sewn together
tablecloth cloth for covering a table, used especially at meals
wedding huppa cloth supported on poles that a couple stands under when being married

Answers to the vocabulary activity:
Weddings: bouquet, bride, celebrate, engaged, husband, wedding huppa
Clothing: apron, babushka, nightdress
Household Objects: table cloth, quilt

LEARN KEY VOCABULARY

Locate and Use Definitions Study the new words. Work with a group. Predict the category for each word. Look up the words in the Glossary and correct your predictions. Use the words to write one or two sentences about each category.

Weddings	Clothing	Household Objects
bride	apron	tablecloth

LEARN TO PREVIEW AND MAKE PREDICTIONS

When you **preview**, you look over parts of the story before you read it. This helps you **predict**, or guess, what the story is about.

READING STRATEGY
How to Preview and Make Predictions
1. Read the title and the introduction.
2. Look at the pictures and think about how they relate to the title.
3. Predict what you think will happen in the story.
4. Read the story. Then check to see if your predictions were correct.

Make a chart to preview each section of "The Keeping Quilt" and check your predictions.

REACHING ALL STUDENTS

Multi-Level Strategies
VOCABULARY OPTIONS

BEGINNING Group students to read ***Families*** or the Key Points Reading on **Master 19**. (See page T79.) Work with the vocabulary, putting words in appropriate categories.

INTERMEDIATE Ask and answer questions to help students predict categories. Have pairs look up words and write sentences together.

ADVANCED Students collaborate to write sentences using two or more words from one category in each sentence.

Transparency 18 / Master 18

HOW TO PREVIEW AND PREDICT

Directions: Take notes about the title, the introduction, and the pictures. Then make a prediction about the story. After you read each section, see if you can confirm your prediction.

Title	The Keeping Quilt
Introduction	family quilt used at wedding a tradition
Pictures	**page 77:** Women are looking at a quilt. **page 79:** Women are sewing a quilt. **page 81:** The quilt is covering a bride and groom. **page 82:** The quilt is covering an old woman.
Prediction	I think this story will be about all the ways a family uses a quilt.
Confirmed?	☐ yes ☐ no

Transparency 18 Level B, Unit 2 | Belonging © Hampton-Brown

The Keeping Quilt

by Patricia Polacco

Anna and her mother make a quilt from old clothes that belonged to family members in their homeland. When the quilt is used at Anna's wedding, a tradition begins. The quilt connects Anna and her family to their past, to their culture, and to one another.

READ THE SELECTION

OBJECTIVES

Reading Strategies:
T Make and Confirm Predictions
Literary Analysis: Family History

INTRODUCE THE SELECTION

4 **Review Predictions** Have students share their predictions. Tell them they will stop after each section to confirm each prediction.

5 **Identify Genre: Personal Narrative** Tell students that writing that covers an event in the writer's life is called a "personal narrative." It often contains personal comments and observations as well as a description of the event. Point out that this selection is a kind of personal narrative in which the author records her family's history. It tells about experiences that helped the writer see how she fits in with her family and other immigrants.

The Keeping Quilt
by Patricia Polacco

Theme Connection This story tells how a quilt connects every generation of one family to its history, customs, and traditions.

Selection Summary and Awards The introduction on page 77 of the student book offers a summary of the selection. *The Keeping Quilt* received The Association of Jewish Libraries' Sydney Taylor Award. Another book by this author received the ALA Notable Children's Book award in 1995.

Background The great influx of Russian and Polish Jews to the United States began in 1881 and, with slight interruption, has continued ever since.

THE BASICS BOOKSHELF

■ ***Families*** by Ann Morris

There are many ways to preserve family memories. In this book, photographs record all the things families share and do. The colorful photos support a simple text that focuses on family activities and provides beginning English learners with an opportunity to learn basic vocabulary about the family.

For Lesson Plans: See the Teacher's Guide for ***The Basics Bookshelf***.

READ PAGES 78–79

OBJECTIVES

Function: Read a Selection
Grammar: Ⓣ Past Tense Verbs
Listening: Listen to a Selection
Reading and Learning Strategies: Set a Purpose for Reading; Use Graphic Organizers (chart); Ⓣ Make and Confirm Predictions
Comprehension: Identify Main Idea and Details; Draw Conclusions; Make Inferences

SET PURPOSE

1 Preview pages 78–79. Set the purpose for reading: *Find out how Anna's family's life changes when they move to New York.*

READ AND THINK

Tape 2A CD 2 Track 1

2 **Strategy Focus: Make and Confirm Predictions** After reading, have students see if they can confirm their predictions. If so, have them use the back of the predictions chart to make a new prediction.

Choose Reading Options in the **Multi-Level Strategies** to tailor the reading to proficiency levels.

The recording of "The Keeping Quilt" on the **Selection Tape/CD** offers an oral language model and the opportunity to build reading fluency.

Red annotations offer opportunities to clarify meaning and check for understanding.

1

THE QUILT IS MADE

When Great-Gramma Anna moves from Russia to New York City, she makes a quilt to remember her family in the homeland.

Build background: Colonial Americans and later immigrants, short on supplies and money, recycled their scraps and old clothing into quilts to use as blankets. Many of these quilts increased in value over the years because of the craftsmanship and the memories attached to them.

When my Great-Gramma Anna came to America, she wore the same thick **overcoat** and big boots she had worn for farm work. But her family weren't dirt farmers anymore. In New York City her father's work was **hauling** things on a **wagon**, and the rest of the family made **artificial flowers** all day.

Everyone was in a hurry, and it was so crowded, not like in backhome Russia. But all the same it was their home, and most of their neighbors were just like them.

When Anna went to school, English sounded to her like **pebbles** dropping into **shallow water**. *Shhhhhh. . . . Shhhhhh . . . . Shhhhhh.* In six months she was speaking English. Her parents almost never learned, so she spoke English for them, too.

The only things she had left of backhome Russia were her dress and the **babushka** she liked to throw up into the air when she was dancing.

Ask: What parts of her culture is Anna leaving behind? What is she adding from her new culture?

And her dress was getting too small. After her mother had sewn her a new one, her mother took her old dress and babushka. Then from a basket of old cloth she took Uncle Vladimir's shirt, Aunt Havalah's **nightdress**, and an **apron** of Aunt Natasha's.

Clarify: Use the two parts of "backhome" to define it.
Have students locate Russia and New York City on a ma

overcoat long coat worn in the winter
hauling carrying
wagon cart with wheels
artificial flowers flowers made of plastic, cloth, or wire
pebbles small stones
shallow water water that is not deep

REACHING ALL STUDENTS

HOME CONNECTION

Family Treasure Hunt Send home a copy of the *High Point Newsletter 3* in the **Teacher's Resource Book**. In this home activity, students go on a treasure hunt, looking for a keepsake, artifact, photo, or story that reflects the history of their family or a special family tradition. They ask family members to explain the treasure's importance. Encourage students to invite the family member to visit the class and share information about the family treasure and its story.

Multi-Level Strategies

READING OPTIONS FOR LESSONS 4–6

BEGINNING Group students to work with ***Families*** or distribute copies of **Master 19** to conduct a Key Points Reading of "The Keeping Quilt." Students can then listen to each section on the **Selection Tape/CD**. Work as a group to fill in the chart on **Transparency 18**. (See page T76.)

INTERMEDIATE Read the story aloud or play the recording on the **Selection Tape/CD**. Use the red annotations on the facsimile pages to clarify meaning. After each part, discuss students' predictions and see which can be confirmed.

ADVANCED After reading each part, pairs check their predictions. Have them note evidence that confirms or refutes their predictions and make a new prediction.

"We will make a **quilt** to help us always member home," Anna's mother said. "It ill be like having the family in backhome ıssia dance around us at night."

And so it was. Anna's mother invited all e neighborhood ladies. They cut out nimals and flowers from the **scraps** of othing. Anna kept the needles threaded and handed them to the ladies as they needed them. The **border** of the quilt was made of Anna's babushka.

On Friday nights Anna's mother would say the **prayers** that started **the Sabbath**. The family ate **challah** and chicken soup. The quilt was the **tablecloth**.

Clarify: The quilt is now used as a tablecloth instead of as a blanket.

BEFORE YOU MOVE ON...

1. **Main Idea and Details** Support this main idea with details: Life in New York was very busy for Anna and her family.
2. **Conclusions** Think of two reasons Anna's mother decided to use old clothes for the quilt.
3. **Inference** Why do you think Anna's mother asked the neighborhood women to help make the quilt?

raps small pieces
rder edge
ayers words spoken to God
the Sabbath Saturday, the Jewish day of rest and worship
challah bread that is shaped by twisting

CHECK COMPREHENSION

3 Answers to "Before You Move On"

1. **Main Idea and Details** Everyone in the family worked while Anna went to school.
2. **Conclusions** Anna's mother used old clothes for the quilt to remind them of their home country. She also probably did not want to waste the old clothes.
3. **Inference** Most of the women in the neighborhood were also Russian immigrants. Working together gave the women a sense of community and belonging.

CLOSE AND ASSESS

Have students who were able to confirm a prediction identify the information in the story that related to their prediction. Ask: *Did previewing the pictures and making predictions help you better understand this portion of the selection? How?*

Transparency 19 / Master 19

KEY POINTS READING

The Keeping Quilt

Great-Gramma Anna and her family move from Russia to New York City. Everything in New York is very new to them. To remember home, she has only her dress and her babushka. Her mother makes a quilt out of the dress, the babushka, and other old clothes from Russia. The quilt helps the family remember their homeland.

When Anna grows up, she marries Great-Grandpa Sasha. Anna uses the quilt in her wedding ceremony. This starts a tradition. Later, Anna wraps her baby daughter Carle in the quilt and teaches her its story. Carle grows up and marries George. The tradition continues.

When Carle and George have a daughter Mary Ellen, she too is wrapped in the quilt. As Anna gets older, the quilt comforts her. Mary Ellen uses the quilt when she marries, and again when she has a child. Baby Patricia loves hearing stories about the quilt. When her daughter, Traci Denise, is born, the quilt wraps her warmly. The quilt connects Patricia and her family to their past and to each other.

Transparency 19 Level B, Unit 2 | Belonging

Grammar Minilesson

▶ PAST TENSE VERBS

TEACH Draw student's attention to the words *invited, handed,* and *needed* on page 79. Point out that all three words are past tense verbs. Remind students that the past tense verb shows that the action happened earlier, or in the past. Review the rules for adding **–ed**.

- For most verbs, add **–ed**: **if needed**.
- For verbs that end in silent **e**, drop the **e** and add **–ed**: **invited**.
- For verbs that end in one vowel and one consonant, double the final consonant and add **–ed**: **snapped**.
- For verbs that end in a consonant and **y**, change the **y** to **i** and add **–ed**: **married**.

PRACTICE Have students write answers to these questions with complete sentences, using past tense verbs.

1. Did English **sound** like shells or like pebbles dropping into water to Anna?
2. At Carle's wedding, did the men and women **celebrate** together or apart?
3. What did Anna **wrap** Carle in?

▶ **Practice Book** page 33

READ PAGES 80–81

OBJECTIVES

Function: Read a Selection
Vocabulary Strategy: Use New Words in Context
Grammar: Ⓣ Irregular Past Tense Verbs
Listening: Listen to a Selection
Reading and Learning Strategies: Set a Purpose for Reading; Use Graphic Organizers (chart); Ⓣ Make and Confirm Predictions
Comprehension: Identify Details; Relate to Personal Experience; Make Comparisons

SET PURPOSE

1 Preview pages 80–81. Set the purpose for reading: *As you read, take note of the customs and traditions of Anna's family. How does the quilt continue a tradition?*

READ AND THINK

Tape 2A
CD 2 Track 1

2 **Strategy Focus: Make and Confirm Predictions** Involve students in reading pages 80–81 of the selection.

See the **Multi-Level Strategies** on page T78 to include students at all proficiency levels.

2

A TRADITION BEGINS

The quilt is used as a huppa at Anna and Sasha's wedding. Many years later, the quilt becomes a wedding huppa for their daughter's wedding.

Anna grew up and **fell in love with** Great-Grandpa Sasha. To show he wanted to be her **husband**, he gave Anna a gold coin, a dried flower, and a piece of **rock salt**, all tied into a **linen handkerchief**. The gold was for **wealth**, the flower for love, and the salt so their lives would **have flavor**.

She accepted the **hankie**. They were **engaged**.

Under the **wedding huppa**, Anna and Sasha promised each other love and understanding. After the wedding, the men and women **celebrated** separately.

Ask: Why do you think the men and women celebrated separately? (traditional Jewish custo

Use visuals: What information can you get from the picture that helps you understand the text?

fell in love with started to care very deeply about
rock salt salt in the shape of a small rock
linen handkerchief square piece of strong cloth
wealth plenty of money and nice things
have flavor be interesting
hankie handkerchief

80 Unit 2 | Belonging

REACHING ALL STUDENTS

Language Development
EXPRESS SOCIAL COURTESIES

Weddings Introduce details of American wedding etiquette and language. Ask students to describe American weddings they have attended or seen on television. Talk about such traditional elements as the clothing of the bride and groom, the toasts, and the cutting of the cake. List common congratulatory expressions such as "We wish you all the best," and "May you have many years of health and happiness," and have students practice the expressions at a mock wedding.

CULTURAL PERSPECTIVES

Home Culture: Symbols
Explain that a symbol represents another thing. Point out the symbols in the story. Have students think of symbols used in their home cultures and record their ideas in a chart. Students should then share their charts to learn about the symbols used in other countries.

Culture	Wedding	Birthday

When my Grandma Carle [w]as born, Anna wrapped her [da]ughter in the quilt to welcome [he]r warmly into the world. Carle [w]as given a gift of gold, flower, [sa]lt, and bread. Gold so she **[w]ould never know poverty**, a [fl]ower so she would always [kn]ow love, salt so her life would [al]ways have flavor, and bread [s]o that she would never [kn]ow **hunger**.

Carle learned to **keep the [S]abbath** and to cook and clean [an]d do washing.

"Married you'll be someday," [A]nna told Carle, and again the [qu]ilt became a wedding huppa, this time [fo]r Carle's wedding to Grandpa George. [M]en and women celebrated together, [bu]t they still did not dance together. In [C]arle's wedding **bouquet** was a gold [co]in, bread, and salt.

Clarify: Now, men and women talk and eat together, but do not dance together.

BEFORE YOU MOVE ON...

1. **Details** What did Sasha give Anna for their engagement? What did each of these items mean?
2. **Personal Experience** When Carle was born, she was given traditional gifts. Describe traditions you know about that welcome babies into the world.
3. **Comparison** How were Anna's and Carle's weddings alike and how were they different?

[w]ould never know poverty would always have [en]ough money

[h]unger the pain of not eating

keep the Sabbath always remember that the Sabbath is a special day

REVIEW KEY VOCABULARY

3 Use New Words in Context Have students work in pairs to create a drawing of each vocabulary word. Then ask them to exchange pictures with another pair and write the vocabulary word illustrated by each picture. The two pairs can then discuss their answers.

CHECK COMPREHENSION

4 Answers to "Before You Move On"

1. **Details** Sasha gave Anna a gold coin for wealth, a dried flower for love, and rock salt so their lives would have flavor.
2. **Personal Experience** Encourage students to share traditions from their home cultures.
3. **Comparison** At Carle's wedding the men and women celebrated together, but they still did not dance together. Students may predict that future generations will celebrate and dance together.

CLOSE AND ASSESS

Ask: *Did the information in this part allow you to confirm your prediction?* Have students complete these sentence starters: *I was right about...; I did not predict....*

Music Connection

WEDDING MUSIC

Play Lohengrin's and Mendelssohn's wedding processionals as two examples of music used in American weddings. Ask students to guess which piece is traditionally played at the beginning of the ceremony (Lohengrin's, because it is more solemn) and which is played at the end (Mendelssohn's, because it is more celebratory). Invite students to share examples of wedding music from their home cultures and to explain the symbolism of the music.

Grammar Minilesson

▶ IRREGULAR PAST TENSE VERBS

TEACH Point out *grew* and *gave* on page 80. Say: *These verbs are in the past tense. Past tense verbs that do not end in* **-ed** *are called irregular verbs.* Display examples.

Present	Past
wear	wore
make	made
go	went
take	took

For more examples, have students look at Handbook pages 450–451.

PRACTICE Dictate the following present tense paragraph. Have students rewrite the paragraph in the past tense.

My aunt and I make quilts together. Everyone gives us old clothes. First we cut them up and make them into patches. Then we sew and sew for months until we have a beautiful quilt.

▶ **Practice Book** page 34

READ PAGES 82–83

OBJECTIVES

Function: Read a Selection
Grammar: Ⓣ Future Tense Verbs
Listening: Listen to a Selection
Reading and Learning Strategies: Set a Purpose for Reading; Use Graphic Organizers (chart); Ⓣ Make and Confirm Predictions
Comprehension and Critical Thinking: Ⓣ Identify Sequence; Identify Narrator's Point of View; Form Generalizations
Literary Analysis: Evaluate Impact of Author's Background

SET PURPOSE

1 Preview pages 82–83. Set the purpose for reading: Ask: *How do you think the quilt will be used in this section?*

READ AND THINK

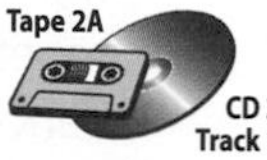

2 **Strategy Focus: Make and Confirm Predictions** Involve students in reading pages 82–83 of the selection.

See the **Multi-Level Strategies** on page T78 to adjust instruction to varying proficiency levels.

3

THE TRADITION CONTINUES

Through the years, the quilt is used to celebrate marriages, welcome babies, and comfort the family in times of sickness.

Have students locate Michigan on a map.

Carle and George moved to a farm in Michigan and Great-Gramma Anna came to live with them. The quilt once again wrapped a new little girl, Mary Ellen.

Mary Ellen called Anna, Lady Gramma. She had grown very old and was sick a lot of the time. The quilt kept her legs warm.

On Anna's ninety-eighth birthday, the cake was a kulich, a **rich cake** with **raisins** and candied fruit in it.

When Great-Gramma Anna died, prayers were said to **lift her soul** to heaven. My mother Mary Ellen was now grown up.

Ask: What traditions is the family keepin[g]? What traditions are changing?

When Mary Ellen left home, she took th[e] quilt with her.

When she became a **bride**, the quilt became her huppa. For the first time, frien[ds] who were not **Jews** came to the wedding. My mother wore a suit, but in her bouquet were gold, bread, and salt.

The quilt welcomed me, Patricia, into th[e] world, and it was the tablecloth for my firs[t] birthday party.

At night I would **trace my fingers** around the edges of each animal on the qui[lt] before I went to sleep. I told my mother

rich cake heavy, sweet cake
raisins dried grapes
lift her soul help her go

Jews people whose religion is Judaism
trace my fingers follow with the tips of my fingers

Clarify: The quilt was used as a baby blanket for Patricia, just as it had been for Carle.

82 Unit 2 | Belonging

REACHING ALL STUDENTS

Language Development
EXPRESS SOCIAL COURTESIES

Birth of a Child Discuss American customs at the time of the birth of a child, such as giving pink clothing to girls and blue to boys, naming ceremonies, and common phrases used when visiting a new baby, such as "He's so cute!" "She has your eyes." "What a sweet baby!" Then have students work in pairs to practice the expressions on an imaginary visit to meet a new baby.

A WORLD OF LANGUAGES

English/Spanish Cognates Point out to students whose first language is Spanish that they already know many words in the selection.

PAGE 78
boots botas
family familia
wagon vagón
flowers flores
day día
Russia Rusia
school escuela
English inglés
air aire

PAGE 79
animals animales
border borde
soup sopa

PAGE 80
tradition tradición
use usar
salt sal
promise promesa
celebrate celebrar

PAGE 81
Anna Ana
George Jorge

PAGE 82
fruit fruta
Patricia Patricia

PAGE 83
cape capa
jungle jungla

See pages T404–T405 for English/Spanish cognates in other selections in *High Point*.

ories about the animals on the quilt. She ld me whose **sleeve** had made the horse, hose apron had made the chicken, whose ess had made the flowers, and whose abushka went around the edge of the quilt.

The quilt was **a pretend cape** when I as in the **bullring**, or sometimes a **tent** in e **steaming Amazon jungle**.

At my wedding to Enzo-Mario, men and omen danced together. In my bouquet were old, bread, and salt.

Twenty years ago I held Traci Denise in e quilt for the first time. Someday she, too, ill leave home and she will take the quilt ith her.

Ask: How do you think the narrator feels about her daughter taking the quilt when she leaves home?

Encourage elaboration: How is this wedding different from the other weddings in the story? How is it the same?

BEFORE YOU MOVE ON...

1. **Sequence** What happened after Carle and George moved to Michigan? Tell the main events in the order in which they happened.
2. **Narrator's Point of View** Who is telling this story? How do you know?
3. **Generalization** What are all the different ways the quilt is used? What do they have in common?

eeve arm of a shirt
pretend cape an imagined piece of othing worn around my shoulders
llring arena in which men fight bulls
nt small temporary shelter made of cloth
eaming Amazon jungle hot, humid, thick rest near the equator in South America

ABOUT THE AUTHOR

Remembering her childhood home in Oakland, California, **Patricia Polacco** says, "All my neighbors came in as many colors, ideas, and religions as there are people on the planet. How lucky I was to know so many people that were so different and yet so alike." As a young girl, she had a learning disability that made it difficult for her to learn to read. She could draw very well, however. Now her drawing and writing come together in her books. Some of them were inspired by listening to the storytellers in her family.

CHECK COMPREHENSION

3 Answers to "Before You Move On"

1. **Sequence** Anna came to live with them. They had a baby, Mary Ellen. Anna died. Mary Ellen left home, got married, and had a daughter, Patricia. Patricia married Enzo-Mario and had a daughter.
2. **Narrator's Point of View** Patricia is telling the story: "The quilt welcomed me, Patricia, into the world. . . ."
3. **Generalization** The quilt is used during weddings, at births, during illness, and at a birthday party. All are important events in the family's history.

ABOUT THE AUTHOR

4 Evaluate Literature: Author's Background Read aloud About the Author. Ask: *How do you think the author learned about the events she tells in this story?* (from the storytellers in her family) Have students give examples of other stories where the author's background and experiences influenced the writing.

CLOSE AND ASSESS

Have students add items to the unit mind map on page T71. Ask: *What has "The Keeping Quilt" taught you about belonging and fitting in?*

INTERNET

SOCIAL STUDIES CONNECTION

Quilting is a craft that is a part of many cultures. Have students use the Internet to research quilt history and styles. The Smithsonian Institution has rich resources on this topic.

Web Sites

Web sites undergo frequent modifications, but here are some you may want to suggest to students:
www.pbs.org
www.si.edu
www.beavton.k12.or.us

Grammar Minilesson

▶ FUTURE TENSE VERBS

TEACH Draw students' attention to this sentence from page 83: *Someday she, too,* ***will leave*** *home and she* ***will take*** *the quilt with her.* Tell students that the **future tense verb** shows action that will happen later, or in the future. Identify *will leave* and *will take* as verbs in the future tense. Explain that there are two ways to show the future tense:

- Use the helping verb *will* along with a main verb: *Traci Denise* ***will leave*** *home.*
- Use the phrase ***going to***: *Someday Traci Denise* ***is going to*** *leave home with the quilt.*

PRACTICE Have students write a paragraph describing how they think Traci Denise will use the quilt. Remind them to use future tense verbs in their descriptions.

▶ **Practice Book** page 35

RESPOND

OBJECTIVES

SUM IT UP

Function: Retell a Story

Reading and Learning Strategies: Ⓣ Confirm Predictions; Review; Summarize; Use Graphic Organizers (chart)

THINK IT OVER

Function: Engage in Discussion

Critical Thinking and Comprehension: Draw Conclusions; Make Inferences; Identify Author's Purpose; Relate to Personal Experience

EXPRESS YOURSELF

Function: Ⓣ Ask and Answer Questions

Speaking and Listening: Questions and Answers

CHECK YOUR UNDERSTANDING

1 **Sum It Up** Students should show these generations in the family tree: Anna's mother and father; Great-Gramma Anna and Great-Grampa Sasha; Grandma Carle and Grandpa George; Mary Ellen and her husband; Patricia and Enzo-Mario; Traci Denise.

▶ **Practice Book** page 36

2 **Think It Over** Possible answers are:

1. **Conclusions** The quilt provides a link between generations. It is called the "keeping quilt" because it has been kept as a family treasure.
2. **Inference** In the U.S., men and women usually celebrate together. This probably influenced the Russian immigrants.
3. **Author's Purpose** She wanted to show how traditions can develop over time.
4. **Personal Experience** Answers will vary. Elicit elaboration.

3 **Express Yourself** Encourage use of the question words *who, what,* etc.

CLOSE AND ASSESS

Have students work in groups to list as many events from the story as they can, without consulting the text.

Respond to the Family History

Check Your Understanding

SUM IT UP

Confirm Predictions Work with a group. Review your preview-and-prediction chart. Tell how previewing and predicting helped you understand the story.

Review and Retell a Story Create a family tree for Patricia Polacco's family.

Family Tree

Use the family tree to retell the story to a partner. For each generation, tell how the quilt was used.

THINK IT OVER

Discuss and Write Talk about these questions with a partner. Write the answers.

1. **Conclusions** Why is the quilt important? Why do you think it is called the "keeping quilt"?
2. **Inference** The men and women celebrated separately at Anna's wedding. How did this custom change over time? Why do you think it changed?
3. **Author's Purpose** Why do you think the author wrote this story?
4. **Personal Experience** What tradition would you like to start with your family? How would this tradition give your family members a sense of belonging?

EXPRESS YOURSELF

▶ASK AND ANSWER QUESTIONS

Work with a partner. Make up questions about details in the story. Ask and answer each other's questions. Here are some sample questions:

- Whose clothes were used to make the quilt?
- What did Anna give Carle when she was born?
- What were some of the things in Mary Ellen's wedding bouquet?

LANGUAGE ACQUISITION ASSESSMENT
See page 21 of the Assessment Handbook.

REACHING ALL STUDENTS

Multi-Level Strategies

SUM IT UP OPTIONS

BEGINNING Have students work in three groups. Assign a picture from each part of the story to each group, asking them to use their picture to list the family members and tell how they used the quilt. Work together to build a family tree.

INTERMEDIATE / **ADVANCED** Students should work in mixed pairs to create the family tree. Then have partners get together to retell the story to each other. Advanced students can then write a summary of the story and read it to the class.

ASSESSMENT
Selection Test 5 on page 23 of the Assessment Handbook tests students' mastery of the reading strategies and the vocabulary, comprehension, and language arts skills taught with this selection.

ıguage Arts and Literature

RAMMAR IN CONTEXT

: VERB TENSE

rn About Verb Tense The tense of a verb ws when an action happens.

present tense shows that the action is pening now.

Anna **wears** a dress.

past tense shows that the action happened ıe past. To form the past tense of most verbs, **-ed**.

Anna **learned** English in school.

ıe verbs form the past tense in different 's. These are called **irregular verbs**. Handbook pages 450–451 for a list of gular verbs.

Anna **wore** a thick overcoat.

future tense shows a time in the future. re are two ways to form the future tense:

We **will make** a quilt.

We **are going to** make a quilt.

ctice Copy the sentences. Choose the correct) to complete each sentence.

ong ago, Anna and her mother nakes / made a quilt.

low, Patricia Polacco owns / owned the quilt.

wenty years ago, Patricia holds / held her aughter in the quilt.

omeday, Traci will take / took the quilt vith her.

LITERARY ANALYSIS

SPEAKING/LISTENING

LEARN ABOUT SYMBOLISM

A **symbol** is an image or object that represents an idea or value. When Sasha asked Anna to marry him, he gave her gold as a symbol of wealth. Follow these steps to create your own symbols.

1. **Think of a Symbol** Work with a partner. Choose an important value, such as strength, happiness, or friendship. Think of a symbol that best represents or stands for that value.
2. **Make the Symbol** Use cloth, clay, paper, or other materials to create your symbol. You may also use objects you find around your home or classroom, such as a food or a plant.
3. **Explain Your Symbol** Show your symbol to the class. Explain the meaning of the symbol, and tell why it is a good symbol. Make a chart to show all the symbols created by the class.

Symbol	Represents	Reason
a rock	strength	Rocks are hard and can't be broken easily.

For tips on giving an **oral presentation**, see Handbook pages 401–402.

Multi-Level Strategies

OPTIONS FOR LEARNING ABOUT SYMBOLISM

BEGINNING Show students pictures of common symbols and the concepts they represent. Divide students into groups, allowing each to choose a symbol to create and explain to the class. Offer assistance with both the making and the explanation of the symbol.

INTERMEDIATE Have students work with a partner to choose and create a symbol that represents a concept. Have the pairs show their completed symbols to the class and explain the meanings of their symbols.

ADVANCED Students should work in pairs to choose a concept and think of a symbol to represent this concept. Encourage students to create original symbols and write explanations for them. Allow the class to try to guess the concept represented by the symbol. Then have pairs read their explanation to the class.

RESPOND

OBJECTIVES

VERB TENSE

Grammar:
T Present, Past, and Future Tense Verbs

SYMBOLISM

Function: Define and Explain
Speaking and Listening: Explanation
Literary Analysis: Symbolism
Representing: Chart; Symbol

LANGUAGE ARTS AND LITERATURE

1 **Use Verb Tense** Answers to the Practice items are:

Practice

1. made
2. owns
3. held
4. will take

▶ **Practice Book** page 37

2 **Learn About Symbolism** Help students grasp the concept that symbols represent important values.

List the following items: salt, bread, gold, apple, heart, dove. Review the first three symbols from the story with the class and invite students to explain what each represents. (flavor, food, prosperity) Next, elicit and verify the symbolism of the next three items. (knowledge, love, peace)

Before working on their own, invite students to generate a list of other common symbols and the values they represent.

CLOSE AND ASSESS

Have pairs of students write a sentence on an index card explaining what they have learned about symbols. Have them circle the verb and tell its tense. Students can then sign and turn in the cards before they leave class.

RESPOND

OBJECTIVES

KEEPING QUILT

Critical Thinking and Research Skills: Relate to Personal Experience; Use Parts of a Book; Gather Information; Take Notes

Representing: Quilt

WEDDING TRADITIONS

Function: Give Information

Concepts and Vocabulary: Wedding Words—*vow, ceremony, custom, symbol*

Speaking and Listening: Interview

Learning Strategies, Critical Thinking, and Research Skills: Formulate Research Questions; Gather Information; Use Parts of a Book; Use Graphic Organizers (chart); Make Comparisons; Form Generalizations

Technology/Media: Multimedia Presentation

Representing and Writing: Chart and Research Report

CONTENT AREA CONNECTIONS

1. **Make a Keeping Quilt** Prompt students to recall funny, interesting, happy, or unusual class events.

2. **Compare Wedding Traditions** Prepare students by teaching content area vocabulary:

   - ***vow, ceremony, custom, symbol*:** Tell students that these are all words that have to do with wedding traditions in the U.S.

   Give examples of vows: love, honor, cherish; sickness/health; richer/poorer. Explain customs: gifts, Father's dance, toasts. List symbols: white dress, ring, flowers. Describe the ceremony: music, readings, vows.

   Brainstorm possible questions to research and model appropriate interviewing techniques. Suggest that students consult the book *Weddings* by Ann Morris (Morrow).

CLOSE AND ASSESS

Ask students to share the most interesting thing they learned from this lesson.

Respond to the Family History, continued

Content Area Connections

FINE ARTS

TECHNOLOGY/MEDIA

MAKE A KEEPING QUILT

Making quilts is a tradition in many parts of the world. Quilts are often passed from generation to generation. Make a keeping quilt that represents your class.

1. **Research Quilts** Use sewing books and magazines to research the kind of quilt you want to make. Also check the Internet. New Web sites appear every day, but these sites are good places to start. Take notes and download photos of quilts.

INTERNET

INFORMATION ON-LINE

Key Word:
quilt

Web Sites:
➤ **Quilts**
- www.historic-american.com
- quiltorama.com

2. **Create a Class Quilt** Follow these steps:
   - Choose a special experience you had in class to be the subject of your quilt square.
   - Cut a square out of paper, and then draw your special memory with markers.
   - Tape the squares together to make one large quilt. If possible, create a pattern.

   Display the quilt in the classroom.

SOCIAL STUDIES

TECHNOLOGY/MEDIA

COMPARE WEDDING TRADITIONS

With a group, research wedding ceremonies an traditions across cultures. Prepare a multimedia report to share with your class.

1. **Gather Information** Make a list of the questions you want to answer. Use encyclopedias and books about wedding traditions. You might also want to interview married couples from different backgrounds. Organize your information into categories such as **symbols**, **customs**, **vows**, and **clothir** Record your findings on a chart.

2. **Prepare a Multimedia Report** Use a combination of written text, pictures, videotapes and audiotapes, charts, and items used in different weddings to create your report.

3. **Make Generalizations** Listen to each group's report. Make a list that summarizes the information. Tell what the wedding traditions from different cultures have in common.

   Examples:
   Most weddings use symbols.
   Many weddings involve a religious ceremony.

For help with **multimedia presentations**, see Handbook pages 390–391.

REACHING ALL STUDENTS

Research Skills

▶ USING PARTS OF A BOOK

TEACH Display a nonfiction book. Show how pages at the front and back can help students find information.

- The **title page** gives the title, author, and publisher.
- The **copyright page** shows when the book was published.
- The **table of contents** shows the organization of the book.
- The **index** alphabetically lists subjects and their page numbers.

PRACTICE Provide pairs of students with nonfiction books about quilts or wedding traditions for the above activities. They should:

1. List the title, author, publisher, and copyright date.
2. Scan the table of contents and write one question the book might answer.
3. Write the pages listed in the index for a subject related to their question.

▶ **Practice Book** page 38

Human Family

poem
by Maya Angelou

Prepare to Read

THINK ABOUT WHAT YOU KNOW

Make a Venn Diagram With a partner, make a Venn diagram. Show how you are the same and different.

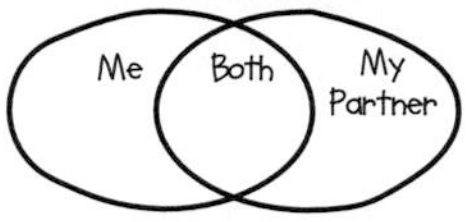

ke like one another
mmon ordinary
light make very happy
vious clear
ious thoughtful
ive grow or do well
alike different
riety number of erent kinds

LEARN KEY VOCABULARY

Relate Words Study the new words and their definitions. Choose a synonym and an antonym for each word in the chart.

Synonyms have the same meaning: **alike, same.**
Antonyms have opposite meanings: **alike, unalike.**

Vocabulary	Choose from these words:			Synonym	Antonym
common	special	small	ordinary	ordinary	special
delight	show	please	anger	please	anger
obvious	clear	serious	hidden	clear	hidden
variety	size	likeness	difference	difference	likeness

LEARN TO READ POETRY

A **stanza** is a group of lines in a poem. Each stanza expresses an idea. If you understand each stanza, you will understand the whole poem.

READING STRATEGY

How to Read a Poem with Stanzas

1. Read the poem to yourself.
2. Stop reading after each stanza.
3. Ask yourself: What does the stanza mean?
4. Think about what the whole poem means.

Now read "Human Family." Stop after each stanza and think about what it means.

Multi-Level Strategies

VOCABULARY OPTIONS

BEGINNING Work with everyday vocabulary to establish the meanings of *synonym* (loud/noisy) and *antonym* (early/late).

INTERMEDIATE Offer a sentence that gives a synonym and an antonym for one vocabulary word. (***alike***: People are the **same** in some ways and **different** in other ways.)

ADVANCED Have students find additional synonyms and antonyms for each vocabulary word in the chart.

Transparency 20 / Master 20

READ A POEM WITH STANZAS

Directions: Read the poem one stanza at a time. Think about what each stanza is saying. Write your ideas next to each stanza. Then finish the sentence at the bottom of the page.

What Do I Care?

How big is your nose?
I really don't care.
Are your ears too small?
They're lost in your hair.

How big is your heart?
That's important to me.
How large are your thoughts?
That's what I want to see.
— *Sweet P*

Ideas

Stanza 1
The poet doesn't care how a person looks.

Stanza 2
The poet cares about how a person thinks and feels.

The meaning of the poem is:
The poet values what's inside a person more than what's outside.

Transparency 20 Level B, Unit 2 | Belonging © Hampton-Brown

PREPARE TO READ

OBJECTIVES

THINK ABOUT WHAT YOU KNOW

Reading and Learning Strategies: Relate to Personal Experience; Use Graphic Organizers (Venn diagram)

Critical Thinking: Make Comparisons

LEARN KEY VOCABULARY

Vocabulary Strategy: Relate Words (synonyms and antonyms)

LEARN TO READ POETRY

Reading Strategy: Use Text Structures (stanzas)

THINK ABOUT WHAT YOU KNOW

1 **Make a Venn Diagram** Have students work with a partner to show their similarities and differences.

LEARN KEY VOCABULARY

2 **Relate Words** Have students read each vocabulary word and its definition. After clarifying meanings, conduct the activity.

Use the Vocabulary Options in the **Multi-Level Strategies** to tailor the activity to proficiency levels.

▶ **Practice Book** page 39

LEARN TO READ POETRY

3 **Model How to Read a Poem with Stanzas** Demonstrate the steps in the box with **Transparency 20**:

- Read each stanza, stopping at the end of each to discuss meaning(s).
- Write students' ideas on the lines at the right.
- Work as a group to finish the sentence starter.

CLOSE AND ASSESS

Ask: *Why is it important to read each stanza carefully?* (If you understand each part, you will understand the overall meaning.)

READ PAGES 88–89

OBJECTIVES

Function: Read a Poem
Listening: Listen to a Poem
Reading and Learning Strategy: Set a Purpose for Reading; Use Text Structures (stanzas)
Critical Thinking: Synthesize Information; Summarize

SET PURPOSE

1 Read aloud the title and ask students to look at the photograph. Set the purpose for listening to the poem: *As you listen, ask yourself what the poet means by the term "human family."*

LISTEN AND READ

Tape 2A
CD 2 Track 2

2 **Strategy Focus: Use Text Structures (stanzas)** Play "Human Family" on the **Selection Tape/CD** or read the poem aloud one stanza at a time. Then play or read the poem again, asking students to read along silently.

Students should then study the stanzas and reflect on the meaning of the poem.

Choose Activity Options in the **Multi-Level Strategies** to include all proficiency levels.

from Human Family

by Maya Angelou

I note the obvious differences
in the human family.
Some of us are serious,
some thrive on comedy.

The variety of our skin tones
can confuse, bemuse, delight,
brown and pink and beige and purple,
tan and blue and white.

I've sailed upon the seven seas
and stopped in every land,
I've seen the wonders of the world,
not yet one common man.

I know ten thousand women
called Jane and Mary Jane,
but I've not seen any two
who really are the same.

comedy funny things, humor
our skin tones the shades or colors of our skin
confuse puzzle us, seem unclear
bemuse make us think
seven seas seven great oceans of the world

REACHING ALL STUDENTS

CULTURAL PERSPECTIVES

World Cultures: Families Ask students to create a photographic essay entitled "The Human Family." Divide the class into five groups and have each group collect pictures of families who live on different continents: North America, South America, Europe, Asia, and Africa. Have students paste their pictures on large sheets of paper and label them with the names of the continents represented. Bind the pages into a book for display.

Multi-Level Strategies

ACTIVITY OPTIONS FOR STUDYING STANZAS

BEGINNING Divide each stanza of the poem into thought chunks for students. Read each chunk aloud. Ask questions to clarify meaning: *Are all people serious? Do any two people have the same skin color?* Have the group agree on the meaning of each stanza.

INTERMEDIATE Form pairs. Have each pair study one stanza and report back to the group on its meaning. Then have students read the whole poem and agree on a sentence that expresses the meaning of the poem.

ADVANCED Ask students to work as a group. Have them write a one-sentence statement about the meaning of each stanza and another stating the overall meaning of the whole poem. Then ask: *Why does the poet repeat the last lines of the poem?* Have students list reasons why they believe these lines are true.

Respond to the Poem

note the obvious differences
tween each sort and type,
ıt we are more alike, my friends,
an we are unalike.

'e are more alike, my friends,
an we are unalike.

'e are more alike, my friends,
an we are unalike.

....

rt kind of person
e kind of person

THINK IT OVER

Discuss Talk about this question with a partner.

1. **Summary** What is the poet's message? Do you agree with the poet? Explain.

LITERARY ANALYSIS

SOUNDS OF POETRY

Learn About Alliteration and Assonance Poets choose words for the way they sound together. Sometimes they use words that begin with the same sound:

*I've **s**ailed upon the **s**even **s**eas*

This is called **alliteration**.

Sometimes they choose words with the same vowel sound:

*Some **o**f **u**s are seri**ou**s*

This is called **assonance**.

Recite the Poem Form five groups. Each group recites one stanza. All of you recite the last two stanzas. What other examples of assonance and alliteration did you hear?

BOUT THE POET

ya Angelou has enjoyed a long career as an ress, a film director, a poet, and an author. e often writes about characters trying to make nnections with other people. In this poem, she invites you to beyond the differences and understand that we all belong a larger family.

RESPOND

OBJECTIVES

THINK IT OVER

Function: Engage in Discussion

Critical Thinking and Comprehension: Summarize; Classify; Form Opinions

Literary Analysis: Evaluate Impact of Author's Style on Meaning

SOUNDS OF POETRY

Speaking and Listening: Recite a Poem; Listen to a Poem

Literary Analysis: Alliteration; Assonance

ABOUT THE POET

Literary Analysis: Evaluate Literary Quality

THINK IT OVER

3 A possible answer is:

1. **Summary** While the world is full of unique people, we all belong to the human family. Ask students to give examples from observation.

SOUNDS OF POETRY

4 Possible answers are:

Alliteration: **c**an **c**onfuse; **b**rown and **p**ink and **b**eige and **p**urple

Assonance: del**i**ght, wh**i**te; J**a**ne, s**a**me; t**y**pe, unal**i**ke

ABOUT THE POET

5 **Evaluate Literary Quality** Point out that Maya Angelou was nominated for a Pulitzer Prize in 1972 and a National Book Award in 1970. Ask: *Would you give this poem an award? Why or why not?*

CLOSE AND ASSESS

Have students choose a favorite stanza and explain what it means to them.

INTERNET

SOCIAL STUDIES CONNECTION

Have students search the Internet for information about the Seven Wonders of the World and create a fact sheet about each one. There is a variety of listings for such categories as natural wonders, manmade wonders, and wonders of the eastern hemisphere.

Use the following key word or web address to find information:

Key Word
"Seven Wonders of the World"

Web Site
ce.eng.usf.edu/pharos/wonders

PREPARE TO READ

OBJECTIVES

THINK ABOUT WHAT YOU KNOW
Reading Strategies:
Relate to Personal Experience

LEARN KEY VOCABULARY Ⓣ
Vocabulary Strategy:
Locate and Use Definitions

LEARN ABOUT FACTS AND OPINIONS
Reading Strategy:
Ⓣ Distinguish Between Facts and Opinions

THINK ABOUT WHAT YOU KNOW

1 Idea Exchange Write the headings *Words, Customs,* and *Ways of Life.* Make class lists as students share their ideas.

LEARN KEY VOCABULARY

2 Locate and Use Definitions Read each word aloud and use it in a sentence. Then conduct the activity.

Use the Vocabulary Options in the **Multi-Level Strategies** to help all students participate.

▶ **Practice Book** page 40

LEARN ABOUT FACTS AND OPINIONS

3 Model How to Distinguish Between Facts and Opinions Define *fact* and *opinion.* Demonstrate the steps in the box with **Transparency 21**:

- Read each statement aloud.
- Ask: *Can this statement be proven, or does it show what a person thinks?* Point out any signal words.

Write statements under the appropriate headings. Then invite students to add more facts and opinions to the chart.

CLOSE AND ASSESS

Ask each student to share one fact and one opinion about his or her home culture.

BEYOND the COLOR LINES

self-portraits
by Janell, Jenny, and Christian

Prepare to Read

THINK ABOUT WHAT YOU KNOW

Idea Exchange Think about people you know from different cultures. What words, customs, and ways of life have you learned from them?

adjust get used to

ceremony formal event

culture arts, beliefs, customs, and traditions

custom way of acting that is special to a nation or culture

elder older person or leader

feast large meal served for a special event

privilege something special you get to do

respect feel or show a high opinion of something

right something that is allowed by law

tradition way of acting that is passed from one generation to the next

For the vocabulary activity, students should locate definitions similar to the above annotations in red.

LEARN KEY VOCABULARY

Locate and Use Definitions Study the new words. Work with a partn to make a vocabulary log for each word.

Vocabulary Log

Word:	ceremony
Definition Prediction:	church service
Dictionary Definition:	formal event on a special occasion
Examples:	wedding, graduation, birthday
Sentence:	A wedding ceremony marks the beginning of a marriage.

LEARN ABOUT FACTS AND OPINIONS

A **fact** is a true statement that can be proven. An **opinion** is a person's belief. It cannot be proven. When you read an opinion, you can decide if you agree or disagree with what the writer says.

READING STRATEGY
How to Distinguish Between Facts and Opinions
1. Ask yourself: Can the information in the statement be checked?
2. Ask yourself: Does the statement express a person's thoughts, ideas, or feelings? Are there signal words like *think, feel,* or *believe*?

As you read "Beyond the Color Lines," decide which statements are facts and which are opinions. Do you agree with the opinions?

REACHING ALL STUDENTS

Multi-Level Strategies
VOCABULARY OPTIONS

BEGINNING Group students to read ***Let's Dance!*** or the Key Points Reading on **Master 22**. (See page T93.) Point out the vocabulary.

INTERMEDIATE Have each student create a Vocabulary Log for two different words. Groups of five students should then work together to share their logs.

ADVANCED Students can work with a partner to write a Vocabulary Log for each word in the list.

Transparency 21 / Master 21

DISTINGUISH FACTS AND OPINIONS

Directions: Read each statement. Decide whether it states a fact or an opinion. Underline any signal words you find. Write each statement in the appropriate column. Then add more facts and your own opinions to the chart.

- Some breads are flat like crackers.
- Whole grain breads are good for you.
- Crackers are delicious with soup.
- I think pita bread is handy.
- Grandma's fry bread tastes the best to me.
- Grandma taught me how to make fry bread.

Facts	Opinions
Some breads are flat like crackers.	Crackers are delicious with soup.
Whole grain breads are good for you.	I think pita bread is handy.
Grandma taught me how to make fry bread.	Grandma's fry bread tastes the best to me.

Transparency 21 Level B, Unit 2 | Belonging © Hampton-Brown

BEYOND *the* COLOR LINES

by Janell, Jenny, and Christian

Three teens look beyond the obvious differences in color and national origin in order to fit in and get along with others.

91

READ THE SELECTION

OBJECTIVES

Reading Strategies: Preview; Predict

INTRODUCE THE SELECTION

4 **Preview and Predict** Read aloud the title, authors' names, and introduction to the selection. Discuss the photos on page 91. Ask: *How are the people in the photos different?* (they are of different ethnicities) *What do they have in common?* (they are all teenagers, they all look happy)

Then have students preview the photos and the Personal Profiles on pages 93, 95, and 97.

Beyond the Color Lines

by Janell, Jenny, and Christian

Theme Connection This selection consists of three teenagers' reflections on the experience of belonging to two different cultures. The writers discuss their views on fitting in.

Selection Summary All three teens offer self-portraits that stress the ways their home languages and traditions enrich their lives and make them feel special. They also note the ways being different can make life more complicated. Janell is Native American, Jenny is Chinese American, and Christian is Romanian American. They each express strong feelings about the need for people to respect one another and accept others for who they are.

THE BASICS BOOKSHELF

■ ***Let's Dance!*** by George Ancona

Dance, like music, is at the heart of many traditions and brings different cultures together in joy and celebration. The colorful photos in this book, combined with simple text, support the acquisition of basic action words and give beginning English learners opportunities to talk about clothing, cultures, and celebrations.

For Lesson Plans: See the Teacher's Guide for ***The Basics Bookshelf***.

READ PAGES 92–93

OBJECTIVES

Function: Read a Selection
Concepts and Vocabulary: Words About Native American Culture
Listening: Listen to a Selection
Viewing: Interpret a Visual Image
Reading and Learning Strategies: Use Graphic Organizers (chart); Set a Purpose for Reading; T Distinguish Between Facts and Opinions
Comprehension: Make Inferences

SET PURPOSE

1 Read aloud the title and photo caption. Say: *As you read, identify the Native American elements in Janell's life.*

READ AND THINK

Tape 2A CD 2 Track 3

2 **Strategy Focus: Distinguish Between Facts and Opinions** Have students identify facts and opinions during the reading process and record opinions on **Master 23**.

Choose Reading Options in the **Multi-Level Strategies** to tailor the reading to proficiency levels.

The recording of "Beyond The Color Lines" on the **Selection Tape/CD** offers an oral language model and the opportunity to build reading fluency.

Janell: "THE SAME AS ANYONE ELSE"

Red annotations offer opportunities to clarify meaning and check for understanding.

Ask: Why do you think Janell chose this as the title to her story?

Janell dances in traditional Native American dress at powwows.

I'm Native American, or Indian. Usually, I say Indian. I have an Indian name I got in the **sweat lodge** when I was **an itty bitty baby**. It means something like *Mother Earth.* I'm proud to be Indian, because that's what **the Creator** brought me down to be. I really enjoy the **traditions** and **customs**, the **feasts**, and the **ceremonies**, like the salmon ceremony. You can't go fishing for salmon unless you have the ceremony first. And I love bein at the **powwows**.

I've been dancing since I first learned to walk. My mom said she made me little outfits to dance in, and I started bouncing around on my tippy toes. I learned by watchir how the older girls moved their fe and arms. They are as beautiful as a butterfly. When I dance, I wear moccasins and leggings, and a dres with a belt, and cape and a shawl. There are bead designs on them. M Auntie Danell made one I wore. It maybe took three months to make. All my aunties and uncles know ho to do beadwork. And my grandma. She be way different than anyone else. I know ho to bead, but I want to do more, maybe wh I'm older.

I think that Native American people ha had dance as a part of their life from their **elders** to their elders to their elders, way

Clarify: Explain the compound word "beadwork" and use of "beads" as a verb.

sweat lodge Native American shelter used for religious ceremonies
an itty bitty baby a very small child
the Creator God, the Great Spirit, the one who created the universe
powwows ceremonial meetings of Native Americans

REACHING ALL STUDENTS

Social Studies Connection
GEOGRAPHY

Have students work in groups to research a Native American tribe that once lived in their state or region of the United States. Students can study such aspects as customs, music, art, housing, and food. Then they create a poster to express what they learned. The poster might include photographs, drawings, charts, and brief explanations.

Multi-Level Strategies
READING OPTIONS FOR LESSONS 13–15

BEGINNING Students should work with ***Let's Dance!*** while the class reads "Beyond the Color Lines." Or distribute copies of **Master 22** to conduct a Key Points Reading of "Beyond the Color Lines." Work together to identify at least one fact and one opinion in each section.

INTERMEDIATE Read the selection aloud or play the recording on the **Selection Tape/CD**. Use the red annotations on the facsimile pages to clarify meaning. Distribute copies of the Structured Opinion Journal on **Master 23**. Have students work in groups to identify and write about the opinions.

ADVANCED Have students read the selection silently at their own pace, referring to a dictionary for the meanings of unfamiliar words. Distribute copies of **Master 23** and have students complete the Structured Opinion Journal independently. Partners should then compare their completed journals.

ıck. When I grow up, I'd like to take my ·ds to powwows so they'll **get the hang of** ıncing. Then they'll be at home bouncing ·ound.

I find I can get along with anyone no ıatter what color or race. At middle school have friends from different groups. A t of my Mexican friends ask questions ĸe, "What do you do down there on e **reservation**?" I tell them about the ›wwows, and watching TV or movies, or **ıooting baskets** at the elementary school. tell them that mainly we like to talk and ıve running races, that we're no different ıan anyone else.

You've got to get to know people first. ıen you'll understand what they're like, ıat they are just the same as anyone else.

Restate: Don't judge people by their looks, dress, or accent. If you get to know how people think and feel, you will realize we are all alike on the inside.

PERSONAL PROFILE

NAME
Janell

COUNTRY of ORIGIN
United States

FAVORITE ACTIVITIES
going to powwows, dancing, doing beadwork, watching TV, shooting baskets

IMPORTANT QUOTE
"You've got to get to know people first. Then you'll understand what they're like, that they are just the same as anyone else."

ıell with her uncle, Foster Kalama.

BEFORE YOU MOVE ON...

1. **Viewing** What colors, patterns, designs, and materials do you see in Janell's outfit?
2. **Inference** Why is dancing an important part of Janell's life? How does Native American dance connect to her past and her future?
3. **Vocabulary** Make a list of words related to Native American culture.

·t the hang of get good at, get used to
servation area of land set apart by the U.S. ·vernment for use by a Native American tribe
ooting baskets throwing a basketball ·rough a hoop

CHECK COMPREHENSION

3 Answers to "Before You Move On"

1. **Viewing** Colors include black, white, pink, yellow, purple, silver. Patterns include stripes and feathers. Materials include fringe, shiny satin, beads, scarf, and belt.
2. **Inference** Dancing is an important part of Janell's life because it is a link to her ancestors, who also danced. She has been dancing since she was a baby and plans to teach her children to dance.
3. **Vocabulary** Words related to Native American culture include *sweat lodge, feast, salmon ceremony, powwows, moccasins, leggings, beadwork,* and *reservation.*

CLOSE AND ASSESS

Have partners write on one side of an index card one fact from the selection and how they know it's a fact. On the other side, have them write an opinion and how they know it's an opinion. The students should sign the card and turn it in as they leave the class.

Transparency 22 / Master 22

KEY POINTS READING

Beyond The Color Lines

Janell is Native American. She enjoys the customs, feasts, ceremonies, and powwows of her Indian culture. Janell has been dancing since she was a baby. Dancing is a large part of Native American life. Janell gets along with all people. She believes you should get to know people. Then you realize we are all the same.

Jenny is a Chinese girl who has lived in America for four years. She is in middle school. She enjoys sports, music, and collecting stamps. Jenny believes everybody is different and some people don't accept others for who they are. She believes people should respect one another.

Christian is Romanian-American. His family tries to keep some Romanian customs, such as speaking Romanian at home. Christian enjoys sports, reading, playing guitar, and writing poetry. He believes that sports help people of different backgrounds get along. He thinks people should think more about how we are alike instead of how we are different.

Transparency 22 Level B, Unit 2 | Belonging © Hampton-Brown

Transparency 23 / Master 23

STRUCTURED OPINION JOURNAL

Directions: Find a sentence in each of the three self-portraits in which the author expresses an opinion. Write the author's name, the author's opinion (taken directly from the text), and the signal words or other clues that helped you identify the statement as an opinion. Then tell if you agree with the opinion.

Beyond the Color Lines

Author	Opinion	Signal Words	Do You Agree? Why or Why Not?

Transparency 23 Level B, Unit 2 | Belonging © Hampton-Brown

READ PAGES 94–95

OBJECTIVES

Function: Read a Selection
Vocabulary Strategy: Use New Words in Context
Grammar: Questions
Listening: Listen to a Selection
Reading and Learning Strategies: Set a Purpose for Reading; Paraphrase; Use Graphic Organizers (chart); Ⓣ Distinguish Between Facts and Opinions
Comprehension: Summarize

SET PURPOSE

1 Read aloud the title. Say: *As you read, notice in what ways Jenny enjoys being a part of two cultures and in what ways she finds it difficult.*

READ AND THINK

Tape 2A
CD 2 Track 3

2 **Strategy Focus: Distinguish Between Facts and Opinions** Involve students in reading pages 94–95.

See the **Multi-Level Strategies** on page T92 to tailor the reading to all proficiency levels.

Jenny: "DIFFERENT ON THE OUTSIDE"

In addition to playing the piano, Jenny has recently started taking clarinet lessons.

Pause to find China on a map.

I was born in the Guangdong area of China, in the southern tip, pretty close to Hong Kong. I don't have any brothers or sisters. You're only supposed to have one child in China.

I've been in America about four years and am now in middle school. I like to play softball and volleyball and other sports. I play the piano, too, and I'm going to be taking clarinet. Bach's my favorite **composer**. I like to **collect** stamps and have a collection of Chinese stamps because we get mail from China sometimes.

When I get home from school I have to do homework. Afterwards, I like to **curl up** in my bedroom and read. I love mysteries. Sometimes I like ghost story mysteries.

I can't read in Chinese, though. I have this **special** book that my mom teaches me out of. I'm memorizing the **characters**. I know probably one hundred. You need to know about two thousand to be able to read the Chinese newspaper.

It's different being Chinese. I feel special. It gives me **privileges**. I can go to different special things that are Chinese, like the Chinese New Year, or special holidays.

I think of myself as more American than Chinese, though. I used to use my Chinese name, Yingyi. But sometimes **I was teased** about it. I tried to just either ignore it, or I said to them, "I bet if you went to China people would tease you about your name, because your name would seem different." Maybe then they'd find out how bad teasing is. But then I thought, Jenny sort of sounds like Yingyi. If I was Jenny, nobody would tease me. So now when people ask, I say my name is Jenny. **Ask:** What are some ways Jenny is American and some ways she is Chinese?

composer person who writes music
collect find and save
curl up get comfortable on a bed or sofa
special uncommon, particular
characters Chinese letters
I was teased others made jokes

REACHING ALL STUDENTS

Vocabulary
MULTIPLE-MEANING WORDS

Demonstrate how one word can have multiple meanings by discussing the word *race* from Janell's portrait. Provide contrasting examples, such as: *The race was 5 miles. I race for the bus every morning. We are all part of the human race.* Then explain other examples of words with multiple meanings (*bead, back, play, stamp, curl, character,* and *right* from Janell's and Jenny's portraits). Have students look up the words and identify which meaning the words have in the story.

CULTURAL PERSPECTIVES

U.S. Culture: Customs Have students identify U.S. customs that differ from those of their home cultures. Begin this discussion by bringing up a topic such as greetings. Have students share how people in their home culture greet each other and compare these with greetings used in the U.S. Students should then discuss some U.S. customs they like and how they might be able to blend these customs with those of their home cultures.

Learning Styles
STRATEGIES FOR CONSTRUCTING MEANING

Have students interpret one of the following quotes: Janell: "You've g get to know people first." Jenny: " people just don't accept you for w you are."

- **Visual Learners** Students make poster or an illustration.
- **Auditory Learners** Students cre poem or a chant.
- **Kinesthetic** Students perform a or mime.

Some people just don't accept you for
ıo you are. Since you don't look like them,
ey think you don't belong with them, like
u're different inside, too. I look Chinese,
d I might have **an accent**. Some people
ake fun of others because they have
accent. I think it's unfair. What would
ey think if they were trying to speak, and
ey had a little accent? Would they want
erybody to laugh at them like they laugh?
Everybody's personality is different.
e way they think is different, and their
ulture is different. But just because they
ok different on the outside, they are still
ıman beings. You just have to **respect**
her people's **rights**. If you see someone
ho is really different, you should try to
friends. It might be really interesting. It
ight open you to another world.

Clarify: You can learn a lot from other people.

nny's family celebrates traditional Chinese holidays, ch as the Chinese New Year. She likes to compare her aditions with those of her friends who come from fferent countries.

PERSONAL PROFILE

NAME
Jenny

COUNTRY of ORIGIN
China

FAVORITE ACTIVITIES
playing softball and volleyball, playing the piano and clarinet, collecting stamps, reading mysteries

IMPORTANT QUOTE
"You just have to respect other people's rights."

BEFORE YOU MOVE ON...

1. **Summary** What is Jenny's background and family history?
2. **Paraphrase** According to Jenny, why do some people have trouble accepting others? What advice does she give?
3. **Making Decisions** What might you say or do if you saw people laughing at someone?

accent a different way to pronounce rtain words

ake fun of laugh at, make jokes about

REVIEW KEY VOCABULARY

3 Use New Words in Context Have students work in pairs to come up with a written example or an illustration for each of the vocabulary words. For a noun such as *ceremony,* students might give the example of a wedding or a tea ceremony. For a verb such as *adjust,* students might give an example of a situation in which a person must adjust, such as attending a new school.

CHECK COMPREHENSION

4 Answers to "Before You Move On"

1. **Summary** Jenny was born in China and has lived in America for four years. She is an only child. Jenny enjoys sports, collecting stamps, and playing the piano.
2. **Paraphrase** Some people think that if you don't look the way they do, you are different inside too. Jenny believes you should show respect for all people.
3. **Making Decisions** Answers will vary. Encourage students to imagine themselves in the person's place.

CLOSE AND ASSESS

Have students work in pairs to write two facts and two opinions Jenny mentioned in her self-portrait.

Language Development

EXPRESS SOCIAL COURTESIES

Model a formal introduction such as "I would like to introduce _____. He/She is/likes/lives/studies _____." Then have students work with a partner to describe themselves, their heritage, and their interests. Point out specific passages in the self-portraits as models. Then have each student formally introduce his or her partner to the class, using the information provided by the partner.

Grammar Minilesson

▶ QUESTIONS

TEACH Ask students to generate a list of words that are used to start questions, such as *Is, Did, Can, When, Who,* and *How.* List their responses and then help students categorize them into words that ask for a yes/no answer and those that ask for more information.

Draw students' attention to the first sentence on page 94 and show them how to create a question for the information in that sentence: *Where were you born?*

Then explain how to form tag questions such as:

You were born in China, weren't you? (Yes, I was.)

You don't have any brothers or sisters, do you? (No, I don't.)

PRACTICE Have students make up more questions that are answered in Jenny's essay on pages 94–95. Then have partners role-play an interview with Jenny using their questions.

READ PAGES 96–97

OBJECTIVES

Function: Read a Selection
Concepts and Vocabulary: Words About Culture/National Origins
Grammar: Transitive and Intransitive Verbs
Listening: Listen to a Selection
Reading and Learning Strategies: Set a Purpose for Reading; Use Graphic Organizers (chart); Ⓣ Distinguish Between Facts and Opinions
Comprehension: Make Comparisons; Identify Details
Literary Appreciation: Respond to Literature

SET PURPOSE

1 Say: *Read to find out what customs Christian has kept from his home culture and what interests he is pursuing in his new culture.*

READ AND THINK

Tape 2A
CD 2 Track 3

2 **Strategy Focus: Distinguish Between Facts and Opinions** Involve students in reading pages 96–97.

See the **Multi-Level Strategies** on page T92 to tailor the reading to varying proficiency levels.

Christian: "THE TEAM SPIRIT"

Christian takes the subway home from school.

My father's grandmother was Greek and his father was Albanian. I'm Romanian, but I should say I'm Romanian American. My father and his family moved to Romania after World War II.

We try to keep some Romanian customs like going to the **Greek Orthodox church** where they have a **mass** in the Romanian **liturgy**. I speak Romanian at home, but it's hard to find others to speak with outside my home.

Clarify: Twelfth grade is the last in high school, also called the senior year.

Next year, instead of going to twelfth grade, I'll be going to St. John's University. I'm in this program that lets me take advanced classes my junior year so I'm able to go into college my senior year. I'm excited about it. After school I play sports, do some reading, play a little guitar—I'm pretty bad actually—and I write. I love writing, especially poetry.

I think if an immigrant family leaves a country that is politically undesirable and their kids are young, the kids will **adjust** pretty easily. For **an adult**, it's something totally different. You come as an adult, you

Define *immigrant*: person who moves into a different country.

Define *politically undesirable*: not safe for people who do not agree with the government.

Greek Orthodox church Christian church to which most of the people in Greece belong
mass Christian religious service
liturgy forms or rituals for public worship
an adult a fully grown person

REACHING ALL STUDENTS

Cooperative Learning

FOR LANGUAGE DEVELOPMENT: Ask and Answer Questions

Create Cultural Profiles Have students create a T-chart. On one side, have them use words, symbols, and images to represent their cultural background, interests, and modes of expression. On the other side, have them show connections they make, or would like to make, to different cultures and traditions.

Interview and Report Have students interview each other about their profiles. Then have students share information about their partners with the group.

Debrief the Content Direct students to share insights they gained from the activities. Ask: *What did you learn about your partner that surprised you? What do you have in common with your partner?*

Debrief the Cooperative Process Have students evaluate the quality of their individual participation. Ask: *What questions helped/did not help you learn about your partner?*

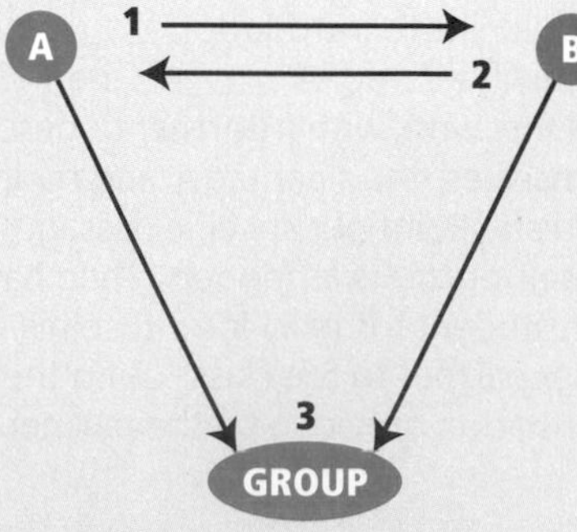

Cooperative Learning Structure: Three-Step Interview

on't know the language, and you are trying
hard to support a family. There is a lot
—a tremendous amount of—stress parents
through trying to adjust and fit into
merican culture, and at the same time
arn a living.

Ask: Why does Christian think it's harder for parents to adjust to American culture?

I think in general too many people
pend their energies on looking at what
e differences are between us instead
what the similarities are.

Sport is **the great equalizer**. When
m playing soccer, we have to play and
ommunicate as a team. We are black,
panish, Greek, Irish, Romanian, Polish
nd Indian on the team. I don't care what
nyone eats at home, what church they go
, or what their skin color is, if they can't
ribble the soccer ball or defend a goal
ey are no help to us.

Ask: How has soccer helped Christian fit in?

PERSONAL PROFILE

NAME
Christian

COUNTRY of ORIGIN
Romania

FAVORITE ACTIVITIES
playing soccer, reading, playing guitar, writing poetry

IMPORTANT QUOTE
"Sport is the great equalizer. When I'm playing soccer, we have to play and communicate as a team."

many sports, like soccer, every player has an
nportant role.

BEFORE YOU MOVE ON...

1. **Comparison** According to Christian, how do children and adults differ in adjusting to a new country?
2. **Details** On a soccer team, skin color is not important. What is?
3. **Vocabulary** Write all the words on pages 96–97 that are related to culture and national origin.

arn a living make money by working at a job
e great equalizer something that makes all eople feel they are the same
dribble the soccer ball move the ball toward the goal with their feet

CHECK COMPREHENSION

3 Answers to "Before You Move On"

1. **Comparison** Children adjust more easily than adults. Adults have to support a family and deal with a new language and culture.
2. **Details** Communicating, dribbling a soccer ball, and defending a goal are important.
3. **Vocabulary** Words include: *Greek, Albanian, Romanian, customs, Greek Orthodox church, black, Spanish, Irish, Polish, Indian.*

ABOUT THE AUTHORS

4 Respond to Literature The self-portraits raise questions of personal importance to the writers. Refer students to the three Important Quotes. Ask: *How are the quotes similar and different? Do you agree or disagree with each one?* Then ask students to write or dictate an Important Quote of personal importance to themselves.

CLOSE AND ASSESS

Have each student write a fact or an opinion statement about Christian. Then have students choose the statements from a container and identify them as fact or opinion.

Social Studies Connection

WORLD CULTURES

Refer students to the first paragraph of Christian's self-portrait to find the three countries of his heritage—Greece, Albania, and Romania. Locate these countries on a map. Then ask students to work in groups of three. Each student should research one of the countries and its customs. Students should then work together to identify similarities among these cultures. Have groups give oral reports on their findings.

Grammar Minilesson

▶ TRANSITIVE AND INTRANSITIVE VERBS

TEACH Tell students they will learn about two types of action verbs. Write:

Christian plays soccer.

His team wins.

Draw an arrow from *plays* to *soccer* and say: *This action verb needs an object to complete its meaning. The object* soccer *receives the action of the verb. This kind of verb is called a* transitive verb.

Then explain that *wins* does not need an object to complete its meaning. This kind of verb is called an *intransitive verb*.

Discuss whether each verb below is transitive or intransitive:

Christian *loves* soccer. (transitive)

The player *runs*. (intransitive)

The fans *cheer*. (intransitive)

PRACTICE Have students add objects to complete these sentences.

1. Christian kicks ______.
2. A player makes ______.
3. The goalie stops ______.

▶ **Practice Book** page 41

RESPOND

OBJECTIVES

SUM IT UP

Function: Write; Express Opinions

Reading and Learning Strategies: Use Signal Words; Use Graphic Organizers (chart); Ⓣ Distinguish Between Facts and Opinions

Critical Thinking: Analyze Information; Form Opinions

Writing: Opinion

THINK IT OVER

Function: Engage in Discussion

Comprehension and Critical Thinking: Draw Conclusions; Make Comparisons; Form Generalizations; Make Judgments

EXPRESS YOURSELF

Function: Dramatize

Speaking and Listening: Role-Play

CHECK YOUR UNDERSTANDING

1 **Sum It Up** Students may write about learning a new language, adapting to new customs, and enjoying special cultural traditions.

▶ **Practice Book** page 42

2 **Think It Over** Possible answers are:

1. **Conclusions** Janell: Get to know people and you will see we are all the same. Jenny: People may be different on the outside, but they are still human. Christian: Look for similarities, not differences.
2. **Comparison** They all belong to two cultures. They have different backgrounds and interests.
3. **Generalization** They learn new languages and customs. They make new friends.
4. **Judgments** People will respect your rights if you respect theirs.

3 **Express Yourself** Model asking questions of the role-player that will help students guess the identity.

CLOSE AND ASSESS

Have students revisit the unit mind map and add ideas from the selection about how it feels to belong and not to belong.

Respond to the Self-Portraits

Check Your Understanding

SUM IT UP

Distinguish Between Facts and Opinions Use a chart to record the authors' opinions about living in two cultures. What signal words helped you distinguish between the facts and opinions? Did you agree with all of the opinions? Why or why not?

Author	Opinion	Signal Words	Do you agree? Why or Why Not?
Jenny	I think it's unfair that some people make fun of others because they have an accent.	I think	I agree. You should respect other people's feelings.

Write an Opinion The authors expressed their opinions about living in two cultures. Use the signal words *think, feel, believe, should, agree,* and *disagree* to write your own opinions. How is living in two cultures difficult? What are the benefits of living in two cultures?

THINK IT OVER

Discuss and Write Talk about these questions with a partner. Then write the answers.

1. **Conclusions** What is the main message of each self-portrait?
2. **Comparison** What do Janell, Jenny, and Christian have in common? How is each person different from the other two?
3. **Generalization** What are some ways that people adjust to new cultures?
4. **Judgments** Why is it important to respect other people's rights and feelings?

EXPRESS YOURSELF ▶DRAMATIZE

Form small groups. Take turns pretending that you are Janell, Jenny, or Christian. Give more details about your self-portrait. See if your group members can guess who you are.

98 **Unit 2** | Belonging

REACHING ALL STUDENTS

Multi-Level Strategies

SUM IT UP OPTIONS

BEGINNING Have students work in groups to identify opinions in the Key Points Reading of "Beyond the Color Lines" on **Master 22**. Work together to complete the chart in Sum It Up. Provide sentence frames to help students complete the writing activity: *I think /believe/feel living in two cultures is easy/difficult because* _____.

INTERMEDIATE Have groups discuss the signal words and opinions on their chart and express agreement or disagreement with each opinion. They should then discuss their opinions on the subject of living in two cultures and write a group opinion.

ADVANCED Have students compare charts with a partner and then write individual opinions. After sharing, they can take a poll about agreement and disagreement with their opinions.

ASSESSMENT
Selection Test 6 on page 25 of the Assessment Handbook tests students' mastery of the reading strategies and the vocabulary, comprehension, and language arts skills taught with this selection.

nguage Arts and Literature

GRAMMAR IN CONTEXT

E HELPING VERBS

arn About Helping Verbs Some verbs are ade up of more than one word. The last word the **main verb**. The verb that comes before it is e **helping verb**. The helping verb agrees with e subject. The main verb shows the action.

me helping verbs have a special purpose. Study e examples in this chart.

elping Verb	Purpose	Example
n, could	to tell about an ability	Janell **can** get along with anyone.
ay, could, ight	to tell about a possibility	There **might** be a powwow tonight.
ust	to tell about a need	We **must** prepare for the powwow.
ould	to tell what someone wants to do	I **would** like to know Janell.
ould	to tell what someone ought to do	You **should** respect other people's rights.

actice Answer these questions.

Janell can dance well. What can you do well?

Janell would like to take her future children to powwows. What would you like to do?

Jenny must do her homework after school. What must you do after school?

Christian might go to a university. What might you do after high school?

WRITING

TECHNOLOGY/MEDIA

WRITE A SELF-PORTRAIT

Use the self-portraits you have read as a model for writing your self-portrait. Include three paragraphs:

- Tell who you are, where you are from, and what activities you enjoy.
- Describe traditions and customs that are unique to your culture.
- Express your opinions about the advantages and difficulties of living in two cultures.

1 Write a Draft Use the outline to write your draft. Use the words *I think, I feel,* and *I believe* to signal some of your opinions.

2 Edit and Publish Your Self-Portrait Check your draft for mistakes. Then prepare a final draft. Include photos or drawings to illustrate your self-portrait. If you have a scanner, you may want to scan in a photo of yourself or a picture of an object that is meaningful to you. Include captions for your visuals.

All About Anil
by Anil Naik

Learn to use **word-processing software** to write your self-portrait. See Handbook pages 383–389.

Research Skills

USING A THESAURUS

TEACH Explain that a thesaurus lists synonyms for words. Tell students that as they write their self-portraits, they can consult a thesaurus to find more specific or descriptive words to use. Discuss how different types of thesauri are organized (by simple alphabetical listings or in the traditional style, with an index and guide numbers). Model finding *custom* in a classroom thesaurus. Discuss the differences in meaning for the entries.

PRACTICE Have pairs of students use a thesaurus to find synonyms for words used in "Beyond the Color Lines." Suggest *ceremony, different, special, privilege, adjust* or let students choose their own. If two different thesauri are available, have two pairs look up the same words and compare entries.

▶ **Practice Book** page 44

RESPOND

OBJECTIVES

HELPING VERBS
Grammar: Helping Verbs

WRITE A SELF-PORTRAIT
Function:
Describe; T Express Likes and Dislikes; Express Opinions; Write
Critical Thinking: Form Opinions
Research Skills: Use a Thesaurus
Writing: Self-Portrait

LANGUAGE ARTS AND LITERATURE

1 Use Helping Verbs Answers to Practice items will vary.

Possible answers include:

1. I can play soccer well.
2. I would like to go to the beach.
3. I must take care of my little brother.
4. I might go to art school.

▶ **Practice Book** page 43

2 Write a Self-Portrait Read aloud the instructions. Prompt students to give examples of information that could be included in each paragraph.

▶ **Practice Book** page 45

CLOSE AND ASSESS

Ask students how the instructions and the models in the selection helped them write their self-portraits. Then have them write sentences about their portraits and include helping verbs.

INTRODUCE THEME 2

OBJECTIVES

Function: Engage in Discussion
Concepts and Vocabulary: Connections—*bridge, gap, distance*
Viewing: Interpret a Visual Image
Learning Strategies: Relate to Personal Experience; Use Graphic Organizers (list)
Critical Thinking: Make Inferences; Generate Ideas

TAP PRIOR KNOWLEDGE

1 **Discuss Connections** Ask: *What does* connection *mean? What kinds of things can be connected?* Have students draw or find pictures of things that are connected. (railway cars, telegraph poles, networked computers, people joined by hands) Invite students to share their pictures with the class.

Ask students how people can be connected. (love, friendship, family ties, history, responsibilities, culture, nationality)

VIEW AND DISCUSS

2 **Explore the Benefits of Bridges** After students view the photograph, ask them to think about the purpose of a bridge and the ways it might improve the quality of people's lives. List ideas.

A bridge can:
- connect two pieces of land
- make it possible to cross over water
- allow goods to be transported to the other side
- allow people to work or visit on the other side

Use the Discussion Prompts in the **Multi-Level Strategies** to help all students generate ideas.

The Golden Gate Bridge connects San Francisco to other cities in northern California.

100 Unit 2 | Belonging

REACHING ALL STUDENTS

Multi-Level Strategies

DISCUSSION PROMPTS

BEGINNING Prompt students to describe what they see in the picture. Ask them questions requiring short answers: *Can cars cross a bridge? Can people walk across it? Is it helpful to people?* Advanced beginners can be asked more open-ended questions, such as *How is a bridge helpful?*

INTERMEDIATE Ask students to think about why this bridge was built and what purposes it serves. Ask: *Why would a person use this bridge? What would happen if there were no bridge?* Broaden the discussion beyond this particular bridge: *Why are bridges important?*

ADVANCED Encourage students to discuss how the bridge can be seen as a metaphor for human connections: *The bridge connects two pieces of land. What types of things act as a "bridge" to connect people?* (interests, family, neighborhood) *Why are these bridges important?*

nnotations offer strategies for
Beginning students

THEME 2

Bridging the Gap

- How do people create connections with each other and find a sense of belonging?
  B Ask: What activities help people get to know each other?
- What kinds of thoughts, feelings, words, and actions put distance between people? What helps people bridge the gap?
- What is one step you can take toward bridging the gap with people who are different from you? Explain your answer. **B Restate:** What can you do to make friends with people who are different from you?

B Restate: What makes people angry or upset with each other? What helps them understand each other?

HEME-RELATED BOOKS

he Bicycle Man
y Allen Say
Jot long after World War II, wo American soldiers make riends with a group of children t a school in Japan.
BEGINNING

Seedfolks
by Paul Fleischman
People of different backgrounds get together and change an ugly city lot into a beautiful garden.
INTERMEDIATE

Oh, Freedom!
by Casey King and Linda Barrett Osborne
Young people interview adults about their involvement in the civil rights movement.
ADVANCED

101

DISCUSS THE GUIDING QUESTIONS

3 Set the Theme Some key points to develop during the discussion are:

- People create connections and a sense of belonging by discovering what they have in common (backgrounds, interests, values, and even our senses of humor).
- Negative thoughts, feelings, and words can put distance between people. Making assumptions based on stereotypes without taking time to get to know a person can also create distance. Showing an interest in differences helps reduce the feeling of distance.
- When people seem different from us, we should take the time to ask questions and learn more. We may find that we have more in common than we expected. This effort can be an important step in bridging the gaps between us.

Form groups and use the **Multi-Level Strategies** so all students can participate.

CLOSE AND ASSESS

Ask students to draw the outline of a bridge, then write what they have learned about bridging gaps inside the drawing.

Multi-Level Strategies

GROUPING GUIDELINES

BEGINNING Group students so you can define words and pose choices for responses. See suggestions in red on the facsimile for page 101.

INTERMEDIATE Have students work in groups to gather a variety of answers to each question. Then ask groups to summarize their answers for the class.

ADVANCED Have students work in pairs to discuss their answers. For the last question, have students tell about a time they "bridged the gap" with someone.

THEME LIBRARY

■ ***Seedfolks*** by Paul Fleischman

Invite students to read *Seedfolks.* Ask them to think about the different characters and decide which character they particularly admired. Invite them to write that character a letter in their notebooks, journals, or reflection logs. Letters should include statements about how the character's story demonstrates ways people can bridge the gap between age groups, backgrounds, and cultures and why this is important.

BUILD LANGUAGE AND VOCABULARY

OBJECTIVES

Function: Listen Actively; Sing a Song; Ⓣ Express Likes and Dislikes

Concepts and Vocabulary: Words About Likes and Dislikes

Patterns and Structures: Ⓣ Pronouns

Learning Strategy: Use Graphic Organizers (bar graph)

Critical Thinking: Make Comparisons

Writing: Paragraph

START WITH A COMMON EXPERIENCE

Tape 1A

CD 1 Track 3

1. **Listen and Sing** Play "In Music Meeting" on the **Language Tape/CD** or read aloud the song on page 102. Have students sing the song several times. When they feel comfortable with the words, divide the class into groups and recite or sing the poem as a round.

2. **Clarify Meaning** Discuss the illustration and lyrics to help students understand the song.

   Use the Discussion Prompts in the **Multi-Level Strategies** to involve all students in the discussion.

3. **Model How to Express Likes and Dislikes** Point out that people's likes and dislikes differ. Then use this model:

   How to Express Likes and Dislikes
   - Tell one thing you like: *I like rap music.*
   - Tell why you like it: *The lyrics are about personal feelings I can relate to.*
   - Tell one thing you dislike: *I do not like classical music.*
   - Tell why you don't like it: *It's hard to understand.*

Build Language and Vocabulary

EXPRESS LIKES AND DISLIKES

Listen to the song and sing it together as a group. Let your voices "meet" in the music!

REACHING ALL STUDENTS

Multi-Level Strategies

DISCUSSION PROMPTS

BEGINNING To help students understand the meaning of the song, ask: *What kinds of music do you like? How does music bring people together?* As students respond, record their answers in a chart.

INTERMEDIATE Point out specific references to music in the poem: *What is the "silent, unsung greeting" mentioned by the poet?* (the idea that music can bring people together) *How do "voices touch"?* (The singers feel united by singing.)

ADVANCED Have students speculate about the songwriter's creative process: *Why do you think the songwriter decided to write this song? What is the message the songwriter hoped to communicate?*

AKE CLASS GRAPHS

old a sheet of paper into thirds. Use the ections to tell:

- one thing you like to do
- one thing you do not like to do
- your most important value

hen compare your papers and make bar graphs to ummarize the class's likes, dislikes, and values.

Bar Graph

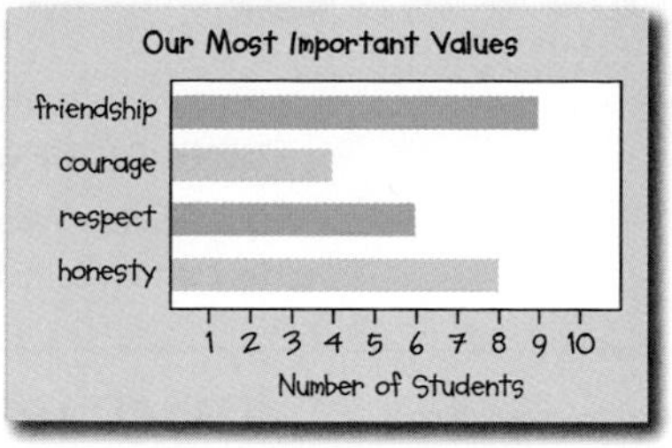

UILD YOUR VOCABULARY

'ays to Tell About Your Likes and Dislikes Form groups according to the alue you have in common. Then brainstorm different ways to say that you ke or do not like something. Make a long list.

I love to . . .
I enjoy . . .
I don't like . . .
There's nothing better than . . .
I really have fun when I . . .

SE LANGUAGE STRUCTURES ▶ PRONOUNS

'riting: Express Likes and Dislikes Work with a partner. Write a short aragraph telling about the likes, dislikes, and values you both have. Use t least three pronouns in your paragraph.

Example:
We both like team sports. **I** enjoy baseball most, but **my** partner prefers volleyball. **We** agree with **our** classmates that good sportsmanship is an important value.

CONDUCT THE ACTIVITIES

4 Make Class Graphs After students write individually, invite volunteers to take turns building the summary bar graphs.

5 Build Your Vocabulary: Ways to Tell About Your Likes and Dislikes Have students share favorite activities, types of music, foods. Encourage them to paraphrase their classmates' statements.

6 Use Language Structures: Pronouns Present the skill, using the definitions and examples on **Transparency 24**. Explain the pronouns in steps 3 and 4 before asking students to complete the sentences in Try It!

Writing: Express Likes and Dislikes Conduct the activity at the bottom of page 103. Have students use the class bar graphs to find ideas for their paragraphs.

Use the Writing Activity Options in the **Multi-Level Strategies** to adjust instruction.

▶ **Practice Book** page 46

CLOSE AND ASSESS

Have students rewrite these sentences, replacing the proper nouns with pronouns: *Jed loves to play soccer. Brianne enjoys basketball. Jed and Brianne like to watch baseball together. Jed and Brianne and I think friendship is an important value.*

Multi-Level Strategies

WRITING ACTIVITY OPTIONS

BEGINNING Help pairs of students by providing the following sentence frames: *We both like* ______. *I like* ______ *most, but my partner likes* ______ *better. We both agree that one important value is* ______ *because* ______. Encourage students to add phrases to complete each sentence and to change the pronouns when necessary.

INTERMEDIATE Students can work in pairs and ask each other questions about their likes and dislikes. Remind students to use pronouns from the charts in writing their answers.

ADVANCED Ask students to share their paragraphs with the class in oral presentations. Encourage classmates to ask questions such as: *Why do you like team sports so much? What do you dislike about board games? Why is loyalty your most important value?*

Transparency 24 / Master 24

LEARN ABOUT PRONOUNS

1. A **pronoun** is a word that takes the place of a noun.
   Ben plays soccer. **He** proudly puts on **his** uniform.
2. The pronouns *he* and *his* tell about *Ben*. The noun *Ben* is called the **antecedent**.
   Ben plays soccer. He proudly puts on his uniform.
   (antecedent: Ben; subject pronoun: He; possessive pronoun: his)
3. Use these pronouns in the subject of a sentence.
   I you he she it we they
4. Use these pronouns to show who owns something.
   my your his her its our their

Try It!

Write each sentence. Add a pronoun.

1. Jane likes to use ______ own paints to create a mural.
2. ______ draws huge fish and other sea life.
3. Jane's parents can't wait to see ______ daughter's mural.
4. Jane's dad says, "______ mural is fantastic!"
5. Jane's mom says, "______ are both so proud of you!"

Transparency 24 Level B, Unit 2 | Belonging © Hampton-Brown

PREPARE TO READ

OBJECTIVES

THINK ABOUT WHAT YOU KNOW
Reading Strategy: Activate Prior Knowledge

LEARN KEY VOCABULARY T
Vocabulary Strategy: Use Context Clues

CONNECT NEW INFORMATION TO WHAT YOU KNOW
Reading Strategy: Preview; Connect New Information to Known

THINK ABOUT WHAT YOU KNOW

1 **Quickwrite** Clarify understanding of the phrase *stand by.* Have students do the quickwrite; then ask them to share what they wrote.

LEARN KEY VOCABULARY

2 **Use Context Clues** Have students read each vocabulary word and its definition. Clarify meanings. Then conduct the activity.

Use the Vocabulary Options in the **Multi-Level Strategies** to tailor the activity to proficiency levels.

▶ **Practice Book** page 47

CONNECT NEW INFORMATION TO WHAT YOU KNOW

3 **Model How to Connect New Information to What You Know** Explain that *what you know* is information you already know before reading, and that *new information* is what you learn from the reading.

Preview "Teammates" and demonstrate steps 1–3 in the Strategy Box with **Transparency 25.** Distribute **Master 25** and have students fill in the "K" and "W" columns of the chart.

CLOSE AND ASSESS

Ask students why it is helpful to connect new information to what they already know. (It helps you learn information more easily.)

Teammates

Prepare to Read

biography
by Peter Golenbock

THINK ABOUT WHAT YOU KNOW

Quickwrite What does it mean to "stand by your teammate"? Write a few sentences to tell what you think.

LEARN KEY VOCABULARY

Use Context Clues Study the new words and their definitions. Write t[he] paragraph and replace the bold words with vocabulary words.

In the 1940s, black baseball players were allowed to join white players on Major League teams. Still, black players had to live with a lot of **hateful actions** from fans and other players. Some tried to **scare** them. Much of the **mean treatment** did hurt the black players. But by the 1950s, blacks and whites began to **take a stand against** this treatment. They thought blacks should be able to compete in sports and other jobs. Some even sent a **form that asks for change** to the government. In the United States many people are still working to stop **bad feelings toward people because of their race.**

abuse mean words or treatment

challenge disagree with, take a stand against

compete try to win a contest or game

cruel mean

hostility hateful actions, mean thoughts

humiliation feeling of shame or embarassment

intimidate frighten

petition form asking for change

racial prejudice dislike of people because of their race

threat words that tell of future harm

Replacement answers to the vocabulary activity in the order they appear:
1. hostility or abuse
2. intimidate
3. abuse or hostility
4. challenge
5. petition
6. racial prejudice

CONNECT NEW INFORMATION TO WHAT YOU KNOW

You will learn new information more easily when you **connect** it to wha[t] you already know. Use a K-W-L chart to make these connections.

READING STRATEGY
How to Connect New Information to What You Know
1. Read the title and look at the illustrations.
2. Write what you know in the first column of your chart.
3. Write questions in the second column.
4. After you read, write the answers in the last column.
5. Review what you wrote to see the connections.

Complete a K-W-L chart as you read "Teammates."

104 **Unit 2** | Belonging

REACHING ALL STUDENTS

Multi-Level Strategies

VOCABULARY OPTIONS

BEGINNING Group students to read ***More Than a Meal*** or the Key Points Reading on **Master 26.** (See page T107.) Work with the vocabulary in those selections.

INTERMEDIATE Have students work in pairs to decide which vocabulary words to substitute in the paragraph.

ADVANCED Students can work alone to substitute vocabulary words in the paragraph. Then have them work with partners to check answers.

Transparency 25 / Master 25

HOW TO CONNECT INFORMATION

Directions: Preview the selection. In the first column, write what you already know about baseball and segregation in the 1950s. Write what you want to know about this topic in the second column. After you finish reading the selection, fill in the last column.

K-W-L Chart

K What I Know	W What I Want to Know	L What I Learned
There used to be separate baseball leagues for African American players and white players.	Who was the first African American player for the Brooklyn Dodgers?	

Transparency 25 Level B, Unit 2 | Belonging © Hampton-Brown

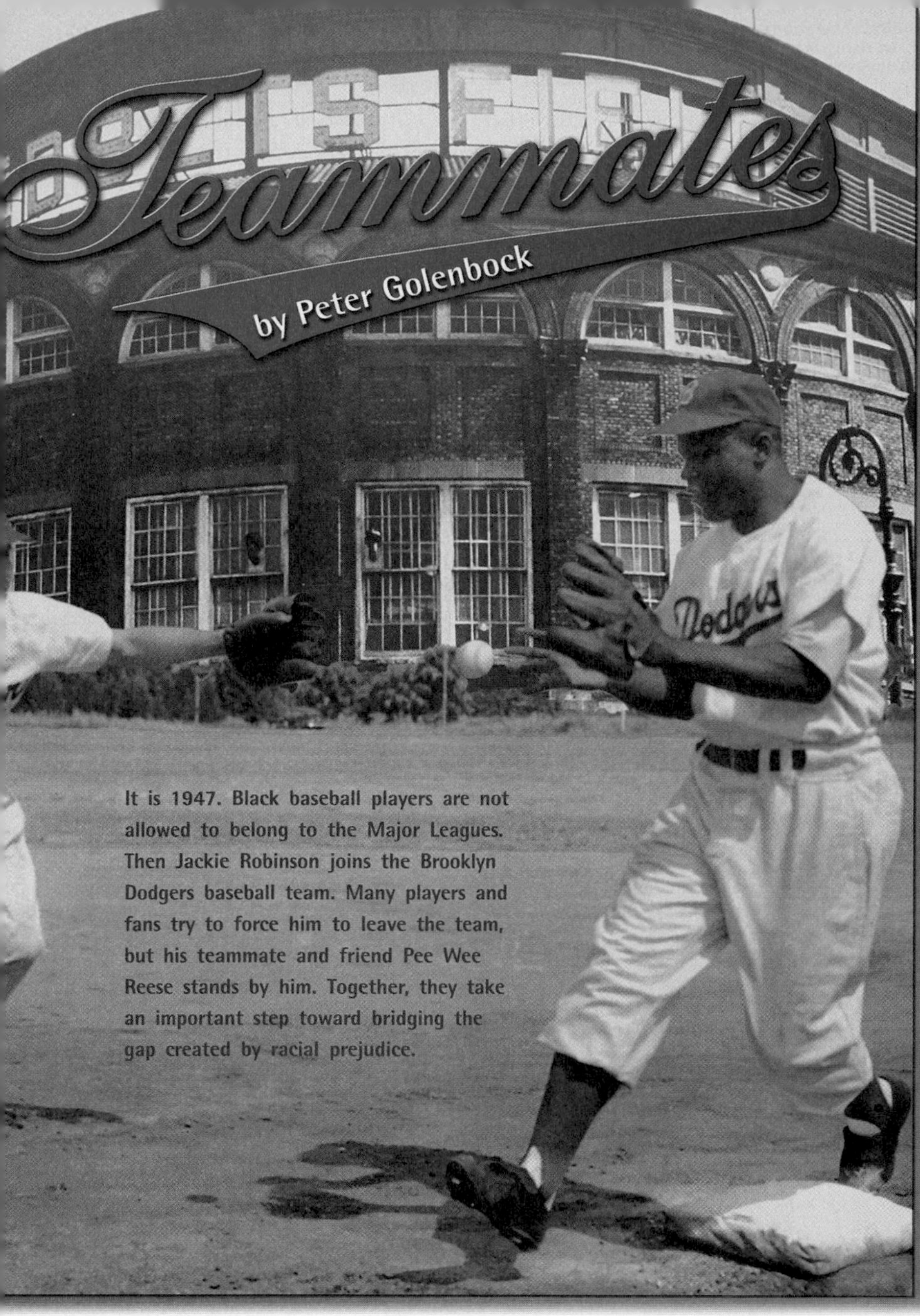

Teammates

by Peter Golenbock

It is 1947. Black baseball players are not allowed to belong to the Major Leagues. Then Jackie Robinson joins the Brooklyn Dodgers baseball team. Many players and fans try to force him to leave the team, but his teammate and friend Pee Wee Reese stands by him. Together, they take an important step toward bridging the gap created by racial prejudice.

READ THE SELECTION

OBJECTIVES

Reading Strategies: Build Background
Literary Analysis: Biography

INTRODUCE THE SELECTION

4 **Build Background** Have students share what they wrote in the "K" column of their charts. Use this idea exchange and the introduction on page 105 to acquaint students with baseball in the 1940s, Jackie Robinson, and Pee Wee Reese.

5 **Identify Genre: Biography** Ask students whom the story is about. Ask: *Is this person real or fictional? Did the events in the story really happen or were they made up by the author?* Explain that a text about the life of a real person is called a biography. Have students tell about other biographies they have read.

Teammates
by Peter Golenbock

Theme Connection This selection describes how two teammates of different races bridge the gap of prejudice. It illustrates how having a common purpose can help people overcome superficial differences.

Selection Summary and Awards The introduction on page 105 of the student book offers a summary of the selection. *Teammates* was the winner of the *Redbook* Children's Picturebook Award and named a *Parents'* Magazine "Best Kids' Books of '90" selection.

Background Jackie Robinson was the first African American baseball player in the Major Leagues. After retiring, Robinson became a leading advocate for African American civil rights. In 1962 he became the first African American inducted into the Baseball Hall of Fame.

THE BASICS BOOKSHELF

■ ***More Than a Meal*** by Suzy Blackaby

Helping out neighbors in a community is one way to bridge the gap between young and old. In this story, a young man delivers "Meals on Wheels" to shut-ins and, when he can, helps out in other ways. Patterned text introduces prepositions and names of places in a neighborhood. A community map and strong visual support for the text increase access for beginning English learners.

For Lesson Plans: See the Teacher's Guide for ***The Basics Bookshelf***.

READ PAGES 106–107

OBJECTIVES

Function: Read a Selection
Grammar: Ⓣ Pronouns
Listening: Listen to a Selection
Reading and Learning Strategies: Set a Purpose for Reading; Use Graphic Organizers (K-W-L chart); Connect New Information to Known
Comprehension: Make Comparisons; Identify Cause and Effect, Character's Traits

SET PURPOSE

1 Read aloud the introduction to pages 106–107. Set the purpose for reading: *Look for ways that black baseball players were treated differently from white players.*

READ AND THINK

Tape 2B
CD 2
Track 4

2 **Strategy Focus: Connect New Information to What You Know** Have students use the "L" column on **Master 25** (see page T104) to take notes on information relevant to the questions they posed in the "W" column.

Choose Reading Options in the **Multi-Level Strategies** to tailor the reading to proficiency levels.

The recording of "Teammates" on the **Selection Tape/CD** offers an oral language model and the opportunity to build reading fluency.

Red annotations offer opportunities to clarify meaning and check for understanding.

1

BASEBALL BEGINS TO CHANGE

In the 1940s, black baseball players are not allowed to play in the Major Leagues. The general manager of the Brooklyn Dodgers decides to change things.

Build background: From the middle of the 1880s until the year of this story (1947), black players were not allowed to compete in the Major Leagues. Instead, teams made up completely of black players formed leagues that were known as the Negro Leagues.

Once upon a time in America, when automobiles were black and looked like tanks and laundry was white and hung on clotheslines to dry, there were two wonderful **baseball leagues** that no longer exist. They were called the Negro Leagues.

The Negro Leagues had **extraordinary** players, and **adoring fans** came to see them wherever they played. They were heroes, but players in the Negro Leagues didn't make much money and their lives **on the road** were hard.

Life was very different for the players in the Major Leagues. They were the leagu for white players. Compared to the Negro League players, white players were very w paid. They stayed in good hotels and ate i fine restaurants. Their pictures were put o baseball cards and the best players becam famous all over the world.

Clarify: "Negro" was a term used to refer to black people at the time of this story. This word is rarely used now; "black" and "African American" are preferred terms.

Satchel Paige was an outstanding pitcher. However, he was not allowed to play in the Major Leagues for many years.

Baseball cards show photos of baseball players and give information about them. Baseball fans collect cards and, sometimes, trade or sell them. This card shows Ted Williams, a player who joined the Boston Red Sox in 1939.

baseball leagues groups of professional baseball teams
extraordinary extremely good, excellent
adoring fans people who loved the players on the teams
on the road while traveling

REACHING ALL STUDENTS

Multi-Level Strategies

READING OPTIONS FOR LESSONS 4–6

BEGINNING Students may work with ***More Than a Meal*** while the class reads "Teammates." Or, distribute copies of **Master 26** and work with students to fill in the "L" column of the chart on **Transparency 25** (see page T104) as you conduct the Key Points Reading.

INTERMEDIATE Read the selection aloud or play the **Selection Tape/CD**. Pause to use the red annotations on the facsimile pages. Students can work in pairs to fill in the "L" column of the chart on copies of **Master 25**. (See page T104.)

ADVANCED Students should work on their own to fill in what they learn in the "L" column of the chart on copies of **Master 25** (see page T104).

Encourage elaboration: Why is racial prejudice wrong? What kinds of things could people have done to challenge racial prejudice?

Many Americans knew ıat **racial prejudice** was ˈrong, but few dared to ·**hallenge** openly the way ıings were.

The general manager f the Brooklyn Dodgers aseball team was a man by ıe name of Branch Rickey. :e was not afraid of change. [e wanted to treat the •odger fans to the best layers he could find, ·egardless of the color of ıeir skin.

To do this, the Dodgers ıeeded one special man.

Jackie Robinson joined the Brooklyn Dodgers in 1947. He is shown here with Branch Rickey, general manager of the Dodgers.

Define *general manager*: a team's leader, responsible for strategy and behavior. He or she decides who joins the team, who plays what position, and what team members play in each game.

Branch Rickey **launched search** for him. He was looking for star player in the Negro Leagues who ᵥould be able to **compete** successfully espite **threats** on his life or attempts to ıjure him. He would have to possess the elf-control not to fight back when **opposing layers** tried to **intimidate** or hurt him. ˈ this man **disgraced himself** on the field, :ickey knew, **his opponents** would use it s **an excuse** to keep blacks out of Major eague baseball for many more years.

Rickey thought Jackie Robinson might e just the man.

BEFORE YOU MOVE ON...

1. **Comparison** How was life for baseball players in the Negro Leagues different from life for players in the Major Leagues?
2. **Cause and Effect** Why did Branch Rickey look for black players to join his team?
3. **Character's Traits** What kind of player did Branch Rickey want to find?

ıunched a search started to look
pposing players players on the other team
isgraced himself made himself look bad
is opponents the people against him
n excuse a reason

CHECK COMPREHENSION

3 Answers to "Before You Move On"

1. **Comparison** Players in the Negro Leagues made less money and had harder lives on the road than Major League players.
2. **Cause and Effect** Branch Rickey wanted to please his team's fans by bringing the best players to his team, regardless of the players' skin color.
3. **Character's Traits** He wanted to find a star player in the Negro Leagues who could handle intimidation with courage and self-control and still play a successful game.

CLOSE AND ASSESS

Have students discuss with a partner their answers in the "L" column for this part of the selection.

Transparency 26 / Master 26

KEY POINTS READING

Teammates

In the 1940s, black baseball players cannot play in the Major Leagues. They must play in the Negro Leagues. Players in the Negro Leagues make less money than Major League players. In 1947, the manager of the Brooklyn Dodgers makes a big decision. He decides not to worry about the color of a player's skin. He looks for a special player from the Negro leagues. He invites Jackie Robinson to join his team.

Jackie starts spring training with the Dodgers. He is treated badly by many of the players on the team. But Jackie never gives up. When the season begins, he is a member of the team. On the road, Jackie feels lonely. Sometimes he is scared. One of Jackie's teammates speaks up for Jackie. Pee Wee Reese says that Jackie is a good player who will help the team win.

During a game in Cincinnati, the fans scream terrible things at Jackie. Pee Wee knows that this is wrong. He decides to show his support for Jackie. Pee Wee walks over to Jackie. He smiles at him and puts his arm around Jackie's shoulders. The crowd is surprised. The people stop yelling. They see that Pee Wee Reese is standing by Jackie.

Transparency 26 Level B, Unit 2 | Belonging

Grammar Minilesson

▶ PRONOUN AGREEMENT

TEACH Read the second paragraph on page 107 aloud and ask students to whom the word *he* refers. (Branch Rickey)

Explain that *he* is a pronoun, or a word that takes the place of a noun. Subject pronouns, like *he*, take the place of subjects in a sentence and object pronouns, like *him*, take the place of objects.

Give more examples: *The Dodgers needed one special man. Branch Rickey searched for* ***him***.

Subject Pronouns		Object Pronouns	
I	we	me	us
you	you	you	you
he, she, it	they	him, her	them

Have students find other pronouns in the story and identify the antecedents.

PRACTICE Have students use the pronouns *he* and *him* in a description of one photo on page 106 or 107.

READ PAGES 108–109

OBJECTIVES

Function: Read a Selection
Vocabulary Strategy: Relate Words
Grammar: Ⓣ Subject, Possessive, and Reflexive Pronouns
Listening: Listen to a Selection
Reading and Learning Strategies: Set a Purpose for Reading; Use Graphic Organizers (K-W-L chart); Connect New Information to Known
Comprehension: Identify Details, Character's Traits, Character's Motive

SET PURPOSE

1 Read aloud the introduction to pages 108–109. Set the purpose for reading: *Read to learn how Jackie is treated by many players and fans and how Pee Wee Reese supports him.*

READ AND THINK

Tape 2B
CD 2 Track 4

2 **Strategy Focus: Connect New Information to What You Know** Involve students in reading pages 108–109 of the selection. Remind them to take notes in the "L" column of their K-W-L charts.

See the **Multi-Level Strategies** on page T106 to tailor the reading experience to all proficiency levels.

2

JACKIE MAKES THE TEAM

Jackie Robinson joins the Brooklyn Dodgers. Many players and fans treat him badly. His teammate Pee Wee Reese, however, supports him.

At spring training with the Dodgers, **Jackie was mobbed by blacks**, young and old, as if he were **a savior**. He was the first black player on a Major League team in almost fifty years. If he **succeeded**, they knew, others would follow.

Initially, life with the Dodgers was for Jackie a series of **humiliations**. The players on his team who came from the South, men who had been taught to **avoid** black people since childhood, moved to another table whenever he sat down next to them. Many opposing players were **cruel** to him, calling him nasty names from their dugouts. A few tried to hurt him with their spiked shoes. Pitchers aimed at his head. And he received threats on his life.

Restate: At first Jackie had many uncomfortable and unhappy experiences with the Dodgers.

Define *dugout*: the area where players and other team members in uniform sit while they are not playing on the field.

Despite all the **difficulties**, Jackie Robinson didn't give up. He made the Brooklyn Dodgers team.

Making the Dodgers was only the beginning. Jackie had to face **abuse** and **hostility** throughout the season, from Apr through September. His worst pain was insic Often he felt very alone. On the road he ha to live by himself, because only the white players were allowed in the hotels in towns where the team played.

A team photo of the Brooklyn Dodgers, taken in 1947. Pee Wee Reese and Jackie Robinson are circled.

Build background: Baseball players were not the only peo who suffered discrimination. Black citizens weren't allowed stay in the same hotels and ea meals in the same restaurants as whites until 1964, when the U.S. Congress passed laws guaranteeing these rights to all citizens.

Jackie was mobbed by blacks black fans crowded around Jackie
a savior someone who could keep bad things from happening to them
succeeded accomplished this goal
Initially At first
avoid stay away from
difficulties problems

REACHING ALL STUDENTS

Social Studies Connection
U.S. HISTORY

Have students work in small groups to research the Negro Leagues, using encyclopedias, books and magazine articles, and the Internet. Each student can concentrate on a different aspect of the Leagues, such as their origin, daily lives of the players, famous players, or how and why the leagues disappeared. The group should then work together to tell the story of the Negro Leagues through a series of posters that include text, illustrations or photos, and charts.

COMMUNITY CONNECTION

Recreational Opportunities Have students explore recreational facilities available in their communities and make a chart to organize the information, showing such details as locations, schedules, and fees for the activities offered. If possible, students should visit these sites and then make evaluative statements about the facilities. Provide optional sentence frames, such as *In my opinion, this facility is _____ because it offers/doesn't offer _____.*

Vocabulary
IDIOMS

Define *idiom* as an expression that has a special meaning that is not clear from the meanings of the individual words. Present *stealing home* as an example. Define *stealing* as "taking something that is not yours." Explain that *home plate* is the place a baseball player must reach in order to score a run. Put the words together and lead students to the idiomatic meaning. Have students practice with other idioms from the selection, such as *stand by*, *bridging the gap*, and *on the road*.

Build background: Until 1956, black people were forced to sit in the back seats on buses in many states.

The whole time Pee Wee Reese, the odger **shortstop**, was growing up in ouisville, Kentucky, he had **rarely** even een a black person, unless it was in the ack of a bus. Most of his friends and latives hated the idea of his playing on e same field as a black man. In addition, ee Wee Reese **had more to lose** than the ther players when Jackie joined the team.

Jackie had been a shortstop, and veryone thought that Jackie would take ee Wee's job. Lesser men might have felt nger toward Jackie, but Pee Wee was ifferent. He told himself, "If he's good nough to take my job, he deserves it."

When his Southern teammates **circulated petition** to throw Jackie off the team and sked him to sign it, Pee Wee responded, I don't care if this man is black, blue, or triped"—and **refused to sign**. "He can play nd he can help us win," he told the others. That's what counts." **Ask:** How does Pee Wee feel about Jackie's skin color? Why?

Harold "Pee Wee" Reese, the shortstop for the Brooklyn Dodgers, was only 5 feet 9 inches tall and weighed 140 pounds when he began his professional baseball career.

BEFORE YOU MOVE ON...

1. **Details** What happened to Jackie during spring training?
2. **Character's Traits** What words can you think of to describe Jackie Robinson?
3. **Character's Motive** Why did Pee Wee refuse to sign the petition?

hortstop player who stands between second nd third bases on the baseball field
arely almost never
ad more to lose had more reasons to be gainst Jackie
irculated passed around
efused to sign would not write his name on it

REVIEW KEY VOCABULARY

3 Relate Words Make index cards with one key vocabulary word written on each. Have students work in pairs. One student selects an index card at random and uses synonyms, antonyms, or examples to give clues about the word. The partner tries to guess the word. Each time a word is guessed, the partners change roles.

CHECK COMPREHENSION

4 Answers to "Before You Move On"

1. **Details** Jackie was mobbed by black fans, who saw him as a kind of savior because he was the first black player trying out for a Major League team in almost fifty years.
2. **Character's Traits** Answers may include: *courageous, determined, even-tempered, resilient.*
3. **Character's Motive** Pee Wee felt that Jackie's ability to play the game well and help his team win was more important than his race.

CLOSE AND ASSESS

Have students revisit the mind map created at the beginning of the unit and add details that tell how Jackie felt about being treated as if he did not belong. Also ask students to predict to what groups Jackie may belong in the future.

HOME CONNECTION

Baseball Memories Send home a copy of *High Point Newsletter 4* in the **Teacher's Resource Book**. In this home activity, students interview an older member of their family or a friend about a time when they made a connection with a person from a different background. Students ask how the people involved bridged the gaps between them. Then students illustrate the story and share it with the class.

Grammar Minilesson

▶ SUBJECT, POSSESSIVE, AND REFLEXIVE PRONOUNS

On page 108, point out *his worst pain* and ask to whom *his* refers. (Jackie Robinson) Explain that *his* is a possessive pronoun.

Then read *He had to live by himself. . . .* Explain that *himself* is a reflexive pronoun, used when referring to a person previously named in a sentence.

PRACTICE Have students develop a chart like the one at the right and create sentences with the various pronouns.

Subject	Possessive	Reflexive
I	my	myself
you	your	yourself
he	his	himself
she	her	herself
it	its	itself
we	our	ourselves
they	their	themselves

READ PAGES 110–111

OBJECTIVES

Function: Read a Selection
Vocabulary: Roots
Listening: Listen to a Selection
Reading and Learning Strategies: Set a Purpose for Reading; Use Graphic Organizers (K-W-L chart); Connect New Information to Known; Paraphrase
Literary Analysis: T Narrator's Point of View

SET PURPOSE

1 Read aloud the introduction to pages 110–112. Set the purpose for reading: *Read to find out how Pee Wee shows his support for Jackie.*

READ AND THINK

Tape 2B
CD 2 Track 4

2 **Strategy Focus: Connect New Information to What You Know** Involve students in reading pages 110–112 of the selection. Remind them to take notes in the "L" column of their K-W-L charts.

Use the **Multi-Level Strategies** on page T106 to address all proficiency levels.

3

PEE WEE TAKES A STAND

When the Dodgers play against Cincinnati, fans scream hateful things at Jackie. Pee Wee supports Jackie, and their friendship causes baseball to change forever.

Very early in the season, the Dodgers traveled west to Ohio to play Cincinnati. Cincinnati is near Pee Wee's hometown of Louisville.

Cincinnati played in a small ballpark where the fans sat close to the field. The players could almost feel the breath of the fans on the backs of their necks. Many who came that day screamed terrible, hateful things at Jackie when the Dodgers were on the field.

Pee Wee Reese and Jackie Robinson shocked the nation through their simple acts of friendship, causing many people to rethink their prejudices.

More than anything else, Pee Wee Rees believed in doing what was right. When he heard the fans yelling at Jackie, Pee Wee decided to **take a stand**.

With his head high, Pee Wee walked directly from his shortstop position to where Jackie was playing first base. The **taunts** and shouting of the fans were ringi in Pee Wee's ears. It saddened him, becaus he knew it could have been his friends and neighbors. Pee Wee's legs felt heavy, but he knew what he had to do.

As he walked toward Jackie wearing the gray Dodger uniform, he looked into his teammate's **bold, pained eyes**. The firs baseman had done nothing to **provoke the hostility** except that he sought to be treate as an equal. Jackie was **grim with anger**. Pee Wee smiled broadly as he reached Jackie. Jackie smiled back.

Restate: It was a difficult thing for him to do
Ask: What kinds of thoughts might have bee going through Pee Wee's mind at this mome

take a stand do what he thought was right
taunts mean words
bold, pained eyes eyes that showed hurt
provoke the hostility make people angry
grim with anger very upset and mad

REACHING ALL STUDENTS

INTERNET

SOCIAL STUDIES CONNECTION

Familiarize students with the positions on a baseball team (pitcher, catcher, shortstop, etc.). Have them conduct research on player profiles and statistics. Ask students to design a team that includes baseball's all-time greatest players. When students have completed their all-star teams, have them determine the percentage of players from various ethnic groups and create pie charts to show the ethnic breakdown.

Web Sites
Web Sites undergo frequent change, but here are some to suggest:
www.majorleaguebaseball.com
www.baseballhalloffame.org

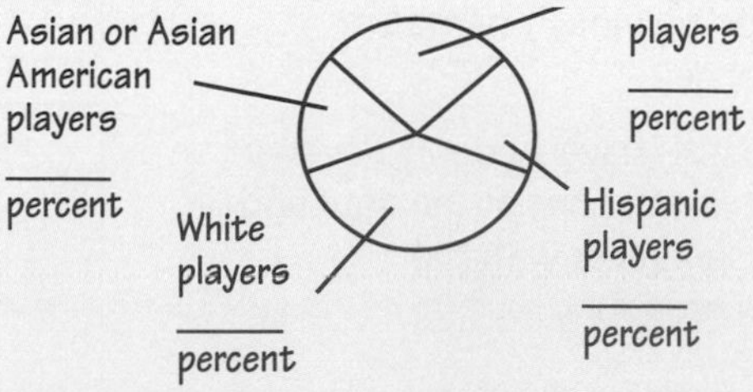

Language Development

JUSTIFY

Have students work in groups to write all the reasons why Branch Rickey made the right decision in hiring Jackie Robinson. Remind students to use pronouns in their sentences. Have each group share their ideas with the class. Model ways that students might introduce their ideas:

- *Mr. Rickey did the right thing because he…*
- *Branch Rickey had good reason to…*
- *I can understand why Mr. Rickey…*

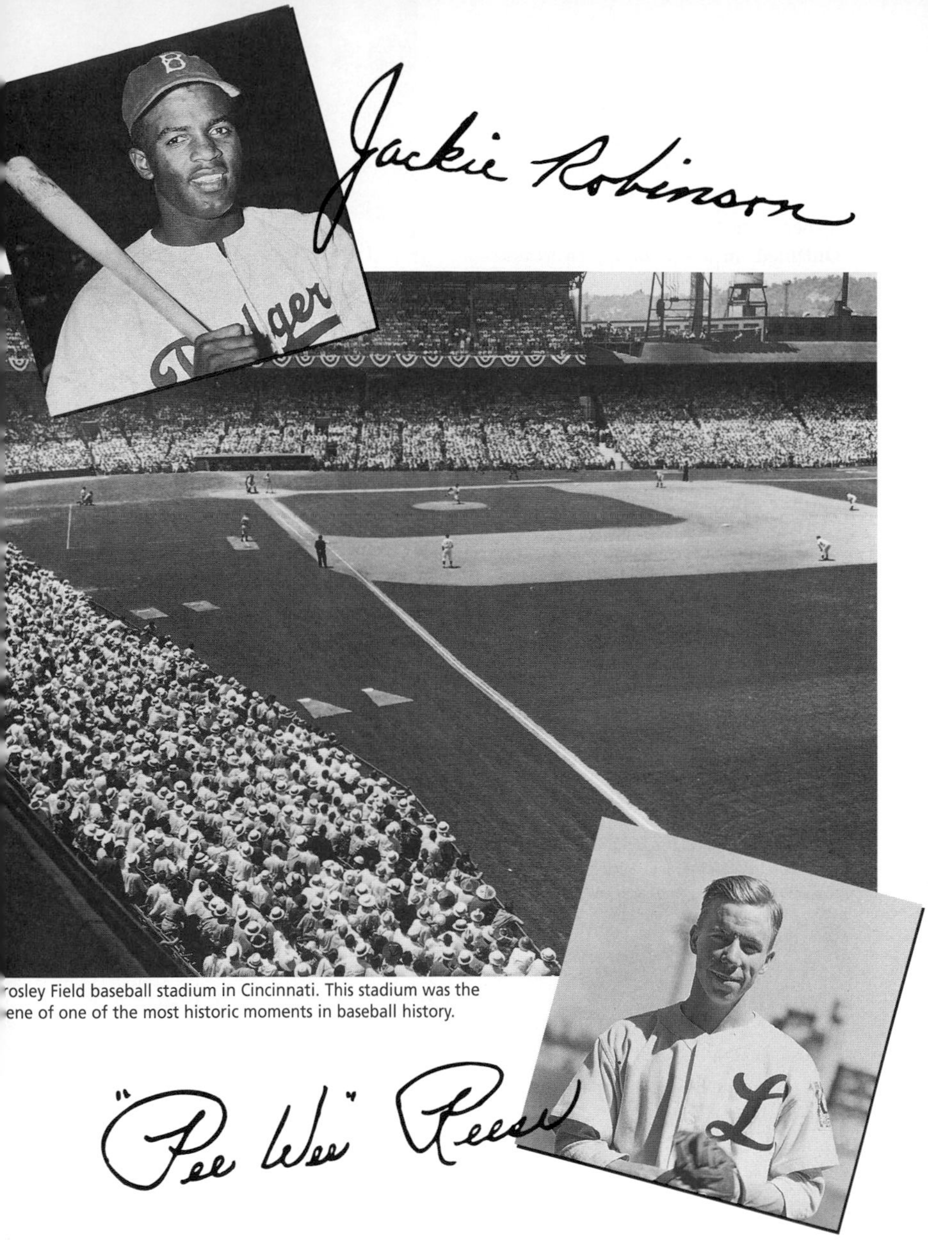

rosley Field baseball stadium in Cincinnati. This stadium was the ene of one of the most historic moments in baseball history.

MONITOR YOUR READING

3 Paraphrase Have students work with a partner to retell the events in the story up to this point. The listening partner should point out any inaccuracies in the speaker's telling and add any important details that the speaker omits.

EXPAND VOCABULARY

4 Roots Teach the meaning of the roots *bio* (life) and *graph* (write). Write the word *biography* and show how knowing the roots can help students unlock the meaning of the word. Have students collect more words with these roots. *(autograph, paragraph, biology, biosphere)*

Art Connection

BALLPARK DESIGNS

Have students work in small groups to draw a famous ballpark (such as Fenway Park or Yankee Stadium). Students can research ballparks in the library or on the Internet and use a computer graphics program to produce the final drawing. Groups should present their drawings and explain their designs. Groups should present their drawings and explain their designs. Encourage students to explain how different parts of the ballpark are connected, using prepositions such as *above, below, beside, between,* and *across from.*

Literary Analysis Minilesson

▶ NARRATOR'S POINT OF VIEW

TEACH Ask: *Is this selection about the writer or about someone else?* (someone else) Say: *Stories that tell about other people's lives are called third-person stories. The narrator uses third-person pronouns, such as* he, she, *and* they.

Next, have students read the first sentence of each paragraph on pages 92–93. Say: *Is this story about Janell or someone else?* (Janell) *Stories that describe the writer's own life are called first-person stories. The narrator uses first-person pronouns, such as* I *and* we. Summarize the pronouns in a chart.

Point of View	Singular	Plural
First-person	I	we
Second-person	you	you
Third-person	he/she/it	they

PRACTICE Have one team of students rewrite the first paragraph of page 108 in the first person. Have another team rewrite the first paragraph of Janell's story in the third person.

▶ **Practice Book** page 48

READ PAGE 112

OBJECTIVES

Function: Read a Selection
Reading Strategy and Comprehension: Paraphrase; Identify Character's Motive; Draw Conclusions
Literary Analysis: Respond to Literature

CHECK COMPREHENSION

5 Answers to "Before You Move On"

1. **Paraphrase** The fans screamed terrible things at Jackie. Pee Wee put his arm around him.
2. **Character's Motive** Answers include: Pee Wee felt the fans' reaction was wrong. He took a stand for what he knew was right.
3. **Conclusions** The fans were surprised. The event helped bridge the gap racial prejudice had caused in baseball.

ABOUT THE AUTHOR

6 Respond to Literature Read About the Author. Then discuss how personal interests influence what people read. Ask: *What do you think the author reads?* (books about baseball and sports) *What do you enjoy reading?*

CLOSE AND ASSESS

Ask: *What did you learn that helped you complete your K-W-L chart?*

Stopping beside Jackie, Pee Wee put his arm around Jackie's shoulders. **An audible gasp rose up** from the crowd when they saw what Pee Wee had done. Then there was silence. **Ask:** Why do you think the crowd fell silent?

Outlined on a sea of green grass stood these two great athletes, one black, one white, both wearing the same team uniform.

"**I am standing by him,**" Pee Wee Reese said to the world. "This man is my teammate."

Role-Play: Have students act out the last event in the story. Two students can play Jackie and Pee Wee and the rest of the class can act as the fans.

Today's Major League teams have players of different races and players from around the world.

BEFORE YOU MOVE ON...

1. **Paraphrase** In your own words, tell how the fans treated Jackie. Tell how Pee Wee reacted.
2. **Character's Motive** Why did Pee Wee take a stand?
3. **Conclusions** Why did the fans gasp when Pee Wee put his arm around Jackie's shoulders?

An audible gasp rose up The sound of people sucking in their breaths could be heard

Outlined on a sea of green grass stood Plainly seen on the baseball field were

I am standing by him I will be his friend no matter what happens

ABOUT THE AUTHOR

Peter Golenbock, one of America's best-selling sportswriters, has written several books about legendary baseball players and teams, including histories of the Brooklyn Dodgers, the New York Yankees, and the Boston Red Sox. In "Teammates," he shows us that star athletes are als ordinary human beings, facing life's challenges and trying to connect with people who may be different from themselves.

REACHING ALL STUDENTS

Mathematics Connection

AVERAGES

Have students compare RBI averages for three baseball players. Explain that an RBI, or Run Batted In, is earned for each run scored when a player gets a hit. The figures in the chart represent RBI totals for each of three years. Have students calculate each player's average and then compare the results to determine which player had the highest RBI average. (*Answer: Jackie Robinson had the highest with a 3-year RBI average of 86*)

Player	1951 RBIs	1952 RBIs	1953 RBIs	Av. RBIs
Jackie Robinson (Dodgers)	88	75	95	86
Randy Jackson (Cubs)	76	34	66	58.7
Alvin Dark (Giants)	69	73	88	76.7

Learning Styles

STRATEGIES FOR CONSTRUCTING MEANING

- **Visual Learners** Have students create a collage that expresses the theme of the selection.
- **Auditory Learners** Invite students to write a rap or a song about the friendship between Pee Wee Reese and Jackie Robinson.
- **Kinesthetic Learners** After finishing the story, have two students role-play scenes from the story.

Respond to the Biography

Check Your Understanding

UM IT UP

onnect New Information to What You now Review your K-W-L chart. Share your art with a group.

K What I Know	W What I Want to Learn	L What I Learned
There used to be separate baseball leagues for black players and white players.	Who was the first African American player for the Brooklyn Dodgers?	Jackie Robinson left the Negro Leagues and joined the Brooklyn Dodgers.

sk More Questions What do you still ant to know about Jackie Robinson, the egro Leagues, or the Major Leagues? rainstorm questions with a group. Discuss ays that you can find answers to your uestions. Then get the answers and share ose with your group.

LANGUAGE ACQUISITION ASSESSMENT
See page 21 of the Assessment Handbook.

THINK IT OVER

Discuss and Write Talk about these questions with a partner. Write the answers.

1. **Conclusions** How did Branch Rickey, Jackie Robinson, and Pee Wee Reese change baseball today?
2. **Judgment** What is the most important idea in this selection?
3. **Inference** The Shawnee leader Tecumseh said "Show respect to all men, but grovel to none." How does this quote apply to "Teammates"?
4. **Opinion** In your opinion, does racial prejudice still exist today? Give reasons to support your answer. What can people do to bridge the gap of racial prejudice?

EXPRESS YOURSELF ▶DESCRIBE

Take the role of a sportscaster at the game in Cincinnati. How would you describe Pee Wee's actions to your listeners? Tape record your sportscast, and then play it for your classmates.

Multi-Level Strategies

SUM IT UP OPTIONS

BEGINNING Work with students to review the answers they wrote in the "L" column of the K-W-L chart. Read some of the questions in the "W" column and have students take turns restating the answers. Help them formulate one additional question.

INTERMEDIATE Have students exchange charts with a partner and compare similarities and differences in the charts. Then have them add any new information to their own charts.

ADVANCED Have students exchange charts with a partner and analyze whether the information in the "L" column of their partner's chart clearly answers the questions in the "W" column. Have each student suggest one way the partner's chart could be expanded or improved. Encourage students to go back to the reading to scan for further information.

RESPOND

OBJECTIVES

SUM IT UP
Function: Give Information; Ⓣ Ask Questions
Reading and Learning Strategies: Review; Use Graphic Organizers (K-W-L chart); Connect New Information to Known

THINK IT OVER
Function: Engage in Discussion
Critical Thinking and Comprehension: Draw Conclusions; Make Judgments; Make an Inference; Form Opinions

EXPRESS YOURSELF
Function: Describe
Speaking and Listening: Role-Play

CHECK YOUR UNDERSTANDING

1 **Sum It Up** Have students compare and discuss their charts, then continue to work in pairs to help clarify, confirm, and complete the information.

▶ **Practice Book** page 49

2 **Think it Over** Possible answers are:

1. **Conclusions** They showed that being a good player and teammate is what matters.
2. **Judgment** Some possible answers: Stand up for what you know is right. Individuals can made a difference.
3. **Inference** Possible answer: Jackie Robinson always kept a strong sense of dignity and self-respect.
4. **Opinion** Answers will vary. Ask students for specific evidence to support their answers.

3 **Express Yourself** Encourage the use of descriptive adjectives and action verbs. If possible, play a real sportscast such as *The Crowd Goes Wild.*

CLOSE AND ASSESS

Ask students to complete the following sentence: *The most surprising thing I learned about Jackie Robinson is. . . .*

RESPOND

OBJECTIVES

PRONOUN AGREEMENT

Grammar: Ⓣ Pronouns

EVALUATE LITERATURE

Functions: Write; Express Opinions

Comprehension and Critical Thinking: Ⓣ Distinguish Between Facts and Opinions

Literary Analysis: Evaluate Literary Quality

Writing: Opinion Essay

LANGUAGE ARTS AND LITERATURE

1 **Use Pronouns** Answers to the Practice items are:

1. they

2. he

3. his

4. him

▶ **Practice Book** page 50

2 **Evaluate Literature** Read the instructions aloud. Pause after each step in the plan to clarify meaning and generate ideas about what students might include in the paragraph. Remind students to check pronoun agreement as they edit their writing.

CLOSE AND ASSESS

Ask students to show you an example of pronoun agreement in their essays and explain why it is correct.

ASSESSMENT
Selection Test 7 on page 27 of the Assessment Handbook tests students' mastery of the reading strategies and the vocabulary, comprehension, and language arts skills taught with this selection.

Respond to the Biography, continued

Language Arts and Literature

GRAMMAR IN CONTEXT

USE PRONOUNS

Learn About Pronoun Agreement A **pronoun** is a word that takes the place of a noun. The noun that it replaces is called its **antecedent**. See Handbook pages 437–440 for a complete list of pronouns.

> **Jackie** tried out for the Brooklyn Dodgers. **He** made the team.
>
> Many did not want **Jackie** on the team. Some players were cruel to **him**.
>
> Pitchers aimed at **Jackie's** head. Jackie received threats on **his** life.

Replace Nouns with Pronouns Write the paragraph. Use pronouns in place of the underlined nouns.

> Jackie faced abuse throughout the season. <u>Jackie's</u> worst pain was inside. <u>Jackie</u> often felt very alone.

Practice Copy these sentences. Complete each sentence with the correct pronoun.

1. Some fans hated Jackie, and it / they yelled hateful things.
2. When Pee Wee heard the fans, he / she decided to take a stand.
3. Pee Wee walked with his / their head high.
4. Pee Wee went up to Jackie. Then Pee Wee smiled at him / you .

WRITING
LITERARY ANALYSIS

EVALUATE LITERATURE

Do you think "Teammates" is well written? Write a five-paragraph essay to give your opinion.

❶ **Write** Use this plan for your draft.

- In the first paragraph, give your **opinion** of the biography. Is it interesting and informative?
- In the second paragraph, discuss the **background information** at the start of the biography. Is there enough information? Is there too much? Explain.
- In the third paragraph, discuss how the author uses **facts and opinions**. Are there enough facts? Do the facts support the opinions? Give examples.
- In the fourth paragraph, discuss the **photos and other illustrations**. Do they add information? Do they help tell the story?
- The fifth paragraph is the **conclusion**. Sum up your opinion of the biography.

❷ **Edit Your Work** Check for correct spelling and pronoun agreement. Write the final draft.

❸ **Share Your Work in a Group** Read your essay aloud. Discuss your opinions.

Review **pronouns** on Handbook pages 437–440.

REACHING ALL STUDENTS

Multi-Level Strategies

WRITING OPTIONS FOR EVALUATING LITERATURE

BEGINNING Work with students to elicit one or two sentences for each section of the essay plan, so that students write an opinion paragraph rather than an essay. Give students sentence frames for each section. For example: *I think the biography is _____. I felt there was/wasn't enough background information because _____.*

INTERMEDIATE Have students work on their essays in pairs. Help them discuss each section of the essay plan and to take notes on important ideas during this discussion. Students then use these notes as the kernels for building each paragraph of their essay.

ADVANCED Have students work on their own to write first drafts of their essays. Then have students exchange drafts. Students should read and give feedback on their partner's essay, noting two things they like about the essay and suggesting at least one addition and one edit to the essay.

Content Area Connections

SOCIAL STUDIES
REPRESENTING/SPEAKING

MAKE AN HISTORICAL EVENTS CHART

Find out what was happening in the 1940s and 1950s. Put your findings in a chart.

1. **Gather Information and Take Notes** You can use a variety of sources to do research:
   - Encyclopedias, almanacs, or history books
   - Old newspapers and news magazines
   - Documentary videos about the 1940s and 1950s
   - People who were young adults during those years
2. **Organize Your Information** Make a chart to show the important events.

Historical Events, 1940s–1950s

Year	Historical Event
1945	World War II ends.
1947	Jackie Robinson joins the Dodgers.
1954	Singer Elvis Presley begins recording his first songs.
1955	Rosa Parks refuses to give up her bus seat, an important event in the Civil Rights movement.

3. **Give an Oral Report** Show your chart to your class. Tell about the events in each year.

For tips on giving an **oral report**, see Handbook pages 401–402.

TECHNOLOGY/MEDIA
SPEAKING/LISTENING

INVESTIGATE MEDIA

Television programs have sound and moving pictures. A radio broadcast uses sound only. News articles use printed words, photographs, and other graphics. How do these differences affect a news report? Find out in a group project.

1. **Form Media Discussion Groups** Group 1 will research TV and videos; Group 2, radio; and Group 3, newspaper and other print.
2. **Choose a Media Event** Choose an event such as a sports game that is covered by all three types of media. Then, take notes on how your type of media helps you understand the event.
3. **Compare Media** Was one report more factual than the others? How did each type of media help you know what happened? Which was most effective? What differences did you find between a live report and one that was produced later?

Sports events are covered by all types of media.

Research Skills

▶ USING AN ALMANAC

TEACH Explain that almanacs are reference books that provide facts and figures about a wide range of topics. They are updated every year, so the latest information is always available. Demonstrate how to look up a key word in the index to find a desired entry. Explain that students should skim the headings and text of the entry to determine whether it includes information relevant and useful to the students' research needs.

PRACTICE Have students use an almanac to research information for their historical events chart. Instruct students to work in groups to:

- Brainstorm a list of subjects.
- Use the index to find entries on these subjects.
- Take notes on information that can be used in their historical events chart.

▶ **Practice Book** page 51

RESPOND

OBJECTIVES

HISTORICAL EVENTS CHART

Function: Give Information

Speaking: Oral Report

Learning Strategies, Critical Thinking, and Research Skills: Use an Almanac; Gather Information; Take Notes; Organize Information; Ⓣ Relate Events in a Sequence

Representing and Writing: Chart

INVESTIGATE MEDIA

Functions: Engage in Discussion; Make Comparisons

Concepts and Vocabulary: Media—*broadcast, print, video*, etc.

Learning Strategies, Critical Thinking, and Research Skills: Gather, Evaluate, and Synthesize Information; Make Comparisons

Technology/Media: Explain How Media Affects the Message

CONTENT AREA CONNECTIONS

1. **Make an Historical Events Chart** Suggest that students give special emphasis to ideas related to the selection, such as the civil rights movement and the contributions of African American artists, athletes, and leaders. Remind students to include events occurring in other parts of the world as well.
2. **Investigate Media** Show students how to use the newspaper to find listings of TV and radio programs about the same event. Then collect print reports in newspapers and magazines released after the event.

   Introduce content area vocabulary:

   - ***broadcast, print, video:*** Explain that a *broadcast* is a radio or TV transmission, while a *video* is the visual part of a broadcast. *Print* refers to printed materials, such as newspapers, magazines, and books.

▶ **Practice Book** page 52

CLOSE AND ASSESS

Ask students to summarize what they have learned in this lesson. Have them write these summaries in their learning logs.

PREPARE TO READ

OBJECTIVES

THINK ABOUT WHAT YOU KNOW

Reading and Learning Strategies:
Activate Prior Knowledge;
Use Graphic Organizers (T-chart)

LEARN KEY VOCABULARY Ⓣ

Vocabulary Strategy:
Use New Words in Context

LEARN TO SEQUENCE EVENTS

Reading Strategy:
Ⓣ Relate Sequence of Events

THINK ABOUT WHAT YOU KNOW

1 **Create a Chart** Draw a T-chart with the headings *City Life* and *Country Life*. Together, brainstorm a few ideas for the chart. Ask students to work in groups to add to the chart.

LEARN KEY VOCABULARY

2 **Use New Words in Context** Have students read each vocabulary word and its definition. Clarify meanings. Then conduct the matching activity.

Use the Vocabulary Options in the **Multi-Level Strategies** to allow all students to participate.

▶ **Practice Book** page 53

LEARN TO SEQUENCE EVENTS

3 **Model How to Sequence Events** Explain the phrase *sequence events*. Demonstrate the steps in the box with **Transparency 27**:

- Read the sentences. Point out signal words for sequencing.
- Paraphrase and write the events in order on the time line.

CLOSE AND ASSESS

Have students work in pairs to write a sentence or two explaining how to sequence events. Have them sign and turn in their sentences before leaving class.

Amir

Prepare to Read

realistic fiction
by Paul Fleischman

THINK ABOUT WHAT YOU KNOW

Create a Chart How are city and country life different? Think of whe
food comes from or the buildings, for example. Write your ideas in a cha

benefit good result or reward for doing something

community group of people who live in the same neighborhood

conversation friendly talk between two or more people

excuse reason given for doing something

harvest festival celebration that takes place when harvest is over

provide give or supply

recognize know someone when you see him or her again

trade give one thing and take another in its place

LEARN KEY VOCABULARY

Use New Words in Context Study the new words and their definition
Then match the beginning of each sentence with its ending.

1. Everyone in my **community**	to eat, dance, and sing.
2. The garden **provides**	with friends about the garden.
3. After the growing season	a place for neighbors to meet.
4. My friends **recognize**	works in the city garden.
5. We **trade** vegetables	me even though I cut my hair.
6. The festival is a good **excuse**	we have a **harvest festival**.
7. We have **conversations**	a **benefit** of having a garden.
8. Good, fresh food is	for fruit.

Answers to the vocabulary activity:

1. Everyone in my **community** works in the city garden.
2. The garden **provides** a place for neighbors to meet.
3. After the growing season we have a **harvest festival**.
4. My friends **recognize** me even though I cut my hair.
5. We **trade** vegetables for fruit.
6. The festival is a good **excuse** to eat, dance, and sing.
7. We have **conversations** with friends about the garden.
8. Good, fresh food is a **benefit** of having a garden.

LEARN TO SEQUENCE EVENTS

When you **sequence** events, you put them in time order. This helps you remember when the events in the story happened.

READING STRATEGY

How to Sequence Events

1. Look for words that tell, or signal, when something happens.
   Examples: *first, second, before, next, now, later, still*
   dates, days of the week, and months
2. As you read, use signal words to put story events in order.

Now read "Amir." Make a time line and put the events in order.

REACHING ALL STUDENTS

Multi-Level Strategies

VOCABULARY OPTIONS

BEGINNING Group students to read ***More Than a Meal*** or the Key Points Reading on **Master 28**. (See page T119.) Work with the vocabulary in those selections.

INTERMEDIATE Ask students *who/what/where/when* questions that lead them to the correct sentence endings. For example: *Everyone in my community does what?*

ADVANCED Have students match the sentences on their own.

Transparency 27 / Master 27

HOW TO SEQUENCE EVENTS

Directions: Read the sentences. Number them to show the correct sequence.
Then create a time line of the events.

The School Garden

☐ After a few weeks, we start to harvest vegetables and flowers.

☐ Then we water and weed the beds, and wait for the garden to grow.

☐ In the spring, we prepare the soil in the garden and plant seeds.

☐ After the fall clean-up, we plan our garden and order seeds from catalogues.

1 We clean up the garden after the summer's harvest and get it ready for the next year.

☐ After our harvest, we give food to local charities that help feed the homeless and other needy people.

clean up garden	plan and order seeds	prepare soil and plant seeds	water and weed	harvest vegetables and flowers	give food to needy

Transparency 27 Level B, Unit 2 | Belonging

READ THE SELECTION

OBJECTIVES

Reading Strategies: Preview; Predict
Literary Analysis: Realistic Fiction

INTRODUCE THE SELECTION

4 **Preview and Predict** Read the title, author's name, and introduction to the story. Talk about the illustration on this page. Have students page through the story, reading the summary statements for each part and looking at the pictures. Ask: *How do you think the garden will help Amir become friends with his neighbors?*

5 **Identify Genre: Realistic Fiction** Discuss what students know about the story from their preview. Ask: *When and where does the story take place?* (a garden in the city in the present) *What makes you think this place could be real?* (The characters look like real people.) *Might you find characters like these in a real city?* Explain that "Amir" is an example of realistic fiction, a made-up story that could really happen.

"Amir" from Seedfolks
by Paul Fleischman

Theme Connection This selection tells about an immigrant from India who finds that he and his neighbors can bridge the gap of their different backgrounds by working alongside one another in a community garden.

Selection Summary and Background The introduction on page 117 of the student book offers a summary of the selection. Community gardens are often organized by neighborhood groups to beautify unused parcels of land.

Author Awards Paul Fleischman is the winner of the Newbery Medal for his book of poems, *Joyful Noise*, and has written many award-winning novels, poems, short stories, and picture books.

THE BASICS BOOKSHELF

■ ***More Than a Meal*** by Suzy Blackaby

Real community is like a garden. It needs nurturing and care to thrive. In this story, a young man delivers "Meals on Wheels" to shut-ins in his neighborhood and, when he can, helps out in other ways. Patterned text introduces prepositions and names of places in a neighborhood. A community map and strong visual support for the text increase access for beginning English learners.

For Lesson Plans: See the Teacher's Guide for ***The Basics Bookshelf***.

READ PAGES 118–119

OBJECTIVES

Function: Read a Selection
Grammar: Possessive Nouns;
Ⓣ Possessive Pronouns
Listening: Listen to a Selection
Reading and Learning Strategies:
Ⓣ Relate Sequence of Events;
Use Graphic Organizers (time line);
Visualize
Comprehension: Make an Inference
Literary Analysis: Foreshadowing

SET PURPOSE

1 Read aloud the introduction to pages 118–119. Set the purpose for reading: *Read to see how knowing his neighbors makes Amir feel less alone.*

READ AND THINK

Tape 2B
CD 2
Track 5

2 **Strategy Focus: Relate Sequence of Events** Have students focus on signal words and the sequence of events as they read each part of the story.

Choose Reading Options in the **Multi-Level Strategies** to include all proficiency levels.

The recording of "Amir" on the **Selection Tape/CD** offers an oral language model and the opportunity to build reading fluency.

Red annotations offer opportunities to clarify meaning and check for understanding.

1

THE WORLD IS FULL OF NEIGHBORS

Even in a large city Amir feels alone. After he gets to know his neighbors, they become part of his world.

Build background: A vacant city lot that had been neglected and used as a trash dump was gradually cleaned up and converted to garden space by local residents.

Clarify: People living isolated lives in the crowded city are being compared to crabs living in crevices.

In India we have many **vast** cities, just as in America. There, too, you are one among millions. But there at least you know your neighbors. Here, one cannot say that. Here you have a million crabs living in a million **crevices**.

When I saw the garden for the first time, so green among the dark brick buildings, I thought back to my parents' Persian rug. It showed climbing vines, rivers and waterfalls, grapes, flower beds, singing birds, everything a desert dweller might want. The garden's green was as **soothing to the eye** as the deep blue of that rug. I'm aware of color—I **manage** a fabric store. But, the garden's greatest **benefit**, I feel, was not **relief to the eyes**, but to make the eyes see our neighbors.

Have students draw Amir's impression of the garden.

I grew eggplants, onions, carrots, and cauliflower. When the eggplants appeared in August they were **pale** purple, a strange and eerie shade. Very man people came over to ask about them and talk to me I **recognized** a few from the neighborhood. Not one had spoken to me before— and now how friendly they turned out to be.

Restate: He discovers that peop who had never spoken to him before are friendly, once they ha something to talk about.

I grew eggplants . . . many people came over to ask about them.

vast huge, big
crevices cracks
soothing to the eye nice to look at
manage am in charge of
relief to the eyes being nice to look at
pale light

BEFORE YOU MOVE ON...

1. **Inference** How do you think Amir feels at the beginning of the story? Explain.
2. **Visualizing** Amir says that the garden reminded him of a Persian rug. Write a sentence to describe how you imagine the garden looked.
3. **Foreshadowing** What hint does Amir give about what the garden will come to mean to him?

REACHING ALL STUDENTS

CULTURAL PERSPECTIVES

Home Culture: Food Sources Talk about various places where people obtain food, such as home gardens, farmers' markets, and supermarkets. Invite students to describe a garden or market their family has used recently or in the past. Ask them to imagine they are in the market and are describing the foods for a news report. Ask questions, such as: *What kinds of food can you buy? What colors do you see? What do you smell? What is in your shopping basket?*

Multi-Level Strategies

READING OPTIONS FOR LESSONS 11–13

BEGINNING Students should work with ***More Than a Meal*** while the class reads "Amir." Or distribute copies of **Master 28** to conduct a Key Points Reading of "Amir." Students can then listen to each part of the recording on the **Selection Tape/CD**. Work together to identify signal words that help indicate the sequence of events.

INTERMEDIATE Read each two-page section aloud, then have students read the same section silently. Use the red annotations on the facsimile pages to clarify meaning. Ask groups to identify signal words and record events on a group time line.

ADVANCED Read the story aloud, or play the Selection Reading on the **Selection Tape/CD**. Then have students read the entire selection silently. Ask them to work as a group to identify signal words and record events in the story on a time line.

CHECK COMPREHENSION

3 Answers to "Before You Move On"

1. **Inference** Amir feels alone because he doesn't know his neighbors.
2. **Visualizing** Answers will vary but should include some details from the story.
3. **Foreshadowing** Amir explains that after he started growing vegetables, people became friendly toward him.

CLOSE AND ASSESS

Review the sequence of events on these pages, asking individual students questions such as: *What happened first? What happened next?*

Transparency 28 / Master 28

KEY POINTS READING

Amir

Amir is from a large city in India. Back home, Amir knows his neighbors. Here in America, he doesn't know his neighbors. Amir feels alone. But after he grows eggplants in the community garden, many people come to ask him about them. Then he gets to know his neighbors. They become part of his world.

Amir and his neighbors help each other clean trash out of the garden. Then they catch a thief near the garden. They discover that the garden helps them feel they belong to a community.

There are many immigrants in the city of Cleveland where Amir lives. Some of them come from Poland. Amir doesn't know much about them. Then he meets a Polish woman in the garden. He learns about her life and they become friends.

Later, the gardeners celebrate the end of the harvest. People bring food and drinks and music. Amir brings his family to join the celebration. Many people speak to Amir. They ask where he is from. Amir's circle of friends grows. He recognizes a woman who was angry at him in his store last year. Now she is friendly. Amir and his neighbors become a community of friends.

Transparency 28 Level B, Unit 2 | Belonging

Grammar Minilesson

▶ POSSESSIVE NOUNS AND PRONOUNS

TEACH Tell students that in English there are three ways to show who owns something:

1. **Use a possessive noun.** Point out *parents'* and *garden's* on page 118 and explain the rules. See Handbook page 436 for support.
2. **Use the pronouns *my, your, his, her, its, our, your, their.*** Explain that these pronouns come before a noun: *our neighbors, my eggplants, their garden.*
3. **Use the pronouns *mine, yours, his, hers, ours, theirs.*** Explain that these pronouns stand alone. They take the place of a person's name and what the person owns:

   Which one is Mrs. Wong's pumpkin?

   The big one is hers.

PRACTICE Have students use possessive nouns and pronouns in a paragraph describing a project they worked on with a group of classmates.

▶ **Practice Book** page 54

THEME 2 **LESSON 12**

READ PAGES 120–121

OBJECTIVES

Function: Read a Selection
Vocabulary Strategy: Use New Words in Context
Grammar: Negative Sentences
Listening: Listen to a Selection
Reading Strategy: Ⓣ Relate Sequence of Events; Use Graphic Organizers (time line)
Comprehension and Critical Thinking: Ⓣ Identify Sequence; Identify Cause and Effect; Form Generalizations

SET PURPOSE

1 Read aloud the introduction to pages 120–121. Set the purpose for reading: *Note the events involving the garden that help Amir and his neighbors create a sense of community.*

READ AND THINK

Tape 2B
CD 2 Track 5

2 **Strategy Focus: Relate Sequence of Events** Have students focus on the sequence of events as they read pages 120–121 of the selection. Ask: *What signal words should you look for?*

See the **Multi-Level Strategies** on page T118 to tailor the reading experience to all proficiency levels.

Amir and his neighbors catch a thief near the garden. They help each other and, in the process, form a community.

Those **conversations tied us together**. In the middle of summer someone **dumped a load** of tires on the garden at night, as if it were still filled with trash. A man's four rows of young corn were crushed. In an hour, we had all the tires by the curb. We were used to helping each other by then. A few weeks later, early in the evening a woman screamed, down the block from the garden. A man with a knife had taken her purse. Three men from the garden ran after him. I was surprised that I was one of them. Even more surprising, we caught him. A teenager named Royce held the man to a wall with his pitchfork until the police arrived. I asked the others. Not one of us had ever chased a criminal before. And most likely we wouldn't have except near the garden. There, you felt part of a **community**. **Ask:** Why does the garden feel like a community?

I came to the United States in 1980. Cleveland is a city of immigrants. The **Pole** are especially well known here. I'd always heard that the Polish men were tough **steelworkers** and that the women cooked lots of cabbage. But I'd never known one—until the garden. She was an old woman whose space bordered mine. She had a seven-block walk to the garden, the same **route I took**. We spoke quite often. We both planted carrots. When her hundreds of seedling came up in a row, I was very surprised that she did not thin them—pulli out all but one healthy-looking plant each few inches, to give them room to grow. I asked her. She looked down at them and said she knew she ought to do it, but that this **task** reminded her too closely of her

Clarify: Point out the context definition *thin.* When plants grow too close togeth they don't grow as large as they do whe they're spaced out by thinning.

tied us together brought us closer to one another
dumped a load dropped a lot, left a lot
Poles people from Poland, Polish people
steelworkers people who work in places where steel is made
route I took way I walked
task job, chore

REACHING ALL STUDENTS

Science Connection

BIOLOGY

Ask students to name living organisms found in gardens, such as worms, weeds, and butterflies. Offer a range of pictures to prompt ideas. Instruct students to make a 3-column chart with the headings *Insects, Plants,* and *Animals* and to work in small groups to list organisms in the appropriate columns. Invite students to create other groupings for organisms, such as *Vertebrate* and *Invertebrate.* Have them explain the reasons for their groupings.

INTERNET

HEALTH CONNECTION

Explain that many plants are used to make medicines. Have students use the Internet to research plants in the temperate zone or rain forests that can be used for medicinal purposes. Start students off with a couple of ideas: quinine is a plant product used to prevent and cure malaria; foxglove is the basis of a heart medicine. Ask students to report their findings creatively, with a poster, a multimedia slide show, or a skit.

Web Sites

Web sites undergo frequent modifications, but here are some you may want to suggest to students:

whyfiles.news.wisc.edu
www.brainpop.com
www.awesomelibrary.org

ɔncentration camp, where the prisoners ·ere inspected each morning and divided ·to two lines—the healthy to live and ·e others to die. Her father, an orchestra ·olinist, had spoken out against the ·ermans, which had caused her family's ·rest. When I heard her words, I realized ·ow **useless** was all that I'd heard about ·oles, how much **richness** it hid, like ·e **worthless shell** around an almond. ·still do not know, or care, whether she ·oks cabbage.

Ask: What is Amir comparing to the worthless shell around an almond? What does he mean by this comparison?

·eless unimportant, of little value
·chness goodness, value, worth
·orthless shell shell that is good for nothing

BEFORE YOU MOVE ON...

1. **Sequence** Three events take place here. Describe them in the order in which they happen.
2. **Cause and Effect** Why did Royce and the others run after the man who took the purse?
3. **Generalization** What did Amir learn after working in the garden with the Polish woman?

REVIEW KEY VOCABULARY

3 Use New Words in Context Have Advanced students write a cloze exercise for the key vocabulary words: *I know lots of people in my* _____. (community) *This morning, I had a* _____ *with my neighbor.* (conversation) Intermediate and Beginning students work in pairs to complete the exercise, then read aloud their sentences.

CHECK COMPREHENSION

4 Answers to "Before You Move On"

1. **Sequence** Someone dumps a load of tires on the garden. Three men chase and catch a thief. Amir learns about a painful time in a Polish neighbor's life.
2. **Cause and Effect** The man had stolen from a neighbor. They felt part of a community that they wanted to protect.
3. **Generalization** Amir learned that everything he had heard about Poles was useless because it hid the true worth and richness of individual people.

CLOSE AND ASSESS

Ask students to explain how events in this section helped people bridge the gaps between them.

Vocabulary

COUNTRIES AND NATIONALITIES

Explain how names of countries, which are proper nouns, change into adjectives to identify the people who live in the countries. Ask students to list the countries mentioned in the selection (America, India, Poland, Italy, Germany, Mexico), as well as the students' home countries. Ask students the adjective for a person from Italy. (Italian) Have students work in groups to write the adjectives for each country.

Grammar Minilesson

▶ NEGATIVE SENTENCES

TEACH Introduce the following negative words:

no	isn't	hasn't
none	aren't	shouldn't
not	weren't	couldn't
never	nobody	didn't
neither	nothing	can't
hardly	nowhere	won't

Then draw students' attention to this sentence from page 120: *Not one of us had ever chased a criminal before.*

Rewrite the sentence, changing *Not one of us had ever* to *We had never.* Explain that both versions mean the same and are correct because only one negative word is used in each sentence.

PRACTICE Have students rewrite these sentences to make them negative.

1. There is a community garden in my neighborhood.
2. All of the children liked carrots.
3. We can pick all the vegetables.

THEME 2 **LESSON 13**

READ PAGES 122–123

OBJECTIVES

Function: Read a Selection

Listening: Listen to a Selection

Reading Strategies: Ⓣ Relate Sequence of Events; Use Graphic Organizers (time line); Visualize

Comprehension: Make Inferences; Identify Cause and Effect

Literary Analysis: Evaluate Impact of Author's Background on Meaning; Flashback

SET PURPOSE

1 Read aloud the introduction to pages 122–123. Set the purpose for reading: *Read to understand why the woman had been angry at Amir and why she no longer feels angry.*

READ AND THINK

Tape 2B CD 2 Track 5

2 **Strategy Focus: Relate Sequence of Events** Have students focus on the sequence of events as they read pages 122–123 of the selection. Remind them to add events to their time lines.

See the **Multi-Level Strategies** on page T118 to help all students participate in the reading.

3

STRANGERS CAN BE NEW FRIENDS

The gardeners celebrate the end of harvest. Amir's circle of friends grows and even includes a woman who was once angry at him.

Ask: Why do you think they built a barbecue?

In September Royce and a Mexican man collected many bricks from up the street and built a big **barbecue**. A bit later their friends began arriving. One brought a guitar, another played violin. They filled a folding table with food.

It was a **harvest festival**, like those in India, though no one had planned it to be. People brought food and drinks and drums. I went home to get my wife and son. Watermelons from the garden were **sliced open**. The gardeners proudly showed off what they'd grown. We **traded** harvests, as we often did. And we gave food away, as we often did also—even I, a businessman, **trained** to give away nothing, to always **make a profit**. The garden **provided** many **excuses** for breaking that **particular** rule.

Encourage elaboration: How is the garden changing Amir?

Many people spoke to me that day. Several asked where I was from. I wonder if they knew as little about Indians as I ha known about Poles. One old woman, Italia I believe, said she'd admir my eggplants for weeks and told me how happy she was to meet me. Something bothered me. Then I remembered. A yea before she'd claimed that she'd received **the wrong change** in my store. She'd gotten quite angry and called me—despite her ow accent—a dirty foreigner. Now that we were so friendly with each other I **dared** to **remind her of this**. Her eyes became huge. She **apologized to me** over and over again. She kept saying, "Back the I didn't know it was you. . . ."

Pose choices: After this, did Amir tr the woman differently or the same?

barbecue outdoor fire used for cooking
sliced open cut open with a knife
trained taught
make a profit make more money than I spend
particular specific
the wrong change an incorrect amount of money given back after buying something
dared was brave enough
remind her of this cause her to remember it
apologized to me told me she was sorry

REACHING ALL STUDENTS

Cooperative Learning

FOR LANGUAGE DEVELOPMENT: Dramatize

Assign Roles Have students work in groups to select a scene from the story to rewrite and act out. Assign roles to students: Script Writers, Performers, Director, and Set Designers. Encourage students to include dialogue among Amir and his neighbors.

Perform a Skit Allow time for students to prepare, offering help as necessary. Invite another class to view a performance of the skit.

Debrief the Content Ask students what they learned from this experience. Ask: *What details do you understand better after acting the scene out? What did you learn about the characters?*

Debrief the Cooperative Process Encourage students to think about their participation in this activity. Ask: *How did your role help the group complete the project? How did other roles help? What role would you like to take next time? Why?*

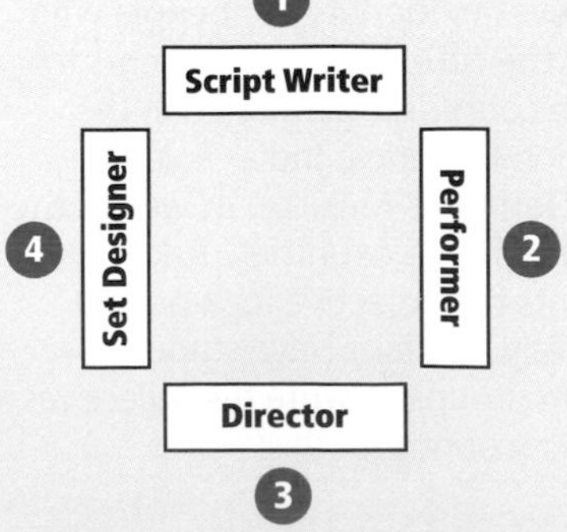

Roles for Cooperative Groups

BEFORE YOU MOVE ON...

1. **Visualize** Imagine you are at the harvest festival. What do you hear? What are people doing? What foods do you see?
2. **Inference** How is the harvest festival an example of neighbors becoming a community?
3. **Cause and Effect** The Italian woman told Amir, "Back then, I didn't know it was you." Why did her opinion of Amir change?

ABOUT THE AUTHOR

Paul Fleischman is familiar with gardening—he grew up in a family of gardeners in Santa Monica, California. "Amir" is a chapter from *Seedfolks,* a book he wrote while spending a summer in North Carolina growing rows and rows of green beans. Paul Fleischman is a native of Monterey, California, and has written many award-winning novels, poems, short stories, and picture books, including *Joyful Noise: Poems for Two Voices,* winner of the Newbery Award.

CHECK COMPREHENSION

3 Answers to "Before You Move On"

1. **Visualize** Answers will vary. Encourage thoughtful responses and discussion.
2. **Inference** Answers will vary, but should include: At the harvest festival, neighbors talked to each other and became friends.
3. **Cause and Effect** Her opinion of Amir changed because now he is no longer a stranger. She thinks of him as a neighbor and friend.

ABOUT THE AUTHOR

4 Evaluate Literature: Author's Background Read aloud About the Author. Point out the author's background in gardening. Ask: *How do you think the author feels about gardening? How does this come through in the story? What are some examples of the way the author compares gardening to life in general?*

CLOSE AND ASSESS

Have students retell events from this part of the selection in sequence.

Literary Analysis Minilesson

▶ FLASHBACK

TEACH Read aloud or have students read the paragraph on page 122 that begins *Many people spoke to me that day.* Ask: *What event does Amir remember?* (A woman claimed she'd received the wrong change.) *When did this event happen?* (before this story began)

Define *flashback*: *Sometimes a character in a story remembers something that happened earlier. The part of the story that tells about the memory is called a* flashback. Clarify that flashbacks can be memories of people, places, events, feelings, sights, smells, and sounds.

Flashback

What happened before...	What happens now...
The woman had visited Amir's shop and claimed she'd received the wrong change.	Amir talks to the woman.

PRACTICE Ask students to look for another example of flashback in "Amir." Remind them that flashbacks are not always events.

RESPOND

OBJECTIVES

SUM IT UP
Reading and Learning Strategies: Ⓣ Relate Sequence of Events; Use Graphic Organizers (time line)
Critical Thinking: Analyze Characters; Form Generalizations
Literary Analysis: Characterization

THINK IT OVER
Function: Engage in Discussion
Critical Thinking and Comprehension: Draw Conclusions; Make Predictions; Identify Character's Point of View; Form Generalizations

EXPRESS YOURSELF
Function: Ⓣ Express Likes and Dislikes

CHECK YOUR UNDERSTANDING

1 Sum It Up The order of events is:

1. Amir came to the United States.
2. The Italian woman said she got the wrong change.
3. Amir started working in the garden.
4. Someone dumped a load of tires in the garden.
5. Men from the garden stopped a thief.
6. Royce and a friend built a barbecue.

▶ **Practice Book** page 55

2 Think It Over Possible answers are:

1. **Conclusions** Amir realized that before the garden, people had known little about each other.
2. **Prediction** There may be more people involved next year.
3. **Character's Point of View** Answers will vary.
4. **Generalization** Answers will vary.

3 Express Yourself Encourage students to give specific examples.

CLOSE AND ASSESS

Ask students to write three events from the selection in sequential order.

Respond to the Story

Check Your Understanding

SUM IT UP

Sequence Events Read this list of events from "Amir."

- Someone dumped a load of tires in the garden.
- Men from the garden stopped a thief.
- Amir started working in the garden.
- Amir came to the United States.
- Royce and a friend built a barbecue.
- The Italian woman said she got the wrong change.

Pretend that Amir started gardening in 1982. Put the events in order on a time line.

Time Line

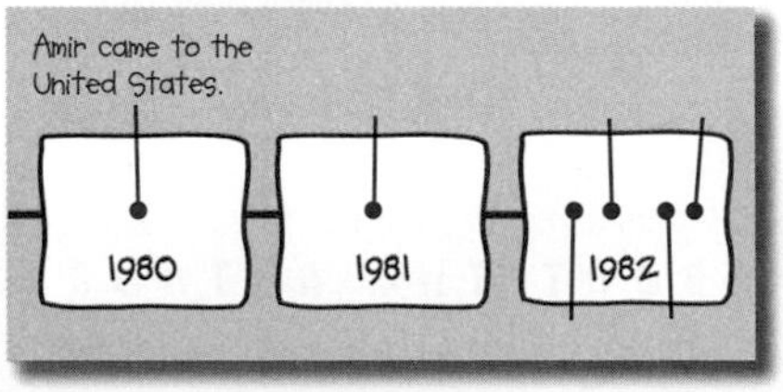

Analyze How Characters Change Look at the time line and think about the story. What changes does Amir experience? How do other characters change? Share your ideas with a group.

Make a Generalization How do you think the garden changed the way Amir looks at people? Do you think he sees strangers in the same way as before? Explain your answer.

THINK IT OVER

Discuss and Write Talk about these questions with a partner. Write the answers.

1. **Conclusions** Why is the garden important to Amir? What did he learn?
2. **Prediction** How might the community garde change in the next year?
3. **Character's Point of View** Imagine what othe people in the community would say about th garden. What would Royce, the Polish woman, or the Italian woman say?
4. **Generalization** How could you get to know other people in your community?

EXPRESS YOURSELF

▶EXPRESS LIKES AND DISLIKES

Work with a partner. Tell what you liked about this selection. Tell what you didn't like. Explain why.

✓ **LANGUAGE ACQUISITION ASSESSMENT**
See page 22 of the Assessment Handbook.

REACHING ALL STUDENTS

Multi-Level Strategies

SUM IT UP OPTIONS

BEGINNING Have students make sentence strips of the events from the Key Points Reading of "Amir" on **Master 28**. (See page T119.) Draw a large replica of the time line on page 124. Ask students to work together to correctly order the sequence of the strips. Once all students have agreed on the sequence, they tape the strips onto the time line. Have students read aloud the completed time line.

INTERMEDIATE / **ADVANCED** Read the list of events on page 124 aloud. If students made the time line during reading (see Reading Options on page T118), have them check to see if these events are represented. If not, have them make a time line of these events now. Students should compare their time lines and review the story to verify sequences that differ.

ASSESSMENT
Selection Test 8 on page 29 of the Assessment Handbook tests students' mastery of the reading strategies and the vocabulary, comprehension, and language arts skills taught with this selection.

GRAMMAR IN CONTEXT

SE INDEFINITE PRONOUNS

ɪarn About Indefinite Pronouns When you ɒn't know the name of a specific person, place, thing, use an **indefinite pronoun**.

ɒost indefinite pronouns are singular. Use them ɪth a **singular verb.**

Everything **looks** good to eat.
Someone **picks** the beans every morning

few indefinite pronouns are plural. Use them th a **plural verb.**

Several of the tomatoes **are** ripe.
Many of us **work** in the garden.

e Handbook page 440 for a list of more definite pronouns.

ɪactice Choose one word or phrase from each ɪlumn. Use the words to make as many ɪntences as you can.

Indefinite Pronouns	Verbs	Phrases
Someone	is talking	green beans
Everything	can grow	very friendly
Anybody	is	tasty vegetables
Many	might be	ready to eat
Several	is cutting	about the garden

LITERARY ANALYSIS
WRITING/SPEAKING

WRITE A STORY

A story's **point of view** is the position or angle from which the story is told. In "Amir," the author tells the story from Amir's point of view, so we get to know Amir's thoughts and opinions. Retell the story using another character's point of view.

1. **Write Your Draft** Make sure to use the pronouns *I, me,* and *my* in your story.
2. **Edit Your Work** Did you give lots of details to make your story believable? Did you use the correct pronouns? Make sure you used capital letters for the names of people, countries, months, and days.
3. **Share Your Work in a Group** Read your story aloud. Ask your group to tell whose point of view you have described.

Sample Story

Emily's Story

I was scared when the man took my purse. Then Royce, Amir, and Marcus ran after the thief. They were so brave! Royce is the nicest teenager I know. I'm lucky to have such caring neighbors.

Develop your skills in the **writer's craft.** See Handbook pages 414–423.

RESPOND

OBJECTIVES

USE INDEFINITE PRONOUNS
Grammar: Ⓣ Indefinite Pronouns

WRITE A STORY
Function: Write
Listening and Speaking: Read Aloud; Listen for a Purpose
Literary Analysis: Characterization; Ⓣ Narrator's Point of View
Writing: Story

LANGUAGE ARTS AND LITERATURE

1 Use Indefinite Pronouns Answers will vary. Possible responses are:

Someone is talking about the garden.
Everything is ready to eat.
Anybody can grow tasty vegetables.
Many can grow green beans.
Several might be ready to eat.

▶ **Practice Book** page 56

2 Write a Story This is a good opportunity to familiarize students with word processing software. When students edit their work, encourage them to use the spelling and grammar check features to highlight incorrect pronoun agreement and missing capital letters.

▶ **Practice Book** page 57

CLOSE AND ASSESS

Ask: *What did you learn from this lesson?* Have students write their answers and then work with a partner to compare them.

Multi-Level Strategies

PRACTICE OPTIONS FOR INDEFINITE PRONOUNS

BEGINNING Ask questions that can be answered with an indefinite pronoun: *What looks good to eat?* (everything!) *Do you want one strawberry or several?* (several!) *Who wants to play softball?* (few, many, everybody, several, no one, etc.) Encourage students to act out their choices of pronouns. For example, spreading the arms when using *everyone* and making a small circle with the hands when using *few.*

INTERMEDIATE Have students work with a partner to write sentences using information from the chart. Then pairs can share their sentences with those of other pairs to discover and critique differences among them.

ADVANCED After students write sentences on their own, they can compare them with a partner's. Encourage students to write original sentences using indefinite pronouns.

RESPOND

OBJECTIVES

FOOD CHAINS

Function: Give Information

Concepts and Vocabulary: Words about Food Chains

Learning Strategies, Critical Thinking, and Research Skills: Gather Information; Take Notes; Relate Steps In a Process

Technology/Media: Evaluate Media; Select Appropriate Media; Make a Multimedia Presentation

Representing: Food Chain

CONTENT AREA CONNECTIONS

1 **Research Food Chains** Before students begin their research, conduct the following activities to develop vocabulary:

- ***herbivores, carnivores, omnivores*:** Have students name animals and tell what they eat. Categorize them into three columns without explanation. Then write the category names above each and teach their meanings.
- ***interdependence*:** Define the root word *depend* (to rely on; to trust) and its prefix *inter-* (among). Ask students to explain why a food chain is a good example of interdependence.

Prepare a Multimedia Presentation To help students get ideas, show a multimedia presentation about a related topic. Include print, video, audio, and/or computer graphics.

▶ **Practice Book** page 58

CLOSE AND ASSESS

Ask students to tell one thing they learned from each multimedia presentation.

Respond to the Story, continued

Content Area Connections

TECHNOLOGY/MEDIA

SCIENCE

RESEARCH FOOD CHAINS

The plants and animals in the community garden are part of a **food chain**. A food chain is a kind of sequence in which each plant or animal is eaten by the one above it. Learn more about food chains, and report your findings in a multimedia presentation.

1 **Gather Information and Take Notes**
Research the answers to these questions:

- What do plants need to grow? Where do these things come from?
- Which animals eat plants, and which animals eat animals? Do any animals eat both?
- When plants and animals die, how are they still part of the food chain?

Choose an environment such as the desert, ocean, mountains, or your backyard! Research food chains in that environment. Use science books, encyclopedias, and the Internet. Take notes as you read. Make copies of helpful charts and illustrations.

2 **Create a Model** Draw a food chain, or use drawing program on a computer. Make sure you show how living things in the food chai are all connected.

Sample Poster

3 **Prepare a Multimedia Presentation** Here are some ways to present your food chain:

- Write a report and create graphics on the computer. You can create a class Web site to post your report.
- Make a diorama. Play recordings of anima and other sounds from nature.
- Draw a poster. Play a videotape of the plants and animals shown on the poster.

For more about the **research process**, see Handbook pages 394–399. For help with **multimedia presentations**, see pages 390–39

126 **Unit 2** | Belonging

REACHING ALL STUDENTS

Multimedia Presentation Skills

▶ **EVALUATING MEDIA**

Evaluate Media Show students a multimedia presentation about a related topic. Point out the various types and purposes of media used. Ask: *How did* (type of media) *help you learn about* (topic)?

Select Appropriate Media Ask students to think about how they could use different types of media in their food chain presentations. Ask: *What might be the best way to show what plants need to grow? How could you show what you learned about animals that eat plants?*

Design and Create a Multimedia Presentation Suggest that students think about the sequence of information in their presentations. What will they show first? What can they do to make the information easy to understand and remember?

Starting a
ommunity
GARDEN

how-to article
DyAnne DiSalvo-Ryan

Prepare to Read

THINK ABOUT WHAT YOU KNOW

Idea Exchange In a group, talk about gardens you have grown or seen.

money paid to do
ething

gine see something in
mind

ormation facts

erested caring

al close to where you
work, or go to school

small piece of land

ner person to whom
ething belongs

mission approval to do
ething

er direct, guide

**swers to the
cabulary activity:**
imagine
lot
permission
fee
local; information
interested
steer

LEARN KEY VOCABULARY

Use New Words in Context Study the new words and their definitions. Write these sentences. Replace each boldface word with a new word.

1. In my mind, I could **see** a beautiful garden.
2. My friends made a community garden on that **small piece of land.**
3. Mr. Gupta, **the man who owns the land,** gave his **approval.**
4. He said there would be no **money charged** for using the land.
5. The **neighborhood** newspaper printed **facts** about our garden.
6. **Caring** people in the community got involved.
7. I can **guide** you toward resources you will need to plant a garden.

LEARN TO SET A PURPOSE AND READING RATE

Sometimes you read to get information. Other times you read for entertainment. Your reason for reading is your **purpose**. Once you know your purpose, you can decide how fast to read.

READING STRATEGY

How to Set a Purpose and Reading Rate

1. Preview the selection.
2. Ask yourself: Will I read this selection to get information? If so, you may want to read more slowly and take notes.
3. Ask yourself: Will I read this selection for entertainment? If so, you can probably read the selection faster.

Now preview "Starting a Community Garden." Will you read this selection quickly or slowly? Why?

Multi-Level Strategies

VOCABULARY OPTIONS

BEGINNING Work with students as a group to determine the right word to substitute in each sentence.

INTERMEDIATE Have students work with a partner to complete the substitution activity. Review the answers with students and discuss any items answered incorrectly.

ADVANCED Students should complete the activity on their own, then compare their answers with a partner. Partners should discuss whether there could be more than one correct answer.

PREPARE TO READ

OBJECTIVES

THINK ABOUT WHAT YOU KNOW
Reading Strategies: Activate Prior Knowledge

LEARN KEY VOCABULARY Ⓣ
Vocabulary Strategy: Use New Words in Context

LEARN TO SET A PURPOSE FOR READING
Reading Strategies: Set a Purpose and Reading Rate

THINK ABOUT WHAT YOU KNOW

1 **Idea Exchange** Create a word web with *gardens* as the label in the center circle. On the outer rays, write students' suggestions.

LEARN KEY VOCABULARY

2 **Use New Words in Context** Have students read each vocabulary word and its definition. Clarify meanings. Then conduct the substitution activity.

Use the Vocabulary Options in the **Multi-Level Strategies** to include all proficiency levels.

▶ **Practice Book** page 59

LEARN TO SET A PURPOSE AND READING RATE

3 **Model How to Set a Purpose and Reading Rate** Have students reread the last paragraph on page 52 of "Fat Men from Space" and the last two paragraphs on page 106 of "Teammates." Before they begin each reading, ask: *Would you read this for entertainment or information?* (page 52: entertainment; page 106: information) *How would this affect your reading rate?* (page 52: I'd read quickly; page 106: I'd read slowly and carefully.)

CLOSE AND ASSESS

Ask students why it is helpful to set a purpose for reading. (Setting a purpose helps you decide on a reading rate.)

READ PAGES 128–129

OBJECTIVES

Function: Read a Selection
Grammar: Progressive Forms of Verbs
Listening: Listen to a Selection
Viewing: Interpret a Visual Image
Reading Strategy: Set a Purpose and Reading Rate
Comprehension: Identify Author's Purpose

SET PURPOSE

1 Read aloud the title and have students view the photos. Then set the purpose for reading: *Read to understand the steps in starting a community garden.*

READ AND THINK

Tape 2B
CD 2 Track 6

2 **Strategy Focus: Set a Purpose and Reading Rate**
Ask: *Will you read for entertainment or information?* (information) *How will this affect your reading rate?* (I'll read slowly and carefully.)

Choose Reading Options in the **Multi-Level Strategies** to tailor the reading to proficiency levels.

The recording of "Starting a Community Garden" on the **Selection Tape/CD** offers an oral language model and the opportunity to build reading fluency.

Starting A Community GARDEN

a how-to article by DyAnne DiSalvo-Ryan

All across America people have joined together to turn ugly lots into beautiful gardens. You may not imagine that you can do it—but you can. If there is already a community garden in your neighborhood, ask your neighbors how they got started. If you are the first on your block to "make something happen," this is what you can do:

1. Find an **interested** grown-up who wants to help you: a parent or **guardian** a teacher, a librarian, or a neighbor.
2. Find out the address of the **lot**. This is very important. You may have to talk to neighbors or look at the address of the buildings next door. Example: The lot I am interested in is on Main Street. It is between 75 and 81 Main Street.
Ask: Why do you think it's importa to find out the address of the lot?
3. While you are finding out the address of the lot, **get in touch with** the **local** gardening program in **your area**

guardian person who takes care of you
get in touch with call or write, contact
your area the place where you live

128 Unit 2 | Belonging

REACHING ALL STUDENTS

COMMUNITY CONNECTION

Composting Have students research composting and its value for gardening. Help students contact the local parks department, community garden clubs, or the state Department of Agriculture for helpful information. Then help them plan how to create a compost heap at school or in their neighborhood. After students have completed their research, have them create a how-to article for a school or local newspaper.

Multi-Level Strategies

READING OPTIONS FOR LESSON 18

BEGINNING Read aloud the article one step at a time. Work with students to create a drawing that represents each numbered step. (a mailbox for step 2, a picture of City Hall for step 5, etc.) Help students put the drawings together to form a visual sequence.

INTERMEDIATE Play the recording of "Starting a Community Garden" on the **Selection Tape/CD**. Then have students work with a partner to read the article again, reminding students to read slowly and carefully. Ask the pairs to turn the steps into a flow chart. They should then compare their charts with another pair.

ADVANCED Have students read the selection slowly and carefully on their own, making a flow chart of the steps. Then have them compare their charts with a partner.

(see end of this note). Say that you are interested in starting a garden. Since every city is different, your local program will be able to **steer you in the right direction.**

4. Find out who the **owner** is. The Department of Records at your local **city hall** can help. Look in the telephone book for the address of city hall in your area.

5. If the lot is owned by the city, the people at city hall can help you get **permission** to use the lot. **Usually** there is a small **fee**. If the lot is owned by an individual person or group, you will need to get permission from that person or group to use the lot.

Encourage elaboration: What might happen if you don't get permission before starting a garden?

6. Once you get permission to use the lot, **it's yours to name**!

There are hundreds of gardening programs that are ready to help community gardeners with **information**, soil, seeds, **fencing**, and more.

To find out the community gardening program that is nearest you, write to:

American Community Gardening Association
100 N. 20th Street, 5th Floor
Philadelphia, PA 19103-1495
web address: www.communitygarden.org

Community gardens bring people together. Join the work and join the fun!

BEFORE YOU MOVE ON...

1. **Author's Purpose** What reason did the author have for writing this article?
2. **Viewing** What do the photographs add to the information you read?

steer you in the right direction tell you what you need to do to get started

city hall building where your city's government is located

Usually Most of the time

it's yours to name you get to decide what to call it

fencing materials for building a gate or a fence

CHECK COMPREHENSION

3 Answers to "Before You Move On"

1. **Author's Purpose** She wanted to encourage young people to help turn ugly lots into beautiful gardens. She wanted to give helpful information.
2. **Viewing** Sample answers include: The photos show that children can work in a community garden. They show it can be fun to work together with friends.

CLOSE AND ASSESS

Have students return to the unit mind map they began on page T71. Ask them to add ideas that tell how joining a community gardening program can help people feel like they belong.

Language Development

GIVE AND CARRY OUT COMMANDS

Have students give a partner directions for completing a multiple-step task. Explain that the follower must follow the directions as stated, not infer what is meant. Show how the command "Fold the paper." could result in many different shapes. As the commands are followed, the giver improves the directions to get the desired result. Then partners reverse roles. Possible tasks include washing a chalkboard, finding a hidden object, rearranging books on shelves, or drawing an object.

Grammar Minilesson

▶ **PROGRESSIVE FORMS OF VERBS**

TEACH Ask students to role-play a scene: *You are digging a hole.* Explain that to describe an action that is in progress, use the **present progressive form** of the verb. This form consists of the present participle, or *-ing* form of the main verb, and the helping verb *am, are,* or *is: I am pruning.*

Point to the photograph on page 128 and ask: *What were these people doing in the garden?* Elicit the response: *They were planting.* Point out that *were planting* is the **past progressive form** of the verb *plant*.

PRACTICE Have students rewrite each sentence using the present or past progressive form of the verb.

1. A month ago, we _____ the trash out of the vacant lot. **(take)**
2. Today the gardeners _____ to us about their plans. **(speak)**
3. Last week I _____ through the community garden. **(walk)**
4. All the flowers _____ at that time. **(bloom)**

▶ **Practice Book** page 60

RESPOND

OBJECTIVES

SUM IT UP

Function: Write

Reading and Learning Strategies: Summarize; Use Graphic Organizers (T-chart)

Comprehension: Analyze Information (important and unimportant information)

Representing: T-chart

THINK IT OVER

Function: Engage in Discussion

Comprehension and Critical Thinking: Draw Conclusions; Make and Support Judgments; Relate to Personal Experience

EXPRESS YOURSELF

Function: Describe

Speaking and Listening: Guessing Game

CHECK YOUR UNDERSTANDING

1 **Sum It Up** Students should have chosen these items as important:

- Find an interested grown-up who wants to help you.
- Find out the address of the lot.
- Find out who the owner is.

▶ **Practice Book** page 61

2 **Think It Over**

1. **Conclusions** Sample answers are: to beautify the neighborhood; to meet people; to get fresh food and flowers.
2. **Judgments** List and compare all suggestions.
3. **Personal Experience** Ask students to elaborate.

3 **Express Yourself** Prompt the use of colorful adjectives in the descriptions.

CLOSE AND ASSESS

Ask students to name one important thing they learned from this lesson.

Respond to the How-to Article

Check Your Understanding

SUM IT UP

Distinguish Between Important and Unimportant Information You and your friends have decided to start a community garden. You've found a good lot, and you have made this list to show the things you need to do.

List of Things to Do

How to Start a Community Garden

Find an interested grown-up who wants to help you.

Make two entrances to the garden.

Find out the address of the lot.

Find out who the owner is.

Name the garden.

Buy gardening shoes and hats.

Which things on your list are important to getting your garden started? Make a T-chart. Work with a partner to compare charts. Do you agree on which information is important and which is not important?

Important Things	Unimportant Things
Find out who the owner is.	

THINK IT OVER

Discuss and Write Talk about these questions with a partner. Write the answers.

1. **Conclusions** What are some good reasons for starting a community garden?
2. **Judgments** What would you name a community garden? Why would you give it that name?
3. **Personal Experience** Have you ever been involved in a community project? What was the project about? Describe your role in it.

EXPRESS YOURSELF ▶DESCRIBE

Work with a group. List different vegetables and flowers that grow in a garden. Take turns describing one of them. See if anyone in the group can guess what you are describing.

REACHING ALL STUDENTS

Multi-Level Strategies

SUM IT UP OPTIONS

BEGINNING Read each item aloud and have students vote on whether it is important or unimportant. Then write the items in a group chart.

INTERMEDIATE Have students work with a partner to decide if each item is important or unimportant as they complete their T-charts. Invite students to give reasons for any differences.

ADVANCED Have students work with a partner to share their T-charts and to discuss any differences. Then ask partners to list details related to each important step.

ınguage Arts and Content Area Connections

REPRESENTING/SPEAKING
ECHNOLOGY/MEDIA

IVE A SPEECH ABOUT FOOD BANKS

od banks give food to people who need it. ith a group, use the Internet or other resources prepare a speech about a food bank.

Find Information This Web site is a good place to start, but new sites appear every day! Use key words and look for links.

INTERNET
INFORMATION ON-LINE
Key Words:
"food bank"
"second harvest"
Web Site:
Information About Food Banks
- www.secondharvest.org

Choose Roles Some members can make posters and other visuals. Others can write the speech.

Give Your Speech Here are some tips:

- Say your name and tell your topic.
- Speak in a loud, clear voice. Look at your audience when you talk.
- At the end of the talk, ask if there are any questions. Thank the audience for listening.

For tips on giving a **speech**, see Handbook pages 401–402.

SCIENCE
SOCIAL STUDIES

COMPARE COUNTRY AND CITY GARDENS

Work in teams of four. Two members research city, or urban, gardens. The other two research country, or rural, gardens. Each set of partners makes a chart to show what they find out.

Answer questions like these:

- Where is a good place to start the garden?
- How big can the garden be?
- What grows best in this kind of garden? What combination of plants is possible?
- What kinds of insects or animals exist in this habitat? How do they affect the plants?
- Can pesticides be used? Why or why not?
- What steps must be taken to protect the plants?
- How does pollution affect the plants?

Compare the charts and define the three most important considerations in planting a garden in each place.

Learn about **charts** on Handbook pages 370–371.

Multi-Level Strategies

ACTIVITY OPTIONS FOR GIVING A SPEECH

BEGINNING Help students brainstorm ideas for a group speech and record them on the web. Then help them create a sentence for each important idea and arrange them in a logical sequence. Assign one or two sentences from the speech to each student for a group presentation.

INTERMEDIATE Have students use the information in **Give Your Speech** on page 131 to create a checklist of what to do when giving a speech. Have listeners provide constructive feedback according to the checklist.

ADVANCED Have students focus on developing strong introductions and conclusions for their speeches. Explain that the introduction should grab the listeners' attention and the conclusion should sum up what they want listeners to remember. Ask students to take notes as their classmates deliver their speeches and offer constructive feedback.

RESPOND

OBJECTIVES

FOOD BANK SPEECH
Function: Give Information
Speaking: Speech
Technology/Media: Use the Internet
Representing: Poster

COMPARE GARDENS
Function: Give Information
Critical Thinking: Make Comparisons; Evaluate Information; Relate Steps in a Process
Representing: Chart

LANGUAGE ARTS AND CONTENT AREA CONNECTIONS

1 Give a Speech About Food Banks
Support suggestions are:

- Direct students to library and community resources. Have them find out where food for those in need is collected or distributed.
- Suggest roles and responsibilities for various tasks.
- Discuss what information could be represented in a chart or graphic.
- Direct students to rehearse their speeches and have group members provide feedback based on tips on page 131.
- Encourage listeners to give constructive criticism.

2 Compare Country and City Gardens
Clarify the meanings of *habitat* (the place where a plant or an animal lives and thrives), *urban* (having to do with a city), and *rural* (having to do with the country).

▶ **Practice Book** page 62

CLOSE AND ASSESS

Have students write a sentence stating what they learned in this lesson. Have students read their sentences aloud to show the variety of concepts they learned.

BUILD WRITING SKILLS

OBJECTIVES

Function: Engage in Discussion; Listen Actively

Reading Strategy and Critical Thinking: Use Text Structures (sequential order); Analyze and Evaluate Information

Listening: Listen Critically

Literary Analysis and Writing: **T** Expressive (personal history); Sequence of Events; Point of View

INTRODUCE WRITING FOR PERSONAL EXPRESSION

1. **Discuss Expressive Writing** Read the introduction and ask students what kind of expressive writing they have done.
2. **Study the Professional Model** Ask students how they know the excerpt is a personal history. (It tells about Patricia Polaco's family history.) Ask for examples of first person point of view. (pronouns *my, me, I*)
3. **Explore Text Structure** Explain that a personal history often relates a series of events in a writer's life. Use the time line to teach one way to structure a personal history.

Use the Options for Studying Text Structure in the **Multi-Level Strategies** to adjust instruction.

Writing for Personal Expression

Expressive writing tells a writer's personal feelings about a subject. Some expressive writing, like a journal or diary entry, is private. Poems and memoirs are published to share with everyone.

PROFESSIONAL WRITING MODELS

In "The Keeping Quilt," Patricia Polacco expresses her feelings about a special family quilt that has been passed down for many generations. Notice that she uses the first person because she is part of the story.

***from* "The Keeping Quilt"**

> When my grandma Carle was born, Anna wrapped her daughter in the quilt to welcome her warmly into the world. . . .
>
> The quilt welcomed me, Patricia, into the world, and it was the tablecloth for my first birthday party.
>
> At night I would trace my fingers around the edges of each animal on the quilt before I went to sleep. . . .

AN EXPRESSIVE PERSONAL HISTORY

When writers express their feelings in a personal history, they may write about events that take place over a long period of time. To help readers follow the order of events, the writer uses words that signal sequence, such as *after, then, many years later, when,* and *now.* Discuss the sequence of events in "The Keeping Quilt."

A Time Line of Personal History

REACHING ALL STUDENTS

Transparency 29 / Master 29

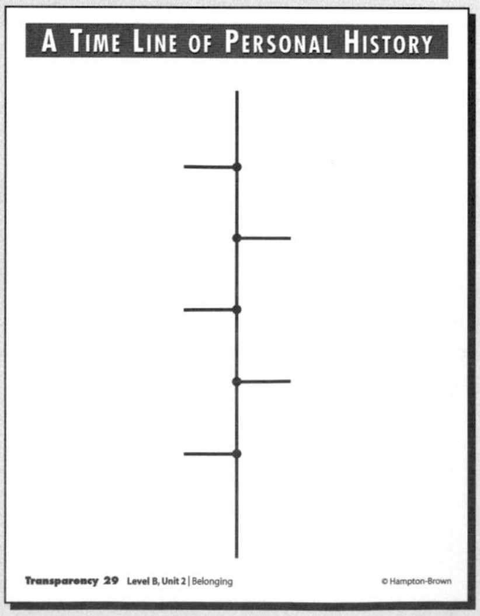

Multi-Level Strategies

OPTIONS FOR STUDYING TEXT STRUCTURE

BEGINNING Display **Transparency 29** and lead students through a simple shared experience by plotting events on the time line. Use events that have occurred during the school year, such as a class field trip, a school play, and so on. Restate students' ideas and record them in simple phrases. Then use the art on page 132 to present the events in "The Keeping Quilt."

INTERMEDIATE / **ADVANCED** Say: *In a personal history, the author often describes events in the order in which they happened.* Work through a Time Line of Personal History for "The Keeping Quilt." To check understanding of the structure, ask students to explain why the events are ordered as they are. Then have them work in pairs to fill out **Master 29** with events from their own lives.

DENT WRITING MODEL

onal History

he Two Worlds of Imara

y Imara Guerrero

I am sitting in my room in my house in America with a hoto album on my lap. I look out the window at a bright full noon shining down on silvery snow. This is the world I live in ow. But at this moment, I am dreaming about my first world—Vicaragua.

I grew up in a town called José Dolores, in a big house with ix rooms and a garden. I lived there with my parents and my randmother Socorro. All around us was family.

When I was five, my parents left our home and came to the J.S.A. I stayed in Nicaragua with my grandmother. I missed my nother and father so much. I didn't understand why they had left ne behind. Now I know they were working hard to send back noney and gifts for me and other family members.

Two years later, I came to the U.S.A., too. I was sad to leave ny friends and family, especially my grandmother and my cousin María. But I was very happy to be with my parents again in an xciting new land—at first.

Then came my first day at school. I had no friends. I had a ard time understanding what the teacher said and what I was upposed to do. That night, I cried.

As time passed, things got better. I made new friends. I learned o be comfortable with English. I learned to eat new foods, like izza, and to listen to new music, like Britney Spears. But I still njoy things from my first world. I often ask my mother to make *allopinto* and *maduro frito*, my favorite Nicaraguan foods. I listen o Selena sing in Spanish. She is still my favorite singer.

So here I am in my second world, sitting in a room in a house n America. My name is Imara, and I love both my worlds.

Imara tells about her own experiences and feelings. She speaks directly to the reader, using **first-person point of view.**

Time order words help the reader follow the sequence of events.

Past tense verbs show which actions happened earlier. **Present tense verbs** show what Imara does today.

STUDY A STUDENT WRITING MODEL

4 Listen for Sequence of Events Have students take notes on copies of **Master 29** as you read the Student Model aloud. Go over their notes together to identify the significant events in the writer's personal history.

5 Analyze and Evaluate Personal Histories Display **Transparency 30** and lead students in studying the features of a personal history. Students should then evaluate the Student Model against the rubric on the transparency.

Use the Roles for Cooperative Groups in the **Multi-Level Strategies** to involve all students.

CLOSE AND ASSESS

Call on a different **Reporter** to summarize the group conclusions for each feature on **Master 30.** Encourage students to add other relevant information, either verbally or by drawing quick sketches to represent their ideas.

Multi-Level Strategies

ROLES FOR COOPERATIVE GROUPS

BEGINNING / **INTERMEDIATE** / **ADVANCED** Distribute **Master 30** to groups of three students with varying proficiencies and have them compare the model to the rubric. Assign these roles:

- **Finder**
- **Recorder**
- **Reporter**

Before groups begin, work through the title and the first feature, pointing out the sample answer. Groups should then discuss each feature of a personal history. The **Finder** can point out the section(s) in the Student Model relevant to the feature; the **Reporter** chooses and reads aloud phrases for that feature; and the **Recorder** checks the box and writes the information in the chart to be read aloud to the whole group later.

Transparency 30 / Master 30

FEATURES OF EXPRESSIVE WRITING

Directions: Read "The Two Worlds of Imara" and compare it to the features of a personal history. Check the box if "The Two Worlds of Imara" shows the feature. Then give an example.

A Personal History. . . The Two Worlds of Imara

describes a person's **thoughts** and **feelings.**	☑ Imara missed her parents when they went to the U.S.A.
tells when events happened using **time order words.**	☑ When I was five Two years later Then came my first day at school As time passed
has **well-organized paragraphs** with topic sentences.	☑ topic sentence in second paragraph names where she grew up in Nicaragua; details tell more about her home there
is written in the **first-person** point of view.	☑ uses first-person pronouns *I*, *me*, and *my*

Transparency 30 Level B, Unit 2 | Belonging

BUILD WRITING SKILLS

OBJECTIVES

PREWRITE

Function: Write

Learning Strategies and Critical Thinking: Plan; Generate Ideas; Interact with Peers; Use Graphic Organizers; Organize Ideas; Self-Assess

Representing: Chart, Time Line

Writing: T Writing Process

PRESENT THE WRITING PROCESS AND PROMPT

Read the prompt together. Then leaf through pages 134–138 to review the stages in the Writing Process.

For more about the Writing Process, refer students to pages 408–413 in the Handbook.

PREWRITE

Before students begin their prewriting, preview the steps with the group and discuss the sample FATP chart.

Use the Prewriting Support in the **Multi-Level Strategies** to tailor this stage to proficiency levels.

CLOSE AND ASSESS

Have students work with a partner to answer the questions in Reflect and Evaluate.

The Writing Process

WRITING PROMPT

Write a personal history to tell an elementary school class about your experiences. Be sure to express your feelings.

PREWRITE

1 **Brainstorm Ideas** Get together with a partner, and discuss some things you might include in your personal history. As you talk, take notes in a chart.

People, Places, and Events	Why They Are Important	My Feelings
Ajay, my friend in India	We liked the same things. We played sports and helped each other.	He was my best friend. I miss him the most of all my friends.
New Delhi, India	My first home. I lived there until I was nine.	I miss my family there. I miss playing cricket. I don't miss the noisy, crowded city.
going to a professional cricket match	It was a special trip with my mom and dad.	I miss going to games with Mom and Dad. I also miss watching and playing cricket. No one in the U.S. even knows how to play the game!

2 **Unlock the Writing Prompt** Before you begin your personal history, fill out an **FATP** chart to help guide your writing.

3 **Organize Your Ideas** The way you organize your ideas depends on what you plan to write about. Here are some possibilities:

- Use a time line to list important events in your life.
- Use a chart to compare your life in the U.S. with your life in the country you came from.
- Make a list of things you liked as you were growing up.

See pages 370–375 of the Handbook for more graphic organizers.

FATP Chart

HOW TO UNLOCK A PROM

Form: *personal history*

Audience: *3rd grade class*

Topic: *things I used to do in India and things I do now in the U.S.*

Purpose: *to tell about my experiences and how I feel about them*

Reflect and Evalua

- How did listening to your partner's ideas help you form your ideas?
- Have you listed enough information?
- Are your dates, place names, and people's nam correct? Check with a family member.

REACHING ALL STUDENTS

Multi-Level Strategies

PREWRITING SUPPORT

BEGINNING Invite students to use drawings (or photos, if possible) to show various experiences from their lives. Have them choose an experience and draw a few feelings about it. Help them fill out FATP charts. Then have students create a storyboard or fill in the time line on **Master 29** (see page T132) with pictures showing the events they choose to write about.

INTERMEDIATE Students can work together to collect ideas and fill out FATP charts. Check the charts and help them sequence events they will write about on copies of **Master 29**. (See page T132.)

ADVANCED Encourage students to ask family and friends for details about the events they choose to focus on. To organize their ideas, they can use **Master 29** (see page T132) or make a chart. Help them decide which organizer best fits the kinds of memories they want to relate.

[DR]AFT

[Use] your **FATP** chart to help you focus your writing. Write quickly to [cap]ture your ideas. Don't worry about making mistakes. If you think of [new] ideas and details, add those to your draft.

Write the Beginning In your first paragraph, introduce yourself. Write in the first person, using the pronouns *I, my, me, we, our,* and *us.*

Tell About Your Life Come up with a topic for each paragraph. State your topic in a topic sentence. Then give the details.

Writer's Craft: Paragraph Structure

Make sure each paragraph tells about only one topic.

Not OK	OK
When I came to Los Angeles, I was surprised that no one played cricket. I liked to eat hamburgers. My sister got some new jeans.	When I came to Los Angeles, I was surprised that no one played cricket. It was my favorite game in India. I wondered if I would ever get to play it again.

Make sure your details support the main idea in your topic sentence.

Not OK	OK
I was amazed by the freeways in Los Angeles. They are bigger than any roads I had ever seen. My mother drives me to the movies.	I am amazed at how enormous the freeways in Los Angeles are! Some are twelve lanes wide! Though there is a lot of traffic in India, the roads there do not take up nearly as much room as the LA freeways.

Write an Ending As you finish your personal history, leave your reader with a final thought to sum up your experiences. Express your feelings about them.

Reflect and Evaluate

- Read through your draft. Does it let your reader know how you feel about your experiences?
- Are your paragraphs well-organized, with topic sentences and supporting details?

OBJECTIVES

DRAFT

Function: Ⓣ Express Feelings; Write

Learning Strategies and Critical Thinking: Generate Ideas; Self-Assess

Writer's Craft: Ⓣ Paragraph Structure

Writing: Ⓣ Writing Process

DRAFT

Before students begin their drafts, discuss the Writer's Craft models in **Step 2**. Ask volunteers to explain why the first model in each pair is "Not OK," while the second model is "OK."

Use the Drafting Support in the **Multi-Level Strategies** to tailor this stage to proficiency levels.

For more about the Writer's Craft, refer students to pages 414–423 in the Handbook.

CLOSE AND ASSESS

Have small groups discuss the questions in Reflect and Evaluate while you work with those who may need more support in assessing their drafts.

Multi-Level Strategies

DRAFTING SUPPORT

BEGINNING To draft their personal histories, guide students in writing one sentence for each image they included in their storyboard or on their time line. Encourage them to indicate sequential structure in their sentences: *Your first sentence should tell about the first event in your personal history. Use sequence words as you add each of the other events.* Offer individual assistance, such as support in forming simple captions, to students who need help.

INTERMEDIATE / **ADVANCED** Have students work in pairs to apply the Writer's Craft skill as they create the "OK" examples on **Master 31**. Then encourage students to draft a paragraph and have a partner check that it tells about just one topic and includes details to support the main idea.

Transparency 31 / Master 31

PARAGRAPH STRUCTURE

Directions: Read each writing tip and the example that is "Not OK." Change the example to make it "OK."

Writing Tips	Not OK	OK
Make sure each paragraph tells about only one topic.	I grew up in José Dolores, Nicaragua. My parents went to the U.S.A. to work. I like pizza and music. Our house in Nicaragua was big. I missed my parents when they left. I had lots of friends.	I grew up in José Dolores, Nicaragua. My parents, grandmother, and other family members lived there, too. Our house in Nicaragua was big. It had six rooms. We also had a large garden.
Make sure your details support the main idea in your topic sentence.	As time passed, things got better. I made friends. I missed my old favorite foods. At night I dreamed about Nicaragua.	As time passed, things got better. I made friends. I learned to eat new foods and to listen to new music.

Transparency 31 Level B, Unit 2 | Belonging

OBJECTIVES

REVISE

Function: Write; Engage in Discussion

Learning Strategies and Critical Thinking: Generate Ideas; Review; Clarify; Interact with Peers; Self-Assess

Listening and Speaking: Peer-Conferencing

Technology and Media: Use Word-Processing Software

Writing: Ⓣ Writing Process

REVISE

First have students reread their drafts. They should turn the entries on their FATP charts into questions to answer as they assess their work. For example: *Did I include my feelings about the experiences I described?*

Next model how to evaluate someone else's writing in a peer conference by asking questions about the draft. Also model how a writer makes revisions. Students can then conduct the peer conferences and revise their drafts.

Use the Peer Conference Support in the **Multi-Level Strategies** to model how to evaluate and revise writing.

CLOSE AND ASSESS

Have peers discuss the questions in Reflect and Evaluate.

REVISE

1. **Reread Your Draft** Review your **FATP**. Is your form, audience, topic, and purpose clear? Did you express your feelings?

2. **Conduct a Peer Conference** Share your writing with a partner or group. Did you use first person throughout your writing? Did you use correct verb tenses? The guidelines on Handbook page 411 can help you conduct peer conferences.

   Look at the questions a partner asked Babu during a Peer Conference. Read what he thinks about the changes he will make.

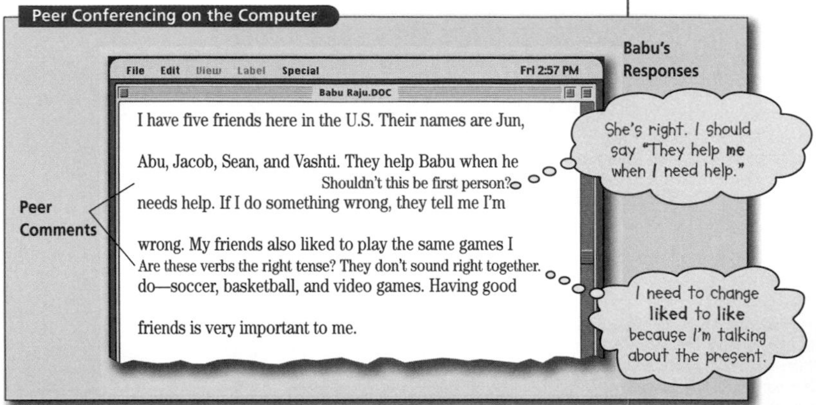

3. **Mark Your Changes** Decide what changes you will make. See Handbook page 411 for a list of Revising Marks. For how to make changes in a word-processed document, see pages 386–387 in the Handbook.

Key In TO Technology

During your peer conference, notes, questions, or comment another color to make them to see.

Reflect and Evalu

- Did your peers like wha you wrote? What did t suggest you change?
- Did you find that you h to do a lot of rewriting
- Did you include all the thoughts and feelings y wanted to?

REACHING ALL STUDENTS

Transparency 32 / Master 32

REVISING

Red annotations show changes related to the sample questions. Revisions should vary to reflect questions students propose.

When I was five, My parents left our home and came to the U.S.A. I missed my mother and father so much. I stayed in Nicaragua with my grandmother. I didn't understand why they left me behind. Now she I knows they were working hard to send back money and gifts for me and other family members.

Revising Marks

^	Add.
↺	Move to here.
⌐	Replace with this.
⤼	Take out.

Ask Questions During a Peer Conference

1. Ask about anything that is unclear.
   - *I don't understand—when did your parents leave?*
   - Students' questions will vary.
2. Ask about details that could be added.
   - *Can you tell how you felt when your parents left?*
   - Students' questions will vary.
3. Think about the writing. Ask a question to make a suggestion.
   - *Don't you want to use the first person here?*
   - Students' questions will vary.

Transparency 32 Level B, Unit 2 | Belonging © Hampton-Brown

Multi-Level Strategies

PEER CONFERENCE SUPPORT

BEGINNING Display **Transparency 32** and read the paragraph. Support students' comprehension by displaying maps of Nicaragua and the United States and role-playing with students the parents moving to the U.S. while the girl stays behind with her grandmother. Then model how to conduct a peer conference. Provide sample questions and have volunteers supply other questions. Next, model how to revise the paragraph, based on the questions.

INTERMEDIATE / **ADVANCED** Read the paragraph on **Transparency 32**, and have students identify parts they want to know more about or parts that are not clear. Invite them to phrase their ideas as questions like the models. Finally, ask volunteers to suggest revisions, based on the questions.

AMMAR IN CONTEXT

B TENSES

tense of a verb shows when an action happens.

se the **present tense** to talk about something that is happening now or
at happens all the time.

Examples: I **live** in the U.S.A.
I **walk** to school every day.

se the **past tense** to talk about something that happened earlier, or in
e past. Past tense verbs are often formed by adding **-ed**.

Examples: I **lived** in New Delhi, India, before.
My best friend and I **played** sports together.

ome verbs have special forms to show past tense.

Examples: We **went** to cricket games together, too.
We **knew** the name of every cricket player.

se the **future tense** to talk about something that will happen later, or in
e future.

Examples: I **will visit** India this summer.
We **are going to stay** with my grandparents.

I play cricket with my friend.

Irregular Verbs

Present	Past
are	were
bring	brought
go	went
is	was
know	knew
say	said
send	sent

tice Write each sentence and add the correct form of the verb
arentheses.

/hen I was in India, I ________ to play cricket. (like)
also ________ soccer. (play)
ow that I am in America, I ________ to be a basketball star. (want)
oday I ________ to practice my foul shots. (need)
ext summer, I ________ to basketball camp. (go)
t basketball camp, I ________ my cousin Manjeet. (see)
e ________ me an e-mail with information about the camp. (send)
the message, Manjeet ________ he practices every day, too. (say)

OBJECTIVES

GRAMMAR IN CONTEXT
Grammar: T Verb Tenses

GRAMMAR IN CONTEXT

1 **Teach Verb Tenses** Work with students to read the definitions and study the examples.

2 **Use Verb Tenses** Involve students in determining verb tenses for sentences:

- Name a verb, such as *look, jump,* or *chase.* Ask students to suggest sentences using that verb in the present, past, and future tense.
- Conduct the cooperative learning activity below.

3 **Answers to Practice Items**

1. liked	**5.** will go
2. played	**6.** will see
3. want	**7.** sent
4. need	**8.** said

CLOSE AND ASSESS

Have partners each write a sentence and then trade and identify the verb tense in their partner's sentence.

Cooperative Learning

FOR LANGUAGE DEVELOPMENT: Verb Tenses

Materials: chart paper, markers

List Verbs Divide students into four "expert" groups. Assign one verb tense to each of three groups, letting the fourth group choose a verb tense. Students can write sentences showing the use of the verb tense. Students in each "expert" group then reconfigure and teach their material to their new group. Invite individuals to share sample sentences and tell the verb tenses.

Debrief the Skill Refer to some of the sentences students share. Ask: *How did you know which verb tense to use? How can you change the sentence to use a different tense?*

Debrief the Cooperative Process Have students reflect on the activity: *How did working with a group make it easier to choose the correct verb tense? How did teaching others the skill help you understand it better?*

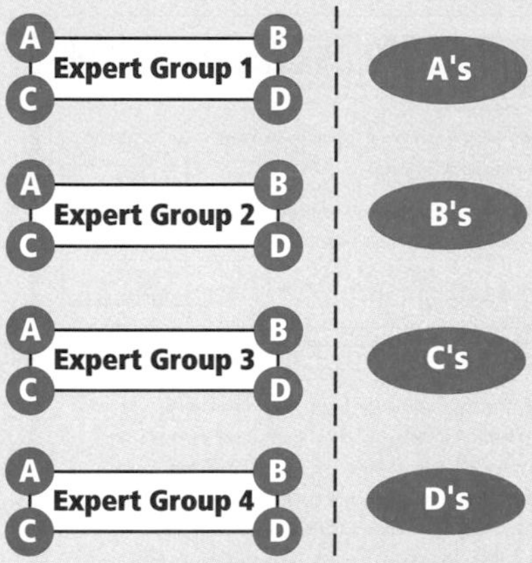

Cooperative Learning Structure: Jigsaw

BUILD WRITING SKILLS

OBJECTIVES

EDIT AND PROOFREAD

Learning Strategies and Critical Thinking: Review; Clarify; Self-Assess

Technology and Media: Use Word-Processing Software

Writing: T Writing Process

PUBLISH

Learning Strategies and Critical Thinking: Interact with Peers; Self-Assess; Make Decisions

Speaking: Read Aloud

Technology and Media: Use Desktop Publishing Software; Use Tape Recorder

Writing: T Writing Process

EDIT AND PROOFREAD

Use **Transparency 33** to model editing and proofreading.

PUBLISH

Ask volunteers to share publishing ideas or have students choose from those suggested on page 138.

Use the Editing and Publishing Support in the **Multi-Level Strategies** to adjust instruction.

CLOSE AND ASSESS

Have groups discuss the questions in Reflect and Evaluate. Monitor how students complete the checklist.

WRITING ASSESSMENT
Use the Writing Rubric on page 31 of the Assessment Han
to evaluate this writing assignment.

Writing for Personal Expression, continued

EDIT AND PROOFREAD

1. **Check for Mistakes** Look through your writing and correct any mistakes in capitalization, punctuation, and spelling. If you need help, see Handbook pages 459–469.
2. **Check Your Verbs** Check to see that you used the correct verb tense.
3. **Make a Final Copy** Copy your personal history, making all the corrections you need to make. If you are working on a computer, make your final edits and print out a clean copy.

PUBLISH

Use one of these ideas for publishing your writing, or come up with an idea of your own.

- If you are using a computer, scan in photos from your family photo album. Import them into your personal history. Be sure to include a caption for each picture. The caption should identify who, what, and where.

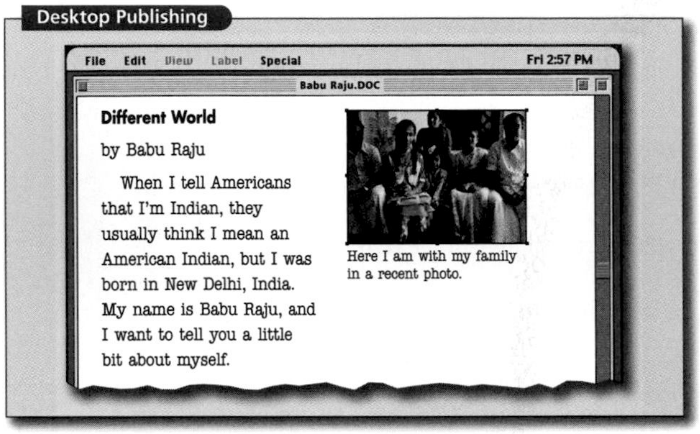

- Make a copy of your personal history to send to a friend or relative who lives in your native country.

I will go everywhere and see everything. I will mee all the people I can. I wil think all the thoughts, fe all the emotions I am abl and I will write, write, write . . .

— Thomas Wolfe

Reflect and Evalu

- Do you feel you did a g job "expressing yourself Does your personal hist
  - ☑ have well-organized paragraphs with topi sentences?
  - ☑ tell important events your life in a sequen that is easy to follow
  - ☑ express your feelings
- What did you learn abo yourself from writing yo personal history?
- Will this work go in you portfolio? Why or why r

REACHING ALL STUDENTS

Transparency 33 / Master 33

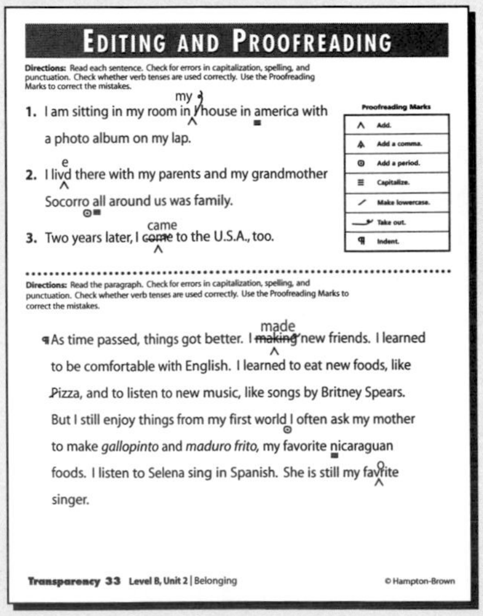
EDITING AND PROOFREADING

Directions: Read each sentence. Check for errors in capitalization, spelling, and punctuation. Check whether verb tenses are used correctly. Use the Proofreading Marks to correct the mistakes.

1. I am sitting in my room in (my) / house in america with a photo album on my lap.
2. I livd (e) there with my parents and my grandmother Socorro all around us was family.
3. Two years later, I ~~come~~ (came) to the U.S.A., too.

Proofreading Marks	
^	Add.
^,	Add a comma.
⊙	Add a period.
≡	Capitalize.
/	Make lowercase.
—↩	Take out.
¶	Indent.

Directions: Read the paragraph. Check for errors in capitalization, spelling, and punctuation. Check whether verb tenses are used correctly. Use the Proofreading Marks to correct the mistakes.

¶ As time passed, things got better. I ~~making~~ (made) new friends. I learned to be comfortable with English. I learned to eat new foods, like Pizza, and to listen to new music, like songs by Britney Spears. But I still enjoy things from my first world I often ask my mother to make *gallopinto* and *maduro frito,* my favorite nicaraguan foods. I listen to Selena sing in Spanish. She is still my favrite (o) singer.

Transparency 33 Level B, Unit 2 | Belonging © Hampton-Brown

Multi-Level Strategies

EDITING AND PUBLISHING

BEGINNING Model finding and correcting errors in the top section of **Transparency 33**. After marking the edits, have students write out the corrected sentences. For publishing, help students scan the art from their storyboards or time lines and import it into a word-processing document with their writing.

INTERMEDIATE Guide students in finding and correcting the errors in the paragraph at the bottom of **Transparency 33**. For publishing, students can bind their personal histories and then include them in the classroom library.

ADVANCED Distribute copies of **Master 33** and have students work on the activities individually or with partners. Students may wish to tape record their personal histories and then make the written and audiotape versions available for check-out by other students.

Debrief A Sense of Place

UNIT 2

✓ **ASSESSMENT**
The Unit 2 Test on page 33 of the Assessment Handbook measures students' progress in reading, language arts, literary study, and writing. Additional forms in the Assessment Handbook allow for:
- **Self Assessment on page 32**
- **Peer Assessment on page 101**
- **Portfolio Evaluation on page 103**

Look Back at the Unit

Make a Word Quilt In this unit you read these selections about belonging.

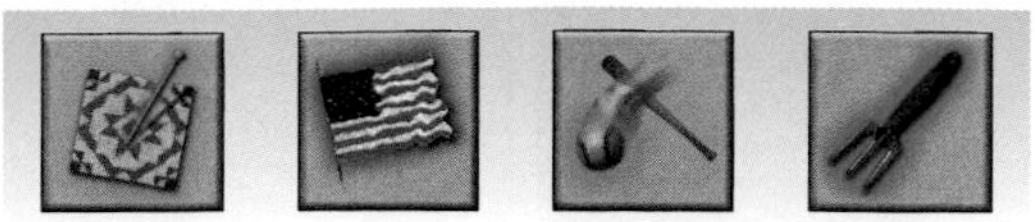

The Keeping Quilt | Beyond the Color Lines | Teammates | Amir

Work with a group. Choose a quote from each selection that tells about belonging. Write each one on a square of colored paper. Then read your quotes to the class. Connect the squares to make a word quilt. Talk about how the quotes work together to make a statement about belonging.

Show What You Know

Sum It All Up Expand and organize your ideas on this mind map. Share your ideas about belonging with a partner.

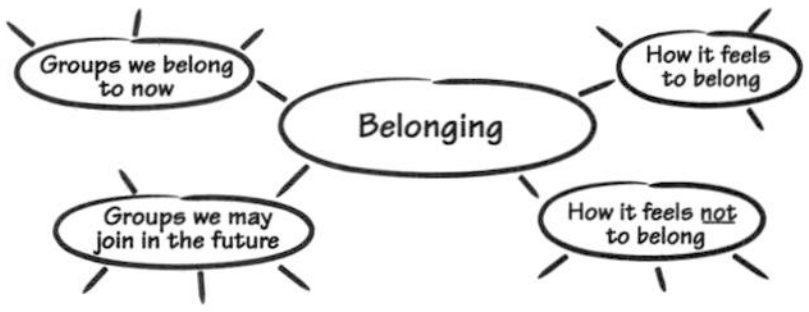

Reflect and Evaluate Write a sentence about a place where you feel like you belong. Then tell why you belong there. Add this writing to your portfolio, along with work from the unit that shows what you learned.

Make Connections

To Your School Think of ways to help new students feel a sense of belonging. Make care packages that include maps of your school, lists of teachers, and school activities. Offer your help as a tour guide or translator for new students.

DEBRIEF UNIT 2

OBJECTIVES

Function: Engage in Discussion; Express Opinions

Learning Strategies and Critical Thinking: Interact with Peers; Generate Ideas; Form Opinions; Summarize; Self-Assess; Synthesize Information; Use Graphic Organizers (mind map)

Literary Analysis: Respond to Literature; Compare Literature

EXPLORE "A SENSE OF PLACE"

1. **Look Back at the Unit** Use this question to help students choose quotations: *Does it help me understand what it means "to belong"?* Then conduct the Cooperative Learning Activity.
2. **Show What You Know** Suggest that students think about what helps them when they feel lonely.
3. **Make Connections** Begin by brainstorming questions students have had or might have when starting at a new school.

CLOSE AND ASSESS

Have students tell you the most important thing they learned in the unit.

Cooperative Learning

FOR CRITICAL THINKING: Synthesize Information

Choose Quotations During think and talk time, students review the selections and choose possible quotations. Groups discuss what the quotations say about belonging. Then they compose a statement to represent all the selections.

Discuss Quotations Call a number and have the student in each group with that number read a quotation, explaining why the group chose it.

Debrief the Content Ask students what they learned about belonging from the unit, for example: *I realized I belong to many different kinds of groups.*

Debrief the Cooperative Process Have students reflect on how working in a group helped them summarize. Ask: *What new ideas about belonging did you learn from other group members?*

Cooperative Learning Structure: Numbered Heads

Resources

For Success in Language, Literature, and Content

Student Book pages 140–211

For Skills Practice

Practice Book
pages 63–101

For Planning and Instruction

Teacher's Edition
pages T140a–T211

For Vocabulary and Language Development

Language Tape Side B
Language CD Track 4

For Selection Readings

Selection Tape 3
Selection CD 3

For Technology Support

Inspiration
Visual Learning Software
with Graphic Organizers

For Classroom Activities

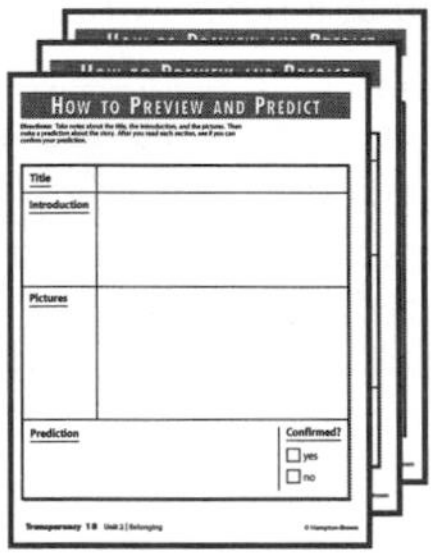

Transparencies or Masters 34–51

For Home-School Connections

High Point Newsletters 5 and 6

For Comprehensive Assessment

Language Acquisition Assessment, Selection Tests, Unit Test, Writing Assessment, Self-Assessment

In the Theme Library

The Lotus Seed
by Sherry Garland

The Milkman's Boy
by Donald Hall

From *The Basics Bookshelf*

- ***Friends Are Like That***
- ***Who Was Martin L. King, Jr.?***

Theme-related books with simple text for including newcomers

UNIT 3 Dreams and Decisions

FOLLOW YOUR DREAMS

Another Place, Another Time, Chris Van Allsburg, pencil. Copyright © 1996.

IMAGINATION AND DETERMINATION FUEL OUR DREAMS, GIVING US HOPE THAT ANYTHING IS POSSIBLE. THIS UNIT INVITES STUDENTS, WHO ARE FORMING THEIR OWN DREAMS FOR THE FUTURE, TO EXPLORE HOW FOLLOWING ONE'S DREAMS FIRST MEANS DETERMINING WHAT'S MOST IMPORTANT AND THEN SETTING GOALS TO ACHIEVE IT.

THEME 1 What Matters Most

Students learn that knowing what is important in life helps people achieve their dreams and goals.

THEME 2 Toward a Better Future

Students discover that setting goals and believing in oneself can help make anything possible.

Activity Planner

THEME 1: What Matters Most

LESSONS

1

THEME 1 OPENER
▶ pages T142–T143

Function	Learning Strategy	Vocabulary	Critical Thinking
Engage in Discussion	Make a Chart	Words About Life Experience	Classify

2

BUILD LANGUAGE AND VOCABULARY
▶ pages T144–T145

Function	Learning Strategy	Vocabulary	Patterns and Structures
Ⓣ Tell a Story	Make a Story Map	Descriptive Words	Ⓣ Adjectives, Adverbs, and Prepositional Phrases

PACING SUGGESTIONS

LESSONS	45–55 MINUTE PERIODS	BLOCK SCHEDULE SESSIONS
1	1 period	1 session (lessons 1–2)
2	1 period	
3–9	6 periods	3 sessions
10–16	6 periods	3 sessions

3–9

Ginger for the Heart by Paul Yee
HISTORICAL FICTION ▶ pages T146–T157

PREPARE TO READ
page T146

Activate Prior Knowledge
Discuss Dreams and Goals

Vocabulary Ⓣ
Use New Words in Context

Reading Strategy
Ⓣ Relate Goals and Outcomes

READ THE SELECTION
pages T147–T154

Pre-Reading Strategies
Preview and Predict

Identify Genre: Historical Fiction

Set Purpose

Strategy Focus
Ⓣ Relate Goals and Outcomes

Vocabulary
Use Context Clues to Meaning

Use Negative Prefixes

Self-Monitoring and Comprehension
Ⓣ Confirm Word Meaning

Before You Move On: Think and Discuss

Literary Analysis Minilessons:
Description

Characterization and Dialogue

RESPOND
pages T155–T157

CHECK YOUR UNDERSTANDING

Critical Thinking and Comprehension
Sum It Up:
Ⓣ Identify Goals and Outcomes; Generate Ideas

Think It Over: Discuss and Write

Function
Express Yourself: Agree or Disagree

LANGUAGE ARTS AND LITERATURE

Grammar in Context
Ⓣ Use Adjectives

Writing/Speaking
Write an Outcome

CONTENT AREA CONNECTIONS

Social Studies
Research the Gold Rush

Mathematics
Compare Travel Times

10–16

Twins by Debra and Lisa Ganz
ARTICLE ▶ pages T158–T167

PREPARE TO READ
page T158

Activate Prior Knowledge
Pantomime

Vocabulary Ⓣ
Use New Words in Context

Reading Strategy
Ⓣ Paraphrase

READ THE SELECTION
pages T159–T164

Pre-Reading Strategies
Preview and Predict

Identify Genre: Article

Set Purpose

Strategy Focus
Ⓣ Paraphrase

Vocabulary
Relate Words

Comprehension
Before You Move On: Think and Discuss

Grammar Minilessons:
Compound Predicates

Compound Subjects

RESPOND
pages T165–T167

CHECK YOUR UNDERSTANDING

Critical Thinking and Comprehension
Sum It Up:
Ⓣ Paraphrase; Compare and Evaluate Literature

Think It Over: Discuss and Write

Function
Express Yourself: Demonstrate Non-Verbal Communication

LANGUAGE ARTS AND LITERATURE

Grammar in Context
Ⓣ Use Adjectives that Compare

Technology/Media and Writing
Write to a Twin

CONTENT AREA CONNECTIONS

Social Studies
Research Contributions of the Hearing Impaired

Technology/Media and Science
Research Twins

Ⓣ = Assessed on **Unit 3 Test** Ⓣ = Assessed on **Unit 3 Language Acquisition Assessment**

THEME 2: Toward a Better Future

LESSONS

PACING SUGGESTIONS

LESSONS	45–55 MINUTE PERIODS	BLOCK SCHEDULE SESSIONS
1	1 period	1 session (lessons 1–2)
2	1 period	
3–10	7 periods	4 sessions
11–13	2 periods	1 session
14–20	6 periods	3 sessions

1 THEME 2 OPENER
▶ pages T168–T169

Function
Engage in Discussion

Learning Strategy
Make a Chart

Vocabulary
Words About Goals

Critical Thinking
Generate Ideas

2 BUILD LANGUAGE AND VOCABULARY
▶ pages T170–T171

Function
Ⓣ Describe

Learning Strategy
Generate ideas

Vocabulary
Synonyms

Patterns and Structures
Ⓣ Complex Sentences

3–10 *The Great Migration* by Jacob Lawrence
ART ESSAY ▶ pages T172–T184

PREPARE TO READ page T172

Activate Prior Knowledge
Quickwrite

Vocabulary Ⓣ
Relate Words

Reading Strategy
Ⓣ Make Comparisons

READ THE SELECTION pages T173–T180

Pre-Reading Strategies
Preview and Predict
Identify Genre: Essay
Set Purpose

Strategy Focus
Ⓣ Make Comparisons

Vocabulary
Use Words in Context
Identify Prefixes

Self-Monitoring and Comprehension
Reread
Before You Move On: Think and Discuss

Grammar Minilessons:
Ⓣ Complex Sentences
Prepositional Phrases

RESPOND pages T181–T184

CHECK YOUR UNDERSTANDING

Critical Thinking and Comprehension
Sum It Up:
Ⓣ Make Comparisons;
Summarize
Think It Over:
Discuss and Write

Function
Express Yourself:
Describe

LANGUAGE ARTS AND LITERATURE

Grammar in Context
Use Phrases and Clauses

Viewing/Writing
Describe an Event

CONTENT AREA CONNECTIONS

Social Studies
Research City Jobs

Representing/Speaking and Fine Arts
Create a Message Without Words

Technology/Media and Social Studies
Study Population Shifts

11–13 *Follow the Drinking Gourd* by Jeanette Winter
TRADITIONAL SONG ▶ pages T185–T189

PREPARE TO READ page T185

Activate Prior Knowledge
Idea Exchange

Vocabulary
Use Words in Context

Reading Strategy
Ask Questions and Clarify Meaning

READ THE SONG pages T186–T188

Pre-Reading Strategies
Listen Actively; Set Purpose

Strategy Focus
Ask Questions and Clarify Meaning

Vocabulary
Multiple-Meaning Words

Comprehension
Before You Move On: Think and Discuss

Grammar Minilesson:
Indefinite Adjectives

RESPOND page T189

CHECK YOUR UNDERSTANDING

Critical Thinking and Comprehension
Sum It Up:
Distinguish Between Apparent Message and Hidden Agenda;
Ⓣ Make Comparisons;
Ⓣ Draw Conclusions
Think It Over: Discuss and Write

Function
Express Yourself: State A Goal

14–20 *A House of My Own* by Sandra Cisneros
STORY ▶ pages T190–T203

PREPARE TO READ page T190

Activate Prior Knowledge
Describe Places

Vocabulary Ⓣ
Relate Words

Reading Strategy
Ⓣ Confirm Word Meanings

READ THE SELECTION pages T191–T200

Pre-Reading Strategies
Preview and Predict
Identify Genre: Story
Set Purpose

Strategy Focus
Ⓣ Confirm Word Meanings

Vocabulary
Use Words in Context
Word Origins
Idioms

Comprehension
Before You Move On: Think and Discuss

Grammar Minilessons:
Modals
Two-Word Verbs
Ⓣ Complex Sentences

Literary Analysis Minilesson:
Style and Word Choice

RESPOND pages T201–T203

CHECK YOUR UNDERSTANDING

Critical Thinking and Comprehension
Sum It Up:
Ⓣ Confirm Word Meanings;
Make Inferences;
Predict Outcomes
Think It Over:
Discuss and Write

Function
Express Yourself:
Express Probability

LANGUAGE ARTS AND LITERATURE

Literary Analysis
Ⓣ Use Similes

Writing
Write a House Poem

CONTENT AREA CONNECTIONS

Fine Arts
Create a Dream House

Technology/Media
Evaluate Web Sites

BUILD WRITING SKILLS — WRITING THAT DESCRIBES
DESCRIPTIVE: CHARACTER SKETCH ▶ Pages T204–T210

Writing Mode/Form
Ⓣ Descriptive Writing
Character Sketch

Writing Process Ⓣ
Prewrite; Draft; Revise; Edit and Proofread; Publish

Writer's Craft
Ⓣ Introductory Sentence
Ⓣ Word Choice

Grammar in Context
Ⓣ Adjectives, Adverbs, and Prepositional Phrases

Reflect and Evaluate
Self-Assessment

Ⓣ = Assessed on **Unit 3 Test** Ⓣ = Assessed on **Unit 3 Language Acquisition Assessment**

Theme-Related Resources

THEME 1: What Matters Most

MORE RESOURCES

THEME LIBRARY

The Lotus Seed
by Sherry Garland
[B] A lotus seed that travels from Vietnam to America helps a family remember its heritage. (Available from Hampton-Brown)

Mandela
by Floyd Cooper
[I] The life story of Nelson Mandela, who has spent his life making a better future for South Africa. (Philomel)

Going Home
by Nicholasa Mohr
[A] While on vacation in Puerto Rico, Felita realizes that what matters most is family and friends. (Penguin)

The Gold Coin
by Alma Flor Ada
[I] Set in Central America, this is a story about Juan, a thief who discovers that there are things in life more valuable than gold. (Macmillan)

The Dragon Prince
by Laurence Yep
[A] In this tale by an award-winning author, a farmer's daughter discovers that inner beauty is more important than what appears on the surface. (HarperCollins)

The Miracle Worker
[B] [I] [A] The inspiring story of Helen Keller, struck deaf and blind by a tragic childhood illness, who learns to communicate through the tireless efforts of her teacher, Annie Sullivan. **Film/Video**

THEME 2: Toward a Better Future

MORE RESOURCES

THEME LIBRARY

The Milkman's Boy
by Donald Hall
[I] A family crisis convinces a family to update their dairy business using the new pasteurization process. (Available from Hampton-Brown)

Follow the Drinking Gourd
by Jeanette Winter
[B] The story of Peg Leg Joe, an old man with a wooden leg who leads slaves north to freedom. (Knopf)

The House on Mango Street
by Sandra Cisneros
[A] Young Esperanza dreams of leaving her rundown neighborhood to make a better life for herself. (Knopf)

Dreaming of America: An Ellis Island Story
by Eve Bunting
[A] Annie Moore sails from Ireland with her two young brothers to be reunited with their parents in America, and is the first immigrant to be processed through Ellis Island. (Troll)

The Bus Ride
by William Miller
[I] This story, by an award-winning author, tells how Sara's courage changes her future. (Lee & Low)

Life in Pioneer America
[B] [I] [A] First-person accounts and musical selections enliven the interactive story of pioneers in search of a better future on America's western frontier. Capture cursor allows instant note-taking. (Queue) **CD-ROM**

[B] Beginning [I] Intermediate [A] Advanced

UNIT 3

Assessment Options

ONGOING, INFORMAL ASSESSMENT

Check for understanding and achieve closure for every lesson with the targeted questions and activities in the **Close and Assess** boxes in your Teacher's Edition.

INDIVIDUAL AND GROUP-ADMINISTERED TESTS

The **Assessment Handbook** includes these comprehensive assessment tools for Unit 3:

- **Selection Tests**
  Test students' mastery of reading strategies and the vocabulary, comprehension, and language arts skills taught with each main selection of Unit 3.
- **Unit Test in Standardized Test Format**
  The multiple-choice sections of this test measure students' cumulative understanding of the skills and language developed in Unit 3. A Writing Prompt measures progress in writing skills and fluency. The Read, Think, and Explain section offers open-ended items to measure strategies and comprehension.
- **Language Acquisition Assessment**
  To verify students' ability to use the vocabulary and grammar structures taught in Unit 3, conduct these performance assessments.

UNIT 3 ASSESSMENT OPPORTUNITIES

	Assessment Handbook Pages
Unit 3 Language Acquisition Assessment	41–42
Selection Tests	
Ginger for the Heart	43–44
Twins	45–46
The Great Migration	47–48
A House of My Own	49–50
Unit 3 Writing Assessment	51
Unit 3 Self-Assessment Form	52
Unit 3 Test	53–60
Peer-Assessment Form	101
Portfolio Evaluation Form	103

SELF- AND PEER-ASSESSMENT

Students use the Unit 3 Self-Assessment Form in the **Assessment Handbook** to evaluate their own work and develop learning strategies appropriate to their needs. Students offer feedback to their classmates with the Peer-Assessment Form.

WRITING ASSESSMENT / PORTFOLIO OPPORTUNITIES

You can evaluate students' writing using the rubrics and scoring guidelines provided in the **Assessment Handbook**. Then collaborate with students to choose work for their portfolios.

INTRODUCE UNIT 3

OBJECTIVES

Function: Engage in Discussion

Concepts and Vocabulary: Dreams—*problems, decisions, goals, results, outcome, future*

Viewing: Interpret a Visual Image

Critical Thinking and Learning Strategies: Use Graphic Organizers (map); Relate Goal and Outcome; Preview; Build Background

INTRODUCE UNIT CONCEPT

1 **Read the Title and Visualize** Ask: *What does it mean to follow your dream? If you close your eyes and imagine following your dreams, what do you see?*

2 **Interpret the Illustration** Direct students' attention to the castle in the illustration. Say: *Imagine that your dream is locked in that castle. Pretend you are in the cart, traveling toward your dream.*

Ask students to brainstorm what is locked in the castle, what problems might be encountered *en route* and decisions they will make to overcome them. Record ideas.

Use the Brainstorm Prompts in the **Multi-Level Strategies** to involve all students.

3 **Create Maps of the Journey** Point out the map behind the illustration. Have students draw an imaginary map, representing the train tracks, water, and castle. Then invite them to record other problems and mark their path to the castle, showing how they overcame the problems.

4 **Summarize Learning in a Mind Map** Invite students to share their maps and discuss their decisions. Then have them vote on one dream to record in a class mind map. Instruct them to leave the rest of the map open to add other dreams as they go through the unit, both their own and ones they read about. Then, discuss the last question on page 141.

UNIT 3 **Dreams and Decisions**

Another Place, Another Time, Chris Van Allsburg, pencil. Copyright © 1996.

140

REACHING ALL STUDENTS

Multi-Level Strategies

BRAINSTORM PROMPTS

BEGINNING Ask questions about the illustration: *Where do these tracks go before they get to the castle—over the water, land, or mountains? Will it be easy or hard to get to the castle?* Prompt students to contribute ideas about problems that could be encountered.

INTERMEDIATE To begin the brainstorm, prompt students to describe what is locked up in the castle: *What would you want to find in the castle? What is most important to you? What might make it difficult to get to your dream?*

ADVANCED Encourage students to expand the brainstorm by providing ideas about how to overcome problems mentioned by others. Elicit information about the decisions that would be made as part of this process.

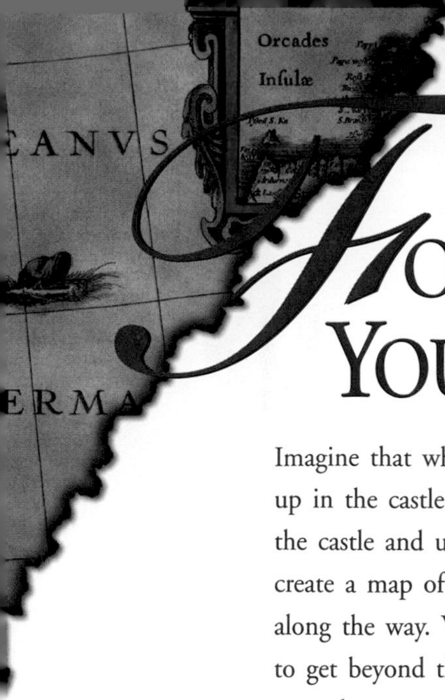

Follow Your Dreams

Imagine that what matters most to you is locked up in the castle in this picture. You must get to the castle and unlock it. Work with a partner to create a map of your journey. Include problems along the way. What decisions must you make to get beyond them? What does it take to reach your dreams?

THEME 1

What Matters Most

Knowing what is important in life can help you reach your dreams and achieve your goals.

THEME 2

Toward a Better Future

Courage and determination can help build a better future.

141

UNIT 3 Mind Map

Dream:	Problem:	Decision:	Outcome:
1. Get something from the castle.	1. Castle is far away across the water.	1. Put a sail on the cart.	1.
2.	2.	2.	2.
3.	3.	3.	3.

Technology Support
See **Inspiration** Visual Learning software for support in creating the mind map.

PREVIEW UNIT THEMES

5 Preview Theme 1: What Matters Most Read aloud the theme statement. Define *dreams* as "what we hope will happen" and *goals* as "plans we make for the future."

Point out that reaching one's dreams and goals can be difficult and may take a long time. Ask: *What are your goals in life? How do you plan to reach your dreams?*

Invite students to leaf through pages 142–164. Discuss the illustrations that show examples of dreams and goals.

6 Preview Theme 2: Toward a Better Future Read the theme title and statement. Ask students what the statement means to them. Invite students to share some of their ideas about a better future. Then leaf through pages 168–200 to find out about some dreamers who worked toward a better future.

7 Set up Student Mind Maps Have students draw the mind map in their notebooks or start the map in the **Practice Book**. Encourage them to record:

- a dream they have for their future
- a problem that might stand in their way
- decisions they can make to overcome the problem
- the expected outcome

Students can record other dreams, problems, and decisions as they move through the unit.

▶ **Practice Book** page 63

CLOSE AND ASSESS

Ask:
- *What will this unit be about?* (dreams and decisions)
- *Why are dreams important?* (because they can help you think of new possibilities)
- *How do you make decisions based on dreams?* (You make decisions that will help make your dreams become reality.)

PREPARE TO READ

OBJECTIVES

Function: Engage in Discussion

Concepts and Vocabulary: Life Experience—*decisions, influences, values*

Viewing: Interpret a Visual Image

Learning Strategies: Relate to Personal Experiences; Use Graphic Organizer (chart)

Critical Thinking: Classify; Generate Ideas

Representing: Collage

TAP PRIOR KNOWLEDGE

1 Share What Matters Most Ask: *What things matter most to you?* Brainstorm categories and write them in a chart. Have students write at least one important item for each category.

Category	Item
People	parents
Talents	
Beliefs	honesty

Say: *In this unit, you'll learn about decisions that people have made to achieve what is most important to them.*

VIEW, DISCUSS, AND PRESENT

2 Interpret a Visual Image Invite students to look at the illustration. Read the caption aloud. Ask: *Who are these people?* (mother, father, child) *How do you know?* (caption and posture of figures) *What do you think matters most to this family? What do you think matters most to the baby? To the mother? To the father?*

3 Present a Collage of Things That Matter Have students make collages of the things that are important to them using original drawings, photos, and pictures cut from magazines.

Use the Presentation Options in the **Multi-Level Strategies** to help all students participate.

Family Group, Henry Moore, bronze. Copyright © 1948–49.

142 **Unit 3** | Dreams and Decisions

REACHING ALL STUDENTS

Multi-Level Strategies

PRESENTATION OPTIONS

BEGINNING Point out specific pictures or drawings in the collages and ask questions, such as: *I see a young woman carrying books and going into a building. Is going to college important to you? Do you know what you want to study in college? Are you thinking about being a doctor?*

INTERMEDIATE Invite students to display their collages to partners and to ask each other questions: *Arun, why did you include a picture of a dog? What does the mountain in your picture mean?* As a group, relate what is revealed in the collages to the mind maps students have begun.

ADVANCED Invite students to describe their collages to the class and explain how each picture relates to their dreams and goals. Encourage elaboration about the problems and decisions they will need to address.

Annotations offer strategies for
B Beginning students

THEME 1

What Matters Most

- How do life's experiences help us find out what matters most? **B Restate:** How do things that happen to us show us what matters to us?
- How do other people influence what we think is important? **B Pose choices:** Do your friends influence what you value? Your parents? Who else?
- How do you think people's dreams affect their decisions? **B Encourage elaboration:** Have students name dreams they have.

HEME-RELATED BOOKS

he Lotus Seed
y Sherry Garland
lotus seed that travels from ietnam to America helps a amily remember its heritage.

EGINNING

Mandela
by Floyd Cooper
The story of Nelson Mandela, who has spent his life making a better future for South Africa.

INTERMEDIATE

NOVEL

Going Home
by Nicholasa Mohr
While on vacation in Puerto Rico, Felita realizes that what matters most is family and friends.

ADVANCED

143

DISCUSS THE GUIDING QUESTIONS

4 Set the Theme Some key points to develop during the discussion are:

- When we evaluate each life experience we can discover what matters most to us. We can see how events and experiences help us set our goals.
- People influence us by what they say and do. If we admire someone, we tend to value what they value. Before letting the opinions of others influence us, we must be sure they have our best interests at heart.
- People will make decisions that will move them toward their dreams. If the dream is strong enough, a person will make very difficult decisions to reach it. For example, if getting an education is important to you, you will make the difficult decision to do your homework instead of going out with your friends.

Form groups and use the **Multi-Level Strategies** so all students can participate.

CLOSE AND ASSESS

Have students draw a backpack shape, and then write words that represent what is most important to them inside it.

Multi-Level Strategies

GROUPING GUIDELINES

BEGINNING Group these students so you can define words and pose choices for responses. See suggestions in red on the facsimile for page 143.

INTERMEDIATE Have partners work together to answer the questions. Invite students to identify people who have influenced them and decisions those people made to reach their dreams. Have pairs of students explain to the group how these people helped them discover what matters most.

ADVANCED Have students write a journal entry that answers the guiding questions and describes one important life experience they have had.

THEME LIBRARY

■ ***The Lotus Seed*** by Sherry Garland
Encourage students to read *The Lotus Seed* and compare it to "Ginger for the Heart" and "Twins." Points of comparison may include: similarities and differences between a lotus seed and a ginger root; the significance of each plant in the lives of characters; what mattered most to Grandmother and to Yenna.

BUILD LANGUAGE AND VOCABULARY

OBJECTIVES

Function: Listen Actively; Ⓣ Tell a Story
Concepts and Vocabulary: Descriptive Words
Patterns and Structures: Ⓣ Adjectives, Adverbs, and Prepositional Phrases
Speaking: Storytelling
Viewing: Interpret Visual Information
Learning Strategy: Use Graphic Organizers (story map)
Critical Thinking: Generate Ideas; Classify

START WITH A COMMON EXPERIENCE

Tape 1B
CD 1 Track 4

1 Listen to a Story Play "The Rooster and the Jewel" on the **Language Tape/CD** or read aloud the folk tale on page T413 as students view the illustrations. Then discuss the story.

Use the Questioning Techniques in the **Multi-Level Strategies** to involve all students.

2 Model How to Tell a Story Present these guidelines.

How to Tell a Story
- Begin by introducing the characters.
- Tell when and where the story takes place.
- Tell about a problem the character has.
- Tell what happens next.
- Tell how the problem gets solved and end the story.

Then play the tape again as a model of telling a story. Ask students to write key events on notecards. Use them to create a story map that traps the information about character, setting, and story events.

Build Language and Vocabulary

TELL A STORY

Listen to this tale from Vietnam about a rooster who learns what matters most to him.

The Rooster and the Jewel

A VIETNAMESE TALE

REACHING ALL STUDENTS

Multi-Level Strategies

QUESTIONING TECHNIQUES

BEGINNING Clarify the meanings of *rooster, jewel,* and *kernel of corn.* Have students look at the illustrations as you ask questions: *Who is the main character? What is he doing? Does he have a problem? Can a jewel help him?*

INTERMEDIATE Have students identify key story events and answer questions about the sequence of the story: *What happened first? Next?* Then encourage heterogeneous small groups to ask one another questions about the story: *What was the rooster looking for? Why didn't the rooster want the jewel?*

ADVANCED Have students speculate about the storyteller's reason for telling this story. *What lesson does the story teach? Why does the rooster believe the jewel is worth less than a kernel of corn? Would you keep the jewel if you were hungry?*

AKE A STORY MAP

ɔrk with a group to plan a story about something that matters most you. Choose the object or event. Then fill out a story map to name e characters, tell the setting, and outline the events in the plot.

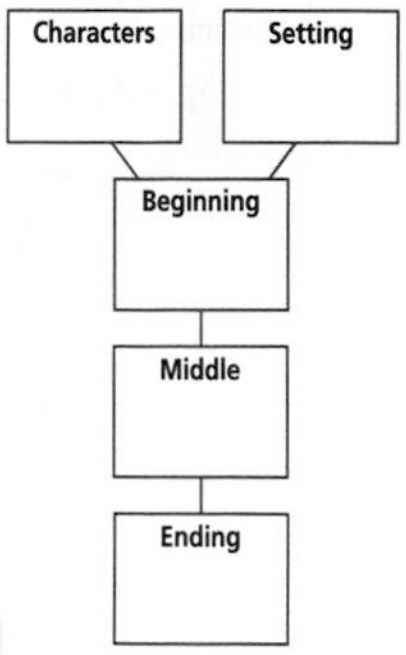

JILD YOUR VOCABULARY

scriptive Words Think of words you will use to describe the story's aracters and setting. Collect them in the charts.

Character	What is the character like?	What does the character do?	How, when, and where does the character do things?
Yolanda	young smart	She skates. She seems to fly.	quickly before dark through the park

Setting	What can you see?	What can you hear?	What can you smell?	What can you taste?	What can you touch?
n afternoon in a park	trees lake	birds traffic	smoke food cooking	hamburger	earth grass

E LANGUAGE STRUCTURES

ADJECTIVES, ADVERBS, AND PREPOSITIONAL PHRASES

eaking: Tell a Story Use your story map and the descriptive words in your arts to tell your story. Divide the story into parts so that each member of ur group will have a part to tell.

Example:

Yolanda **quickly** gathered her skates and went **to the park**. She wanted to skate all **around the lake before dark**. She seemed to fly **through the park**, but then made a **sudden** stop. There **in the trees** she saw flames and smelled smoke. . . .

CONDUCT THE ACTIVITIES

3 Make a Story Map Review the terms *characters, setting,* and *events* with students. Then allow brainstorming time to plan the story.

4 Build Your Vocabulary: Descriptive Words Point out that telling about what we can see, hear, touch, taste, and smell helps a reader appreciate a story.

5 Use Language Structures: Adjectives, Adverbs, and Prepositional Phrases Present the skill, using the definitions and examples on **Transparency 34.** Point out that adverbs and prepositional phrases can both be used to tell where or when. Then have students add details to the sentences in Try It!

Speaking: Tell a Story Conduct the activity at the bottom of page 145.

Use the Speaking Activity Options in the **Multi-Level Strategies** to adjust instruction.

▶ **Practice Book** page 64

CLOSE AND ASSESS

Ask students to list words to describe the way their favorite animal looks and acts. Then have them complete these sentences, using adjectives, adverbs, and prepositional phrases: *My favorite animal is a ______. It is ______, and ______. It has ______. It moves ______.*

Multi-Level Strategies

SPEAKING ACTIVITY OPTIONS

BEGINNING Have students draw pictures to show the main events in their part of the story. Ask yes/no questions about the pictures and record key words. *Is there a dog?* (yes) *Is the dog spotted?* (yes) Write *spotted dog.* Ask students to label their pictures by copying the key words.

INTERMEDIATE Have partners from each group work together and agree on the best way to retell their section of the story. Let them spend time practicing before the class presentation.

ADVANCED These students can act as directors. They can help students compile their story map ideas and then lead the rehearsals for each section of the storytelling. Encourage student directors to plan props and gestures for the groups to incorporate into the presentation.

Transparency 34 / Master 34

ADD DETAILS TO SENTENCES

You can add adjectives, adverbs, or prepositional phrases to a sentence to make it more interesting.

A squirrel scrambles.

A red squirrel scrambles quickly across the garden.
(red: adjective; quickly: adverb; across the garden: prepositional phrase)

1. An **adjective** describes a noun or pronoun.
   The **huge** barn has a **blue** door. It is **full** of animals.
2. An **adverb** tells "how," "where," or "when." Adverbs usually tell more about a verb.
   We pet the bull **carefully**. The chickens live **outside**.
3. A prepositional phrase also tells "where" or "when." It starts with a **preposition** and ends with a noun or pronoun.
   The pigs live **across** the barnyard. (prepositional phrase)

Try It!

Add details to these sentences. Use adjectives, adverbs, and prepositional phrases.

1. The rooster ran home.
2. I lost the jewel.
3. The chicks found nothing to eat.
4. I saw the animals.

Transparency 34 Level B, Unit 3 | Dreams and Decisions © Hampton-Brown

PREPARE TO READ

OBJECTIVES

THINK ABOUT WHAT YOU KNOW

Reading Strategy:
Activate Prior Knowledge

LEARN KEY VOCABULARY Ⓣ

Vocabulary Strategy:
Use New Words in Context

LEARN TO RELATE GOALS AND OUTCOMES

Reading Strategy:
Ⓣ Relate Goals and Outcomes

THINK ABOUT WHAT YOU KNOW

1. **Discuss Dreams and Goals** Present a two-column chart labeled *Dreams* and *Goals*. Write key words on the chart as students give examples.

LEARN KEY VOCABULARY

2. **Use New Words in Context** Read the vocabulary words. Clarify meanings and conduct the cloze activity.

   Use the Vocabulary Options in the **Multi-Level Strategies** to tailor the activity to proficiency levels.

▶ **Practice Book** page 65

LEARN TO RELATE GOALS AND OUTCOMES

3. **Model How to Relate Goals and Outcomes** Demonstrate the steps in the box with **Transparency 35**:
   - Read the first paragraph aloud.
   - Fill in columns 1 and 2 on the chart. Define *goal* as what you want to accomplish. There might be several goals. Then record the actions the character takes to reach her goal.
   - Define *outcome* as the result of trying, whether or not you succeed. Have students think about the goal and actions, and then predict the outcome.
   - Read the second paragraph together. Add information to the chart.

CLOSE AND ASSESS

Ask students to write an example of a personal goal and an outcome on an exit slip.

Ginger *for the* Heart

Prepare to Read

historical fiction
by Paul Yee

THINK ABOUT WHAT YOU KNOW

Discuss Dreams and Goals Talk about how a person's dreams and goals show what matters to that person.

craftsmanship skill or ability to do special work

debt money that is owed to another person

epidemic sickness or disease that affects most of the people in a place

garment piece of clothing

ginger root part of ginger, a spice plant, that grows underground

gold field place where gold is found

merchant person who sells things to make money

miner worker who digs in the earth for minerals

tailor person who makes and mends clothes to earn money

tower tall and narrow structure or building

Answers to the vocabulary activity:
1. epidemic
2. miners
3. debts
4. tower
5. Merchants
6. craftsmanship
7. garments

LEARN KEY VOCABULARY

Use New Words in Context Study the new words and their definitio[n]
Then write the paragraph, adding the missing words.

In 1849, gold fever spread like an ___(1)___ around the world. Chinese immigrants and many others rushed to California. They worked as ___(2)___ in the gold fields. Some of them had to repay huge ___(3)___ when they arrived. In their dreams, they saw gold coins stacked as high as a ___(4)___. Some of the new immigrants did not become miners, however. ___(5)___ opened stores and sold goods. Tailors used their ___(6)___ to sew ___(7)___.

LEARN TO RELATE GOALS AND OUTCOMES

In a story, a **goal** is what a person wants to do. The **outcome** tells if the person reaches the goal. When you know the goals and outcomes of a story, you understand the main events of the plot.

READING STRATEGY

How to Relate Goals and Outcomes
1. Look for what the people want to do.
2. Pay attention to the actions they take to reach their goals.
3. Predict the outcome. Then see if the outcome at the end of the story matches your prediction.

As you read "Ginger for the Heart," take notes on the characters' goals, their actions, and the final outcome of the story.

REACHING ALL STUDENTS

Multi-Level Strategies

PRACTICE OPTIONS FOR USING ADJECTIVES

BEGINNING Group students to read ***Friends Are Like That*** or the Key Points Reading on **Master 36**. (See page T149.) Work with the vocabulary in those selections.

INTERMEDIATE Work with students as a group to decide where to place vocabulary words in the paragraph.

ADVANCED Encourage students to write the paragraph on their own, and then read it aloud with a partner.

Transparency 35 / Master 35

RELATE GOALS AND OUTCOMES

Directions: Read the first paragraph. Record the character's goals and actions. Predict an outcome. Read the second paragraph. Add information to the chart. Check your prediction.

In 1849, Fu Tien was living with her parents in China. She heard s[tories] about gold in California. Fu Tien wanted to be rich. She sold her cart [to] get the money for the trip. In California she worked hard digging for [gold]. After a year, the money was almost gone and she had found no gold.

Character	Goal	Actions	Outcome
Fu Tien	to be rich	• sold her cart • went to California • dug for gold • built a cart • made dumplings to sell	opened three restaurants in San Francisco and became r[ich]

Then Fu Tien had an idea. She took the last of her money and bui[lt a] cart. She made dumplings and sold them to people in the mining ca[mps]. She earned enough money to move to San Francisco and start a sma[ll] restaurant. Soon she owned three very large restaurants. Fu Tien did[n't] find gold in the mines, but she did find gold in San Francisco.

Transparency 35 Level B, Unit 3 | Dreams and Decisions © Hampt[on-Brown]

Ginger for the Heart

by Paul Yee

Yenna and a young man fall in love. Before he leaves on a journey, she gives him a ginger root to remind him of her. When he returns four years later, they are both amazed that the ginger has remained firm and fragrant—a symbol of their love and devotion. They learn that what means the most to them is always being together.

READ THE SELECTION

OBJECTIVES

Reading Strategies: Preview; Predict
Literary Analysis: Historical Fiction

INTRODUCE THE SELECTION

4 **Preview and Predict** Read aloud the title, author's name, and introduction to the story. Lead a discussion about the introduction. Ask: *How do you think Yenna and the young man learned what means most to them?* Next, have students page through the story and read the summary statements for each section.

5 **Identify Genre: Historical Fiction** Use the illustration to help students establish the setting for the story (19th century Chinatown, San Francisco). Explain that historical fiction is usually set in the past in a real time and place. Many of the characters and events are based in reality, while others may be invented by the author. Encourage students to look for both historical and fictional elements in the selection.

Ginger for the Heart
by Paul Yee

Theme Connection When Yenna and her young man discover what matters most to them, they overcome all obstacles to make their dream come true.

Selection Summary and Background The introduction on page 147 of the student book offers a summary. When word of gold in California reached China at the end of the 19th century, many young men emigrated. Some looked for gold; others opened laundries and stores around San Francisco. Later they sent for their wives and children to join them.

Author Awards Author Paul Yee received the Governor General's Literary Award for Children's Literature in 1996 and Honorable Mention for the Canada Council Literature Prize in 1986.

THE BASICS BOOKSHELF

■ ***Friends Are Like That*** by Daphne Liu

Trust is at the very heart of real friendship. That is what the friends in this story learn when a misunderstanding threatens their special relationship. The simple text describing their confrontation and reconciliation builds basic vocabulary about feelings, while the illustrations provide opportunities to talk about familiar teen pastimes and interests.

For Lesson Plans: See the Teacher's Guide for ***The Basics Bookshelf***.

READ PAGES 148–149

OBJECTIVES

Function: Read a Selection
Listening: Listen to a Selection
Vocabulary Strategy:
Use Context Clues to Meaning
Reading and Learning Strategies:
Set a Purpose for Reading;
Use Graphic Organizers (chart);
T Relate Goals and Outcomes
Comprehension: Identify Details; Identify Cause and Effect; Make an Inference

SET PURPOSE

1 Read aloud the introduction. Set the purpose: *Look for the details that show how Yenna and the young man meet and how they feel about each other.*

READ AND THINK

Tape 3A CD 3 Track 1

2 **Strategy Focus: Relate Goals and Outcomes** As students read this section, have them use the Goal-and-Outcome Chart to record information on characters' goals and actions.

Choose Reading Options in the **Multi-Level Strategies** to tailor the reading to proficiency levels.

The recording of "Ginger for the Heart" on the **Selection Tape/CD** offers an oral language model and the opportunity to build reading fluency.

Red annotations offer opportunities to clarify meaning and check for understanding.

1

YENNA FALLS IN LOVE

Yenna meets a young man in the store where she works, and he visits her often. They fall in love, but he must leave for the gold fields so he can earn money.

Build background: This story tells about a time long ago. Chinese immigrants had to make difficult decisions as they tried to follow their dreams.

The buildings of **Chinatown** are **stoutly constructed** brick. While some are **broad** and others thin, they rise no higher than four solid **stories**.

Only one building stands above the rest. Its **tower is visible** even from the harbor, because the cone-shaped roof is made of copper.

In the early days, Chang the **merchant tailor** owned this building. He used the main floor for his store and rented out the others. But he kept the tower room for his own use, for the sun filled it with light. This was the room where his wife and daughter worked.

Ask: What is the tower room used for?

His daughter's name was Yenna, and her beauty was **beyond compare**. She had ivory skin, sparkling eyes, and her hair hung long and silken, shining like **polished ebony**. All day long she and her mother sat by the tower window and sewed with silver needles and **silken** threads. They sang songs while they worked, and their voices **rose in wondrous harmonies**.

In all Chinatown, the **craftsmanship** of Yenna and her mother was considered the finest. Buttonholes never stretched out of shape, and **seams** were **all but invisible**.

One day, a young man came into the store **laden with garments** for **mending**. His shoulders were broad and strong, yet his eyes were soft and caring. Many times he came, and many times he saw Yenna. For hours he would sit and watch her work. They fell deeply in love, though few words

Ask: How do Yenna and her mother make work more pleasant?

Chinatown the part of town where Chinese people live and work
stoutly constructed well built
broad wide
stories floors in a building
is visible can be seen
beyond compare greater than any other's
polished ebony very smooth dark wood
silken smooth, very fine
rose in wondrous harmonies sang beautiful, enjoyable music
seams the parts of clothing where two pieces of cloth are sewn together
all but invisible very hard to see
laden with carrying a lot of
mending sewing, patching up, or restoring

REACHING ALL STUDENTS

Vocabulary
DESCRIBING WORDS

Point out the many vivid descriptive terms in the story, such as *cone-shaped roof, sparkling eyes,* and *silken threads.* Elicit students' visualizations of the terms. Divide the class into groups. Have each group select an object from the classroom and make a web of descriptive terms for the object.

Multi-Level Strategies
READING OPTIONS FOR LESSONS 4–6

BEGINNING Students can work with ***Friends Are Like That*** while the class reads "Ginger for the Heart." Or, distribute copies of **Master 36** to conduct a Key Points Reading of "Ginger for the Heart." Work as a group with **Transparency 37** to construct one or two notes about the characters' goals, actions, and the final outcome in the story.

INTERMEDIATE Read the story aloud, or play the recording on the **Selection Tape/CD**, pausing to clarify meaning. Use the red annotations on the facsimile pages. Have pairs of students record characters' goals, actions, and outcomes on copies of **Master 37** as the group reading progresses.

ADVANCED Have students read the selection with a partner. Distribute copies of **Master 37** and invite students to record characters' goals, actions, and outcomes independently as they read.

ere spoken between them.

Spring came and boats bound for the orthern **gold fields** began to sail again. was time for the young man to go. e had borrowed money to pay his way over to the New World, and now he had to repay his **debts**. Onto his back he threw his blankets and tools, food and warm jackets. Then he set off with **miners** from around the world, clutching **gold pans** and shovels.

Ask: Why does the young man leave? Where is he going?

BEFORE YOU MOVE ON...

1. **Details** What special skills and qualities did Yenna have?
2. **Inference** Did Yenna and her mother enjoy working together? How do you know?
3. **Cause and Effect** Why did the young man have to go to the gold fields?

old pans metal dishes used to separate gold from ater, gravel, and dirt

REVIEW KEY VOCABULARY

3 Use Context Clues to Meaning

With students, identify the new vocabulary words on pages 148–149. Read aloud the sentences containing the words: *tower, merchant tailor, craftsmanship, garments, gold fields, debts,* and *miners.* Suggest that students read other words and phrases near the new word for clues to its meaning. Then have students look up the new words in a dictionary to verify definitions.

CHECK COMPREHENSION

4 Answers to "Before You Move On"

1. **Details** Yenna was a very fine tailor. She was very beautiful and had a pleasant singing voice.
2. **Inference** Yes, they did enjoy working together. We know this because they sang together.
3. **Cause and Effect** The young man had to go to the gold fields to pay back the money he had borrowed to come to the New World.

CLOSE AND ASSESS

Have students share the information they wrote on their Goal-and-Outcome Chart. Check to make sure they have included information for both Yenna and the young man.

Transparency 36 / Master 36

KEY POINTS READING

Ginger for the Heart

A young girl named Yenna works in her father's store in San Francisco. She meets a young man and they fall in love. The young man goes to northern California to look for gold. He says he will come back and marry her. She decides to wait for him.

Yenna gives the young man a ginger root to take with him. Every night Yenna lights a lamp in the window and thinks of the young man. As the years pass, her mother dies, and her father becomes blind.

After four years, the young man returns. He shows her the ginger root. It is still new and fresh. The young man is rich now. He asks Yenna to move to a big, new house in the country. Yenna says she must stay with her father. The young man is angry. He throws the ginger root in the fire, but it doesn't burn. It stays new and fresh, just like their love for each other.

Yenna and the young man decide to stay together. They have a big wedding and Yenna's father is very happy. Soon after, he dies and the couple moves to their new house in the country.

Transparency 36 Level B, Unit 3 | Dreams and Decisions © Hampton-Brown

Transparency 37 / Master 37

GOAL-AND-OUTCOME CHART

Directions: Fill in the chart as you read each section of the selection. When you finish, check your prediction.

Ginger for the Heart

Character	Goal	Actions	Outcome
Yenna	• be with the young man	• waits for young man • refuses to marry	Her father dies, and Yenna marries the young man.
	• care for her father	• refuses to leave with the young man	
Young man	• repay his debts	• goes to the gold fields	The young man marries Yenna and stays in her house until her father dies.
	• marry Yenna	• buys farm and builds house for Yenna • asks her to move to the farm	

Transparency 37 Level B, Unit 3 | Dreams and Decisions © Hampton-Brown

HOME CONNECTION

Parting Gifts Send home a copy of *High Point Newsletter 5* in the **Teacher's Resource Book.** In this home activity, students ask about gifts that family members received when they parted from someone. These gifts may be treasured family mementos that have special stories behind them. Students create an illustration to tell about a family treasure of this sort.

READ PAGES 150–151

OBJECTIVES

Function: Read a Selection
Listening: Listen to a Selection
Reading and Learning Strategies: Set a Purpose for Reading; Use Graphic Organizers (chart); Ⓣ Relate Goals and Outcomes
Comprehension: Identify Character's Motive, Traits; Ⓣ Make Comparisons
Literary Analysis: Description

SET PURPOSE

1 Read aloud the introduction to the second section and briefly discuss the picture. Set the purpose for reading: *As you read, notice what happens while the young man is away in the gold fields.*

READ AND THINK

Tape 3A
CD 3 Track 1

2 **Strategy Focus: Relate Goals and Outcomes** Involve students in reading pages 150 and 151 of the selection and in adding more information to the Goal-and-Outcome Chart.

See the **Multi-Level Strategies** on page T148 to tailor the reading experience to all proficiency levels.

2

THE GINGER ROOT

Yenna gives the young man a ginger root as a goodbye gift. He promises to come back. For four years she works hard and waits patiently for his return.

Ask: What message does Yenna give to the young man?

Yenna had little to give him **in farewell**. All she found in the kitchen was a **ginger root** as large as her hand. As she stroked its brown **knobs** and bumpy eyes, she whispered to him, "This will warm you in the cold weather. I will wait for you, but, like this piece of ginger, I, too, will age and grow dry." Then she pressed her lips to the ginger, and turned away.

"I will come back," the young man said. "The fire burning for you in my heart can never be **extinguished**."

Thereafter, Yenna lit a lamp at every nightfall and set it in the tower window. Rains **lashed against** the glass, snow piled low along the ledge, and ocean winds rattled the frame. But the flame did not **waver**, even though the young man never sent letters. Yenna did not weep uselessly, but continued to sew and sing with her mother.

Pose choices: Will the young man come back or will he forget Yenna?

in farewell to say goodbye, as a goodbye gift
knobs bumps, hard lumps
extinguished put out
lashed against hit hard on
waver seem to go out, flicker

REACHING ALL STUDENTS

CULTURAL PERSPECTIVES

U.S. and World Cultures: Chinatowns
In U.S. cities such as San Francisco and New York—and in other cities around the world—Chinese immigrants settled close to each other to preserve links to their homeland. These Chinatowns still attract Chinese immigrants, as well as tourists, and are cultural centers. Have each group of students find out about various aspects of life in one Chinatown. Then they explain their information as they record it on a class chart.

Links to the Homeland

	San Francisco	New York
Foods		
Customs		
Education		
Businesses		

Language Development
EXPRESS FEELINGS

Explain that people often give gifts to friends and loved ones who are going away. Have students identify a symbolic gift, to whom they would give it, and what they would say to explain its symbolism. Teach farewell expressions, such as: *Good-bye. Take this with you for good luck; I brought this from my homeland;* and *I hope you will remember me when you use this.*

There were few unmarried women in hinatown, and many men came to seek enna's hand in marriage. ich gold miners and sons f successful merchants owed before her, but she ways looked away. They ave her grand gifts, but ill she shook her head, ntil **finally** the men grew eary and called her crazy. China, parents arranged ll marriages, and daughters ecame the property of their usbands. But Chang the erchant tailor **treasured** his daughter's appiness and let her be.

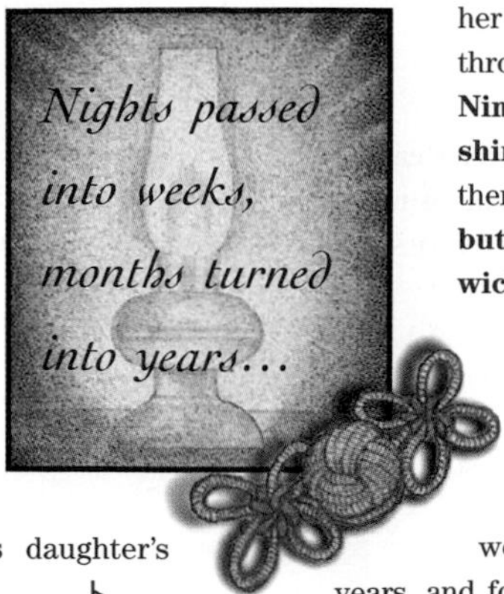

One winter, an **epidemic ravaged** the ty. When it was over, Chang had lost his ife and his **eyesight**. Yenna led him up to e tower where he could feel the sun and rifting clouds move across his face. She egan to sew again, and while she sewed, e sang for her father. The lamp continued burn **steadily** at the tower window as she worked. With twice the amount of work to do, she labored long after **dusk**. She fed the flame more oil and sent her needle **skimming** through the heavy **fabrics**. **Nimbly** her fingers **braided shiny cords** and **coiled** them into **butterfly buttons**. And when the **wick sputtered** into light each evening, Yenna's heart soared **momentarily** into her love's memories. Nights passed into weeks, months turned into years, and four years quickly flew by.

Ask: How is Chang different from other Chinese fathers?

Define *soared*: flew high. **Ask:** How does Yenna feel when she looks at the light? Why?

BEFORE YOU MOVE ON...

1. **Character's Motive** Why did Yenna give the young man the ginger root?
2. **Character** How did Yenna and her father show how much they cared for each other?
3. **Comparison** How were the burning lamp and Yenna's love for the young man similar?

nally at last
easured valued, cared a lot about
vaged destroyed, did great damage to
vesight ability to see
eadily all the time
usk the time between sunset and night
kimming moving quickly
brics cloth
Nimbly Easily and quickly
braided shiny cords wove or wrapped together three or more bright strings
coiled twisted and turned
butterfly buttons buttons made with twisted string
wick sputtered flame on the candle began to burn
momentarily for a very short time

CHECK COMPREHENSION

3 Answers to "Before You Move On"

1. **Character's Motive** Yenna wanted the young man to keep a remembrance of her with him. The ginger root was the only gift she could find.
2. **Character** Yenna stayed with her father and took care of him. Her father respected her desires and did not force her to marry someone she did not love.
3. **Comparison** The lamp kept burning brightly, and Yenna's love for the young man remained strong.

CLOSE AND ASSESS

Have students revisit the mind maps they created at the beginning of the unit and add a row showing Yenna's and the young man's dreams, problems, decisions, and outcomes.

Literary Analysis Minilesson

▶ DESCRIPTION

TEACH Tell students that writers often use descriptions to give the reader a clear picture of a person, place, or thing. Readers can use all five senses to help them visualize the description.

Read aloud the first paragraph on page 150. Ask students to visualize the way the ginger and Yenna look when they are young, and how Yenna says they will look as they age. Invite students to tell which senses they used in their visualizations.

PRACTICE Have pairs of students look through the story for descriptive passages, discuss their visualizations, make a chart to record their findings, and share their charts with the class.

Description	Visualization	Senses Used
Rains lashed. . .	Noisy, heavy rain; fresh	Sight, sound, touch, smell

▶ **Practice Book** page 66

READ PAGES 152–153

OBJECTIVES

Function: Read a Selection
Vocabulary Strategy: Structural Clues (prefixes)
Listening: Listen to a Selection
Reading and Learning Strategies: Set a Purpose for Reading; Ⓣ Relate Goals and Outcomes; Use Graphic Organizers (chart); Confirm Word Meaning
Literary Analysis: Characterization; Dialogue

SET PURPOSE

1 Read aloud the introduction to pages 152–154. Set the purpose for reading: *Read to find out if Yenna and the young man achieved their goals.*

READ AND THINK

Tape 3A
CD 3 Track 1

2 **Strategy Focus: Relate Goals and Outcomes** Involve students in reading pages 152–154 of the selection. Be sure they add information about the outcome to the Goal-and-Outcome Chart.

Use the **Multi-Level Strategies** on page T148 to tailor the reading experience to proficiency levels.

3

THE YOUNG MAN RETURNS

The young man asks Yenna to marry him, but she can't leave her father. The still-fresh ginger is a sign that they should stay together.

Pose choices: While the young man was gone, did he relax or work hard?

One day a dusty traveler came into the store and flung a bundle of **ragged** clothes onto the counter. Yenna shook out the first shirt, and out rolled a ginger root. Taking it into her hand, she saw that pieces had been nibbled off, but the core of the root was still firm and **fragrant**.

She looked up. There stood the man she had promised to wait for. His eyes appeared older and wiser.

"Your gift saved my life several times," he said. "The fire of the ginger is powerful indeed."

"Why is the ginger root still firm and heavy?" she wondered. "Should it not have dried and **withered**?"

"I kept it close to my heart and my sweat **coated** it. In lonely moments, my tears soaked it." His **calloused** hands reached out for her. "Your face has not changed."

Encourage elaboration: How might the gift have saved his life?

"Nor has my heart," she replied. "I have kept a lamp burning all these years."

"So I have heard," he smiled. "Will you come away with me now It has taken many years to gather enough gold to buy a farm. I have bui you a house on my land."

For the first time since his departure, tears **cascaded** down Yenna's face. She shook her head. "I cannot leave. My father needs me."

"Please come with me," the young man pleaded. "You will be very happy, I promise"

Yenna swept the **wetness** from her cheeks. "Stay with me and work this store instead," she **implored**.

Pose choices: Should Yer go or stay? Why?

ragged torn and ripped
fragrant had a strong, pleasant smell
withered lost its firm shape
coated covered
calloused rough, hard
cascaded fell, poured
wetness tears
implored begged

REACHING ALL STUDENTS

Health Connection

MEDICINAL PLANTS

Have students research the medicinal uses of plants such as ginger, aloe vera, garlic, or cinnamon. Students can find information in reference and medical texts, on Web sites, or by interviewing an herbalist or health care professional. They can display information on an individual poster and record data on a class chart. To help students express their findings, provide sentence frames as necessary.

Class Chart

Name of Plant	Medicinal Uses
Aloe vera	Heals burns
Ginger	Aids digestion

Sentence Frames

The plant _____ grows in _____.

The (leaves, roots, berries) are useful for _____.

I found my information by _____.

Ask: How do you think Yenna feels when he throws the ginger root into the fire?

The young man stiffened and stated roudly, "A man does not live in his wife's ouse." And the eyes that she remembered) well gleamed with determination.

"But this is a new land," she cried. Must we forever follow the old ways?"

She reached out for him, but he brushed er away and **hurled** the ginger root into e fireplace. As the flames leapt up, enna's eyes **blurred**. The young man **clenched and unclenched** his fists in anger. They stood like stone.

At last the man turned to leave, but suddenly he knelt at the fireplace. Yenna saw him reach in with the tongs and pull something out of the flames.

"Look!" he whispered in amazement. "The ginger refuses to be burnt! The flames cannot touch it!"

Ask: Why do you think the root isn't burning?

urled angrily threw
urred could not see clearly
enched and unclenched tightened nd let go

EXPAND VOCABULARY

3 Use Negative Prefixes Read aloud this sentence on page 153: *The young man clenched and unclenched his fists in anger.* Ask students to demonstrate the two actions and explain how the prefix *un-* changes the meaning of a word. Discuss other examples of negative prefixes from the story: page 148, *seams were all but invisible;* page 151, *There were few unmarried women in Chinatown.* Then ask students to give other examples they have encountered elsewhere.

MONITOR YOUR READING

4 Confirm Word Meaning Point out the words defined at the bottom of each page of the story. If students have difficulty understanding a paragraph containing several unfamiliar words, suggest that they reread it aloud, substituting the definition for the original wording.

Learning Styles

STRATEGIES FOR CONSTRUCTING MEANING

Arrange groups that include students with various learning styles. Invite each group to choose a scene from the story to act out as a skit.

- **Visual Learners** Have students design and create a set and program art.
- **Auditory Learners** Encourage students to select and produce music and sound effects for the skit.
- **Kinesthetic Learners** Have students write stage directions and act out the scene.

Literary Analysis Minilesson

▶ CHARACTERIZATION AND DIALOGUE

TEACH Read the paragraph on page 152 that begins *For the first time.* Tell students that writers often use dialogue, or words spoken by a character, to show the character's personality. Ask: *What do you learn about Yenna from what she says?*

PRACTICE Have teams of students look for dialogue spoken by Yenna, her father, and the young man, and discuss what it reveals about each speaker. Teams can share their information with the class and record it on a chart.

Character	Dialogue	Characterization
Yenna	I cannot leave. My father needs me.	Yenna is loyal to those she loves.
Father		
Young Man		

▶ **Practice Book** page 67

READ PAGE 154

OBJECTIVES

Comprehension: Form Opinions; Identify Character's Motive; Summarize

Literary Analysis: Evaluate Impact of Author's Background on Literature

CHECK COMPREHENSION

5 **Answers to "Before You Move On"**

1. **Opinion** Answers will vary. Students may say the request is fair since Chinese women often leave their families when they marry.
2. **Character's Motive** Yenna felt that her father needed her.
3. **Summary** After their marriage and the death of Yenna's father, the couple goes away together.

ABOUT THE AUTHOR

6 **Evaluate Literature: Author's Background** Read About the Author. Ask: *How did the author show his feelings about being "caught between two worlds"?*

CLOSE AND ASSESS

Have students add the final outcomes to their Goal-and-Outcome Charts and share the information they recorded.

Yenna looked and saw black burn marks charring the root, but when she took it in her hand, she found it still firm and moist. She held it to her nose, and found the **fragrant sharpness** still there.

The couple embraced and vowed to stay together. They were married at a **lavish banquet** attended by all of Chinatown. There, the father passed his fingers over his son-in-law's face and nodded in satisfaction.

Ask: What changed the young man's mind?

Shortly after, the merchant Chang died, and the young couple moved away. Yenna sold the business and locked up the tower room. But on nights when boats pull in from far away, they say a **flicker** of light can still be seen in that high window. And Chinese women are reminded that ginger is one of their best friends.

Pose choices: Does the tower light comfort people or frighten them?

BEFORE YOU MOVE ON...

1. **Opinion** Was it fair for the young man to ask Yenna to leave her father? Explain your answer.
2. **Character's Motive** Why did Yenna refuse to leave her father?
3. **Summary** Tell how the story ends.

ABOUT THE AUTHOR

Paul Yee grew up in Chinatown in Vancouver, British Columbia, Canada, where he felt "caught between two worlds." His stories are a mix of history and his imagination. The Chinese folk tales he heard as a child blend with his true accounts of Chinese immigrants contributions to settling North America. Yee says that in his writing, he looks ahead with hope. His motto is "From the past, for the future."

fragrant sharpness strong smell
lavish banquet large meal served to entertain and celebrate a special event
flicker small or faint glow

REACHING ALL STUDENTS

Cooperative Learning

FOR CRITICAL THINKING: Make and Support Judgments

Consider Questions Model stating a judgment and finding information to support it in the text. Then have students consider: *Who is the strongest character? Wisest? Most faithful?*

Think and Talk Allow Think Time for students to privately process and reflect. Then have them formulate group answers during Talk Time.

State and Support Judgments During Share Time, call on one student from each group to give the group's answers and support them.

Debrief the Content Direct students to share insights they gained from the discussion, for example: *What new information about a character did you find? Did you change your initial judgment? Why? Why not?*

Debrief the Cooperative Process Have students share examples of how Think and Talk Times helped them support their judgments.

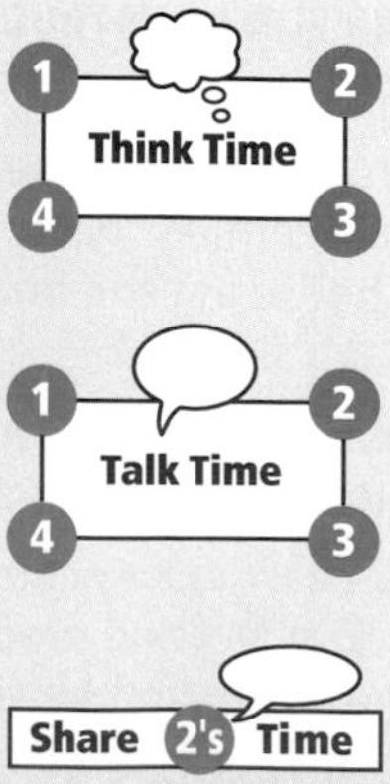

Cooperative Learning Structure: Numbered Heads

Respond to the Story

Check Your Understanding

UM IT UP

elate Goals and Outcomes in a Retelling omplete a Goal-and-Outcome Chart like this ne and use it to retell the story to a partner.

Character	Goal	Actions	Outcome
Yenna			
the young man			

enerate Ideas Discuss actions the characters ould have taken. How might these new actions hange the outcome of the story? Choose your est idea, think of a new story ending, and share with the class.

THINK IT OVER

Discuss and Write Talk about these questions with a partner. Write the answers.

1. **Summary** Tell what matters most to Yenna. How do you know? Is it the same for the young man? Use details from the story to support your answer.
2. **Conclusions** Why do you think this story is called "Ginger for the Heart"? What would be another good title?
3. **Opinion** Do you think Yenna and the young man will have a long and happy marriage? Identify details in the story that support your opinion.
4. **Judgment** Yenna had to wait four years for the young man to return. What things do you think are worth waiting for?

EXPRESS YOURSELF ▸AGREE OR DISAGREE

As a class, act out part of the story in which two characters disagree and later agree on something. Take turns with different actors playing the scene. You might also choose different scenes for different pairs of actors. If possible, bring some ginger root and other props to include in your dramatizations.

Ginger for the Heart **155**

Multi-Level Strategies

SUM IT UP OPTIONS

BEGINNING Use the Key Points Reading on **Master 36**. (See page T149.) Write phrases that indicate the goals and have students match them with descriptions of the outcomes. Ask volunteers to read aloud one goal and outcome.

INTERMEDIATE Have pairs compare their Goal-and-Outcome Charts and retell the story to each other. Partners then brainstorm how the outcome might have differed if the characters had made different decisions.

ADVANCED Students use their Goal-and-Outcome Charts to retell the selection. Then have each student change two specific decisions in the story, one by Yenna and one by the young man. The partners then tell the story to each other, showing how the suggested changes influence the final outcome.

RESPOND

OBJECTIVES

SUM IT UP

Functions: Retell a Story; Engage in Discussion

Reading Strategy: Ⓣ Relate Goals and Outcomes; Use Graphic Organizers (chart)

Critical Thinking: Synthesize Information; Generate Ideas

THINK IT OVER

Function: Engage in Discussion

Critical Thinking and Comprehension: Summarize; Ⓣ Draw Conclusions; Form Opinions; Make Judgments

EXPRESS YOURSELF

Function: Agree or Disagree

Speaking and Listening: Dramatize

CHECK YOUR UNDERSTANDING

1 **Sum It Up** Annotations on the Goal-and-Outcome Chart on **Transparency 37** (see page T149) provide sample answers.

▶ **Practice Book** page 68

2 **Think It Over** Possible answers are:

1. **Summary** Yenna: honor; stayed with her father; stayed true to her young man. Young man: money and Yenna; worked hard; lived in Yenna's house when he did not want to.
2. **Conclusions** Yenna gave the ginger root to represent the love in her heart. Other titles will vary.
3. **Opinion** The marriage is likely to last because Yenna and her husband care enough to make difficult decisions.
4. **Judgments** Answers should reflect high or difficult goals.

3 **Express Yourself** Prompt the use of new vocabulary and convincing arguments in the dramatization.

CLOSE AND ASSESS

Ask: *What did you learn from Yenna and the young man about reaching your goals?* Students write their answers on an exit card.

RESPOND

OBJECTIVES

ADJECTIVES

Grammar: Adjectives

WRITE AN OUTCOME

Function: Write; Engage in Discussion

Critical Thinking: Generate Ideas;
T Relate Goals and Outcomes

Representing: Goal-and-Outcome Chart

Writing: Story

LANGUAGE ARTS AND LITERATURE

1 **Use Adjectives** Possible answers for "Add Adjectives" are:

1. Yenna sewed with **silver** needles and **silk** thread.
2. The **handsome** man held the **fragrant** ginger in his **strong** hand.

A possible paragraph for "Practice" is:

The **noisy** streets of Chinatown are interesting to see. There are **many ancient** buildings in this part of the city. Some have **brick** walls and **tall, narrow** windows. One building has a **high, round** tower with a **copper** roof.

▶ **Practice Book** page 69

2 **Write an Outcome** Some ideas for changes in action are:

- Yenna leaves her father.
- The young man stays in the fields.

▶ **Practice Book** page 70

CLOSE AND ASSESS

Ask students to write a sentence using adjectives to describe a character in light of new actions and outcomes.

ASSESSMENT
Selection Test 9 on page 43 of the Assessment Handbook tests students' mastery of the reading strategies and the vocabulary, comprehension, and language arts skills taught with this selection.

Respond to the Story, continued

Language Arts and Literature

GRAMMAR IN CONTEXT

USE ADJECTIVES

Learn About Adjectives An **adjective** is a word that describes, or tells about, a noun.

Adjectives can tell how many or how much.

Yenna waited **four** years.
Yenna had **little** interest in marrying.

Adjectives can tell which one.

Yenna shook out the **first** shirt.

Adjectives can tell what something is like.

The ginger was **fragrant** and **moist**.
The **young** man asked Yenna to marry him.

Proper adjectives come from proper nouns. They begin with a capital letter.

Chang was from China. He was **Chinese**.

Add Adjectives Expand these sentences with adjectives.

1. Yenna sewed with ________ needles and ________ thread.
2. The ________ man held the ________ ginger in his ________ hand.

Practice Write this paragraph. Add an adjective in each blank.

The ________ streets of Chinatown are interesting to see. There are ________ buildings. Some have ________ walls and ________ windows. One building has a ________ tower with a ________ roof.

WRITING/SPEAKING

WRITE AN OUTCOME

Think of the new endings to the story you discussed with your group in the Sum It Up activity on page 155. How would the characters actions change in order to cause a new outcome? Would their goals also change? Make a chart to organize your ideas. Then write the new outcome.

1. **Complete a Chart** Fill in a new Goal-and-Outcome Chart like the one you made on page 155.
2. **Write a Draft** Write the main events of the beginning, middle, and end of the new story. Include dialogue that shows what the characters' goals are.
3. **Edit Your Work** Add, change, or take out text to make your story more interesting. Do the characters have believable goals? What is the final outcome? Finally, check for correct spelling, punctuation, and grammar.
4. **Read and Discuss** Read your work in a group. Discuss the goals and actions that caused the new outcomes.

For more about the **writing process**, see Handbook pages 408–413.

LANGUAGE ACQUISITION ASSESSMENT
See page 41 of the Assessment Handbook

REACHING ALL STUDENTS

Multi-Level Strategies

PRACTICE OPTIONS FOR USING ADJECTIVES

BEGINNING List additional examples of each type of adjective in a chart with headings. Draw examples from the classroom: *three students, red sweater, long hair, last book, Spanish music.* Complete Practice exercises with students. Provide choices for answers or identify the type of adjective needed for each blank.

INTERMEDIATE Have students work with a partner to complete the Practice exercises. Review the answers with students. Discuss their choices.

ADVANCED Students can complete the Practice exercises independently and trade papers with a partner for review. Partners should make any necessary revisions together.

ontent Area Connections

SOCIAL STUDIES

:SEARCH THE GOLD RUSH

arn About the Gold Rush A gold rush is the dden movement of people to a place where ld has been discovered. Chinese immigrants ere among those who came to California in the 00s in search of gold. Create a class bulletin ard display about this event in U.S. history.

rite Questions What would you like to know out the California gold rush? Write questions ch as:

Where did people come from?

How long did the gold rush last?

How did the gold rush change California?

splay Answers Work in groups. Use ference books and the Internet to find answers your questions. Make a poster with the formation you find. Include art and photos. en display your poster.

Prospectors panned for gold in rivers and streams.

MATHEMATICS

COMPARE TRAVEL RATES

In the 1800s, many Chinese immigrants came from Hong Kong to San Francisco by boat. Today you can travel between the two cities by plane. With a partner, calculate the rates of travel.

1. **Set Up a Data Grid** In 1851, the *Solida* reached San Francisco from Hong Kong, a distance of over 6,955 miles. The trip took 48 days or about 1,152 hours.

   Contact an airline and ask how long a flight from Hong Kong to San Francisco takes. Ask the distance (miles or kilometers) of the flight. Use this information to make a data grid.

Means of Travel	Distance	Time	Rate
Boat—1851	6,955 miles	1,152 hours	6 mi/hr
Plane—today	6,915 miles	14 hours	494 mi/hr

The time it takes to travel by plane might vary slightly.

2. **Calculate the Rate of Travel** To get the rates, divide the distance by the time. Add the rates to your chart.

$$\frac{\text{500 miles}}{\text{5 hours}} = \text{100 miles per hour}$$

3. **Make Comparisons** Share your charts with another pair. How many times longer did it take to travel in the 1800s than it does today? What other conclusions can you reach?

Research Skills

USING MAPS

TEACH Display a map of the United States. Explain how the compass rose (or north arrow) helps people understand directions. Point out cities to the east, west, north, or south of another feature (river, state line).

Point out the scale and explain its use: *One inch on the map equals ____ miles (kilometers) on the ground.* Explain that each map has a unique scale for the area it depicts.

Model using the scale. Locate your town and another city. Measure the map distance between them and guide students in applying the scale to determine the distance.

PRACTICE Have pairs of students choose places of interest and use a map to determine the distance between them. Then have them give directions to the location (go south ____ miles, then east ____ miles).

▶ **Practice Book** page 71

RESPOND

OBJECTIVES

RESEARCH THE GOLD RUSH

Function: Give Information

Critical Thinking, Learning Strategies and Research Skills: Formulate Questions; Gather Information; Use Maps

Representing: Bulletin Board Display

Writing: Questions; Poster

COMPARE TRAVEL RATES

Function: Give Information

Learning Strategies and Research Skills: Gather Information; Take Notes; Organize and Synthesize Information; T Make Comparisons

Representing: Chart

CONTENT AREA CONNECTIONS

1 **Research the Gold Rush** Brainstorm questions and post a list.

For Multi-Level Strategies: Guide Beginners to locate appropriate reference materials. Model how to use key words. Work as a group to find pictures and write captions.

Encourage Intermediate students to turn answers to the questions into captions for their pictures.

Advanced students can conduct the research in pairs and write short paragraphs for their pictures.

2 **Compare Travel Rates** Model how to:

- use the formula with several different sets of data
- complete the chart with the results of your models

Have pairs of students exchange papers to check calculations.

▶ **Practice Book** page 72

CLOSE AND ASSESS

Ask each student: *What is one thing you learned about the Chinese immigration during the Gold Rush?*

PREPARE TO READ

OBJECTIVES

THINK ABOUT WHAT YOU KNOW

Reading Strategy: Activate Prior Knowledge

LEARN KEY VOCABULARY T

Vocabulary Strategy: Use New Words in Context

LEARN TO PARAPHRASE

Reading Strategy: T Paraphrase

THINK ABOUT WHAT YOU KNOW

1 **Pantomime** You might set up this activity as a game of charades with two teams competing to guess the words first. Then discuss which words were the most difficult or easiest to communicate.

LEARN KEY VOCABULARY

2 **Use New Words in Context** Have students read each vocabulary word and its definition. Clarify meanings. Then conduct the activity.

Use the Vocabulary Options in the **Multi-Level Strategies** to tailor the activity to proficiency levels.

▶ **Practice Book** page 73

LEARN TO PARAPHRASE

3 **Model How to Paraphrase** Demonstrate the steps in the box with **Transparency 38**:

- Read the first sentence of the paragraph aloud and identify unfamiliar words or phrases.
- Say: Hereditary *looks like* inherit. *I think this means that some people are deaf because their parents are also deaf.*
- Continue reading and have students paraphrase each sentence with a partner. Have the class agree on the paraphrase and write it on the chart.

CLOSE AND ASSESS

Ask: *What new fact about deafness did you learn from this lesson? What are you still curious about?*

TWINS

article
by Debra and Lisa Ganz,
with Alex Tresniowski

Prepare to Read

THINK ABOUT WHAT YOU KNOW

Pantomime Take turns drawing an index card with the names of different activities on it. Act out each word. Discuss how people communicate without speaking.

advanced up-to-date, the most recent

condition health or physical state

confident feeling sure of yourself, believing in yourself

determined have one's mind set on doing something

excel do something extremely well and better than others

extraordinary very unusual, special

hearing-impaired unable to hear or hear well

independent able to do things alone or without help

opportunity chance to do something

secure safe, without worry or fear

Answers to the vocabulary activity will vary.

LEARN KEY VOCABULARY

Use New Words in Context Study the new words and their definitions. Choose two words that go together, and write them in the same sentence.

Sample Sentence

There are many advanced technologies to help hearing-impaired people.

LEARN TO PARAPHRASE

When you **paraphrase** something, you repeat it in your own words. Use this strategy to help you understand difficult words or phrases.

READING STRATEGY

How to Paraphrase

1. As you read, think about the words and phrases mean.
2. Use your own words to tell what you just read.

As you read "Twins," stop and paraphrase each section of the article.

REACHING ALL STUDENTS

Multi-Level Strategies

VOCABULARY OPTIONS

BEGINNING Group students to read ***Friends Are Like That*** or the Key Points Reading on **Master 39**. (See page T161.) Work with the vocabulary in those selections.

INTERMEDIATE Challenge small groups of students to write as many sentences that use two or more of the words as they can.

ADVANCED After students have completed the activity independently, invite them to compare original sentences with a partner.

Transparency 38 / Master 38

HOW TO PARAPHRASE

Directions: Read the paragraph one sentence at a time. Write unfamiliar words and phrases in the chart under "What It Says." Paraphrase sentences that are difficult to understand and write your own words in the chart under "What It Means."

Sometimes deafness is hereditary. Sometimes it is a result of trauma or illness. Some people are born deaf, and some lose their hearing later in life. Deaf people can learn to communicate with each other and with hearing people. Some deaf people speak, and others don't. Some deaf people read lips. Most hearing-impaired people use their hands to "talk" in sign language.

Not every hearing person uses the same spoken language. Likewise, not every deaf person uses the same sign language. There are many sign languages throughout the world. For instance, American Sign Language uses different symbols, words, and phrases than British Sign Language or Australian Sign Language.

What It Says (Quotation)	What It Means (Paraphrase)
Sometimes deafness is hereditary.	Some people are deaf because their parents are deaf.
Sometimes it is a result of trauma or illness.	Sometimes it is because of accidents or being sick.
Most hearing-impaired people...	Most deaf people...

Transparency 38 Level B, Unit 3 | Dreams and Decisions

TWINS

by Debra and Lisa Ganz, with Alex Tresniowski

What matters most to twins Neshmayda and Suzette is staying close to each other. Born deaf, they helped each other learn sign language to communicate. They went to school and played sports together. Now that they are both married and will soon live in different cities, their goal is to maintain their extraordinary closeness.

159

READ THE SELECTION

OBJECTIVES

Reading Strategies: Preview; Predict
Literary Analysis: Article

INTRODUCE THE SELECTION

4 **Preview and Predict** Read aloud the title and introduction. Ask: *What are the symbols under the title?* (the word *twins* spelled in sign language) *What are the girls doing with their hands?* (communicating in sign language) Have students page through the article and predict what it will be about.

5 **Identify Genre: Article** Explain that the authors of this article interviewed real people to find out about the lives of these deaf twins. Ask: *What did the authors write about?* (what they learned from the twins and their parents) *Is everything in the article true?* (yes) An article is nonfiction when it relates facts about a topic.

Twins
by Debra and Lisa Ganz, with Alex Tresniowski

Theme Connection This article tells of the dreams of deaf twins and how they help each other make decisions to achieve what they want in life.

Selection Summary The introduction on page 159 of the student book offers a summary of the selection.

Background Hearing people may believe that deaf people can't talk, learn, write, and draw. They may think they can't enjoy music or watch TV. It is important for students to understand that deaf people can do everything hearing people can do, except hear. Decoders that print captions on television screens allow deaf people to watch TV. Hearing aids can help some deaf people hear.

THE BASICS BOOKSHELF

■ ***Friends Are Like That*** by Daphne Liu

Two girls, more like sisters than friends, share everything, until one of them suspects the other of also sharing her feelings for her boyfriend. The simple text describing their confrontation and reconciliation introduces basic vocabulary about feelings, while the realistic illustrations provide opportunities to talk about familiar teen pastimes and interests.

For Lesson Plans: See the Teacher's Guide for ***The Basics Bookshelf***.

THEME 1 **LESSON 11**

READ PAGES 160–161

OBJECTIVES

Function: Read a Selection
Grammar: Compound Predicates
Listening: Listen to a Selection
Reading and Learning Strategies: Set a Purpose for Reading; Ⓣ Paraphrase; Make Predictions
Comprehension: Make an Inference; Identify Cause and Effect

SET PURPOSE

1 Read aloud the introduction on page 160. Set the purpose for reading: *Find out how the family coped with the twins' deafness when they were young.*

READ AND THINK

Tape 3A CD 3 Track 2

2 **Strategy Focus: Paraphrase** Involve students in reading and paraphrasing text on pages 160–161 of the selection. Have them record the difficult words and their paraphrases in two columns labeled "What It Says" and "What It Means."

Choose Reading Options in the **Multi-Level Strategies** to include students at all proficiency levels.

The recording of "Twins" on the **Selection Tape/CD** offers an oral language model and the opportunity to build reading fluency.

Red annotations offer opportunities to clarify meaning and check for understanding.

1

THE SILENT YEARS

The twins' parents discover that Suzy and Neshy are deaf. They all learn sign language so everyone in the family can communicate with each other.

Build background: It is often said that twins have a special ability to communicate with each other. To Suzy and Neshy, this ability proved to be especially important.

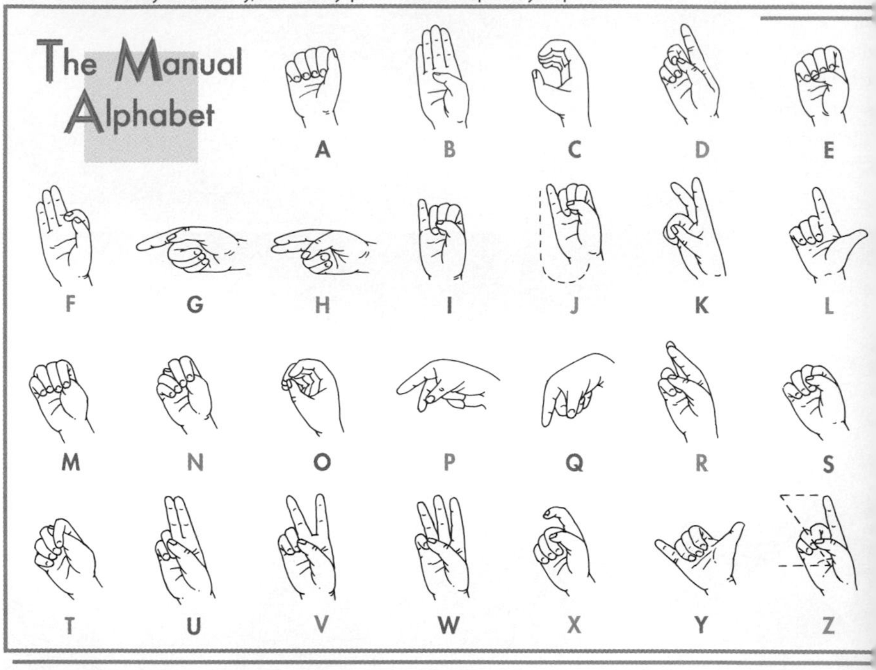

Pause to allow students to practice the manual alphabet.

Early on they knew they were different from other children, because they were the only ones who shared a face. "They loved that about themselves," says Maria Aguayo, mother of Neshmayda and Suzette. "They had a way of communicating that no one else understood. One of them would point at something or make some noise and the other would go and get what she wanted." Two kids **cavorting through** happy world of their own, experiencing life surprises as one—in other words, twins.

But Suzy and Neshy were different for a much greater reason—they were born **deaf**

Clarify: From the time they were very young, they knew they were different from other children because they were the only ones who looked alike.

cavorting through having fun in

deaf without the ability to hear

REACHING ALL STUDENTS

Health Connection

PRENATAL CARE

Invite a health professional to talk about prenatal health and effects of illnesses in pregnant women. Plan the presentation with the guest to make the content comprehensible for students. Use pictures, articles, key words, and definitions to prepare students. Brainstorm questions for the speaker with them. Ask each student to prepare a question. Provide question starters: *What if _____ ? Should a mother _____ ? How can a pregnant woman protect _____ ?*

Multi-Level Strategies

READING OPTIONS FOR LESSONS 11–13

BEGINNING Have students work with ***Friends Are Like That*** while the class reads "Twins." Or distribute copies of **Master 39** to conduct a Key Points Reading of "Twins." As a group, read each paragraph. Together, record paraphrases on a What it Says/What it Means chart.

INTERMEDIATE Read the article aloud, clarifying meaning with the red annotations on the facsimile pages. As partners reread the selection, they can stop after each section to identify difficult sentences, put the sentences into their own words, and record their work on a What it Says/What it Means chart.

ADVANCED Have pairs read the article together, stopping after each section to identify difficult sentences and complete the What It Says/What It Means chart.

Ask: What context clue tells you the meaning of the word *denial*?

Ve did not know it for their first two-and-half years," says Maria, who **contracted** erman measles during her first **trimester**. ıe technology in her native Puerto Rico as not as **advanced** as it is today, so her vins' deafness was not **diagnosed** until ey were nearly three. "And when we first scovered they were deaf, I did not want believe it. It was a mother's denial."

Maria soon accepted her daughters' **ondition**, and as soon as she and her ısband, Joaquin, heard about the Gallaudet :hool for the deaf in Washington, D.C., they oved their family and enrolled the twins, then five years old. "We all learned **sign language** so we could communicate with the girls," says Maria. "We started to talk about all the things that had happened to them in their first five years. I learned all these things that I had not known. For instance, Suzette had once been with her grandmother and **wound up** in the emergency room **getting stitches**. Her grandmother didn't know how she got hurt. Suzy later told me that she had fallen, that she was scared, that she wanted me there with her in the hospital **so badly**. When I discovered these things, I cried and cried."

Pose choices: Did the mother cry because she was happy or sad?

zette (left) and Neshmayda (right) at age six. The ins are wearing hearing aids strapped to their chests they enjoy a day at Baltimore's Inner Harbor.

BEFORE YOU MOVE ON...

1. **Inference** What do you think helped the twins form their own way of communicating?
2. **Cause and Effect** What caused the twins' deafness, and why did it take so long to diagnose?
3. **Prediction** Do you think the twins will remain close as they grow up? Why or why not?

ntracted got, caught
mester three months of being pregnant
ıgnosed discovered by doctors
ɪn language a way to communicate with our hands
wound up in the end was
getting stitches having her cut or wound closed by sewing
so badly so much

CHECK COMPREHENSION

3 Answers to "Before You Move On"

1. **Inference** Answers will vary but should include references to necessity, the need to feel connected, and being the same age. Elicit elaboration.
2. **Cause and Effect** Encourage students to use *because* and *so* in their answers. (The twins are deaf because their mother got German measles while she was pregnant with them. Technology in Puerto Rico was not as advanced as it is today, so they were not diagnosed until they were almost three.)
3. **Prediction** Students' answers will vary but should tend to be positive, based on the tone of the article.

CLOSE AND ASSESS

Ask: *How does paraphrasing help you understand what you read?* Ask students to offer a specific example.

Transparency 39 / Master 39

KEY POINTS READING

Twins

Neshmayda and Suzette are twins. When the twins are two-and-a-half years old their parents discover that Suzy and Neshy are deaf. Now everyone in the family talks using their hands to sign words and feelings.

The twins are never lonely because they have each other. They go to school together. They play sports together. They make friends together. It is important to them to stay close to each other.

Suzy and Neshy both go to college. Now they are planning to marry. Suzy's fiance is a hearing-impaired teacher. He is from Wisconsin. Neshy's fiance is a deaf legal assistant. He lives in Washington, D.C. Neshy and Suzy face living apart for the first time. But the twins know they will always keep their special closeness.

Transparency 39 Level B, Unit 3 | Dreams and Decisions © Hampton-Brown

Grammar Minilesson

▶ COMPOUND PREDICATES

TEACH Remind students that the verb in a sentence tells what the subject is, does, or has. Then write:

The twins' parents moved their family to Washington.

Identify the verb and explain that some sentences have two or more verbs. These verbs are joined by a conjunction and are called a *compound predicate*. Extend the sentence:

The twins' parents moved their family to Washington and enrolled the girls in a school for the deaf.

Have a volunteer underline the two verbs. Point out that both verbs agree with the subject *parents*.

PRACTICE Have students combine sentences, creating a compound predicate.

1. The twins kicked the soccer ball. The twins ran fast.
2. Suzy earns a master's degree. Suzy moves to Wisconsin.

▶ **Practice Book** page 74

READ PAGE 162

OBJECTIVES

Function: Read a Selection
Listening: Listen to a Selection
Reading and Learning Strategies:
Set a Purpose for Reading; Ⓣ Paraphrase
Comprehension:
Form Opinions; Ⓣ Draw Conclusions

SET PURPOSE

1 Set the purpose: *Find out how the twins began to socialize.*

READ AND THINK

Tape 3A
CD 3 Track 2

2 **Strategy Focus: Paraphrase**
Read and paraphrase page 162.

See the **Multi-Level Strategies** on page T160 to involve all students in the reading experience.

CHECK COMPREHENSION

3 **Answers to "Before You Move On"**

1. **Opinion** Elicit elaboration.
2. **Evidence and Conclusion** Answers may vary but should include reference to their doing sports together.

CLOSE AND ASSESS

Have students write a paraphrase of "They are very secure and confident about who they are," on exit slips.

2

SIGNS OF HOPE

The twins are never lonely because they have each other. They learn to play sports and to mix in with other children.

Ask: What was the best thing about being twins?

Ask: What do you think Maria means by a "wall between them and the rest of the wor

The twins helped each other learn signs—more and more signs—**ecstatic** at the **opportunity** to explore each other's feelings in a new way. "Being deaf twins is a very special thing," explains Neshy. "A deaf child in a hearing world can feel very lonely and **secluded**, but we never experienced that. We were always together, never alone. We learned from each other every day, and we still do."

Their parents **exposed them to** hearing children from a very early age, **determined** to **foster their self-sufficiency**. "We would take them to soccer practice, and they would stay behind a little, not daring to go on the field," remembers Maria. "They put up this wall between them and the rest of the world. But after a while they would feel more comfortable. They might get a ball and start kicking it between them, and then before we knew it they were mixing in with the other children."

The twins **excelled** at a number of sports, particularly soccer, and together the helped **establish** a women's varsity team at Gallaudet. They tried waterskiing, they hit t mountain slopes, they talked about one day diving from a plane. "They feel that they ca do anything that they want to do, **except** hear," says their mother. "They are very **secure** and **confident** about who they are and that has come from them being two."

Define *hit the mountain slopes*: they went s

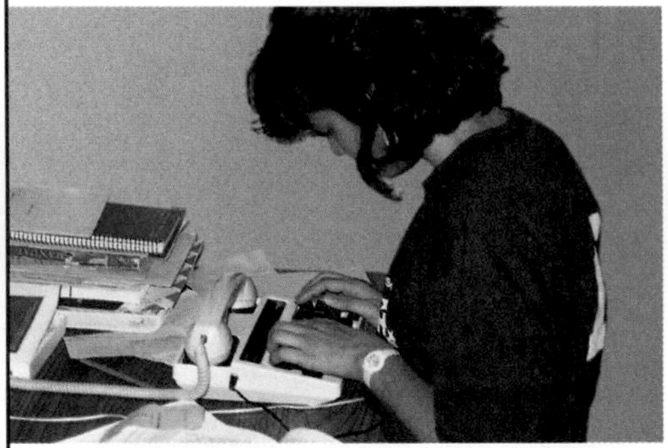

Suzette, age 14, uses a TDD (Telecommunication Device for the Deaf) to talk with a friend. Messages sent and received appear on the screen below the receiver.

BEFORE YOU MOVE ON...

1. **Opinion** Do you think that being deaf helped the twins become closer to each other? Explain.
2. **Evidence and Conclusion** How did playing sports help the twins become secure and confident?

ecstatic very happy
secluded cut off from others
exposed them to kept them around, brought them into contact with
foster their self-sufficiency encourage their ability to take care of themselves
establish start
except but not

REACHING ALL STUDENTS

Mathematics Connection
CAUSES OF DEAFNESS

Ask: *How many people do you know that use a hearing aid?* Explain that hearing loss has many causes. Guide students to resources with statistics about the causes of deafness: print and electronic encyclopedias, Internet, literature from local organizations. Have small groups research topics and make pie charts of their findings. Display their work. Discuss the major causes of deafness: congenital, viral infections, injury, noise.

Vocabulary
LATIN ROOTS

Write words such as *audiocassette, auditorium,* and *audience.* Point out that all of these words contain the root word *aud-*. Ask: *How are the meanings of these words similar?* (They are all related to some sort of listening activity.) Start a list of *aud-* words. Help students discover other related words and their meanings, such as *audit, audible, audition, audiologist,* and add them to the list. Encourage students to add to their clues or individual dictionaries a chart of *aud-* words and their defintions.

3

CLOSER THAN EVER

Even as they prepare to live apart for the first time, the twins know they will always maintain their special closeness.

It is a closeness that will be tested ›w that the twins are facing their first ›**paration**. Suzy and Neshy—who both **ırned master's degrees** in social work— ere also both recently married, Suzy to a **earing-impaired** teacher, and Neshy to a ›af legal assistant. Suzy and her husband ill live in Wisconsin, while Neshy plans to ay behind in Washington, D.C. "Of course, e'll miss each other terribly," says Neshy. Vhen one of us is not present, we feel half npty, so it's going to be really difficult." ır the last few months, "they have been **›eparing themselves** for the separation," ys Maria. "To even start talking about it as **extremely** painful, but they have been tting ready."

Not long ago, when Suzy spent a few eeks in Wisconsin, the twins got a chance see how the separation would go. "It was ally **tough** not being able to communicate th her **regularly**," says Suzy. "I would ite her letters, but by the time she'd read em, it was old news. Thank goodness for e Internet. Now we talk for hours and ›urs on the computer. We need to be able

Suzette (left) and Neshmayda (right) on their wedding day in 1999. In a double ceremony conducted both by speaking and in signing, each twin married a man who is deaf.

to share our feelings all the time, and this way we can."

Busy social lives, dreams of having children, a **passion** for the Internet—perhaps the Aguayo twins are not so different after all. "They are so incredibly **independent**," says their mother. "I can't remember the last time I had to do something for them."

Ask: How does the Internet help the twins cope with being so far apart?

›aration time of not being together
ṙned master's degrees completed advanced lege courses
›paring themselves getting ready
tremely very

tough difficult, hard
regularly every few days or every week, often
passion love

READ PAGE 163

OBJECTIVES

Function: Read a Selection
Grammar: Compound Subjects
Listening: Listen to a Selection
Reading and Learning Strategies: Set a Purpose for Reading; Ⓣ Paraphrase

SET PURPOSE

1 Read aloud the introduction on page 163. Set the purpose for reading: *Read to find out what the future holds for the twins.*

READ AND THINK

Tape 3A CD 3 Track 2

2 **Strategy Focus: Paraphrase** Involve students in reading and paraphrasing pages 163–164 of the selection.

See the **Multi-Level Strategies** on page T160 to involve all students in the reading experience.

INTERNET

SOCIAL STUDIES CONNECTION

Suggest that students use the Internet to prepare a report about the phenomenon of twins. Encourage them to explore such questions as: *How many twins are born in the U.S. today? In the past?* Web sites undergo frequent modification, but here are some to suggest.

Web Sites
www.nomotc.org/incid.htm
www.twinsworld.com
www.multiplebirth.com/first.htm

Grammar Minilesson

▶ **COMPOUND SUBJECTS**

TEACH Remind students that the subject of a sentence tells whom or what the sentence is about. Then, write:

Suzy and Neshy send messages on the Internet.

Underline *Suzy and Neshy* and identify the words as a compound subject. Say: *A* compound subject *has two or more simple subjects joined by* and *or* or.

Use page 428 of the Handbook to teach agreement between a verb and a compound subject.

PRACTICE Have students combine each pair of sentences to make a new sentence with a compound subject.

1. Suzy loves to water-ski. Neshy loves to water-ski.
2. The parents were born in Puerto Rico. The girls were born in Puerto Rico.
3. Scientists study how twins grow. Pediatricians study how twins grow.

▶ **Practice Book** page 75

READ PAGE 164

OBJECTIVES

Vocabulary Strategy: Relate Words

Reading Strategy: Ⓣ Paraphrase

Comprehension: Identify Character's Point of View; Ⓣ Make Comparisons; Make Predictions

REVIEW KEY VOCABULARY

3 Relate Words Form groups. Ask a volunteer in each group to spell a vocabulary word in sign language.

CHECK COMPREHENSION

4 Answers to "Before You Move On"

1. **Character's Point of View** They haven't been separated before; communication will be harder.
2. **Comparison** Talking by computer is faster, but writing letters can feel more personal.
3. **Prediction** Answers will vary.

CLOSE AND ASSESS

Have students paraphrase "A life without sounds has had no impact on the extraordinary love that exists between them."

Neshmayda (left) and Suzette (right) at Gallaudet University in their first year of graduate school.

A life without sounds has had no **impact** on the **extraordinary** love that **exists** between them—they simply found a way to share the quiet music of their souls. What chance do time and distance have of changing the way they feel? "It's true we are becoming more independent of each other," Neshy says. "But it really doesn't matter. The longer we are apart, the closer we become."

Encourage elaboration: How do you think the twins can become closer even though they are apart?

impact effect
exists is

BEFORE YOU MOVE ON...

1. **Character's Point of View** Why will separation be so difficult for Suzy and Neshy?
2. **Comparison** Compare writing letters with "talking" by computer. How are they alike, and how are they different?
3. **Prediction** Do you believe the twins will always remain close? Why or why not?

ABOUT THE AUTHORS

Identical twins **Debbie and Lisa Ganz** know a lot about the special joys and challenges of twinship. They share their experience with other twins, multiples, and their parents through their website and helpline. In addition, they raise funds for twins in need and help reunite twins who have grown up apart. When they opened Twins, a New York City restaurant that is staffed entirely by identical twins, critics called it a silly idea. The Ganz were determined, however, and today their restaurant is a success.

164 Unit 3 | Dreams and Decisions

REACHING ALL STUDENTS

Science Connection

SENSES

Have five groups each research one of the five senses and prepare a report that shows how the sense "works" and how the structure of the human body helps it to work. Encourage students to use multiple sources in their research and to present their findings in ways that relate to their sense. For instance, the sense of sight would be best presented in a visual display, hearing in an oral or audio presentation, touch with tactile props, and so on.

A WORLD OF LANGUAGES

Non-Verbal Language In any language, communication is both verbal and nonverbal. Misunderstandings may result if people are not aware of the traditions of other cultures. Demonstrate the following gestures and explain their meaning in the United States.

GESTURE	MEANING IN THE UNITED STATES
"OK" sign with fingers	"That's great"; "Well done"
placing the fingers to the lips	"Be quiet"
thumbs down	"Poor work"; "I/we disapprove"
shaking the index finger at someone	"Don't do that"; "That's bad to do"

Respond to the Article

Check Your Understanding

IM IT UP

raphrase What mattered most to the uayos? Make a chart to paraphrase the ormation in the selection. Then add specific amples to support your statements.

The Aguayo Family	What Matters Most?	How Do You Know?
aría and oaquin guayo	to help the twins become independent	The text says the parents were "determined to foster their self-sufficiency."
eshy and uzy Aguayo	to stay close no matter what	Neshy says, "The longer we are apart, the closer we become."

mpare and Evaluate Literature Use your arts to compare "Twins" with another ection you have read. You might:

Compare Yenna from "Ginger for the Heart" with the twins.

Compare the genre with "Talking Walls."

Compare the problem and solution with "Teammates."

rite three paragraphs. In the first paragraph, ll how the two selections are alike. In the cond, tell how they are different. In the last ragraph, tell which selection you think is onger and why.

THINK IT OVER

Discuss and Write Talk about these questions with a partner. Write the answers.

1. **Prediction** Do you think Suzy and Neshy will be happy living in two different cities? How might their relationship change?
2. **Opinion** What are the advantages and disadvantages of being a twin?
3. **Inference** Do you think the twins feel that they are "missing out" because they are deaf? How can you tell?
4. **Characters' Motives** What are the twins' dreams? What kinds of decisions did they have to make to follow their dreams?

EXPRESS YOURSELF

▶DEMONSTRATE NON-VERBAL COMMUNICATION

People around the world use gestures to give extra meaning to their words. In a group, demonstrate different kinds of movements and ways of standing. Discuss the meanings of these gestures. How do eye contact and physical closeness affect communication? Compare these gestures with those from other countries.

Multi-Level Strategies

SUM IT UP OPTIONS

BEGINNING Use the Key Points Reading of "Twins" on **Master 39** (see page T161) to help students make their statements. Ask students to find words in the reading to support their statements. Paraphrase the words. Have students echo your paraphrase and write it on the chart.

INTERMEDIATE Have students work in small groups to complete their charts. Students should debate the question of what matters most to Mr. and Mrs. Aguayo and the twins until they agree on an answer. Then they skim the reading to find and paraphrase supporting sentences.

ADVANCED Have students work on the chart on their own. After they complete their charts, they can orally present their statements and sentences from the selection that support them. Students should paraphrase these sentences during their presentation.

RESPOND

OBJECTIVES

SUM IT UP

Function: Write

Reading and Learning Strategies: Ⓣ Paraphrase; Use Graphic Organizers (chart)

Critical Thinking: Ⓣ Make Comparisons

Literary Analysis: Compare Literature; Evaluate Literary Quality

THINK IT OVER

Function: Engage in Discussion

Comprehension and Critical Thinking: Make Predictions; Ⓣ Make Comparisons; Make Inferences; Make Decisions

EXPRESS YOURSELF

Function: Demonstrate Non-Verbal Communication

Speaking and Listening: Gestures

CHECK YOUR UNDERSTANDING

1 **Sum It Up** Students can create a Venn diagram to help compare "Twins" to another selection.

▶ **Practice Book** page 76

2 **Think It Over** Possible answers are:

1. **Prediction** They will miss each other but will communicate often.
2. **Opinion** Advantages: help each other, have fun together Disadvantages: being stared at by others and asked about being twins
3. **Inference** Elicit elaboration.
4. **Characters' Motives** Their dreams are to grow and excel at what they do. They completed their educations and agreed to move apart with their husbands.

3 **Express Yourself** Define *gesture* and model common gestures such as shrugging shoulders to mean "I don't know." Elicit common gestures from home cultures.

CLOSE AND ASSESS

Have partners share and discuss their literary comparisons. Ask students to use the feedback to make changes.

RESPOND

OBJECTIVES

ADJECTIVES THAT COMPARE

Grammar:
T Comparative and Superlative Adjectives

WRITE TO A TWIN

Function: Write

Technology/Media: Use E-mail; Use Word-Processing Software

Writing: Letters

LANGUAGE ARTS AND LITERATURE

1 Use Adjectives That Compare
Answers to the Practice items are:

1. greater
2. finest
3. more confident
4. most difficult

▶ **Practice Book** page 77

2 Write to a Twin Demonstrate using e-mail software. If possible, set up e-mail boxes for partners to send and receive e-mail at different computer stations. Arrange time for students to use computers.

If e-mail is not available, encourage students to write letters using word-processing software, and either print them or save them electronically for their partners to read.

CLOSE AND ASSESS

Ask students to compare written communications with spoken conversations. Encourage them to use comparative and superlative adjectives in their comparisons.

ASSESSMENT
Selection Test 10 on page 45 of the Assessment Handbook tests students' mastery of the reading strategies and the vocabulary, comprehension, and language arts skills taught with this selection.

Respond to the Article, continued

Language Arts and Literature

GRAMMAR IN CONTEXT

USE ADJECTIVES THAT COMPARE

Learn About Comparative Adjectives A **comparative adjective** compares two things. To make the comparison, add **–er** to the adjective and use the word **than.**

Neshy's hair is **longer than** Suzy's.

If the adjective is a long word, use **more** or **less.**

Neshy is **more independent than** Suzy.

Learn About Superlative Adjectives A **superlative adjective** compares three or more things. Add **–est** to the adjective. Use **the** before the adjective.

Suzy is **the fastest** runner in her class.

If the adjective is long, use **the most** or **the least.**

The most important thing to the twins is staying in touch.

Practice Write these sentences. Use the correct form of the adjective in parentheses.

1. Some hearing-impaired people have a (great) hearing loss than others do.
2. Gallaudet is perhaps the (fine) school in the world for hearing-impaired students.
3. When they learned sign language, the twins were (confident) than before.
4. The (difficult) time of all came after the twins were separated.

TECHNOLOGY/MEDIA
WRITING

WRITE TO A TWIN

With a partner, take the roles of Suzy and Neshy. Pretend that you have been apart for one month. Write a series of letters or e-mails to each other.

1. **Choose a Topic** Here are some possible topics for your first letters:
   - future dreams or plans
   - life in your new city or home
   - an upcoming visit
   - family and friends
2. **Start the Series** One partner writes the firs letter or e-mail. The other partner reads it and writes back. Write several more letters o e-mails back and forth.
3. **Check Your Work** Check your work before sending it to your "twin." Check for correct spelling and punctuation.

For more about **e-mail**, see Handbook page 382.

REACHING ALL STUDENTS

Multi-Level Strategies

PRACTICE OPTIONS FOR COMPARATIVE AND SUPERLATIVE ADJECTIVES

BEGINNING Give students additional examples of comparative and superlative forms. Elicit examples from students or prompt them by writing equations: *soft + er = softer.* Complete the Practice exercises with students. Identify the type of adjective needed for each blank and provide two choices for each answer.

INTERMEDIATE Students can work with a partner to complete the Practice items. Discuss and revise the exercises together.

ADVANCED Students can complete the Practice items independently and compare their papers with a partner for review. Have students look back at the selection and use comparative and superlative adjectives in three new sentences about the twins.

ntent Area Connections

IAL STUDIES

'ARCH CONTRIBUTIONS OF THE
RING IMPAIRED

:e a class book with the information
find about the contributions of the
'ng impaired.

hoose a Person With a group, choose a
earing-impaired artist, teacher, or leader
at you would like to know more about.
ere are a few suggestions:

Ludwig van Beethoven, composer

Helen Keller, author

I. Jordan King, President of
Gallaudet University

Marlee Matlin, actress and spokesperson

ather Information You can find
formation about the person you chose in
ooks and encyclopedias or through a search
n the Internet.

lake a Class Book Write a short biography
article about the person. Tell about his or
er challenges and achievements. Then put all
f the groups' papers together in a class
ook. Give the book a cover, table of
ntents, and title page.

TECHNOLOGY/MEDIA

SCIENCE

RESEARCH TWINS

Use the Internet and other resources to learn interesting facts about twins. Present your findings in a question-and-answer fact sheet.

1. **Plan Your Research** With a group, brainstorm questions such as:
   - What is the difference between fraternal twins and identical twins?
   - What percentage of the population is twins?
   - Is a twin likely to be the parent of twins?
2. **Locate Information** Use key words in your search and look for links. Download helpful information.

INTERNET

INFORMATION ON-LINE

Key Word:
twins

Web Sites:
> **Information about Twins**
- www.eblast.com
- encarta.msn.com

3. **Make a Fact Sheet** Write your questions in one column and the answers in another column. Share your fact sheet with the class.

Learn to use the **Internet** on Handbook pages 392–393.

Research Skills

USING THE INTERNET

TEACH Gather small groups of students around a large computer monitor and demonstrate how to use Internet browser software. Introduce the term *search engine* as a way to locate information on the Internet. Type www.yahooligans.com to access this kids-oriented search engine. Enter the key word "deafness" to show how a search engine works. Choose an appropriate Web site and demonstrate skimming and taking notes from this site.

PRACTICE Click on the Back button to return to the Yahooligans list. Ask students to take turns checking the Web sites on the list for relevant information. Invite students to continue using the Internet in pairs as they conduct research for their fact sheets. Schedule computer time so that everyone gets a turn. Remind students to use the Web site addresses on page 167 as well as results from the search engine.

RESPOND

OBJECTIVES

CONTRIBUTIONS OF HEARING IMPAIRED

Function: Give Information; Write

Learning Strategies, Critical Thinking, and Research Skills: Locate Resources; Plan; Gather Information; Interact with Peers

Representing and Writing: Biography; Article

RESEARCH TWINS

Function: Give Information; Write

Concepts and Vocabulary: Twins—*fraternal, paternal, maternal*

Learning Strategies, Critical Thinking, and Research Skills: Locate Resources; Plan; Gather and Synthesize Information

Technology/Media: Use the Internet

Representing: Fact Sheet

CONTENT AREA CONNECTIONS

1 **Research Contributions of the Hearing Impaired** Share the class book with visitors and parents. Invite students to present the book by summarizing the topic.

2 **Research Twins** To prepare students for this activity, present the following science vocabulary:

- ***fraternal, paternal, maternal*:** Challenge small groups to look up the meanings of the words. Then ask what these words have in common. (They describe roles and relationships in families.)

  Have students use the words in sentences that describe their family. Provide sentence frames.

  My _____ aunt lives in. . . .

  My _____ uncle is. . . .

  My brother and I are not _____ twins.

▶ **Practice Book** page 78

CLOSE AND ASSESS

Ask: *What have you learned from this lesson?* Have students write one sentence and post it on a class chart.

INTRODUCE THEME 2

OBJECTIVES

Function: Write; Engage in Discussion
Concepts and Vocabulary: Goals—*decisions, rewarding, future*
Viewing: Respond to a Photograph
Learning Strategies: Relate to Personal Experience; Use Graphic Organizers (chart)
Critical Thinking: Generate Ideas; Make Inferences

TAP PRIOR KNOWLEDGE

1 **Quickwrite about a Better Future** Ask: *What does the theme title mean to you?* Elicit that most people want to make the future better for themselves and others. Then ask: *What are some things you hope for in the future? What can you do to work toward these things?* Have students quickwrite on the theme topic.

2 **Make a "Working Toward the Future" Chart** Ask students to share their quickwrites in groups. Then invite them to complete a chart like the following.

Hopes for the Future	What I Can Do Now
good job	study hard in school

VIEW AND DISCUSS

3 **Discuss Graduates** Have students view the picture. Ask: *Of what kind of better future might these graduates be thinking? What kinds of decisions have they made to help them achieve their goals?*

Use the Discussion Prompts in the **Multi-Level Strategies** to involve all students.

168

REACHING ALL STUDENTS

Multi-Level Strategies

DISCUSSION PROMPTS

BEGINNING Invite students to help you label details in the photograph. (caps, gowns, physical characteristics of the graduates) Then students can draw pictures depicting the futures of the graduates.

INTERMEDIATE Have students work in groups to describe the people in the photograph. Then ask students to imagine what the graduates might do to realize their dreams. Ask: *In what ways might their futures be better?*

ADVANCED To encourage critical thinking, ask: *What event does this photograph show? Who else might be present at the graduation?* Tell students to make a list of decisions the graduates might need to make to achieve better futures.

Annotations offer strategies for
B Beginning students

THEME 2

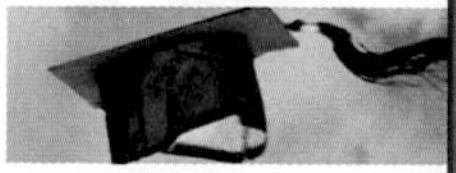

Toward a Better Future

- Who are the people that you admire for reaching their goals? Explain how they did it.

  B Encourage elaboration: List the people and goals that students cite. Then invite students to tell each admired person's story.

- What does it take to reach an important goal?

  B Pose choices: Does it take hard work or luck to reach a goal?

- What decisions can you make to build a rewarding future for yourself?

  B Restate: What choices will help you reach your dreams?

THEME-RELATED BOOKS

Follow the Drinking Gourd
by Jeannette Winter
The story of Peg Leg Joe, an old man with a wooden leg who leads slaves north to freedom.

BEGINNING

The Milkman's Boy
by Donald Hall
A family crisis convinces a family to update their dairy business using the new pasteurization process.

INTERMEDIATE

NOVEL

The House on Mango Street
by Sandra Cisneros
Young Esperanza dreams of leaving her rundown neigborhood to make a better life for herself.

ADVANCED

169

DISCUSS THE GUIDING QUESTIONS

4 Set the Theme Some key points to develop during the discussion are:

- We may have family members or friends who changed their lives for the better. They may have overcome illness or some other difficulty, put themselves through school, or achieved success in their work or profession.
- Reaching a goal takes knowledge, skill, courage, perseverance, and hard work. Suggest role models who represent these qualities, such as: sports figures, political leaders, teachers, business people.
- Getting a good education, staying healthy, and cultivating networks all can contribute to building a rewarding future. Decisions that lead to these qualities would include: staying in school, learning as much as you can, eating right and getting exercise, meeting people who can serve as guides.

Form groups and use the **Multi-Level Strategies** so all students can participate.

CLOSE AND ASSESS

Have students state examples of dreams for a better future most people have.

Multi-Level Strategies

GROUPING GUIDELINES

BEGINNING Group students so you can define words and pose choices for responses. See suggestions in red on the facsimile for page 169.

INTERMEDIATE Invite students to brainstorm examples of people who have built better futures for themselves or their families. Ask: *What qualities do these people have that help them reach their goals? What do you need to do to make a better future for yourself?* Have pairs identify and share decisions they can make to reach personal goals.

ADVANCED Encourage students to identify people who have reached lofty goals that made a better future for the world. Have pairs of students trace decisions a specific person made to achieve success. Ask students to identify decisions in specific areas, such as: education, perseverance, courage, self-confidence, service to others, and support systems.

THEME LIBRARY

■ ***The Milkman's Boy*** by Donald Hall

After students read *The Milkman's Boy*, ask them to write a summary of the story and tell about something they learned from the book. Students may comment on:

- how the family worked together to make a better future for themselves
- historical and/or scientific information given through the story
- how the family adapted to changes in technology.

BUILD LANGUAGE AND VOCABULARY

OBJECTIVES

Function: Ⓣ Describe
Concepts and Vocabulary: Synonyms
Patterns and Structures: Ⓣ Complex Sentences
Viewing: Interpret Visual Information
Learning Strategy: Use Graphic Organizers (chart)
Critical Thinking: Make Inferences; Generate Ideas
Writing: Description

START WITH A COMMON EXPERIENCE

1 **View and Describe** View the painting, encouraging students to tell what is happening. Then model how to give an effective description.

How to Describe
- Name something: *the pioneers*
- Tell more: *The brave pioneers are going west in their wagons.*
- Use sensory words: *The wooden wagons bumped along the rough roads.*
- Compare it to something else: *The wagons moved slowly, like turtles that also carry their homes on their backs.*

2 **Discuss the Quotation** Have students speculate on what the quotation means and how it relates to the painting. Through the discussion, develop the idea that like the pioneers, we each have within ourselves the power to carry out our dreams for a better future.

Use the Discussion Prompts in the **Multi-Level Strategies** to involve all proficiency levels.

Build Language and Vocabulary

DESCRIBE

Study the painting. Then read the quotation. What do you think the future holds for these people?

Pioneers of the West, Helen Lundeberg, oil on canvas. Copyright © 1934

WE ARE SUCH STUFF AS DREAMS ARE MADE ON.

—*William Shakespeare*

REACHING ALL STUDENTS

Multi-Level Strategies

DISCUSSION PROMPTS

BEGINNING Help students describe concretely what they see in the illustration: *Where are the pioneers? Where are they going? What is their dream?* Restate the answers as you record key words on a word web.

INTERMEDIATE / **ADVANCED** Have students elaborate on the pioneers' dream. Ask: *What do they hope for? Why are they heading west? Did they achieve their dreams by themselves?* Then have students complete this sentence: *The pioneers are such stuff as dreams are made on because* ______. Advanced students can use the sentence to start a paragraph and add more details about what it takes to be a pioneer.

MAKE A DRAWING OF THE FUTURE

ook at the painting again. At a signal from your teacher, start drawing all the ifferent things that might be in the future for these pioneers. Stop when you re given the next signal. You will have three minutes.

BUILD YOUR VOCABULARY

ynonyms A synonym is a word that has the same or almost the same meaning s another word. Study the chart. The pairs of words about the pioneers are ynonyms. Work with a partner to list more pairs of synonyms about the ainting. Take turns adding words to the chart and writing a synonym for each.

Subjects	Adjectives	Verbs	Adverbs
pioneers	brave courageous	traveled journeyed	boldly fearlessly

USE LANGUAGE STRUCTURES ▶ COMPLEX SENTENCES

Writing: Describe in Detail Write complex sentences to describe the ioneers in your drawing. Use conjunctions from the **Word Bank**.

Examples:

When the brave pioneers got to Oklahoma, they built their homes. They made them out of sod **because** there were few trees for lumber.

Word Bank

Some Subordinating Conjunctions

although
because
if
since
unless
until
when
where
while

CONDUCT THE ACTIVITIES

3 Make a Drawing of the Future
Invite volunteers to share their drawings and talk about what they included and why.

4 Build Your Vocabulary: Synonyms
Before students begin, review definitions and examples of adjectives, verbs, and adverbs.

5 Use Language Structures: Complex Sentences Present the skill, using the definitions and examples on **Transparency 40**. Clarify the meaning of each subordinating conjunction in the Word Bank and explain how a conjunction alters the meaning of a sentence, for example: *You can use* because *to tell why something happens.* Then have students form complex sentences in Try It!

Writing: Describe in Detail
Conduct the activity at the bottom of page 171.

Use the Writing Activity Options in the **Multi-Level Strategies** to adjust instruction.

▶ **Practice Book** page 79

CLOSE AND ASSESS

Have students tell what a complex sentence is. Then ask them to create a clause that completes this sentence: *I like popular music* ______.

Multi-Level Strategies

WRITING ACTIVITY OPTIONS

BEGINNING Help students pick one of the ideas from their drawings to describe in a sentence. Provide a frame: *The pioneers* _____ *because* _____.

INTERMEDIATE Students can work in pairs to ask each other questions about their drawings. *What are the pioneers like?* (brave) *Why?* (because they left everything they knew to find a better future) Show students how to turn the answers into a complex sentence: *The pioneers are brave because they left everything they knew to find a better future.*

ADVANCED Encourage students to write several complex sentences with a variety of subordinating conjunctions. Point out the different points of view that emerge by using different conjunctions.

Transparency 40 / Master 40

LEARN ABOUT COMPLEX SENTENCES

1. A **complex sentence** has one independent clause and one dependent clause.

   The pioneers will continue west (independent clause) when the rain stops. (dependent clause)

2. An **independent clause** can stand alone as a sentence.

   Sentence: The pioneers will continue west.
   Not a sentence: when the rain stops

3. The connecting word in a complex sentence is called a **subordinating conjunction**. It shows how the two parts of the sentence are related.

   The pioneers went west **because** they wanted a better future. (**because** tells *why*)

   They will build homes **when** they get to Oklahoma. (**when** tells *at what time*)

Try It!

Complete each sentence by finishing the clause.

1. We follow the setting sun because ______.
2. The men must hunt for food until ______.
3. We will plant crops when ______.
4. The horses can go all day if ______.

Transparency 40 Level B, Unit 3 | Dreams and Decisions

PREPARE TO READ

OBJECTIVES

THINK ABOUT WHAT YOU KNOW
Reading Strategy: Activate Prior Knowledge

LEARN KEY VOCABULARY Ⓣ
Vocabulary Strategy: Relate Words

LEARN TO MAKE COMPARISONS
Reading Strategy: Ⓣ Make Comparisons

THINK ABOUT WHAT YOU KNOW

1 **Quickwrite** Call on volunteers to read their answers aloud to the class.

LEARN KEY VOCABULARY

2 **Relate Words** Read aloud and clarify vocabulary words and definitions. Assign each of three groups one question from the word map.

Use the Vocabulary Options in the **Multi-Level Strategies** to tailor the activity to proficiency levels.

▶ **Practice Book** page 80

LEARN TO MAKE COMPARISONS

3 **Model How to Make Comparisons** Define *migration*. Demonstrate the steps with **Transparency 41**:

- Help students preview the title and headings.
- Ask: *What topic will be discussed in the article? What two aspects will be compared?* Write answers in the chart as headings for the columns and rows.
- Read the selection. Ask: *What is the same or different about the two time periods?*
- Read the selection again, one paragraph at a time, and complete the chart.

CLOSE AND ASSESS

Ask students to give two examples each of similarities and differences in northern industry before and during WW I.

THE GREAT MIGRATION
art essay
by Jacob Lawrence

Prepare to Read

THINK ABOUT WHAT YOU KNOW

Quickwrite Why do people move from one area to another?

adversity hard times, difficult situation

exodus move of a very large number of people from an area

migration move from one place to another by a group of people

newcomer person who has recently come to an area

population shift change in the number of people living in a certain area

replace put one thing in place of another

segregation separation of one group of people from another

shortage too small a number or amount

triumph success, victory

Answers to the vocabulary activity:
What are some reasons for it?
adversity
shortages
segregation
What happens?
There is a population shift.
Many newcomers arrive.
There are personal triumphs.
People throw away a lot of things before they move and replace them later.

LEARN KEY VOCABULARY
Relate Words Study the new words and their definitions. With your group, use the vocabulary words to complete a word map.

Word Map

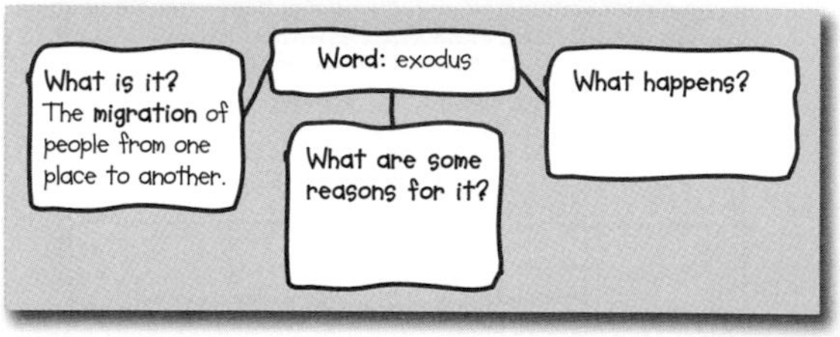

LEARN TO MAKE COMPARISONS
When you **make comparisons**, you see how things are alike and differen
This strategy will help you understand information.

READING STRATEGY
How to Make Comparisons

1. Preview the selection by looking at pictures, captions, and headings. Decide what you want to compare.
2. Set up a comparison chart. Show what you plan to compare in the headings.
3. Read each part of the selection. Take notes on your chart.
4. Look over your chart. How are things alike and different?

As you read "The Great Migration," compare life for African Americans
the South and in the North.

REACHING ALL STUDENTS

Multi-Level Strategies

VOCABULARY OPTIONS

BEGINNING Group students to read ***Who Was Martin Luther King, Jr.?*** or the Key Points Reading on **Master 42**. (See page T175.) Work with the vocabulary in those selections.

INTERMEDIATE Work with students as a group to complete the word maps.

ADVANCED Students complete the word maps on their own and compare their answers in groups.

Transparency 41 / Master 41

HOW TO MAKE COMPARISONS

Directions: Read the paragraphs. Complete the boxes for Workers and Products for each time period.

Northern Industries

Before 1916 Before 1916, many workers in northern factories were immigrants from other countries. These workers produced cars in automobile factories. In the steel mills, they made railroad tracks for the nation's railroads and farm machinery.

World War I During World War I many people joined the military to fight in the war. No immigration was allowed to the United States. For these reasons, there was a shortage of workers in the North. Many African Americans from the South joined the movement north to find jobs. In addition, many women took factory jobs. The northern factories now produced ships, ammunition, and planes for the war.

Northern Industries	Workers	Products
During World War I	African Americans from the South Women	ships ammunition planes
Before 1916	Immigrants	cars railroad tracks farm machinery

Transparency 41 Level B, Unit 3 | Dreams and Decisions

THE GREAT MIGRATION
AN AMERICAN STORY
by JACOB LAWRENCE

It is 1916. Segregation divides the South. Living conditions are difficult for all southerners, but especially for blacks. Many African Americans travel north in search of a better life. This chapter of American history, known as the "Great Migration," inspired painter Jacob Lawrence to tell the story of this journey.

173

READ THE SELECTION

OBJECTIVES

Reading Strategies: Preview; Predict
Literary Analysis: Essay

INTRODUCE THE SELECTION

4 **Preview and Predict** Read aloud the title, author's name, and introduction. Ask: *How might a painter tell a story?* Have students read the introductory statements and captions on each page to preview the selection.

5 **Identify Genre: Essay** Ask students to recall "Talking Walls" and what they learned about essays. Elicit a definition. Tell students that "The Great Migration" includes the ideas and opinions of the author as well as some of his paintings.

THE BASICS BOOKSHELF

■ ***Who Was Martin Luther King, Jr.?***
by Shirleyann Costigan

Years after southern slaves were granted freedom, their struggle for civil rights continued. The simple text in this biography of civil rights leader, Martin Luther King, Jr., introduces social studies vocabulary related to civil rights issues, while the photos of events in the life of this great leader give beginning English learners access to the literature.

For Lesson Plans: See the Teacher's Guide for ***The Basics Bookshelf***.

The Great Migration: An American Story
by Jacob Lawrence

Theme Connection The essay is about African Americans who dream of a better life and move north during World War I.

Selection Summary and Background The introduction on page 173 of the student book offers a summary. Jacob Lawrence described the events recounted in this selection as "a great epic drama." Between 1890 and the1960s the African American population in the United States moved from being 95% in the South to 90% outside the South.

Author Awards Jacob Lawrence won the National Medal of Arts and was an elected member of the National Academy of Arts and Letters.

READ PAGES 174–175

OBJECTIVES

Function: Listen Actively

Vocabulary Strategy: Use Context Clues; Use New Words in Context

Grammar: T Complex Sentences

Listening: Listen to a Selection

Reading and Learning Strategies: Build Background; Identify Author's Purpose

Literary Analysis: Setting

SET PURPOSE

1 Read aloud the introduction to pages 174–175. Set the purpose for listening: *Find out what the great migration was and what Jacob Lawrence wanted to show in his paintings.*

LISTEN AND READ

Tape 3B
CD 3 Track 3

2 **Strategy Focus: Build Background** Play the recording of pages 174–175 or read them aloud to develop the concept of migration and learn about the artist's purpose in creating the paintings.

Choose Options for Building Background in the **Multi-Level Strategies** to include all students.

Red annotations offer opportunities to clarify meaning and check for understanding.

1

AN AMERICAN STORY

Jacob Lawrence's family moves to the North during the great migration. Many years later, he decides to paint the story to share with all Americans.

Build background: Jacob Lawrence not only describes what it was like to be part of the Great Migration, he *shows* us, through his paintings.

This is the story of an **exodus** of African Americans who left their homes and farms in the South around the time of World War I and traveled to northern **industrial cities** in search of better lives. It was **a momentous journey**. Their **movement** resulted in one of the biggest **population shifts** in the history of the United States, and the **migration** is still going on for many people today.

Clarify: "I" refers to Jacob Lawre

The great migration is a part of my lif I grew up knowing about people on the move from the time I could understand what words meant. There was always talk my house of other families arriving from the South. My family was part of the first **big wave of the migration**, which occurred between the years 1916 and 1919

To me, migration means movement. While I was painting, I thought about train and people walking to the stations. I thoug about field hands leaving their farms to become factory workers, and about the families that sometimes got left behind. Th choices made were hard ones, so I wanted to show what made the people get on thos northbound trains. I also wanted to show just what it cost to ride them. **Uprooting** yourself from one way of life to make

Clarify: By "cost," he means the emotional pain of leaving behind what you know and love about a plac

Jacob was born in 1917 in New Jersey after his family moved to the North. Here he is with his mother, baby brother, and sister.

industrial cities cities with large factories
a momentous journey an important trip
big wave of the migration movement of a large number of people
Uprooting Moving

REACHING ALL STUDENTS

Mathematics Connection
LIFE EXPECTANCY

Read aloud the caption to the photograph on page 174. Ask: *In what year was Jacob Lawrence born?* (1917) Have students look in a reference book or on the Internet to find out how long a person born in that year would be expected to live. Ask students to compare this information with the life expectancy of a child born in 2000 and in various other years. Then have students answer this question in a paragraph: *Why do you think there is a difference in life expectancies?*

Multi-Level Strategies
OPTIONS FOR BUILDING BACKGROUND

BEGINNING Work with ***Who Was Martin Luther King, Jr.?***, or distribute copies of **Master 42** to read aloud the first paragraph of the Key Points Reading for "The Great Migration." Focus on the concept of migration, using examples and illustrations of other mass movements, such as those of animals.

INTERMEDIATE / **ADVANCED** As you play the recording on the **Selection Tape/CD**, invite students to read along quietly. Emphasize key vocabulary words and use the red annotations on the facsimile pages to clarify meaning. Invite volunteers to read aloud, one paragraph at a time. Discuss the metaphor Lawrence employs on page 174, "the first big wave of migration," and relate it to his comments about migration meaning "movement." Have students jot down all the words that have to do with movement. *(exodus, journey, movement, migration, wave, trains, walking, uprooting, quest)*

This is a self-portrait by Jacob Lawrence. It shows the artist in his studio, surrounded by his paintings and tools.

The Studio, Jacob Lawrence, lithograph. Copyright © 1996.

our way in another involves onflict and struggle. But out of ie struggle comes a kind of ower, and even beauty. I tried to **onvey** this in the rhythm of the ictures, and in the repetition of ertain images.

"And the migrants kept oming" is a **refrain** of **triumph** ver **adversity**. My family and thers left the South on a **quest** or freedom, **justice**, and **dignity**. our story **rings true** for you oday, then it must still **strike a hord** in our American experience.

—*Jacob Lawrence, 1992*

Use visuals: Pause to look at the paintings and discuss the repetition Lawrence refers to.
Encourage elaboration: How can pictures have rhythm?

onvey show
efrain repeated saying, common phrase
uest search
stice fair treatment
gnity sense of honor and worth
ngs true has the sound of truth
rike a chord be deeply felt, be understood

BEFORE YOU MOVE ON...

1. **Setting** When and where did the great migration take place?
2. **Context Clues** What does *migration* mean to the author? Give examples from the text.
3. **Artist's Purpose** Why did Jacob Lawrence decide to paint the story of the great migration?

REVIEW KEY VOCABULARY

3 Use New Words in Context
Assign specific vocabulary words to different groups. Ask groups to find examples of art in this essay that illustrate their words. Invite each group to explain their choices to the class. Encourage discussion and other opinions.

CHECK COMPREHENSION

4 Answers to "Before You Move On"

1. **Setting** The Great Migration took place in the United States during World War I, from the farms in the South to the cities in the North.
2. **Context Clues** To the author, migration means moving at a cost. (examples: "migration means movement"; "Uprooting yourself"; "involves conflict and struggle.")
3. **Artist's Purpose** He wanted to show why people left the South, as well as the struggle and beauty of the great migration.

CLOSE AND ASSESS

Ask students to draw what they see when they think of migration and write a sentence about their drawing.

Transparency 42 / Master 42

KEY POINTS READING

The Great Migration

This essay tells the story of a huge population move in the United States. African Americans leave their homes in the South. They move to cities in the North to find a better life. So many people move that it is called a "migration."

Northern factories don't have enough workers because people are fighting in the First World War. They promise jobs to African Americans from the South.

Life in the South is hard for African Americans. There are floods and ruined farms in the South. Food is expensive, and there is no justice for African Americans. There is segregation in the South and not much education. So, people from the South move North.

Life in the North is a little better. But African Americans find segregation in the North, too. They also find crowded, unhealthy housing. Some southerners fight with northern workers.

People from the South learn to depend on each other. They set up churches. Doctors and lawyers move north. Children go to school. Adults have the right to vote. Life is better in many ways.

Transparency 42 Level B, Unit 3 | Dreams and Decisions

Grammar Minilesson

▶ COMPLEX SENTENCES

TEACH Have students recall and share what they have learned about independent and dependent clauses. Ask: *What are some words that can signal a dependent clause?* Refer students to page 429 of the Handbook to verify their review.

Call students' attention to the sentence on page 175 that begins *If our story rings true for you. . . .* Identify this sentence as a complex sentence. Have students study the explanation on page 430 of the Handbook. Point out the words *if* and *then* and explain that these words relate two ideas in the two clauses. Have students identify the two clauses in the example.

PRACTICE Have students create oral sentences about the story using *if* and *then* clauses. Begin by providing a frame: *"If your life is very difficult in one place, then. . . . "* Have students suggest *if* and *then* clauses for others to finish.

▶ **Practice Book** page 81

READ PAGES 176–177

OBJECTIVES

Function: Read a Selection
Vocabulary Strategy: Structural Clues (prefixes)
Grammar: Prepositions
Listening: Listen to a Selection
Reading and Learning Strategies: Set a Purpose for Reading; Use Graphic Organizers (comparison chart); Reread; Ⓣ Make Comparisons

SET PURPOSE

1 Read aloud the introduction to pages 176–178. Set the purpose for reading: *Find out what the conditions were like in the South during the Great Migration.*

READ AND THINK

Tape 3B
CD 3 Track 3

2 **Strategy Focus: Make Comparisons** Involve students in reading pages 176–178 and writing important facts in their comparison charts.

Choose Reading Options in the **Multi-Level Strategies** on this page to include all students.

The recording of "The Great Migration" on the **Selection Tape/CD** offers an oral language model and the opportunity to build reading fluency.

2

THE SEGREGATED SOUTH

Life in the South is difficult for African Americans. They begin leaving in great numbers in search of a better life in the North.

This painting captures the feeling of a busy train station during the great migration. The travelers are crowded together, and they are all leaning toward their destination. You can almost hear their scuffling feet and feel their bodies pressing close together.

Around the time I was born, many African Americans from the South left home and traveled to cities in the North in search of a better life. My family was part of this great migration.

There was a **shortage** of workers in northern factories because many had left their jobs to fight in the First World War. The factory owners had to find new worke[rs] to **replace** those who were marching off [to] war. Northern industries offered southern blacks jobs as workers and lent them money, to be repaid later, for their railroad tickets. The northbound trains were packe[d] with **recruits**.

Ask: How did the war help cause the migration?

recruits new workers

REACHING ALL STUDENTS

HOME CONNECTION

Family Migration Maps Send home a copy of *High Point Newsletter 6* in the **Teacher's Resource Book**. In this home activity, students interview family members about family migrations. On a world map, students can trace how their families have moved, using arrows to show the directions from place to place. Encourage students to ask family members to help put dates alongside the arrows. Ask students to describe their family migration maps to the class and then display them.

Multi-Level Strategies

READING OPTIONS FOR LESSONS 5–6

BEGINNING Have students work with the Key Points Reading. After each sentence, ask: *Is this an important fact?* In groups, have students write important phrases on copies of **Master 43**, then read the information back to you. Point out similarities and differences in the two columns.

INTERMEDIATE Use the red annotations on the facsimile pages to clarify meaning. Then divide the group into "North" and "South" teams. Each team completes a section of the comparison chart on **Transparency 43**. Then the group discusses similarities and differences.

ADVANCED Have students fill in copies of **Master 43** individually. Then have partners exchange charts and ask each other questions about the information: *Where was there a shortage of workers? What surprised you about conditions in the North?* Encourage pairs to discuss similarities and differences.

ese paintings show the damaging effects of
ods and boll weevils on southern crops.

Nature had ravaged the South. Floods ined farms. The boll weevil destroyed tton crops.

Use visuals: Pause to discuss details in the paintings of crops.

The war had **doubled the cost of** food, aking life even harder for the poor. ilroad stations were so crowded with grants that guards were called in to **keep der**. The flood of migrants northward left ops back home to dry and **spoil**. For rican Americans, the South was **barren** in any ways. There was no justice for them the courts, and their lives were often in nger. Although slavery had long been **olished,** white landowners treated the ack tenant farmers **harshly** and unfairly.

And so the migration grew.

Ask: Why did the migration keep growing?

ubled the cost of made the price twice as high for
ep order make sure everyone followed the rules
il go bad, rot
rren lifeless, without happiness, empty
olished ended
rshly in a mean or cruel way

For much of the twentieth century, many African Americans did not own cars. Most traveled to the North by train. Some even walked part of the way.

MONITOR YOUR READING

3 Reread Have students reread these two pages and check their comparison charts for accuracy. Invite volunteers to read from their charts. Ask: *What is one important fact about life in the South? In the North?*

EXPAND VOCABULARY

4 Identify Prefixes Remind students of the meaning of *replace.* Explain that the prefix *re-* means "again." Point out the word *repaid* (page 176) and its meaning. Elicit other examples of words with this prefix and help students define them. Point out other selection words with prefixes: *uprooting* (page 174), *unfairly* (page 177). Help students discover the meanings of these prefixes. Have them list the words and their meanings in their class or individual dictionaries. Encourage them to add other words with prefixes as they read the rest of the selection.

Transparency 43 / Master 43

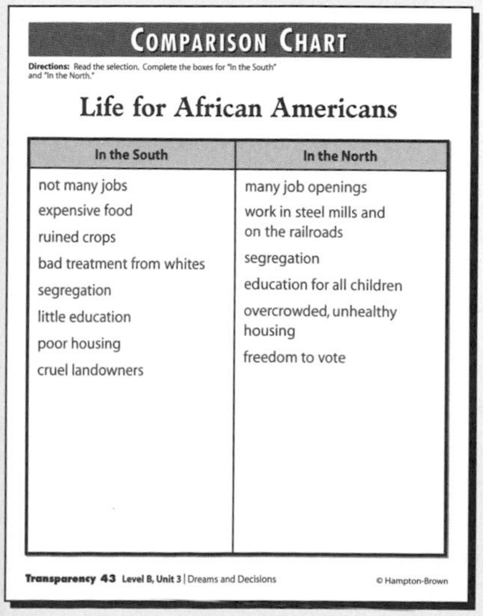

COMPARISON CHART

Directions: Read the selection. Complete the boxes for "In the South" and "In the North."

Life for African Americans

In the South	In the North
not many jobs	many job openings
expensive food	work in steel mills and on the railroads
ruined crops	segregation
bad treatment from whites	education for all children
segregation	overcrowded, unhealthy housing
little education	freedom to vote
poor housing	
cruel landowners	

Transparency 43 Level B, Unit 3 | Dreams and Decisions © Hampton-Brown

Grammar Minilesson

▶ PREPOSITIONAL PHRASES

TEACH Draw students' attention to the sentence containing the prepositional phrase *for the poor* in the second paragraph on page 177. Explain that prepositions are words such as *on, in, for, with, from, above, below, before,* or *after.* Prepositional phrases start with a preposition and end with a noun or pronoun. They include all the words in between. Tell students that prepositional phrases are used to add details to writing.

Refer students to page 456 in the Handbook. Have them work in groups to clarify the uses of prepositional phrases.

PRACTICE As an oral game, have students add details to these sentences by inserting prepositional phrases.

1. Many families moved _____.
2. They traveled north _____.
3. Many migrants arrived _____.
4. Life was hard _____.
5. The children could go _____.

▶ **Practice Book** page 82

READ PAGE 178

OBJECTIVES

Comprehension and Critical Thinking: Identify Details; Identify Cause and Effect; Form Opinions

CHECK COMPREHENSION

5 Answers to "Before You Move On"

1. **Details/Viewing** In the South, farms were ruined, cotton crops were destroyed, and food was expensive. African Americans had no justice and were often in danger. The artist paints floods, damaged crops, and separate drinking fountains.
2. **Cause and Effect** Reasons should include: harsh treatment of black tenant farmers by white landowners, expensive food, segregation, little opportunity for education, and child labor.
3. **Opinion** Answers will vary. Encourage thoughtful responses.

CLOSE AND ASSESS

Refer students to the unit mind map they started on page T141. Have them add information about dreams, decisions, and actions they have learned about in "The Great Migration."

Trains were an important means of transportation in the early part of the twentieth century. The trip to the North took a long time, so many travelers took plenty of food and extra clothing.

Use text features: Why did Lawrence show a river in the middle of the painting? Have students use the caption to answer.

Segregation divided the South. The black newspapers told of better housing and jobs in the North. **Agents** from northern factories **flocked** into southern counties and towns, looking for laborers. Families often gathered to discuss whether to go north or to stay south. The promise of better housing in the North **could not be ignored**. The railroad stations were crowded with migrants.

And the migrants kept coming.

In the South there was little opportunity for education, and children **labored** in the fields. These were more reasons for people to move north, leaving some communities **deserted**. There was much excitement and discussion about the great migration.

Many migrants arrived in Chicago. In Chicago and other cities they labored in the **steel mills** . . . and on the railroads. **Ask:** What kind of work did the migrants do?

Here Lawrence shows what life was like under segregation. He uses a river to divide the painting in order to show how blacks and whites were separated in their daily activities. In the two parts of the painting, black women and white women drink at separate water fountains.

BEFORE YOU MOVE ON...

1. **Details/Viewing** What was life like in the South for African Americans? How do the paintings help you better understand?
2. **Cause and Effect** Why did African Americans decide to move to the North?
3. **Opinion** Do you think migrating was an easy decision to make? Explain.

Agents People acting for others
flocked came in great numbers
could not be ignored attracted attention
labored worked
deserted without any people
steel mills factories where steel, a very strong metal, is produced

REACHING ALL STUDENTS

Vocabulary

WORD FAMILIES

Write *migration* and *immigration*. Point out *migr-*, from the Latin root *migrare*, which means "move." Make a list of other words with this root *(migrate, emigrant, emigration, migrant, migratory)*. Tell students to look up their definitions and discuss similarities and differences in meanings. Then have students use each word in a sentence. Invite students to share their sentences.

CULTURAL PERSPECTIVES

U.S. Culture: Regional Identities
Point out that, within the United States, people identify themselves by regions, even after they have relocated elsewhere. For example: *I'm a southerner. Her house has that southwest flavor.* Have students research various regions of the United States to discover identifying characteristics of the regions. Then students can report their findings, using visual aids to illustrate concepts.

3

LIFE IN THE NORTH

ɿfrican Americans continue migrating to the North. Many of them find the jobs they were ooking for, but they also find that there are many problems and prejudices to overcome.

Ask: What statement is being repeated? Why?

And the migrants kept coming. Southern landowners, **stripped of** eap labor, tried to stop the migration jailing the labor agents and the grants. Sometimes the agents guised themselves to avoid arrest, t the migrants were often taken m railroad stations and jailed until trains departed. Black and white uthern leaders met to discuss ways improve conditions to stop the w of workers north.

Although life in the North was tter, it was not **ideal**. Many grants moved to Pittsburgh, which s a great industrial center at time.

Although they were promised tter housing in the North, some nilies **were forced** to live in over-owded and unhealthy **quarters**. e migrants soon learned that gregation was not **confined to** South.

Many northern workers were gry because they had to compete h the migrants for housing and s. There were **riots**. Longtime African American residents living in the North did not welcome the **newcomers** from the South and often treated them with **disdain**. The migrants had to **rely on** each other.

Ask: What do you think surprised the migrants about the North?

Newcomers were excited about the opportunities waiting for them in steel mills in the North. As they approached the great northern cities, they eagerly looked out the train windows at the exciting new landscapes.

ipped of left without any
al perfect
re forced had no other choice but
rters places to live or sleep
confined to found only in
riots violent actions by a crowd of people
disdain disapproval
rely on depend on or trust

READ PAGE 179

OBJECTIVES

Function: Read a Selection
Grammar: Ⓣ Complex Sentences
Listening: Listen to a Selection
Reading and Learning Strategies: Set a Purpose for Reading; Use Graphic Organizers (comparison chart); Ⓣ Make Comparisons

SET PURPOSE

1 Read aloud the introduction to pages 179–180. Ask students to set the purpose for reading: *Look for problems African Americans found in the North.*

READ AND THINK

Tape 3B
CD 3
Track 3

2 **Strategy Focus: Make Comparisons** As they read this section, have students write important facts in their comparison charts.

See the **Multi-Level Strategies** on page T176 to help all students participate.

Social Studies Connection

AFRICAN AMERICAN HISTORY

Have students research some important events in African American history, for example: slavery, the Emancipation Proclamation, World War I, World War II, and the Civil Rights Act. Suggest that students find sources in the library and on the Internet. Encourage them to create a time line that shows major milestones in history as well as lapses of time between significant events. Have students work in groups to write statements about each entry on the time line.

Grammar Minilesson

▶ COMPLEX SENTENCES

TEACH Point out the sentences on page 179 that begin *Although life in the North was better . . .* and *Many northern workers were angry because. . . .* Remind students that a complex sentence has one independent clause and one dependent clause. Ask them to identify the dependent clauses.

Point out the subordinating conjunctions *(although, because)*. Refer to the charts on pages 429 and 458 of the Handbook for more examples of subordinating conjunctions.

PRACTICE Have students orally finish these sentences by adding another clause.

1. Although Southern landowners tried to stop the migration, ______.
2. The migrants learned to depend on each other ______.
3. Since housing was more available in the North, ______.
4. Life in the South was difficult ______.

▶ **Practice Book** page 83

READ PAGE 180

OBJECTIVES

Reading Strategy: Ⓣ Make Comparisons
Comprehension and Critical Thinking: Make Inferences; Identify Cause and Effect
Literary Analysis: Evaluate Impact of Medium on Meaning

CHECK COMPREHENSION

3 Answers to "Before You Move On"

1. **Inference** All farmland was in bad shape. They thought the North offered more opportunities.
2. **Cause and Effect** They put northern labor agents and some migrants in jail.

ABOUT THE AUTHOR

4 Evaluate Literature: Medium Read About the Author. Discuss how Lawrence tells his story. Ask: *How do the pictures help tell the story? What do you learn from them that you don't learn from the words?*

CLOSE AND ASSESS

Ask students to write test questions that require making comparisons. For example: *How were work opportunities different in the North and the South?*

Children could go to better schools in the North. Notice how each girl is reaching higher than the one to her left. Lawrence wanted to show that better schools provided the education needed to open up new opportunities. **Ask:** How would you explain this painting in your own words?

The **storefront church** was a **welcoming** place and the center of their lives, in joy and in sorrow. Black professionals, such as doctors and lawyers, soon followed **their patients** and **clients** north. Female workers were among the last to leave.

Life in the North brought many challenges, but the migrants' lives had changed for the better. The children were able to go to school, and their parents gained the freedom to vote.

And the migrants kept coming.

Theirs is a story of African American strength and courage. I share it now as my parents told it to me, because their struggl and triumphs ring true today. People all over the world are still on the move, tryin to build better lives for themselves and for their families.

Pose choices: In the end, were the migrants better off in the North or in the South? Explain.

storefront church small church in a building that is used as a store at other times
welcoming warm and inviting
their patients the people they (doctors) cared for
clients customers; people who pay for the services of other people

BEFORE YOU MOVE ON...

1. **Inference** Why didn't African Americans move to other farmlands in the South?
2. **Cause and Effect** How did southern landowners and leaders react to the great migration?

ABOUT THE AUTH

When he was thirteen, **Jacob Lawrence** moved with his family to New York City. He began taking art lessons after school. He decided then that he wanted to use painting to tell the history of African Ame In his long career, Jacob Lawrence has crea many paintings of famous African America as Frederick Douglass and Harriet Tubman an art professor at the University of Wash before he retired.

REACHING ALL STUDENTS

Art Connection
COMPARE ART FORMS

Materials: photographs or pictures of photographs

Have students review the paintings in the selection. Display a few photographs of people and activities. Ask: *How are paintings and photographs different?* (photographs capture a real moment; paintings show the artist's view of it) Tell students to make a list of strengths and weaknesses of using photographs and of using paintings to document history. Have students write summary statements about each art form.

INTERNET

ART CONNECTION

Point out how, in the U.S. and around the world, African Americans have influenced culture, especially the cultures of cities. Have students research information about the Harlem Renaissance, Langston Hughes, jazz, or blues. Pose this question to help prompt students' research and discussion: *How do you think the African American community produced such talented writers and musicians in the midst of adversity and the struggle for human rights?*

On-line Encyclopedias
Web sites undergo frequent modifications, but here are some you may want to suggest to students:

britannica.com
ipl.org
si.edu

Key Word Search
"Harlem Renaissance"
jazz
"Langston Hughes"
"The Great Migration"

Respond to the Essay

Check Your Understanding

UM IT UP

lake Comparisons Work with a partner to eview the comparison chart you made while eading. Be sure to consider elements such as mployment, education, and financial situations. dd any missing details.

Life for African Americans

In the South	In the North
not many jobs	many job openings

ummarize Use the details in your chart to rite a short paragraph that compares what life as like for African Americans in the South and ose in the North.

nswers to the comparison chart:

n the South
treated badly by some whites
no justice
segregation
lives were in danger

n the North
better schools
crowded housing
some segregation
treated badly by some blacks and whites

THINK IT OVER

Discuss and Write Talk about these questions with a partner. Write the answers.

1. **Inference** Why do you think some African Americans in the North treated the newcomers badly?
2. **Evaluate Information** From the details in the selection, do you think the migrants were better off in the South or in the North? Explain your answer.
3. **Conclusions** What do people move to get away from? What do people move toward?
4. **Prior Knowledge** What other large migrations of people do you know about?

EXPRESS YOURSELF ▶ DESCRIBE

Which painting in the selection do you like most? Describe it to a group of classmates. Tell about the colors, how people and things appear in the painting, and how it makes you feel.

LANGUAGE ACQUISITION ASSESSMENT
See pages 41 and 42 of the Assessment Handbook.

Multi-Level Strategies

SUM IT UP OPTIONS

BEGINNING Work with students to complete their comparison charts. If necessary, reread aloud sections of the selection. Then have students cut apart the statements in their charts and arrange them to make a summary. Invite volunteers to read or tell about their summaries.

INTERMEDIATE Have students share their comparison charts in groups and add ideas from each other's charts. Then groups can list the facts they want to include in their summary paragraphs before they write them.

ADVANCED Allow time for students to review their comparison charts individually for completeness and share them with the group. Then they use their charts to list the categories of ideas to include in their summary paragraphs (work, food, living conditions, segregation). Students can share these ideas before they write.

RESPOND

OBJECTIVES

SUM IT UP

Function: Write

Critical Thinking and Learning Strategies: Use Graphic Organizers (comparison chart); Ⓣ Make Comparisons

Writing: Summary Sentences; Paragraph

THINK IT OVER

Function: Engage in Discussion

Critical Thinking, Learning Strategies, and Comprehension: Make Inferences; Evaluate Information; Ⓣ Draw Conclusions; Relate to Prior Knowledge

EXPRESS YOURSELF

Function: Ⓣ Describe

Speaking and Listening: Description

CHECK YOUR UNDERSTANDING

1 **Sum It Up** Encourage students to discuss their charts before writing.

▶ **Practice Book** page 84

2 **Think It Over** Possible answers are:

1. **Inference** They were afraid the newcomers might take their jobs.
2. **Evaluate Information** They were better off in the North where life wasn't perfect, but they had more opportunities.
3. **Conclusions** People move away from adversity and toward opportunities.
4. **Prior Knowledge** The California Gold Rush; the migration west during the Great Depression; people leaving Cuba for Florida; the exodus of ethnic Albanians from Kosovo.

3 **Express Yourself** Students can work in groups to describe the paintings. Encourage them to imagine the stories behind the paintings.

CLOSE AND ASSESS

Call out categories *(food, work, housing, segregation)* and ask students to make comparisons between North and South in each category.

RESPOND

OBJECTIVES

PHRASES AND CLAUSES

Grammar: Phrases and Clauses

DESCRIBE AN EVENT

Function: Write

Viewing: Interpret a Visual Image

Critical Thinking and Reading Strategies: Visualize

Writing: Description

LANGUAGE ARTS AND LITERATURE

1 **Use Phrases and Clauses** Answers to the Practice will vary but should be written as compound or complex sentences.

▶ **Practice Book** page 85

2 **Describe an Event** Help students focus their viewing and writing by offering these suggestions:

- Choose a painting that you have a strong feeling about.
- Imagine that you are a person in the painting. It has come alive and the people are in motion.
- Use sensory phrases *(I feel... ; I see... ; That sounds like...).*

Encourage students to use complex sentences in their descriptions.

▶ **Practice Book** page 86

CLOSE AND ASSESS

Ask students to underline phrases and clauses in their descriptions.

ASSESSMENT
Selection Test 11 on page 47 of the Assessment Handbook tests students' mastery of the reading strategies and the vocabulary, comprehension, and language arts skills taught with this selection.

Respond to the Essay, continued

Language Arts and Literature

GRAMMAR IN CONTEXT

USE PHRASES AND CLAUSES

Learn About Phrases A **phrase** is a group of related words that does not have a subject and a predicate.

in the South

A phrase can be part of a complete sentence.

Many blacks lived **in the South**.

Learn About Clauses A **clause** is a group of words that has a subject and a verb. An **independent clause** can stand alone as a sentence.

The **South experienced** a drought.
Pests ruined the cotton crop.

Two independent clauses can be combined into a **compound sentence**. Join the clauses with a **conjunction** : *and, but, or, for, nor,* or *yet*.

The South experienced a drought, **and** pests ruined the cotton crop.

A **dependent clause** is not a complete sentence.

although slavery was abolished

A dependent clause can be combined with an independent clause to make a **complex sentence**.

Although slavery was abolished, white landowners treated black farmers harshly.

Practice Work with a partner to write three compound sentences and three complex sentences.

VIEWING/WRITING

DESCRIBE AN EVENT

Imagine that you are a character in one of Jacob Lawrence's paintings. Write a description of the event shown in the painting.

1. **Write Your Draft** Put yourself in the painting. What are you doing? Describe what you see, hear, and smell. How does the scene make you feel? Write a colorful, interesting description.
2. **Edit Your Work** Does your description make the event seem like it really happened? Did you use descriptive words and phrases? Check for correct spelling and punctuation. Check that all your sentences are complete.
3. **Share Your Work** Take turns reading your description aloud to a partner. Guess which painting you each described. Then look at the paintings together.

Sample Description

It's cold outside, but I feel warm because we are all pressed close together. The smell of hot chocolate is mixed with the smell of burning coal. I can't wait for the trip to start!

Review **sentences** on Handbook pages 424–430.

REACHING ALL STUDENTS

Multi-Level Strategies

PRACTICE OPTIONS FOR PHRASES AND CLAUSES

BEGINNING First, focus on using phrases. Draw examples of sentences with phrases from the classroom: *I write my name on the board.* Provide frames: *I write my name* _____. Model combining two simple sentences into a compound one. *I ask for the book. Micah hands it to me; I ask for the book and Micah hands it to me.* Provide frames for students' original compound sentences. *The bell* _____ *but we* _____.

INTERMEDIATE Provide simple frames for partners to work with. *The migrants traveled* _____. *They lived* _____. Encourage students to combine sentences to create compound sentences. (The migrants traveled to the north and lived in large cities.)

ADVANCED Students can complete the Practice independently and trade papers with a partner for review.

SOCIAL STUDIES

SEARCH CITY JOBS

d out about jobs in today's large cities. Use ıat you learn to make a career notebook.

Choose a Category Select one of these fields to research:

communications/publishing
education
hospitality/service
manufacturing
retail
transportation
technology

Research Jobs in Your Category Use the Internet, the "Help Wanted" section in your local newspaper, or library books about careers. Take notes as you read.

Make a Career Notebook Summarize your research in a paragraph. Put copies of all your classmates' paragraphs in your own career notebook.

REPRESENTING/SPEAKING

FINE ARTS

CREATE A MESSAGE WITHOUT WORDS

How shapes and figures are arranged in a picture is called the **composition**. A good composition can clearly express the picture's message without words. Draw your own picture that speaks for itself.

1. **Choose a Subject** Decide what you want to draw. Think about a subject that is important or meaningful to you. What message do you want to convey about it?
2. **Create the Composition** Experiment by sketching different compositions. Choose one. Then use pencils, crayons, chalk, or paint to draw your final picture.
3. **Take a Gallery Walk** Display your picture with those of your classmates. Walk around the room, and discuss how the composition in each picture helps convey the message of the artist.

For tips on **representing**, see Handbook pages 404–405.

Research Skills

USING A NEWSPAPER

TEACH Before students begin the Research City Jobs activity, introduce them to the "Help Wanted" section of a newspaper. Display a newspaper and demonstrate how to find the "Help Wanted" section. Explain that most newspapers list job ads by type (high tech, professional, sales, health care, etc.).

For different ads, model how to find the company name, job description, required qualifications, and how to contact the company. Ask: *If you want to work in a department store, which ad would you use?*

PRACTICE Have partners find ads in different categories. They should:

- identify the company, job description, qualifications, and contact information for each job
- explain how they would answer each ad.

RESPOND

OBJECTIVES

RESEARCH CITY JOBS

Function: Give Information

Learning Strategies, Critical Thinking, and Research Skills: Use a Newspaper; Gather and Organize Information; Take Notes; Evaluate Information

Representing and Writing: Paragraph

CREATE A MESSAGE WITHOUT WORDS

Viewing: Interpret a Visual Image

Representing: Drawing

CONTENT AREA CONNECTIONS

1. **Research City Jobs** Group students according to job interests and have them search for information together. As they research jobs, have students look in area phone books for the names of companies in the fields listed in the student book. Suggest that students make a list of companies with names that relate to their fields of interest.

▶ **Practice Book** page 87

2. **Create a Message Without Words** Make available a variety of drawing tools (paints, markers, colored pencils). Encourage students to comment on and question each other about their drawings: *What does this color mean? Why did you choose this shape?*

CLOSE AND ASSESS

Ask students to write a message on an index card that tells one thing they learned in this lesson.

RESPOND

OBJECTIVES

POPULATION SHIFTS

Function: Give Information

Concepts and Vocabulary: Words About Population—*population, census, demographics, race, ethnic group*

Learning Strategies, Critical Thinking, and Research Skills: Gather Information; Take Notes; Form Generalizations

Technology/Media: Use the Internet

Representing: Observation and Data Chart

CONTENT AREA CONNECTIONS, CONTINUED

1 **Study Population Shifts** To prepare for and support the activity, group students according to specific migrations and have them share resources and information for their charts. Invite groups to present their charts and explain them to the class. Then the class can compare and contrast the various migrations.

Introduce these terms about population shifts:

- ***population, census, demographics*:** Define population as *"all the people that live in a certain area."* Explain that, when governments take a *census,* they count the population of an area. *Demographics* refers to information about the characteristics of human populations, such as: growth; density; gender, ethnicity, and age distribution; and birth and death rates.
- ***race, ethnic group*:** Explain that *race* has two meanings. We are all members of the human race. A person's race might also mean "physical characteristics passed on genetically" (Caucasian, African American). An *ethnic group* has at least one characteristic in common: race, nationality, religion, or cultural background.

CLOSE AND ASSESS

Ask each student: *What is one thing you learned in this lesson?*

Respond to the Essay, continued

Content Area Connections

TECHNOLOGY/MEDIA

SOCIAL STUDIES

STUDY POPULATION SHIFTS

Many African Americans moved north during the early 1900s. Use the Internet, encyclopedias, and almanacs to learn about other population shifts in U.S. history. Make a class chart of what you learn.

1 **Choose an Event** Find out about population shifts in U.S. history like the Westward Movement, the California gold rush, and the Dust Bowl. Be sure to find out when the migration occurred, too. Choose a topic that interests you.

2 **Prepare to Research** Write questions you'd like to answer such as:
- Why did the migration happen?
- Who migrated?
- What were the effects of the migration?

3 **Gather Information and Take Notes** These Web sites might be good places to fi[nd] answers. Use the name of the migration as key word in your search. Download helpful information.

INTERNET

INFORMATION ON-LINE

Web Sites:
- **Search Engine**
  - www.yahooligans.com
- **Encyclopedia Articles**
  - www.encarta.com

4 **Make a Class Chart** Combine the information you and your classmates learne[d] into a class chart. Discuss the effects of the migrations.

Population Shifts in U.S. History

Name of Migration	Time Period	Reasons	Effects
Great Migration			
Gold Rush			

Learn more about **charts** on Handbook pages 370–371. For more about the **research process,** see pages 394–399.

REACHING ALL STUDENTS

Research Skills

▶ TAKE NOTES

Materials: Index Cards

TEACH Before students begin the Study Population Shifts activity, elicit that taking notes will help students remember and organize the information they find while they read and research. Point out that notes will also help them remember where they found the information.

Model taking notes from current reading in a science or social studies text.

- Write a sample research question.
- Read a passage and write answers to the question.
- Write information about the source (title, author, page number).

PRACTICE Distribute index cards and have students continue using their textbooks to ask and answer a research question. Or they could write a research question using another classroom reference, such as an almanac.

▶ **Practice Book** pages 88–89

OLLOW THE RINKING GOURD

traditional song
with text support
by Jeanette Winter

Prepare to Read

THINK ABOUT WHAT YOU KNOW

Idea Exchange Tell about groups of stars you know. Do you know how to find the Big Dipper? Why is it called that?

ture take or catch
orce

ductor leader or guide
trip

ape break loose or
free

edom state of not
g under the control of
her person

rney trip

work group of people
hings that work together
ne

ard money or a
given for something
rson does

away slave person
tries to get away from
one who owns him or her

very custom or practice
wning slaves

wers to the
abulary activity:
avery
scape
unaway slave
etwork
ourney
apture
onductor
eedom
eward

LEARN KEY VOCABULARY

Use New Words in Context Study the new words and their definitions. Then write the paragraph, adding the missing words.

In the early history of the United States, ____(1)____ was legal. Some African American slaves tried to ____(2)____. A ____(3)____ often used the Underground Railroad. It was a ____(4)____ of people and places that helped these slaves. The ____(5)____ on the Underground Railroad was dangerous. Slave hunters tried to ____(6)____ some slaves. So the slaves needed a ____(7)____ to guide them north. There, they hoped to find ____(8)____. This was the ____(9)____ that waited for them at the end of their long journey.

LEARN TO ASK QUESTIONS AND CLARIFY MEANING

When you read, you can stop and **ask questions**. This helps you **clarify**, or understand what you read.

READING STRATEGY

How to Ask Questions and Clarify Meaning

1. Read part of the selection.
2. Ask yourself: What does this mean? What questions do I have about it?
3. Use resources to answer your questions.
4. As you read the next part, look for answers to your questions, and ask new questions about what you've read.

Now read "Follow the Drinking Gourd." Stop after each verse or section and ask questions to clarify meaning.

Multi-Level Strategies

VOCABULARY OPTIONS

BEGINNING Read the paragraph aloud to students as a group and stop at each blank. Suggest two possible answers, one correct and one incorrect. Elicit the correct choice.

INTERMEDIATE Work with students as a group to try out vocabulary words in the paragraph. Then guide them to the correct choices.

ADVANCED Students can complete the paragraph individually and compare answers with a partner.

Transparency 44 / Master 44

ASK QUESTIONS AND CLARIFY

Directions: Ask yourself questions about words and ideas in the song; then try to answer the questions.

Follow the Drinking Gourd

Follow the drinking gourd!
Follow the drinking gourd.
For the old man is awaiting
for to carry you to freedom
If you follow the drinking gourd.

Questions	Answers
1. What is a drinking gourd?	a dried, hollowed out fruit shell, used as a drinking utensil
2. Who is the old man?	someone who will take people to freedom

Transparency 44 Level B, Unit 3 | Dreams and Decisions © Hampton-Brown

PREPARE TO READ

OBJECTIVES

THINK ABOUT WHAT YOU KNOW
Reading Strategy:
Activate Prior Knowledge

LEARN KEY VOCABULARY T
Vocabulary Strategy:
Use New Words in Context

LEARN TO ASK QUESTIONS AND CLARIFY
Reading Strategies:
Ask Questions and Clarify Meaning

THINK ABOUT WHAT YOU KNOW

1 **Idea Exchange** Have students locate the Big Dipper on a map of the constellations.

LEARN KEY VOCABULARY

2 **Use New Words in Context** Read the words and definitions. Conduct the cloze activity.

Use the Vocabulary Options in the **Multi-Level Strategies** to include students at all proficiency levels.

▶ **Practice Book** page 90

LEARN TO ASK QUESTIONS AND CLARIFY MEANING

3 **Model How to Ask Questions and Clarify Meaning** Demonstrate the steps using **Transparency 44**:

- Read aloud the lines from the song. Model asking the question in the first column of the chart.
- Then model how to clarify. First, look up the word *gourd* and write its definition. Then say: *Now I know what a gourd is, but that doesn't make sense. You can't follow a gourd. Maybe you follow something that looks like a gourd. I bet the drinking gourd is the Big Dipper I see in the illustration.*
- Continue by asking *Who is the old man?* and using context clues to answer the question.

CLOSE AND ASSESS

Ask students for examples of questions that clarify meaning. (What does this word mean?)

READ PAGES 186–187

OBJECTIVES

Function: Listen Actively
Vocabulary Strategy: Context Clues (multiple-meaning words)
Grammar: Indefinite Adjectives
Listening: Listen to a Selection
Reading and Learning Strategies: Set a Purpose for Reading; Ask Questions and Clarify Meaning

SET PURPOSE

1 Read aloud the introduction. Set the purpose for listening: *Discover the meaning of the song.*

LISTEN AND READ

Tape 3B
CD 3 Track 4

2 **Strategy Focus: Ask Questions and Clarify Meaning** Play the song once. Then read aloud "A Note About the Song." Play the song again, pausing after each stanza. Encourage students to ask questions and clarify meaning, using the song lyrics as well as what they learned in the Note.

Choose Reading Options in the **Multi-Level Strategies** to include students at all proficiency levels.

FOLLOW THE DRINKING GOURD

A TRADITIONAL SONG
WITH TEXT SUPPORT BY JEANETTE WINTER

The migration of African Americans began long before the Great Migratio From the earliest days of slavery, African American traveled north to find a lif of freedom and opportunit

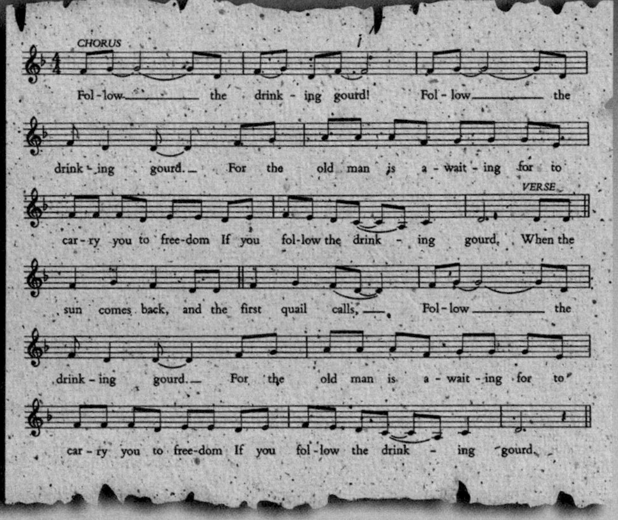

The riverbank makes a very good road,
The dead trees will show you the way.
Left foot, peg foot, traveling on,
Follow the drinking gourd.

(*repeat chorus*)

The river ends between two hills,
Follow the drinking gourd.
There's another river on the other side,
Follow the drinking gourd.

(*repeat chorus*)

When the great big river meets the little river,
Follow the drinking gourd.
For the old man is a-waiting for to carry you to freedom
If you follow the drinking gourd.

riverbank ground by the side of the river
peg foot wood used in place of the missing right foot
a-waiting ready and waiting; an old-fashioned way of saying "waiting"
for to carry to carry

186 **Unit 3** | Dreams and Decisions

REACHING ALL STUDENTS

Science Connection
CONSTELLATIONS

Encourage students to find out about different constellations. Suggest these research questions: *What do they look like? How did they get their names? How have they been used?* Students can look in the library or on the Internet for information. Then ask students to choose one constellation and observe it in the sky. Have students draw the constellation, label it, and tell the class something they have learned about it. Display the drawings in the classroom.

Multi-Level Strategies
READING OPTIONS FOR LESSON 12

BEGINNING Use the visuals, gestures, and restatements to explain the literal meaning of each line. Provide a question frame: What *does* _____ *mean?* As students ask questions, read aloud sections in the Note that pertain to their questions. Restate answers as necessary and record on **Transparency 44**. (See page T185.)

INTERMEDIATE / **ADVANCED** Use **Transparency 44** (see page T185) to continue recording students' questions about unclear phrases and lines. Write their questions, then prompt them about ways to clarify meaning: *Try looking up* quail *in the dictionary. How can the picture help you? Think about what it says in the Note.*

A Note About the Song

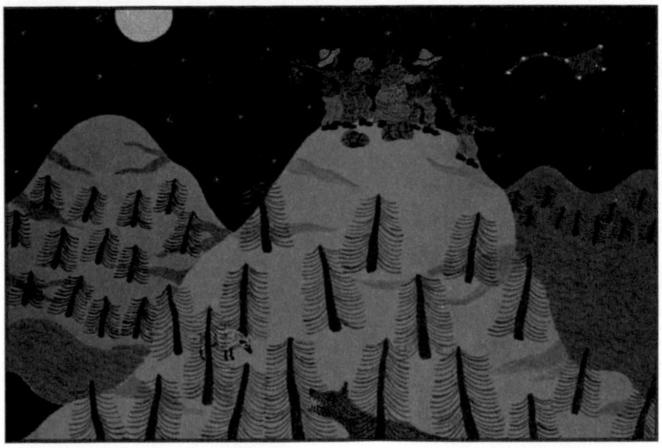

In the early days of **slavery** in the Jnited States many slaves tried to **escape** heir cruel **bondage** by fleeing north—sually to Canada—to **freedom**. By the 840s a loosely organized group of free lacks, slaves, and white **sympathizers** ormed a secret **network** of people and laces that hid escaped slaves on their angerous **journey** to freedom—a network hat came to be known as the Underground Railroad.

Traveling along darkened roads at night, iding out by day, moving slowly upriver long hundreds of miles of **connecting waterways,** the **fugitive** slaves **endured many hardships**. Slave catchers hunted them down with dogs. Many were shot or hanged. And even after crossing into the "free" states, **runaway slaves** could still be **captured** and returned to their masters for a **reward**.

The most famous **conductor** on the Underground Railroad was Harriet Tubman, a runaway slave herself, who led hundreds of her people to freedom. Among other conductors, there was a one-legged sailor named Peg Leg Joe. Joe hired himself out to plantation owners as a handyman. Then he made friends with the slaves and taught them what seemed a harmless folk song—

ondage slavery, enslavement
ympathizers people who cared about the slaves
onnecting waterways rivers and streams that are short distance apart yet joined together
fugitive escaping
endured many hardships had to put up with many problems and hard times

REVIEW KEY VOCABULARY

3 Multiple-Meaning Words Have students look up *capture, conductor,* and *network* in a dictionary, noting definitions different from those given on page 185. (*capture* a scene on film; *conductor* of an orchestra; *network* of computers) Ask students to use the words in sentences with the different meanings. Invite volunteers to read their sentences aloud.

Language Development
GIVE DIRECTIONS

Have students create codes for messages that tell how to get someplace. First, they brainstorm a list of command words (*walk, go right, cross the hall, open the door*). Then invite students to make up codes for each command word, for example, *up arrow = go straight.* In partners, have one student make up directions in code and the other student carry them out. Allow time for students to discuss whether they were able to follow the code words.

Grammar Minilesson

▶ INDEFINITE ADJECTIVES

TEACH Draw students' attention to the word *many* in the sentence on page 187 that begins *In the early days of slavery. . . .* Identify *many* as an indefinite adjective. Explain that indefinite adjectives tell about "how many" or about "how much." They do not identify a definite, or exact, number or amount.

Have students turn to page 442 in the Handbook. Use the explanation and examples to clarify the concept.

PRACTICE Choose from these words to complete the sentences:

some *much* *many*

1. How _____ information do you have about the Underground Railroad?
2. The runaway slaves endured _____ hardships.
3. _____ people were caught even after they reached "free" states.

▶ **Practice Book** page 91

READ PAGE 188

OBJECTIVES

Comprehension: Identify Characters' Motives, Details; Make an Inference

Literary Analysis: Evaluate Impact of Author's Qualifications on Meaning

CHECK COMPREHENSION

4 Answers to "Before You Move On"

1. **Characters' Motives** Freedom mattered most to the slaves.
2. **Details** They could be shot or hanged, or they could be returned to their masters for a reward.
3. **Inference** The conductors were brave people who risked their lives to help slaves escape.

ABOUT THE AUTHOR

5 Evaluate Literature: Author's Qualifications Read About the Author. Ask: *Why do you think this author understands what the escape to freedom meant to the slaves?* (She has written books about people who traveled far to reach their dreams.)

CLOSE AND ASSESS

Read aloud or play a line from the song and ask: *What does this mean?* Use different lines for different groups.

"Follow the Drinking Gourd." But hidden in the **lyrics of the song** were directions for following the Underground Railroad. The Drinking Gourd is the Big Dipper, which points to the North Star. "When the sun comes back, and the first **quail** calls" meant spring, when travel might be least **hazardous**. As the runaway slaves followed the stars north, they would come across marks Peg Leg Joe had made in mud or in charcoal on dead trees—a left foot and a peg foot—and they would know they were on the right trail.

The river that "ends between two hills" was the Tombigbee River. The second was the Tennessee River and the "great big river" was the Ohio River, where Peg Leg Joe would be waiting to **ferry** them across to the free states on the other side. From there the fugitives were guided from one hiding place to the next until—with luck—they made it to Canada or other safe places in the North.

— Jeanette Winter

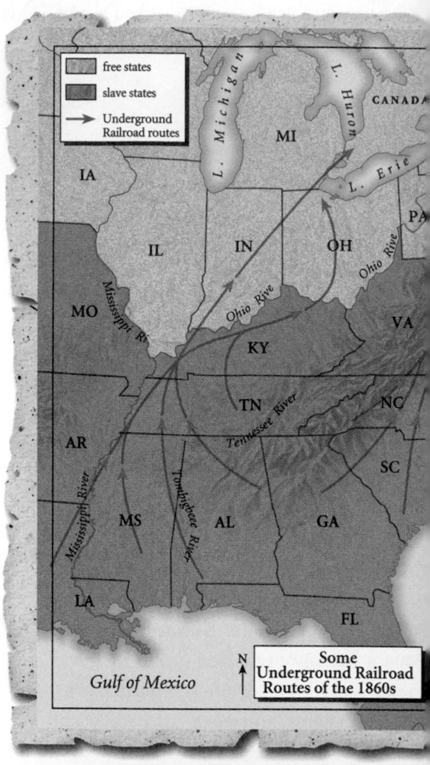

Some Underground Railroad Routes of the 1860s

BEFORE YOU MOVE ON...

1. **Characters' Motives** What mattered most to the slaves who tried to escape?
2. **Details** What could happen to runaway slaves who were captured?
3. **Inference** What can you tell about the character of the conductors?

ABOUT THE AUTHOR

Jeanette Winter is an award-winning children's book author and illustrator. Among her many books are *Cowboy Charlie: The Story of Charles M. Russell* and *My Name Is Georgia: A Portrait by Jeanette Winter*. Both are stories about artists who traveled long distances to achieve their goals and live their dreams. Jeanette Winter lives with her husband in Pipe Creek, Texas.

lyrics of the song words in the song
quail bird; small, fat bird with brown feathers and white spots
hazardous dangerous
ferry carry; carry in a small boat

REACHING ALL STUDENTS

Social Studies Connection

UNDERGROUND RAILROAD

Invite students to find out more about the Underground Railroad. Suggest questions to guide research: *How did passengers know where to go next? What kinds of people served as conductors?* Have students look for information in the library and on the Internet. Suggest that they present reports to the class in the form of posters, skits, and storytelling.

CULTURAL PERSPECTIVES

World Cultures: Songs and Poems

Tell students that many songs and poems communicate information about political or social topics. For example, "Ring Around a Rosie" is about the Plague, which caused circular lesions on the skin. Have students find historical or patriotic songbooks and poems in the library, choose one song or poem, and look for information about it in magazine indexes or on the Internet. They can tell the class what they learned about its background and message.

Vocabulary

SUFFIXES

Call students' attention to the word *bondage* on page 187. Say: *There is a suffix at the end of this word. A suffix is a special word ending that changes the meaning of a word.* Point out several words with different suffixes on this page and the next: *hardship; harmless; hazardous.* Help them discover the meanings of the suffixes. Encourage students to note these words in their individual or class dictionaries.

Respond to the Song

Check Your Understanding

'M IT UP

**stinguish Between Apparent Message and
dden Agenda** An **apparent message** is the
act meaning of the words in a selection. This
ng appears to be about a river through
e woods.

metimes a selection also has a **hidden agenda**,
another meaning. The hidden agenda for
s song is a series of directions for the
derground Railroad.

ke a chart that shows the details of the
parent message and hidden agenda.

Apparent Message	Hidden Agenda
he riverbank makes very good road,	Walk along the riverbank

aw Conclusions Tell why knowing the
dden agenda in the song would be important
a slave. Why would it be important to a slave
ner? Share your ideas in a group.

THINK IT OVER

Discuss and Write Talk about these questions with a partner. Write the answers.

1. **Inference** Why was the Underground Railroad given that name? How was it like a real railroad?
2. **Comparisons** What did the Underground Railroad and the Great Migration have in common?
3. **Inference** Songs were one way for slaves to communicate. What might have been other ways for them to communicate their hidden agenda for escaping to freedom?
4. **Judgments** Peg Leg Joe and other conductors on the Underground Railroad were in great danger. Why do you think they took such risks to help runaway slaves?

EXPRESS YOURSELF ▶ STATE A GOAL

What were the goals of the people you have learned about in this selection? Role-play Harriet Tubman, Peg Leg Joe, a runaway slave, or a slave owner. Tell about your goal to a group.

ne by line interpretation of the song could be:
orus)
low the Big Dipper, keep going north.
g Leg Joe is waiting to ferry you across the Ohio
ver to the free states
ou follow the Big Dipper, and keep going north.
vel in the spring
epeat first three lines>

lk along the riverbank,
rks on dead trees will show you which way to go.
e marks will be a left foot and a peg foot.
low the Big Dipper, keep going north.

Follow the Tombigbee River,
Follow the Big Dipper, keep going north.
Go to the Tennessee River,
Follow the Big Dipper, keep going north.

When you get to the Ohio River,
Follow the Big Dipper, keep going north.
Peg Leg Joe will ferry you across to the free states
If you follow the Big Dipper, keep going north.

Multi-Level Strategies

SUM IT UP OPTIONS

BEGINNING Encourage students to ask questions about meaning after each entry in column 1 of the chart. *(What is this secret meaning?)* Guide students to use the map on page 188 to find places mentioned in the song and the Note. Have students answer conclusion questions with a partner.

INTERMEDIATE Have students discuss hidden agenda meanings and complete the chart in groups. Then have them exchange charts, check answers, and discuss any differences. Encourage students to share conclusions.

ADVANCED After students complete their charts individually, have them exchange charts and compare their information. Ask volunteers to read aloud each statement in column 1 and explain its hidden meaning. Have students write their answers to conclusion questions.

RESPOND

OBJECTIVES

SUM IT UP
Function: Write
Learning Strategy:
Use Graphic Organizers (chart)
Critical Thinking and Comprehension:
Analyze Information (apparent message and hidden agenda); Ⓣ Make Comparisons; Ⓣ Draw Conclusions

THINK IT OVER
Function: Engage in Discussion
Comprehension and Critical Thinking:
Make Inferences; Ⓣ Make Comparisons; Make Judgments

EXPRESS YOURSELF
Function: State a Goal
Speaking and Listening: Role-Play

CHECK YOUR UNDERSTANDING

1 **Sum It Up** Read aloud or play the song before students begin. Let them use "A Note About the Song" to check their charts.

If slave owners knew the song, they would know slaves singing it were planning to escape. For slaves, the song contained directions to freedom.

▶ **Practice Book** page 92

2 **Think It Over** Possible answers are:

1. **Inference** It was secret. It had a route, conductors, and passengers.
2. **Comparisons** Both were about African Americans' journeys north in search of a better life.
3. **Inference** Ways to communicate include leaving markings on trails; hanging quilts outside with messages hidden in their designs; leaving a lamp burning at night.
4. **Judgments** These people believed it was the right thing to do.

3 **Express Yourself** Students can write notes about the people to help with their role-plays.

CLOSE AND ASSESS

Have students write three important things they learned in this lesson.

PREPARE TO READ

OBJECTIVES

THINK ABOUT WHAT YOU KNOW
Reading Strategy:
Relate To Personal Experience

LEARN KEY VOCABULARY Ⓣ
Vocabulary Strategy: Relate Words

LEARN TO CONFIRM WORD MEANINGS
Reading Strategy:
Ⓣ Confirm Word Meanings

THINK ABOUT WHAT YOU KNOW

1 Describe Places Have students label parts of their dream homes. Encourage listeners to ask questions about their partners' dream homes.

LEARN KEY VOCABULARY

2 Relate Words Read aloud and clarify words and definitions. Then conduct the activity.

Use the Vocabulary Options in the **Multi-Level Strategies** to tailor the activity to proficiency levels.

▶ **Practice Book** page 93

LEARN TO CONFIRM WORD MEANINGS

3 Model How to Confirm Word Meanings Define *confirm* as "make sure." Use **Transparency 45** to demonstrate the steps:

- Point out that *painful* has two parts: *pain* and the suffix *-ful.*
- Elicit that the meaning of *emerge* can be determined from context clues.
- Model predicting the meaning of *commercial* from personal experience.
- Look up words in a dictionary to confirm meanings.

CLOSE AND ASSESS

Invite students to choose any difficult word in the paragraph and confirm its meaning. Have them write a sentence explaining how they confirmed it.

A House of My Own

story
by Sandra Cisneros

Prepare to Read

THINK ABOUT WHAT YOU KNOW

Describe Places Draw a picture of your dream home and describe it to a partner. Tell about all the details that make it perfect for you.

flat apartment

landlord person who owns a building and takes money from others who live in it

laundromat place of business with self-service washing machines and dryers

ordinary not special, regular

own have, possess

real true, not imagined

rent money paid to live in an apartment or house that another person owns

temporary not permanent, for a limited time

washroom bathroom or small room with a sink

LEARN KEY VOCABULARY

Relate Words Study the new words and their definitions. Then use th new words to complete these charts.

Antonyms	
false	real
permanent	temporary
own	borrow
special	ordinary

Synonyms	
apartment	flat
bathroom	washroom
laundry	laundromat
rent	payment

LEARN TO CONFIRM WORD MEANINGS

When you read, stop to figure out the meanings of words you don't know.

READING STRATEGY
How to Confirm Word Meanings

1. Look for parts of the word that you know. Use these word parts to help you guess what the word means.
2. Read the words around the new word. Do they give you clues about the meaning of the new word?
3. Predict the meaning of the word.
4. Look the word up in a dictionary, glossary, or thesaurus. Find th meaning that fits the sentence you are reading.

Confirm the meaning of the new words you read in "A House of My Ow

REACHING ALL STUDENTS

Multi-Level Strategies
VOCABULARY OPTIONS

BEGINNING Group students to read ***Who Was Martin Luther King, Jr.?*** or the Key Points Reading on **Master 46.** (See page T193.) Work with the vocabulary in those selections.

INTERMEDIATE Work with students as a group to determine the placement of words in the chart.

ADVANCED Students complete the charts on their own and explain their decisions to a partner. Then they write a sentence relating two of the vocabulary words.

Transparency 45 / Master 45

CONFIRM WORD MEANINGS

Directions: Read the paragraph. Use the strategies below to figure out the meanings of the words in bold.

The House on Mango Street includes a story about Mamacita. She and her son arrive from her country to be with her husband. Coming to this new place is **painful** for her. She is homesick and she misses her old home. She arrives with overflowing suitcases. Then she doesn't **emerge** from the building again and no one sees her. Sometimes people hear her yelling. Her son sings a **commercial** from the TV. Mamacita yells at him not to speak English, a language that is foreign to her ears. She feels misplaced in this country.

1. Look for parts of words that you know. Suffix *–ful* means "full of." *painful*: full of pain.
2. Look for context clues. Context clues: "from the building," "no one sees her." *emerge*: come out.
3. Predict the meaning. *commercial*: something on radio or television.
4. Look up the words in a dictionary to confirm meanings.

Transparency 45 Level B, Unit 3 | Dreams and Decisions

READ THE SELECTION

OBJECTIVES

Reading Strategies: Preview; Predict
Literary Analysis: Story

INTRODUCE THE SELECTION

4 **Preview and Predict** Read aloud the title, author's name, and introduction. Ask: *What do you think Esperanza dreams about?* Then page through the selection with students, reading the introduction to each section. Ask: *Do you think Esperanza's dreams come true?*

5 **Identify Genre: Story** Tell students that a story is an example of fiction writing. It is an invented narrative, although some characters, settings, and even events may be based on fact. Remind them that a story always has a plot, which the characters move forward, and a theme.

A House of My Own
by Sandra Cisneros

Theme Connection In "A House of My Own," a young girl dreams of moving toward a better future and finding a place of her own.

Selection Summary and Awards The introduction on page 191 of the student book offers a summary of the selection. *The House on Mango Street* won the American Book Award from Before Columbus Foundation, 1985.

Background Author Sandra Cisneros feels that her writing gains an extra dimension from her bilingual background. She has said: "I think that incorporating the Spanish language... allows me to create new expressions in English—to say things in English that have never been said before."

THE BASICS BOOKSHELF

■ ***Who Was* Martin Luther King, Jr.?** by Shirleyann Costigan

The dreams of one person who is willing to make necessary changes can lead to a better future. One great example is Martin Luther King, Jr. and his dream of equal rights for all. The simple text in this biography introduces social studies vocabulary related to civil rights issues, while the photos of events in the life of this great leader give beginning English learners access to the literature.

For Lesson Plans: See the Teacher's Guide for ***The Basics Bookshelf***.

READ PAGES 192–193

OBJECTIVES

Function: Read a Selection
Vocabulary Strategy: Use New Words in Context
Grammar: Modals
Listening: Listen to a Selection
Reading and Learning Strategies: Set a Purpose for Reading; Ⓣ Confirm Word Meanings

SET PURPOSE

1 Read aloud the introduction to pages 192–195. Set the purpose for reading: *Find out what the new house is like and what Esperanza thinks of it.*

READ AND THINK

2 Strategy Focus: Confirm Word Meanings Students make 3-column charts with difficult words in column 1 and predictions of meanings in column 2. Working with a partner, they use a dictionary to confirm meanings and write them in column 3.

Choose Reading Options in the **Multi-Level Strategies** to allow all students to participate.

Red annotations offer opportunities to clarify meaning and check for understanding.

1

A HOUSE BUT NOT A HOME

Although Esperanza and her family finally own a house, it's not the large, beautiful one they had hoped for. It doesn't feel like home.

Build background: To some people, a house is just a place to live; to others a house expresses who we are, what we have accomplished, what we dream of doing.

The House on Mango Street

We didn't always live on Mango Street. Before that we lived on Loomis on the third floor, and before that we lived on Keeler. Before Keeler it was Paulina, and before that I can't remember. But what I remember most is moving a lot. Each time it **seemed** there'd be one more of us. By the time we got to Mango Street we were six—Mama, Papa, Carlos, Kiki, my sister Nenny and me.

The house on Mango Street is ours, and we don't have to pay **rent** to anybody, or share the yard with the people downstairs, or be careful not to make too much noise, and there isn't a **landlord** banging on the ceiling with a broom. But even so, it's not the house we'd thought we'd get.

We had to leave the **flat** on Loomis quick. The **water pipes** broke and the landlord wouldn't fix them because the house was too old. We had to leave fast. We were using the **washroom** next door and carrying water over in empty milk gallons. That's why Mama and Papa looked for a house, and that's why we moved into the house on Mango Street, far away, on th other side of town.

Restate: Every time they moved, there was one more family member because another child had been born.

They always told us that one day we would move into a house, a **real** house that would be ours for always so we wouldn't have to move each year. And our house would have running water and pipes that worked. And inside it would have real stairs, not **hallway stairs**, but stairs inside like the houses on TV. And we'd have a **basement** and at least three washrooms so when we took a bath we wouldn't have to tell everybody. Our house would be white with trees around it, a great big yard and grass growing without a fence. This was th house Papa talked about when he held a **lottery ticket** and this was the house Mama dreamed up in the stories she told us before we went to bed.

Pose choices: Who cared about having a drea house—just Esperanza or the whole family?

Ask: How is the house different from the other places they've lived?

seemed looked as if
water pipes metal or plastic tubes used for directing water through the building
hallway stairs outside stairs like in an apartment building
basement storage room under the house
lottery ticket numbered piece of paper in a contest to win money

REACHING ALL STUDENTS

Vocabulary
CONTRACTIONS

Materials: Index cards

Write these contractions from the selection on one side of index cards: *didn't, can't, there'd, isn't, it's, that's, wouldn't, we'd.* On the backs, write the whole term (*did not*). Explain how to use an apostrophe to form a contraction. Have students take turns showing contractions, stating the complete term, and naming the missing letter(s). Invite them to add cards for other contractions. Then have them write a sentence for each contraction and one for its complete term.

Multi-Level Strategies
READING OPTIONS FOR LESSONS 15–17

BEGINNING Students can work with ***Who Was* Martin Luther King, Jr.?** while the class reads "A House of My Own." Or distribute copies of **Master 46** to conduct a Key Points Reading. Students can follow along as you read aloud, one paragraph at a time. Help students create their charts. Help them confirm meanings using a dictionary or glossary.

INTERMEDIATE Read the story aloud. Use the red annotations on the facsimile pages to clarify meaning. Work as a group to choose words from the selection to add to their charts. Confirm meanings together.

ADVANCED Students create their charts in pairs. Then pairs compare their charts with other pairs. Remind students to use a dictionary to confirm meanings.

Use visuals: What can you tell about Esperanza from this picture?

REVIEW KEY VOCABULARY

3 Use New Words in Context Have students complete this paragraph with vocabulary words:

Roger lived in an <u>ordinary</u> apartment building that looked like many others. He used the <u>laundromat</u> to wash his clothes. The <u>rent</u> he paid was high. Roger said the apartment was <u>temporary</u> until he found a house. He was saving money because he wanted to <u>own</u> the place where he lived.

Transparency 46 / Master 46

KEY POINTS READING

A House of My Own

Esperanza and her family used to move often. Now they live in a house they own on Mango Street. In this house, there is no landlord. They don't have to share the yard. But this is not the house Esperanza and her family dreamed about.

The house on Mango Street is small, and the front door is hard to open. There is no front yard, and there is only one washroom. Esperanza's father says the house on Mango Street is temporary. "For the time being," her Mama says.

Esperanza understands the trees in front of her house. She feels they understand her, too. They grow and grow in the middle of concrete. They are strong, like Esperanza. Esperanza's mom is strong, too. And smart. She wants Esperanza to to go school and be somebody. She says she was "a smart cookie" when she was young.

Esperanza likes to tell stories. She dreams of someday telling this story. She will say goodbye to Mango Street. But she will always come back for the ones she left behind.

Transparency 46 Level B, Unit 3 | Dreams and Decisions

Grammar Minilesson

▶ MODALS

TEACH Point out the sentence on page 192 that begins *They always told us that one day. . . .* Explain that verbs like *would* tell about things that are possible, not things that are definite.

Provide examples of sentences with modals: *We might move next year. We would have a nicer house. My parents may decide about it soon.*

PRACTICE Write these words:

could	may	might
should	will	would

Have students choose a word from the list to complete these sentences:

1. Esperanza _____ like her own house.
2. She _____ make that her goal.
3. She _____ reach her goal some day.
4. Esperanza _____ be happy with her house.

▶ **Practice Book** page 94

PAGES 194–195

OBJECTIVES

Vocabulary Strategy: Locate Word Origins (borrowed words, coined words)
Grammar: Two-Word Verbs
Reading Strategies: Reduce the Amount Read
Comprehension: Ⓣ Make Comparisons; Identify Character's Point of View; Make an Inference

MONITOR YOUR READING

4 **Reduce the Amount Read** Read aloud the first two paragraphs on page 194. Allow time for students to add to their charts and work with meanings. Read paragraph three and stop again. Finish the page. Ask: *Is it easier to think about meanings if you read a smaller section at a time?* Encourage discussion.

EXPAND VOCABULARY

5 **Word Origins** Use *landlord* to explain how a word created in one set of circumstances is later adapted. (Land owners in old England were members of the gentry and called lords.) Explain that another way to create new words is to put two words together, as in *laundromat* (laundry + automatic). Elicit others, such as *e-mail* (electronic + mail), *apartment* (separate living spaces, apart, yet within one building).

Ask: What was disappointing about the house on Mango Street?

But the house on Mango Street is not the way they told it at all. It's small and red with **tight** steps in front and windows so small you'd think they were holding their breath. Bricks are **crumbling** in places, and the front door is so **swollen** you have to push hard to get in. There is no front yard, only four little **elms** the city planted by the **curb**. Out back is a small garage for the car we don't **own** yet and a small yard that looks smaller between the two buildings on either side. There are stairs in our house, but they're **ordinary** hallway stairs, and the house has only one washroom. Everybody has to share a bedroom—Mama and Papa, Carlos and Kiki, me and Nenny.

Once when we were living on Loomis, a nun from my school passed by and saw me playing out front. The **laundromat** downstairs had been boarded up because it had been robbed two days before and the owner had painted on the wood YES WE'RE OPEN so as not to **lose business**.

Where do you live? she asked.

Define *nun*: a woman whose job is to work as part of a religious organization (in this case, the Catholic church).

Use visuals: What details in the pictures help you understand what Esperanza's house was like?

tight small or narrow
crumbling breaking off in little pieces
swollen big beyond its normal size
elms shade trees
curb edge of the street
lose business have fewer customers than before

194 **Unit 3** | Dreams and Decisions

REACHING ALL STUDENTS

Cooperative Learning
FOR LANGUAGE DEVELOPMENT: Describe and Explain

Brainstorm Ideas Ask: *What is the most important thing about a house?* Encourage students to list as many ideas as they can. Have students vote to determine the four opinions to consider.

Think About Choices Assign one opinion to each corner. Allow five minutes for students to think about each opinion. Then ask students to stand in one corner and tell their reasons for choosing it. One student from each corner shares reasons with the class. Continue sharing from the four corners until at least three reasons for each opinion have been stated.

Debrief the Content Instruct students to share what they learned during the activity. Ask: *What is the best reason for your opinion?*

Debrief the Cooperative Process Have students reflect on the value of their participation, for example, ask: *How did your corner-mates help you choose a reason?*

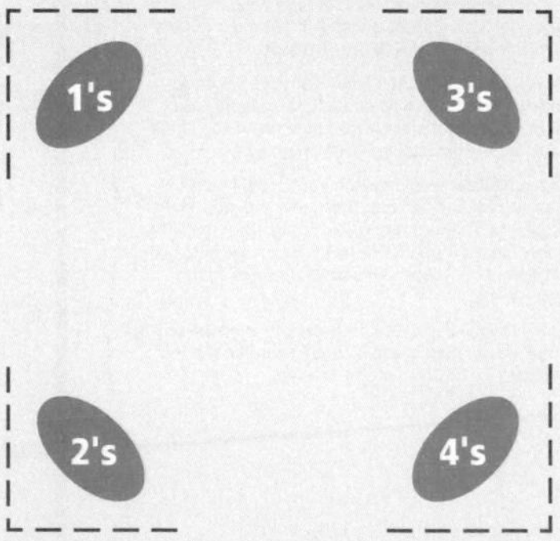

Cooperative Learning Structure: Corners

There, I said pointing up to the
rd floor.
You live *there*?
There. I had to look to where she
nted—the third floor, the paint **peeling**,
oden bars Papa had nailed on the
ndows so we wouldn't fall out. You live
re? The way she said it made me feel like
thing. *There*. I lived *there*. I nodded.
I knew then I had to have a house.
real house. One I could point to. But
s isn't it. The house on Mango Street

Restate: The way the nun said it made her feel embarrassed and belittled.

Pose choices: Does "one I could point to" mean one she could point her finger at or one she could be proud of?

isn't it. **For the time being**, Mama says. **Temporary**, says Papa. But I know how those things go.

BEFORE YOU MOVE ON...

1. **Comparison** How is the house on Mango Street better than the flat on Loomis? How is it similar?
2. **Character's Point of View** Does it matter to Esperanza what other people think about her house? Explain.
3. **Inference** Does Esperanza believe her parents when they say the Mango Street house is temporary? Explain your answer.

ling coming off in pieces and strips
the time being For right now

CHECK COMPREHENSION

6 Answers to "Before You Move On"

1. **Comparison** The house on Mango is better because it doesn't have broken water pipes or a shared washroom next door. It's similar because it's small, has no front yard, and only hallway stairs.
2. **Character's Point of View** It does matter. When people point at her house in surprise, she says she "feels like nothing."
3. **Inference** She may not believe her parents because no place they have lived was their dream house.

CLOSE AND ASSESS

Refer students to the mind map on page T141 and have them add to the dreams and decisions chain.

COMMUNITY CONNECTION

Map Skills Encourage students to walk around the school or another local neighborhood. Tell them to take notes about the street names, the kinds of houses, and any stores or other landmarks they see. Then get community maps from the town or city hall and have students compare them to the notes they took. Finally, tell students to create their own maps of the neighborhood they walked, labeling streets and important landmarks. Display the maps and discuss them.

Grammar Minilesson

▶ TWO-WORD VERBS

TEACH Draw students' attention to the sentence on page 194 that begins *Once when we were living on Loomis....* Have students identify the action verb *passed by*. Explain that some verbs are made up of a verb and a small word like *by*, *in*, or *out*. Tell students the meaning of the verb *passed by* is different from the meaning of *passed*. For more examples, write:

passed in   passed over
passed out   passed up

Use each in a sentence, and discuss its meaning. Refer students to pages 452–453 in the Handbook to see more two-word verbs.

PRACTICE Have students work in groups. Assign a set of two-word verbs to each group and have them become experts in their meanings. Then they can create sentences about the story using those two-word verbs.

▶ **Practice Book** page 95

READ PAGES 196–197

OBJECTIVES

Function: Read a Selection
Grammar: Complex Sentences
Listening: Listen to a Selection
Reading and Learning Strategies: Set a Purpose for Reading;
Ⓣ Confirm Word Meanings
Comprehension: Ⓣ Make Comparisons; Make an Inference; Form Opinions

SET PURPOSE

1 Read aloud the introduction to pages 196–197. Set the purpose for reading: *Find the ways that Esperanza learns strength and wisdom.*

READ AND THINK

2 **Strategy Focus: Confirm Word Meanings** Involve students in reading pages 196–197. Direct them to make entries in their charts and confirm meanings with each other and a dictionary.

See the **Multi-Level Strategies** on page T192 to tailor the reading experience to all proficiency levels.

2

LIVING AND LEARNING

Esperanza compares herself to the skinny trees that survive by the city street. She listens to the advice her mother gives about life.

Four Skinny Trees

They are the only ones who understand me. I am the only one who understands them. Four skinny trees with skinny necks and pointy elbows like mine. Four who do not belong here but are here. Four **raggedy** excuses planted by the city. From our room we can hear them, but Nenny just sleeps and doesn't appreciate these things.

Their strength is secret. They send **ferocious** roots beneath the ground. They grow up and they grow down and grab the earth between their hairy toes and bite the sky with violent teeth and never quit their anger. This is how they **keep**.

Let one forget his reason for **being**, they'd all droop like tulips in a glass, each with their arms around the other. Keep, keep, keep, trees say when I sleep. They teach.

When I am too sad and too skinny to **keep keeping**, when I am a tiny thing against so many bricks, **then it is** I look at trees. When there is nothing left to look at on this street. Four who grow **despite concrete**. Four who reach and do not forget to reach. Four whose only reason is to be and be.

Restate: Esperanza sees the trees as models for how to hang on against all odds. By "keep" she means they persevere, hope, look toward the future.

Pose choices: Does Esperanza admire or despise the trees?

raggedy unevenly shaped
ferocious mean and angry
keep stay alive
being living
keep keeping go on trying
then it is at that time
despite concrete even though the ground around them is covered with rock-hard material

REACHING ALL STUDENTS

Vocabulary
DENOTATION AND CONNOTATION

Explain that *denotation* is a word's literal definition and *connotation* is another meaning suggested by a word. Give the examples *eat* and *devour*: *He ate his lunch.* (no special image) *He devoured his lunch.* (He ate quickly and seemed very hungry.) Point out selection words with connotations: *grab the earth* (hold tightly); *bite the sky* (fierce, angry touch). Have students find more examples from the selection and write them in a chart. Encourage them to write sentences using the words with their connotations.

Word or Phrase	Denotation	Connotation
tight steps	small, close together	poor, uncomfortable space

Language Development
GIVE INFORMATION

Reread page 197 and ask students why Esperanza's mother says, "I could've been somebody, you know?" Elicit that she was advising Esperanza to follow her dreams and become "somebody." Then ask: *Has anyone encouraged you to reach a goal? Who was the person? What was the goal?* Allow time for students to discuss their ideas with partners or write notes. Then ask students to tell the class about the person. Offer these sentence starters: *I wanted to. . . ; _____ helped me.*

arify: Even though the author's yle is to not use quotation marks, ou can tell who is speaking. Here, speranza's mother is speaking.

A Smart Cookie

I could've been somebody, you know? y mother says and sighs. She has lived in is city her whole life. She can speak two nguages. She can sing **an opera**. She nows how to fix a TV. But she doesn't now which subway train to take to get owntown. I hold her hand very tight while e wait for the right train to arrive.

She used to draw when she had time. ow she draws with a needle and thread, ttle knotted rosebuds, tulips made of silk read. Someday she would like to go to the allet. Someday she would like to see a play. he borrows opera records from the public brary and sings **with velvety lungs owerful as morning glories**.

Today while cooking oatmeal she is **adame Butterfly** until she sighs and oints the wooden spoon at me. I could've een somebody, you know? Esperanza, you o to school. Study hard. That Madame utterfly was a fool. She stirs the oatmeal. ook at my *comadres*. She means Izaura hose husband left and Yolanda whose usband is dead. Got to take care all your wn, she says shaking her head.

Then **out of nowhere**:

Shame is a bad thing, you know. It keeps ou down. You want to know why I quit

Ask: How does Esperanza feel about her mother? How can you tell?

school? Because I didn't have nice clothes. No clothes, but I had brains.

Yup, she says **disgusted**, stirring again. I was a smart cookie then.

BEFORE YOU MOVE ON...

1. **Comparison** In what ways is Esperanza like the four skinny trees?
2. **Inference** What does Esperanza's mother mean when she says, "Got to take care all your own"?
3. **Opinion** Do you think that "shame is a bad thing"? Why or why not?

n opera a musical play in which words are sung ther than spoken

ith velvety lungs powerful as morning glories noothly, beautifully, and forcefully

Madame Butterfly the main character of a famous opera

out of nowhere suddenly

disgusted unhappy at the thought of it

CHECK COMPREHENSION

3 Answers to "Before You Move On"

1. **Comparison** Esperanza has a skinny neck and pointy elbows. She feels she does not belong where she is. She grows and survives despite her surroundings.
2. **Inference** She means you have to take care of yourself and make your own dreams come true.
3. **Opinion** Students will probably say that you should be proud of yourself and your family and keep your inner pride.

CLOSE AND ASSESS

Have groups share the entries they have made in their word meanings charts.

Grammar Minilesson

▶ COMPLEX SENTENCES

TEACH Point out this question from page 197: *You want to know why I quit school?* Have students answer the question with a complex sentence and the subordinating conjunctions *because* or *since*. (*I quit school because. . . .*)

Remind students that a complex sentence has one independent clause and one dependent clause. Ask them to identify the dependent clause in each sentence they create. Refer them to page 429 in the Handbook for examples of other words that signal a dependent clause.

PRACTICE Have students use a complex sentence to answer the question: *What happened to that Esperanza?* For Beginning students, provide sentence frames:

1. Since she never liked the house on Mango Street, Esperanza _____.
2. Esperanza tells stories because _____.
3. Because Esperanza wants a house of her own, she _____.

▶ **Practice Book** page 96

READ PAGES 198–199

OBJECTIVES

Function: Read a Selection
Vocabulary Strategy: Idioms
Grammar: Complex Sentences
Listening: Listen to a Selection
Reading and Learning Strategies: Set a Purpose for Reading; Ⓣ Confirm Word Meanings
Literary Analysis: Author's Style; Word Choice

SET PURPOSE

1 Read aloud the introduction to pages 198–200. Set the purpose for reading: *Find out what Esperanza dreams about.*

READ AND THINK

2 **Strategy Focus: Confirm Word Meanings** Involve students in reading pages 198–200. Remind them to make entries in their charts.

See the **Multi-Level Strategies** on page T192 to tailor the reading experience to all proficiency levels.

3

ESPERANZA'S DREAM

Esperanza dreams of having a wonderful house all her own, and she sets her goals. She plans to go away from Mango Street, but she won't forget her past.

Use visuals: How do you think this house is like Esperanza's dream house?

A House of My Own

Not a flat. Not an apartment in back. Not a man's house. Not a daddy's. A house all my own. With my **porch** and my pillow, my pretty purple **petunias**. My books and my stories. My two shoes waiting beside the bed. Nobody to shake a stick at. Nobody's garbage to pick up after.

Only a house quiet as snow, a space for myself to go, clean as paper before the poem.

Define *nobody to shake a stick at*: nobody to be concerned about.

porch covered area in front of the entrance
petunias flowers that are shaped like trumpets

REACHING ALL STUDENTS

CULTURAL PERSPECTIVES

U.S. Cultures: Latino Writers, Artists, and Musicians Many Latino writers, artists, and musicians show American, Hispanic, and other influences in their work. This group includes the writers Sandra Cisneros, Julia Alvarez, and Gloria Anzaldúa; Los Angeles artists Gronk and Judy Baca; and musicians Gloria Estefan and Ricky Martin. Suggest that students choose a Latino writer, artist, or musician and bring to class a sample of his or her work to share.

Vocabulary

SENSORY IMAGES

Point out that Sandra Cisneros uses colorful phrases in her writing (*hairy toes; clean as paper*). These phrases appeal to different senses. Ask students to work in groups to make a Sensory Images chart. They should look for other colorful phrases in the story, including *arms around the other; pretty purple petunias; house as quiet as snow.* Invite students to illustrate some of the phrases and share their charts with the class.

Sense	Sensory Images	Drawings
sight	pretty purple petunias	
hearing	quiet as snow	

Mango Says Goodbye Sometimes

I like to tell stories. I tell them inside y head. I tell them after the mailman says, ere's your mail. Here's your mail he said.

I make a story for my life, for each step y brown shoe takes. I say, "And so she **udged** up the wooden stairs, her sad brown oes taking her to the house she never liked."

I like to tell stories. I am going to tell u a story about a girl who didn't want belong.

We didn't always live on Mango Street. fore that we lived on Loomis on the ird floor, and before that we lived on eeler. Before Keeler it was Paulina, but hat I remember most is Mango Street, d red house, the house I belong but do t belong to. **Ask:** Why does she describe the Mango Street house as a sad house?

I put it down on paper and then the ost does not ache so much. I write it wn and Mango says goodbye sometimes. e does not hold me with both arms. She ts me free. **Encourage elaboration:** How does writing set Esperanza free?

udged walked slowly, as if she were tired

EXPAND VOCABULARY

3 Idioms Use phrases from page 197 *(could've been somebody, take care all your own,* and *smart cookie)* to elicit an explanation of idioms. Ask: *What other phrases could you use in place of these? Why does the author use these particular phrases?* (to give a flavor of her culture and family) Lead students to define *idiom* as "words or phrases used in a unique way by a particular group of people." Encourage students to identify examples they encounter in school or their neighborhoods and record the idioms and their meanings in individual or class dictionaries.

Literary Analysis Minilesson

▶ AUTHOR'S STYLE AND WORD CHOICE

TEACH Have students look for figurative language in Esperanza's description of the trees on page 196, such as "four raggedy excuses planted by the city." Point out the author's word choices on page 198:

- *My two shoes waiting beside the bed.* (compressed language)
- *pretty purple petunias; a house quiet as snow* (sensory images)

Elicit that the author's use of such language shows her poetic style.

PRACTICE Have students form groups. Each group can take one paragraph on page 196 and rewrite it as a poem, with one line under another. Tell students to invent their own sensory images. Invite groups to read their poems to the class. Encourage discussion about the differences between their poems and the author's original text.

▶ **Practice Book** page 97

READ PAGE 200

OBJECTIVES

Comprehension: Identify Details;
Ⓣ Draw Conclusions; Make an Inference
Literary Analysis: Evaluate Impact of Author's Background on Meaning

CHECK COMPREHENSION

4 **Answers to "Before You Move On"**

1. **Details** She wants a house with a garden, a porch, quiet space, and her possessions inside.
2. **Conclusions** By graduating, she has fulfilled her mother's dream of education. She will use it as a way out of poverty.
3. **Inference** They don't know that when I leave, I'll be planning to come back.

ABOUT THE AUTHOR

5 **Evaluate Literature: Author's Background** Read aloud About the Author. Ask: *How do you think the author's favorite book influenced her writing?*

CLOSE AND ASSESS

Ask students to work in pairs to come up with one sentence that summarizes what they learned in this lesson.

One day I will pack my bags of books and paper. One day I will say goodbye to Mango. I am too strong for her to keep me here forever. One day I will go away.

Friends and neighbors will say, What happened to that Esperanza? Where did she go with all those books and paper? Why did she march so far away?

They will not know I have gone away to come back. For the ones I left behind. For the ones who cannot out.

Encourage elaboration: Why will Esperanza come back to the old neighborhood someday?

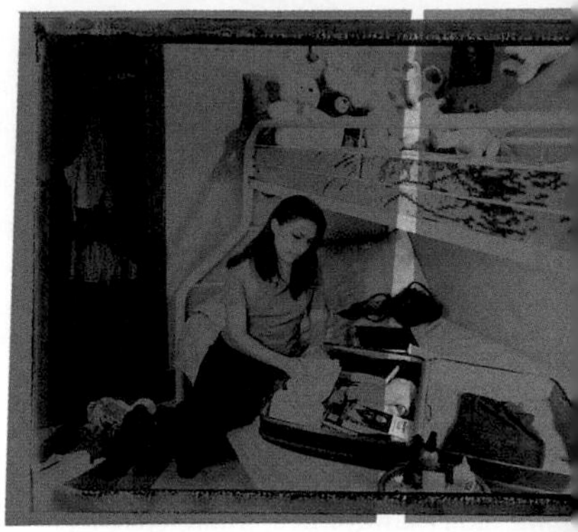

BEFORE YOU MOVE ON...

1. **Details** Describe the house that Esperanza wants.
2. **Conclusions** Look at the photographs on page 199. How has Esperanza fulfilled her mother's dream as well as her own?
3. **Inference** What do you think Esperanza means when she says, "They will not know I have gone away to come back"?

ABOUT THE AUTHOR

As a girl, **Sandra Cisneros** moved frequently with her family between Mexico City and Chicago. She didn't have much chance to make friends, so books became her friends. Her favorite book described the kind of house she wanted. Unlike the large apartment houses she was used to, it was a single-famil[y] house. Later, the books Sandra Cisneros wrote about her experiences as a Mexican American woman helped her move to th[e] home of her dreams. She now lives and writes in her Texas home that is painted a vivid purple.

REACHING ALL STUDENTS

Social Studies Connection

URBAN RENEWAL

Invite students to find out about projects in major cities to clean up rundown areas and make them more useful and pleasant. Suggest such cities as Boston, Chicago, Atlanta, San Francisco, and Seattle. Brainstorm research questions with students: *What is the purpose of the project? What needs does it hope to meet? What problems are related to the project?* Suggest that students go to the library or look on the Internet for information. They can present their findings on maps, posters, in oral reports, or with scale models.

INTERNET

SOCIAL STUDIES CONNECTION

Sandra Cisneros lived part of her childhood in Mexico City. Invite students to find out about this city that boasts the largest population of any city in the world. Suggest that students choose an aspect to research on the Internet, such as climate, history, or culture. Students can assemble their information in a class presentation that might include posters and charts.

Web Sites

Web sites often undergo changes, but here are a few to suggest:

encarta.msn.com
britannica.com
letsfindout.com
encyclopedia.com

Respond to the Story

Check Your Understanding

UM IT UP

onfirm Meanings and Make Inferences ›ok at the chart. Confirm the meanings of the nderlined words. Write how you confirmed ach meaning. Then, once you understand the ords, reread each passage. What inferences n you make about the characters?

Story Passage	How I Confirmed Meaning	Inference
Out back is a small garage for the car we don't own yet.	context	They cannot afford to buy a car.
And so she trudged up the wooden stairs, her sad brown shoes taking her to the house she never liked.	dictionary	Esperanza was sad because she didn't like the house.
But she doesn't know which subway train to take to get downtown.	word parts	Her mother isn't good at getting around town on her own.

redict Outcomes Use what you learned bout Esperanza to predict what will happen hen she grows up. Will she come back to Mango Street? Why or why not? Share your leas in a group.

THINK IT OVER

Discuss and Write Talk about these questions with a partner. Write the answers.

1. **Conclusions** What did Esperanza discover about herself? Why is it so important for her to have a place of her own?
2. **Theme** How does this selection relate to the theme Dreams and Decisions?
3. **Opinion** Think about this selection and "The Great Migration." How do you think people make a home wherever they go?
4. **Author's Background** Sandra Cisneros was the only girl among seven children. Her six brothers were so bossy that she says she felt as if she had "seven fathers." In what ways do you think the author's background influenced her life and her work as a fiction writer?

EXPRESS YOURSELF ▶EXPRESS PROBABILITY

Do you think Esperanza will get the house she wants? How will she find her dream home? Form a group to discuss your ideas.

Multi-Level Strategies

SUM IT UP OPTIONS

BEGINNING Review the steps in the Reading Strategy Box on page 190. Invite students to draw pictures of what the words mean. Then have students complete the chart as a group and read their notes aloud.

INTERMEDIATE Have students review with a partner the steps in the Reading Strategy Box on page 190. Instruct groups to ask who? what? where? how? and yes/no questions about word meanings and inferences as they complete the chart: *Do they own a car?* (no) *How did she feel when she went up the stairs?* (sad) *Does she find her own way around the city very often? (no)*

ADVANCED Suggest that Advanced students find other passages in the selection and add ideas to the chart.

RESPOND

OBJECTIVES

SUM IT UP
Function: Write
Reading and Learning Strategies: Ⓣ Confirm Word Meanings; Use Graphic Organizers (chart)
Critical Thinking: Make Inferences; Make Predictions

THINK IT OVER
Function: Engage in Discussion
Critical Thinking and Comprehension: Ⓣ Draw Conclusions; Form Opinions
Literary Analysis: Theme; Evaluate Impact of Author's Background on Meaning

EXPRESS YOURSELF
Function: Express Probability
Speaking and Listening: Discussion

CHECK YOUR UNDERSTANDING

1 **Sum It Up** Have students explain inferences. Students can share predictions as oral stories.

▶ **Practice Book** page 98

2 **Think It Over** Possible answers are:

1. **Conclusions** She learned she wants to write and needs privacy.
2. **Theme** To follow dreams may mean hard decisions. Esperanza may choose to leave her family.
3. **Opinion** They take their ideas and feelings about home with them.
4. **Author's Background** It made her want to be independent and have her own place.

3 **Express Yourself** Students should base their ideas on what they know about Esperanza from the story and support their ideas.

CLOSE AND ASSESS

Have students write a question based on this lesson on a card. Partners trade cards and write the answers on the backs. After checking answers, cards can be used to quiz other students.

RESPOND

OBJECTIVES

USE SIMILES

Critical Thinking: Ⓣ Make Comparisons

Literary Analysis: Ⓣ Simile

WRITE A HOUSE POEM

Function: Write

Critical Thinking: Ⓣ Make Comparisons

Writing: Poem

LANGUAGE ARTS AND LITERATURE

1 **Use Similes** Annotations on the student page show possible answers to the practice items.

▶ **Practice Book** page 99

2 **Write a House Poem** Have students reread page 198. Compare it to the Sample Poem. To help students get started, provide a frame:

A House of My Own

Not a(n) _________.
Not a(n) _________.
(kinds of houses you don't want)

Not a(n) _________'s.
(name of a property owner)

A(n) _________.
(the kind of house you do want)

With my _________ and my
_________, my _________.
(things you want in your house)

My _________.
(a special thing waiting for you)

Nobody to _________.
(something that people do that bothers you)

Nobody's _________.
(something that belongs to someone else)

Only a(n) _________ as _________
as _________.
(your dream house and a simile to describe it)

CLOSE AND ASSESS

Have students name the two things they are comparing through the simile in their poem.

ASSESSMENT
Selection Test 12 on page 49 of the Assessment Handbook tests students' mastery of the reading strategies and the vocabulary, comprehension, and language arts skills taught with this selection.

Respond to the Story, continued

Language Arts and Literature

LITERARY ANALYSIS

USE SIMILES

Learn About Similes Writers often use adjectives to describe a person or thing:

The house was **small**.

To help the reader get a better picture of the house, a writer might compare the size to something else:

The house was **as small as a closet**.

The house was **like a box**.

These comparisons, which use the words *like* and *as*, are called **similes**. A simile compares two different things that are alike in some way.

Find Similes What two things are compared in this sentence?

The bricks crumbled like stale cookies.

Practice Create similes to complete these sentences. Possible answers are:

1. The yard was as __big__ as __a ball field__.
2. The front door was as __shiny__ as __the sun__.
3. The water pipes burst like __popcorn__.

WRITING

WRITE A HOUSE POEM

Look at how Sandra Cisneros uses a poetic quality in her writing on page 198. Write a poem with lines like these about your dream house. Tell what it is and isn't.

Sample Poem

A House of My Own

Not an apartment.
Not a trailer.

Not a landlord's.

A big house.

With my dog and my sofa,
My books stacked high.

My door opened to greet me.

Nobody to tell me to get off the phone.

Nobody's toys to trip over.

Only a big house as cozy as fuzzy slippers.

Develop your skill in the **writer's craft**, see Handbook pages 414–423.

REACHING ALL STUDENTS

Multi-Level Strategies

PRACTICE OPTIONS FOR SIMILES

BEGINNING Draw pictures as you give additional examples of similes: *The bedroom was as bright as the sun.* Have students draw pictures to fill in these blanks and create similes about houses:

The windows are as wide as _____.
The steps creak like _____.
The driveway is as smooth as _____.

INTERMEDIATE Students make rebus sentences for the Practice by cutting pictures out of magazines, pasting them into the blanks, and "reading" them.

ADVANCED After students complete the Practice individually, have them exchange papers with a partner. Students then name the two things being compared in each item of their partner's practice sentences.

:ontent Area Connections

FINE ARTS

REATE A DREAM HOUSE

›rm a team and design a dream house.

Choose an Architectural Style As a class, collect pictures of various homes and decorated rooms in magazines. Cut out the pictures and note the various styles you found. Then select the style to use as a model for your home.

Organize Your Design Team Have each member of your team choose a task:

- Draw the outside of the home in the architectural style you have chosen.
- Use graph paper to draw the floor plan of each room. Also decide how many square feet the house has.
- Use photos of furniture and other furnishings to decorate each room.
- Write a description of the special features, such as a patio or skylight.
- Include some facts about the distinguishing features of the style.

Share Your Design Paste drawings, photos, and descriptions on a large poster. As a class, conduct a "dream house conference." Listen to each presentation. Then discuss the advantages of each team's design.

TECHNOLOGY/MEDIA

EVALUATE WEB SITES

Where do you dream of living? Find Web sites with information about two cities you'd like to live in. Then compare and evaluate the sites.

1. **Visit Sites** Work with a partner to choose your two dream cities. Use the names of the cities and their states as key words, for example "Tallahassee, Florida."

   Find sites that are about the city itself and not about specific businesses or organizations in the city. Explore links through the sites. Take notes about features, such as how the site looks, the amount of information presented, and the value of the links provided.

INTERNET

INFORMATION ON-LINE

Web Sites:

- **Some Search Engines**
  - www.google.com
  - www.goto.com
  - www.altavista.com

2. **Evaluate Sites** Use your notes to make a comparison chart. Present the information to the class.

Learn about **charts** on Handbook pages 370–371.

Research Skills

▶ USING CHARTS

TEACH Tell students that a chart is useful for organizing information in a small space. Explain that details are presented in columns and rows, which makes it easy to compare or review them.

Display a chart from a classroom text or reference book. Point out the column heads and how information in the columns relates to the heads. Show how all the columns relate to the item in the first row.

PRACTICE Have students make a chart about the class. Draw a grid and help them choose headings. Invite students to take turns filling in information about themselves on the chart.

Name	Favorite Food	Favorite Music
Anna	Pizza	Salsa

▶ **Practice Book** page 100

RESPOND

OBJECTIVES

DREAM HOUSE

Function: Give Information

Learning Strategies, Critical Thinking, and Research Skills: Gather and Organize Information

Representing: Poster

EVALUATE WEB SITES

Function: Give Information

Learning Strategies, Critical Thinking, and Research Skills: Use Charts; Evaluate Information; Ⓣ Make Comparisons

Technology/Media: Use the Internet; Evaluate Information from Electronic Resources

Representing: Comparison Chart

CONTENT AREA CONNECTIONS

1 **Create a Dream House** Have students list house-related words. Beginning students can organize words in a word web with one branch for each room of the house. Then they can expand their web with new words from a thesaurus.

Guide Intermediate and Advanced students in classifying words by features and defining the terms:

- exterior features: *roof line, bay window, patio, balcony, exterior finish*
- interior features: *open-beam ceiling, light fixture, skylight, walk-in closet*
- furnishings: *bookcase, counter, shelf*

2 **Evaluate Web Sites** Review how to print pages from Web sites. Help students interpret information from any charts that appear at the sites. Encourage students to use printouts as visuals to support their charts.

▶ **Practice Book** page 101

CLOSE AND ASSESS

Have students work in heterogeneous groups to create a sentence that tells what they learned in this lesson. Each group then shares with the class.

BUILD WRITING SKILLS

OBJECTIVES

Function: Engage in Discussion; Listen Actively

Reading Strategy and Critical Thinking: Use Text Structures (character map); Analyze and Evaluate Information

Listening: Listen Critically

Literary Analysis and Writing: Ⓣ Descriptive (character sketch); Sensory Details

INTRODUCE WRITING THAT DESCRIBES

1. **Discuss Descriptive Writing** Read the introduction. Model using descriptive words to describe a classroom object.
2. **Study the Professional Model** Read the excerpt and ask students how they know it is a character sketch. (Students should identify sensory details, such as ivory skin; sparkling eyes; long, silken hair; and wondrous harmonies.)
3. **Explore Text Structure** Explain that descriptions often use comparisons, such as similes, to tell about a character. Use the Character Map to teach one way to structure a character description.

Use the Options for Studying Text Structure in the **Multi-Level Strategies** to adjust instruction.

Writing That Describes

In descriptive writing the author uses words to help the reader picture what someone or something is like.

PROFESSIONAL WRITING MODEL

Descriptive writing uses sensory details. Then readers can see, smell, hear, taste, and touch things in the story. They can imagine that they are standing right beside the characters.

from **"Ginger for the Heart"**

> His daughter's name was Yenna, and her beauty was beyond compare. She had ivory skin, sparkling eyes, and her hair hung long and silken, shining like polished ebony. All day long she and her mother sat by the tower window and sewed with silver needles and silken threads. They sang songs while they worked, and their voices rose in wondrous harmonies.

A DESCRIPTION OF A CHARACTER

In a description of a character, a writer tells what the character is like. Sometimes an author uses similes—comparisons using *like* or *as*—to help the reader understand the character. Study the character map and discuss the description of Yenna in "Ginger for the Heart."

Character Map

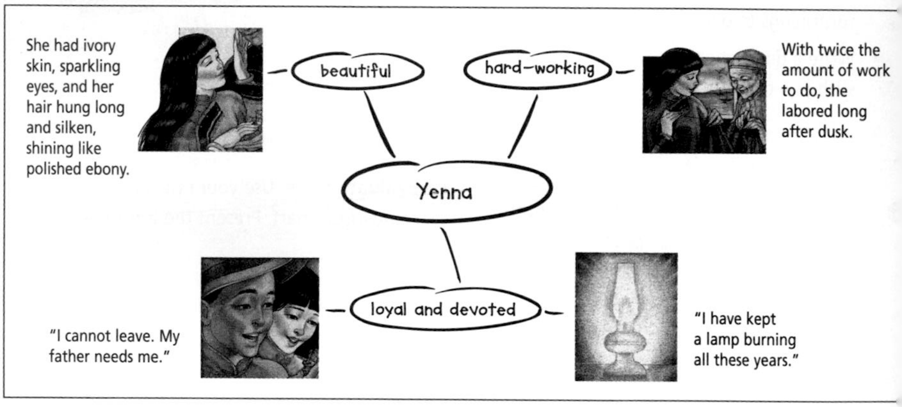

REACHING ALL STUDENTS

Transparency 47 / Master 47

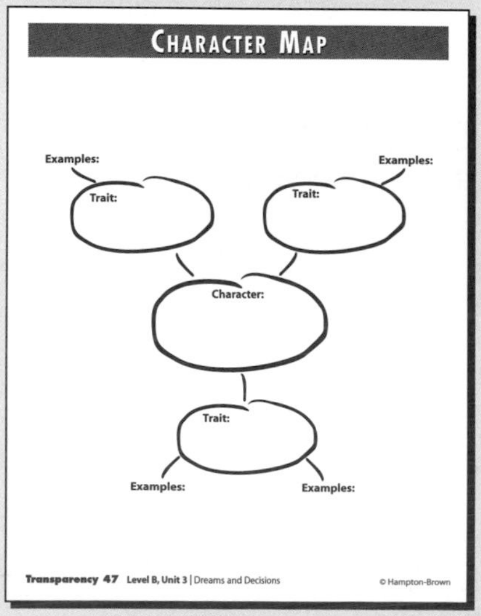

Multi-Level Strategies

OPTIONS FOR STUDYING TEXT STRUCTURE

BEGINNING Display **Transparency 47**. Work with students to choose a familiar character, such as a fictional character they have all read about. Have students sketch or act out that person's traits. Record the traits and examples to support them on the map. Then use the images on page 204 to present the description of Yenna in "Ginger for the Heart."

INTERMEDIATE / **ADVANCED** Use the Character Map to explore Yenna's character traits and the examples that support those traits. Then invite partners to fill out **Master 47** showing traits of a character they have read about and examples to support the traits.

DENT WRITING MODEL

acter Sketch

Dream Come True

y David Yoo

Jun Kim could tackle the most difficult computer games. He asily slipped through twisted mazes, glided around threatening pponents, and swooped up the glittering treasure. He wanted to esign a new, harder computer game.

However, Jun had just come to the United States from Korea nd did not speak English well. Because Jun wanted to study ith the best American computer programmers, he needed to now how to speak English.

Like a runner in a long distance race, Jun pushed himself arder than he sometimes thought possible. His fingers were ramped and throbbing by the time he dropped into bed every ght. As he slept, Jun dreamed of the game he would design ne day.

One summer, Jun stayed in his dark room with his fingers ued to the keyboard until late at night. Slowly, his Technicolor eam game became vivid three-dimensional computer images ashing on the screen.

After three months of hard, lonely work, Jun presented s masterpiece to the world. In an instant, the game became golden trophy everyone wanted. Several computer ogrammers asked to work with him.

The morning Jun heard of his game's success, he smiled. Then e turned his head back to the computer screen and continued esigning his next game.

A **character sketch** uses colorful words and descriptive details to tell what someone is like.

SENSORY DETAILS
Some of the details appeal to the reader's senses. This **sensory imagery** tells how Jun Kim's fingers felt after studying.

COMPARISONS
David uses a **simile** and a **metaphor** to help the reader imagine what's being described.

STUDY A STUDENT WRITING MODEL

4 **Listen for Character Traits** Have students take notes on copies of **Master 47** as you read the Student Model aloud. Go over their notes together to identify sensory details and comparisons that describe Jun Kim.

5 **Analyze and Evaluate Character Sketches** Display **Transparency 48** and lead students in studying the features of a character sketch. Students should then evaluate the Student Model against the rubric on the transparency.

Use the Roles for Cooperative Groups in the **Multi-Level Strategies** to involve all students.

CLOSE AND ASSESS

Call on each **Note Taker** to report the group's conclusions for each feature on **Master 48**. Invite students to add other relevant information and opinions, either verbally or using pantomime to express their ideas.

Multi-Level Strategies

ROLES FOR COOPERATIVE GROUPS

BEGINNING / **INTERMEDIATE** / **ADVANCED** Distribute **Master 48** to groups of three students with varying proficiencies and have them compare the model to the rubric. Assign these roles:

- ▶ **Searcher**
- ▶ **Reader**
- ▶ **Note Taker**

Before groups begin, work through the title and the first feature, pointing out the sample answer. Groups should then discuss each feature of a character sketch. The **Searcher** looks for section(s) in the Student Model relevant to the feature; the **Reader** chooses and reads aloud phrases from those sections; and the **Note Taker** checks the box and writes the information in the chart to be read aloud to the whole group later.

Transparency 48 / Master 48

FEATURES OF DESCRIPTIVE WRITING

Directions: Read "A Dream Come True" and compare it to the features of a character sketch. Check the box if "A Dream Come True" shows the feature. Then give an example.

A Character Sketch. . . A Dream Come True

tells **what someone is like.**	☑ Jun Kim likes computer games. He's very good on the computer.
introduces the person in an **interesting way.**	☑ says he could tackle the most difficult computer games
uses **sensory details,** and **colorful words.**	☑ He easily slipped through twisted mazes, glided around threatening opponents, and swooped up the glittering treasure.
includes **vivid comparisons.**	☑ like a runner in a long distance race; the game became a golden trophy

Transparency 48 Level B, Unit 3 | Dreams and Decisions © Hampton-Brown

BUILD WRITING SKILLS

OBJECTIVES

PREWRITE

Function: Write

Learning Strategies and Critical Thinking: Plan; Generate Ideas; Interact with Peers; Identify Character Traits; Organize Ideas; Self-Assess

Representing: Chart, Character Map

Writing: Ⓣ Writing Process

PRESENT THE WRITING PROCESS AND PROMPT

Read the prompt together. Then leaf through pages 206–210 to review the stages in the Writing Process.

For more about the Writing Process, refer students to pages 408–413 in the Handbook.

PREWRITE

Before students begin their prewriting, preview the steps with the group and discuss the sample FATP chart.

Use the Prewriting Support in the **Multi-Level Strategies** to tailor this stage to proficiency levels.

CLOSE AND ASSESS

Have students work with a partner to answer the questions in Reflect and Evaluate.

The Writing Process

WRITING PROMPT

Now you will write a character sketch—a description of someone. You can write about a real or an imaginary person. Your audience will be your classmates. Make the person come alive for them!

PREWRITE

1. **Collect Ideas and Choose a Subject** Think about people you know or would like to know. Or, imagine an unusual character you may meet someday. Make a chart to show your ideas.

People I Know Today	People I Remember	People I'd Like to Meet	Imaginary People
friend Aman cousin Hector baby sister	grandmother first teacher	NFL quarterback U.S. President	120-year-old man myself in the future an alien

Then choose the subject you can describe in the most interesting way.

2. **Unlock the Writing Prompt** Before you begin writing, fill out an FATP chart to help guide your writing.

3. **Collect the Details** What does your character like to do or say? What does he or she look like? Observing someone is a great way to gather details. If you can, interview the person you are writing about. Then use a Character Map like the one on page 204 to list character traits and examples.

4. **Choose a Focus** Check off the details that you think are most important. Decide what you will describe first, next, and last, and then number your details.

FATP Chart

HOW TO UNLOCK A PRO

Form: *character sketch*

Audience: *classmates*

Topic: *cousin Hector*

Purpose: *to describe Hector's traits*

Reflect and Evalu

- Why do you want to describe this character?
- Do you have enough examples of your character's traits?
- How do you want your readers to feel about yo character?

REACHING ALL STUDENTS

Multi-Level Strategies

PREWRITING SUPPORT

BEGINNING Students can find or draw pictures of people or characters they wish to describe. Have them dictate their FATP charts. Encourage students to create a collage showing descriptive details about their subject. Assist them in adding captions.

INTERMEDIATE Guide students to resources for information about real people. Point out that students might also choose fictional characters they have read about. Have partners work together to fill out FATP charts. Then help them use **Master 47** (see page T204) to organize ideas.

ADVANCED Encourage students to expand their research, if possible, by interviewing any real subject in person or by e-mail. To organize their ideas, they can use **Master 47** (see page T204) or another graphic representation such as an outline or labeled sketch.

AFT

your **FATP** chart to remind you of whom and why you are writing. rst draft is not supposed to be final, so write just to get your ideas n. Expect to make changes later.

Introduce Your Character The beginning should introduce your character in a way that grabs your readers' attention.

Writer's Craft: Introductory Sentence

> My cousin Hector goes after information like a wolf stalking its prey.

Develop the Details Turn the details from your Character Map into sentences and paragraphs. To make your character come alive, use lots of descriptive details.

Writer's Craft: Describing

Use specific, colorful words and images.

Just OK	Much Better
Hector loves chess; he thinks a lot when he plays it.	Hector will never refuse a chess match. His eager eyes dart about the board as he makes a mental note of every possible move.

Use similes.

Overused Comparison	Fresher Comparison
Hector is as sharp as a tack.	Hector absorbs information like a sponge absorbs water.

Make It Personal Put yourself in your writing so your character can be seen through your eyes. Your personal voice and style come from the words you choose and the kinds of sentences you write.

The best advice on writing I've ever received is, "Knock 'em dead with that lead sentence."

— Whitney Balliett

Reflect and Evaluate

- Read your draft. How well do you think you've captured your character's traits?
- Does your draft have an interesting beginning?
- Have you included descriptive details that will help your readers form sharp pictures?

OBJECTIVES

DRAFT

Function: Ⓣ Describe; Write

Learning Strategies and Critical Thinking: Generate Ideas; Self-Assess

Writer's Craft: Ⓣ Introductory Sentence; Describing

Writing: Ⓣ Writing Process

DRAFT

Before students begin their drafts, discuss the Writer's Craft models:

- In **Step 1**, encourage volunteers to explain why the sample introductory sentence is an effective way to begin a character sketch.
- In **Step 2**, ask volunteers to tell why the second model in each set of descriptions is better.

Use the Drafting Support in the **Multi-Level Strategies** to tailor this stage to proficiency levels.

For more about the Writer's Craft, refer students to pages 414–423 in the Handbook.

CLOSE AND ASSESS

Have small groups discuss the questions in Reflect and Evaluate while you work with those who may need more support in assessing their drafts.

Multi-Level Strategies

DRAFTING SUPPORT

BEGINNING Guide students as they draft a sentence that introduces their character. Then work with them to generate a sentence for each picture they included in their collage. Help students use comparisons by providing the following frames: _____ *is like* _____ ; _____ *is as* _____ *as* _____. For students who need individual support, ask questions about their pictures and assist them in forming simple sentences.

INTERMEDIATE / **ADVANCED** Have partners work together to apply the Writer's Craft skill as they revise the examples on **Master 49**. Then encourage students to draft describing sentences that include comparisons and review them with a partner to identify which ones they will use.

Transparency 49 / Master 49

WRITING DESCRIPTIONS

Directions: Read each writing tip and the example that is "Just OK." Change the example to make it "Much Better."

Writing Tips	Just OK	Much Better
Use specific, colorful words and images.	Jun Kim set a goal for himself. Jun Kim worked hard on his game.	Jun Kim dreamed of designing the computer game to top all games. Jun Kim hibernated in his room for three months while he made his dream a reality.
Use similes.	Jun Kim can figure out a computer game as quick as a wink. The game sold like hot cakes.	Jun Kim figures out a computer game as fast as the speed of sound. The game sold like ice cream on a hot day.

Transparency 49 Level B, Unit 3 | Dreams and Decisions © Hampton-Brown

BUILD WRITING SKILLS

OBJECTIVES

REVISE

Function: Write; Engage in Discussion

Learning Strategies and Critical Thinking: Generate Ideas; Review; Clarify; Interact with Peers; Self-Assess

Listening and Speaking: Peer-Conferencing

Technology and Media: Use Word-Processing Software

Writing: Ⓣ Writing Process

REVISE

First have students reread their drafts. They should turn the entries on their FATP charts into questions to answer as they assess their work. For example: *Does my character sketch describe Hector's traits?*

Next model how to evaluate someone else's writing in a peer conference by asking questions about the content and clarity of the draft. Also model how a writer makes revisions. Students can then conduct the peer conferences and revise their drafts.

Use the Peer Conference Support in the **Multi-Level Strategies** to model how to evaluate and revise writing.

CLOSE AND ASSESS

Have peers discuss the questions in Reflect and Evaluate.

REVISE

❶ **Reread Your Draft** Review your **FATP**. Does your writing match your form, audience, topic, and purpose? Have you given a clear picture of your character?

❷ **Conduct a Peer Conference** Talk to a partner or group about your writing. Discuss word choice. How can you make your descriptions more colorful and exact? Should you add or change describing words or phrases? Use the guidelines on Handbook page 411 for help.

Look at the question a reviewer asked during a Peer Conference. Then read what Tina thinks about the changes she will make.

Peer Conferencing on Computer

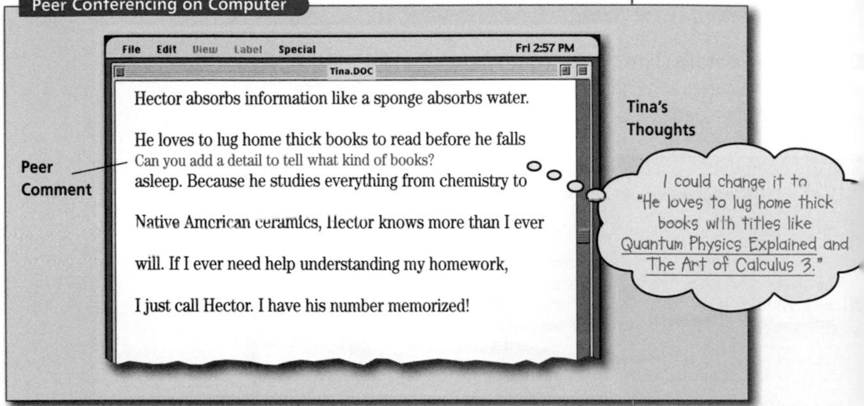

❸ **Mark Your Changes** Look at your notes and decide how you want to change your writing. Revising Marks appear on Handbook page 411. For how to make changes in a word-processed document, see Handbook pages 386–387.

Key In TO Technology

Your word-processing softwa[re may] have a **Comments** feature tha[t] allows your reviewers to add comments. The comments re[main] hidden until you point to the highlighted words.

Reflect and Evalua[te]

- Were your peer reviewe[rs] able to picture your character clearly?
- Did you include all the descriptive details and examples you wanted to[?]
- Are you pleased with yo[ur] writing?

REACHING ALL STUDENTS

Transparency 50 / Master 50

REVISING

Red annotations show changes related to the sample comments. Revisions should vary to reflect comments students make.

After three months of ~~work~~ [hard, lonely work], Jun presented his masterpiece to the world. [In an instant,] The game became ~~the one~~ [a golden trophy] everyone wanted. Several computer programmers asked to work with him.

Revising Marks	
^	Add.
↻	Move to here.
↖	Replace with this.
⤳	Take out.

Ask Questions in a Peer Conference

1. Ask about anything that isn't clear.
   - *Can you add some detail about his work?*
   - Students' comments will vary.
2. Ask about what you want to know more about.
   - *How quickly did the game became popular?*
   - Students' comments will vary.
3. Ask when you think descriptions can be made more colorful or exact.
   - *Can you make this description of his game more colorful?*
   - Students' comments will vary.

Transparency 50 Level B, Unit 3 | Dreams and Decisions © Hampton-Brown

Multi-Level Strategies

PEER CONFERENCE SUPPORT

BEGINNING Display **Transparency 50**. Read the paragraph and support students' comprehension by role-playing Jun Kim working hard at a computer, finding out that his game is a success, and so on. Then model how to evaluate the writing and formulate questions to express suggestions. Have volunteers dictate other sample questions. Model how to revise the paragraph, based on the comments.

INTERMEDIATE / **ADVANCED** Read the paragraph on **Transparency 50** together and have students identify parts that are not clear or that could include more detail. Model with the sample questions and then ask students to suggest questions of their own. Call on volunteers to suggest revisions to the paragraph, based on the comments.

AMMAR IN CONTEXT

IECTIVES, ADVERBS, AND PREPOSITIONAL PHRASES

ectives, adverbs, and prepositional phrases add details to sentences. y can make your descriptions stronger.

djectives describe nouns and tell more about a person, place, thing, r idea.

Examples: My cousin is **hilarious**.

His **outrageous** jokes make everyone laugh.

dverbs usually describe a verb. They can also tell more about an djective or another adverb.

Examples: My cousin **always** makes funny comments.

He is **really** clever.

repositional phrases begin with a preposition and end with a noun or pronoun. Prepositional phrases may act as adjectives or adverbs.

Example: A joke about some penguins made me laugh for ten minutes!
(about some penguins: **adjective phrase**; for ten minutes: **adverb phrase**)

Questions Answered by Adjectives

What is it like?
Which one?
How many?
How much?

Questions Answered by Adverbs

How?
Where?
When?
How much?
How often?

ctice Choose the correct word or phrase from the box at the right. n write the whole sentence.

__________ my cousin told me a joke.
adverb

was a story __________.
prepositional phrase

he man was supposed to take the penguins __________.
prepositional phrase

he next day a friend saw the man __________.
prepositional phrase

We had an __________ time at the zoo. So today we're going to e beach!"
adjective

Word Box

to the zoo
incredible
about a man and two penguins
with the penguins
Yesterday

OBJECTIVES

GRAMMAR IN CONTEXT

Grammar: Ⓣ Adjectives, Adverbs, and Prepositional Phrases

GRAMMAR IN CONTEXT

1 **Teach Adjectives, Adverbs, and Prepositional Phrases** Work with students to read the definitions and study the examples. Then conduct the cooperative learning activity below.

2 **Answers to Practice Items**

1. Yesterday my cousin told me a joke.
2. It was a story about a man and two penguins.
3. The man was supposed to take the penguins to the zoo.
4. The next day a friend saw the man with the penguins.
5. "We had an incredible time at the zoo. So today we're going to the beach!"

CLOSE AND ASSESS

Have partners each write a simple sentence about a familiar character. Partners should then exchange sentences and add an adjective, an adverb, or a prepositional phrase.

Cooperative Learning
FOR LANGUAGE DEVELOPMENT:
Adjectives, Adverbs, and Prepositional Phrases

Materials: picture of a person, large sheet of paper, markers

Write Sentences Display the picture of the person. Post a list of questions about the person answered by adjectives and adverbs. Form groups of four and give each group paper and markers. Each group member writes a sentence that contains an adjective, adverb, or prepositional phrase about the person in the picture. Encourage group members to assist one another.

Debrief the Skill As groups share sentences, list adjectives, adverbs, and prepositional phrases they used. Ask: *What do the descriptive words add to the sentences? How did the questions help you choose words to include?*

Debrief the Cooperative Process Lead students to reflect on the activity: *Did working as a team make it easier to write sentences with descriptions? What did you learn from other team members?*

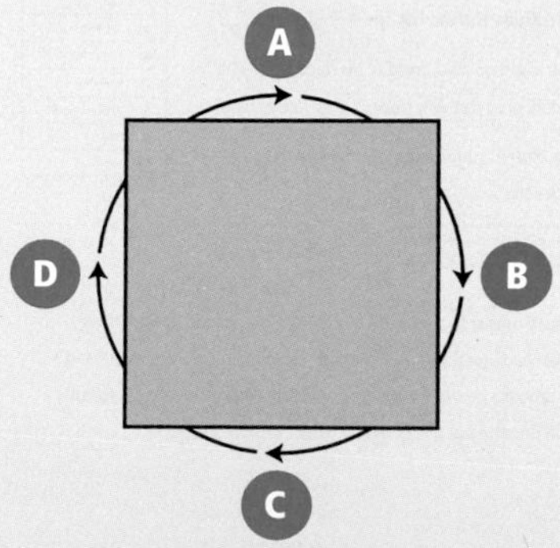

Cooperative Learning Structure: Team Word Webbing

BUILD WRITING SKILLS

OBJECTIVES

EDIT AND PROOFREAD

Learning Strategies and Critical Thinking: Review; Clarify; Self-Assess

Technology and Media: Use Word-Processing Software

Writing: Ⓣ Writing Process

PUBLISH

Learning Strategies and Critical Thinking: Interact with Peers; Self-Assess; Make Decisions

Speaking: Read Aloud

Technology and Media: Use Desktop Publishing Software

Writing: Ⓣ Writing Process

EDIT AND PROOFREAD

Before students edit and proof their own writing, use **Transparency 51** to model the process.

PUBLISH

Ask volunteers to share publishing ideas or choose from those suggested on page 210.

Use the Editing and Publishing Support in the **Multi-Level Strategies** to meet the varying needs of all students.

CLOSE AND ASSESS

Have groups discuss the questions in Reflect and Evaluate. Monitor how students complete the checklist.

LANGUAGE ACQUISITION ASSESSMENT
See page 42 of the Assessment Handbook.

WRITING ASSESSMENT
Use the Writing Rubric on page 51 of the Assessm
Handbook to evaluate this writing assignment.

Writing That Describes, continued

EDIT AND PROOFREAD

1. **Check for Mistakes** Look through your writing and correct any mistakes in capitalization, punctuation, and spelling. If you need help, use Handbook pages 459–469.

2. **Check Your Sentences** Have you used adjectives, adverbs, and prepositional phrases correctly? Make sure you haven't used an adjective where an adverb belongs.

3. **Make a Final Copy** If you are working on a computer, print out the corrected copy of your work. If not, make the corrections as you rewrite a neat, final version.

PUBLISH

Use these ideas for publishing your writing, or come up with your own idea.

- If you are using a desktop publishing program, scan a photo of your subject into your document. Add a caption. Also think of a great title for your work, and show it in a display font.

Desktop Publishing

File Edit View Label Special Fri 2:57 PM

Hector Vega.DOC

Hector Vega: The Human Computer

My cousin Hector goes after knowledge like a wolf stalking its prey. With a smile on his face, he untangles the most difficult math problem in a matter of minutes. To relax, Hector would rather conquer a chemical equation than watch TV. Hector prides himself on knowing all of Mozart's symphonies. He knows everything. He is a human computer.

Cousin Hector

- Read your character sketch aloud to your classmates while they close their eyes and form images. Can your classmates "see" your subject?

Key In TO Technology

Don't use the adverb *very* too often. Use the **Find** feature to for every use of the word *very*. Then delete it or replace it wit stronger word.

Reflect and Evalua

- Are you pleased with yo character sketch? Have y
  - ☑ introduced your character in an interesting way?
  - ☑ included sharp descriptive details?
  - ☑ made some vivid comparisons?
- What do you like best about your writing? Wh still needs work?
- Will this character sketc go in your portfolio? Wh or why not?

REACHING ALL STUDENTS

Transparency 51 / Master 51

EDITING AND PROOFREADING

Directions: Read each sentence. Check for errors in capitalization, spelling, and punctuation. Use the Proofreading Marks to correct the mistakes

1. However, Jun had just come to the United states from Korea and did not speak English well?
2. One summer, jun stayed in his dark room with his fingers glud to the keyboard until late at night.
3. The Morning Jun heard of his game's success, he smiled.

Proofreading Marks	
^	Add.
^,	Add a comma.
⊙	Add a period.
≡	Capitalize.
/	Make lowercase.
⟿	Take out.
¶	Indent.

Directions: Read the paragraph. Check for errors in capitalization, spelling, and punctuation. Check whether adjectives and adverbs are used correctly. Use the Proofreading Marks to correct the mistakes.

¶ Like a runner in a long distance race, Jun pushed himself hard ^er than he sometimes ~~thot~~ ^thought possible. His fingers were cramped and throbbing by the time he dropped into bed ~~all~~ ^every night as he slept, Jun dreamed of the game he would design one day.

Transparency 51 Level B, Unit 3 | Dreams and Decisions © Hampton-Brown

Multi-Level Strategies

EDITING AND PUBLISHING SUPPORT

BEGINNING Model finding and correcting errors in the top section of **Transparency 51**. After marking the edits, have students write out the corrected sentences. For publishing, help students scan their photos and import them in a word processing program to include with their character sketches.

INTERMEDIATE Guide students in finding and correcting the errors in the paragraph at the bottom of **Transparency 51**. Offer students the opportunity to practice reading their character sketches aloud to you before they share them with the group.

ADVANCED Distribute copies of **Master 51** and have students work on the activities individually or with partners. Students may wish to make an entertainment magazine by combining their character sketches.

ebrief

Follow Your Dreams

UNIT 3

ASSESSMENT
The Unit 3 Test on page 53 of the Assessment Handbook measures students' progress in reading, language arts, literary study, and writing. Additional forms in the Assessment Handbook allow for:
- **Self Assessment on page 52**
- **Peer Assessment on page 101**
- **Portfolio Evaluation on page 103**

Look Back at the Unit

Rank Decisions In this unit, you read about people whose decisions helped make their dreams come true.

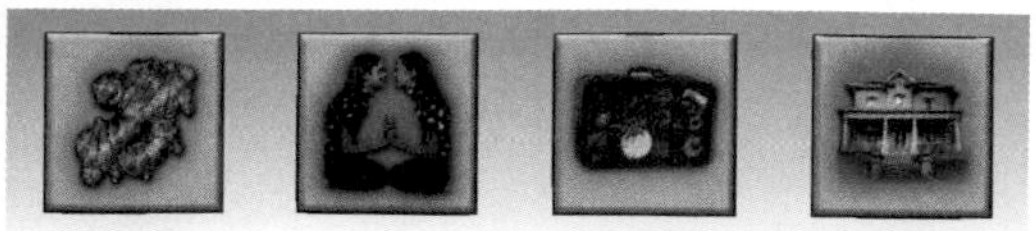

Ginger for the Heart — Twins — The Great Migration — A House of My Own

Write the title of each selection and a character's decision on an index card. Then rank the decisions according to how difficult they were to make. Share and defend your ranking.

Show What You Know

Sum It All Up Expand and organize your ideas on this mind map. Share your ideas about dreams and decisions with a partner.

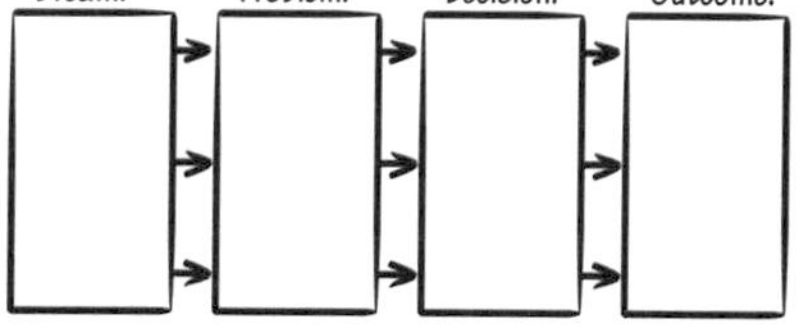

Reflect and Evaluate Finish these sentences:
- Something that matters a lot to me is ________.
- To make my dreams come true, I will have to ________.

Add this writing to your portfolio. Include work from the unit that shows what you learned.

Make Connections

To Your Community Invite friends, family, or members of the community to your class. Ask them to share dreams they have, problems they have faced, and decisions they have made in their lives.

DEBRIEF UNIT 3

OBJECTIVES

Function: Engage in Discussion; Express Opinions

Learning Strategies and Critical Thinking: Interact with Peers; Generate Ideas; Form Opinions; Summarize; Self-Assess; Evaluate Information; Justify; Use Graphic Organizers (mind map)

Literary Analysis: Respond to Literature; Compare and Evaluate Literature

EXPLORE "FOLLOW YOUR DREAMS"

1 **Look Back at the Unit** Discuss criteria for determining the difficulty of a decision, for example: *leaving a loved one.* Then conduct the Cooperative Learning Activity.

2 **Show What You Know** Encourage students to choose work that helps them recognize and value their own dreams.

3 **Make Connections** After students hear about other dreams, have them consider their own dreams.

CLOSE AND ASSESS

Have students tell you the most important thing they learned in the unit.

Cooperative Learning

FOR CRITICAL THINKING: Evaluate and Justify

Grade Decisions After establishing criteria, provide time to think about the decisions in each selection. Then have students discuss their ideas with a partner and determine the most difficult decision.

Sharing Ideas Discuss the decisions made in each selection. During the discussion, partners should take turns sharing their ideas. The class may want to combine their ideas to reach a class consensus.

Debrief the Content Ask students what they learned about dreams and goals from the unit. Model a response: *I learned that the first step toward reaching my dream is to believe in myself.*

Debrief the Cooperative Process Have students evaluate how working with a partner helped them make evaluations. Ask: *How did discussing your ideas with a partner help you better understand them?*

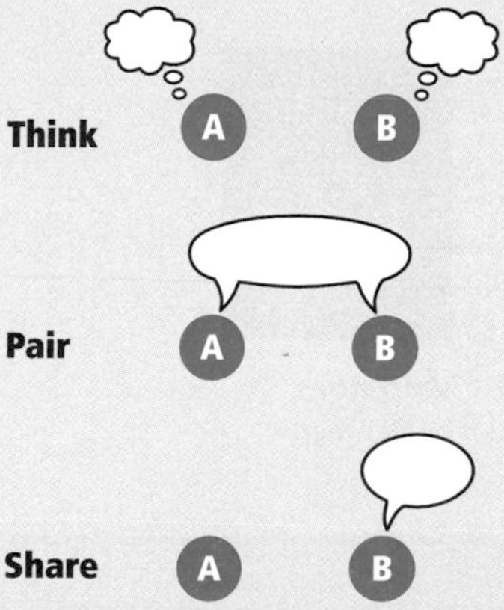

Cooperative Learning Structure: Think, Pair, Share

Resources

For Success in Language, Literature, and Content

Student Book pages 212–289

For Skills Practice

Practice Book
pages 102–137

For Planning and Instruction

Teacher's Edition
pages T212a–T289

For Vocabulary and Language Development

Language Tape Side B
Language CD Track 5

For Selection Readings

Selection Tape 4
Selection CD 4

For Technology Support

Inspiration
Visual Learning Software
with Graphic Organizers

For Classroom Activities

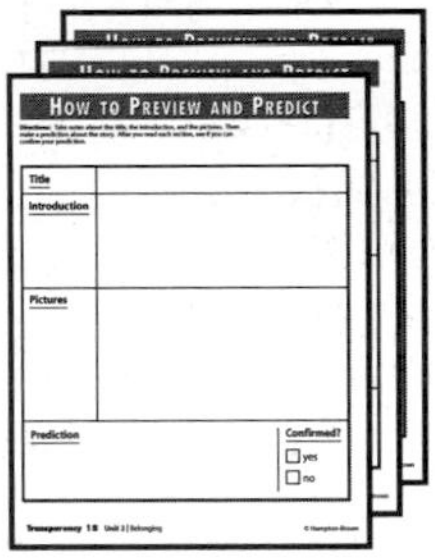

Transparencies or Masters 52–73

For Home-School Connections

High Point Newsletters 7 and 8

For Comprehensive Assessment

Language Acquisition Assessment, Selection Tests, Unit Test, Writing Assessment, Self-Assessment

In the Theme Library

Volcanoes
by Neil Morris

Nine Spoons: A Chanukah Story
by Marci Stillerman

From *The Basics Bookshelf*

- ***The Eagle and the Moon Gold***
- ***Explore!***
- ***The Children We Remember***

Theme-related books with simple text for including newcomers

and Change

Coming Full Circle

CHANGE, WHETHER WROUGHT BY NATURE OR BY HUMANKIND, OFTEN BRINGS DESTRUCTION, FOLLOWED BY RENEWAL. THIS UNIT CHALLENGES STUDENTS, WHO EXPERIENCE TRANSITIONS DAILY, TO EXAMINE THE DYNAMICS OF CHANGE AND DISCOVER HOW IT CAN SOMETIMES LEAVE AN ENDURING LEGACY.

THEME 1 The Certainty of Change

Students learn that changes in nature are always occurring, whether they are cyclical or random.

THEME 2 An Enduring Legacy

Students discover that, in the midst of life's cruelest changes, things of enduring value can survive.

THEME 1: The Certainty of Change

LESSONS

1 — THEME 1 OPENER ▶ pages T214–T215

Function	Learning Strategy	Vocabulary	Critical Thinking
Engage in Discussion	Form Generalizations	Words About Continuity and Change	Form Generalizations

2 — BUILD LANGUAGE AND VOCABULARY ▶ pages T216–T217

Function	Learning Strategy	Vocabulary	Patterns and Structures
Ⓣ Give Information	Make a Mind Map	Words About Change	Ⓣ Relative Clauses

PACING SUGGESTIONS

LESSONS	45–55 MINUTE PERIODS	BLOCK SCHEDULE SESSIONS
1	1 period	1 session (lessons 1–2)
2	1 period	
3–9	7 periods	4 sessions
10–12	2 periods	1 session
13–19	7 periods	4 sessions

3–9 *The Mother Who Lost Her Daughter* by Anne Rockwell

GREEK MYTH/PLAY ▶ pages T218–T230

PREPARE TO READ
pages T218–T219

Activate Prior Knowledge
Idea Exchange

Vocabulary Ⓣ
Relate Words

Reading Strategy
Ⓣ Analyze Story Elements (characters and plot)

READ THE SELECTION
pages T220–T227

Pre-Reading Strategies
Preview and Predict
Identify Genre: Play
Set Purpose

Strategy Focus
Ⓣ Analyze Story Elements (characters and plot)

Vocabulary
Use New Words in Context

Comprehension
Before You Move On: Think and Discuss

Grammar Minilessons:
Ⓣ Relative Clauses

Literary Analysis Minilesson:
Foreshadowing

RESPOND
pages T228–T230

CHECK YOUR UNDERSTANDING

Critical Thinking and Comprehension
Sum It Up:
Ⓣ Analyze Story Elements (characters and plot)
Think It Over: Discuss and Write

Function
Express Yourself: Negotiate

LANGUAGE ARTS AND LITERATURE

Literary Analysis
Ⓣ Make a Plot Diagram

Writing and Literary Analysis
Write a Myth

CONTENT AREA CONNECTIONS

Science
Study Behavior and Nature

Science and Representing/Writing
Create a Botanical Journal

10–12 *Chrysalis Diary* by Paul Fleischman

POEM ▶ pages T231–T235

PREPARE TO READ
page T231

Activate Prior Knowledge
Discuss Life Stages

Vocabulary
Use Context Clues

Reading Strategy
Ⓣ Relate Steps in a Process

READ THE POEM
pages T232–T234

Pre-Reading Strategies
Set Purpose

Strategy Focus
Ⓣ Relate Steps in a Process

Vocabulary
Relate Words

Literary Analysis Minilesson:
Alliteration and Consonance

RESPOND
page T235

Critical Thinking and Comprehension
Sum It Up:
Ⓣ Relate Steps in a Process; Make Predictions
Think It Over: Discuss and Write

Function
Express Yourself: Recite a Poem for Two Voices

13–19 *The Big Blast* by Patricia Lauber

SCIENCE ARTICLE ▶ pages T236–T249

PREPARE TO READ
pages T236–T237

Activate Prior Knowledge
Idea Exchange

Vocabulary Ⓣ
Use New Words in Context

Reading Strategy
Ⓣ Skim and Take Notes

READ THE SELECTION
pages T238–T246

Pre-Reading Strategies
Preview and Predict
Identify Genre: Science Article
Set Purpose

Strategy Focus
Ⓣ Skim and Take Notes

Vocabulary
Relate Words
Sensory Words

Self-Monitoring and Comprehension
Use Text Features: Sidebars
Before You Move On: Think and Discuss

Grammar Minilessons:
Adverbs
Ⓣ Relative Clauses

Literary Analysis Minilesson:
Similes

RESPOND
pages T247–T249

CHECK YOUR UNDERSTANDING

Critical Thinking and Comprehension
Sum It Up:
Ⓣ Relate Causes and Effects; Compare Literature
Think It Over: Discuss and Write

Function
Express Yourself: Ask for and Give Information

LANGUAGE ARTS AND LITERATURE

Vocabulary
Ⓣ Use Latin and Greek Roots

Writing
Write News Stories

CONTENT AREA CONNECTIONS

Technology/Media and Science
Make a Volcano Report

Ⓣ = Assessed on Unit 4 Test Ⓣ = Assessed on Unit 4 Language Acquisition Assessment

THEME 2: An Enduring Legacy

LESSONS

1 **THEME 2 OPENER** ▶ *pages T250–T251*

Function	Learning Strategy	Vocabulary	Critical Thinking
Engage in Discussion	Make a Chart	Words About Continuity and Change	Draw Conclusions

2 **BUILD LANGUAGE AND VOCABULARY** ▶ *pages T252–T253*

Function	Learning Strategy	Vocabulary	Patterns and Structures
Ⓣ Define and Explain	Make a Comparison Chart	Wartime Words	Ⓣ Present Perfect Tense

PACING SUGGESTIONS

LESSONS	45–55 MINUTE PERIODS	BLOCK SCHEDULE SESSIONS
1	1 period	1 session (lessons 1–2)
2	1 period	
3–10	8 periods	4 sessions
11–17	6 periods	3 sessions

3–10 ***Anne Frank*** by Yona Zeldis McDonough — BIOGRAPHY ▶ *pages T254–T269*

PREPARE TO READ pages T254–T257

- **Activate Prior Knowledge**: Idea Exchange
- **Vocabulary** Ⓣ: Use New Words in Context
- **Reading Strategy**: Ⓣ Use Graphic Organizers

READ THE SELECTION pages T258–T265

- **Pre-Reading Strategies**: Preview and Predict; Identify Genre: Biography; Set Purpose
- **Strategy Focus**: Ⓣ Use Graphic Organizers
- **Vocabulary**: Use New Words in Context
- **Self-Monitoring and Comprehension**: Clarify; Before You Move On: Think and Discuss
- **Grammar Minilessons:** Helping Verbs; Two-Word Verbs
- **Literary Analysis Minilesson:** Evaluate Literary Quality

RESPOND pages T266–T269

CHECK YOUR UNDERSTANDING

- **Critical Thinking and Comprehension**: Sum It Up: Ⓣ Identify Sequence; Make Comparisons; Form Generalizations; Think It Over: Discuss and Write
- **Function**: Express Yourself: Define and Explain

LANGUAGE ARTS AND CONTENT AREA CONNECTIONS

- **Grammar in Context**: Ⓣ Use the Present Perfect Tense
- **Social Studies and Representing/Speaking**: Give an Oral Report

CONTENT AREA CONNECTIONS

- **Social Studies and Representing**: Make a War Effort Poster
- **Science and Technology/Media**: Report on Nuclear Weapons

11–17 ***The Diary of a Young Girl*** by Anne Frank — DIARY ▶ *pages T270–T281*

PREPARE TO READ page T270

- **Activate Prior Knowledge**: Brainstorm
- **Vocabulary** Ⓣ: Use New Words in Context
- **Reading Strategy**: Monitor Your Reading

READ THE SELECTION pages T271–T278

- **Pre-Reading Strategies**: Preview and Predict; Identify Genre: Diary; Set Purpose
- **Strategy Focus**: Monitor Your Reading
- **Vocabulary**: Use New Words in Context
- **Comprehension**: Before You Move On: Think and Discuss
- **Literary Analysis Minilessons:** Point of View; Compare Literature

RESPOND pages T279–T281

CHECK YOUR UNDERSTANDING

- **Critical Thinking and Comprehension**: Sum It Up: Identify Important Information; Ⓣ Relate Causes and Effects; Think It Over: Discuss and Write
- **Function**: Express Yourself: Give Information

LANGUAGE ARTS AND LITERATURE

- **Grammar in Context**: Ⓣ Use the Present Perfect Tense
- **Writing**: Keep a Diary

CONTENT AREA CONNECTIONS

- **Technology/Media**: Evaluate and Use Web Sites
- **Social Studies**: Explore Legacies

BUILD WRITING SKILLS **WRITING THAT INFORMS AND EXPLAINS** — EXPOSITORY: CONTENT-AREA REPORT ▶ *Pages T282–T288*

Writing Mode/Form	Writing Process Ⓣ	Writer's Craft	Grammar in Context	Reflect and Evaluate
Ⓣ Expository Content-Area Report	Prewrite Draft Revise Edit and Proofread Publish	Ⓣ Sentence Variety Ⓣ Elaboration	Complex Sentences	Self-Assessment

Ⓣ = Assessed on **Unit 4 Test** Ⓣ = Assessed on **Unit 4 Language Acquisition Assessment**

Theme-Related Resources

THEME 1: The Certainty of Change

MORE RESOURCES

THEME LIBRARY

Volcanoes
by Neil Morris
I This book explains everything about volcanoes. It describes how they change and how they change the areas around them. (Available from Hampton-Brown)

Cactus Hotel
by Brenda Z. Guiberson
B A huge cactus grows to be nearly two hundred years old. Over the course of its long life, it provides a place to live for many small animals. (Holt)

The Time Machine
by H. G. Wells
A A time-traveler explores the future, then returns to his own time to tell about the changes humankind has experienced. (Bantam)

To Everything There is a Season
illustrated by Leo and Diane Dillon
B Illustrations from diverse cultures show a common bond between different peoples. (Scholastic)

Felita
by Nicholasa Mohr
A Felita returns to her old neighborhood to find that many things have changed since she moved away, including herself. (Bantam Doubleday Dell)

Volcanoes
B I A Spectacular video clips along with interviews, computer graphics, and simulations bring "Big Blasts" to life for students. (Discovery Channel) **CD-ROM**

THEME 2: An Enduring Legacy

MORE RESOURCES

THEME LIBRARY

Nine Spoons: A Chanukah Story
by Marci Stillerman
B A few prisoners in a Nazi camp risk everything to gather together nine spoons to make a menorah for Chanukah. (Available from Hampton-Brown)

So Far from the Sea
by Eve Bunting
I A family brings special mementos to a grandfather who died in a Japanese internment camp. (Clarion)

Number the Stars
by Lois Lowry
A During WW II, Annamarie Johansen goes on a dangerous mission to save the life of her best friend, Ellen Rosen. (Bantam Doubleday Dell)

Sadako and the Thousand Paper Cranes
by Eleanor Corr
I A Based on a true story, the bravery of a young Japanese girl touches those around her and makes her a heroine. (Dell)

TimeLiner 4.0
B I A Enables students to create, illustrate, and print time lines to accompany their research projects about World War II. (Tom Snyder Productions) **Software**

The Diary of Anne Frank
B I A This sensitive classic, directed by George Stevens in 1959, captures the elements of hope and tragedy embodied in Anne Frank's self-told story. **Film/Video**

B Beginning I Intermediate A Advanced

UNIT 4

Assessment Options

ONGOING, INFORMAL ASSESSMENT

Check for understanding and achieve closure for every lesson with the targeted questions and activities in the **Close and Assess** boxes in your Teacher's Edition.

INDIVIDUAL AND GROUP-ADMINISTERED TESTS

The **Assessment Handbook** includes these comprehensive assessment tools for Unit 4:

- **Selection Tests**
  Test students' mastery of reading strategies and the vocabulary, comprehension, and language arts skills taught with each main selection of Unit 4.
- **Unit Test in Standardized Test Format**
  The multiple-choice sections of this test measure students' cumulative understanding of the skills and language developed in Unit 4. A Writing Prompt measures progress in writing skills and fluency. The Read, Think, and Explain section offers open-ended items to measure strategies and comprehension.
- **Language Acquisition Assessment**
  To verify students' ability to use the vocabulary and grammar structures taught in Unit 4, conduct these performance assessments.

UNIT 4 ASSESSMENT OPPORTUNITIES

	Assessment Handbook Pages
Unit 4 Language Acquisition Assessment	61–62
Selection Tests	
The Mother Who Lost Her Daughter	63–64
The Big Blast	65–66
Anne Frank	67–68
The Diary of a Young Girl	69–70
Unit 4 Writing Assessment	71
Unit 4 Self-Assessment Form	72
Unit 4 Test	73–80
Peer-Assessment Form	101
Portfolio Evaluation Form	103

SELF- AND PEER-ASSESSMENT

Students use the Unit 4 Self-Assessment Form in the **Assessment Handbook** to evaluate their own work and develop learning strategies appropriate to their needs. Students offer feedback to their classmates with the Peer-Assessment Form.

WRITING ASSESSMENT / PORTFOLIO OPPORTUNITIES

You can evaluate students' writing using the rubrics and scoring guidelines provided in the **Assessment Handbook**. Then collaborate with students to choose work for their portfolios.

INTRODUCE UNIT 4

OBJECTIVES

Function: Engage in Discussion
Concepts and Vocabulary: Continuity and Change—*certainty, enduring, legacy*
Viewing: Interpret a Visual Image
Learning Strategies and Critical Thinking: Preview; Build Background; Use Graphic Organizers (mind map)

INTRODUCE UNIT CONCEPT

1. **Discuss the Title** Define *continuity* as "continuing over time." Ask: *How does a circle represent both continuity and change?* Explain what it means to "come full circle" (to come back to where you started).
2. **Explore the Phases of the Moon** Use **Transparency 52** to explain the phases of the moon: *waxing* (from new to full) and *waning* (from full to new). Then have students make the calculations.
3. **Discuss Continuity and Change** Invite students to discuss:
   - what things change
   - what things have continuity
   - why change is important
   - why continuity is important.

   Use the Questioning Techniques in the **Multi-Level Strategies** to create a class mind map.

UNIT 4 Continuity and Change

212

REACHING ALL STUDENTS

Transparency 52 / Master 52

PHASES OF THE MOON

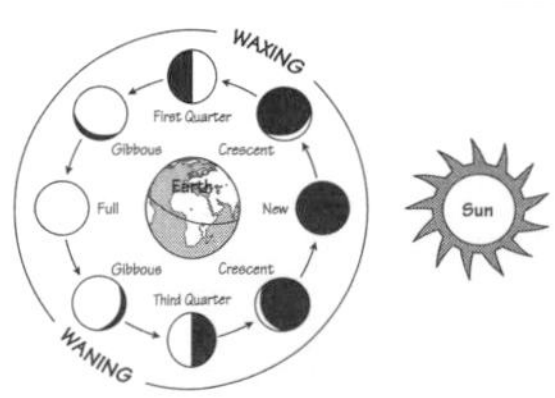

How Many Full Moons?

The moon completes this cycle once every 29½ days.

1. How many full moons appeared last year?
   365 days ÷ 29.5 days in the cycle = 12.4
2. How many full moons were seen over the last 100 years?
   36,500 days in 100 years ÷ 29.5 = 1237.3
3. How many appeared in the last millennium (1000 years)?
   [illegible]

Transparency 52 Level B, Unit 4 | Continuity and Change © Hampton-Brown

Multi-Level Strategies

QUESTIONING TECHNIQUES

BEGINNING Ask students questions that will elicit short answers: *How does the moon appear to change over time? How does it continue? What other things change yet continue?* Have students work together to make a mind map of things that change and have continuity.

INTERMEDIATE Ask students open-ended questions: *What are some examples of things in nature that change? What things show continuity? What are examples of change and continuity from your own life?* Have students incorporate answers into the mind map.

ADVANCED Use questions that lead students to examine the importance of change and continuity: *Why is it important to understand the phases of the moon? What other examples of change and continuity are important to people?* Incorporate students' ideas into the mind map.

Coming Full Circle

WE SEE DIFFERENT PHASES OF THE MOON AS IT ORBITS THE EARTH ONCE EVERY 29½ DAYS. HOW MANY TIMES DID THE FULL MOON APPEAR IN THE LAST YEAR? IN THE LAST CENTURY? IN THE LAST MILLENNIUM? WHAT DOES THIS TELL YOU ABOUT HOW NATURE WORKS IN CYCLES? WHAT CHANGES? WHAT STAYS THE SAME?

THEME 1
The Certainty of Change
Nature changes in cycles or by surprise. Only one thing is certain—change happens.

THEME 2
An Enduring Legacy
The human spirit can survive life's cruelest changes—and leave a legacy for generations to come.

UNIT 4 Mind Map

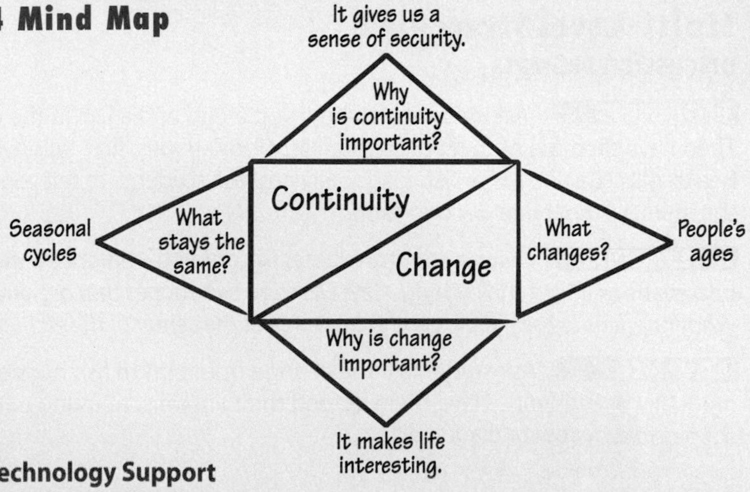

Technology Support
See **Inspiration** visual learning software for support in creating the mind map.

PREVIEW UNIT THEMES

4 **Preview Theme 1: The Certainty of Change** Read aloud the theme title. Define *certainty* as "something that is sure." Ask students: *Are you certain the seasons will change? Are you certain you will be different in five years? Why?*

Invite students to leaf through pages 214–246. Have them tell you about some of the changes they will be reading about.

5 **Preview Theme 2: An Enduring Legacy** Read aloud the theme title. Define *enduring* as "lasting and permanent" and *legacy* as "something passed on to the next generation." Ask: *What kinds of legacies might be enduring?* Read the theme statement and develop the idea that legacies are not always physical—they can be emotional or spiritual as well.

Invite students to leaf through pages 250–278 to identify legacies they will explore.

6 **Set up Student Mind Maps** Have students draw the mind map in their notebooks or start the map in the **Practice Book**. Encourage them to add to the map as they move through the unit.

▶ **Practice Book** page 102

CLOSE AND ASSESS

Ask:

- *What will this unit be about?* (continuity and change)
- *What new ideas about continuity and change did you learn in this lesson?* (Change occurs constantly in nature and in life. Even in things that change, there can be a pattern of continuity.)

INTRODUCE THEME 1

OBJECTIVES

Function:
Engage in Discussion; Dramatize
Concepts and Vocabulary: Continuity and Change—*cycles, predict*
Viewing: Interpret a Visual Image
Learning Strategies:
Relate to Personal Experience
Critical Thinking:
Form Generalizations; Generate Ideas

TAP PRIOR KNOWLEDGE

1 **Pantomime the Seasons** Divide the class into four heterogeneous groups. Assign a season to each group. Have students create a pantomime to represent their season. Remind groups to show both continuity and change.

VIEW AND DISCUSS

2 **Interpret an Image** Point out that art is another way to express the theme of change and continuity. Direct students to page 214 and ask: *Does this etching show continuity or change?* First, ask students to look "on the surface" and note how the birds change into fish.

Use the Discussion Prompts in the **Multi-Level Strategies** to help students interpret the etching.

Read the title and ask students how the etching also shows continuity. (The birds and fish appear to be moving continually forward in the repeating pattern of nature.)

3 **Form Generalizations** Have students think about their pantomimes, the activities they did on pages 212–213, and the etching. Have them list common elements and work as a group to agree on a generalization about continuity and change.

Generalization: Life continues in repeating cycles of change. Both change and continuity are important parts of life.

Sky and Water I, M.C. Escher, woodcut. Copyright © 1938.

REACHING ALL STUDENTS

Multi-Level Strategies

DISCUSSION PROMPTS

BEGINNING Ask students to show you a bird and a fish in the etching. Then have them point to features, such as: body shapes, fins, tails, wings, beaks, gills. Track birds or fish diagonally and ask students to tell you when the animal is no longer recognizable.

INTERMEDIATE Invite students to state, in complete sentences, their observations about the etching. Say: *Describe two shapes that are similar. What happens to the pictures of the creatures at the center of the etching?*

ADVANCED Ask students if the change from bird to fish happens gradually or suddenly. Have them defend their answers, pointing to the shapes row by row or diagonally.

ınotations offer strategies for
Beginning students

THEME 1

The Certainty of Change

- What kinds of things change in the natural world? Describe these changes.
  B **Pose choices:** Which things change—seasons, the appearance of the moon and the sun?
- What kinds of changes happen in cycles? How can we predict these changes?
- What kinds of changes happen suddenly? Can we predict these kinds of changes, too? Explain.
  B **Provide an example:** Think about changes caused by storms. Can we predict storms?

Define *cycle*: a quence of events at repeats in a regular ttern. **Ask:** What are me examples of anges that happen er and over?

HEME-RELATED BOOKS

actus Hotel
y Brenda Z. Guiberson
huge cactus grows to be nearly o hundred years old. Over the ourse of its long life, it provides a ace to live for many small animals.

EGINNING

Volcanoes
by Neil Morris
This book explains everything about volcanoes. It describes how they change and how they change the areas around them.

INTERMEDIATE

NOVEL

The Time Machine
by H. G. Wells
A time-traveler explores the future, then returns to his own time to tell about the changes humankind experiences.

ADVANCED

215

DISCUSS THE GUIDING QUESTIONS

4 **Set the Theme** Some key points to develop during the discussion are:

- The natural world is in a state of constant change. These changes affect the weather, the seasons, and all living things.
- Examples of changes that repeat in cycles include the phases of the moon, the changing tide, the changing seasons, animal migration, and the life cycle. These cycles repeat themselves so consistently that we can predict them.
- Changes that are difficult to predict include weather and natural disasters. Although we try to predict such things as blizzards, droughts, floods, tornadoes, and earthquakes, our predictions are often inaccurate because the cycles of these events are less consistent.

Form groups and use the **Multi-Level Strategies** to allow all students to participate.

CLOSE AND ASSESS

Have students work with a partner to compose a two-sentence summary of what they learned in this lesson.

Multi-Level Strategies

GROUPING GUIDELINES

BEGINNING Group students so you can define words and pose choices for responses. See suggestions in red on the facsimile for page 215.

INTERMEDIATE Have students work in groups to list answers to the guiding questions. Ask students to brainstorm as many answers as they can for each question.

ADVANCED As students discuss the questions with a partner, encourage them to consider their lives as well as the natural world. Say: *Identify and discuss changes in your life that occur in cycles and those that occur more randomly.* Students should summarize the important points in their discussion for the class.

THEME LIBRARY

■ ***Volcanoes*** by Neil Morris

Invite students to read *Volcanoes* and discuss how it relates to the theme. After reading "The Big Blast" (see pages T238–T246), ask: *How do the selections complement each other? What did you learn from each about continuity and change?* Students could then research Vulcan, the Roman god of fire, or the Greek god Hephaestus, and work together to create a myth that explains volcanoes.

BUILD LANGUAGE AND VOCABULARY

OBJECTIVES

Function: Ⓣ Give Information
Concepts and Vocabulary: Words About Change
Patterns and Structures: Ⓣ Relative Clauses
Viewing: Interpret a Visual Image
Learning Strategy: Use Graphic Organizers (mind map; chart)
Critical Thinking: Analyze Information; Generate Ideas
Writing: Sentences

START WITH A COMMON EXPERIENCE

1 **View and Give Information** Have students study the images and tell about the changes they see in the Temple of Artemis from ancient times to today. Model how to give information:

How to Give Information
- Name the topic: *the Temple of Artemis*
- Give details that answer the questions who, what, where, when, why, or how: *The Temple of Artemis is in Greece.*
- Tell more: *In ancient times, the temple had a stone roof and tall columns.*

2 **Discuss the Quotation** Define *permanent* as "lasting for a long time." Have students speculate on how changes could be permanent. Through the discussion, develop the idea that changes can be considered to be permanent if they are long lasting.

Use the Questioning Techniques in the **Multi-Level Strategies** to include all students.

Build Language and Vocabulary

GIVE INFORMATION

The philosopher Heraclitus lived in ancient Greece about 2,500 years ago. He discussed many important ideas in his speeches. What do you think he meant about change being permanent?

NOTHING IS SO PERMANENT AS CHANGE.
—*Heraclitus*

Today, tourists from all over the world visit the Temple of Artemis and other ruins to learn more about ancient Greece.

REACHING ALL STUDENTS

Multi-Level Strategies

QUESTIONING TECHNIQUES

BEGINNING Point out different features in the images such as the people, the roof, and the columns in the temple. Ask students how the features have changed from ancient times to today. For example: *Does the roof look the same today as it did in ancient Greece?* (no) *How did it change?* (The roof is gone.) *Was the roof permanent?* (no)

INTERMEDIATE / **ADVANCED** Have partners work together to compare the similarities and differences in the two images. Then ask pairs: *What has changed between the two images? When the temple was built, do you think the builders thought that it would be permanent? What could have happened to change the temple over the years?*

AKE A MIND MAP

ink of different kinds of changes. What kinds of changes happen in cycles? hat kinds happen slowly over time? What kinds happen suddenly? Add two amples of each kind of change to the mind map.

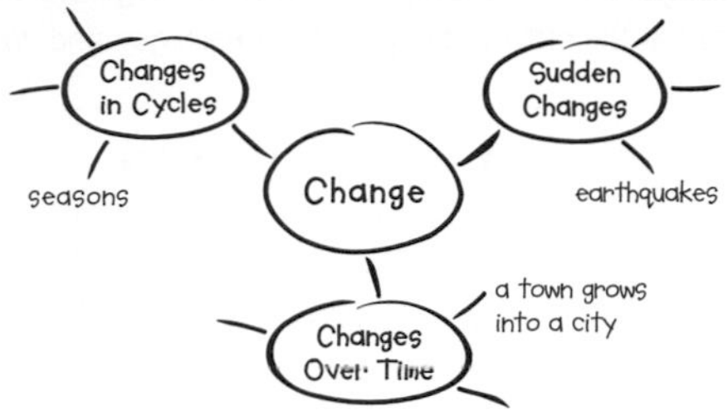

JILD YOUR VOCABULARY

ords About Change Work with a group. Choose an example of change om your mind map and collect words that describe it. Organize your words to a chart.

Town to City

Then	Now
dirt roads	paved streets
small houses	skyscrapers

SE LANGUAGE STRUCTURES ▶RELATIVE CLAUSES

riting: Tell About Changes Write two complex sentences about a ange. Each sentence should have a clause that begins with a word from e **Word Bank**.

Word Bank

who
whose
whom
that
which

Example:

The people **who** settled Chicago would be surprised to see today's skyscrapers.

CONDUCT THE ACTIVITIES

3 **Make a Mind Map** Have students work in small groups to brainstorm ideas for their maps.

4 **Build Your Vocabulary: Words About Change** Suggest students classify the words they put in the chart into several categories.

5 **Use Language Structures: Relative Clauses** Present the skill, using the definitions and examples on **Transparency 53**. Then have students complete the relative clauses in Try It!

Writing: Tell About Changes Conduct the activity at the bottom of page 217. Remind students to use their mind maps and charts for ideas.

Use the Writing Activity Options in the **Multi-Level Strategies** to adjust instruction.

▶ **Practice Book** page 103

CLOSE AND ASSESS

Ask students to name five relative pronouns. (*who, whom, whose, that, which*) Have students add a relative clause to complete this sentence: *This is the student editor* ______.

Multi-Level Strategies

WRITING ACTIVITY OPTIONS

BEGINNING Have students write two simple sentences: *My mother is a gardener. My mother loves warm weather.* Provide a frame: *My mother is a gardener* ______ *loves warm weather.* Students can add a relative pronoun to form a complex sentence.

INTERMEDIATE Encourage students to use their mind maps and word charts to help them brainstorm their sentences. Then have them exchange papers with a partner and look for the relative clauses in each sentence.

ADVANCED After students have written their sentences, have them help other students formulate their sentences. Advanced students might also help others find suitable subjects in the mind maps and charts to inspire sentence building.

Transparency 53 / Master 53

LEARN ABOUT RELATIVE CLAUSES

1. A complex sentence has one independent clause and one dependent clause.

   We visited the ruins (independent clause) that are the closest to Athens. (dependent clause)

2. A relative clause is one kind of dependent clause. It begins with a **relative pronoun.**

   We visited the ruins **that** are the closest to Athens. (relative clause)

3. The relative pronoun connects the clause to a word in the sentence. Use **who**, **whom**, or **whose** to describe a person.

   We met the archaeologist **who** discovered the tiled wall.

   Use **which** for things. Use **that** for people or things.

   The wall, **which** I have seen, is beautiful.

   Tourists **that** visit the wall are impressed.

Try It!

Complete the relative clause in each sentence.

1. The tourists who ______ learned a lot about Greece.
2. Photography is an activity that ______.

Transparency 53 Level B, Unit 4 | Continuity and Change © Hampton-Brown

PREPARE TO READ

OBJECTIVES

THINK ABOUT WHAT YOU KNOW
Reading Strategy: Build Background
LEARN KEY VOCABULARY Ⓣ
Vocabulary Strategy: Relate Words
LEARN ABOUT CHARACTERS AND PLOT
Reading Strategy:
Ⓣ Analyze Story Elements (characters and plot)

THINK ABOUT WHAT YOU KNOW

1 **Idea Exchange** Assign each of the deities on page 219 to a different group. Groups study and discuss the picture, then brainstorm ideas about events in nature and human life that might be explained by the god or goddess. The groups then share ideas.

LEARN KEY VOCABULARY

2 **Relate Words** Read each vocabulary word and its definition aloud. Clarify meanings. Then conduct the activity.

Use the Vocabulary Options in the **Multi-Level Strategies** to help all students participate.

▶ **Practice Book** page 104

LEARN ABOUT CHARACTERS AND PLOT

3 **Model How to Analyze Characters and Plot** Define *character* and *plot*. Demonstrate the steps in the box with **Transparency 54**:

- Read aloud the story.
- Model filling in the boxes for Character, Traits or Feelings, and Problem.
- Then note the action and explain how Hades' traits and problem caused him to abduct Persephone.

CLOSE AND ASSESS

Ask students to agree on why a character map is helpful. (It helps you to understand a character's actions.)

THE MOTHER WHO LOST HER DAUGHTER

play based on a Greek myth retold by Anne Rockwell

Prepare to Read

THINK ABOUT WHAT YOU KNOW

Idea Exchange Skim "The Origin of Myths" on page 219. In a group, talk about what the pictures tell you about each god and goddess.

bear fruit produce ripe fruit in time for harvest

damp slightly wet, moist

dull not shiny

gloomy sad, not cheerful

shiver shake with cold, fear, or excitement

shrivel up become dry and smaller in size

sprout begin to grow

underworld to the ancient Greeks, the underground home for the dead

wither become dry

Students' diagrams should show illustrations that correspond with the text in the graphic. Sample text is presented below, although students' work will vary.

Summer is when plants **sprout** and trees **bear fruit**.

Winter is **damp**, cold, and **gloomy**, and sometimes makes you **shiver**. Plants **wither** and **shrivel up**.

LEARN KEY VOCABULARY

Relate Words Study the new words and their definitions. Then draw a picture of summertime in the upper part of a circle and a picture of wintertime in the lower part. Write a sentence about each half of the circle. Use as many of the new words as you can.

Drawing

LEARN ABOUT CHARACTERS AND PLOT

A **character** is a person, animal, or imaginary creature in a story or play. The **plot** is the sequence of events that happen. The plot is often about a problem that the main character must solve. The words and actions of the characters move the plot along.

READING STRATEGY

How to Analyze Characters and Plot

1. Preview the selection and find the names of the characters.
2. As you read, ask yourself: What are the character's traits? What is the character's problem?
3. Think about how the character will act. See if these actions show up in the plot.

As you read "The Mother Who Lost Her Daughter," identify the characters. Think about how their traits and problems affect the events in the plot.

REACHING ALL STUDENTS

Multi-Level Strategies

VOCABULARY OPTIONS

BEGINNING Group students to read ***The Eagle and the Moon Gold*** or the Key Points Reading on **Master 55**. (See page T220.) Work with the vocabulary in those selections.

INTERMEDIATE Have students work in pairs to decide which words and phrases are associated with which season, then complete the activity.

ADVANCED Students should complete the activity independently, then use a thesaurus to find other words associated with these seasons.

Transparency 54 / Master 54

ANALYZE STORY ELEMENTS

Directions: Read the story. Identify the character. List the character's traits or feelings. Identify the character's problem. Tell about an action that relates to the problem.

Hades, Ruler of the Underworld

The three sons of Kronos and Rhea drew lots to see which part of the world each would rule. Zeus got the sky; Poseidon won the seas; and Hades drew the underworld.

Hades was very lonely in the lifeless underworld. He needed to share his kingdom with someone special. He kidnapped Persephone to bring life to the underworld.

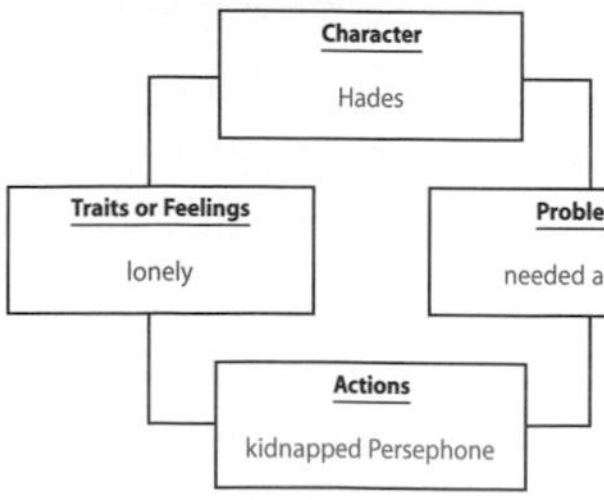

Transparency 54 Level B, Unit 4 | Continuity and Change © Hampton-Brown

REFERENCE POINT

THE ORIGIN OF MYTHS

In ancient Greece, over 3,000 years ago, people did not understand events in the natural world such as the changing seasons or the rising and setting of the sun. They made up stories called myths to explain these **mysteries**. In the myths they told how different gods and goddesses made events happen.

Here are five of the Greek gods and goddesses and the parts of the world they controlled.

steries things not known or understood

The Mother Who Lost Her Daughter 219

MORE TO EXPLORE

Greek Mythology Students can learn more about Greek mythology and its principal gods and goddesses. Have them consult:

- a print or on-line encyclopedia
- a classic literary anthology
- Web sites, such as:

  www.hsa.brown.edu/~maicar

  www.geocities.com/Athens/Agora/9542/mythology

  www.geocities.com/Yosemite/7371/greekgods.html

Have students expand upon the profiles of the major deities included on page 219 of the student book.

THE BASICS BOOKSHELF

- ***The Eagle and the Moon Gold: A Fable from the Hmong People*** adapted by Yeemay Chan

It is winter, and it is cold. A poor orphan boy starts to cut down a tree to build a fire, when an eagle offers to fly the boy to the moon where there is gold for the taking. The simple text for this delightful tale introduces words with opposite meanings, while the beautiful illustrations provide picture support for the beginning English learners.

For Lesson Plans: See the Teacher's Guide for ***The Basics Bookshelf***.

READ THE SELECTION

OBJECTIVES

Reading Strategies: Preview; Predict
Literary Analysis: Play

INTRODUCE THE SELECTION

1. **Preview and Predict** Read aloud the title, author's name, and introduction to the play. Next, have students page through the selection and look at the pictures in each section. Encourage students to make predictions about the plot, based on the pictures.
2. **Identify Genre: Play** Have students look at the list of characters on page 220 and the first page of the script on page 221. Point out that the lines of the script are to be spoken by the choruses and the characters. Explain that this kind of writing is called a play and that it is intended to be performed in front of an audience. Elicit examples of other plays.

THE MOTHER WHO LOST HER DAUGHTER

A PLAY BASED ON A GREEK MYTH
RETOLD BY ANNE ROCKWELL

The goddess Demeter is deeply saddened when her daughter Persephone is taken from her by the god of the underworld. In her sadness, Demeter takes her gifts of fruit and flowers from Earth, but restores them when Persephone is returned to her. Demeter's joy and sadness are reflected in the cycle of the seasons.

CHARACTERS

In ancient Greek drama, the chorus provided narration and commentary on the action. These characters are in the chorus and should read their parts aloud.

FIRST CHORUS
SECOND CHORUS
SINGLE FEMALE VOICE
SINGLE MALE VOICE

These are the actors in the play. The actors should act out their parts as they say their lines.

DEMETER
PERSEPHONE
TRIPTOLEMUS
HADES
HERMES

220

The Mother Who Lost Her Daughter
A play based on a Greek myth
retold by Anne Rockwell

Theme Connection This play tells the myth of Demeter, the goddess of growing things. The story is a way of explaining the continuity and change of the seasons.

Selection Summary The introduction on page 220 of the student book offers a summary of the selection.

Author Awards Anne Rockwell's work has been honored as one of *Redbook*'s top 10 children's picture books (1985) and as the Child Study Association's children's book of the year (1976).

REACHING ALL STUDENTS

Transparency 55 / Master 55

KEY POINTS READING

The Mother Who Lost Her Daughter

Demeter is the goddess of growing things. She is kind and happy. She makes plants grow. Because of her, it is always summertime on Earth. One day, Hades (the god of the underworld) hears Demeter's daughter, Persephone, picking flowers. He steals Persephone to make her his queen. He drags her down to the underworld.

Persephone is very sad. She eats a pomegranate and swallows one seed. Demeter cannot find her daughter. She is so sad she forgets to tell things to grow. It is the first winter on Earth.

Demeter goes to Zeus for help. He tells Hades to return Persephone to Earth. Demeter is happy and makes things grow again. It is the first springtime. But Persephone must go back to the underworld for part of every year because she ate the pomegranate, the fruit of the dead. When she leaves, winter comes back. Spring returns each time Persephone comes home.

Transparency 55 Level B, Unit 4 | Continuity and Change © Hampton-Brown

Transparency 56 / Master 56

CHARACTER MAP

Directions: Make a map for each character in the myth. Fill in the character's name, traits or feelings, problems, and actions.

The Mother Who Lost Her Daughter

Character:

Traits or Feelings:
1.
2.
3.

Problems:
1.
2.
3.

Actions:
1.
2.
3.

Transparency 56 Level B, Unit 4 | Continuity and Change © Hampton-Brown

1

DEMETER LOSES HER DAUGHTER

One day, Demeter's daughter Persephone sees a strange flower and picks it. She falls through an opening in the ground into the underworld.

d annotations offer opportunities clarify meaning and check for derstanding.

RST CHORUS: The Mother Who Lost Her Daughter

COND CHORUS: A play based on a Greek myth retold by Anne Rockwell

RST CHORUS: Demeter was the goddess of green and growing things. She was good and kind and beautiful, and she had a young daughter named Persephone. No mother ever loved a child as much as Demeter loved her Persephone.

COND CHORUS: In those days, it was always summertime, and people on Earth were never cold or hungry. But they did not know how to plant seeds.

RST CHORUS: Only Demeter could make things grow. Without her, people would have had no fruit and flowers, or wheat and barley with which to make their bread. But Demeter saw to it that the fields were high and golden with wheat and barley and the trees always bore sweet fruit. **Ask:** How were the people dependent on Demeter?

One day, her daughter Persephone was picking flowers in a meadow.

RSEPHONE: [*singing softly in background*]

SECOND CHORUS: Persephone danced and sang as she picked the flowers. Suddenly she stopped dancing and said, . . .

PERSEPHONE: Ohhh, how beautiful!

FIRST CHORUS: For Persephone saw a strange flower she had never seen before. She ran over to pick it, singing and dancing as she added it to her bouquet.

SECOND CHORUS: [*deep voice*] Far down below in the **chilly, dank** underworld Hades . . .

SINGLE MALE VOICE: [*heavily*] the god who ruled the land of the dead . . .

FIRST CHORUS: [*deep voice*] heard Persephone's sweet singing and the sound of her dancing feet.

He decided he wanted the young girl to be his queen. She was full of laughter and joy, and Hades often grew **gloomy** and lonely in his dark and **dismal** kingdom, with only the dead for company. He made up his mind to steal Persephone away from the flower-filled meadow. **Ask:** Who was Hades and what did he want?

[*Sound Effect: cracking and breaking sound in background, growing from soft to thunderous*]

illy, dank cold, wet
mal depressing

The Mother Who Lost Her Daughter 221

READ PAGE 221

OBJECTIVES

Function: Read a Selection
Listening: Listen to a Selection
Reading and Learning Strategies: Set a Purpose for Reading; Ⓣ Analyze Story Elements (character and plot); Use Graphic Organizers (character map)

SET PURPOSE

3 Read aloud the introduction to pages 221–222. Set the purpose for reading: *Read to understand why Hades wants to bring Persephone into the underworld.*

READ AND THINK

Tape 4A
CD 4 Track 1

4 **Strategy Focus: Analyze Characters and Plot** As students read, have them complete a character map for each character, using **Master 56.**

Choose Reading Options in the **Multi-Level Strategies** to tailor the reading to proficiency levels.

The recording of "The Mother Who Lost Her Daughter" on the **Selection Tape/CD** offers an oral language model and the opportunity to build reading fluency. Listening frequently to this tape will help students perform the play later with effective expression. (See page T226.)

Multi-Level Strategies

READING OPTIONS FOR LESSONS 4–6

BEGINNING Students should work with ***The Eagle and the Moon Gold*** while the class reads "The Mother Who Lost Her Daughter." Or distribute copies of **Master 55** to conduct a Key Points Reading of the selection. Work together to complete the character map on **Transparency 56** for Demeter.

INTERMEDIATE Have students listen to the play on the **Selection Tape/CD** as they read. Use the red annotations on the facsimile pages to clarify meanings. Work together to complete character maps on **Transparency 56** for Hades, Demeter, and Persephone.

ADVANCED Have students read the play silently. Distribute three copies of **Master 56** and invite students to fill in the character maps independently. Have them compare their work with a partner.

READ PAGE 222

OBJECTIVES

Comprehension: Identify Character's Motive; Analyze Information (fantasy and reality)
Literary Analysis: Setting

CHECK COMPREHENSION

5 **Answers to "Before You Move On"**

1. **Setting** In this part of the myth there is only one season. It is always summertime because Demeter makes plants and trees grow all the time.
2. **Fantasy and Reality** A person could pick flowers in a meadow. A hole could open up in the earth. A person could not be dragged down into the earth by a chariot.
3. **Character's Motive** Hades was lonely. His only company in the underworld was the dead. He wanted the lively Persephone to keep him company.

CLOSE AND ASSESS

Have students write in their notebooks what they think Hades' problem is, and how his feelings led to his actions.

SECOND CHORUS: [*quickly*] All at once there was a terrible cracking sound. The earth where Persephone danced opened wide. Hades rose up from the dark underworld, driving a **golden chariot** pulled by black horses.

SINGLE MALE VOICE: [*forcefully*] He grabbed Persephone, lifted her into his chariot . . .

FIRST CHORUS: [*quickly*] and galloped back to the black hole where the earth had ripped open. **Encourage elaboration:** What would it be like in Hades' kingdom?

PERSEPHONE: [*frantic*] Mother! Mother! Help me!

SECOND CHORUS: The poor girl **shrieked** as loudly as she could. But Persephone had danced so far from where her mother was, that Demeter could not hear her calling.

SINGLE FEMALE VOICE: Only a little **swineher[d] tending his pigs** saw what happened.

FIRST CHORUS: He began to cry as loudly as Persephone, because all his pigs tumble[d] into the black opening in the earth. The[n] the hole closed behind them.

Ask: Why was the swineherd cryi[ng]

BEFORE YOU MOVE ON...

1. **Setting** Were there seasons in this part of the myth? Explain your answer.
2. **Fantasy and Reality** Which events could happen in real life? Which could not?
3. **Character's Motive** Why did Hades take Persephone down into the underworld?

golden chariot kind of cart made of gold
shrieked yelled, screamed, let out a loud cry
swineherd tending his pigs boy who takes care of pigs

REACHING ALL STUDENTS

HOME CONNECTION

Favorite Myths Send home a copy of *High Point Newsletter 7* in the **Teacher's Resource Book**. In this home activity, students interview family members to learn about favorite myths or stories that explain natural phenomena. Students take notes and use these notes to retell the myth to the class.

Science Connection
EARTHQUAKES

Discuss the scene in the selection in which the ground opens up and swallows Persephone. Ask students whether this could actually happen during an earthquake. Have students work in groups to research something about earthquakes such as plate tectonics, fault lines, causes of earthquakes, or famous earthquakes. Each group should give an oral report on what they researched. Encourage students to ask questions after each presentation.

2

DEMETER LOOKS FOR PERSEPHONE

Demeter cannot find her daughter. She learns that Hades has pulled her down into the underworld. Demeter demands her return.

ECOND CHORUS: Demeter searched for her daughter.

IRST CHORUS: [*agitated*] She ran everywhere calling for her, and when she could not find her, she began to **sob and wail**. No laughing girl's voice called back to her, . . .

NGLE FEMALE VOICE. [*faint as if far away*] I am coming, Mother.

ECOND CHORUS: Persephone could not answer, for she was far, far away.

IRST CHORUS: [*slow and gloomy*] Day after day she sat, sad and silent, next to Hades on the throne he had given her in the land of the dead. Her tan and rosy cheeks grew pale and cold. She ate nothing, until one day when she tasted a **pomegranate** and . . .

SINGLE MALE VOICE: [*slow and measured*] swallowed one of its tiny, blood-red seeds.

SECOND CHORUS: Demeter traveled all over the world searching for her lost child. Her beautiful golden hair, which had been the color of **ripe** wheat, turned **dull** and gray. In her **grief**, the goddess forgot to tell the wheat and barley to grow.

Clarify: This isn't actually Persephone's voice, it's only the voice that Demeter hopes to hear.

b and wail cry loudly without control
megranate red fruit with juicy, sour-tasting seeds
ripe ready to harvest
grief great sadness

READ PAGE 223

OBJECTIVES

Function: Read a Selection
Grammar: Ⓣ Relative Clauses
Listening: Listen to a Selection
Reading and Learning Strategies: Set a Purpose for Reading; Ⓣ Analyze Story Elements (characters and plot); Use Graphic Organizers (character map)

SET PURPOSE

1 Read aloud the introduction to pages 223–224. Set the purpose for reading: *Read to find out the effect Demeter's unhappiness has on the natural world.*

READ AND THINK

Tape 4A
CD 4 Track 1

2 **Strategy Focus: Analyze Characters and Plot** Involve students in reading pages 223–224.

See the **Multi-Level Strategies** on page T221 to tailor the reading to all proficiency levels.

Language Development

EXPRESS CERTAINTY, PROBABILITY, POSSIBILITY

Have students read and listen to weather reports for one week. Instruct students to use the information to create statements on slips of paper about what is certain, probable, and possible regarding the week's weather. Provide sentence frames such as: *I am sure that* (it will be warm). *It is likely that* (it will rain). *There's a possibility that* (it will snow). Have students share and compare their statements.

Grammar Minilesson

▶ RELATIVE CLAUSES

TEACH Review independent and dependent clauses with students. Then say: *A relative clause is one kind of dependent clause. It begins with a relative pronoun like* that *or* which. Show students how to combine two sentences into a complex sentence with a relative clause. Write:

Demeter's beautiful hair turned gray.
Her hair had been the color of ripe wheat.

Then combine the sentences:

Demeter's beautiful hair, which had been the color of ripe wheat, turned gray.

Circle the word *which* and show how it connects the clause to the word *hair.* Repeat with an example for *that.*

PRACTICE Have students join each pair of sentences with a relative pronoun to make a complex sentence.

1. Persephone picked a flower.
   She had never seen it before.
2. Hades drove a chariot.
   It was pulled by black horses.

▶ **Practice Book** page 105

READ PAGE 224

OBJECTIVES

Vocabulary Strategy: Use New Words in Context
Comprehension: Ⓣ Identify Cause and Effect; Ⓣ Identify Details; Ⓣ Identify Sequence
Literary Analysis: Ⓣ Plot (foreshadowing)

REVIEW KEY VOCABULARY

3 **Use New Words in Context** Have students draw pictures to represent as many vocabulary words as possible in one picture.

CHECK COMPREHENSION

4 **Answers to "Before You Move On"**

1. **Cause and Effect** Demeter could not find her daughter. The first winter came.
2. **Foreshadowing** Students may notice that the First Chorus and the Single Male Voice emphasize this event.
3. **Details/Sequence** Triptolemus told Demeter, and she went to Hades' powerful brother, Zeus.

CLOSE AND ASSESS

Have partners use their character maps to discuss Demeter's problem and how her feelings led to her actions.

Encourage elaboration: What is the world like without Demeter's attention?

FIRST CHORUS: So all the stalks of wheat and barley **withered.** She forgot to tell the trees to **bear fruit.**

SECOND CHORUS: So the fruit trees **shed** their green leaves, and their apples and pears and figs **shriveled up** and died.

SINGLE MALE VOICE: The first cold winter in the world came.

SINGLE FEMALE VOICE: All the people were hungry.

ALL VOICES: Their children cried, for they had no bread or fruit to eat and they were cold, besides.

FIRST CHORUS: [*quickened pace*] Demeter kept on searching for Persephone. She asked everyone she met if they had seen her child. But everyone said no until at last the goddess met a boy called Triptolemus.

SINGLE FEMALE VOICE: Triptolemus was the older brother of the little swineherd.

Ask: Who is Triptolemus?

SECOND CHORUS: Demeter asked Triptolemus, as she asked everyone she met, . . .

DEMETER: Have you seen my lovely child who is lost? Have you seen dear Persephone with her golden **braids** and dancing feet?

FIRST CHORUS: And Triptolemus answered, . . .

TRIPTOLEMUS: I have not seen her, but I kno where she is.

SECOND CHORUS: Then he told the goddess what his brother had seen that **dreadful** day. **Ask:** What did his brother s

FIRST CHORUS: When Demeter heard what Triptolemus told her, she grew very angry. Since Hades was the brother of Zeus, she went straight up to Mount Olympus and said to **mighty** Zeus, . .

Clarify: Zeus was the king of the go

DEMETER: Your **wicked** brother has stolen my child! Make him give her back to me!

SECOND CHORUS: And Demeter, who had always been so kind and gentle, screamed at Zeus so that even he was afraid. Besides, he was sad to see the fruits and grains and grasses of the earth all withered and gone. It was no fun for him to watch the mortals belo when they just sat and **shivered** wit cold and hunger. **Encourage elaboration** How did Zeus feel abou the mortals?

BEFORE YOU MOVE ON...

1. **Cause and Effect** Why was Demeter so sad? What changes happened on Earth because of her sadness?
2. **Foreshadowing** Do you think it is important that Persephone ate a pomegranat seed? Why or why not?
3. **Details/Sequence** How did Demeter find out where Persephone was? What happened next?

shed dropped
braids hair tied and twisted like rope
dreadful bad, horrible, awful
mighty powerful
wicked bad, mean, evil

REACHING ALL STUDENTS

Vocabulary

GREEK ROOTS

Tell students that the ancient Greeks gave us many things besides myths. Explain that many of the roots of English words also come from the ancient Greeks. Give the example of the root *cycl.* Tell students that this root means *circle.* Then elicit English words with this root, such as *cycle, bicycle,* and *cyclone.* Have students explain the meanings of these words and how they relate to the Greek root. Use a chart to introduce and explore other Greek roots.

Greek root	Greek meaning	Related English word	Meaning of English word
ast	star	astronomy	study of stars
graph	written		
phon	sound		
photo	light		
therm	heat		

3

PERSEPHONE RETURNS

Zeus makes Hades return Persephone to Earth for part of every year. When she arrives, she brings spring. When she goes back, it is winter.

IRST CHORUS: So Zeus sent Hermes down to the underworld kingdom. Hermes told Hades that Zeus **commanded** him to return Persephone to her mother. Hades could not **refuse to obey** the orders of his brother, for Zeus was even more powerful than he. But Hades knew that the girl had eaten the pomegranate seed.

INGLE MALE VOICE: The blood-red pomegranate was the fruit of the dead.

ECOND CHORUS: Anyone who tasted it had to return, sooner or later, to Hades' underworld kingdom.

ADES: I will let her go, since Zeus commands me, . . .

FIRST CHORUS: said Hades to the messenger god.

HADES: But because of the pomegranate seed she ate, she must return to me for part of the year to sit beside me as my wife and queen. **Ask:** Where must Persephone spend part of each year?

SECOND CHORUS: Persephone returned to her mother. [*lively*] Demeter was glad and happy again. Once more she told the wheat and barley to grow. She made red poppies **appear** among the golden wheat and made the trees bear apples and pears and figs. She made the earth **put forth** all the good things that people needed.

SINGLE FEMALE VOICE: It was the first springtime in the world. And everyone was happy again. **Ask:** What changes occur in the springtime?

Encourage elaboration: What is the world like when Persephone returns from the underworld?

ommanded told, ordered
efuse to obey say no to
ppear come up, show, become visible
ut forth grow

READ PAGE 225

OBJECTIVES

Function: Read a Selection
Grammar: Ⓣ Relative Clauses
Listening: Listen to a Selection
Reading and Learning Strategies: Set a Purpose for Reading; Ⓣ Analyze Story Elements (characters and plot); Use Graphic Organizers (character map)

SET PURPOSE

1 Read aloud the introduction on page 225. Set the purpose for reading: *As you read, note details about how Demeter's emotions bring about the cycle of seasons.*

READ AND THINK

Tape 4A
CD 4 Track 1

2 **Strategy Focus: Analyze Characters and Plot** Involve students in reading pages 225–227.

See the **Multi-Level Strategies** on page T221 to tailor the reading to varying proficiency levels.

Health Connection

FOODS IN SEASON

Have students research and compare the nutritional values of fresh versus preserved fruits and vegetables. Suggest that they read food labels in the supermarket and at home and refer to books about nutrition. Invite students to work in groups to research foods that are plentiful in a chosen country at a particular season of the year. Then ask: *How do people who live in that country get adequate nutrition when those foods are out of season?*

Grammar Minilesson

▶ RELATIVE CLAUSES

TEACH Review the relative pronouns *that* and *which* from the Grammar Minilesson on page T223. Then introduce *who* and explain that this relative pronoun connects a relative clause to a noun or pronoun in the sentence. Write:

> Demeter, who had always been so kind, screamed at Zeus.

Circle *who* and identify the relative clause. Then have a volunteer draw an arrow from *who* to the noun it describes.

Have students substitute other relative clauses in the sentence, for example:

> Demeter, who wanted her child back, screamed at Zeus.

PRACTICE Have students write complex sentences with relative clauses about Persephone, Hades, and Hermes.

▶ **Practice Book** page 106

READ PAGES 226–227

OBJECTIVES

Function: Read a Selection; Dramatize

Comprehension and Critical Thinking: Ⓣ Identify Cause and Effect; Make an Inference; Identify Character's Point of View; Draw Conclusions

Literary Analysis: Plot (foreshadowing); Respond to Literature

PERFORM A PLAY

Have students perform this selection as a play for parents or other classes. Students can brainstorm and sign up for roles, such as costume designers, set designers, props people, stage manager, director, and actors. Students working on costumes, sets, and props should conduct research about styles, architecture, and designs of the ancient Greeks.

The stage manager and director can plan rehearsal schedules and assign roles. Encourage actors to speak their roles clearly and slowly.

FIRST CHORUS: But after eight months, Persephone had to say goodbye to her mother and return to her throne beside her husband, King Hades. She had to **remain** in the cold, **damp**, dark underworld for four long months. While she was there, she seemed as cold and lifeless as the dead around her, and her husband did not understand why she would not dance and sing for him.

ALL VOICES: Throughout those four months of every year, Demeter **mourns** for her child. The wheat and barley wither and die. The red poppy petals fall away, and the trees bear no more fruit.

SINGLE MALE VOICE: [*heavy, deep voice*] Winter comes. **Ask:** What changes are brought by winter?

ALL VOICES: Demeter's tears fall as cold rain and **sleet** until at last the happy day arrives when her daughter returns to her and springtime begins.

SECOND CHORUS: [*lightly*] Demeter rewarded Triptolemus well for his help. She gave him a chariot pulled by dragons . . .

SINGLE FEMALE VOICE: a bag of seeds . . .

SINGLE MALE VOICE: and a wooden plow.

remain stay, wait
mourns shows her sadness by crying
sleet frozen raindrops

REACHING ALL STUDENTS

CULTURAL PERSPECTIVES

World Cultures: Seasonal Celebrations Have groups research the seasonal holidays or celebrations of a culture. For example, explain that most cultures have holidays to celebrate the harvest season in the fall. Have students research the special foods, dress, dance, music, and other traditions associated with each holiday. Students can present their findings to the class as posters, essays, multimedia shows, or with guest speakers.

Science Connection

SEASONAL CHANGE

Have students work in groups to discuss the common changes we observe with the changes of season. Then ask them to discuss the mythological explanation for a season and compare it to the scientific explanation.

Students then record their ideas in charts. Encourage groups to compare their completed charts, making note of similarities and differences.

Season: FALL

What we see...	Days get shorter. Weather gets cooler. Plants scatter seeds. Animals gather food for winter.
Myth says...	Persephone goes to the underworld.
Science says...	The Earth tilts away from the sun.

RST CHORUS: Then she whispered to him the secrets of how to make things grow and how to harvest them and save them so that people would have food to eat through the long winter months.

COND CHORUS: Triptolemus traveled all over the world in his dragon chariot. He taught the people who would listen to him how to plant and how to harvest and **preserve** what they had grown. All over the world, people planted the seeds Triptolemus gave them—

SINGLE FEMALE VOICE: the gifts of Demeter.

SINGLE MALE VOICE: The people had bread for the long winter.

ALL VOICES: When springtime comes, people on Earth **rejoice** with Demeter. Persephone returns to her mother and sings and dances through the fields. Demeter is filled with joy and all the green things **sprout** and grow again.

PERSEPHONE: *[softly singing, fade out voice]*

Ask: What are the gifts of Demeter? **Encourage elaboration:** How do her gifts help the people?

BEFORE YOU MOVE ON...

1. **Cause and Effect** Why did Persephone have to return to the underworld?
2. **Inference** Why do you think that Persephone felt "cold and lifeless" in the underworld?
3. **Conclusions** How does this myth explain the change of seasons?

eserve keep fresh, protect
joice become happy or joyful, celebrate

ABOUT THE AUTHOR

Anne Rockwell says that she loved rainy days as a child. "I didn't have to go outside to play. Instead, I could stay indoors reading. . . ." Her feelings about the outdoors have changed since then. Now she gets ideas for her books while walking on the beach with her dog and sketchbook. Nature's forces of waves and winds, in Connecticut, where Anne Rockwell lives, give her a different beach to observe each day.

CHECK COMPREHENSION

3 Answers to "Before You Move On"

1. **Cause and Effect** Persephone had eaten the pomegranate, the fruit of the dead. Anyone who eats it has to return to the underworld at some time.
2. **Inference** The underworld was a gloomy place where she was surrounded by the dead.
3. **Conclusions** This myth explains that winter is a result of Demeter's sadness while her daughter is away, and that spring is a result of her joy when Persephone returns.

ABOUT THE AUTHOR

4 Respond to Literature Read aloud or have students read About the Author. Ask: *How does this story affect your appreciation of nature and the seasons? How does it affect your opinions about Greek myths?*

CLOSE AND ASSESS

Ask: *What have you learned about ancient Greek beliefs from this play?*

Literary Analysis Minilesson

▶ FORESHADOWING

TEACH Tell students that foreshadowing is a device used by writers to introduce an idea that will take on greater significance later in the story. Explain that writers use foreshadowing to give important clues and to prepare the reader for a future event in the plot. Ask students to identify an example of foreshadowing in the myth. (On page 223, the First Chorus and the Single Male Voice give great emphasis to Persephone eating the pomegranate.) Discuss how this event becomes more important later in the plot.

PRACTICE Ask students how the author might have foreshadowed the coming of the first winter. Have them work in groups to come up with as many ideas as they can. (Perhaps on the morning Persephone will disappear, Demeter could wake up with a gray streak in her hair, a leaf could fall from a tree, or a cold breeze could blow.)

RESPOND

OBJECTIVES

SUM IT UP

Reading and Learning Strategies: Ⓣ Analyze Story Elements (characters and plot); Use Graphic Organizers (character map, chart)

Comprehension: Identify Problem and Solution

THINK IT OVER

Function: Engage in Discussion

Critical Thinking and Comprehension: Make Inferences; Make Judgments; Draw Conclusions

Literary Analysis: Ⓣ Plot

EXPRESS YOURSELF

Function: Negotiate

Speaking and Listening: Role-Play

CHECK YOUR UNDERSTANDING

1 **Sum It Up** The character maps should include the kind of information shown in the example.

▶ **Practice Book** page 107

2 **Think It Over** Possible answers are:

1. **Plot** By the end of the myth, Persephone sings and dances and Demeter makes green things grow, just as they did at the beginning.
2. **Conclusions** She made things grow so that people would not be hungry. She also taught humans how to grow food themselves.
3. **Judgments** Answers will vary.
4. **Inference** People create myths to explain the forces of nature.

3 **Express Yourself** Teach typical phrases of negotiation such as *"If you. . . , I'll. . . "; "Would you consider. . . "; "How about. . . ".*

CLOSE AND ASSESS

Have students revisit the unit mind map and add ideas about continuity and change from the selection.

Respond to the Play

Check Your Understanding

SUM IT UP

Analyze Characters Complete character maps for Demeter, Hades, and Persephone.

Character Map

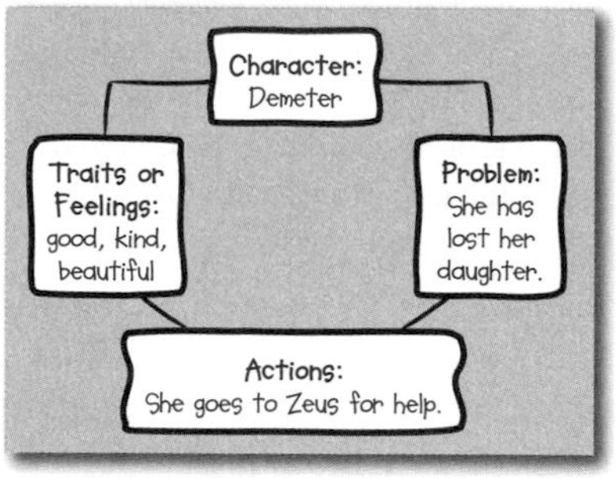

Relate Problems, Solutions, and Consequences Make a chart like this one for each character. For the last two rows, work with a partner to think of another possible solution and consequence.

Problem	Hades is lonely.
Solution	He kidnaps Persephone.
Consequence	Persephone is unhappy.
Other Solution	Hades finds a wife who wants to marry him.
Other Consequence	They live happily ever after.

Review your chart with a partner. Discuss how the characters affect the plot.

THINK IT OVER

Discuss and Write Talk about these questions with a partner. Write the answers.

1. **Plot** How is this myth like a circle?
2. **Conclusions** What are all the different ways that Demeter helped people on Earth?
3. **Judgments** In the myth, spring is a time of growth and happiness, and wintertime is sad and lifeless. Do you feel this way about the seasons? Give reasons to support your answer.
4. **Inference** Why do people create myths?

EXPRESS YOURSELF ▶NEGOTIATE

Work with a partner. Act out a scene in which two characters from the play negotiate to reach an agreement.

Example:

Demeter: If you talk to Hades for me, I will let the crops grow again.

Zeus: I will talk to Hades if you make sure the people have food. Agreed?

Demeter: Agreed.

228 **Unit 4** | Continuity and Change

REACHING ALL STUDENTS

Multi-Level Strategies

SUM IT UP OPTIONS

BEGINNING Have students review their Demeter character map. Ask: *What happened because Demeter went to Zeus for help?* (Persephone is released for part of the year; spring returns.) Invite students to dictate entries for a group plot chart focused on Demeter and her problem.

INTERMEDIATE Assign each pair of students one character. Pairs review their character maps and complete the plot chart. Have students discuss other possible solutions and consequences for each character.

ADVANCED After students finish their character maps, have them work in pairs to create a chart of actual and suggested solutions and consequences for each character. Then they share their charts and decide which ones offer the best solutions for each character.

ASSESSMENT
Selection Test 13 on page 63 of the Assessment Handbook tests students' mastery of the reading strategies and the vocabulary, comprehension, and language arts skills taught with this selection.

ınguage Arts and Literature

LITERARY ANALYSIS

AKE A PLOT DIAGRAM

›arn About Plot Use a **plot diagram** to show ›ents in a story. A plot diagram shows these ain elements of the plot:

The **conflict** is the story problem. Most stories start with or are built around a conflict.

Complications are events that make the story problem harder to solve.

The **climax** is the turning point. It is the most important or exciting part of the story where the outcome of the conflict is decided. Actions or events that lead to the climax are the **rising action**. The events that follow the climax are the **falling action**.

The **resolution** comes at the end of the story. It answers the remaining questions.

ot Diagram

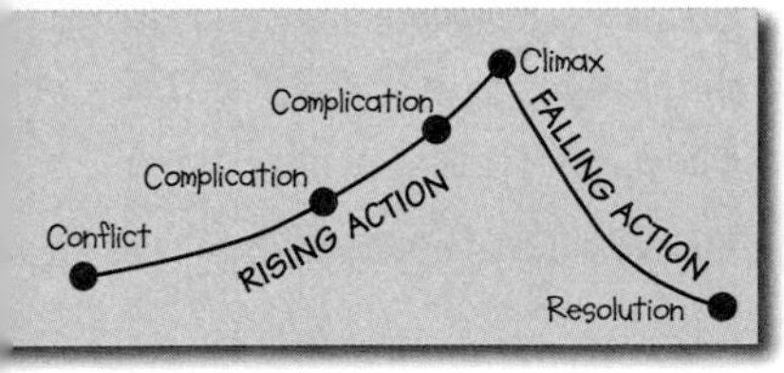

ractice Make a plot diagram for "The Mother /ho Lost Her Daughter." In the diagram, write otes to show the plot's main elements.

WRITING

LITERARY ANALYSIS

WRITE A MYTH

Imagine that you are a storyteller who lives in ancient Greece. Write your own myth about how the natural world changes.

1. **Prepare to Write** Choose a natural event. Then choose a Greek god or goddess, or invent one as a character. Make a character map like the one you made on page 228.
2. **Write Your Draft** Imagine the myth in your mind. Write what you see and hear.
3. **Edit Your Work** Do your characters have personal traits? How is the plot or problem solved in the end? Remember to check for correct spelling and punctuation.
4. **Publish a Book** Put all of the class myths together in a book. Give the book a title, and share it with others.

Develop your skill in the **writer's craft**. See Handbook pages 414–423.

Multi-Level Strategies

ACTIVITY OPTIONS FOR ANALYZING ELEMENTS OF PLOT

BEGINNING Read the myth aloud, pausing after each event to clarify meaning. Have students sketch the event. Select and save one sketch per event. After reading, draw a plot diagram. Review the myth as you place the sketches on the diagram. Create a group sentence about each step in the plot: *A conflict happens when Hades steals Demeter's daughter.*

INTERMEDIATE Read the myth aloud or play its recording. Pause after key events to elicit steps in the plot: *What is the conflict about?* Work as a group to record events on a plot diagram. After reading, partners retell the myth to each other.

ADVANCED As partners read the myth or listen to its recording, have them complete a plot diagram. After reading, students retell the myth to each other. Then have students change an event and revise the plot diagram before telling the story again to see how events in the plot affect the final outcome.

RESPOND

OBJECTIVES

PLOT DIAGRAM
Concepts and Vocabulary: Words About Plot—*conflict, complication, rising action, climax, falling action, resolution*
Literary Analysis: Ⓣ Plot

WRITE A MYTH
Function: Write
Learning Strategy: Use Graphic Organizers (plot diagram)
Literary Analysis and Writing: Myth

LANGUAGE ARTS AND LITERATURE

1. **Make a Plot Diagram** Possible notes for the diagram are:

   Conflict Demeter looks for Persephone, whom Hades has captured.

   Complication Demeter can't find Persephone. She becomes sad, and the first winter comes.

   Complication Persephone eats a pomegranate seed. She cannot leave the underworld permanently.

   Climax Demeter asks Zeus for help. He orders Hades to return Persephone to her mother for part of the year.

   Resolution Persephone returns to her mother for a while, and Demeter makes the crops grow. It is the first spring.

▶ **Practice Book** page 108

2. **Write a Myth** Brainstorm natural events, such as why the moon changes phases, why birds fly south, and why earthquakes happen.

   Remind students that they can incorporate the gods they learned about on page 219 into their myths.

▶ **Practice Book** page 109

CLOSE AND ASSESS

Ask students to identify the elements of plot structure in their myths.

RESPOND

OBJECTIVES

BEHAVIOR AND NATURE

Function: Ⓣ Define and Explain

Concepts and Vocabulary: Scientific Words—*method, hypothesis, data*

Critical Thinking and Research Skills: Formulate Hypotheses; Gather and Analyze Information; Plan Research Methods; Draw Conclusions; Conduct an Observation

BOTANICAL JOURNAL

Function: Write

Learning Strategies, Critical Thinking, and Research Skills: Gather and Organize Information; Classify

Representing: Drawing

Writing: Paragraph

CONTENT AREA CONNECTIONS

1 **Study Behavior and Nature** Preview content area vocabulary:

- ***method*:** Define *method* as a "way of doing something." Ask: *What are your study methods? Do you study with a friend?*
- ***hypothesis*:** Define *hypothesis* as a "theory or prediction based on current information." Explain that the example about people's sleep habits is a hypothesis until it has been proven through research.
- ***data*:** Explain that *data* is information organized for study. Show computer-generated data or data from a scientific journal.

Support students' research by teaching the Research Skills Minilesson.

▶ **Practice Book** pages 110–111

2 **Create a Botanical Journal** Students work in pairs to research their plant and identify its botanical name. Then all students classify their plants in a chart with headings such as *trees, flowers,* and *crops.*

CLOSE AND ASSESS

Ask students to write one or two sentences to summarize what they have learned in this lesson.

Respond to the Play, continued

Content Area Connections

SCIENCE

STUDY BEHAVIOR AND NATURE

How do events in nature affect people's behavior? One way to study these events is by following the **scientific method**. The scientific method is a process for gathering information. With a group, choose one event in the living world that you would like to study.

1. **Form a Hypothesis** A **hypothesis** is a statement that you will try to prove. For example: People sleep more when the days are shorter and the nights are longer. Make a hypothesis about the natural event you chose to study.
2. **Do Your Research** Look at calendars, encyclopedias, and almanacs to get information about your topic. Make observations. If possible, interview people to gather **data**. Data is information that you get from the real, or living, world.
3. **Draw Conclusions and Explain Results** Review the data and information you collected. Draw a conclusion. Was your hypothesis proven to be true? If not, then, like other scientists, you must change your hypothesis to match the data. Explain the results of your study to a group.

SCIENCE
REPRESENTING/WRITING

CREATE A BOTANICAL JOURNAL

Scientists write and draw in botanical journals to collect information about plants. Make a clas botanical journal to record information about plants in the play. Follow these steps:

1. **Sketch** Draw a detailed picture of the plant Compare pictures of the plant to help you.
2. **Label** Use an encyclopedia or field guide to find the botanical name of the plant. The botanical name may be different from the name you use. Write the name under your drawing. Label other parts of the plant.
3. **Write** Write a short paragraph about the lif cycle of the plant. Answer these questions:
   - When does the plant sprout?
   - How does it produce flowers and fruit?
   - How does it produce new plants?
   - Does it go dormant, or rest? When?
4. **Make a Journal of Plants** Classify all the plants. For example, trees are not part of the same group as cactus. Arrange them in groups in the journal. Then create a cover.

For more about the **research process**, see Handbook pages 394–399.

REACHING ALL STUDENTS

Research Skills

▶ **MAKING OBSERVATIONS**

TEACH Explain that observation means "the act of paying attention or noticing." Tell students that observation is a basic and useful research skill. Explain that it requires a clear hypothesis, as well as focus and concentration on the part of the observer. Give students an example: *If your hypothesis is that a certain kind of plant can grow without sunlight, you will need to take that plant out of the sun and make daily observations about its growth.*

PRACTICE Have students work in pairs to formulate hypotheses about events in nature. Then have them determine whether or not each hypothesis is true by using careful observation. Finally, students report back to the class on their findings and explain how observation helped them confirm or refute their hypotheses.

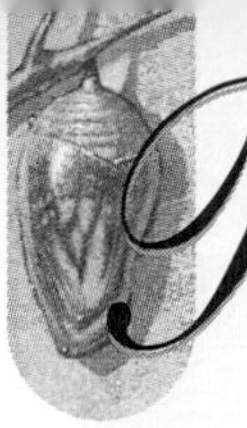

'rysalis
iary

oem for two voices
by Paul Fleischman

Prepare to Read

THINK ABOUT WHAT YOU KNOW

Discuss Life Stages Discuss the stages of human life. Use the stages to make a time line on the board.

pillar worm-like
n the life cycle of a
fly or moth
stop
nicle record of events
order in which they
ned, history
salis stage in the life
e insects when they are
ed in a hard shell
le hang down loosely
notebook in which
thoughts are written
lve disappear
n attach, join, connect
pe change into a
rm
lose by natural
s
h disappear, fade

ers to the
ulary activity:
ronicle
terpillar
stens
eds
rysalis
ngles
shapes
ssolve
ases
nishes

LEARN KEY VOCABULARY

Use Context Clues Study the new words and their definitions. Replace each underlined word in the paragraph with a vocabulary word. You may need to change the form of some words.

The Life Story of a Butterfly

A butterfly starts as a tiny egg, then changes into a worm-like creature. The caterpillar hooks onto a plant. Then it loses its skin and becomes an insect enclosed in a hard shell. The chrysalis hangs down loosely from the plant. Inside, the chrysalis completely changes itself. Its old body parts disappear, and it grows wings. It stops being a caterpillar or a chrysalis. It is now a butterfly. It comes out, flies away, and fades from view.

LEARN ABOUT STEPS IN A PROCESS

A **process** is a series of steps. When you put the steps in order, you can understand the whole process.

READING STRATEGY

How to Relate Steps in a Process

1. Pay attention to the order in which the steps happen. Look for signal words such as *first, second, next, then,* and *finally.*
2. Make a graphic organizer that shows the order of the steps.
3. Reread the selection and check the order.

Complete a diagram to show a butterfly's life cycle as you read "Chrysalis Diary."

Multi-Level Strategies

VOCABULARY OPTIONS

BEGINNING Group students and read aloud the entire paragraph. Then, model how to determine the correct answer. Work with students to complete the paragraph.

INTERMEDIATE Have students complete the activity in pairs, then compare and discuss their answers with another pair.

ADVANCED Invite students to complete the activity independently. Partners can compare answers.

Transparency 57 / Master 57

RELATE STEPS IN A PROCESS

Directions: Read the passage. Record the steps in the diagram.

The Life Cycle of a Frog

A female frog lays many eggs at once. The male fertilizes the eggs, and each egg forms an embryo.

After three weeks, the embryo becomes a tadpole, which breathes with gills and has a long tail. After about five weeks, the tadpole begins to grow legs, and lungs begin to develop.

Next, the tadpole's mouth widens, the gills and tail are absorbed into the body, and the lungs and legs grow. Then, eleven weeks after the egg is laid, the frog is fully developed. It comes out of the water to live mostly on land. After a while it finds a mate. The female lays eggs, the male fertilizes them, and the cycle begins again.

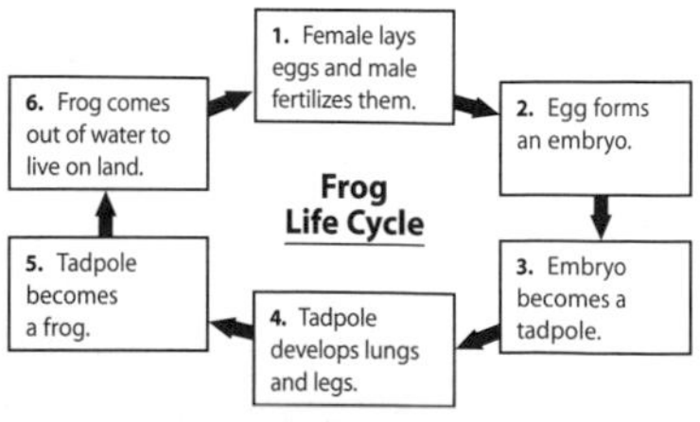

Transparency 57 Level B, Unit 4 | Continuity and Change © Hampton-Brown

PREPARE TO READ

OBJECTIVES

THINK ABOUT WHAT YOU KNOW

Reading and Learning Strategies: Relate to Personal Experience; Use Graphic Organizers (time line)

LEARN KEY VOCABULARY Ⓣ

Vocabulary Strategy: Use Context Clues

LEARN ABOUT STEPS IN A PROCESS

Reading Strategy: Ⓣ Relate Steps in a Process

THINK ABOUT WHAT YOU KNOW

1 **Discuss Life Stages** Write life stages as students call them out. Then have students suggest the order and label the time line.

LEARN KEY VOCABULARY

2 **Use Context Clues** Read each vocabulary word and its definition aloud. Clarify meanings. Then conduct the activity.

Use the Vocabulary Options in the **Multi-Level Strategies** to enable all students to participate.

▶ **Practice Book** page 112

LEARN ABOUT STEPS IN A PROCESS

3 **Model How to Relate Steps in a Process** Define *process.* Demonstrate the steps in the box with **Transparency 57.**

- Read the passage.
- Point out signal words.
- Complete the diagram showing the steps in the process.
- Have students reread to verify the order shown in the diagram.

CLOSE AND ASSESS

Ask: *What clues can help you understand the steps in a process?* (Signal words can tell the order in which events happen.)

READ PAGES 232–233

OBJECTIVES

Function: Read a Poem
Concepts and Vocabulary: Nature Words
Vocabulary Strategy: Relate Words
Listening: Listen to a Poem
Reading and Learning Strategies: Ⓣ Relate Steps in a Process; Use Graphic Organizers (process diagram)
Literary Analysis: Alliteration; Consonance

SET PURPOSE

1 Read aloud the title of the poem. Preview the illustrations and ask: *Why do you think the poet named the poem "Chrysalis Diary"?*

LISTEN AND READ

Tape 4A
CD 4 Track 2

2 **Strategy Focus: Relate Steps in a Process** Play "Chrysalis Diary" on the **Selection Tape/CD** or read the poem aloud. Using **Transparency 58**, explain the life cycle of a butterfly. Point out that the box at the bottom represents the part of the cycle expressed in the poem. Distribute copies of **Master 58**. Play or read the poem again, pausing after the entry for each date to interpret the text and complete the life cycle diagram.

Choose Activity Options in the **Multi-Level Strategies** to involve all students in completing the diagram.

Chrysalis Diary

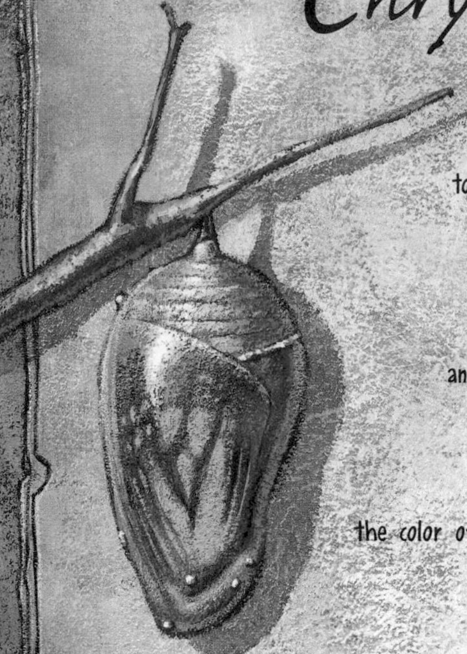

November 13:

Cold told me
to fasten my feet
to this branch,

to dangle upside down
from my perch,

to shed my skin,

to cease being a caterpillar
and I have obeyed.
and I have obeyed.

December 6:

Green,
the color of leaves and life,
has vanished!
has vanished!
The empire of leaves
lies in ruins!
lies in ruins!
I study the
brown new world around me.

I fear the future.

I hear few sounds.

Have any others of my kin
survived this cataclysm?

Swinging back and forth
in the wind,
I feel immeasurably alone.

my perch the branch where I sit
survived this cataclysm lived through this great disaster
immeasurably so very much

REACHING ALL STUDENTS

Transparency 58 / Master 58

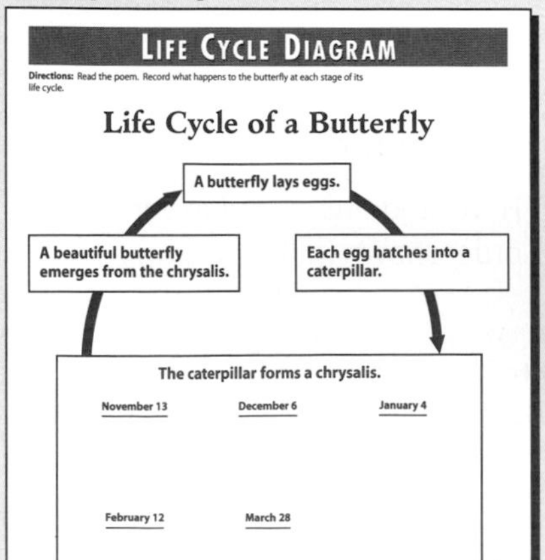

Multi-Level Strategies

ACTIVITY OPTIONS FOR COMPLETING THE DIAGRAM

BEGINNING Ask yes/no and either/or questions to involve students in completing the diagram. Ask: *Are the leaves green now or have they changed color? Has the weather changed? Is it snowing now or is it raining?*

INTERMEDIATE / **ADVANCED** Have students do a think, pair, share to come up with entries for each date. Prompt the thinking with questions, such as: *How do changes outside the chrysalis affect the butterfly? What is happening to the chrysalis that is not described in the poem?*

January 4:

can make out snow falling.

For five days and nights
it's been drifting down.

I find I never tire of
watching the flakes
in their multitudes
passing my window.

The world is now white.

Astounding.
Astounding.

I enter these
wondrous events
in my chronicle

knowing no reader
would believe me.

February 12:

An ice storm last night.

Unable to see out
at all this morning.

Yet I hear boughs cracking

and branches falling.

Hungry for sounds
in this silent world,
I cherish these,

ponder their import,

miser them away
in my memory,

and wait for more.
and wait for more.

fting down slowly falling to the ground
ltitudes great numbers
ndrous events beautiful happenings
ughs large branches
cherish love, care a lot about
ponder their import wonder what they mean
miser them away put them in a secret place for me only

REVIEW KEY VOCABULARY

3 Relate Words Point out that language in poetry is carefully chosen to fit the mood and tone of the poem. Certain words lend a poetic or musical tone. Others are less colorful, or neutral. Invite students to categorize the key vocabulary words as "poetic" or "neutral." Write poetic words in one chart and neutral ones in another.

Poetic	Neutral
cease	
chronicle	
vanish	
dangle	

Poetic	Neutral
	caterpillar
	dissolve
	fasten
	reshape

Invite students to think of a neutral, or more everyday, synonym for each poetic word and a more poetic word for each neutral one.

Science Connection

EXTREME WEATHER

Help students make connections between this poem and their study of the seasons related to "The Mother Who Lost Her Daughter." Read aloud each date in "Chrysalis Diary," and for each date ask: *What kinds of weather do you see in your mind as you read this part of the poem? What season is it?* Have students research and report on how a delicate creature such as a chrysalis can withstand such extremes of weather.

Literary Analysis Minilesson

▶ ALLITERATION AND CONSONANCE

TEACH Read aloud the first five lines of the poem, emphasizing the repeated *f* and *d* sounds. Ask students to identify the sounds that are repeated in these lines. Explain that the repetition of consonant sounds at the beginnings of words is called *alliteration*. Repetition of consonant sounds in the middle or at the ends of words is called *consonance*. Tell students that poets use these devices to create a mood, to enhance the rhythm of the lines, or to emphasize certain words or ideas.

PRACTICE Point out examples of alliteration and consonance in "Chrysalis Diary."

Alliteration

- page 232: leaves, life, lies; fear, future, few, forth, feel

Consonance

- page 232: cold, told; sound, kind

Discuss examples and analyze the feelings created by the alliteration or consonance.

▶ **Practice Book** page 113

READ PAGE 234

OBJECTIVES

Literary Analysis: Evaluate Impact of Point of View on Meaning

ABOUT THE POET

4 **Evaluate Literature: Point of View**
Read aloud About the Poet. Ask: *What experiences helped Fleischman feel close to nature?* Point out that Fleischman tells the story of the chrysalis from the first-person point of view, as if the chrysalis were talking.

Read aloud the entry for March 28. Ask: *How does the first-person point of view affect the reader?* (It makes the reader feel the story is more personal.)

CLOSE AND ASSESS

Ask students to write on an exit slip one thing they learned about a chrysalis and one thing they learned about poetry from this lesson.

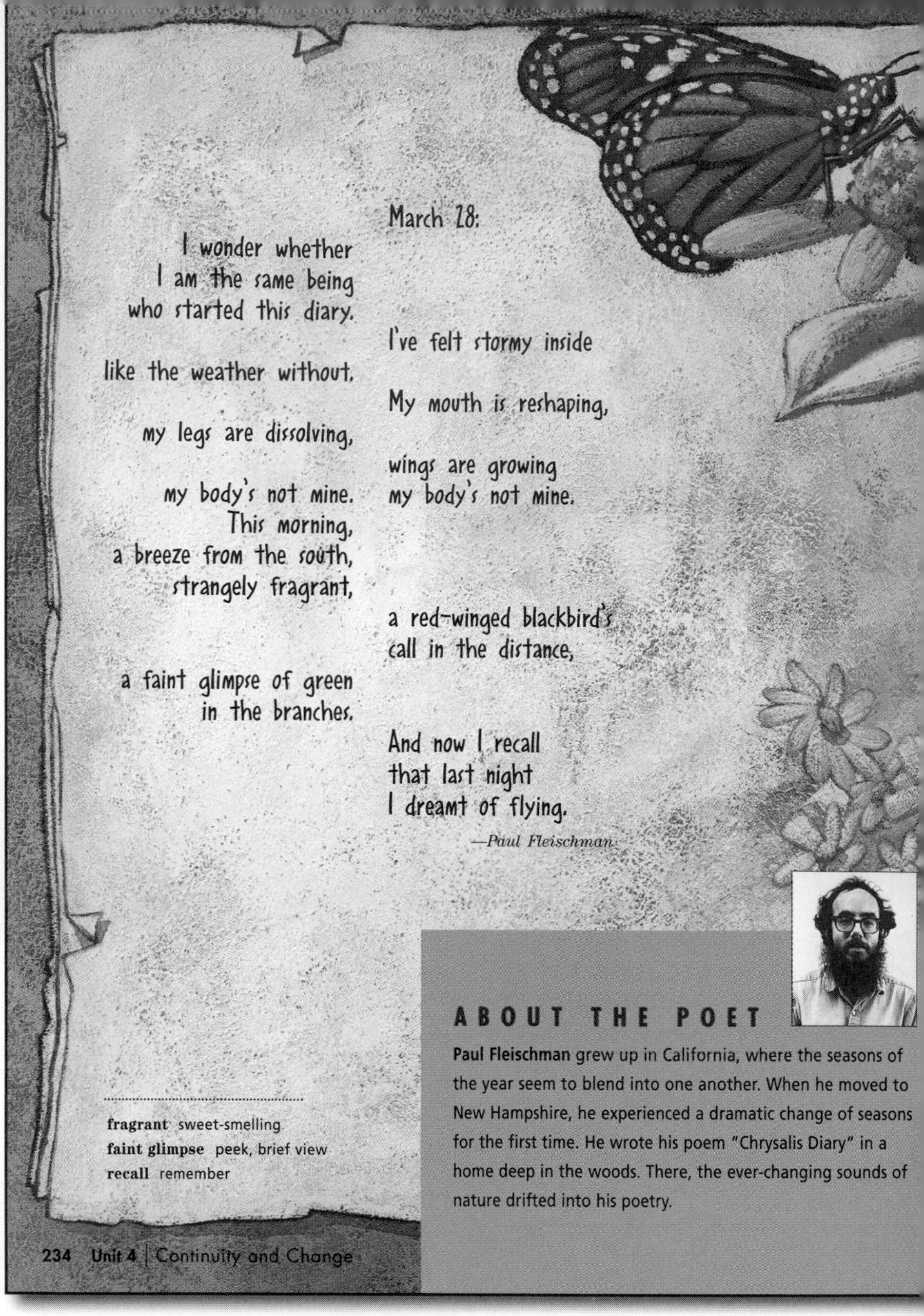

March 28:

I wonder whether
I am the same being
who started this diary.

I've felt stormy inside

like the weather without.

My mouth is reshaping,

my legs are dissolving,

wings are growing

my body's not mine.
my body's not mine.

This morning,
a breeze from the south,
strangely fragrant,

a red-winged blackbird's
call in the distance,

a faint glimpse of green
in the branches.

And now I recall
that last night
I dreamt of flying.

—*Paul Fleischman*

fragrant sweet-smelling
faint glimpse peek, brief view
recall remember

ABOUT THE POET

Paul Fleischman grew up in California, where the seasons of the year seem to blend into one another. When he moved to New Hampshire, he experienced a dramatic change of seasons for the first time. He wrote his poem "Chrysalis Diary" in a home deep in the woods. There, the ever-changing sounds of nature drifted into his poetry.

234 **Unit 4** | Continuity and Change

REACHING ALL STUDENTS

Music Connection
MOOD

Provide some examples of classical music or "nature" music for students to play as they read different sections of the poem. Encourage students to bring in music they like and to create a list that matches musical pieces to the parts of the poem. Discuss how the music expresses and extends the mood of the poem.

Learning Styles
STRATEGIES FOR CONSTRUCTING MEANING

- **Visual Learners** Have students draw pictures of each stage in the process described in the poem.
- **Auditory Learners** Ask students to do a choral reading of the poem. Help them rehearse the two-voice format with particular attention to the overlapping lines.
- **Kinesthetic Learners** Have students show the phases of the process using yarn or string to link the steps on a large graphic organizer as they read.

Respond to the Poem

Check Your Understanding

JM IT UP

elate Steps in a Process Write these steps in e life cycle of a butterfly. Add the missing steps.

A butterfly lays eggs.

Each egg hatches into a caterpillar.

The caterpillar forms a chrysalis.

Inside the chrysalis, the caterpillar becomes a butterfly.

A beautiful butterfly emerges from the chrysalis.

t a check beside the steps described in e poem.

ake Predictions The entry for March 18 ends ith the words "And now I recall that last night I eamt of flying." In a group, discuss why you ink the poet chose to end the poem with these ords. Then, choose a date later in March and ite a new entry for the diary that shows what u are experiencing as a butterfly.

THINK IT OVER

Discuss and Write Talk about these questions with a partner. Write the answers.

1. **Mood** What is the mood, or feeling, of the poem? What words in the poem support your answer?
2. **Author's Style** Why do you think the poet wrote this poem as if he were the chrysalis?
3. **Personal Experience** People also go through many changes in their lives. What kinds of changes have you experienced? Compare yourself now to the way you were as a very young child or baby.

EXPRESS YOURSELF

▸RECITE A POEM FOR TWO VOICES

Paul Fleischman wrote this poem to be read aloud by two readers. Sometimes the readers take turns, and sometimes they read together.

Practice in pairs first, and then form two groups with the whole class. Each group reads one column of the poem aloud. The groups join together when the same words appear on the same line in each column. Listen to see if your voices go together and are clearly understood.

Multi-Level Strategies

SUM IT UP OPTIONS

BEGINNING Have students work in a group to complete the list. Then ask either/or questions to relate the steps to the poem. For example: *Does the poem describe how an egg turns into a caterpillar or how the caterpillar becomes a chrysalis?* (how a caterpillar becomes a chrysalis) Invite students to compose a group entry for the diary.

INTERMEDIATE Encourage students to work with a partner to complete the list and identify the steps described in the poem. Then invite each pair to compose one line for the diary entry. Finally, combine the lines into a group entry.

ADVANCED Have students work independently to complete the list. Brainstorm with the group possible information to be included in the diary entry. Encourage them to compose their own entries and share them with the class.

RESPOND

OBJECTIVES

SUM IT UP

Function: Write

Reading and Learning Strategies: Ⓣ Relate Steps in a Process; Make Predictions

Writing: Diary Entry

THINK IT OVER

Function: Engage in Discussion

Critical Thinking: Relate to Personal Experience

Literary Analysis: Mood; Style

EXPRESS YOURSELF

Function: Recite

Speaking and Listening: Choral Reading

CHECK YOUR UNDERSTANDING

1 **Sum It Up** See red annotations on page 235 for the missing steps and checks. A sample diary entry is:

March 30:

Dry wings	Dry wings
I fly	I flutter
I sit in the sun.	
	I sit on a flower.

▸ **Practice Book** page 114

2 **Think It Over** Possible responses are:

1. **Mood** Words like *stormy* show fear. Words like *study* show curiosity.
2. **Author's Style** He wanted to make the experience more immediate.
3. **Personal Experience** Answers will vary.

EXPRESS YOURSELF

3 **Recite a Poem for Two Voices** Remind groups that when lines appear side-by-side ("and I have obeyed") they are to be spoken by both groups at the same time.

CLOSE AND ASSESS

Have students read aloud and describe appealing images in the poem.

PREPARE TO READ

OBJECTIVES

THINK ABOUT WHAT YOU KNOW
Reading Strategy: Activate Prior Knowledge; Build Background

LEARN KEY VOCABULARY Ⓣ
Vocabulary Strategy: Use New Words in Context

LEARN TO SKIM AND TAKE NOTES
Reading and Learning Strategies: Ⓣ Skim and Take Notes

THINK ABOUT WHAT YOU KNOW

1 **Idea Exchange** Before reading page 237 together, invite students to jot down their ideas about how volcanoes erupt. After reading, they can revise, if necessary.

LEARN KEY VOCABULARY

2 **Use New Words in Context** Read aloud each vocabulary word and its definition. Clarify meanings. Then conduct the four-square activity.

Use the Vocabulary Options in the **Multi-Level Strategies** to include all proficiency levels.

▶ **Practice Book** page 115

LEARN TO SKIM AND TAKE NOTES

3 **Model How to Skim and Take Notes** Demonstrate the steps in the box with **Transparency 59:**

- Model how to skim the passage and diagram. Then say: *I think this selection will be about predicting eruptions, so my question will be "What are the warning signs of a volcanic eruption?"*
- Then take notes on the card as you read the passage aloud.

CLOSE AND ASSESS

Ask students why it is helpful to skim and take notes. (Skimming helps you formulate questions for your reading; taking notes helps you keep track of the answers you find.)

The Big Blast

science article
by Patricia Lauber

Prepare to Read

THINK ABOUT WHAT YOU KNOW

Idea Exchange Read about volcanoes on page 237. Tell a partner one thing you learned.

avalanche sudden falling of snow or rock down a mountain

colonizer plant or animal that moves to a new place to live

crater bowl-shaped hole at the top of a volcano

dome large, round top

earthquake sudden movement of the earth

eruption strong, sudden release of something

flow stream, steady movement

force power, energy; make something move

lava hot, melted rock that comes out of a volcano

magma hot, melted rock below the earth's surface

pressure energy used to press one thing against another

survivor animal or plant that lives through a dangerous event

Student pictures and sentences in the vocabulary activity will vary, but definitions should match those above.

LEARN KEY VOCABULARY

Use New Words in Context Study the new words and their definitio[ns.] Make a four-square diagram for each word.

Word: dome	Picture 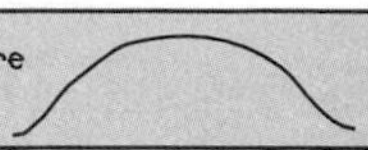
Definition: large, round top	Sentence: Mount St. Helens' dome is very large.

LEARN TO SKIM AND TAKE NOTES

When you **skim** a selection, you look at the headings, photos, and diagrams before you read the whole selection. This strategy can help you form questions and get ready to **take notes.**

READING STRATEGY
How to Skim and Take Notes
1. Read the headings.
2. Look at the diagrams, photos, captions, and charts. Think about how these graphics relate to the headings.
3. Form questions you hope to answer as you read. Write each question at the top of a notecard.
4. As you read, write down the answers to your questions.

Skim "The Big Blast." Prepare notecards before you read, and write the answers to your questions as you read.

REACHING ALL STUDENTS

Multi-Level Strategies
VOCABULARY OPTIONS

BEGINNING Group students to read ***Explore!*** or the Key Points Reading on **Master 60.** (See page T239.) Work with the vocabulary in those selections.

INTERMEDIATE Work with the group to write words and definitions. Then allow time to draw pictures and write sentences independently.

ADVANCED Students can complete the activity on their own, and then categorize the words into groups, such as parts of a volcano.

Transparency 59 / Master 59

HOW TO SKIM AND TAKE NOTES

Directions: Skim the selection. Write your research question and the source at the top of a notecard. Read the selection and take notes that answer your question.

Predicting Volcanic Eruptions

Ground Bulges Volcanoes that are about to erupt give warning signs. Bulges, or swellings, in the ground show that something may happen soon. Bulges are monitored by devices called *tiltmeters.*

Earth Tremors Small earthquakes, called earth tremors, also indicate activity. Tremors become stronger and more numerous before an eruption. They can be monitored by instruments called *seismometers.*

Sulfur Dioxide Clouds of this gas are released before an eruption. It can be measured with a device called a *correlation spectrometer.*

What are the warning signs of a volcanic eruption?
All About Volcanoes by Quynh Nguyen, page 35
—The bulges in the ground show that something might happen.
—Small earthquakes get stronger before an eruption.
—Sulfur dioxide is released before an eruption.

Transparency 59 Level B, Unit 4 | Continuity and Change

REFERENCE POINT

Sleeping Giants

Many volcanoes are quiet and still for years, even centuries. When they do awake, or become active, the once-sleeping giants shake the earth with their great power.

IAT HAPPENS IN AN ERUPTION

temperature deep inside the earth is very —so hot that it can melt rock. Melted rock alled **magma**. When rock melts, gases are ased and become mixed with the magma. gma rises and melts surrounding rock to ate and fill a **magma chamber**. Pressure 1 causes the magma to melt a path through k lying above. An **eruption** occurs when gma, gases, and other materials are forced ough openings to the earth's **surface**.

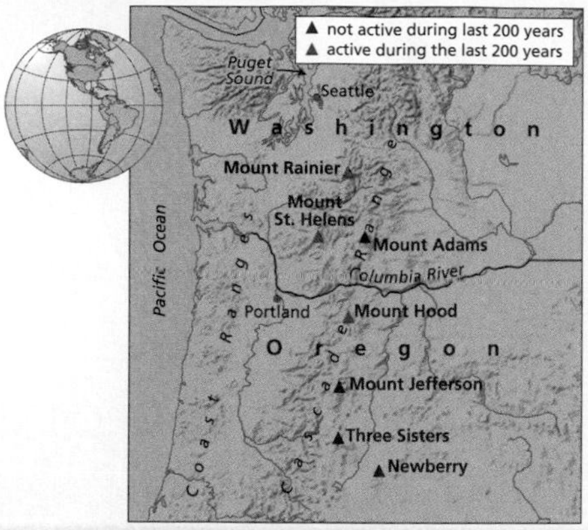

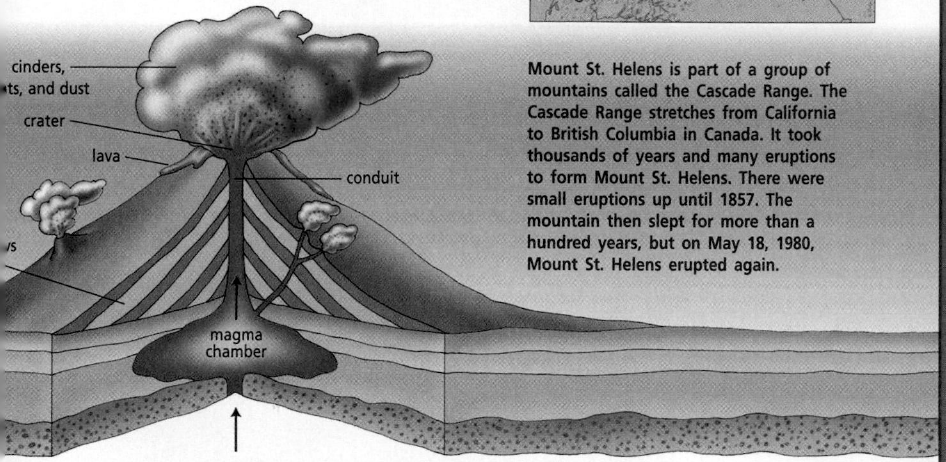

Mount St. Helens is part of a group of mountains called the Cascade Range. The Cascade Range stretches from California to British Columbia in Canada. It took thousands of years and many eruptions to form Mount St. Helens. There were small eruptions up until 1857. The mountain then slept for more than a hundred years, but on May 18, 1980, Mount St. Helens erupted again.

ma chamber space that contains magma
ace upper or outer boundary

MORE TO EXPLORE

Updates on Volcanoes After reading page 237, ask: *How can you evaluate the accuracy of the information on this page?* (check it against other sources such as encyclopedias, books, the Internet) Elicit that the most up-to-date information can be found on the Internet. Invite students to locate several sources of information about volcanic eruptions and compare their findings with the information in "The Big Blast."

Web Sites

Web sites undergo frequent modifications, but here are some you may want to suggest to students:

surfnetkids.com/volcano.htm
library.thinkquest.org/17457
www.geol.ucsb.edu/~fisher/

THE BASICS BOOKSHELF

■ ***Explore!*** by Janine Wheeler

Visit a volcano and other interesting places around the world. This colorful book uses patterned text to introduce each locale and a vehicle for exploring it, providing opportunities to develop basic vocabulary about weather and landforms. Photographs and illustrations, including maps, support the text and increase access for beginning English learners.

For Lesson Plans: See the Teacher's Guide for ***The Basics Bookshelf***.

Science Connection

ERUPTIONS

Give a demonstration of an eruption by boiling a teakettle of water. As steam begins to escape, ask students to describe, informally, what is happening. Then have students give accurate scientific explanations. Write the explanations as a step-by-step process. Invite comparisons with volcanic eruptions.

READ THE SELECTION

OBJECTIVES

Reading Strategies: Preview; Predict
Literary Analysis: Science Article

INTRODUCE THE SELECTION

1 **Preview and Predict** With students, read the title, the author's name, and the introduction to the selection. Ask: *What do you expect to find out about volcanoes in this selection?* (the effects of a volcanic eruption)

2 **Identify Genre: Science Article** Say: *This selection is a science article. From that name, do you think this will be a fiction or nonfiction selection?* Explain that a science article is nonfiction writing that describes and explains scientific details. Point out that graphics are often included in science articles. Have students page through the selection to preview these special features.

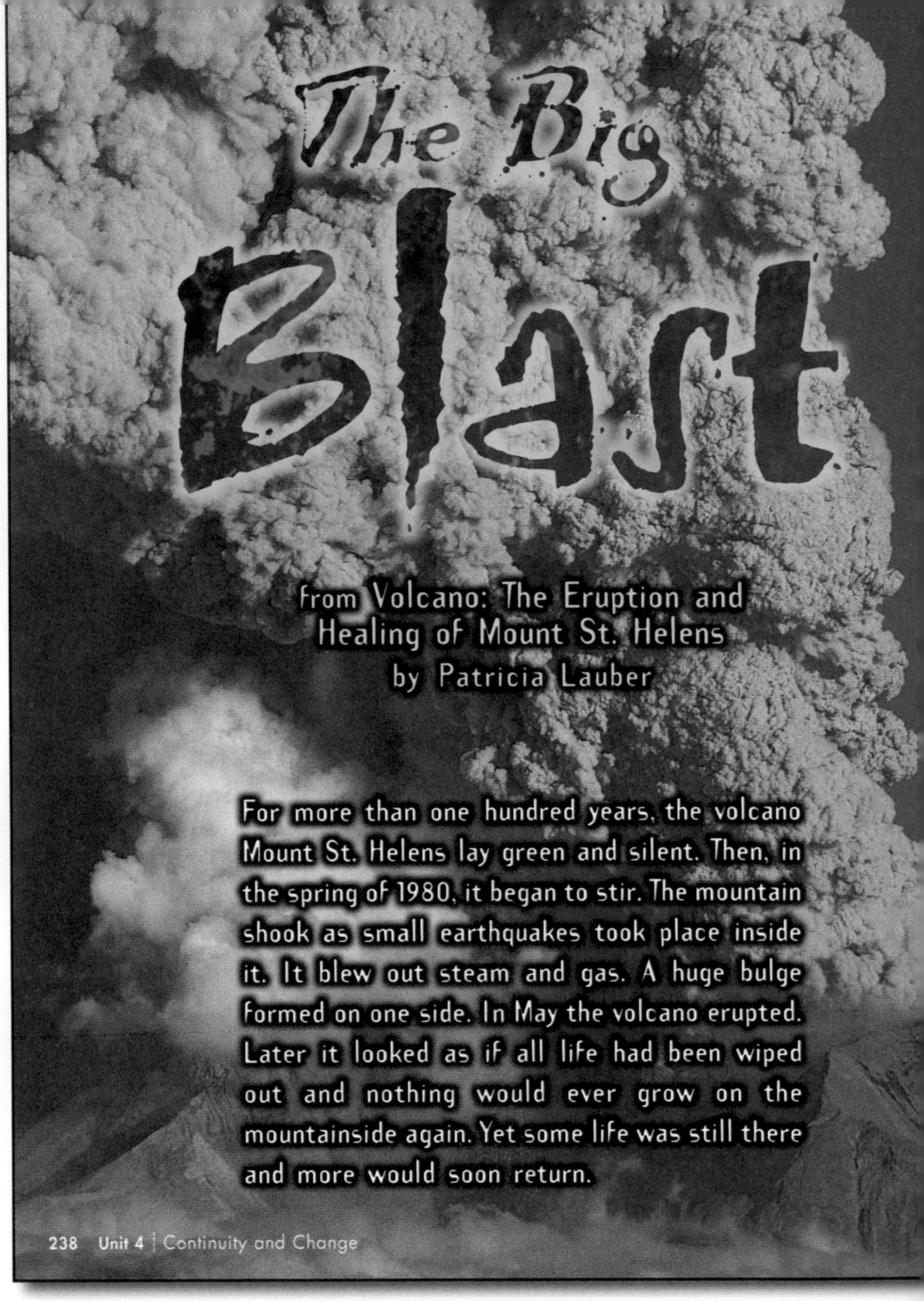

The Big Blast

from Volcano: The Eruption and Healing of Mount St. Helens
by Patricia Lauber

For more than one hundred years, the volcano Mount St. Helens lay green and silent. Then, in the spring of 1980, it began to stir. The mountain shook as small earthquakes took place inside it. It blew out steam and gas. A huge bulge formed on one side. In May the volcano erupted. Later it looked as if all life had been wiped out and nothing would ever grow on the mountainside again. Yet some life was still there and more would soon return.

238 **Unit 4** | Continuity and Change

The Big Blast
from *Volcano: The Eruption and Healing of Mount St. Helens*
by Patricia Lauber

Theme Connection In this selection, a violent volcanic eruption causes devastating changes, but even in the midst of destruction, life continues.

Selection Summary and Awards The introduction on page 238 of the student book offers a summary of the selection. Patricia Lauber won a Newbery Honor Book award for *Volcano: The Eruption and Healing of Mount St. Helens.* Other books by this author were nominated as ALA Notable Books, and for the American Book Award.

REACHING ALL STUDENTS

Math Connection
STATISTICS

Have students work in groups to research and report on statistics about the 1980 Mount St. Helens eruption. One group may concentrate on the lava and mudflows, answering questions like: *How many tons of earth were moved by the eruptions?* Another group may research the ash fall: *How big was the area covered with ash?* Encourage students to use print and electronic resources.

Build background: Because the Mount St. Helens volcano had not been active in the twentieth century, the surrounding forests and lakes became a popular spot for hiking, camping, fishing, and boating.

he First Blast

d annotations offer opportunities to clarify meaning and check for understanding.

ıe May 18 eruption of Mount St. Helens ·gan with an **earthquake** that **triggered** . **avalanche**. At 8:32 A.M. instruments ıat were miles away **registered** a strong ·rthquake. The pilot and passengers of ·small plane saw the north side of the ·ountain rippling and churning. Shaken by ·e quake, the **bulge** was tearing loose. It ·gan to slide, in a huge avalanche that ·rried along rock ripped from deep inside ·ount St. Helens. **Ask:** What caused the avalanche?

The avalanche tore open the mountain. **scalding blast** shot sideways out of the ·ening. It was a blast of steam, from water ·ated by rising magma.

Normally water cannot be heated beyond ; boiling point, which is 212 degrees ·hrenheit at sea level. At boiling point, ·ater turns to a gas, which we call steam. ıt if water is kept under **pressure**, it can · heated far beyond its boiling point and ·ill stay liquid. (That is how a pressure ·ooker works.) If the pressure is removed, is superheated water suddenly turns, or ·ashes, to steam. As steam, it takes up much more room—it expands. The sudden change to steam can cause an explosion.

Explain: A pressure cooker is a pot with a tight fitting lid that has a valve to control the pressure that builds up inside the pot as the contents are heated.
Define *superheated water*: water that is hotter than the boiling point because it is under pressure.

Before the eruption Mount St. Helens was like a giant pressure cooker. The rock inside it held superheated water. The water stayed liquid because it was under great pressure, sealed in the mountain. When the mountain was torn open, the pressure was suddenly **relieved.** The superheated water flashed to steam. Expanding violently, it **shattered** rock inside the mountain and exploded out the opening, traveling at speeds of up to 200 miles an hour.

The blast **flattened** whole forests of 180-foot-high firs. It snapped off or uprooted the trees, scattering the trunks as if they were straws. At first, this damage **was puzzling**. A wind of 200 miles an hour is not strong enough to **level forests of giant trees**. The explanation, **geologists** later discovered, was that the wind carried rocks ranging in size from grains of sand to blocks as big as cars. As the blast roared out of the volcano, it swept up and carried along the rock it had shattered.

Ask: Why were the scientists puzzled? What actually broke and uprooted the trees? (the rocks carried in the wind)

iggered caused
gistered recorded, measured
ılge huge bump
alding blast very hot and powerful stream air, gas, or steam
·lieved let out, lessened
shattered broke up
flattened knocked down
was puzzling caused questions
level forests of giant trees make the big trees in a forest fall down and lie flat
geologists scientists who study the earth

READ PAGE 239

OBJECTIVES

Function: Read a Selection
Listening: Listen to a Selection
Reading and Learning Strategies: Set a Purpose for Reading; Ⓣ Skim and Take Notes

SET PURPOSE

3 Read the heading and set the purpose for reading: *What inference can you make from this heading?* (There will be more than one blast.)

READ AND THINK

Tape 4A
CD 4 Track 3

4 **Strategy Focus: Skim and Take Notes** Have students skim the selection and set up notecards with the questions they want to answer.

Use the Reading Options in the **Multi-Level Strategies** to guide the note-taking.

The recording of "The Big Blast" on the **Selection Tape/CD** offers an oral language model and the opportunity to build reading fluency.

Multi-Level Strategies

READING OPTIONS FOR LESSONS 14–16

BEGINNING Students should work with ***Explore!*** while the class reads "The Big Blast." Or distribute copies of **Master 60** to conduct a Key Points Reading of "The Big Blast." As a group, use notecards to record questions and take notes about each paragraph.

INTERMEDIATE Read the selection aloud or play the recording on the **Selection Tape/CD**, pausing to clarify meaning. Also use the red annotations on the facsimile pages. Students can work in pairs to take notes.

ADVANCED Read the selection aloud or play the recording on the **Selection Tape/CD**, stopping at the end of each page for students to record notes. Encourage students to jot down any new information that seems important. Have them use their notecards to restate the main ideas of the selection.

Transparency 60 / Master 60

KEY POINTS READING

The Big Blast

On May 18, 1980, the Mount St. Helens volcano begins to erupt. A bulge tears loose from the side of the mountain. Very hot steam blasts out the opening. Boulders and dirt slide down the mountain in an avalanche.

A "stone wind" of rocks and sand snaps off every tree. The avalanche splits apart. One part pours into Spirit Lake. Water sloshes up the slope. Trees slide back down into the lake. Most of the avalanche sweeps down the Toutle River valley and stops there.

Next, Mount St. Helens erupts upward. Ash and ground-up rock shoot into the sky. The sky goes dark for miles around. Ash falls like snow. Melted snow and ice mix with rocks and dirt to form mudflows. The largest mudflow tears out steel bridges and rips houses apart.

The next day, the mountain is 1,300 feet shorter. The area around it is a barren wasteland. The volcano erupts six more times that year. Afterward, scientists study how life returns to the mountain. Some plants, small animals, and insects survive underground. Larger animals return later.

Transparency 60 Level B, Unit 4 | Continuity and Change © Hampton-Brown

READ PAGES 240–241

OBJECTIVES

Concepts and Vocabulary: Words About Destruction; Sensory Words
Reading and Learning Strategies: Predict; Use Text Features (sidebars)
Comprehension:
T Identify Cause and Effect
Literary Analysis: Simile

EXPAND YOUR VOCABULARY

5 Sensory Words Have students close their eyes and visualize the scene as you read aloud pages 240–241. Then ask students to skim the text and identify the vivid verbs that helped them picture the action. Make a chart.

Sensory Words	Associations
trees snapped	cracking sound; broken pencils
wind rushed	whooshing sound; loud; force; push; fast
It stripped bark	peeled bare; fast; forceful
uprooted	strong force; bare roots; dying trees and plants
scorched and killed	burned quickly; blackened; dead
water sloshed up	water splashing; wet; sloppy

The result was what one geologist described as "a stone wind." It was a wind of steam and rocks, traveling at high speed. The rocks gave the blast its great **force**. Before it, trees snapped and fell. Their stumps looked as if they had been **sandblasted**. The wind of stone rushed on. It stripped bark and branches from trees ar uprooted them, leveling 150 square miles of countryside. At the edge of this area other trees were left standing, but the heat of the blast **scorched** and killed them.

The stone wind was traveling so fast that it overtook and passed the avalanche. On its path was Spirit Lake, one of the most beautiful lakes in the Cascades. The blast stripped the trees from the **slopes** surrounding the lake and moved on. Meanwhile the avalanche had hit a **ridge**

Encourage elaboration: Name as many things as you can that are being changed at this time.

Clarify: Different things were happening a the same time: both the avalanche and the stone wind were causing destruction.

These photos (top to bottom) show the first few minutes of the eruption on May 18, 1980. An earthquake, an avalanche, and a violent blast closely followed one another.

sandblasted stripped clean by powerfully blown sand
scorched burned
slopes sides of the mountain
ridge narrow area of higher ground

REACHING ALL STUDENTS

Vocabulary
VOLCANIC WORDS

Point out that the author uses powerful words to describe the volcanic eruption. Tell students that organizing these words into categories can help them use powerful words in their own descriptions. Have small groups create word clusters around topics, such as: *pressure, temperature, movement, sound, plant,* and *geography*.

Post the clusters for students to refer to as they speak and write about volcanoes.

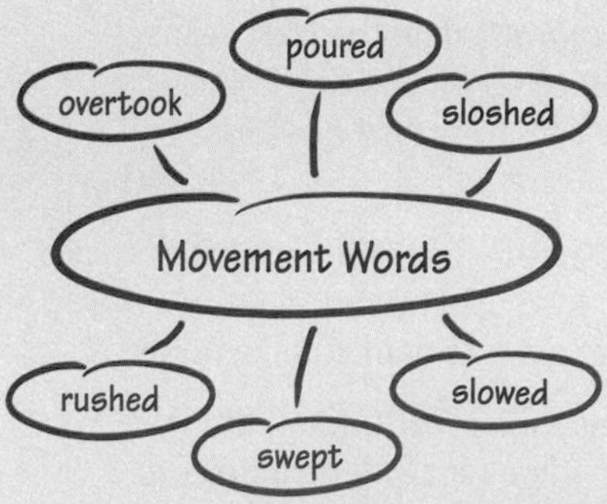

Science Connection
WATER POWER

Materials: plates, toothpicks, water

Point out the first paragraph on page 241, which describes the power of sloshing water during an avalanche. Have several groups of students conduct an experiment demonstrating this idea. Tell them to place water in the center of a plate, and place toothpicks on the rim of the plate. They then gently slosh the water from side to side and observe how the water drags the toothpicks off the rim and into the center of the plate. Discuss the experiment and its implications.

ıd split. One part of it poured into Spirit ıke, adding a 300-foot layer of rock and ırt to the bottom of the lake. The slide of ·alanche into the lake **forced** the water ıt. The water **sloshed** up the slopes, en fell back into the lake. With it came ousands of trees **felled** by the blast.

The main part of the avalanche swept ɔwn the valley of the North Fork of the ɔutle River. There, in the valley, most ' the avalanche slowed and stopped. It ɔvered 24 square miles and averaged 50 feet thick.

POINT-BY-POINT

Change Comes to Mount St. Helens

An earthquake causes an avalanche.

Mount St. Helens loses part of its north side in the first blast.

The blast breaks off rocks and carries them at high speed. It damages everything in its path.

Clarify: The 150-foot thick deposit from the avalanche would be taller than a five-story building. **Ask:** How many stories deep was the layer that poured into Spirit Lake? (a 300-foot layer would be taller than a ten-story building)

ıe blast leveled whole forests of huge firs. The tiny figures of ʋo scientists (lower right) give an idea of the scale.

Use visuals: Read the caption. Invite students to locate the two scientists and compare them to the lengths of the trees and the height of the debris deposit.

BEFORE YOU MOVE ON...

1. **Cause and Effect** What effect did the avalanche have on the mountain?
2. **Vocabulary** Make a list of words that describe something that has been damaged or destroyed. Example: *shattered*
3. **Prediction** What might happen if material continues to flow into the lake and river?

oshed splashed
lled knocked down

MONITOR YOUR READING

6 Use Text Features: Sidebars
Direct students' attention to the Point-by-Point sidebar. Explain that it can help them remember details and the sequence of events.

CHECK COMPREHENSION

7 Answers to "Before You Move On"

1. **Cause and Effect** It leveled the trees and added a thick layer of debris to the bottom of the lake, which forced the water to slosh up the slopes and then carry felled trees back into the lake.
2. **Vocabulary** Responses will vary but may include: *snapped, sandblasted, stripped, uprooted, leveling, scorched, felled.*
3. **Prediction** Responses will vary but may include flooding or changing the course of the river.

CLOSE AND ASSESS

Have students share their notecards for pages 239–241. Check for focus: Do the notes answer the questions?

Language Development

DESCRIBE EVENTS

Have students imagine that they are reporters observing the Mount St. Helens eruption from a safe vantage point. Cameras cannot be used because of the thick dust, so they are phoning in a description of what is happening. As they relate their stories, encourage students to use specific vocabulary and expressions from the selection. Invite students to describe their feelings as they "watch" the destruction.

Literary Analysis Minilesson

▶ SIMILES

TEACH Tell students that similes are comparisons of things that have some quality in common. Point out the simile on page 239: "Mount St. Helens was like a giant pressure cooker." Elicit that this simile gives the reader a mental image of the force building up inside the mountain. Similes use the words *like* or *as* to make a comparison. Similes often appeal to the senses and create memorable mental images.

PRACTICE Ask students to find other similes in the selection and create a chart in their class or individual dictionaries. The chart should include similes in one column and comparison words in another.

Simile	Comparison Word
Mount St. Helens was like a giant pressure cooker.	like

▶ **Practice Book** page 116

READ PAGES 242–243

OBJECTIVES

Function: Read a Selection
Grammar: Adverbs
Listening: Listen to a Selection
Reading and Learning Strategies: Set a Purpose for Reading; Ⓣ Skim and Take Notes; Paraphrase
Comprehension: Ⓣ Identify Cause and Effect; Summarize

SET PURPOSE

1 Read aloud the heading and the photo captions. Set the purpose for reading: *As you read, look for details that show the effects of the mudflows.*

READ AND THINK

Tape 4A
CD 4 Track 3

2 Strategy Focus: Skim and Take Notes Involve students in reading pages 242–243. Remind them to continue taking notes.

See the **Multi-Level Strategies** on page T239 to tailor the reading experience to all proficiency levels.

The Upward Eruption

The blast itself continued for 10 to 15 minutes, then stopped. Minutes later Mount St. Helens began to erupt upwards. A dark column of ash and ground-up rock rose miles into the sky. Winds blew the ash eastward. Lightning flashed in the ash cloud and started forest fires. In Yakima, Washington, some 80 miles away, the sky turned so dark that streetlights went on at noon. Ash fell like snow that would not melt. This eruption continued for nine hours.

Shortly after noon the color of the ash column changed. It became lighter, a sign that the volcano was now throwing out mostly new magma. Until then much of the ash had been made of old rock.

Ask: What changes occurred because of the ashes?

At the same time the volcano began giving off huge **flows** of **pumice** and ash. The material was very hot, with temperature of about 1,000 degrees Fahrenheit, and it traveled down the mountain at speeds of 10 miles an hour. The flows went on until 5:30 in the afternoon. They formed **a wedge-shaped plain** of pumice on the side of the mountain. Two weeks later temperatures in the pumice were still 780 degrees.

Finally, there were the mudflows, which started when heat from the blast melted ice and snow on the mountaintop. The water mixed with ash, pumice, ground-up rock, and dirt and rocks of the avalanche. The result was a thick mixture that was like

Support comprehension: Point out the sequen clues in the paragraphs on this page. (*Shortly afte noon; At the same time; Two weeks later; Finally*)

Melted snow and ice caused this mudflow. The smaller part of the flow went into Spirit Lake (lower left), while the larger part traveled down the Toutle River.

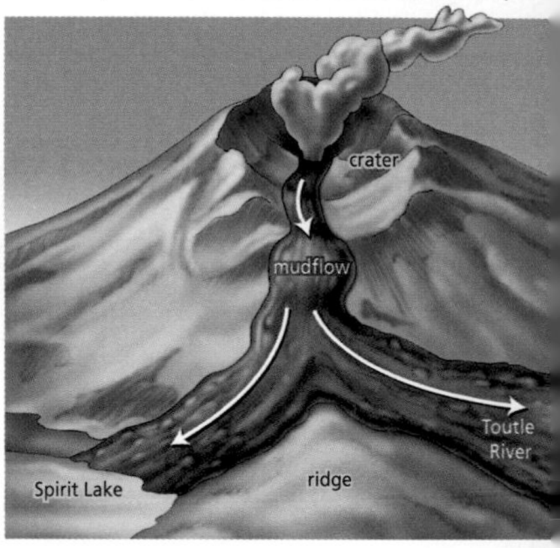

pumice rock from the volcano
a wedge-shaped plain an area shaped like a triangle

REACHING ALL STUDENTS

A WORLD OF LANGUAGES

Borrowed Words All languages change through contact with other languages. See how many of these words students recognize, and point out their origins.

WORD	ORIGIN	MEANING
avalanche	French	ice, snow, or earth that moves down a mountain
cascade	Italian; French	a small waterfall
glacier	French	a huge mass of ice
volcano	Vulcan, the Roman god of fire	a mountain that spews molten rock and steam

The mudflow swept up and carried along huge boulders and tore out bridges.

POINT-BY-POINT

Change Comes to Mount St. Helens

- **Mount St. Helens erupts again. This time the blast comes out of the top.**
- **Very hot flows of volcanic rock and ash move down the mountain.**
- **Melted snow and ice mix with rocks and dirt. These mudflows cause great damage.**

ret concrete, a mudflow. The mudflows raveled fast, **scouring** the landscape nd **sweeping** down the slopes into river alleys. Together their speed and thickness id great damage.

The largest mudflow was made of valanche material from the valley of the orth Fork of the Toutle River. It **churned** own the river valley, tearing out steel bridges, ripping houses apart, picking up boulders and trucks and carrying them along. Miles away it **choked** the Cowlitz River and blocked **shipping channels** in the Columbia River.

Ask: What was the sequence of events that started with the second eruption and ended with the mudflows?

Ask: What kinds of damage were caused by the mudflow?

BEFORE YOU MOVE ON...

1. **Cause and Effect** How did lightning affect the forest?
2. **Paraphrase** Explain how the avalanche material became a mudflow.
3. **Summary** Compare your prediction to what actually happened as mud and rocks flowed into the lake and river.

couring clearing away
weeping moving quickly
hurned moved with great force
hoked blocked, stopped
hipping channels deep areas that ships pass through

CHECK COMPREHENSION

3 Answers to "Before You Move On"

1. **Cause and Effect** Lightning caused forest fires.
2. **Paraphrase** Answers should indicate that melted snow and ice mixed with ash, rocks, and dirt.
3. **Summary** Responses will vary. Descriptions should mention the destruction of structures and the blockage of waterways.

CLOSE AND ASSESS

Ask: *Which answer on your notecard suprised you most?*

Vocabulary

GEOLOGY WORDS

Materials: index cards

Have students choose from the selection ten words representing key geological concepts (stone, slope, crater, ridge, etc.) and make an index card for each word. On one side of the card, the student writes the word; on the other side, the student draws a diagram to show its meaning and writes a definition below the drawing. Students can then use the cards as flashcards to quiz each other on the meanings of the words.

Grammar Minilesson

▶ ADVERBS

TEACH Point out this sentence on page 242: *Minutes later Mount St. Helens began to erupt* ***upwards****.* Identify *upwards* as an adverb that tells *where*. Write these examples:

> The pumice and ash flowed <u>rapidly</u> down the mountain. (how)
>
> It is time to escape <u>now</u>. (when)
>
> The scientists waited <u>nearby</u>. (where)

Explain that adverbs usually tell more about a verb—*how, when,* and *where*. Adverbs that tell *how* usually end in *-ly*.

PRACTICE Have students use adverbs to add details to these sentences.

1. Rescuers looked for survivors. (how)
2. The scientists study. (when)
3. The hottest pumice was found. (where)
4. Steam shot out. (how)
5. Winds blew the ash. (where)

▶ **Practice Book** page 117

READ PAGES 244–245

OBJECTIVES

Function: Read a Selection
Vocabulary Strategy: Multiple-Meaning Words
Grammar: Ⓣ Relative Clauses
Listening: Listen to a Selection
Reading and Learning Strategies: Set a Purpose for Reading; Ⓣ Skim and Take Notes
Comprehension: Make Comparisons; Draw Conclusions

SET PURPOSE

1 Read aloud the heading. Ask: *What changes do you think will be described?*

READ AND THINK

2 **Strategy Focus: Skim and Take Notes** Involve students in reading pages 244–246. Remind them to pay attention to topic sentences as they take notes.

See the **Multi-Level Strategies** on page T239 to tailor the reading to all proficiency levels.

Restate: Scientists studied the events leading up to the eruption so they could recognize danger signs before another eruption occurred

Many Changes for Mount St. Helens

When the sun rose on May 19, it showed a greatly changed St. Helens. The mountain was 1,300 feet shorter than it had been the morning before. Most of the old top had slid down the mountain in the avalanche. The rest had erupted out as shattered rock. Geologists later figured that the volcano had lost three quarters of a cubic mile of old rock.

The north side of the mountain had changed from a green and lovely slope to a **fan-shaped wasteland**.

At the top of Mount St. Helens was a big, new **crater** with the shape of a horseshoe. Inside the crater was the vent, the opening through which rock and gases erupted from time to time over the next few years.

In 1980 St. Helens erupted six more times. Most of these eruptions were explosive—ash **soared** into the air, pumice swept down the north side of the mountain. In the eruptions of June and August, thick **pasty lava** oozed out of the vent and built a **dome**. But both domes were destroyed by the next eruptions. In October the pattern changed. The explosions stopped, and thick lava built a dome that was not destroyed. Later eruptions added to the dome, making it bigger and bigger.

Ask: What was the top of the mountain now composed of?

During this time, geologists were learnin to read the clues found before eruptions. They learned to predict what St. Helens was going to do. The predictions helped to protect people who were on and near the mountain.

Among these people were many **natura scientists**. They had come to look for **survivors**, for plants and animals that had lived through the eruption. They had come to look for **colonizers**, for plants and animals that would move in. Mount St. Helens had erupted many times before. Eac time life had returned. Now scientists woul have a chance to see how it did. They woul see how nature **healed itself**.

Ask: What is the differe between a natural scie and a geologist?

May 17, 1980. Mount St. Helens before the big eruptior

fan-shaped wasteland large area of land, shaped like a fan, where everything is dead
soared flew high
pasty rough and sticky
natural scientists scientists that study the earth and living things
healed itself returned itself to health

REACHING ALL STUDENTS

Cooperative Learning

FOR CRITICAL THINKING: Generate Ideas

Brainstorm Roles Have students brainstorm people (teacher, letter carrier, student, etc.) who might have lived near Mount St. Helens and write the roles on index cards, one per student.

Role-Play Students face each other in two concentric circles, as shown in the diagram. Give each outside person an index card naming a role to play. Each inside person asks the outside person questions, such as: *Where were you when the volcano blew? What was the first thing you heard/felt?* The circles rotate to change partners.

Debrief the Content Have students share insights they gained about how the volcano might have affected people's lives.

Debrief the Cooperative Process Ask students to evaluate individual participation, for example: *What responses seemed most realistic? Why?*

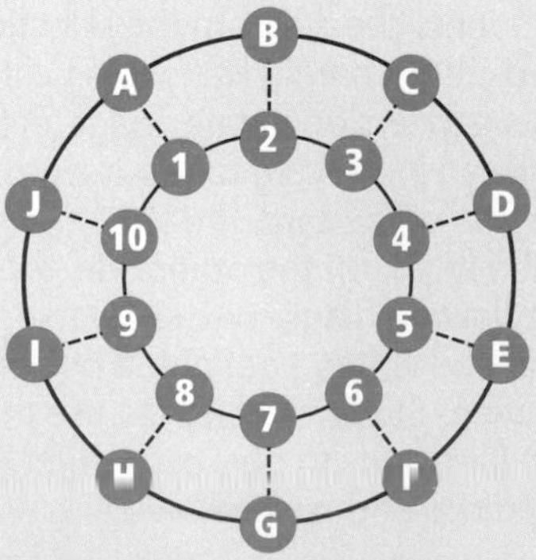

Cooperative Learning Structure: Inside-Outside Circle

eptember 9, 1980. Mount St. Helens after the big eruption.

se visuals: Look at the photographs on pages 244 and 245 and ead the captions. Compare them, using your own words.

POINT-BY-POINT

Change Comes to Mount St. Helens

- An earthquake causes an avalanche.
- Mount St. Helens loses part of its north side in the first blast.
- The blast breaks off rocks and carries them at high speed. It damages everything in its path.
- Mount St. Helens erupts again. This time the blast comes out of the top.
- Very hot flows of volcanic rock and ash move down the mountain.
- Melted snow and ice mix with rocks and dirt. These mudflows cause great damage.
- Mount St. Helens becomes 1,300 feet shorter in one day.
- The mountain erupts six more times and then stops.
- Signs of life return to the mountain.

BEFORE YOU MOVE ON...

1. **Comparison** After October, how did the eruptions affect the mountain differently than before?
2. **Conclusions** What could scientists learn from the eruptions of Mount St. Helens? Explain how this knowledge might be helpful.

REVIEW KEY VOCABULARY

3 Relate Words Invite students to sort key vocabulary words into categories. First, review the words as a class and brainstorm as many categories as possible. Then suggest that students work with a partner to sort the words. Encourage them to find a category for every key vocabulary word, if possible.

Possible categories to suggest include:

- words starting and ending in a vowel: *avalanche, earthquake*
- two-syllable words: *crater, lava, magma, pressure*
- words that describe parts of a volcano: *crater, dome*
- words related to volcanic activity: *eruption, flow, force, pressure*
- words related to animals or plants: *survivor, colonizer*

CHECK COMPREHENSION

4 Answers to "Before You Move On"

1. **Comparison** The explosions stopped, and eruptions only added lava to the dome, making it bigger.
2. **Conclusions** They could learn how to predict future eruptions, which would protect the people in the area.

Grammar Minilesson

▶ RELATIVE CLAUSES

TEACH Write these sentences from page 244 and underline the relative clauses:

> The predictions helped to protect people who were on and near the mountain.
>
> They had come to look for survivors, for plants and animals that had lived through the eruption.

Circle the relative pronouns. Explain that *who* is used to connect a clause to a noun that names a person. Have students draw an arrow from *who* to the noun it describes. (people)

Explain the use of *that* to connect a clause to a noun that names a person or a thing. Have students draw a line from *that* to the nouns it describes. (plants and animals) Replace *who* with *that* in the first sentence to show the use of *that* to refer to people.

PRACTICE Have students write complex sentences with relative clauses about Mount St. Helens, Spirit Lake, and the scientists who studied the eruption.

▶ **Practice Book** page 118

READ PAGE 246

OBJECTIVES

Literary Analysis:
Evaluate Literary Quality

ABOUT THE AUTHOR

5 **Evaluate Literary Quality** Read aloud About the Author. Ask: *How effectively do you think the author conveys the devastation and renewal on Mount St. Helens? What features of the text make you feel this way?*

CLOSE AND ASSESS

Ask students to add ideas about continuity and change to the unit mind map, based on what they have learned in this science article.

In 1982, 110,000 acres were set aside as Mount St. Helens National Volcanic Monument. Trails, viewpoints, and information centers have been established so that visitors can enjoy the mountain.

Afterword: Twenty Years Later

After the eruption, the north side of Mount St. Helens looked as lifeless as the moon. It looked like a place where nothing could be alive or ever live again. Yet life was there, and more life would soon appear.

Some plants had **survived** under the snow. Some survived as roots, bulbs, and stems underground.

Clarify: Even though the aboveground parts of the plants were destroyed, the underground parts were able to grow again.

Some small animals also survived under the snow or in the ground. There were chipmunks, squirrels, deer mice, ants. Eggs laid by insects also survived underground. Fish in ice-covered lakes survived. In time, larger animals wandered through. Deer and elk fed on some of the plants, but they also brought in seeds. Some were stuck in their coats. Some were in their **droppings**.

Ask: How did animals help restore the beauty of the area?

Scientists knew that Mount St. Helens had erupted in the past and that each time life had returned to the mountain. Watching after the 1980 eruption, they were surprised at how quickly life began to come back. Someday the volcano will erupt again, and then, once again, life will return.

—Patricia Laub

survived lived through the eruption
droppings waste from digested food

ABOUT THE AUTHOR

Patricia Lauber has always liked reading and writing about volcanoes. She had not, however, thought of writing about Mount St. Helens until she saw a photograph of a hardy green plant that had pushed its way through a crack in the ash and put out a pink flower. "Suddenly," she says, "I knew that I wanted to write a book about the eruption and also about the return of life." After making two research trips to the volcano, she wrote her book.

REACHING ALL STUDENTS

COMMUNITY CONNECTION

Emergency Services Ask students to research agencies in the local community that help people when natural disasters occur. They might start by contacting the Red Cross to find out what other agencies would be involved. Students can prepare a brochure that shows all the agencies, the services they provide, telephone numbers, and general emergency precautions and procedures.

Science Connection

PLANT AND ANIMAL SPECIES

Have students research the responses of animals and plants to the kind of destruction caused by volcanic eruptions. Suggest categories for research:

- species most likely to survive
- order in which species begin to colonize
- length of time for recolonization to be complete

Students should use a variety of forms for reporting their research: before-and-after maps and photographs, diagrams or illustrations, time lines, and graphs.

Respond to the Article

Check Your Understanding

UM IT UP

elate Causes and Effects An event has a ause and effect. The **cause** is what made it appen. The **effect** is the result of the event.

eview your notecards. Add more notes if you eed to. Then use your notes to write causes and ffects in a chart.

Causes	Effects
An earthquake happens.	An avalanche tears open the mountain.
Steam blasts from the volcano.	A "stone wind" flattens trees.
Heat from the eruption melts ice and snow.	There are huge mudflows.
Lava flows out of the vent.	A dome is formed.
The volcano erupts several more times.	The dome gets bigger.

ompare Literature "The Mother Who Lost er Daughter" is a myth, and "The Big Blast" is onfiction. Still, they both tell about change. rite a few sentences to compare how these vo selections relate to the topic of change.

THINK IT OVER

Discuss and Write Talk about these questions with a partner. Write the answers.

1. **Prediction** Do you think Mount St. Helens will look the same in the year 2100 as it did in the year 2000? Why or why not?
2. **Inference** After the big blast, how do you think life changed for people who lived near Mount St. Helens?
3. **Personal Experience** What should people know if they live near a volcano? What can people do to prepare in the event of an earthquake or eruption?

EXPRESS YOURSELF

▶ ASK FOR AND GIVE INFORMATION

With a partner, look through the article and find words about volcanoes. Write each word on a piece of paper, and put the papers in a box. Take turns drawing words and using them to ask each other questions.

LANGUAGE ACQUISITION ASSESSMENT
See page 61 of the Assessment Handbook.

The Big Blast 247

Multi-Level Strategies

SUM IT UP OPTIONS

BEGINNING Work with students to use their note cards to complete the Cause-and-Effect Chart as a group.

INTERMEDIATE Have pairs of students share with the group the notes they completed during the reading of the selection. They can arrange their notes to create a chronology of events and then complete the Cause-and-Effect Chart together.

ADVANCED Ask students to compare with a partner the notes they took during the reading. The pair should synthesize their notes to create as comprehensive a Cause-and-Effect Chart as they can. Encourage the pairs to skim the reading again to find more information to add to their charts.

RESPOND

OBJECTIVES

SUM IT UP
Function: Write
Reading and Learning Strategies: Use Graphic Organizers (cause/effect chart)
Comprehension and Critical Thinking: Ⓣ Relate Cause and Effect
Literary Analysis: Compare Literature
Writing: Comparison

THINK IT OVER
Function: Engage in Discussion
Critical Thinking and Comprehension: Make Predictions; Make Comparisons; Make Inferences; Relate to Personal Experience

EXPRESS YOURSELF
Function: Ask for Information; Ⓣ Give Information
Speaking and Listening: Question Game

CHECK YOUR UNDERSTANDING

1 **Sum It Up** See annotations on the facsimile of page 247 for chart answers. When students compare the literature, they should note that both selections address an important change and both deal with continuity and renewal.

▶ **Practice Book** page 119

2 **Think It Over** Possible responses are:

1. **Prediction** Responses will vary, but should be supported by reasons based on the selection.
2. **Inference** Responses will vary.
3. **Personal Experience** Responses should address knowing warning signs, planning evacuation routes, and keeping supplies ready.

3 **Express Yourself** Extend the activity by drawing two words at a time and using both in one question.

CLOSE AND ASSESS

Ask students to describe one important effect of the Mount St. Helens eruption.

RESPOND

OBJECTIVES

LATIN AND GREEK ROOTS
Vocabulary: Ⓣ Structural Clues (Latin and Greek roots)

NEWS STORIES
Function: Ⓣ Give information; Write
Writing: Newspaper Article

LANGUAGE ARTS AND LITERATURE

1 Use Latin and Greek Roots Answers to the Find Words activity are: eruption, survivor.

Answers to the Practice items are:

1. geologist
2. predict
3. scientists
4. survive

▶ **Practice Book** pages 120–121

2 Write News Stories To provide support, you may want to suggest:

- a list of activities and occupations from which to choose, such as fishing, camping, rock climbing, forest ranger, tour guide, naturalist
- story starters, such as *On May 17, the Miller family hiked. . . .*

▶ **Practice Book** page 122

CLOSE AND ASSESS

Ask students: *What did you learn in this lesson?*

ASSESSMENT
Selection Test 14 on page 65 of the Assessment Handbook tests students' mastery of the reading strategies and the vocabulary, comprehension, and language arts skills taught with this selection

Respond to the Article, continued

Language Arts and Literature

VOCABULARY

USE LATIN AND GREEK ROOTS

Learn About Root Words Many words in English come from Latin and Greek, as well as other languages. **Root words** can help you understand what the whole word means in the English language. Study the chart.

Root	Meaning	Example
geo	earth	geologist
photo	light	photograph
graph	written	autograph
rupt	to break	erupt
dict	to say	predict
viv	to live	survive
sci	knowledge	scientists

Find Words Look at the vocabulary list on page 236. Which words have Greek or Latin roots?

Practice Add a word from the chart to complete each sentence.

1. A ________ studies the earth.
2. People try to ________ when volcanoes might erupt.
3. Other ________ are interested in life forms found near volcanoes.
4. They study the plants and animals that ________ volcanic eruptions.

WRITING

WRITE NEWS STORIES

Write a news article about an event at Mount St. Helens before the eruption. You may want to write about an outdoor activity, for example hiking. Then write another news story about what happened the day after the eruption.

1. **Write Your Draft** Write headlines that give the main ideas of your two stories. In th stories, answer the questions *Who? What? When? Where? Why?* and *How?*
2. **Edit Your Work** Did you answer all six questions in your articles? Did you include facts and interesting details? Check your work for correct spelling and punctuation.
3. **Publish a News Story** Rewrite or type you article on the computer in the style of a news article.

Sample Article

The Daily News
May 17, 1980

A Busy Day for Mount St. Helens
Today was a perfect day to enjoy the outdoors at Mount St. Helens. It was 75 degrees with no wind. Hundreds of campers came to look at the beautiful scenery and breathe the fresh air.

248 Unit 4 | Continuity and Change

REACHING ALL STUDENTS

Multi-Level Strategies

OPTIONS FOR WRITING NEWS STORIES

BEGINNING As a group, students can create pictorial essays to tell their news stories. Help students list the events for the before-and-after stories. Divide up the illustration tasks. Then students come together as a group to sequence the pictures and write explanatory captions.

INTERMEDIATE Have students work with a partner to complete the news stories. Partners will agree on the foci of their stories, and one partner will write the "before" story while the other writes the "after" story. Have partners exchange papers for peer review and editing.

ADVANCED Instruct students to work independently to create the two articles. They should then exchange their articles with other students to give and get feedback on the articles. Have students revise their articles, based on their partner's suggestions.

ontent Area Connections

LANGUAGE ACQUISITION ASSESSMENT
See page 61 of the Assessment Handbook.

TECHNOLOGY/MEDIA

SCIENCE

AKE A VOLCANO REPORT

lcanoes have erupted many times and in many fferent places. With a group, use the Internet other resources to research one eruption. esent your findings to the class, using a map d chart.

Gather Information Choose a volcano like Etna, Kilauea, Krakatoa, Mauna Loa, Mount Shasta, or Vesuvius. Use the name of the volcano as the key word in your search. These Web sites might be a good place to start, but remember that new sites appear every day!

INTERNET

INFORMATION ON-LINE

Web Sites:
- **Volcano Sites**
  - volcano.und.nodak.edu
  - www.geol.ucsb.edu/~fisher
- **Online Encyclopedia**
  - www.letsfindout.com

Download helpful articles and take notes for your presentation.

❷ **Make a Map** Create a map to show the location of the volcano. Label the country, closest city, and any bodies of water.

Sample Map

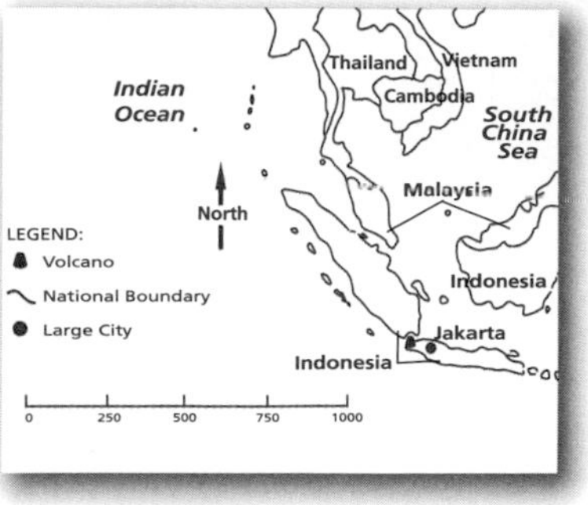

❸ **Summarize Information** Present your map to the class, and tell about the effects of the eruption. Summarize each group's presentation in a class chart. Include the volcano's name, location, date of eruption, and its effects.

Learn to use the **Internet** on Handbook pages 392–393.

Research Skills

USING MAPS

TEACH Point out the map on page 249. Explain that a *general reference map* usually shows geographic features (mountains, oceans) and political features (state, national boundaries). Model using the legend to find the location of the volcano in Indonesia and the nearest large city (Jakarta).

Display a local or state road map. Elicit comparison to the map on page 249. (A *road map* shows major roads; both types of maps show locations of cities.)

PRACTICE Distribute copies of the road map and have students locate general reference maps in texts. Invite students to work in pairs to identify specific information about areas they choose:

- major city or capital
- two different numbered highways and towns linked by them
- a lake or river.

▶ **Practice Book** page 123

RESPOND

OBJECTIVES

VOLCANO REPORT

Function: Ⓣ Give Information

Concepts and Vocabulary: Volcanoes—*active, dormant, extinct*

Learning Strategies, Critical Thinking, and Research Skills: Gather, Organize, and Synthesize Information; Ⓣ Take Notes; Summarize; Use a Map

Technology/Media: Use the Internet

Representing and Writing: Map; Chart

CONTENT AREA CONNECTIONS

1 **Make a Volcano Report** Prepare students by previewing the following content area vocabulary:

- ***active, dormant, extinct*:** List the three words. Next to each, draw an outline of a volcano. For the active volcano, draw lines and circles coming from the top to represent an explosion. Tell students an active volcano is one that has erupted during the last few hundred years and is considered likely to erupt again.

  Show the dormant volcano with "Z-Z-Z-Z" coming from the top to represent sleep. Explain that *dormant* means "sleeping"; it has not erupted for a few hundred years, but it has erupted during recorded history.

  At the top of the extinct volcano, draw a tombstone with the inscription "R.I.P." Tell students that a volcano that has not erupted during recorded history is considered extinct.

▶ **Practice Book** page 124

CLOSE AND ASSESS

Ask students to formulate three questions based on this lesson, number each question, and write it on an index card. They should write the answers on the backs of the cards. Students trade cards with a partner and quiz each other.

INTRODUCE THEME 2

OBJECTIVES

Function: Engage in Discussion

Concepts and Vocabulary: Continuity and Change—*enduring, legacy, progress*

Viewing: Interpret a Visual Image

Reading and Learning Strategies: Relate to Personal Experience; Build Background; Use Graphic Organizers (chart)

Critical Thinking: Draw Conclusions; Generate Ideas

TAP PRIOR KNOWLEDGE

1 **Quickwrite About Enduring Legacies** Read the title. Explain that a legacy may be an object, a belief, even a song—anything passed from one generation to the next. Have students list as many legacies as they can think of in one minute. Students can then share their lists.

VIEW AND DISCUSS

2 **Interpret a Photograph** Ask students to view the photograph and read the caption. Explain the significance of D-Day: The Allies' surprise invasion of German-held territory on June 6, 1944, marked the beginning of the end of World War II. Ask: *What change resulted from D-Day?* (end of WW II)

Use the Discussion Prompts in the **Multi-Level Strategies** to help all students interpret the photograph.

3 **Draw Conclusions** Pose the question: *How can deeds such as this be a kind of legacy?* List conclusions in a chart.

D-Day: An Enduring Legacy
• part of world history
• reminds people of heroic deeds
• later generations learn from it
• might help prevent another world war

D-Day: American soldiers land in Normandy during World War II

Unit 4 | Continuity and Change

REACHING ALL STUDENTS

Multi-Level Strategies

DISCUSSION PROMPTS

BEGINNING Ask questions that will elicit short answers: *What shows that these people are soldiers? Did the soldiers come by land or by sea? Did these soldiers land in the U.S. or in another country?*

INTERMEDIATE Ask questions about details in the photograph: *What details give information about where the invasion took place?* (water, boats) *What detail shows that these soldiers plan to be here for several days?* (bed rolls) *How do you think these soldiers are feeling?*

ADVANCED Have students make observations beyond the photograph: *If you had lived during World War II, how might you have felt on D-Day? How can remembering events like D-Day improve our lives today?*

otations offer strategies for
eginning students

THEME 2

An Enduring Legacy

B Encourage elaboration: What changes in the world would you like to see happen? How can you help?

- What changes in history have had a lasting effect on you? What kinds of changes can you bring about that will have a lasting effect on the future?

Define *progress*:
ady improvement.
: What are some
mples of changes
ociety? Can such
nges be controlled?

- Does change always represent progress? Is change always within your control?
- What can you learn about yourself by the way you respond to change?

B Pose choices: Does change make you feel anxious, happy, excited, worried?

EME-RELATED BOOKS

Spoons: A Chanukah Story
Marci Stillerman
w prisoners in a Nazi camp
everything to gather together
spoons to make a menorah for
nukah.

INNING

So Far from the Sea
by Eve Bunting
A family brings special mementos to a grandfather who died in a Japanese internment camp.

INTERMEDIATE

NOVEL

Number the Stars
by Lois Lowry
During World War II, Annamarie Johansen goes on a dangerous mission to save the life of her best friend, Ellen Rosen.

ADVANCED

251

DISCUSS THE GUIDING QUESTIONS

4 **Set the Theme** Some key points to develop during the discussion are:

- Wars and disasters can change the lives of individuals. For example, people may move to new lands to escape dangerous situations. As individuals, we can bring about changes by working as scientists or teachers, by creating jobs, or by participating in government or private efforts to improve lives.
- Change can be for the better or the worse. It may represent progress, but at what cost? We can always react to change in positive ways and try to make changes that help us fulfill our hopes and dreams.
- Some people feel more secure when everything remains the same. Others are constantly in search of change to make life more interesting. We can learn how adaptable we are from the way we respond to change.

Form groups and use the **Multi-Level Strategies** so all students can participate.

CLOSE AND ASSESS

Ask students to give examples of enduring legacies and support their choices.

Multi-Level Strategies

GROUPING GUIDELINES

BEGINNING Group these students so you can define words and pose choices for responses. See suggestions in red on the facsimile for page 251.

INTERMEDIATE Invite students to work in groups. Have them focus their conversation on situations in which they have personally responded to change. Ask: *Was the change related to changing schools? A move your family made? What did you learn about yourself from this situation?* Have students share ideas from their discussion with the class.

ADVANCED Ask pairs of students to make a Pro-and-Con Chart about whether change tends to be a good thing or a bad thing. Have them summarize their conclusions for the class.

THEME LIBRARY

■ ***Nine Spoons*** by Marci Stillerman
Invite students to read *Nine Spoons.* After they read, remind them that the story of the children's menorah is based on events that really happened. Ask: *How did the author make the women seem real? How does a menorah represent an enduring legacy to the women in the story?* After reading the Anne Frank biography and the excerpt from her diary, invite students to compare Anne's legacy with the legacy of the menorah.

THEME 2 **LESSON 2**

BUILD LANGUAGE AND VOCABULARY

OBJECTIVES

Function: Listen Actively; Ⓣ Define and Explain
Concepts and Vocabulary: Ⓣ Wartime Words
Patterns and Structures: Ⓣ Present Perfect Tense Verbs
Learning Strategy: Use Graphic Organizers (chart)
Critical Thinking: Generate Ideas; Make Comparisons
Writing: Paragraph

START WITH A COMMON EXPERIENCE

Tape 1B
CD 1 Track 5

1. **Listen to a Song** Play "The House I Live In" on the **Language Tape/CD.** Explain to students that during World War II, when most young American men were overseas fighting in the war, Americans of all ages and backgrounds joined together to help the war effort at home.

2. **Model How to Define and Explain** Ask volunteers to tell how the songwriter defines "America." Then, model how to define and explain:

How to Define and Explain
- Name the word: *America*
- Tell what its dictionary meaning is: *America is a country.*
- Tell what it is like: *America is a democratic country.*
- Tell more about it: *America is a democratic country. People of all races and religions live here.*

3. **Interpret the Song** Play the song again and discuss how the songwriter defines America.

Use the Discussion Prompts in the **Multi-Level Strategies** to involve all students in the discussion.

Build Language and Vocabulary
DEFINE AND EXPLAIN

In 1941, the U.S. entered World War II. Americans from all parts of the country joined the war effort. Listen to the song and read the words. How do you think this song made Americans feel during the war years?

from The House I Live In

What is America to me?
A name, a map, or a flag I
A certain word, democracy
What is America to me?

The house I live in
A plot of earth, a street
The grocer and the butche
Or the people that I meet.

The children in the playgro
The faces that I see
All races and religions,
That's America to me.

—performed in the 1940s to support the war effort, written Lewis Allen and Earl Robinson

REACHING ALL STUDENTS

Multi-Level Strategies
DISCUSSION PROMPTS

BEGINNING List all the images described in the song that help to define the name *America*. Have students answer the question *What is America to me?* by choosing one image from the song and completing the statement: *America is* _____. Restate the responses as you record them in a web.

INTERMEDIATE Point out specific images in the song to prompt comment from students: *What flag does the songwriter refer to and why? How does the word* democracy *relate to the definition of America? Why does the songwriter feel that the faces he sees help to define America for him?*

ADVANCED Ask students to make observations about the song that go beyond its literal meaning: *What is the songwriter's attitude about life in America? Why do you think that? If you were writing the song, what images would you add?*

AKE A COMPARISON CHART

ake a chart to compare life in the United States in e 1940s with life in the United States today.

Life in the United States

Life in the U.S., 1940s	Life in the U.S., Today
Food and goods are in short supply.	Food and goods are readily available.
Communication is by telephone, telegraph, and letter.	E-mail, Internet, and fax are common means of communication.

JILD YOUR VOCABULARY

artime Words Look at the list of words that relate to the World War II eriod. Find out more about these words by looking in an encyclopedia and dictionary. Take notes.

ally	defeat	ration
buddy system	democracy	sacrifice
citizen	invade	unity
courage	join	victory

SE LANGUAGE STRUCTURES

VERBS IN THE PRESENT PERFECT TENSE

riting: Define and Explain an Historical Term Write a paragraph about nerica during World War II. Define and explain one of the words in the list. e verbs in the present perfect tense.

Example:

A *sacrifice* is giving up one thing for another thing. During World War II, Americans made many sacrifices. Soldiers **have written** stories about the terrible times. If you **have read** about the war years, you know that the people at home made sacrifices, too.

CONDUCT THE ACTIVITIES

4 **Make a Comparison Chart** Before students begin, brainstorm with them aspects of everyday life that might have changed since the 1940s.

5 **Build Your Vocabulary: Wartime Words** Encourage students to add to the list other wartime words they already know.

6 **Use Language Structures: Verbs in the Present Perfect Tense** Present the skill, using the definition and examples on **Transparency 61**. Present several more examples. Then have students complete the sentences in Try It!

Writing: Define and Explain an Historical Term Conduct the activity at the bottom of page 253. Have students refer to their comparison charts for ideas.

Use the Writing Activity Options in the **Multi-Level Strategies** to allow all students to participate.

▶ **Practice Book** page 125

CLOSE AND ASSESS

Have students explain how to use the present perfect tense and give an example that relates to World War II.

Multi-Level Strategies

WRITING ACTIVITY OPTIONS

BEGINNING To help students define and explain a term, provide a frame for each sentence in the paragraph: *In class we have read ______. We have seen ______. We have learned that during World War II, many Americans ______.*

INTERMEDIATE Before students begin their paragraphs, have them work in pairs to ask and answer questions about the wartime words: *Why were gas rations necessary? I have read that much of our country's gas supply went to the war effort. People had to share what was available.*

ADVANCED Students can work independently to write their paragraphs. Encourage them to select at least two words to define and explain, then read their paragraphs aloud to the class.

Transparency 61 / Master 61

PRESENT PERFECT TENSE VERBS

Some actions happened in the past, but the exact time is not known. Use the **present perfect tense** to tell about these actions.

Our teacher **has asked** for a report on WW II.

1. To form the present perfect tense, use a helping verb and a form of the main verb called the past participle.

   We **have** (helping verb) **looked** (past participle) at Marty's photos of World War II.

2. Use the helping verb **has** with *he, she,* or *it.* Use the helping verb **have** with *I, you, we,* or *they.*

   He **has used** the photos in his report.

Try It!

Add the present perfect tense of the verb in parentheses.

1. I ______________ a lot about history from my dad. (learn)
2. He ______________ me find some good books. (help)
3. We ______________ many history programs on a special TV channel, too. (watch)

Transparency 61 Level B, Unit 4 | Continuity and Change

PREPARE TO READ

OBJECTIVES

THINK ABOUT WHAT YOU KNOW
Reading Strategies: Build Background; Use Visuals; Use Text Structures (time line, map)

LEARN KEY VOCABULARY Ⓣ
Vocabulary Strategy: Use New Words in Context

LEARN TO USE GRAPHIC ORGANIZERS
Reading Strategy: Ⓣ Use Graphic Organizers (time line)

THINK ABOUT WHAT YOU KNOW

1 **Idea Exchange** Use the Cooperative Learning Activity and other teaching suggestions from pages T255–T257 to provide additional support for studying the time line.

LEARN KEY VOCABULARY

2 **Use New Words in Context** Have students read each vocabulary word and its definition. Clarify meanings. Then conduct the cloze activity.

Use the Vocabulary Options in the **Multi-Level Strategies** to tailor the activity to proficiency levels.

▶ **Practice Book** page 126

LEARN TO USE GRAPHIC ORGANIZERS

3 **Model How to Use a Graphic Organizer** Define *graphic organizer* and use the time line on pages 255–257 as an example. Demonstrate the steps in the box with **Transparency 62**:

- Read the passage aloud.
- Ask students to notice the dates and order of the events.
- Remind students to look for dates and signal words, such as *then, finally, at that time,* and *later.*

CLOSE AND ASSESS

Ask groups to agree on one reason for using a time line. (A time line helps you understand the order of events.)

Anne Frank

Prepare to Read

biography
by Yona Zeldis McDonough

THINK ABOUT WHAT YOU KNOW

Idea Exchange Read and discuss the information on pages 255–257. What were some of the key events of World War II?

annex part added to a building

concentration camp place where prisoners of war are held

declare war on tell a country of plans to fight against it

discriminate against harm or treat differently from others because of color, race, age, or religion

law rule made by the government that controls what people can and cannot do

power ability to make people do what you want

prisoner person who is held in a place and not allowed to leave

survive live through a dangerous time or event

Answers to the vocabulary activity:
1. power
2. law
3. discriminate against
4. concentration camp
5. survive
6. declare war on
7. annex
8. prisoner

LEARN KEY VOCABULARY

Use New Words in Context Study the new words and their definition Then write the paragraph and add the missing words.

After Adolf Hitler gained ___(1)___ in Germany in 1933, he took awa the freedom of German Jews to live normal lives. Hitler made more than one ___(2)___ that would ___(3)___ the Jews, or treat them differently. He also sent Jews to a cruel kind of prison, or ___(4)___. In that terrible place, it was hard to ___(5)___. In 1939, Hitler invaded Poland. Great Britain decided to ___(6)___ Germany, and World War II began. During the war years, Anne Frank, a young Jewish girl, hid with her family in a building that had a secret ___(7)___ to the house. She wrote in her diar what her life was like. She described her fears of being captured and made a ___(8)___ of the Nazis.

LEARN TO USE GRAPHIC ORGANIZERS

A **graphic organizer** is a diagram that shows how information and ideas are related. It helps you to keep track of what you read.

READING STRATEGY
How to Use a Graphic Organizer
1. Think about how the ideas are related.
2. Create an organizer. For example, if you are reading about history, you might make a time line to show the order of events.

Look at the time line on pages 255–257. As you read "Anne Frank," thir about where you would place the events in her story on the time line.

254 **Unit 4** | Continuity and Change

REACHING ALL STUDENTS

Multi-Level Strategies
VOCABULARY OPTIONS

BEGINNING Group students to read ***The Children We Remember*** or the Key Points Reading on **Master 64**. (See page T258.) Work with the vocabulary in those selections.

INTERMEDIATE Work in groups to decide where to place each vocabulary word in the paragraph.

ADVANCED Have students complete the cloze activity on their own. Then they compare their answers with a partner and discuss answers that differ.

Transparency 62 / Master 62

HOW TO USE A TIME LINE

Directions: Read the passage and think about the way events relate to one another. Put the events from the passage on the time line in the order in which they happened.

World War II

Adolf Hitler was a leader in Germany. He wanted Germany to rule the world. In 1933 he ordered German troops to invade the Rhineland, Austria, Poland, and Czechoslovakia. Britain and France thought these invasions were wrong and declared war on Germany in 1939. The next year Germany invaded six more countries. Then Japan and Italy entered the war to help Germany. Because so many countries were involved, this great conflict was called World War II.

Another of Hitler's goals was to allow only certain types of people to live free in Germany. In 1933, he began to build concentration camps for groups he did not like, including Jews. Many Jews tried to leave Germany to find a better life.

Later, American, British, and Canadian soldiers joined the war. In an invasion called D-Day, in 1944, they began to push the Germans out of France. Finally, the war ended in 1945. At that time, the surviving Jews were released from concentration camps.

1933
German troops invade four countries.
Hitler begins concentration camps.
Jews try to leave Germany.

1939 Britain and France declare war.

1940
More German invasions
Japan and Italy join Germany.

1944 D-Day

1945 The war is over. Jews are released.

Transparency 62 Level B, Unit 4 | Continuity and Change

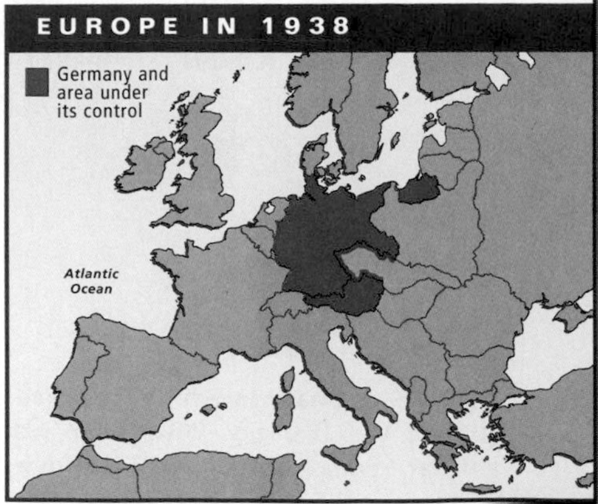

REFERENCE POINT

THE YEARS BEFORE THE WAR

1933–1938

In 1932, the people of Germany have no work and no money. Adolf Hitler blames the Jews for Germany's problems. Many Germans believe that Hitler and his Nazi Party will help them. In 1933, Hitler becomes dictator of Germany. He wants to rule not only Germany but the rest of Europe.

Adolf Hitler tells Germans that Jews have taken all their jobs and money. Many, but not all, Germans believe him. The Nazis force Jews to wear a yellow star with the word "Jew," shown here in Dutch.

1933 Hitler becomes dictator of Germany.

1935 Hitler takes away the freedoms of German Jews. He creates **laws** that **discriminate against** them.

1936 Hitler's troops march into the Rhineland, land that is next to France.

1938 Hitler annexes, or adds, Austria to Germany's territory.

MORE TO EXPLORE

World War II Tell students that World War II was a worldwide military conflict that was the most devastating war in history in terms of lives lost and material destruction. It caused enormous changes in the lives of millions of people. Have students use the Internet or their local library to learn more about World War II. Invite students to share their findings in a report.

Web Sites

Web sites undergo frequent modifications, but here are some you may want to suggest to students:

www.encarta.msn.com

search.corbis.com

www.eblast.com

Key Word Search

World War II

United States History

D-Day

Pearl Harbor

German History

THE BASICS BOOKSHELF

- ***The Children We Remember***
  by Chana Byers Abells

This book describes children who went to school, played games, and celebrated their faith. Then the Nazis came and terrible things began to happen. Simple sentences and powerful black and white photos provide an opportunity to learn basic vocabulary related to home, family, and survival while learning about a central event in WW II.

For Lesson Plans: See the Teacher's Guide for ***The Basics Bookshelf***.

PREPARE TO READ

OBJECTIVES

Reading Strategies: Use Text Structures (time line, map)

USE TEXT STRUCTURES

Interpret a Time Line Tell students that a time line helps show how events relate to one another in time. Direct students' attention to the time line running across the bottom of pages 255–257. Point out the features that make the time line useful:

- events are presented in the order they occurred
- dates are clear and easy to read
- photographs offer visual support
- captions provide more information.

Prepare to Read, continued

REFERENCE POINT

THE WORLD AT WAR

1939–1945

In 1939, Germany invades Poland and World War II begins. Jews who live under German control try to **survive** Hitler's **anti-Jewish laws**. Many Jews find places to hide. Some Jews escape. Others fight back. However, millions of Jews are arrested and sent to **concentration camps** where they are forced to work. Many die there.

Germany takes control of Czechoslovakia. Germany then invades Poland. As a result, Great Britain and France **declare war on** Germany. World War II begins.

Germany invades Denmark, Norway, the Netherlands, Belgium, Luxembourg, and France.

Without warning, on December 7th Japan bombs the United States Navy at Pearl Harbor, Hawaii. The U.S. declares war on Japan the next day.

anti-Jewish laws rules that are unfair to people who are Jewish

REACHING ALL STUDENTS

Cooperative Learning

FOR CRITICAL THINKING: Synthesize Information

Research World War II Tell students that they will work in small groups to become experts about one aspect of World War II. Assign each group one of the topics on **Master 63**.

Give Expert Reports After expert groups have completed their research, place them in new groups consisting of one student from each of the expert groups. These experts give a report on the area they researched with their original group, while the other students in their new group take notes in the appropriate box on **Master 63**.

Debrief the Content Direct students to share information gained from the activities. Ask: *What did you learn about World War II from your own research? From the reports of other experts?*

Debrief the Cooperative Process Have students evaluate the effectiveness of expert groups. Ask: *Which helped you learn the most, being an expert or listening to other students' reports? Why?*

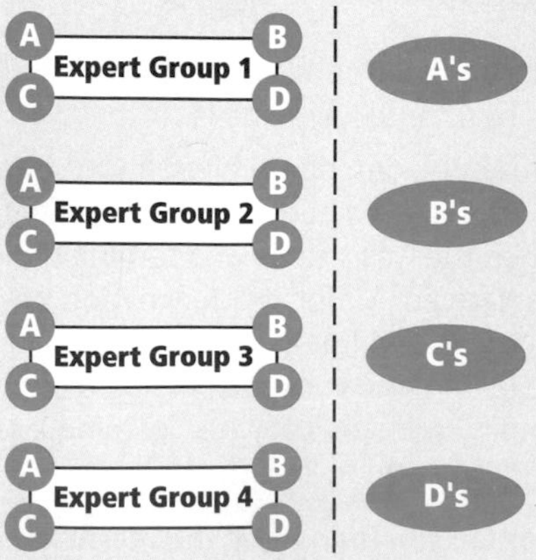

Cooperative Learning Structure: Jigsaw

German soldiers force Jews to leave their homes. Many are loaded into boxcars on trains and taken to concentration camps. Most of them starve or are killed in those camps.

On June 6, 1944, D-Day, more than 150,000 American, British, and Canadian soldiers land on the coast of Normandy in France. They begin to push the Germans out of France.

Germany loses the war. U.S., Soviet, and British soldiers release surviving Jews from the concentration camps.

USE TEXT STRUCTURES

Interpret a Political Map Draw students' attention to the maps on pages 255 and 257. Explain that a political map provides information about the political boundaries of countries at a point in time. On page 255, ask: *What year does this map represent? What does the legend tell you about the use of color on this map?*

These maps allow students to compare the countries under German control before and during World War II. Students can use the maps as starting points to research and list the specific countries under German rule in each year. The contrast in the maps can also be used to encourage students to make inferences about the power of Germany during World War II.

Guide students' comparisons by asking: *About what portion of Europe was under German control in 1938? In 1942? How do you think people in Spain or Norway or Sweden felt about Germany in 1938? In 1942?*

Transparency 63 / Master 63

NOTE-TAKING CHART

Directions: Research one of these World War II topics. Record your findings in the chart. Then use the chart to take notes on the other topics as students who researched these topics report to you on their information.

Causes:
Major Battles:
Political Changes/Outcomes:
Other Changes/Outcomes:

Transparency 63 Level B, Unit 4 | Continuity and Change

Social Studies Connection

MAP SKILLS

Have students work in groups to conduct research leading to a map-making activity. Ask each group to create either a map contrasting European borders before and after World War II or a map showing areas of conflict in Asia, America, and Europe during the war. Encourage groups to share and compare their maps.

READ THE SELECTION

OBJECTIVES

Reading Strategy: Preview; Predict
Literary Analysis: Biography

INTRODUCE THE SELECTION

1 **Preview and Predict** Read aloud the title, author's name, and introduction to the selection. Ask: *What kind of details do you think we will learn about Anne's life in this selection?* Invite students to leaf through the selection, paying careful attention to photo captions, headings, and diagrams. Explain that features like these provide important clues to the content of a selection.

2 **Identify Genre: Biography** Point out the photograph of Anne Frank on page 258. Explain that the subject of this selection was a real person. Remind students that, when an author writes about the life of a real person, the work is called a *biography*.

Anne Frank
by Yona Zeldis McDonough

Theme Connection This selection tells the story of Anne Frank, a young Jewish girl who, with her family, went into hiding from the Nazis during World War II. Although Anne eventually died in a concentration camp, the diary Anne kept while in hiding is an enduring legacy of courage and hope.

Selection Summary The introduction on page 258 of the student book offers a summary of the selection.

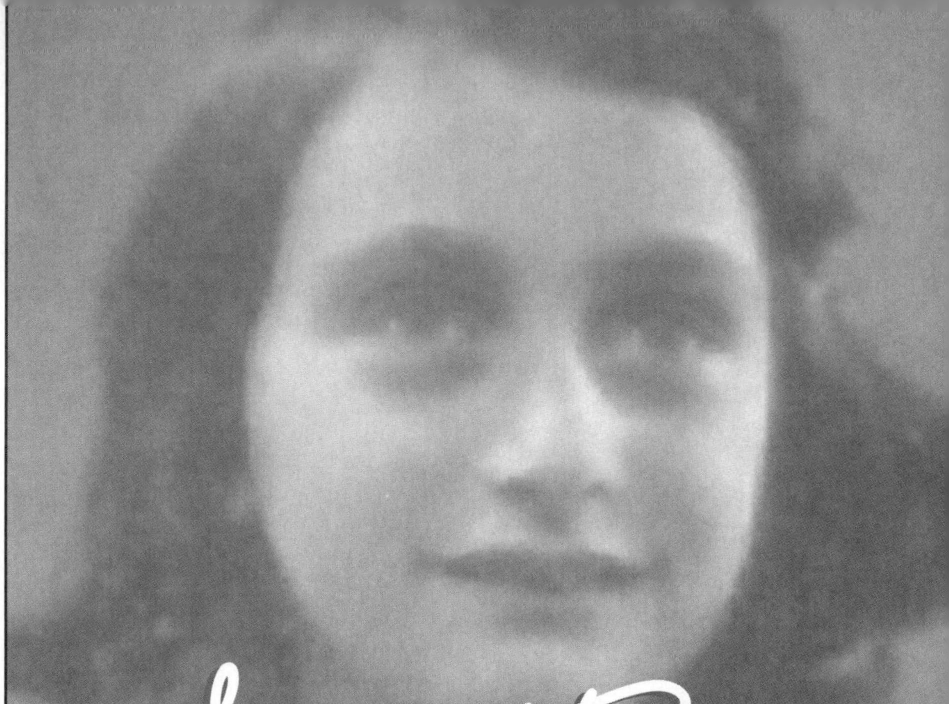

Anne Frank

by Yona Zeldis McDonough

Anne Frank's family lives happily in Germany until Adolf Hitler becomes the leader in 1933. When Hitler begins to treat Jews unfairly, Anne's father decides to move his family to Amsterdam, the Netherlands. The Franks are safe there for a few years, but the family has to hide when Hitler's armies invade the Netherlands. Although hiding is difficult for thirteen-year-old Anne, she tries to stay cheerful and busy. She often writes about her thoughts, dreams, and feelings in a diary. On August 4, 1944, the Nazis discover the Franks' hiding place and send them to concentration camps. Everyone in the family except Anne's father dies.

258 **Unit 4** | Continuity and Change

REACHING ALL STUDENTS

Transparency 64 / Master 64

KEY POINTS READING

Anne Frank

Anne Frank is born in Germany in 1929. Her family has a happy life, but bad things are happening in Germany. People are losing their jobs and there is little money for food or clothes. Adolf Hitler becomes the leader of Germany in 1933. He blames Germany's troubles on the Jewish people.

Anne's father sees that Germany is not safe for Jews. He moves his family to Amsterdam. The Franks are safe for a few years, but Hitler's anti-Jewish laws spread. Jews begin to lose their possessions and jobs. In 1942, the Franks go into hiding in a place called the secret annex.

Hiding is hard for Anne, but she tries to stay cheerful and busy. She writes about her thoughts and dreams in a diary she calls "Kitty." She dreams that someday people all over the world will read her words.

On August 4, 1944, the Nazis discover the Franks' hiding place. The Nazis send the family to concentration camps. Anne's father is the only survivor. After the war, he finds Anne's diary and publishes it.

Transparency 64 Level B, Unit 4 | Continuity and Change © Hampton-Brown

Transparency 65 / Master 65

TIME LINE

Directions: This time line shows important events in World War II. As you read, write the events happening to the Frank family during these same years on the right side of the time line.

		1929	Anne Frank is born.
Hitler becomes dictator of Germany.	1933	1933	The Frank family leaves Germany.
Hitler takes freedoms away from German Jews.	1935		
Great Britain and France declare war on Germany. Hitler declares war on Poland.	1939		
Germany invades six countries, including Denmark and Holland.	1940		
		1942	The Frank family goes into hiding.
D-Day	1944	1944	Nazis raid the secret annex. The Franks are sent to concentration camps. Anne, her sister, and her mother die.
Germany loses the war. Surviving Jews are released.	1945		

Transparency 65 Level B, Unit 4 | Continuity and Change © Hampton-Brown

ed annotations offer
pportunities to clarify
eaning and check for
nderstanding.

1

A TIME OF CHANGE

Adolf Hitler becomes the leader of Germany and begins to treat Jews unfairly.

Anne Frank was born in Germany. er parents, Edith and Otto Frank, were erman Jews. They came from the town of ankfurt am Main, where Otto's family had lived **for generations**. First the Franks had a daughter named Margot. Then, on June 12, 1929, Anne was born. The Franks' house was in a pretty neighborhood where Anne played happily in her sandbox or with the many other children who lived nearby.

ank

rank

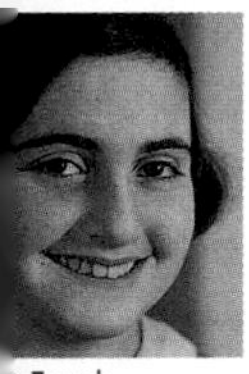
Frank

But outside the loving world of Papa, Mama, and Margot, bad things were happening in Germany. People lost their jobs and had no money for food and clothes. They were scared and angry. They wanted a leader who promised an end to their problems. Adolf Hitler, who **came to power** in 1933, seemed like such a leader. He told the Germans that they were better than all other people on Earth. He blamed Germany's troubles mainly on the Jews. He immediately began passing laws that discriminated against the Jews. Hitler and all the people who **supported** him were called Nazis, a shortened **version** of the German word *Nationalsozialist*, which means **National Socialist**.

About 1935. German people held up signs like this one in front of Jewish stores. The German words mean, "Germans! Watch yourselves! Don't buy from Jews!"

Define *discriminated*: acted unfairly.

Encourage elaboration: How did the Nazis discriminate against Jews?

BEFORE YOU MOVE ON...

1. **Details** Where and when was Anne Frank born?
2. **Cause and Effect** Why did people listen to Adolf Hitler?

Encourage elaboration: Describe life inside Anne's family and compare it to what was happening in their country.

r generations since long before his birth
ame to power became the leader
upported agreed with
version form
National Socialist the government that ruled Germany from 1933 to 1945

Multi-Level Strategies
READING OPTIONS FOR LESSONS 4–7

BEGINNING Students should work with ***The Children We Remember***. Or distribute copies of **Master 64** to conduct a Key Points Reading of "Anne Frank." Work together to note the dates of important events in Anne's life on the time line on **Transparency 65**.

INTERMEDIATE Read the selection aloud or play the recording on the **Selection Tape/CD**, pausing to clarify meaning. Also use the red annotations on the facsimile pages. Distribute copies of **Master 65** and have students work in pairs to record the important dates and events on the time line.

ADVANCED Have students read the selection on their own, identifying unfamiliar words or phrases. Clarify meanings. Distribute copies of **Master 65** and invite students to complete the time line independently. Encourage students to compare and discuss their time lines.

READ PAGE 259

OBJECTIVES

Function: Read a Selection
Listening: Listen to a Selection
Reading and Learning Strategies: Set a Purpose for Reading; T Use Graphic Organizers (time line)
Comprehension: Identify Details; T Identify Cause and Effect

SET PURPOSE

3 Read aloud the introduction on page 259. Set the purpose for reading: *Find out why Hitler begins treating the Jews unfairly.*

READ AND THINK

Tape 4B
CD 4 Track 4

4 **Strategy Focus: Use Graphic Organizers (time line)** As students read the selection, have them note the important events and dates of Anne's life and place them on the time line on **Master 65**.

Choose Reading Options in the **Multi-Level Strategies** to tailor the reading to proficiency levels.

The recording of "Anne Frank" on the **Selection Tape/CD** offers an oral language model and the opportunity to build reading fluency.

CHECK COMPREHENSION

5 **Answers to "Before You Move On"**

1. **Details** Anne was born on June 12, 1929, in Frankfurt am Main.
2. **Cause and Effect** They wanted a leader who promised to end their problems. Hitler seemed to know the reason for their problems and to have the answers to ending these problems.

CLOSE AND ASSESS

Ask students to write three sentences that describe Germany in 1933.

READ PAGES 260–261

OBJECTIVES

Function: Read a Selection
Vocabulary Strategy: Use New Words in Context
Grammar: Helping Verbs
Listening: Listen to a Selection
Reading and Learning Strategies: Set a Purpose for Reading; Ⓣ Use Graphic Organizers (time line)
Comprehension: Identify Characters' Traits and Motives; Identify Details

SET PURPOSE

1 Read aloud the introduction to pages 260–261. Set the purpose for reading: *Read to understand why the family must hide from the Nazis.*

READ AND THINK

Tape 4B
CD 4 Track 4

2 **Strategy Focus: Use Graphic Organizers (time line)** Involve students in reading pages 260–261 of the selection.

See the **Multi-Level Strategies** on T259 to tailor the reading to all proficiency levels.

2

A HIDING PLACE

Anne's family moves to the Netherlands. They are happy until Hitler's armies arrive. Then the Frank family has to hide from the Nazis.

Ask: Are the Franks safe in the Netherland What will they do now to avoid the Germa

Anne's father saw that it was not safe to be a Jew in Nazi Germany so when Anne was four, he took his family to Amsterdam, in the Netherlands. The Franks liked their new home. It was not far from the shore, and they spent happy summer holidays on the beach.

Pause to show the places mentioned on a map.

When Anne started school at the age of five, she quickly learned to read and write. She was a good student and had lots of friends. Because Anne was **outgoing** and lively, she often was given **lead parts** in the school plays.

1939. Margot, Anne, and Grandma Hollander are at the beach in Zandvoort, Holland.

In 1939 Hitler declared war on Poland. War **broke out** across Europe, and soon Hitler's armies **reached** the Netherlands, where Anne and her family lived.

Even with the war going on, Anne still had fun with her friends. History, movie stars, cats, and dogs were among her favorite things. Another favorite thing was the little red-and-white-checked diary she got from her parents as a thirteenth-birthda present. Anne was **thrilled** by the gift and thought of it as her best friend. She wantec to give it a name, so all the **entries** in the diary began with "Dear Kitty."

Writing to Kitty, Anne described how Hitler's anti-Jewish laws had spread to **Holland**. Slowly, Jews had lost their jobs and **their possessions** had been taken away. All Jews over the age of six had to wear a six-pointed yellow Star of David on their clothing. Although Anne did not know it, her father was making plans for the family to **go into hiding**.

Ask: How did Hitle laws affect Jews?

outgoing very friendly, fun-loving
lead parts the most important roles
broke out suddenly began
reached arrived in
thrilled pleased, excited
entries different pieces of writing
Holland the Netherlands
their possessions the things they owned
go into hiding hide

260 Unit 4 | Continuity and Change

REACHING ALL STUDENTS

CULTURAL PERSPECTIVES

Home and World Cultures: Commemorations Define *commemoration* (something that honors or preserves a memory). Explain that many countries have commemorated those who suffered or fought in World War II. Have groups of students research and prepare oral or written reports on different World War II commemorations such as statues, parks, and museums.

Mathematics Connection

DATA ANALYSIS

Invite students to poll others about their knowledge of World War II. First, work together to generate questions about the period, such as *Who was Adolf Hitler? What countries were under his control?* Have students poll other classes and determine the number of correct answers to each question. Display the results in a graph. Students then analyze the information and draw conclusions about how knowledgeable people are about WW II and the importance of studying it.

Encourage elaboration: Describe the Franks' friends.

In July 1942 the Frank amily moved into a hidden partment in the back of the uilding that **housed** Otto rank's business. Anne called it ne secret **annex**. The entrance) their rooms was **blocked by movable bookcase** that was uilt just after they **settled in**.

Ask: How was the annex hidden?

> These friends smuggled food and clothing to the Franks . . .

Only seven people knew nat the family was there. Four of them orked in Otto's office. These friends **muggled** food and clothing to the Franks hen they could. Had they been caught by the Germans, they could have been put to death.

After the Franks had been living in the secret annex for about a week, they were joined by Mr. and Mrs. van Pels and their fifteen-year-old son, Peter. Anne was glad that Peter had brought along his pet cat, Mouschi, since Anne had had to leave her own cat behind when they left home. In November the last member of their little group, a dentist named Fritz Pfeffer, came to stay as well.

Encourage elaboration: How would it feel to be locked away?

942–1944. This is the uilding where Anne's amily was hiding.

This bookcase moved to open the way to the hidden rooms.

BEFORE YOU MOVE ON...

1. **Characters' Motives** Why did the Franks move into a hiding place?
2. **Character** How would you describe Anne's personality?
3. **Details** Who was the last person to join the Franks in the annex?

oused contained
locked by a movable bookcase covered up by bookcase that could be moved
settled in went to live there
smuggled secretly brought in

REVIEW KEY VOCABULARY

3 Use New Words in Context Have partners reread the first two sections of "Anne Frank" and find the key vocabulary words. Have them copy each sentence in which a key word appears and then rewrite the sentence, using a synonym or words from the definition in place of the key word to show their understanding of the word's meaning.

CHECK COMPREHENSION

4 Answers to "Before You Move On"

1. **Characters' Motives** Hitler's anti-Jewish laws had spread to Holland. Jews were losing their jobs and their possessions. They had to wear a Star of David on their clothing. Fear of further problems made the Frank family go into hiding.
2. **Character** Anne was friendly, outgoing, and lively. She had a positive outlook.
3. **Details** A dentist named Fritz Pfeffer was the last person to join the group in the annex.

CLOSE AND ASSESS

Ask students to retell this portion of the story in their own words. Remind them to use signal words, such as *first, next, then,* and *later.*

Grammar Minilesson

▶ HELPING VERBS (MODALS)

TEACH Explain that some verbs are made up of more than one verb. The verb that shows the action is the main verb. The verbs that precede it are called helping verbs. Point out this sentence from page 261: *Had they been caught by the Germans, they could have been put to death.*

Identify *could* and *have* as helping verbs in the sentence. Explain that *would* is also often used when one action depends upon another.

PRACTICE Have students identify the main verbs and helping verbs in these sentences.

1. If the anti-Jewish laws had not spread to Holland, Anne might have lived a normal life.
2. She would have gone to the university.
3. She might even have become a writer.

▶ **Practice Book** page 127

READ PAGES 262–263

OBJECTIVES

Function: Read a Selection
Grammar: Two-Word Verbs
Listening: Listen to a Selection
Reading and Learning Strategies: Set a Purpose for Reading; Ⓣ Use Graphic Organizers (time line); Clarify
Comprehension: Relate to Personal Experience; Make Inferences; Relate Main Idea and Details

SET PURPOSE

1 Read aloud the introduction to pages 262–263. Set the purpose for reading: *As you read, take note of the ways Anne keeps herself busy in the secret annex.*

READ AND THINK

Tape 4B
CD 4 Track 4

2 **Strategy Focus: Use Graphic Organizers (time line)** Involve students in reading pages 262–263 of the selection.

See the **Multi-Level Strategies** on T259 to tailor the reading to all proficiency levels.

3

LIFE IN HIDING

Anne tries hard to stay busy and cheerful in the crowded annex. She writes in her diary and hopes that one day people everywhere will read her words.

Life in hiding was not easy for Anne. She was often bored and lonely. She longed for her friends, her school, and most of all her freedom. Living in such **close quarters** with near-strangers was not easy either. Many times, there were arguments. Anne **quarreled** with her mother and sister. She even felt misunderstood by her beloved father. All of her sadness and **frustration** were poured out into the pages of her diary, Kitty, who was her friend **throughout**.

Anne told Kitty how strange she felt during the first few days in the secret annex. She missed her friends, the black bicycle on which she rode to school, and the room in which she had grown up. Since the Franks were frightened of being discovered, they had to whisper and tiptoe around during the day. Only at night could they relax a little, although they still had to take care not to be seen through the windows. Using scraps of different materials, Anne and her father stitched together some curtains that they pinned to the walls.

Encourage elaboration: What else would a young girl miss?

Ask: How did Anne cope with being in hiding?

Ask: What steps did the Fran[ks] take to avoid being discover[ed]

Yet Anne was brave. She tried hard to sta[y] busy and cheerful. She spent time reading an[d] doing schoolwork, so she wouldn't be too fa[r] behind when she was finally able to return to school. She worked on a detailed **family tree** of all the kings and queens of Europe and she learned **shorthand**.

> The attic was Anne's special place . . .

She loved to look at photos of her favorite movie stars and paste their pictures on the walls of her bedroom. Even in hiding there were still little treats and surprises like the time when Anne, who was growing quickly, outgrew her shoes and was given a pair of red high heels by Miep Gies, one of the **devoted** friends who knew their secret.

The **attic** was Anne's special place, since it had a small window that could be opened to let in a glimpse of the stars, sunshine, or the tower across the street. Anne and Margot often went up there to read. And

Pause to have students find the attic in the layout of the hiding place on page 263.

close quarters a crowded place
quarreled argued, disagreed
frustration a feeling that nothing she could do would make any difference
throughout for the whole time
family tree chart that shows all of the family members
shorthand a shorter way to write using symbols instead of letters to show a word
devoted loving, faithful
attic room at the top of the building

REACHING ALL STUDENTS

Mathematics Connection
PERCENTAGES

Tell students that the Jewish population was severely reduced in many countries as a result of World War II. Invite students to use the Internet and the local or school library to conduct research. Have them compare population statistics before and after the war in specific countries to find out the extent to which the Jewish population decreased or shifted. Students should calculate percentages and present the information in a chart or graph.

HOME CONNECTION

Honoring Heroes Send home a copy of *High Point Newsletter 8* in the **Teacher's Resource Book.** In this home activity, students talk with their family members about a family or cultural hero. Have them find out why the family members consider this person to be a hero. Students should work with their family members on a time line of the person's life, then bring the time line to class and use it to tell the person's story.

Layout for the 3rd and 4th Floor of the Annex

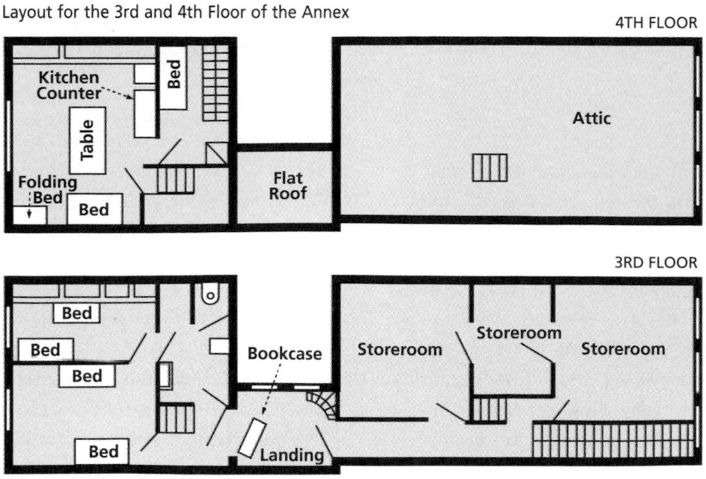

hen Anne and Peter formed a special iendship, the attic was the place where ey got together to talk.

Alone in the attic, Anne often thought oout the life she hoped to lead when the ar ended. She wanted to be a writer. In ldition to her diary, she wrote fairy tales ad other imaginary stories. She even began ork on a book called *Stories and Events om the Secret Annex.*

And when she learned that the Dutch overnment hoped to **publish** all wartime aries, she started to copy hers out neatly, on lined paper. She **cherished** the dream that someday her words would be read by people all over the world.

Ask: What was Anne's goal? What steps did she take to achieve it?

BEFORE YOU MOVE ON...

1. **Personal Experience** Why do you think there were quarrels among the people living in the annex?
2. **Inference** Why did Anne think of her diary as a friend?
3. **Main Idea and Details** Find details to support the main idea: Anne found many ways to keep busy in the annex.

ıblish print and sell to many people
ıerished cared very much about

MONITOR YOUR READING

3 Clarify Have students reread the first sentence on page 262. Explain that there are many clues on the page that clarify the statement. Help students turn the statement into a question. (How was life "not easy" for Anne?) Then ask them to list all the clues they can find to answer that question.

CHECK COMPREHENSION

4 Answers to "Before You Move On"

1. **Personal Experience** Answers will vary.
2. **Inference** It provided a place for her to express her sadness and frustration.
3. **Main Idea and Details** Answers should include that she wrote, made curtains, did schoolwork, made a family tree, looked at photos.

CLOSE AND ASSESS

Have students revisit the mind map created at the beginning of this unit and add ideas about continuity and change generated from reading this selection.

Grammar Minilesson

▶ TWO-WORD VERBS

TEACH Tell students that a phrase can be a two-word verb. Point out the phrase *broke out* at the top of column two on page 260. Define *broke* (split into pieces) and *broke out* (began), and explain how the addition of the small word *out* creates a phrase that means something different from the verb by itself.

Repeat with other two-word verbs in the selection: page 262, *worked on*; page 264, *turn on*; and page 265, *lives on*.

PRACTICE Have students study more two-word verbs on Handbook pages 452–453 and then write sentences with two-word verbs to tell about Anne Frank's life in hiding. Some good two-word verbs to use are:

- **get out**: The Frank family had to get out of their home.
- **go on**: In the annex, the family could go on living together.
- **look forward**: Anne looked forward to the time alone in the attic.

READ PAGES 264–265

OBJECTIVES

Function: Read a Selection

Listening: Listen to a Selection

Reading and Learning Strategies: Set a Purpose for Reading; Ⓣ Use Graphic Organizers (time line)

Comprehension: Ⓣ Identify Sequence; Form Opinions; Identify Character's Motive

Literary Analysis: Evaluate Impact of Author's Background on Meaning; Evaluate Literary Quality

SET PURPOSE

1 Read aloud the introduction to pages 264–265. Set the purpose for reading: *Read to find out about the events leading to Anne's death after their secret annex is discovered by the Nazis.*

READ AND THINK

Tape 4B

CD 4 Track 4

2 **Strategy Focus: Use Graphic Organizers (time line)** Involve students in reading pages 264–265 of the selection.

See the **Multi-Level Strategies** on T259 to tailor the reading to proficiency levels.

4

A TIME OF GREAT SADNESS

The Nazis find the Franks and send them to a concentration camp. Anne, her mother, and her sister die. After the war, Anne's father finds her diary and publishes it.

Although the little group was **cut off from** the rest of the world, they managed to hear news from a radio kept in Otto's office. At night, they would creep into the room and turn it on. When Anne heard that the Germans were losing the war, she felt hopeful. She wrote in her diary that, **despite everything**, she still believed that people were really good at heart.

But someone discovered the Franks' hiding place and told the police. On August 4, 1944, the secret annex was **raide**[d] by German and Dutch Nazis. Anne and the others were now **prisoners**. The Frank[s], the van Pelses, and Fritz Pfeffer were sent to Westerbork, a concentration camp in Holland, where they were made to work for the Nazis.

Define *concentration camp*: a place where prisoners of war, enemies, and political prisoners are locked up.

A month later, they were sent to Auschwitz, a concentration camp in Poland. The **conditions** there were terrible. Anne, Margot, and their mother were forced to work with little food, water, or clothing. Many people around them died of hunger and sickness. Many others were killed outright by the Nazis. In October the two girls were sent to Bergen-Belsen, a camp in Germany. Their paren[ts] were left at Auschwitz, where their mother, Edith, died in the **infirmary**.

It was a long, cold winter and the girls got sick. First Margot died of **typhus** and a short while later Anne died to[o]. She had not yet turned sixtee[n].

Encourage elaboration: Describe th[e] experiences of the Franks in the cam[p]

About 1944. The entrance to Auschwitz concentration camp. The words over the gate mean, "Work will make you free."

cut off from not part of, away from

despite everything even though so many bad things had happened

raided entered suddenly

conditions ways people lived

infirmary place where sick people are kept

typhus a painful sickness

REACHING ALL STUDENTS

Art Connection
DRAWING OR MODELING

Invite students to draw or create a model of one room in the Frank family's secret annex. Encourage students to use their imaginations, adding details that are not included in the biography.

Language Development
NEGOTIATE

Living in the cramped quarters of the annex meant that Anne had to share food, furniture, chores, and even light with others. Have students imagine conflicts between inhabitants of the annex. Ask: *What problems would occur? What matters might need to be resolved? How would the people come to agreements?* Have pairs role-play these negotiations.

bout 1941. Anne Frank at a public hall in Amsterdam.

Anne's little book became extremely popular and it was translated into many languages. Because people were amazed by Anne's courage and maturity, the story of her life was made into a play and the building where she and her family hid **was turned into** a **museum**. Anne Frank **lives on** through her remarkable words, which **are an inspiration to** millions of people all over the world.

Encourage elaboration: How do you think Anne Frank would feel about having her diary read by so many people?

Anne's diary and other papers were found ı the annex by Miep Gies, who kept them. ‌fter the war ended, Anne's father went back ı Amsterdam. He was the only one from the ecret annex who survived the hard winter t Auschwitz. When he read the diary Miep ave him, he decided it should be published.

Clarify: Remember that Miep Gies was one of the people who helped the Franks when they were hiding in the Annex.

BEFORE YOU MOVE ON...

1. **Sequence** Tell what happened to the Franks after the annex was raided.
2. **Opinion** Do you think life in the concentration camps changed Anne's belief that people are good at heart? Explain.
3. **Character's Motive** Why do you think Anne's father decided to publish her diary?

as turned into became
useum place where important objects ‌re kept and shown
ves on continues to live
re an inspiration to encourage, support

ABOUT THE AUTHOR

Yona Zeldis McDonough was born in the Jewish state of Israel and now lives in Brooklyn, New York, with her husband and two children. Although the story of Anne Frank is not a happy one, she feels that it is important for everyone to know what the Nazis did to the Jews and other people in Europe during World War II.

CHECK COMPREHENSION

3 Answers to "Before You Move On"

1. **Sequence** The Franks were sent to Westerbrook and then to Auschwitz. The girls were sent from there to Bergen-Belsen. Anne, her mother, and her sister died in concentration camps. Only Anne's father survived.
2. **Opinion** Answers will vary.
3. **Character's Motive** Possible answers are: He wanted people to remember his daughter; He wanted people to know what happened during the war.

ABOUT THE AUTHOR

4 Evaluate Literature: Author's Background Read aloud About the Author. Point out that the author was born in Israel, which is the birthplace of Judaism, Anne Frank's religion. Ask students how this might have made the author particularly interested in telling Anne Frank's story. Ask: *What kinds of stories are you particularly interested in because of their connection to your background?*

CLOSE AND ASSESS

Distribute index cards. Instruct students to write a summary of the events that occurred after the secret annex was raided. Use the cards as exit slips.

Literary Analysis Minilesson

▶ EVALUATE LITERARY QUALITY

TEACH Explain that literature can be evaluated on various criteria, or standards. Say: *You may judge a selection for its use of language.* (for example, "Chrysalis Diary") *Or you might evaluate how much it teaches you.* (for example, "Starting a Community Garden")

PRACTICE Brainstorm criteria that students can use to evaluate the biography of Anne Frank. Suggest such categories as:

- clarity (How well does the selection explain concepts?)
- relevance (How much does the topic mean to you?)
- depth (How much detail did the selection give?)

Encourage students to rank the biography of Anne Frank in each category on a scale of 1 to 10, with 10 being the highest rating. Then have them compare and defend their ratings with a partner. To obtain an overall class evaluation, graph the individual ratings.

▶ **Practice Book** page 128

RESPOND

OBJECTIVES

SUM IT UP
Function: Make Comparisons
Learning Strategies:
Ⓣ Use Graphic Organizers (time line)
Critical Thinking and Comprehension:
Ⓣ Identify Sequence; Make Comparisons; Form Generalizations

THINK IT OVER
Function: Engage in Discussion
Critical Thinking and Comprehension:
Draw Conclusions; Make Judgments; Make Comparisons; Relate to Personal Knowledge

EXPRESS YOURSELF
Function: Ⓣ Define and Explain

CHECK YOUR UNDERSTANDING

1 Sum It Up See annotations on **Transparency 65** on page T258 for events in the Frank family time line. The generalization should indicate that world events can change the lives of individuals profoundly.

▶ **Practice Book** page 129

2 Think It Over Possible answers are:

1. **Conclusion** Honoring those who suffered and died might prevent it from happening again.
2. **Judgment** Her thoughts, feelings, and experiences have comforted some and moved others to action.
3. **Comparisons** Forms of government, boundaries, and names of some countries have changed.
4. **Personal Knowledge** Student answers will vary.

3 Express Yourself Prompt the use of new vocabulary.

CLOSE AND ASSESS

Ask students to state what they would tell their families about this selection.

Respond to the Biography

Check Your Understanding

SUM IT UP

Compare Sequences Complete a time line to show how the events in the life of the Frank family were connected to the events of World War II.

Time Line

World War II	The Frank Family
	1929 Anne Frank is born.
1933 Hitler becomes dictator of Germany.	

Talk over your time line with a partner. Answer questions like these to compare the events.

- How old was Anne when Hitler became dictator of Germany?
- When did the Frank family leave Germany? Why?
- Why were the Franks no longer safe even in Holland?

Form Generalizations Think about the comparisons you made. Write a sentence or two to tell how world events affect the lives of individuals.

THINK IT OVER

Discuss and Write Talk about these questions with a partner. Write the answers.

1. **Conclusion** Why is it important to remember what happened to Anne and other Jews during World War II?
2. **Judgment** What is Anne Frank's legacy?
3. **Comparisons** What has changed in the world since Anne Frank's time? What has stayed the same?
4. **Personal Knowledge** Anne's diary became her connection to the world. Name other ways that people communicate their thoughts to the world.

EXPRESS YOURSELF ▶ DEFINE AND EXPLAIN

Choose one event from the time line on pages 255–257. In a group, tell about the event and then explain how it affected people like Anne. Next, put yourself in Anne's place and explain how these events made her and other ordinary people feel.

✔ **LANGUAGE ACQUISITION ASSESSMENT**
See page 62 of the Assessment Handbook.

REACHING ALL STUDENTS

Multi-Level Strategies

SUM IT UP OPTIONS

BEGINNING Ask students to underline the key dates in Anne's Frank's life in the Key Points Reading on **Master 64**. (See page T258.) Work together to check for these dates on their time line. In groups, students write sentences that describe what was happening both in the world and in Anne's life during these years. Suggest sequencing words such as *before, after, while,* and *next.*

INTERMEDIATE Have students work with partners to check their time lines of Anne's life and World War II. Students should analyze how events in the world time line may have affected or led to events in Anne's life. Have the pairs write their ideas, then compare these ideas with those of another pair.

ADVANCED Have students exchange time lines of Anne's life and World War II and check for completeness. Then they write paragraphs about how the events of the two sides of the time lines are related.

ASSESSMENT
Selection Test 15 on page 67 of the Assessment Handbook tests students' mastery of the reading strategies and the vocabulary, comprehension, and language arts skills taught with this selection.

anguage Arts and Content Area Connections

GRAMMAR IN CONTEXT

SE THE PRESENT PERFECT TENSE

earn About Helping Verbs Some verbs are ade up of more than one word—a **main verb** nd one or more **helping verbs**. The helping verb grees with the subject of the sentence.

se **has** with *he, she,* or *it*.

Since May, Lisa **has learned** about the Franks.

se **have** with *I, you, we,* or *they*.

I **have enjoyed** reading Anne's diary.

earn About Present Perfect Verbs The resent perfect tense can tell about an action at began in the past and may still be going on.

Millions of people **have learned** about her.

ometimes you don't know when an action appened in the past. Use a verb in the present erfect tense to tell about this action, too.

Mark **has read** the diary twice.

o form the present perfect tense, use the elping verb **has** or **have** with the past articiple. See pages 450–451 in the Handbook or the past participles of irregular verbs.

ractice Write each sentence. Choose the orrect helping verb.

It is November, 1942. Anne and her family have / has been in hiding for four months.

The Franks has / have moved into a hidden apartment.

The young girl has / have started a diary.

SOCIAL STUDIES

REPRESENTING/SPEAKING

GIVE AN ORAL REPORT

What would you like to learn about World War II? With a partner, research and then report on one event from the war.

1. **Form Questions** Choose a battle or event you want to research. Use these words to form questions about your topic: *Who? What? When? Where? Why? How?*
2. **Research the Answers** Use encyclopedias, newspapers, magazines, and the Internet to find the answers to your questions.
3. **Present Your Findings** Share your questions and answers with the class. Use pictures and graphics to support your presentation.

For tips on giving an **oral report**, see Handbook pages 401–402.

Allied paratroopers fill the skies over Europe in 1942.

Multi-Level Strategies

OPTIONS FOR ORAL REPORTS

BEGINNING Have students work in small groups. After the groups form their research questions, each group should be assigned one of the questions to research. Provide simple sentence frames for the groups to use in their oral reports, such as: *The World War II event we researched is _____. This event occurred in _____.*

INTERMEDIATE / **ADVANCED** Challenge students to use and synthesize information from as many sources as possible in their reports. After students give their reports, invite listeners to ask questions. Have pairs of students create quiz questions for one another. Then have students self-assess by answering questions: *Did I adequately answer each of the questions I posed? What did I learn from my listeners' questions?*

RESPOND

OBJECTIVES

PRESENT PERFECT TENSE
Grammar: Helping Verbs; Ⓣ Present Perfect Tense

ORAL REPORT
Function: Ⓣ Give Information
Speaking: Oral Report
Critical Thinking and Research Skills: Choose and Narrow a Topic; Locate Resources; Gather and Synthesize Information

LANGUAGE ARTS AND LITERATURE

1 Use the Present Perfect Tense
Answers to Practice items are:

Practice

1. have

2. have

3. has

▶ **Practice Book** page 130

2 Give an Oral Report Offer support by:

- providing reference books, articles, and lists of Internet sites about World War II
- modeling how to frame possible topics as questions for research
- pairing students with similar interests
- monitoring students' plans and helping them narrow their topics.

CLOSE AND ASSESS

Ask students to use verbs in the present perfect tense to tell what they have learned about Anne Frank or World War II.

RESPOND

OBJECTIVES

WAR EFFORT POSTER

Function: Persuade

Learning Strategies and Critical Thinking: Interact With Peers; Generate Ideas

Representing: Poster

CONTENT AREA CONNECTIONS

1 Make a War Effort Poster Tell students that the goal of this assignment is to convince others to take action. To complete the poster, have students:

- list possible poster topics from library or Internet research
- decide which topic the poster will address
- write a slogan about the topic
- use drawings or collage materials to create a poster that will attract attention and promote the message of the slogan.

Respond to the Biography, continued

Content Area Connections

SOCIAL STUDIES

REPRESENTING

MAKE A WAR EFFORT POSTER

During World War II, the U.S. government needed help from all its citizens. While soldiers fought overseas, there was much work to do at home. The government created posters to ask citizens to join in the war effort. Look at the images and read the slogans in these posters.

In this poster, a popular character called Uncle Sam encourages men to join the U.S. Army. The poster calls to their patriotism, or love for their country.

The government encouraged women to take jobs during the war. Because of the government's slogans—messages that are easy to remember—many women worked for the first time.

Work with a small group. Follow these steps to design your own war effort poster.

1. **Think of a Message** Brainstorm ideas for a war effort poster. You may want to ask people to grow their own food, for example Or, you might want to convince people to sav fuel and metal products. With your group, choose one idea to develop as a message.
2. **Design Your Poster** Use persuasive words and images in your message. Strong colors, simple images, and direct language are very effective.
3. **Display Your Poster** Show your group's poster to the class. Tell about the process of brainstorming and creating your poster. Ther display all of the posters in a class "gallery."

For tips on **representing** ideas, see Handbook pages 404–405.

REACHING ALL STUDENTS

Multi-Level Strategies

OPTIONS FOR MAKING A POSTER

BEGINNING / **INTERMEDIATE** / **ADVANCED** Encourage Advanced students to use the library or the Internet to research issues important to countries at times of war. After these students present possible poster topics to their group, students of all levels should participate in deciding which issue to develop. Using the posters on page 268 as models, Advanced and Intermediate students should work together to create an effective slogan. Beginning students should then contribute to decisions on choice and placement of images to best convey the idea of the slogan. After all posters have been completed and displayed in the "gallery," prompt a class discussion analyzing the ways in which each poster communicates its message through its slogan and art.

SCIENCE

TECHNOLOGY/MEDIA

PORT ON NUCLEAR WEAPONS

e Anne Frank, the scientist Albert Einstein cided to leave Germany in the early 1930s cause of Hitler's anti-Jewish laws. He warned e U.S. that Germany might develop an atomic mb. Scientists who worked for the U.S. built eir own atomic bomb first.

e atomic bomb is a very powerful weapon that built by splitting apart an atom. Weapons that e made with this technology are called nuclear eapons. With a group, research the history and fects of the atomic bomb and other nuclear eapons. Here is a list of questions to help guide ur research:

- When was the first atomic bomb developed? Who invented it?
- Where was the atomic bomb dropped during the war? What were its effects?
- What are some types of nuclear weapons?
- Which countries have nuclear weapons today?

e the Internet and other resources to conduct ur research.

1. **Gather Information and Take Notes** These Web sites might be good places to start, but remember that new sites appear every day! Use key words in your search and look for links.

INTERNET

INFORMATION ON-LINE

Key Words:
"atomic bomb"
"hydrogen bomb"
"nuclear weapons"

Web Sites:
- **Manhattan Project**
  - www.encyclopedia.com
  - www.letsfindout.com

Download helpful information and take notes for your report.

2. **Organize Information** Write key points and facts on a large chart. Use it to present your report to the class.

3. **Present Your Report** Choose a member of the group to tell about the group's findings. Other members can point to related facts on the chart as the speaker gives the report.

For more about the **research process**, see Handbook pages 394–399. For help with the **Internet**, see pages 392–393.

Research Skills

▶ CITING SOURCES

TEACH Define *cite.* Tell students that he writer of a report must include a list of sources for the information cited. Give some examples. Demonstrate the organization of a bibliography:

- author's name
- title of text
- city of publication
- publisher
- copyright date

Format: Author's last name, first name. *Title of text.* City: Publisher, date.

PRACTICE In the school library, show students the locations of periodicals, card catalog, and encyclopedias. Assign students a topic and have them find three sources for that topic. Assign topics that will help them with their research project, such as Los Alamos, Hiroshima, Albert Einstein. Have students use proper form to cite their sources.

OBJECTIVES

NUCLEAR WEAPONS REPORT

Function: Ⓣ Give Information
Speaking: Oral Report
Technology/Media: Use the Internet
Research Skills: Locate Resources; Gather and Synthesize Information; Ⓣ Take Notes; Cite Sources
Representing: Chart

2 Report on Nuclear Weapons Tell students that, in order to prepare this report, they must learn facts and details about specific subjects by asking questions, observing, and reading. The information they share must be well organized and clearly presented. Encourage them to collect and cite the resources they use in their reports.

For Multi-Level Strategies: Guide Beginning students to use notecards to organize their research—one for each question. Title the notecards: *who, what, where, when, why.* Tell students to write key points on these cards.

Encourage Intermediate students to work in pairs to gather data. Have them try out *who, what, where, when, why* questions on one another and agree on a plan to narrow their research.

Ask Advanced students to add a human dimension to the report. Tell them that many of the scientists who worked on nuclear weapons had strong personal feelings about whether the work they were doing was the right thing to do. Ask them to explore that dimension and include some quotes from scientists in their reports.

▶ **Practice Book** page 131

CLOSE AND ASSESS

Have students write a paragraph summarizing what they have learned from this lesson.

PREPARE TO READ

OBJECTIVES

THINK ABOUT WHAT YOU KNOW

Reading Strategy:
Activate Prior Knowledge

LEARN KEY VOCABULARY Ⓣ

Vocabulary Strategy:
Use New Words in Context

LEARN TO MONITOR YOUR READING

Reading Strategy: Monitor Your Reading (clarify, ask questions, summarize, predict)

THINK ABOUT WHAT YOU KNOW

1 Brainstorm Discuss with students how a person's background, culture, and the time and place in which they live might influence diary subjects.

LEARN KEY VOCABULARY

2 Use New Words in Context Read vocabulary words and definitions aloud. Then conduct the activity.

Use Vocabulary Options in the **Multi-Level Strategies** to tailor the activity to proficiency levels.

▶ **Practice Book** page 132

LEARN TO MONITOR YOUR READING

3 Model How to Monitor Your Reading Define *monitor* as "pay close attention to." Demonstrate the steps in the box with **Transparency 66**:

- Read the passage. Stop after *turned upside down* to clarify by pointing out context clues to its non-literal meaning. *(as if; so much has happened)*
- Stop again after *main thing* to question.
- Finish the reading and then summarize and predict.

CLOSE AND ASSESS

Ask students to list at least three ways they can monitor their reading. Students may list three out of four: Clarify, Question, Summarize, Predict.

The Diary of a Young Girl
diary
by Anne Frank

Prepare to Read

THINK ABOUT WHAT YOU KNOW

Brainstorm What do people write in diaries? Make a class list.

agitated nervous, upset, worried

bother make an effort

call-up notice message from the Nazi police that ordered a person to be at a certain place at a certain time

exhausted very tired

impression idea

matter be important

preoccupied thinking about something else, lost in thought

shock great and sudden surprise

stunned greatly surprised

LEARN KEY VOCABULARY

Use New Words in Context Study the new words and their definitions. Then write the paragraph, adding the missing words.

When I read Anne Frank's diary, I get the ___(1)___ that she was a lot like me. I can feel how scared she was when her father got the ___(2)___. Like Anne, I try to write each memory in my personal diary. Sometimes I get so ___(3)___ over a problem that I want to scream! Instead, I write about it. That way, I am not ___(4)___ by the situation, and I can think about other things. All of my diaries ___(5)___ more to me than anything else. I am never too ___(6)___ to write in them. One morning, I didn't even ___(7)___ to eat breakfast because I was writing. That was a real ___(8)___ to my mother! I was ___(9)___ too when I wrote 100 pages in a month.

Answers to the vocabulary activity:
1. impression
2. call-up notice
3. agitated
4. preoccupied
5. matter
6. exhausted
7. bother
8. shock
9. stunned

LEARN TO MONITOR YOUR READING

When you **monitor your reading**, you stop from time to time to be sure you understand the text.

READING STRATEGY

How to Monitor Your Reading

1. **Clarify** Make sure you understand new words and ideas.
2. **Ask Questions** Ask yourself questions about each section.
3. **Summarize** Think about the most important events or ideas. State them in a sentence or two.
4. **Predict** Think about what will happen next.

Use these strategies as you read "The Diary of a Young Girl."

REACHING ALL STUDENTS

Multi-Level Strategies

VOCABULARY OPTIONS

BEGINNING Group students to read ***The Children We Remember*** or the Key Points Reading on **Master 67**. (See page T273.) Work with the vocabulary in those selections.

INTERMEDIATE Work with students as a group to decide where to place each vocabulary word in the paragraph.

ADVANCED Students can complete the paragraph on their own, then compare answers with a partner and discuss differences.

Transparency 66 / Master 66

HOW TO MONITOR YOUR READING

Directions: Read the passage. Then read and answer the questions in the chart below. Try to think of other questions that would help you understand the reading better.

Wednesday, July 8, 1942

Dearest Kitty,

It seems like years since Sunday morning. So much has happened. It's as if the whole world had suddenly turned upside down. But as you can see, Kitty, I'm still alive, and that's the main thing, Father says. I'm alive all right, but don't ask where or how. You probably don't understand a word I'm saying, so I'll begin by telling you what happened Sunday afternoon.

Clarify What words need more explanation? turned upside down	**Ask Questions** What questions did I have while I was reading? Who is Kitty? What does Father say is the most important thing?
Summarize [illegible] remember from this reading? Something serious has happened to Anne.	**Predict** What will the next section of the reading be about? In the next section, Anne will tell about Sunday afternoon.

Transparency 66 Level B, Unit 4 | Continuity and Change

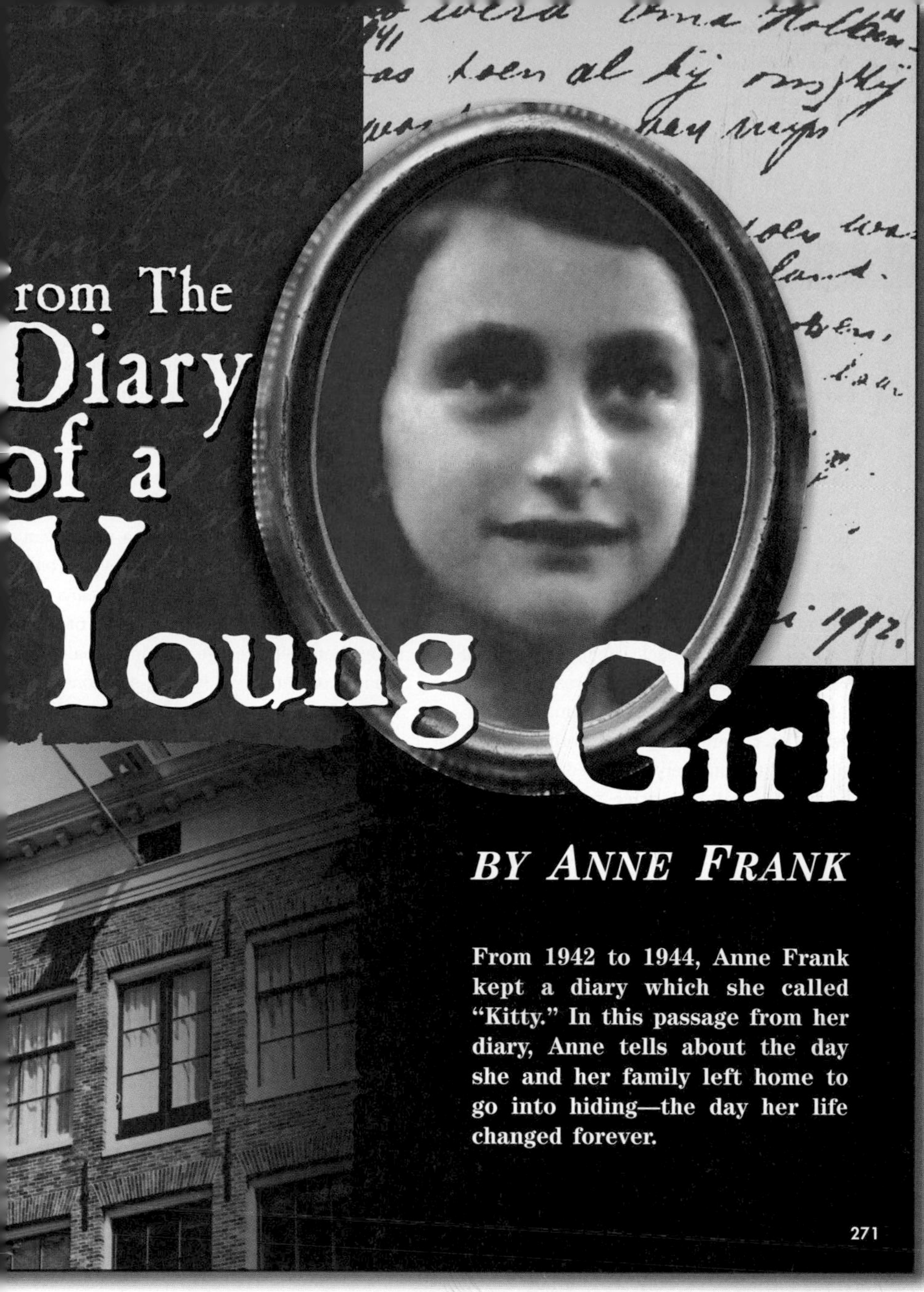

from The Diary of a Young Girl

BY ANNE FRANK

From 1942 to 1944, Anne Frank kept a diary which she called "Kitty." In this passage from her diary, Anne tells about the day she and her family left home to go into hiding—the day her life changed forever.

271

READ THE SELECTION

OBJECTIVES

Reading Strategies: Preview; Predict
Literary Analysis: Diary

INTRODUCE THE SELECTION

4 **Preview and Predict** Read aloud the title, author's name, and introduction to the selection. Ask: *In what ways do you think Anne's life would be changed when the family goes into hiding?* Next, have students page through the selection and read the summary statements for each part. Ask students to make more predictions about the selection based on these statements.

5 **Identify Genre: Diary** Point out that the root word of *diary, di-,* means day. Elicit from students a definition of the word. Verify that a diary is a daily written record of personal experiences. Remind students that this selection is an entry from Anne's diary.

The Diary of a Young Girl
by Anne Frank

Theme Connection This selection is an entry from Anne Frank's diary in which she relates the events that preceded her family's going into hiding from the Nazis during World War II. Anne's diary is a legacy of courage and hope that has touched generations of readers.

Selection Summary The introduction on page 271 of the student book offers a summary of the selection.

THE BASICS BOOKSHELF

- ***The Children We Remember***
  by Chana Byers Abells

Just as Anne Frank's diary tells about a typical teenage girl, this book describes ordinary children who went to school, played games, and celebrated their faith. Then the Nazis came and terrible things began to happen. Simple sentences, combined with powerful black and white photos, provide an opportunity to learn basic vocabulary related to home, family and survival while learning about a central event in WW II.

For Lesson Plans: See the Teacher's Guide for ***The Basics Bookshelf***.

READ PAGES 272–273

OBJECTIVES

Function: Read a Selection

Listening: Listen to a Selection

Reading and Learning Strategies: Set a Purpose for Reading; Monitor Your Reading (clarify, ask questions, summarize, predict)

Comprehension: Ⓣ Identify Cause and Effect; Identify Details; Ⓣ Identify Sequence

SET PURPOSE

1 Read aloud the introduction to pages 272–273. Set the purpose for reading: *Read to find out what happens after Anne's father receives a call-up notice from Hitler's police.*

READ AND THINK

Tape 4B
CD 4 Track 5

2 **Strategy Focus: Monitor Your Reading** After each major paragraph, have students work in groups using the reciprocal reading strategy on the chart on **Master 68**.

Choose Reading Options in the **Multi-Level Strategies** to tailor the reading to proficiency levels.

The recording of "The Diary of a Young Girl" on the **Selection Tape/CD** offers an oral language model and the opportunity to build reading fluency.

Red annotations offer opportunities to clarify meaning and check for understanding.

1

RECEIVING THE CALL-UP

Hitler's police call for Anne's father. His family fears that he will be taken away to a concentration camp.

Build background: Anne Frank dreamed of being a writer, but when she started her diary in 1942, she had no idea of how many people all over the world would read that diary.

WEDNESDAY, JULY 8, 1942

Dearest Kitty,

It seems like years since Sunday morning. So much has happened it's as if the whole world had suddenly turned upside down. But as you can see, Kitty, I'm still alive, and that's the **main thing**, Father says. I'm alive all right, but don't ask where or how. You probably don't understand a word I'm saying, so I'll begin by telling you what happened Sunday afternoon.

At three o'clock (Hello* had left but was supposed to come back later), the doorbell rang. I didn't hear it, since I was out on the balcony, lazily reading in the sun. A little while later Margot appeared in the kitchen doorway looking very **agitated**. "Father has received a **call-up notice** from **the SS**," she whispered. "Mother has gone to see Mr. van Daan." (Mr. van Daan is Father's **business partner** and a good friend.)

Ask: How does Margot feel about the call-up notice?

I was **stunned**. A call-up: everyone knows what that means. **Visions** of concentration camps and lonely **cells** raced through my head. How could we let Father go to such a fate? "Of course he's not going," declared Margot as we waited for Mother in the living room. "Mother's gone to Mr. van Daan to ask whether we can move to our hiding place tomorrow. The van Daans are going with us. There will be seven of us altogether." Silence. We couldn't speak. The thought of Father off visiting someone in the Jewish Hospital and completely **unaware of** what was happening, the long wait for Mother, the heat, the **suspense**—all this **reduced us to silence**.

Encourage elaboration: What emotions w[as] Anne feeling while waiting for her father?

*Hello Silberberg was Anne's close friend. He would often visit Anne at her home.

main thing most important point
the SS Hitler's police force, the *Schutzstaffel*
business partner partner in the work they do
Visions Pictures
cells rooms in a prison
unaware of not knowing
suspense fear, tension
reduced us to silence made us unable to speak

REACHING ALL STUDENTS

Language Development

MAKE COMPARISONS

Have students work in small groups to compare Anne's concerns as a young, European, Jewish teenager alive during World War II with the concerns of modern teenagers in the United States. Suggest that students scan teen magazines to assist them in identifying the concerns of today's teenagers. Together, create a Venn diagram representing similarities and differences between the teenagers.

Multi-Level Strategies

READING OPTIONS FOR LESSONS 12–14

BEGINNING Students should work with ***The Children We Remember***. Or distribute copies of **Master 67** to conduct a Key Points Reading of "The Diary of a Young Girl." After reading each paragraph, have students answer at least one question from each of the boxes on **Master 68**.

INTERMEDIATE Read the selection aloud or play the recording on the **Selection Tape/CD**, pausing to clarify meaning. Also use the red annotations on the facsimile pages. Form groups of four. Cut copies of **Master 68** into four sections. Each student asks questions from one part of **Master 68**. Others in the groups write answers to the questions.

ADVANCED Have students read the selection on their own. Distribute copies of **Master 68** and have students answer the questions on the chart with a partner, then write their answers in a journal. They can also generate new questions for each category.

In her diary, Anne called the van Pels family the van Daans. These pictures show Auguste, Peter, and Hermann van Pels.

nne, left, with her neighbor Hannah Goslar in msterdam before the war. They were separated hen the Franks went into hiding, but they met gain in Bergen-Belsen concentration camp. Hannah rvived the war, and the story of her friendship with nne was later published in a book.

BEFORE YOU MOVE ON...

1. **Cause and Effect** Why did Mrs. Frank go to see Mr. van Daan about moving into the hiding place?
2. **Details** Where was Anne's father while she and Margot waited for him to return home?
3. **Summary/Sequence** Retell the events described on page 272 in the correct time order.

CHECK COMPREHENSION

3 Answers to "Before You Move On"

1. **Cause and Effect** The family received a "call-up" notice from the SS. Because of this, the family began preparations to go into hiding.
2. **Details** Anne's father was visiting someone in the Jewish Hospital.
3. **Summary/Sequence** Answers should include these details: Margot says that Father received a call-up notice; Mother goes to see Mr. van Daan; Anne worries about the call-up; Anne remembers that her father is at the hospital.

CLOSE AND ASSESS

Have groups share their summaries for pages 272–273. Check focus: Do the summary sentences mention that the Franks will go into hiding because they received a call-up notice from Hitler's police?

Transparency 67 / Master 67

KEY POINTS READING

The Diary of a Young Girl

Anne's family gets a call-up notice from Hitler's police. They are worried that Father will be taken away to a concentration camp. But Father is at work. He doesn't know what has happened. Mother asks a friend about a hiding place for the family.

Anne learns that Hitler's police want her sister Margot, not her father. Anne does not know where the hiding place is. Friends help the family start to pack their belongings. Anne is very tired and falls asleep quickly. Her mother wakes her early the next morning.

Anne and her family prepare to leave their home. They wear many layers of clothing but do not carry suitcases. Anne still does not know where the hiding place is. Anne says goodbye to her cat. The family leaves the house in a hurry. They hope to reach their hiding place in safety.

Transparency 67 Level B, Unit 4 | Continuity and Change

Transparency 68 / Master 68

CHART TO MONITOR READING

Directions: As you read the diary, use these questions to monitor your reading. Ask yourself questions about each section. Write your answers in a journal.

The Diary of a Young Girl

Clarify	Ask Questions
• What words or ideas need more explanation? • What new word did I learn, and how did I learn it? What other words can I use in place of it? • Which words have more than one meaning? How did I figure out which meaning to use?	• What questions did I have while I was reading? • For which questions did I find answers? • What did I do when I could not find the answers? • What did I think about as I was reading?
Summarize	**Predict**
• What are the most important events in this section, and why are they important? • What does the author want me to remember or learn? • What kind of "teacher" questions can I ask about the main idea?	• What did I think the selection would be about before I read it? • How did my prediction change after I started reading? • What do I think will happen next? What clues in the section helped me get that idea?

Transparency 68 Level B, Unit 4 | Continuity and Change

READ PAGES 274–275

OBJECTIVES

Function: Read a Selection
Vocabulary Strategy: Use New Words in Context
Listening: Listen to a Selection
Reading and Learning Strategies: Set a Purpose for Reading; Monitor Your Reading (clarify, ask questions, summarize, predict)
Comprehension and Critical Thinking: Draw Conclusions; Make Inferences; Make Decisions
Literary Analysis: Evaluate the Impact of Point of View on Meaning

SET PURPOSE

1 Read aloud the introduction to pages 274–275. Say: *As you read, notice how Anne and her family prepare to go into hiding.*

READ AND THINK

Tape 4B
CD 4 Track 5

2 **Strategy Focus: Monitor Your Reading** Involve students in reading pages 274–275. Have students continue using the reciprocal reading strategy on the chart on **Master 68**. (See page T273.)

See the **Multi-Level Strategies** on T272 to tailor the reading to proficiency levels.

2

PREPARING TO LEAVE

Anne learns that the call-up is for her sister Margot, not her father. The Franks and their friends start packing and prepare to go into hiding.

Suddenly the doorbell rang again. "That's Hello," I said.

"Don't open the door!" exclaimed Margot to stop me. But it wasn't **necessary**, since we heard Mother and Mr. van Daan downstairs talking to Hello, and then the two of them came inside and shut the door behind them. Every time the bell rang, either Margot or I had to tiptoe downstairs to see if it was Father, and we didn't let anyone else in. Margot and I were sent from the room, as Mr. van Daan wanted to talk to Mother alone.

When she and I were sitting in our bedroom, Margot told me that the call-up was not for Father, but for her. At this second **shock**, I began to cry. Margot is sixteen—**apparently** they want to send girls her age away on their own. But thank goodness she won't be going; Mother had said so herself, which must be what Father had meant when he talked to me about our going into hiding. Hiding . . . where would we hide? In the city? In the country? In a house? In a **shack**? When, where, how . . . These were questions I wasn't **allowed** to ask, but they still kept running through my mind.

Margot and I started packing our most important **belongings** into a schoolba[g]. The first thing I stuck in was this diary, and then curlers, handkerchiefs, schoolbooks, a comb and some old letters. **Preoccupied** by the thought of going into hidin[g], I stuck the craziest things in the bag, but I'm not sorry. Memories mean more to me than dresses.

Father finally came home around five o'clock, and we called Mr. Kleiman to ask if he could come by that evening. Mr. van Daan left and went to get Miep. Miep arrived and promised to return later that

Otto Frank

Role-play: Act out this scene.

Ask: Why does Anne say she packed "the crazie[st] things"? What do these things mean to her?

necessary needed
apparently it seems
shack small run-down building
allowed free
belongings things we own, possessions

REACHING ALL STUDENTS

Mathematics Connection

DATA ANALYSIS

Have students study the data about migration destinations of European Jews after World War II. Ask them to use this information to form generalizations about the extent to which war affects the lives of ordinary people and discuss their ideas in class.

Migration Destinations of European Jews 1946–1950

Country	Number	Country	Number
Australia	4,745	The Netherlands	5,000
Belgium	5,000	Sweden	7,200
Brazil	4,837	United Kingdom	1,000
Canada	19,697	United States	105,000
Israel	748,540	Other Latin American Countries	5,046
France	8,000		

ght, taking with her a bag full shoes, dresses, jackets, derwear and stockings. ter that it was quiet in our artment; none of us felt like ting. It was still hot, and erything was very strange.

We had rented our big upstairs om to a Mr. Goldschmidt, a vorced man in his thirties, who parently had nothing to do that ening, since **despite** all our **polite nts** he hung around until ten clock.

Miep and Jan Gies came at eleven. iep, who's worked for Father's company nce 1933, has become a close friend, and has her husband Jan. Once again, shoes, ockings, books and underwear **disappeared** to Miep's bag and Jan's deep pockets. At even-thirty they too disappeared.

I was **exhausted**, and even though I ew it'd be my last night in my own bed, fell asleep right away and didn't wake up atil Mother called me at five-thirty the next orning. **Fortunately**, it wasn't as hot as nday; a warm rain fell throughout the day.

Encourage elaboration: How were Miep and Jan helping the Franks?

1933. Anne Frank and her sister Margot at home in Germany during happier times.

BEFORE YOU MOVE ON...

1. **Conclusions** Why didn't Anne and Margot let anyone into the house except their father?
2. **Inference** Why do you think the Gieses took so many of the Franks' belongings away?
3. **Making Decisions** What would you take with you if you had to go into hiding today?

spite no matter, in spite of
lite hints gentle suggestions
sappeared were put away, went away
rtunately Luckily

REVIEW KEY VOCABULARY

3 Use New Words in Context Have pairs create a sentence or drawing to illustrate the meaning of five vocabulary words. The pairs then join to form groups of four. Have groups compare their work and revise it to improve the expression of each word's meaning.

CHECK COMPREHENSION

4 Answers to "Before You Move On"

1. **Conclusions** They didn't let anyone into the house except their father because they were afraid Hitler's police would arrive to take away a member of the family.
2. **Inference** The Gieses were helping them take more things to the hiding place.
3. **Decisions** Answers will vary. Tell students that they, like Anne, could take only as much as they could fit into a schoolbag.

CLOSE AND ASSESS

Have groups share their summaries for pages 274–275. Each summary sentence should note that many people helped the Franks go into hiding. Have each student make a prediction about the next section.

Literary Analysis Minilesson

▶ POINT OF VIEW

TEACH Remind students that "Anne Frank" on pages 258–265 is a biography. It uses the pronouns *he, she,* and *they* to describe key characters.

Elicit how "The Diary of a Young Girl" differs from the biography because it was written by Anne herself. Sometimes this kind of text is called an autobiography. Anne writes her own story in the form of a diary. Anne uses the pronouns *I* and *we* to describe her experiences. Thus, the diary is written in the first-person point of view.

PRACTICE Have partners create a chart with examples of the narrators' points of view in the two selections.

Anne Frank	Diary of a Young Girl
page 261 "In July 1942 the Frank family moved into a hidden apartment..."	page 272 "Mother's gone to Mr. van Daan to ask whether we can move..."

▶ **Practice Book** page 133

READ PAGES 276–277

OBJECTIVES

Function: Read a Selection
Listening: Listen to a Selection
Reading and Learning Strategies: Set a Purpose for Reading; Monitor Your Reading (clarify, ask questions, summarize, predict)
Comprehension: Make Inferences; Ⓣ Identify Cause and Effect; Relate Main Idea and Details
Literary Analysis: Compare Literature

SET PURPOSE

1 Read aloud the introduction to pages 276–277. Say: *As you read, look for details that show that the family left their home in a hurry.*

READ AND THINK

Tape 4B
CD 4 Track 5

2 **Strategy Focus: Monitor Your Reading** Involve students in reading pages 276–277. Have students continue to monitor their reading using the reciprocal reading strategy on **Master 68**. (See page T273.)

See the **Multi-Level Strategies** on T272 to tailor the reading to proficiency levels.

3

FACING THE UNKNOWN

Anne and her family leave home in a hurry. She doesn't know where the hiding place is; she knows only that they have to reach it safely.

1941. Anne and her family safe and together for a time in Amsterdam.

Encourage elaboration: What would have happened if they had carried suitcases?

The four of us were wrapped in so many **layers** of clothes it looked as if we were going off to spend the night in a refrigerator, and all that just so we could take more clothes with us. No Jew in our **situation** would **dare** leave the house with a suitcase full of clothes. I was wearing two undershirts, three pairs of underpants, a dress, and over that a skirt, a jacket, a raincoat, two pairs of stockings, heavy shoes, a cap, a scarf and lots more. **I was suffocating** even before we left the house, but no one **bothered** to ask me how I felt.

Margot **stuffed** her schoolbag with schoolbooks, went to get her bicycle and, with Miep leading the way, rode off **into the great unknown**. At any rate, that's how I thought of it, since I still didn't know whe our hiding place was.

At seven-thirty we too closed the door behind us; Moortje, my cat, was the only living creature I said good-bye to. Accordin to a note we left for Mr. Goldschmidt, she was to be taken to the neighbors, who would give her a good home.

The **stripped beds**, the breakfast thing on the table, the pound of meat for the cat in the kitchen—all of these **created** the **impression** that we'd left in a hurry. But we **weren't interested in** impressions. We just wanted to get out of there, to get away and **reach our destination** in safety. Nothing else **mattered**.

More tomorrow.

Yours, Ann

Ask: Why weren't the Franks interested in th impression they left?

layers pieces, coverings
situation place
dare take the chance to
I was suffocating I could hardly breathe
stuffed tightly packed, filled up
into the great unknown to where no one knew or could guess
stripped beds beds with all the sheets and covers taken off
created made, produced
weren't interested in didn't care about
reach our destination get to where we were going

REACHING ALL STUDENTS

Technology And Media
COMPARE MEDIA

Have students use the Internet or the library to search for books, movies, and plays based on the story of Anne Frank. Invite students to compare the different media and to assess what impact each has on the story.

Possible references include:

BOOK: *Anne Frank: The Biography.* By Melissa Muller, et al. Henry Holt & Co.

PLAY: *The Diary of Anne Frank.* Goodrich, Frances and Albert Hackett. New York: Random House, 1956.

Language Development
EXPRESS FEELINGS

Draw students' attention to this statement from page 276 of the story: "... no one bothered to ask me how I felt." Have students think about how Anne felt at this moment. Then invite them to take on the role of Anne and express her feelings.

Johannes Kleiman worked in the office below the Annex. He helped to hide Anne's family. When the family was discovered on August 4, 1944, Mr. Kleiman was arrested. Because of his poor health, he was released shortly afterward. He stayed in Amsterdam until his death in 1959.

Miep Gies was a friend and helper of the Franks and the van Pelses. She is still living in Amsterdam. Her husband Jan died in 1993.

BEFORE YOU MOVE ON...

1. **Inference** Explain why Anne and her family could not leave with their belongings in a suitcase.
2. **Cause and Effect** What created the impression that Anne's family left in a hurry?
3. **Main Idea and Details** List three details to support this main idea: The Franks had a lot to do before they went into hiding.

CHECK COMPREHENSION

3 Answers to "Before You Move On"

1. **Inference** The Frank family needed to leave their home without anyone noticing. If they had left with their belongings in a suitcase, someone might have realized that the family was leaving and notified Hitler's police.
2. **Cause and Effect** The stripped beds, the breakfast things on the table, and the meat for the cat in the kitchen all created the impression that the Frank family left in a hurry.
3. **Main Idea and Details** Anne's mother had to go to Mr. van Daan to ask whether they could go into hiding; the family needed to pack quickly; they had to leave a note for Mr. Goldschmidt about their cat.

Literary Analysis Minilesson

▶ COMPARE LITERATURE

TEACH Define *compare* as "to show similarities and differences between two or more things."

Elicit from students that the biographical selection "Anne Frank" and autobiographical selection "The Diary of a Young Girl" can be compared, since they are both about generally the same topic but are different genres.

Guide them to start a chart of attributes that might be compared, including Genre, Characters, Details, and Point of View.

PRACTICE Break the class into teams, one for each attribute. Ask each team to select examples for their part of the comparison chart.

Reconvene and make a class chart that shows an attribute-by-attribute comparison of the two Anne Frank selections. As a follow-up, encourage students to write comparison paragraphs or sentences based on the class activity.

▶ **Practice Book** page 134

READ PAGE 278

OBJECTIVES

Literary Analysis: Respond to Literature

ABOUT THE AUTHOR

4 Respond to Literature Read aloud or have students read About the Author.

Point out that Anne wrote about events that were important not only to her but to the world as well. Ask: *What topics are important to you? What topics are also important to the world?*

Invite students to chart types of literature that deal with topics of personal interest to them.

Topic	Literature
personal challenges	• diaries
space exploration	• textbooks • newspaper articles
real life adventures	• chapter books
sports	• magazine articles

CLOSE AND ASSESS

Have students share their summaries.

The building in which the Franks had hidden is now a museum.

ABOUT THE AUTHOR

Anne Frank is the author of one of the most famous diaries ever written. *The Diary of a Young Girl* has been published in more than fifty languages. Anne wrote her diary with the intention of having it published. During the last year of her life, she rewrote and edited it to improve its quality. She took out some passages that she didn't think were very interesting and added others from memory. In addition to her diary, Anne wrote poems and stories while she was in the annex. She had dreams of becoming a writer after the war was over.

278 **Unit 4** | Continuity and Change

REACHING ALL STUDENTS

Language Development

DEFINE AND EXPLAIN

Have students work with a partner to review information from the selection "Anne Frank" on pages 258–265 about where Anne and her family went after she wrote this diary entry. Partners should define Anne's destination and explain what life would be like living in the family's secret annex. Provide students with sentence starters to elicit detailed definitions and explanations: *Anne and her family went to _____. They went there because _____. The annex was _____.*

Respond to the Diary

Check Your Understanding

JM IT UP

entify Important Information Review "The ary of a Young Girl." Make a list of the portant events in the selection.

late Causes and Effects Some events have a use-and-effect relationship. The **effect** tells hat happens. The **cause** tells why it happened. view your list of important events from "The ary of a Young Girl." Write them in a chart like 's one to show how they are related. Add a use or effect, if necessary, to go with an event.

Cause	Effect
Father receives a call-up notice.	The Family decides to go into hiding.
'eople might come nd take the Frank amily away.	They have to be quiet and not open the door.
he Franks are eaving their home.	They quickly pack up their belongings.
'hey have to get their elongings into their iding place.	Miep and Jan Gies carry the things away in their bags and pockets.
ews cannot be seen vith a suitcase full of lothes.	The Franks wear several layers of clothes when they leave the house.
he Franks leave uickly.	The house is left messy and untidy.

THINK IT OVER

Discuss and Write Talk about these questions with a partner. Write the answers.

1. **Mood or Tone** How does Anne seem to feel about leaving her home and moving into the annex?
2. **Character** What words would you use to describe Anne?
3. **Comparison** Compare an event from Anne's diary to the same event in the Anne Frank biography. How are they similar? How are they different?
4. **Judgments** Why is *The Diary of a Young Girl* an important book for people to read today? What lessons can we learn from it?

EXPRESS YOURSELF ▶Give Information

Work with a team. Choose facts from "Anne Frank" and quotations from "The Diary of a Young Girl." Prepare a report for a radio broadcast on the experiences of the Frank family. Take turns making the broadcast.

Multi-Level Strategies

SUM IT UP OPTIONS

BEGINNING Provide students with one column of causes and another column of effects from the selection. Together review the Key Points Reading on **Master 67** (see page T273) to match the causes with their effects.

INTERMEDIATE Have students work in groups to make a list of important events from the summaries they created during the reciprocal reading. The groups should then chart cause-and-effect relationships and write sentences to explain them. To elicit ideas, provide sentence frames such as *Anne and her family go into hiding because* _____.

ADVANCED Have students work individually to use the summaries they created during the reciprocal reading to complete the activity. Ask students to write sentences explaining the relationships and then discuss them with a partner.

RESPOND

OBJECTIVES

SUM IT UP
Function: Write
Reading and Learning Strategies: Ⓣ Identify Cause and Effect; Use Graphic Organizers (cause/effect chart)

THINK IT OVER
Function: Engage in Discussion
Critical Thinking and Comprehension: Identify Character's Traits; Make Comparisons; Make Judgments
Literary Analysis: Mood and Tone

EXPRESS YOURSELF
Function: Ask and Answer Questions
Speaking and Listening: Oral Report

CHECK YOUR UNDERSTANDING

1 **Sum It Up** Point out that *because* and *since* can signal a cause-and-effect relationship, and that causes and effects can be inferred. See the annotations on page 279 for sample answers.

▶ **Practice Book** page 135

2 **Think It Over** Possible answers are:

1. **Mood or Tone** Anne seems to feel scared and worried.
2. **Character** She is thoughtful and caring. She can act maturely, but she can also act like a teenager.
3. **Comparison** The biography gives mostly factual details, while the diary tells more about Anne's feelings.
4. **Judgments** The diary provides a legacy of courage and hope and reminds us to keep tragedies like this from ever happening again.

3 **Express Yourself** Prompt the use of new vocabulary and language structures in the activity.

CLOSE AND ASSESS

Ask students to give an example of cause and effect from their own lives:
Cause: *I studied hard for the test.*
Effect: *I got the best grade in the class.*

RESPOND

OBJECTIVES

PRESENT PERFECT TENSE

Grammar: Ⓣ Present Perfect Tense Verbs

KEEP A DIARY

Functions: Express Feelings; Write

Writing: Diary

LANGUAGE ARTS AND LITERATURE

1 Use the Present Perfect Tense
Answers to the Practice items are:

Practice

1. has spoken
2. have gone
3. have left

▶ **Practice Book** page 136

2 Keep a Diary Remind students that a diary is a record of daily events, experiences, and observations. Explain that diary writing has a number of benefits: It provides a valuable record of thoughts, dreams, memories, and experiences. It also offers easy and enjoyable writing practice and can serve as a useful resource for future writing ideas.

CLOSE AND ASSESS

Have students work in small heterogeneous groups to create a sentence telling what they learned in this lesson. Each group should share their sentence with the class.

ASSESSMENT
Selection Test 16 on page 69 of the Assessment Handbook tests students' mastery of the reading strategies and the vocabulary, comprehension, and language arts skills taught with this selection.

Respond to the Diary, continued

Language Arts and Literature

GRAMMAR IN CONTEXT

USE THE PRESENT PERFECT TENSE

Learn About the Present Perfect Tense The **present perfect tense** is formed in this way:

has + past participle

have + past participle

Use the present perfect tense when you need to tell about an action that began in the past and may still be going on. You can also use the present perfect tense when you aren't sure of the exact time of the past action.

Learn About Past Participles Most verbs form the past tense and past participle by adding *-ed.*

Verb	Past	Past Participle
happen	happened	happened

Some verbs have irregular forms. Study the examples. See Handbook pages 450–451 for more irregular verbs.

Present	Past	Past Participle
go	went	gone
leave	left	left
speak	spoke	spoken

Practice Write each sentence. Add *has* or *have* and a past participle from the list above.

1. Anne's mother ________ to Mr. van Daan about going into hiding.
2. The Franks ________ to the annex.
3. The Franks ________ their home forever.

WRITING

KEEP A DIARY

Anne enjoyed writing in her diary and wanted to be published. Write in your own diary for one week. Then choose one entry that you would like to share with your classmates.

1. **Prepare to Write** Think about something that is important to you. You may want to write about school, family, friends, or your feelings. Write your first entry. Put the day and date at the top. Use Anne Frank's diary as a model.
2. **Make Daily Entries** Write in your diary every day for a week. Choose a quiet time and place where you can write in private. Use the correct verb tenses in your entries.
3. **Publish** Choose an entry that does not give away any information you don't want to share. Publish your entry in a class diary.

Sample Entry

Tuesday, February 1, 2001

Dear Diary,
Today I made a new friend. His name is Eric, and he's from Guatemala. He's shy but very nice. I hope we become the best of friends!

Yours,
Tara

Review **verbs** on Handbook pages 444–454.

REACHING ALL STUDENTS

Multi-Level Strategies

WRITING OPTIONS FOR KEEPING A DIARY

BEGINNING Provide students with concrete questions to help generate ideas for diary entries: *Did anything interesting happen to you today? What did you do in school? Whom did you talk to? What did you talk about?*

INTERMEDIATE Ask students to write in their diaries, not only describing their daily activities, but also sharing their thoughts and feelings. Provide thought-provoking questions, such as: *What are you most excited about in your life right now? Why? What are you most worried about?*

ADVANCED Encourage students to use descriptive language that will help the diary reader understand the events, thoughts, and feelings recorded in the diary. Instruct students to review and edit their diary entries before sharing them with the class.

Content Area Connections

TECHNOLOGY/MEDIA

EVALUATE AND USE WEB SITES

Web sites differ in quality. Evaluate Web sites and choose one for research.

1. **Visit Web Sites** Find at least five sites about World War II or Anne Frank. Remember that new Web sites appear every day, but these might be a good place to start.

INTERNET

INFORMATION ON-LINE

Key Words:
Anne Frank

Web Sites:
➤ **Sites about Anne Frank**
• www.annefranknm.com
• come.to/annefrank

2. **Evaluate Web Sites** What do the Web sites show? Are they easy to understand and use? Do they give enough information? Summarize your findings.

Example:

Anne Frank Center USA—shows museum exhibits; easy to use; lots of links

3. **Make an Oral Report** With a group, use the best site to conduct more research. Report your findings to the class.

Learn to use the **Internet** on Handbook pages 392–393.

SOCIAL STUDIES

EXPLORE LEGACIES

Anne Frank's life left an important legacy to the world. What other people from World War II left important legacies? Learn more about leaders from this period, then role-play these figures in a class simulation.

1. **Choose a Figure** Here is a list of key figures from World War II. Choose one to research.
   - Winston Churchill, British Prime Minister
   - Franklin Delano Roosevelt, U.S. President
   - Eleanor Roosevelt, First Lady of the U.S.
   - General Dwight D. Eisenhower, Supreme Allied Commander
   - Albert Einstein, scientist
   - A. Philip Randolph, labor activist
   - Hirohito, Emperor of Japan
   - Josephine Baker, member of French resistance
2. **Research** Use encyclopedias, history books, and the Internet to learn about your leader.
3. **Stage a Dinner** Pretend that all the leaders are having dinner together. Take the role of the leader you researched. Answer questions about your participation in the war and your legacy.

Research Skills

▶ USING SEARCH ENGINES

TEACH Explain that a search engine is a tool for finding subject-specific information on the Internet. Point out that there is an enormous amount of information on the World Wide Web, and that search engines make it possible to navigate through this information to target a specific subject. Point out that this makes a search engine an invaluable research tool. Explain how to conduct a search using key words related to a desired topic.

PRACTICE Give each pair of students a topic to research on the Internet. Suggest an age-appropriate search engine, such as www.yahooligans.com. After students have conducted their research, have them give a short oral report on both what they learned about their topic and their experience using the search engine.

RESPOND

OBJECTIVES

WEB SITES

Functions:
T Give Information; Express Opinions
Critical Thinking: Evaluate Information
Technology/Media and Research Skills: Use the Internet; Use Search Engines
Speaking: Oral Report

LEGACIES

Function: Ask and Answer Questions
Learning Strategies and Research Skills: Locate Resources; Gather Information; Interact with Peers
Speaking: Simulation

CONTENT AREA CONNECTIONS

1. **Evaluate and Use Web Sites** Web sites about World War II, the Holocaust, and Anne Frank are frequently of a graphic nature. Preselect the search engines to be sure students visit age-appropriate Web sites for their evaluations.

   For Multi-Level Strategies: Guide Beginning students to use search engines. Read aloud from the sites, clarifying information. Discuss the value and appropriateness of each Web site and summarize findings as a group.

   Encourage each Intermediate student to work with an Advanced student to evaluate Web sites. Give them additional criteria to use: *Are the sites well-designed and easy to follow? Are there pictures or other graphics to help you understand? Are the sentences too long and complex?*

2. **Explore Legacies** Have students use a biographical dictionary to look up basic information about the World War II leaders.

▶ **Practice Book** page 137

CLOSE AND ASSESS

Have students add something about this selection to each side of the unit mind maps they began on page T213.

BUILD WRITING SKILLS

OBJECTIVES

Function: Engage in Discussion; Listen Actively
Reading Strategy and Critical Thinking: Use Text Structures (cause and effect); Analyze and Evaluate Information
Listening: Listen Critically
Literary Analysis and Writing: Ⓣ Expository (content-area report)

INTRODUCE WRITING THAT INFORMS AND EXPLAINS

1. **Discuss Expository Writing** Read the introduction and ask students to think of examples of expository writing. Help them recall specific topics by prompting them in content areas such as science and history.
2. **Study the Professional Model** Read the excerpt and ask students how they know it is an example of expository writing. (Students should identify the scientific facts about trees and wind.)
3. **Explore Text Structure** Explain that expository writing often tells how one event causes another. Use the Cause-and-Effect Chart to teach one way to structure expository writing.

Use the Options for Studying Text Structure in the **Multi-Level Strategies** to adjust instruction.

Writing That Informs and Explains

Expository writing gives information. Often the writer explains facts about a topic. The writer may also explain how something happens, how it works, and why it is important or interesting.

PROFESSIONAL WRITING MODEL

"The Big Blast" is a nonfiction article about a real event—the 1980 eruption of Mount St. Helens. The writer uses scientific facts and descriptions to explain what happened.

***from* "The Big Blast"**

> The blast flattened whole forests of 180-foot-high firs. . . . At first, this damage was puzzling. A wind of 200 miles an hour is not strong enough to level forests of giant trees. The explanation, geologists later discovered, was that the wind carried rocks ranging in size from grains of sand to blocks as big as cars. . . .
> The result was what one geologist described as a "stone wind."

A CAUSE-AND-EFFECT CHART

When writing nonfiction, writers often explain causes and effects. A cause-and-effect chart can help you understand how events are related. Use the chart below to discuss some of the causes and effects in "The Big Blast."

Cause-and-Effect Chart for "The Big Blast"

Cause	 earthquake hits	avalanche occurs	 volcano opens	steam shoots out	rock shatters
Effect	avalanche occurs	tears hole in Mt. St.Helens; volcano opens 	blast of steam shoots out	rock shatters 	a stone wind fo

REACHING ALL STUDENTS

Transparency 69 / Master 69

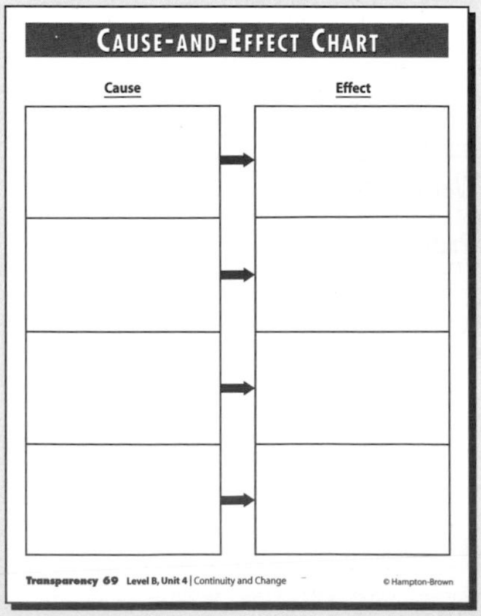
CAUSE-AND-EFFECT CHART

Cause	Effect

Transparency 69 Level B, Unit 4 | Continuity and Change © Hampton-Brown

Multi-Level Strategies

OPTIONS FOR STUDYING TEXT STRUCTURE

BEGINNING Set up a simple demonstration of cause and effect: push a chair into a desk to cause a book to fall, knocking another book over. Then have pairs tell or act out the first event, or cause, and its effect. Record causes and effects on **Transparency 69**. Afterward, use the chart on page 282 to discuss the causes and effects in "The Big Blast."

INTERMEDIATE / **ADVANCED** Go over the Cause-and-Effect Chart for "The Big Blast," pointing out that events are explained as a series of causes and effects. Then have pairs complete **Master 69** about a simple demonstration such as that described above. Ask volunteers to state the relationships between events on their chart in cause-and-effect terms.

ENT WRITING MODEL

nt-Area Report

y Pompeii Is Famous

Claudia Rizo

Pompeii was a city in ancient Italy. It is famous today because a disaster that happened about two thousand years ago.

Pompeii was located near a volcano named Mount Vesuvius. For long as the people of Pompeii could remember, Vesuvius had n quiet. Then in 62 CE, there was a sudden earthquake, causing nage to Pompeii and other nearby towns. People rebuilt the city. ey thought the danger was past, but they were mistaken.

Early in the afternoon of August 24, 79 CE, disaster struck. h a loud roar, Mount Vesuvius erupted so violently that it blew top off. It kept erupting throughout the night. Showers of t ash, stone, and flaming cinder fell on Pompeii. Later on, son gas filled the air.

The residents of Pompeii panicked. Many grabbed what they ild and ran out of the town. The people who stayed in Pompeii not survive. Some were killed by falling stones or hot ash. me hid but died from the poisonous air. When the eruptions led, Pompeii was buried under twelve feet of ash, cinder, and ne. As the years went by, grass covered the site. Pompeii appeared.

For a while, the city was forgotten. But one of the people who l escaped, Pliny the Younger, wrote about the disaster. People ndered where Pompeii was buried. Then in 1748, scientists gan to uncover the ancient city. The ash that buried Pompeii also served it. By pouring plaster into casts, scientists created atues" of those who were left behind. Then they could see actly what the people were like and what they were doing.

Today many people visit Pompeii to see what an ancient city ks like. Some come to study Mount Vesuvius. They hope to rn more about volcanoes so that no one else will have to suffer way the people of Pompeii did almost 2000 years ago.

INTRODUCTION
The **introduction** tells what the report is about, the ancient city of Pompeii.

BODY
The middle paragraphs, or the **body**, give the facts. Here Claudia tells about the volcanic eruption and its effects on Pompeii.

Each paragraph starts with a **topic sentence** that tells one main idea about the subject.

The **information** presented in a report must be accurate. The writer found and checked facts in two or more reliable sources.

CONCLUSION
The **conclusion** sums up the report. Claudia tells how the eruption has affected our lives today.

STUDY A STUDENT WRITING MODEL

4 Listen for Causes and Effects Have students take notes on copies of **Master 69** as you read the Student Model aloud. Go over their notes together to identify the causes and effects of the Pompeii disaster.

5 Analyze and Evaluate Reports Display **Transparency 70** and lead students in studying the features of a content-area report. Students should then evaluate the Student Model against the rubric on the transparency.

Use the Roles for Cooperative Groups in the **Multi-Level Strategies** to involve all students.

CLOSE AND ASSESS

Call on a different **Reporter** to share the group conclusions for each feature on **Master 70.** Encourage students to add other relevant information each time, either verbally or by drawing quick sketches to represent their ideas.

Multi-Level Strategies

ROLES FOR COOPERATIVE GROUPS

BEGINNING / **INTERMEDIATE** / **ADVANCED** Distribute **Master 70** to groups of three students with varying proficiencies and have them compare the model to the rubric. Assign these roles:

▶ **Illustrator** ▶ **Researcher** ▶ **Reporter**

Before groups begin, work through the title and the first feature, pointing out the sample answer. Then prompt groups to continue analyzing the model: the **Researcher** points out one or more examples of each feature; the **Illustrator** provides a diagram or drawing to represent information graphically whenever possible; and the **Recorder** checks the box, writes examples in the chart, and labels the drawings and diagrams.

Transparency 70 / Master 70

FEATURES OF EXPOSITORY WRITING

Directions: Read "Why Pompeii Is Famous" and compare it to the features of a content-area report. Check the box if "Why Pompeii Is Famous" shows the feature. Then give an example.

Content-Area Report. . . Why Pompeii Is Famous

tells about a **real event.**	☑ tells what happened to Pompeii when Mount Vesuvius erupted in 79 CE
has an **introduction** that names the **topic.**	☑ The report is about the ancient city of Pompeii which is famous because of a two-thousand-year-old disaster.
has a **body** that presents **accurate facts.**	☑ On August 24, 79 CE Mount Vesuvius erupted and buried Pompeii. In 1748, the buried city was discovered.
can explain what happened by telling the **causes and effects.**	☑ An earthquake struck, causing damage to Pompeii. Mount Vesuvius erupted and people were killed. Pompeii was buried under ash, cinder, and stone.
has a **conclusion** that sums up the report.	☑ People hope to learn from Pompeii how to avoid similar disasters.

Transparency 70 Level B, Unit 4 | Continuity and Change

BUILD WRITING SKILLS

OBJECTIVES

PREWRITE

Function: Write

Learning Strategies and Critical Thinking: Plan; Generate Ideas; Interact with Peers; Relate Cause and Effect; Organize Ideas; Self-Assess

Representing: Outline

Writing: Ⓣ Writing Process

PRESENT THE WRITING PROCESS AND PROMPT

Read the prompt together. Then leaf through pages 284–288 to review the stages in the Writing Process.

For more about the Writing Process, refer students to pages 408–413 in the Handbook.

PREWRITE

Before students begin their prewriting, preview the steps with the group and discuss the sample FATP chart.

Use the Prewriting Support in the **Multi-Level Strategies** to tailor this stage to proficiency levels.

CLOSE AND ASSESS

Have students work with a partner to answer the questions in Reflect and Evaluate.

The Writing Process

WRITING PROMPT

Write a report for your classmates on a science or social studies topic that includes a cause and its effects. Explain what happened. Tell why it happened.

PREWRITE

1. **Collect Ideas and Choose a Topic** Who or what would you like to learn more about? Brainstorm a list of ideas with a partner. Cross out ideas that do not involve causes and effects. Then choose a topic that would be the most interesting to your audience.
2. **Unlock the Writing Prompt** Before you begin writing, fill out an FATP chart.
3. **Collect Information** Use at least two sources to find information on your topic. Take notes. Keep a list of your sources. Go back to them if you need to. See pages 394–399 of the Handbook for tips on doing research and taking notes.
4. **Get Organized** Look through your notes to identify the causes and effects you want to include in your report. Create an outline. Use Roman numerals for main ideas and capital letters for supporting details.

Topic of Report — Toussaint L'Ouverture, Freedom Fighter

Introduction — I. Who was Toussaint L'Ouverture?

Main Idea — II. What was the early history of the French colony in Haiti?

Supporting Detail — A. What caused the French to set up this colony?

B. Why did they bring over African slaves?

III. What happened during the slave revolt of 1791?

A. What caused this revolt?

B. What was Toussaint's role?

IV. What happened as a result of this revolt?

A. What did the French do?

B. What did Toussaint do?

Conclusion — V. Why is Toussaint important? What is his effect today?

FATP Chart

HOW TO UNLOCK A PROM

Form: *report*

Audience: *classmates*

Topic: *Toussaint L'Ouverture*

Purpose: *to explain what caused him to lead a revo and the effects of his fight for freedom*

Reflect and Evalua

- How did working with a partner help you choose a topic?
- Did you find all the information you need? A your facts accurate?
- As you organized your outline, did you focus or causes and effects?

REACHING ALL STUDENTS

Multi-Level Strategies

PREWRITING SUPPORT

BEGINNING Provide several print resources with numerous illustrations and diagrams. Have students choose one topic from the resources. Ask them to create a two-column chart and label the columns *Cause* and *Effect*. Have them draw the cause-and-effect relationships in the columns. Then they can dictate, write, or illustrate an FATP chart.

INTERMEDIATE Suggest that students look through their textbooks to collect ideas. Then have them fill out FATP charts with partners. Check the charts and recommend further resources for their topics. Students can organize their facts on copies of **Master 69**. (See page T282.)

ADVANCED Encourage students to use the Internet to find ideas and resources for topics they choose. Have them take notes as they go, and then organize the facts on **Master 69** (see page T282) or in an outline.

FT

/our **FATP** chart to focus your writing. Write quickly to get your ideas n on paper. Don't worry about making mistakes on your draft.

ntroduce Your Topic Your title should make clear what your report ; about. The opening paragraph should introduce your topic and park your audience's interest.

Vrite the Body of Your Report Use your outline to write your eport. Make your writing interesting and clear. If you decide you want o add more information, go back to your notes or to your sources.

Writer's Craft: Sentence Variety and Elaboration

Vary the way your sentences begin.

Just OK	Much Better
Toussaint L'Ouverture was a famous freedom fighter. Many people think he is the greatest freedom fighter of all time. Toussaint L'Ouverture was born a slave in the French colony of Saint Domingue. Toussaint led a slave revolt against the slaveholders.	To many people, Toussaint L'Ouverture is the greatest freedom fighter that ever lived. Born a slave in the French colony of Saint Domingue, he led a revolt against the slaveholders.

Add more information to your sentences to make the causes and effects clear.

Just OK	Much Better
Toussaint became the leader of Saint Domingue. The colony did well. Then, in 1802, the French ruler Napoleon sent an army to Saint Domingue.	Toussaint became the leader of Saint Domingue. The colony did well because of his wise leadership. By 1802, the French ruler Napoleon decided he wanted the colony back under French control, so he sent an army to Saint Domingue.

Vrite a Conclusion In your last paragraph, sum up your topic. ell why it is important to know about this person or event.

Reflect and Evaluate

- Look over your draft. Do you want to add more information?
- Have you made it easy for your reader to identify causes and effects?
- Are your sentences varied and interesting?

OBJECTIVES

DRAFT

Function: Ⓣ Give Information; Write

Learning Strategies and Critical Thinking: Generate Ideas; Self-Assess

Writer's Craft: Ⓣ Sentence Variety and Elaboration

Writing: Ⓣ Writing Process

DRAFT

Before students begin their drafts, discuss the Writer's Craft models in **Step 2**. Ask volunteers to explain why the second model in each pair of passages is "Much Better."

Use the Drafting Support in the **Multi-Level Strategies** to tailor this stage to proficiency levels.

For more about the Writer's Craft, refer students to pages 414–423 in the Handbook.

CLOSE AND ASSESS

Have small groups discuss the questions in Reflect and Evaluate while you work with those who may need more support in assessing their drafts.

Multi-Level Strategies

DRAFTING SUPPORT

BEGINNING Guide students in drafting a clear introduction for their reports. For subsequent parts, have them return to their cause-and-effect charts and complete sentence frames to express relationships between events. _____ *because* _____; _____ *caused* _____; *When* _____ *happened*, _____. Help them with wording their ideas to fit the frames. Finally, guide students in writing a strong conclusion.

INTERMEDIATE / **ADVANCED** Have partners apply the Writer's Craft skill as they create the "Much Better" examples on **Master 71**. Encourage students to apply what they have learned about sentence variety and elaboration as they draft their own content-area reports.

Transparency 71 / Master 71

WRITING: VARIETY AND ELABORATION

Directions: Read each writing tip and the example that is "Just OK." Change the example to make it "Much Better."

Writing Tips	Just OK	Much Better
Vary the way your sentences begin.	Pompeii was located near a volcano. The volcano was named Mount Vesuvius.	Pompeii was located near a volcano named Mount Vesuvius.
	The volcano had been quiet for many years. The people did not believe they were in any danger.	Because the volcano had been quiet for many years, the people did not believe they were in any danger.
Add more information to your sentences to make the causes and effects clear.	Many people wanted to know about Pompeii. Today we can see what the city looked like.	Many people wanted to know about Pompeii so scientists uncovered the ancient city in 1748. Today we can see what the city looked like because the ash that buried it also preserved it.

Transparency 71 Level B, Unit 4 | Continuity and Change

BUILD WRITING SKILLS

OBJECTIVES

REVISE

Function: Write; Engage in Discussion
Learning Strategies and Critical Thinking: Generate Ideas; Review; Clarify; Interact with Peers; Self-Assess
Listening and Speaking: Peer-Conferencing
Writing: T Writing Process

REVISE

First have students reread their drafts. They should turn the entries on their FATP charts into questions to answer as they assess their work. For example: *Does my report explain what caused Toussaint to lead a revolt?*

Next, model how to evaluate someone else's writing in a peer conference by asking questions about the content and clarity of the draft. Also model how a writer makes revisions. Students can then conduct the peer conferences and revise their drafts.

Use the Peer Conference Support in the **Multi-Level Strategies** to model how to evaluate and revise writing.

CLOSE AND ASSESS

Have peers discuss the questions in Reflect and Evaluate.

Writing That Informs and Explains, continued

REVISE

1. **Reread Your Draft** Check your draft against your **FATP**. Does it match the form, audience, topic, and purpose you listed? Have you written about causes and effects? Have you checked your facts?

2. **Conduct a Peer Conference** Hold a roundtable discussion to read and evaluate each other's reports. Look at the flow of the sentences: Are they too short and choppy? Do any run on? Use the guidelines on Handbook page 411 to help you.

Read what Marco's group had to say during a Peer Conference. Notice how Marco decides to make changes.

Round Table Peer Conferencing

Lilia: You have 5 short sentences in a row: "It was August 22. The revolt began. Some black slaves rebelled against their owners. Then hundreds joined them. Then thousands joined." Try to combine some of them.

Marco: Is this better? "The revolt began on August 22, when some black slaves rebelled against their owners. Hundreds and then thousands joined them."

Peter: That sounds better.

Veronica: The next sentence is too long, and some of it doesn't make sense. I think it is a run-on.

Marco: You're right! I'll change it to "At first, Toussaint did not fight. He even led his master and mistress to safety. When he finally felt he had to fight, he showed that he was a good leader."

3. **Mark Your Changes** Review your notes and decide how you want to change your writing. Revising Marks appear on Handbook page 411.

Reflect and Evalu

- Did your peers find you report interesting and informative? Were thei suggestions helpful?
- Did you need to revise y sentences? If so, what problems did you corre
- Were you able to inclu most of the interesting facts you found about y topic?

REACHING ALL STUDENTS

Transparency 72 / Master 72

REVISING

Red annotations show changes related to the sample comments.
Revisions should vary to reflect comments students make.

Pompeii was located near a volcano named Mount Vesuvius. [For as long as the people of Pompeii could remember,] Vesuvius had been quiet.

Then, [in 62 CE] there was a sudden earthquake, causing damage to Pompeii and other nearby towns.

People rebuilt the city. They thought the danger was past, [but] they were mistaken.

Revising Marks	
^	Add.
↩	Move to here.
↖	Replace with this.
⤳	Take out.

Ask Questions in a Peer Conference

1. Ask about what else you want to know.
   - How long had Vesuvius been quiet?
   - Students' questions will vary.
2. Ask about any facts that you think are missing.
   - Can you add exactly when the earthquake happened?
   - Students' questions will vary.
3. Ask a question to make a suggestion.
   - Can you combine some of the short sentences at the end?
   - Students' questions will vary.

Transparency 72 Level B, Unit 4 | Continuity and Change © Hampton-Brown

Multi-Level Strategies

PEER CONFERENCE SUPPORT

BEGINNING Display **Transparency 72** and read the paragraph. Support students' comprehension through photos or diagrams, or by sketching the events described. Then model how to evaluate the writing, using the sample questions. Call on volunteers to make other comments. Model how to revise the writing, based on comments and questions.

INTERMEDIATE / **ADVANCED** After you read the paragraph on **Transparency 72**, model how to evaluate the writing, using the sample questions. Invite students to generate questions of their own. Have volunteers suggest revisions, based on the questions. Point out that writers can make revisions in addition to—or instead of those that others suggest.

AMMAR IN CONTEXT

MPLEX SENTENCES

mplex sentence contains one independent clause and one or more endent clauses.

Toussaint L'Ouverture

n **independent clause** expresses a complete thought. It makes sense y itself.

Examples: Toussaint taught himself to read.
He became well-educated.

dependent clause does not express a complete thought. It does not make nse by itself.

Examples: because there were no schools for slaves
although he was a slave for almost 50 years

a **complex sentence,** a subordinating conjunction connects the ependent clause to the independent clause.

Examples:
Toussaint taught himself to read (independent clause) because there were no schools for slaves. (dependent clause)

He became well-educated (independent clause) although he was a slave for almost 50 years. (dependent clause)

the dependent clause comes first, set it off with a comma.

Example:
Although he was a slave for almost 50 years, (dependent clause) he became well-educated. (independent clause)

Some Subordinating Conjunctions

after
although
because
before
if
since
until
when
where
while

ctice Combine each pair of sentences to form a complex sentence. Use bordinating conjunction. Add a comma after the dependent clause if it es first.

oussaint read about the American Revolution. He was a young man.
oussaint was willing to fight for freedom. He did not want to use violence.
he slaves rebelled on August 22, 1791. Many slave owners were killed.
oussaint did not join the rebellion. He first led his master and mistress o safety.
ater Toussaint joined the rebellion. He proved to be a great leader.

OBJECTIVES

GRAMMAR IN CONTEXT
Grammar: T Complex Sentences

GRAMMAR IN CONTEXT

1 **Teach Complex Sentences** Work with students to read the definitions and study the examples. Then conduct the cooperative learning activity below.

2 **Answers to Practice Items** Student answers will vary. These are samples:

1. When he was a young man, Toussaint read about the American Revolution.
2. Toussaint was willing to fight for freedom although he did not want to use violence.
3. Many slave owners were killed when the slaves rebelled on August 22, 1791.
4. Toussaint did not join the rebellion until he first led his master and mistress to safety.
5. After Toussaint joined the rebellion, he proved to be a great leader.

CLOSE AND ASSESS

Have partners each write an independent clause. Then have them switch papers and add a dependent clause to create a complex sentence.

Cooperative Learning

FOR LANGUAGE DEVELOPMENT: Complex Sentences

Materials: index card for each student

Create Complex Sentences Put students in groups of four and give each group member a number. Provide four independent clauses and assign one to each numbered student: Number 1s will start with the sentence *I missed the bus.* Students add a dependent clause and write the resulting complex sentence on an index card. Have students help each other complete their sentences.

Debrief the Skills Call on group members by number to share their sentences. Tally the subordinating conjunctions used. Ask: *Which subordinating conjunction was used most often? Why is that? What does a dependent clause add to a sentence?*

Debrief the Cooperative Process Have students reflect on the process: *Did discussing the sentences help you understand the two kinds of clauses?*

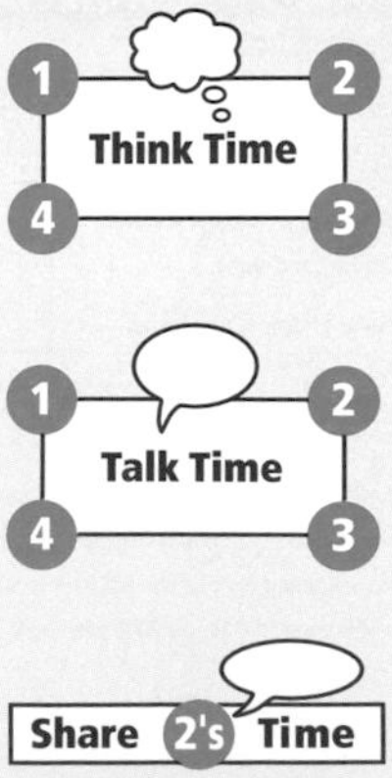

Cooperative Learning Structure: Numbered Heads

BUILD WRITING SKILLS

OBJECTIVES

EDIT AND PROOFREAD

Learning Strategies and Critical Thinking: Review; Clarify; Self-Assess

Writing: Ⓣ Writing Process

PUBLISH

Learning Strategies and Critical Thinking: Interact with Peers; Self-Assess; Make Decisions

Speaking: Read Aloud

Writing: Ⓣ Writing Process

EDIT AND PROOFREAD

Before students edit and proof their own writing, use **Transparency 73** to model the process.

PUBLISH

Ask volunteers to share publishing ideas or choose from those suggested on page 288.

Use the Editing and Publishing Support in the **Multi-Level Strategies** to meet the varying needs of all students.

CLOSE AND ASSESS

Have groups discuss the questions in Reflect and Evaluate. Monitor how students complete the checklist.

WRITING ASSESSMENT
Use the Writing Rubric on page 71 of the Assessment Handbook to evaluate this writing assignment.

Writing That Informs and Explains, continued

EDIT AND PROOFREAD

1. **Check for Mistakes** Carefully read your report and correct any mistakes in capitalization, punctuation, and spelling. If you need help, use Handbook pages 459–469.
2. **Check Your Sentences** Did you combine short sentences to make complex sentences? Did you avoid any run-on sentences?
3. **Make a Final Copy** Neatly hand copy your report. Or, if you are working on a computer, print out a final copy.

PUBLISH

Choose one of these ideas for publishing your report, or come up with your own idea.

- Put your report in a binder. Add drawings, charts, or maps. At the back, list a variety of book titles, magazine articles, movies, and Internet sites on your subject.

To Find Out More About Toussaint...

• Read These Books	• Visit These Sites
Toussaint L'Ouverture–The Fight for Haiti's Freedom by Walter Dean Myers	www.pbs.org/wgbh/aia
	encarta.msn.com
Toussaint L'Ouverture–Lover of Liberty by Laurence Santrey	britannica.com

- Give an oral report. Create a diagram or a 3-D model to show how the causes led to the effects. As part of your report, walk your audience through your display.

Reflect and Evalua[te]

- Are you pleased with how your report turned out? Does it
  - ☑ clearly introduce your topic?
  - ☑ include well-organized sentences and paragraphs that tell about causes and effects?
  - ☑ present accurate facts?
  - ☑ sum up your topic at the end?
- Did you enjoy finding out about your topic? Do you want to find out more—or do you wish you had picked a different topic?
- What was the hardest part of doing research? What part was the most fun?

REACHING ALL STUDENTS

Transparency 73 / Master 73

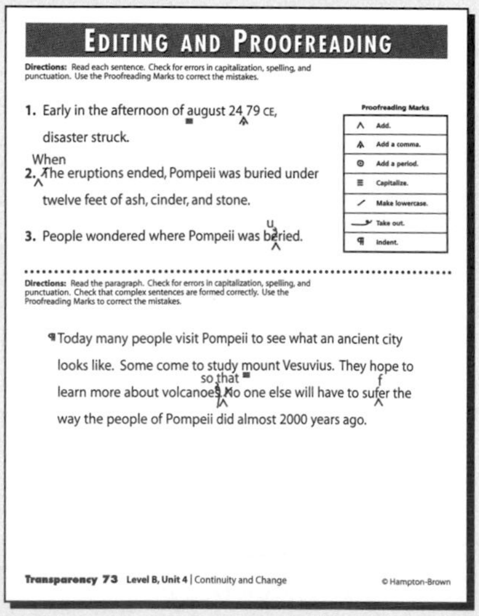

EDITING AND PROOFREADING

Directions: Read each sentence. Check for errors in capitalization, spelling, and punctuation. Use the Proofreading Marks to correct the mistakes.

1. Early in the afternoon of august 24 79 CE, disaster struck.
2. (When) The eruptions ended, Pompeii was buried under twelve feet of ash, cinder, and stone.
3. People wondered where Pompeii was beried. (u)

Proofreading Marks	
^	Add.
^,	Add a comma.
⊙	Add a period.
≡	Capitalize.
/	Make lowercase.
⟿	Take out.
¶	Indent.

Directions: Read the paragraph. Check for errors in capitalization, spelling, and punctuation. Check that complex sentences are formed correctly. Use the Proofreading Marks to correct the mistakes.

¶ Today many people visit Pompeii to see what an ancient city looks like. Some come to study mount Vesuvius. They hope to learn more about volcanoes. (so that) No one else will have to sufer (f) the way the people of Pompeii did almost 2000 years ago.

Transparency 73 Level B, Unit 4 | Continuity and Change © Hampton-Brown

Multi-Level Strategies

EDITING AND PUBLISHING SUPPORT

BEGINNING Model finding and correcting errors in the top section of **Transparency 73**. After marking the edits, have students write out the corrected sentences. Students can use their drawings from the Prewrite stage to include with their reports. Bind their work together with others' in a "Science" or "Social Studies" collection for the class library.

INTERMEDIATE Guide students in finding and correcting the errors in the paragraph at the bottom of **Transparency 73**. For publishing, students may wish to illustrate their reports and display them in the school library.

ADVANCED Distribute copies of **Master 73** and have students work on the activities individually or with partners. Students may want to give an oral report with diagrams or models.

ebrief

Coming Full Circle

UNIT 4

ASSESSMENT
The Unit 4 Test on page 73 of the Assessment Handbook measures students' progress in reading, language arts, literary study, and writing. Additional forms in the Assessment Handbook allow for:
- **Self Assessment on page 72**
- **Peer Assessment on page 101**
- **Portfolio Evaluation on page 103**

Look Back at the Unit

Rate the Selections In this unit, you read about events that are examples of continuity and change. You also read about people who experienced our ever-changing world.

The Mother Who Lost Her Daughter | The Big Blast | Anne Frank | The Diary of a Young Girl

Work with a partner to list the titles in order from your favorite to your least favorite. Share your list with the class. Together discuss the selection that offers the best example of continuity, the one that offers the best example of change, and the one that provides the best example of both.

Show What You Know

Sum It All Up Expand and organize your ideas on this mind map. Share your ideas about continuity and change with a partner.

Reflect and Evaluate Write about an event that has changed your life. Add this writing to your portfolio, along with the work from the unit that shows what you learned.

Make Connections

To Your Community Find a place in your community that has changed over time. Report your findings to the class. Tell whether the change was caused by natural events or by people's decisions to make changes.

DEBRIEF UNIT 4

OBJECTIVES

Function: Engage in Discussion; Express Opinions

Learning Strategies and Critical Thinking: Interact with Peers; Generate Ideas; Make Judgments; Summarize; Self-Assess; Form Opinions; Evaluate Information; Use Graphic Organizers (mind map)

Literary Analysis: Respond to Literature; Compare and Evaluate Literature

EXPLORE "COMING FULL CIRCLE"

1. **Look Back at the Unit** Discuss possible criteria for deciding on a favorite selection, for example: *identifying with story or character.* Then conduct the Cooperative Learning Activity.
2. **Show What You Know** When writing about the impact of an event, students may consider its resonance in the future.
3. **Make Connections** Brainstorm old buildings in town that have been torn down and describe what has replaced them.

CLOSE AND ASSESS

Have students tell you the most important thing they learned in the unit.

Cooperative Learning

FOR CRITICAL THINKING: Make Judgments

Rate Selections Give partners time to rate the selections. Then have them gather in groups according to their top-rated selection. Review the responsibilities of each role: (Supervisor, Recorder, Reporter, and Checker).

Discussing Selections Groups discuss how their selection exemplifies continuity and/or change. After discussions, ask each Reporter to report to the class. Have the class decide together which selections best represent continuity, change, or both.

Debrief the Content Model a response for sharing what was learned from the unit and discussions: *I realized that we cannot stop change from occurring.*

Debrief the Cooperative Process Have students evaluate what they learned by discussing the selections with a group. Ask: *Did your partner or group members give you new reasons for liking your favorite selection?*

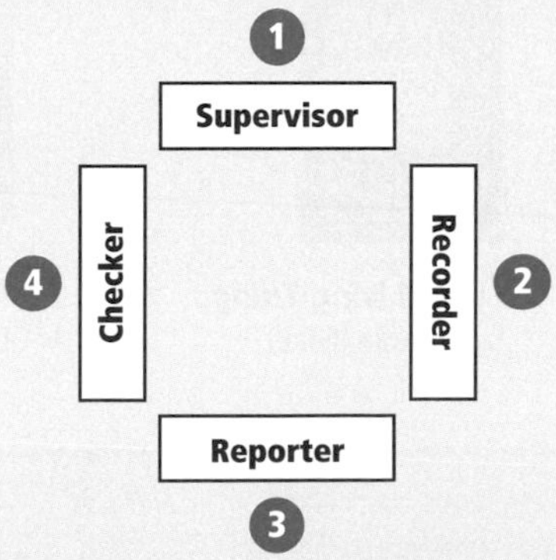

Roles for Cooperative Groups

Resources

For Success in Language, Literature, and Content

Student Book pages 290–363

For Skills Practice

Practice Book
pages 138–172

For Planning and Instruction

Teacher's Edition
pages T290a–T363

For Vocabulary and Language Development

Language Tape Side B
Language CD Tracks 6 and 7

For Selection Readings

Selection Tape 5
Selection CD 5

For Technology Support

Inspiration
Visual Learning Software
with Graphic Organizers

For Classroom Activities

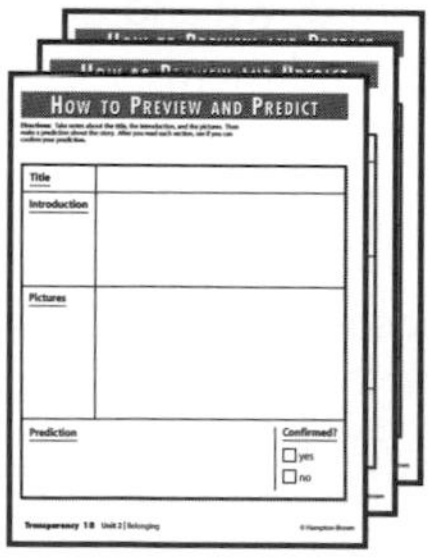

Transparencies or Masters 74–92

For Home-School Connections

High Point Newsletters 9 and 10

For Comprehensive Assessment

Language Acquisition Assessment, Selection Tests, Unit Test, Writing Assessment, Self-Assessment

In the Theme Library

Every Living Thing
by Cynthia Rylant

Wings
by Jane Yolen

From *The Basics Bookshelf*

- ***Rachel Carson: A Woman Who Loved Nature***
- ***Crops***
- ***Sunny and Moonshine: A Love Story***

Theme-related books with simple text for including newcomers

Overcoming Obstacles

CHALLENGES CAN COME FROM FEELINGS WITHIN US OR EVENTS THAT HAPPEN AROUND US. WHATEVER FORM A CHALLENGE TAKES, WHAT'S MOST IMPORTANT IS TO RISE UP AND FACE IT. IN THIS UNIT, STUDENTS, WHOSE LIVES POSSESS ANY NUMBER OF OBSTACLES, EXPLORE HOW MEETING A CHALLENGE CAN MAKE A DIFFERENCE.

THEME 1 Making a Difference

Students learn that getting involved can make the world a better place.

THEME 2 Pushing Past the Limits

Students read about others who pushed past their limits to face challenges.

Activity Planner

THEME 1: Making a Difference

LESSONS

1 — THEME 1 OPENER ▶ pages T292–T293

Function	Learning Strategy	Vocabulary	Critical Thinking
Engage in Discussion	Make a Chart	Words About the Natural Environment	Formulate Hypotheses

2 — BUILD LANGUAGE AND VOCABULARY ▶ pages T294–T295

Function	Learning Strategy	Vocabulary	Patterns and Structures
Ⓣ Persuade	Brainstorm Problems and Solutions	Words Used to Persuade	Ⓣ Past Perfect Tense

PACING SUGGESTIONS

LESSONS	45–55 MINUTE PERIODS	BLOCK SCHEDULE SESSIONS
1	1 period	1 session (lessons 1–2)
2	1 period	
3–10	8 periods	4 sessions
11–16	8 periods	4 sessions

3–10 — *Saving the Peregrine Falcon* by Caroline Arnold — SCIENCE ARTICLE ▶ pages T296–T309

PREPARE TO READ
page T296

Activate Prior Knowledge
Take a Poll

Vocabulary Ⓣ
Relate Words

Reading Strategy
Ⓣ Use SQ3R

READ THE SELECTION
pages T297–T305

Pre-Reading Strategies
Preview and Predict
Identify Genre: Science Article
Set Purpose

Strategy Focus
Ⓣ Use SQ3R

Vocabulary Review
Use Structural Clues to Meaning

Self-Monitoring and Comprehension
Use Text Features in Nonfiction
Before You Move On: Think and Discuss

Grammar Minilessons:
Present Perfect Tense Verbs
Ⓣ Past Perfect Tense Verbs
Active and Passive Verbs

Literary Analysis Minilesson:
Evaluate Literature: Accuracy of Information

RESPOND
pages T306–T309

CHECK YOUR UNDERSTANDING

Critical Thinking and Comprehension
Sum It Up: Review the Article; Respond to Literature;
Ⓣ Draw Conclusions
Think It Over: Discuss and Write

Function
Express Yourself: Verify Information

LANGUAGE ARTS AND LITERATURE

Grammar in Context
Ⓣ Use the Past Perfect Tense

Writing
Write a Thank-You Letter

CONTENT AREA CONNECTIONS

Mathematics and Representing/Speaking
Graph Population Changes

Social Studies and Writing/Viewing
Investigate the Legislative Process

Technology/Media and Science
Make an Informational Poster on an Endangered Animal

11–16 — *A Celebration of the Everglades* by Frank Asch and Ted Levin — ARTICLE AND POEMS ▶ pages T310–T325

PREPARE TO READ
pages T310–T313

Activate Prior Knowledge
Idea Exchange

Vocabulary Ⓣ
Relate Words

Reading Strategy
Ⓣ Identify Author's Point of View and Purpose

READ THE SELECTION
pages T314–T321

Pre-Reading Strategies
Preview
Set Purpose

Strategy Focus
Ⓣ Identify Author's Point of View and Purpose

Vocabulary
Locate and Use Definitions

Comprehension
Before You Move On: Think and Discuss

Grammar Minilesson:
Present Perfect Tense Verbs
Ⓣ Past Perfect Tense Verbs

Literary Analysis Minilesson:
Repetition and Personification

RESPOND
pages T322–T325

CHECK YOUR UNDERSTANDING

Critical Thinking and Comprehension
Sum It Up: Respond to Literature;
Ⓣ Evaluate Literature
Think It Over: Discuss and Write

Function
Express Yourself: Persuade

LANGUAGE ARTS AND LITERATURE

Literary Analysis
Ⓣ Use Figurative Language: Metaphor

Literary Analysis and Writing
Write a Rhyming Poem

LANGUAGE ARTS AND CONTENT AREA CONNECTIONS

Technology/Media and Repesenting/Speaking
Evaluate Propaganda in the Media

Social Studies and Representing/Speaking
Explore Geography (climate zone maps)

Science and Representing
Make a Wildlife Report

Ⓣ = Assessed on **Unit 5 Test** Ⓣ = Assessed on **Unit 5 Language Acquisition Assessment**

THEME 2: Pushing Past the Limits

LESSONS

1 — THEME 2 OPENER ▶ pages T326–T327

- **Function**: Engage in Discussion
- **Learning Strategy**: Make a Chart
- **Vocabulary**: Words about Challenges
- **Critical Thinking**: Classify

2 — BUILD LANGUAGE AND VOCABULARY ▶ pages T328–T329

- **Function**: Ⓣ Elaborate
- **Learning Strategy**: Make a Word Web
- **Vocabulary**: Survival Words
- **Patterns and Structures**: Ⓣ Future Perfect Tense

PACING SUGGESTIONS

LESSONS	45–55 MINUTE PERIODS	BLOCK SCHEDULE SESSIONS
1	1 period	1 session (lessons 1–2)
2	1 period	
3–8	6 periods	3 sessions
9–10	2 periods	1 session
11–16	5 periods	3 sessions

3–8 — *The Circuit* by Francisco Jiménez — AUTOBIOGRAPHY ▶ pages T330–T342

PREPARE TO READ page T330

- **Activate Prior Knowledge**: Share Your Experiences
- **Vocabulary** Ⓣ: Locate and Use Definitions
- **Reading Strategy**: Ⓣ Relate Causes and Effects

READ THE SELECTION pages T331–T339

- **Pre-Reading Strategies**: Preview and Predict; Identify Genre: Autobiography; Set Purpose
- **Strategy Focus**: Ⓣ Relate Causes and Effects
- **Vocabulary**: Use New Words in Context
- **Self-Monitoring and Comprehension**: Visualize; Paraphrase; Relate to Personal Experience; Make Predictions; Before You Move On: Think and Discuss
- **Grammar Minilesson**: Ⓣ Past Perfect and Future Perfect Tense Verbs
- **Literary Analysis Minilessons**: Theme; Respond to Literature

RESPOND pages T340–T342

CHECK YOUR UNDERSTANDING

- **Critical Thinking and Comprehension**: Sum It Up: Ⓣ Relate Causes and Effects; Compare Life Stories; Think It Over: Discuss and Write
- **Function**: Express Yourself: Clarify and Elaborate

LANGUAGE ARTS AND LITERATURE

- **Grammar in Context**: Ⓣ Use the Future Perfect Tense
- **Writing**: Use Logical Order in Writing

CONTENT AREA CONNECTIONS

- **Social Studies**: Explore Geography (maps)
- **Technology/Media and Social Studies**: Study the "Salad Bowl to the World"

9–10 — *Mother to Son* by Langston Hughes — POEM ▶ pages T343–T345

PREPARE TO READ page T343

- **Activate Prior Knowledge**: Share Parents' Sayings
- **Vocabulary**: Relate Words
- **Reading Strategy**: Ⓣ Interpret Metaphors

READ THE POEM page T344

- **Pre-Reading Strategies**: Set Purpose
- **Strategy Focus**: Ⓣ Interpret Metaphors

RESPOND page T345

- **Critical Thinking and Comprehension**: Think It Over: Discuss
- **Function**: Express Yourself: Justify

11–16 — *The Clever Wife* by Carol Kendall and Yao-wen Li — FOLK TALE ▶ pages T346–T355

PREPARE TO READ page T346

- **Activate Prior Knowledge**: Quickwrite
- **Vocabulary** Ⓣ: Relate Words
- **Reading Strategy**: Ⓣ Summarize

READ THE SELECTION pages T347–T353

- **Pre-Reading Strategies**: Preview and Predict; Identify Genre: Folk Tale; Set Purpose
- **Strategy Focus**: Ⓣ Summarize
- **Comprehension**: Before You Move On: Think and Discuss
- **Literary Analysis Minilessons**: Onomatopoeia; Characterization: Protagonist and Minor Characters

RESPOND pages T354–T355

CHECK YOUR UNDERSTANDING

- **Critical Thinking and Comprehension**: Sum It Up: Ⓣ Summarize; Think It Over: Discuss and Write
- **Function**: Express Yourself: Persuade

LANGUAGE ARTS AND LITERATURE

- **Literary Analysis**: Evaluate How Setting Affects Characters
- **Speaking/Listening**: Sing Your Praises
- **Writing**: Ⓣ Evaluate Literature: Write a Review of a Story

BUILD WRITING SKILLS — WRITING THAT PERSUADES — PERSUASIVE: ESSAY AND SPEECH ▶ Pages T356–T362

- **Writing Mode/Form**: Ⓣ Persuasive; 5-Paragraph Essay for a Speech
- **Writing Process** Ⓣ: Prewrite; Draft; Revise; Edit and Proofread; Publish
- **Writer's Craft**: Ⓣ Important Details; Ⓣ Transitions; Effective Conclusions
- **Grammar in Context**: Ⓣ Perfect Tenses
- **Reflect and Evaluate**: Self-Assessment

Ⓣ = Assessed on **Unit 5 Test** Ⓣ = Assessed on **Unit 5 Language Acquisition Assessment**

Theme-Related Resources

THEME 1: Making a Difference

MORE RESOURCES

Every Living Thing
by Cynthia Rylant
A A collection of stories about animals that influence people's lives by causing them to see things in a different way. (Available from Hampton-Brown)

The Shaman's Apprentice
by Lynne Cherry and Mark J. Plotkin
B A young boy and a scientist work to keep the knowledge of a traditional healer alive. (Gulliver Books)

Sawgrass Poems
by Frank Asch and Ted Levin
I Poems and photographs that capture the beauty and wonder of the Everglades and its unusual plants and animals. (Gulliver Books)

Turtle Bay
by Saviour Pirotta
B A story which shows how patience and caring can help nature to take its course. (Farrar, Straus, and Giroux)

Saving the Peregrine Falcon
by Caroline Arnold
I This informative book documents how the efforts of people are rescuing peregrine falcons from extinction. (Carolrhoda)

Discoveries: Explore the Everglades Ecosystem
B I A Students study the Everglades through video, animation, and sound on this interactive CD-ROM. (Sunburst)
CD-ROM

THEME 2: Pushing Past the Limits

MORE RESOURCES

Wings
by Jane Yolen
I The Greek myth of Icarus, who learned the secret of flight. (Available from Hampton-Brown)

Wilma Unlimited
by Kathleen Krull
B Wilma Rudolph could barely walk as a child, but she overcame a crippling disease to become a gold medalist at the Olympics. (Harcourt Brace)

Call It Courage
by Armstrong Sperry
A Determined to conquer his fear of the sea, Mafatu goes to sea all alone, survives a frightening ordeal, and returns to his village a hero. (Aladdin)

Hercules: The Twelve Labors of a Legendary Hero
by Georges Moroz
I The story of Hercules's unparalleled valor as he completes the tasks given him as punishment from the gods. (Bantam Doubleday Dell)

Hatchet
by Gary Paulsen
A Finding himself suddenly alone in the Canadian wilderness, Brian must learn how to survive with only a hatchet for help. (Penguin)

Road Adventures USA
B I A Students work on geography, math, and problem-solving skills as they experience a virtual road trip across the country. (The Learning Company)
CD-ROM

B Beginning I Intermediate A Advanced

Assessment Options

ONGOING, INFORMAL ASSESSMENT

Check for understanding and achieve closure for every lesson with the targeted questions and activities in the **Close and Assess** boxes in your Teacher's Edition.

INDIVIDUAL AND GROUP-ADMINISTERED TESTS

The **Assessment Handbook** includes these comprehensive assessment tools for Unit 5:

- **Selection Tests**
  Test students' mastery of reading strategies and the vocabulary, comprehension, and language arts skills taught with each main selection of Unit 5.
- **Unit Test in Standardized Test Format**
  The multiple-choice sections of this test measure students' cumulative understanding of the skills and language developed in Unit 5. A Writing Prompt measures progress in writing skills and fluency. The Read, Think, and Explain section offers open-ended items to measure strategies and comprehension.
- **Language Acquisition Assessment**
  To verify students' ability to use the vocabulary and grammar structures taught in Unit 5, conduct these performance assessments.

UNIT 5 ASSESSMENT OPPORTUNITIES

	Assessment Handbook Pages
Unit 5 Language Acquisition Assessment	81–82
Selection Tests	
Saving the Peregrine Falcon	83–84
A Celebration of the Everglades	85–86
The Circuit	87–88
The Clever Wife	89–90
Unit 5 Writing Assessment	91
Unit 5 Self-Assessment Form	92
Unit 5 Test	93–100
Peer-Assessment Form	101
Portfolio Evaluation Form	103

SELF- AND PEER-ASSESSMENT

Students use the Unit 5 Self-Assessment Form in the **Assessment Handbook** to evaluate their own work and develop learning strategies appropriate to their needs. Students offer feedback to their classmates with the Peer-Assessment Form.

WRITING ASSESSMENT / PORTFOLIO OPPORTUNITIES

You can evaluate students' writing using the rubrics and scoring guidelines provided in the **Assessment Handbook**. Then collaborate with students to choose work for their portfolios.

INTRODUCE UNIT 5

OBJECTIVES

Function: Engage in Discussion

Concepts and Vocabulary: Challenges—*obstacles, make a difference, face or meet a challenge, get involved*

Viewing: Respond to a Photograph

Critical Thinking and Learning Strategies: Preview; Brainstorm; Build Background; Use Graphic Organizers (mind map)

INTRODUCE THE UNIT

1 **View and Discuss** Define *challenge* as "something that tests abilities and is difficult to do." Use the photograph of people climbing Mount Everest as an example. Ask: *Why would people do something this difficult and dangerous if they didn't have to?* Explain that meeting a challenge can benefit people in some important ways: *They might learn they have some strengths they didn't know about before. They might learn how to do something new. They might help solve a problem.* Then define *obstacles* as "events or conditions that make something difficult to do." Discuss the obstacles faced by the mountain climbers.

2 **Brainstorm Challenges** Ask: *What are some challenges you, your friends, your community, or your country are facing?* List the challenges. Then invite students to work with a partner to discuss and rank five or six challenges from easiest to hardest. Record some of the challenges on a class mind map and involve students in identifying obstacles, ways to meet the challenges, and what they can learn.

Use the Discussion Prompts in the **Multi-Level Strategies** to involve all students in creating mind maps.

3 **Analyze Risks and Rewards** After completing the class mind map, set up a T-chart for recording students' ideas about the positive and negative sides of meeting a challenge.

REACHING ALL STUDENTS

Multi-Level Strategies

DISCUSSION PROMPTS

BEGINNING Have each student choose a challenge they might face. Invite them to draw pictures of themselves facing the challenge. Ask: *What might make this challenge hard for you?* Encourage them to draw pictures of the obstacles and label them. Then they can create a storyboard showing how they will meet the challenge.

INTERMEDIATE / **ADVANCED** After students have ranked challenges on the mind map, invite them to choose one challenge to discuss further with a partner. Give partners a list of discussion questions: *What are the obstacles to meeting this challenge? What can you do to meet the challenge? What might you learn about yourself in the process? What problem might you solve?* Incorporate students' answers into the mind map.

Overcoming Obstacles

Few people ever reach the top of Mount Everest. Those who do have overcome many obstacles—extreme cold, fear of falling. Brainstorm other challenges. Rank them from easy to hard. Find a partner who would accept the same challenge as you. Figure out the obstacles, how you would meet the challenge, and what you would learn. What did you find out about the positive and negative sides of meeting a challenge?

THEME 1
Making a Difference
You can make the world a better place if you are willing to get involved.

THEME 2
Pushing Past the Limits
You can learn a lot about yourself by facing life's challenges and pushing past the limits.

291

PREVIEW UNIT THEMES

4 **Preview Theme 1: Making a Difference** Read aloud the theme statement. Ask students what *get involved* means. (taking an active role in meeting a challenge)

Ask students to think of a time when they got involved in a challenge. For example, the class may have raised money to take a class trip or collected food for the homeless. Ask: *What difference did your involvement make?*

Invite students to leaf through pages 293–321 and tell you who is getting involved (scientists, poets, and photographers) and what they are trying to do (save the peregrine falcon and the Everglades).

5 **Preview Theme 2: Pushing Past the Limits** Read aloud the theme statement. Ask students to brainstorm some things they might discover about themselves through facing challenges. (hidden strengths, new abilities, deep feelings)

Invite students to leaf through pages 326–353 and explain what the challenges are (dealing with family problems) and how they are met (hard work and cleverness).

6 **Set up Student Mind Maps** Have students draw the mind map in their notebooks or start the map in the **Practice Book**. Encourage them to add to the map as they move through the unit.

▶ **Practice Book** page 138

CLOSE AND ASSESS

Ask:

- *What will this unit be about?* (challenges)
- *What positive things can happen when you meet a challenge?* (You can help make the world a better place; you can grow stronger.)
- *What can you learn about yourself when you meet a challenge?* (You can discover new strengths, abilities, and deep feelings.)

UNIT 5 Mind Map

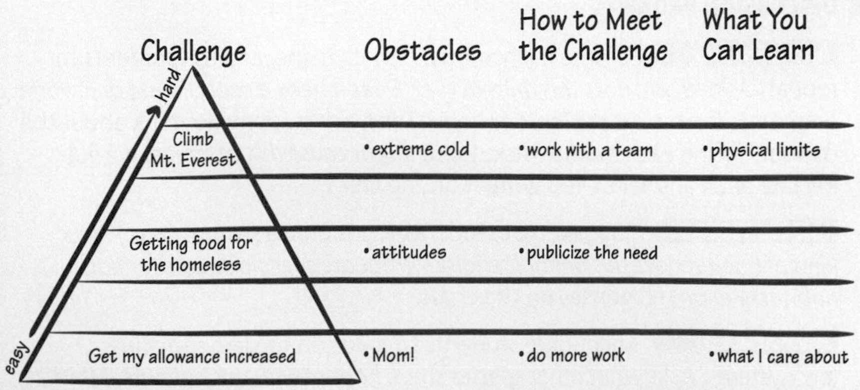

Technology Support
See **Inspiration** Visual Learning software for support in creating the mind map.

INTRODUCE THEME 1

OBJECTIVES

Function: Engage in Discussion
Concepts and Vocabulary: Natural Environment—*environment*
Viewing: Respond to Visual Images
Learning Strategies: Relate to Personal Experience; Use Graphic Organizers (chart)
Critical Thinking: Generate Ideas; Formulate Hypotheses

TAP PRIOR KNOWLEDGE

1 **Compare Challenges** Ask students to think about the challenges faced by characters in previous selections. Give this example: *Yenna in "Ginger for the Heart" met the challenge of loyalty when she refused to abandon her father.*

Ask students to brainstorm a list of other characters who met challenges and tell what differences their actions made.

VIEW AND DISCUSS

2 **Formulate Hypotheses** Read and discuss the caption beneath the picture. Define *endangered.* Then ask: *What obstacles to survival do you think these animals face?* Remind students that animals and humans need the same basic things in order to survive. Start a chart.

Obstacles to Animals' Survival	Examples
• lack of shelter (habitat)	• pollution • logging
• lack of food and water	• pollution • draining wetlands
• threats to health and safety	• hunting • pesticides

Ask questions to prompt students to add to the chart.

Use the Discussion Prompts in the **Multi-Level Strategies** to help all students participate.

Endangered Species, Andy Warhol, silkscreen. Copyright © 1983.

The Siberian tiger, black rhinoceros, and Grevy's zebra are all animals at high risk of dying out. The Pine Barrens tree frog was once endangered but is now at lower risk. People can make a difference by getting involved to help save endangered animals.

REACHING ALL STUDENTS

Multi-Level Strategies

DISCUSSION PROMPTS

BEGINNING Point to each animal, say its name, and ask students to repeat. Ask: *Where does this animal live? Does it need a cool climate or a warm one? Does it eat meat or plants or both?* Then ask students to think about the dangers facing each animal. Ask: *What might cause this animal to die out?* Restate each answer as you write it on the chart.

INTERMEDIATE Suggest that students focus on these questions: *What kind of habitat does this animal require? What are specific threats to that habitat?* Record responses on the chart.

ADVANCED Encourage students to focus on the larger picture (ecosystem). Ask: *What other species share habitat with this animal? If this animal dies out, what could happen to other species in the habitat?*

notations offer strategies for
Beginning students

THEME 1

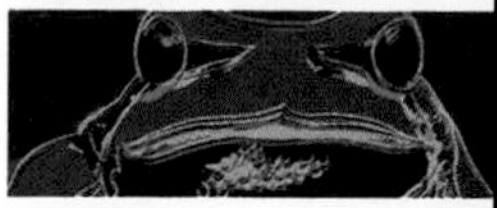

Making a Difference

Clarify: The natural
ironment is the world of
ure. It includes plants,
nals, the air we breathe,
water we drink.

- Think about our natural environment. What are some problems that need to be solved?
- Why is it important to take action as an individual or as part of a group? **B Restate:** Why should you get involved in trying to solve environmental problems?
- What are some ways in which you can make the world a better place?
  B Encourage elaboration: To encourage students to focus their responses, start a web with "solving environmental problems" as the center.

EME-RELATED BOOKS

e Shaman's Apprentice
Lynne Cherry and
rk J. Plotkin
young boy and a scientist
rk to keep the knowledge
a traditional healer alive.

GINNING

Sawgrass Poems
by Frank Asch and Ted Levin
Poems and photographs that capture the beauty and wonder of the Everglades and its unusual plants and animals.

INTERMEDIATE

Every Living Thing
by Cynthia Rylant
A collection of stories about animals that influence people's lives by causing them to see things in a different way.

ADVANCED

293

DISCUSS THE GUIDING QUESTIONS

3 **Set the Theme** Some key points to develop during the discussion are:

- Define *environment* as "the conditions around a plant or animal." Elicit that all living things need clean water, air, and soil to survive, but the pollution in many places affects their survival. Animals need space to live and find food, but with unhealthy living spaces and food sources, many species are dying.
- One person can make a difference by using less water, recycling, and not littering. Groups can make a bigger difference by cleaning up a beach or working with local government to preserve open land.
- We should all take on the challenge of making the world a better place by conserving resources and not polluting. We can raise awareness in others by discussing problems and joining groups that take action.

Form groups and use the **Multi-Level Strategies** so all students can participate.

CLOSE AND ASSESS

Ask students to write one sentence that summarizes what they have learned in this lesson about making a difference in the world and read it to the class.

Multi-Level Strategies

GROUPING GUIDELINES

BEGINNING Group these students so that you can define words and pose choices for responses. See suggestions in red on the facsimile for page 293.

INTERMEDIATE Suggest that students begin their discussion of the questions by looking back at the chart that shows threats to various species. Prompt students to give examples of individual and group actions that have helped improve the environment.

ADVANCED Ask students to write the answers to the questions and share them with a partner. Then have the group discuss the last question together, compiling a list of ideas. Encourage them to share and discuss their list with the class.

THEME LIBRARY

■ ***Every Living Thing***
by Cynthia Rylant

Invite students to read the stories in *Every Living Thing* and discuss them with a partner. Provide the following questions to guide their discussions:

- How did the characters' encounters with the animals change their lives?
- Why do you think the animals have such an impact on people?
- How have animals made a difference in your life?

BUILD LANGUAGE AND VOCABULARY

OBJECTIVES

Function: Listen Actively; Ⓣ Persuade
Concepts and Vocabulary: Words Used to Persuade
Patterns and Structures: Ⓣ Verbs in the Past Perfect Tense
Listening: Listen critically
Speaking: Persuasive Talk
Learning Strategy: Use Graphic Organizers (problem and solution chart)
Critical Thinking: Analyze Information; Solve Problems; Form Opinions

START WITH A COMMON EXPERIENCE

Tape 1B CD 1 Track 6

1 **View Photos and Discuss the Quote** Tell students that Jacques Cousteau was a scientist and environmentalist who fought to clean up pollution of our oceans. Read the quotation and identify it as an example of persuasive language. Then model how to persuade people to take action.

How to Persuade

- Tell your opinion: *We need to stop polluting the oceans now.*
- Give reasons for your opinion: *... so that ocean plants and animals will not die.*
- Use persuasive and emotional words: *The polluted waters are poisonous to wildlife. We must act before it is too late!*

2 **Listen to a Persuasive Message** Play the speech on the **Language Tape/CD** or read it aloud from page T413. Ask what the speech is about. Have students pick out words that the speech writer uses to persuade listeners to take action.

Use the Discussion Prompts in the **Multi-Level Strategies** to involve all students.

3 **Try Out Persuasive Language** Invite volunteers to paraphrase the quotation using different persuasive words to convey the same message.

Build Language and Vocabulary

PERSUADE

Look at the photos and read the quote. Then listen to a persuasive message about protecting the environment.

REACHING ALL STUDENTS

Multi-Level Strategies

DISCUSSION PROMPTS

BEGINNING Ask for information from the persuasive message: *Is the speaker talking about pollution of the water or the air?* (water) *Is the problem toxic wastes or whale hunters?* (toxic wastes) Have students write the key words on notecards.

INTERMEDIATE Point out specific ideas in the message to prompt comment from students: *Where does most of our waste end up?* (in the ocean) *What is the effect of using our oceans as dumps?* (plants and animals die) *What does Jacques Cousteau suggest?* (People need to act on their concern about pollution of the oceans.)

ADVANCED Ask these students to go beyond the literal meaning of the words as they explain the action the speaker wants us to take: *What does Jacques Cousteau mean by "make your opinions known by physical presence"? By "applauding is not enough"?*

:AINSTORM IMPORTANT PROBLEMS AND SOLUTIONS

·hat other problems in the world today require action? Work with a group to ake a list. Tell what actions need to be taken to solve the problems.

Problem-and-Solution Chart

Problem	What Actions Can Solve The Problem?
Sea plants and animals are harmed and killed by pollution.	clean up polluted waters pass laws to prevent further pollution

JILD YOUR VOCABULARY

ords Used to Persuade Work as a class. Collect words that will help you t others to do something about the problem.

Words Used to Persuade

You should. . .
We really must. . .
Let's act now to prevent. . .
The world needs your help.
Time is running out.
If you will do only one small thing each day. . .

SE LANGUAGE STRUCTURES ▶ VERBS IN THE PAST PERFECT TENSE

eaking: Give a Persuasive Talk Give a talk on a problem that concerns u. In the first sentence, state the problem. Then try to persuade others to nk or act as you do. Use at least one verb in the past perfect tense.

Example:
If you **had seen** how many animals **had been** destroyed by the oil spill, you would agree that we must act now to prevent future spills.

CONDUCT THE ACTIVITIES

4 Brainstorm Important Problems and Solutions Have students brainstorm broad categories, such as the environment, cities, and schools, before writing ideas in the chart.

5 Build Your Vocabulary: Words Used to Persuade Suggest that students look at advertisements to collect more words that persuade.

6 Use Language Structures: Verbs in the Past Perfect Tense Present the skill, using **Transparency 74**. Have students look at Handbook pages 450–451 to find past participles of irregular verbs. Then students can use the past perfect tense to complete the paragraph in Try It!

Speaking: Give a Persuasive Talk Conduct the activity at the bottom of page 295, having students use their Problem-and-Solution Charts for ideas.

Use the Speaking Activity Options in the **Multi-Level Strategies** to adjust instruction.

▶ **Practice Book** page 139

CLOSE AND ASSESS

Have students list two words that can be used to persuade. Then have them complete this sentence using the verb *study* in the past perfect tense: *After I ______ the oceans of the world, I realized how many were polluted.*

Multi-Level Strategies

SPEAKING ACTIVITY OPTIONS

BEGINNING Have students draw a picture to portray their issue. Make comments and ask questions about their pictures and record key words from their responses: *I see smog in the sky. Do you think we need fewer cars that pollute the air?* Have students echo as you read the key words aloud.

INTERMEDIATE Ask students yes/no questions followed by an open-ended question to help them formulate their opinions: *Should oil companies be fined for oil spills? How can we prevent threats to sea animals?* Have students record key words and use their notes as they give their talks.

ADVANCED Have students work in pairs to ask each other questions about their issues. Each partner should record key words about their partner's issue and suggested solutions. Students should listen to each other's speeches and note which verbs are in the past perfect tense.

Transparency 74 / Master 74

PAST PERFECT TENSE VERBS

The tense of a verb shows when an action happens. A verb in the **past perfect tense** tells about an action that was completed before some other action in the past.

We had a debate on pollution. Before the debate, I **had done** a lot of research.

1. To form the past perfect tense, use the helping verb **had** plus the past participle of the main verb.

   I **had practiced** my speech three times.

2. The past participle of regular verbs ends in **-ed**. Irregular verbs have special forms for the past participle.

Verb	Past	Past Participle
learn	learned	learned
see	saw	seen
go	went	gone

Try It!

Complete the paragraph with the past perfect tense of the verb.

Last month, our class went to Potter River to study the plant life. Before that, we ___(visit)___ the Long River. We ___(see)___ a lot of pollution there. The plants and animals ___(begin)___ to die. We have now made people aware of these problems.

Transparency 74 Level B, Unit 5 | Challenges

PREPARE TO READ

OBJECTIVES

THINK ABOUT WHAT YOU KNOW
Reading and Learning Strategies: Activate Prior Knowledge

LEARN KEY VOCABULARY Ⓣ
Vocabulary Strategy: Relate Words

LEARN TO USE SQ3R
Reading Strategy: Ⓣ Use SQ3R

THINK ABOUT WHAT YOU KNOW

1 **Take a Poll** As students answer, record responses on a chart or graph.

LEARN KEY VOCABULARY

2 **Relate Words** Have students read each vocabulary word and definition. Clarify meanings and conduct the activity.

Use the Vocabulary Options in the **Multi-Level Strategies** to tailor the activity to proficiency levels.

▶ **Practice Book** page 140

LEARN TO USE SQ3R

3 **Model How to Use SQ3R** Explain the acronym: **S** for Survey, **Q** for Question, **R** for Read, **R** for Recite, and **R** for Review. Conduct a guided practice with **Transparency 75**:

- Help students survey and record questions for pages 298–299 in the chart.
- Read the pages.
- Suggest that students use the Point-By-Point feature for the Recite step.
- Remind students to fill in answers to questions as they find them during the Review step.

CLOSE AND ASSESS

Have students write the SQ3R steps from memory on an exit slip.

SAVING THE Peregrine Falcon
science article
by Caroline Arnold

Prepare to Read

THINK ABOUT WHAT YOU KNOW

Take a Poll Which animals do you think are in danger of dying out? Check your answers on the Internet or in an encyclopedia.

combat fight against
effect result
endangered in danger of dying out or disappearing forever
environment air, land, and water that people, plants, and animals need to live
extinct not living anymore, gone forever
ignorance not having education or knowledge about something
interfere get in the way, block
peregrine falcon, hunting bird with a dark head, gray and white feathers, and a hooked bill
pollution chemicals, dirt, smoke, and garbage that make the air, water, and soil unclean and unsafe
repair fix

Possible answers for what can be done:
Repair and **combat** the effects of **pollution**.
Protect and restore the natural **environment**.
Ask people not to **interfere** with natural habitats.
Make strict laws against people who create **pollution**.

LEARN KEY VOCABULARY

Relate Words Study the new words and their definitions. Then use the words to fill in a map like the one below.

Word Map

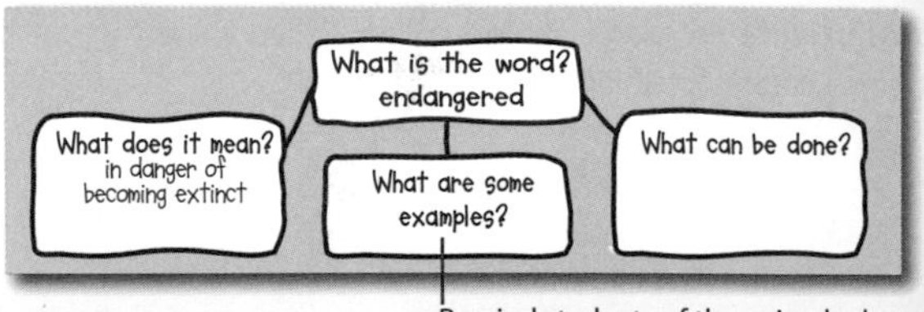

Remind students of the animals shown on page 292. Other animals include: gray whale, brown pelican, Puerto Rican boa, Gila trout.

LEARN TO USE SQ3R

SQ3R is a study strategy, or plan, to use when you read nonfiction. It will help you remember what you read.

READING STRATEGY
How to Use SQ3R

1. **Survey** the selection. Look at the graphs, charts, and section titles.
2. **Question.** Turn the titles into questions. Write them down.
3. **Read** each section slowly and carefully. Look for answers to your questions.
4. **Recite.** Summarize each section in your own words.
5. **Review** what you read. Try to answer your questions.

Use the SQ3R strategy as you read "Saving the Peregrine Falcon."

296 **Unit 5** | Challenges

REACHING ALL STUDENTS

Multi-Level Strategies

VOCABULARY OPTIONS

BEGINNING Group students to read ***Rachel Carson*** or the Key Points Reading on **Master 76**. (See page T299.) Work with the vocabulary in those selections.

INTERMEDIATE Have students complete their word maps in pairs and then compare with another pair.

ADVANCED Encourage students to try to use all of the key vocabulary words as they construct their maps.

Transparency 75 / Master 75

How to Use SQ3R

Directions: Survey "Saving the Peregrine Falcon." Write questions in the first column of the chart. Read the selection. Stop after each section to write answers in the second column.

Questions	Answers
1. How does DDT kill peregrine falcons?	1. Small birds eat seeds covered with DDT, and the falcons eat these birds. The eggs they lay are weak.
2. How do scientists help save falcons?	2. They take eggs to a safe place and make the eggs stronger.
3. How do the eggs get back to the wild?	3. Scientists put the eggs back in the nest and leave as quickly as possible.

Transparency 75 Level B, Unit 5 | Challenges © Hampton-Brown

SAVING THE Peregrine Falcon

In Ithaca, New York; Boise, Idaho; and Santa Cruz, California, teams of scientists make a difference every day of the year. They work to save a beautiful bird, the peregrine falcon, from extinction. The scientists help peregrine falcon eggs to hatch and then release the birds into the wild.

by Caroline Arnold

Photographs by Richard R. Hewett

297

READ THE SELECTION

OBJECTIVES

Reading Strategies: Preview; Predict
Literary Analysis: Science Article

INTRODUCE THE SELECTION

4 **Preview and Predict** Read aloud the title, author's name, and introduction to the article. Lead a discussion about the introduction. Ask: *How do you think scientists help the eggs to hatch? Why do they release the birds instead of keeping them in a zoo?*

5 **Identify Genre: Science Article** Point out the photographs and sidebars throughout the text and the chart on page 298. Tell students that a selection giving factual information about a scientific topic is called a *science article.*

Saving the Peregrine Falcon

by Caroline Arnold

Theme Connection This selection tells how environmentalists decided to make a difference and created a plan to save the endangered peregrine falcon.

Selection Summary and Awards The introduction on page 297 of the student book offers a summary of the selection. In 1985, *Saving the Peregrine Falcon*, the book on which this selection is based, won the ALA Notable Book award, the Outstanding Science Trade Book award from the National Science Teachers Association, and the Children's Book Council Joint Committee Special Achievement Award, PEN, Los Angeles Chapter.

THE BASICS BOOKSHELF

- ***Rachel Carson: A Woman Who Loved Nature*** adapted from *Rachel Carson* by William Accorsi

Rachel Carson was one of the first to recognize that everyone is responsible for protecting wildlife in their natural habitats. In this biography, simple text introduces basic vocabulary for plants and animals on land and sea. Labeled wildlife sketches and photographs increase access for beginning English learners.

For Lesson Plans: See the Teacher's Guide for ***The Basics Bookshelf***.

READ PAGES 298–299

OBJECTIVES

Function: Read a Selection
Grammar:
T Present and Past Perfect Tense Verbs
Listening: Listen to a Selection
Reading and Learning Strategies:
Set a Purpose for Reading; T Use SQ3R; Use Text Features in Nonfiction
Comprehension: T Identify Cause and Effect; T Draw Conclusions; Make Judgments

SET PURPOSE

1 Read aloud the section titles on pages 298 and 299. Set the purpose for reading: *Find out why DDT is a problem. Learn how scientists help the peregrine falcon.*

READ AND THINK

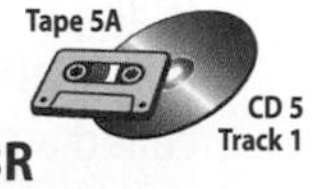

2 **Strategy Focus: Use SQ3R** Involve students in applying the SQ3R strategy as they read.

Choose Reading Options in the **Multi-level Strategies** to tailor the reading to proficiency levels.

The recording of "Saving the Peregrine Falcon" on the **Selection Tape/CD** offers an oral language model and the opportunity to build reading fluency.

Red annotations offer opportunities to clarify meaning and check for understanding.

THE PROBLEM: DDT

Build background: Many species have disappeared fror Earth because of human activities. But thanks to the eff of scientists, some species are being saved from extincti

For **centuries** the **peregrine** was prized by kings and **falconers** who used it to hunt. Bird lovers too have always admired the peregrine. Yet a few years ago it was feared that soon there would be no more peregrines. **Pollution** of the **environment** with the poison DDT had **interfered** with the birds' **ability** to **produce** babies.

Most of the smaller birds that peregrines in the United States eat spend the winter in Central and South America. There they eat grains and insects that have been sprayed with DDT. DDT is a poison used by farmers to kill insects that are harmful to crops. When the birds eat food with DDT on it, the poison is **stored** in their bodies. Later, when the peregrines eat these birds, they eat the poison too. The more birds the peregrines eat, the more DDT they store.

Scientists have found that DDT causes birds to lay eggs with shells that are too thin. When they measure the shells of **hatched** or broken eggs, they find that the thinnest shells are those with the most DDT in them. When parent birds sit on these eggs to keep them warm, the thin shells often break. Thin-shelled eggs also lose moisture faster than thick-shelled eggs. Often the chick growing inside the egg dies because the egg dries out too much.

Ask: How does DDT affect peregrine falcon eggs?

A DEADLY CHAIN

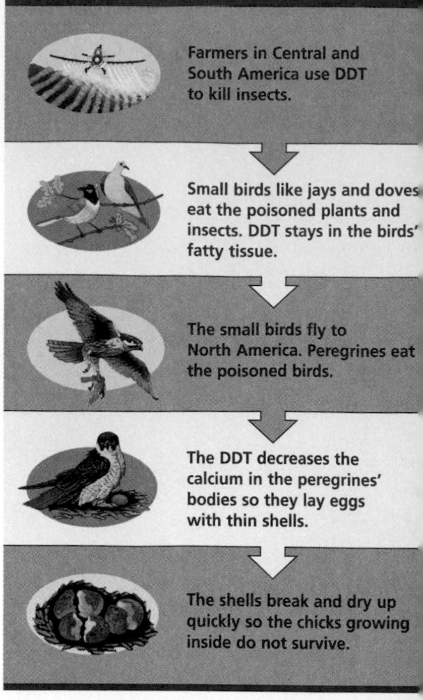

Ask: How do peregrine falcons pick up DDT? **Point out how this graphic contains the same information as the text.**

centuries hundreds of years
falconers people who hunt with hawks and falcons
ability being able
produce make
stored kept
hatched empty

REACHING ALL STUDENTS

Health Connection
PESTICIDES

Ask students to use the library, science textbooks, and the Internet to learn more about DDT and how it affects the lives of animals and humans. You might suggest these questions: *What does DDT stand for? What positive effects does it have? What negative effects does it have? Since the government has banned its use, why is it still a problem?* Divide the class into groups and have each group search for answers using a different medium. Ask each group to write a paragraph telling what they discovered about DDT.

Multi-Level Strategies
READING OPTIONS FOR LESSONS 4–7

BEGINNING Students can work with ***Rachel Carson*** while the class reads "Saving the Peregrine Falcon." Or distribute copies of **Master 76** and use SQ3R with the Key Points Reading of "Saving the Peregrine Falcon." During the Survey step, give question starters: *How is ______? How do ______?* and record the questions on **Transparency 75.** (See page T296.) Read each paragraph and then summarize the information for the Recite step. For the Review step, write answers students find for their questions.

INTERMEDIATE / ADVANCED Distribute three copies of **Master 75.** (See page T296.) Have students work with a partner to write each section title as a question. After they read each section, invite pairs to summarize information together for the Recite step. For the Review step, have students write answers to their questions.

ᵹIVING NATURE A HAND

ɏ helping the eggs with thin shells
› hatch, scientists can **combat** some
' the **effects** of DDT. **Encourage elaboration:** How can the scientists help?
Most wild peregrines nest on high ledges
ɐ rocky cliffs. Scientists carefully watch
ɐch peregrine nest. Then if they feel that
e eggs are **unlikely** to hatch without help,
ey borrow them for a while, but first they
t the birds sit on the eggs for five days.
ɿis seems to **improve** the eggs' chances of
ɐtching in the **laboratory**.

Because the cliffs where peregrines nest
'e so steep, only a mountain climber can
ach a nest. When he approaches the
est, the angry parents screech and swoop
him. The mountain climber quickly and
ɐrefully puts each speckled egg into a
ɐdded box. He then replaces the eggs he
ɐs taken with **plaster eggs** which look just like real peregrine eggs. These fake eggs will fool the parent birds. After the mountain climber leaves, the parents will return to the nest and sit on the plaster eggs as if they were their own.

It is important to keep the parent birds interested in the nest. After the eggs have hatched, the mountain climber will bring the babies back so that the parents can take care of them. **Ask:** Why do the scientists put plaster eggs in the nests?

When the mountain climber gets back down from the top of the cliff, he puts the eggs into a portable **incubator**. The incubator will keep them safe and warm on their ride back to the laboratory.

is climber is in search of a peregrine nest.

Use visuals: From this picture, what can you tell about where peregrine falcons nest?

POINT-BY-POINT

HOW PEOPLE HELP THE PEREGRINE

1. Scientists search for eggs affected by DDT. ▼
2. Climbers take eggs from the nest. They replace them with plaster eggs. ▼
3. They take the real eggs to the laboratory in an incubator. ▼

BEFORE YOU MOVE ON...

1. **Cause and Effect** Why are peregrines in danger of extinction?
2. **Conclusions** Do you think it matters if all the peregrines die out? Why or why not?
3. **Judgments** Is it fair to the peregrines to put fake eggs in their nests? Why or why not?

ɐlikely not expected
ɐprove make better
boratory room where scientists work
plaster eggs fake eggs
incubator warm, moist case used to hatch eggs

MONITOR YOUR READING

3 Use Text Features in Nonfiction
Call attention to the Point-By-Point summaries throughout the selection. Students can use this feature, which provides a cumulative outline of the article, to preview the content and to help with the Recite and Review steps of SQ3R.

CHECK COMPREHENSION

4 Answers to "Before You Move On"

1. **Cause and Effect** The DDT that farmers use to kill insects causes the peregrine falcons' eggs to crack easily. Therefore, many of the baby falcons die before they can hatch.
2. **Conclusions** Answers may vary: Earth would lose a beautiful animal. If the environment is unhealthy for peregrine falcons, then it may be unhealthy for other living things, too.
3. **Judgments** Answers may vary. One response may be that it is fair because it is helping to guarantee their survival as a species.

CLOSE AND ASSESS

Ask groups to present from memory the path DDT takes from the farmer to the peregrine falcon's fragile eggshell.

Transparency 76 / Master 76

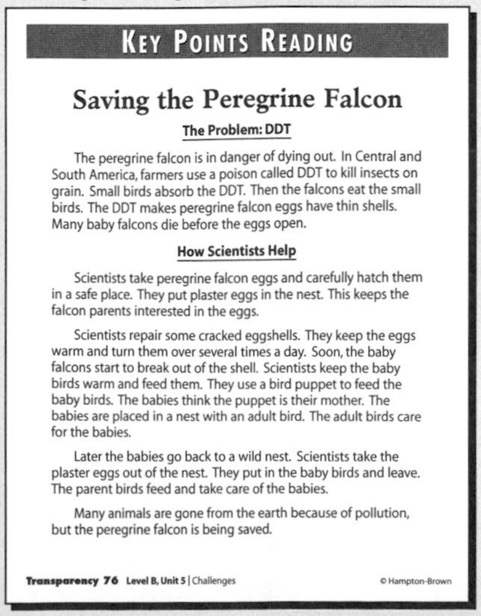

KEY POINTS READING

Saving the Peregrine Falcon

The Problem: DDT

The peregrine falcon is in danger of dying out. In Central and South America, farmers use a poison called DDT to kill insects on grain. Small birds absorb the DDT. Then the falcons eat the small birds. The DDT makes peregrine falcon eggs have thin shells. Many baby falcons die before the eggs open.

How Scientists Help

Scientists take peregrine falcon eggs and carefully hatch them in a safe place. They put plaster eggs in the nest. This keeps the falcon parents interested in the eggs.

Scientists repair some cracked eggshells. They keep the eggs warm and turn them over several times a day. Soon, the baby falcons start to break out of the shell. Scientists keep the baby birds warm and feed them. They use a bird puppet to feed the baby birds. The babies think the puppet is their mother. The babies are placed in a nest with an adult bird. The adult birds care for the babies.

Later the babies go back to a wild nest. Scientists take the plaster eggs out of the nest. They put in the baby birds and leave. The parent birds feed and take care of the babies.

Many animals are gone from the earth because of pollution, but the peregrine falcon is being saved.

Transparency 76 Level B, Unit 5 | Challenges © Hampton-Brown

Grammar Minilesson

▶ PRESENT PERFECT AND PAST PERFECT TENSES

TEACH Remind students that a verb can show when an action happens. Point out the first paragraph on page 298. Explain that the verb *have admired* is in the present perfect tense to tell about an action that happened in the past and is still going on today. Write the following and explain the formation of the present perfect tense:

has + past participle
have + past participle

Identify *had interfered* in the first paragraph as a verb in the past perfect tense. Explain that it shows action that was completed before some other action in the past. Explain its formation:

had + past participle

PRACTICE Have students recite this chant, adding animals they might see in the woods. Ask them to create five or more verses for the chant.

In the past few days
we have seen five ______s.
Before this week ,
we had seen only one ______.

▶ **Practice Book** page 141

READ PAGES 300–301

OBJECTIVES

Function: Read a Selection
Grammar: Active and Passive Verbs
Concepts and Vocabulary: Describing Words
Vocabulary Strategy: Structural Clues (suffixes)
Listening: Listen to a Selection
Reading and Learning Strategies: Set a Purpose for Reading; Ⓣ Use SQ3R
Comprehension: Ⓣ Summarize

SET PURPOSE

1 Read aloud the section titles on pages 300–301. Then point to the titles in turn and say: *First we'll find out what happens in the laboratory. Then we'll learn how the chick breaks out of the egg.*

READ AND THINK

Tape 5A
CD 5 Track 1

2 **Strategy Focus: Use SQ3R** Involve students in reading pages 300–301 of the selection and adding to their SQ3R Charts.

See the **Multi-Level Strategies** on page T298 to tailor the reading experience to all proficiency levels.

IN THE LABORATORY

In the laboratory each egg is carefully weighed. Then it is held in front of a bright light in a dark room. This is called *candling.* When an egg is candled, the shadow of the chick growing inside and a lighter area at the large end of the egg can be seen. The lighter area is called the air pocket.

Then the egg is placed on a **rack** inside an incubator. The incubator keeps the egg warm and **moist**. Each day the egg will be weighed and candled again. As the chick grows, water slowly **evaporates** from the egg, making room for the air pocket to get bigger. The egg's weight shows how much water it is losing. If it is losing water too quickly, the incubator can be made more moist. **Ask:** How does an incubator help the egg?

Wild birds turn their eggs **constantly** as they move around in the nest. But in the laboratory, people must carefully turn each egg four or five times each day. This **prevents** the growing chick from sticking to the inside of the eggshell. If the eggs are not turned, they will not hatch.

Sometimes eggs are found with shells so thin that they have already begun to crack. Then people in the laboratory try to **repair** them with glue. Sometimes eggs are also **waxed** to prevent them from losing moisture. Everything possible is done to make sure that each egg hatches into a healthy peregrine chick.

The eggs are kept in the incubator until they are 31½ days old. Then they are carefully watched for the first signs of hatching.

Ask: What will the scientists do when the eggs hatch?

A scientist uses glue to repair a crack in a peregrine's egg.

rack shelf
moist slightly wet
evaporates becomes water vapor and moves into the air
constantly all the time
prevents stops
waxed covered with wax

REACHING ALL STUDENTS

HOME CONNECTION

Opinion Poll Send home a copy of *High Point Newsletter 9* in the **Teacher's Resource Book**. In this home activity, students poll family members about their feelings regarding the protection of endangered species. Suggest follow-up questions, such as: *Do you know anyone who has helped to protect endangered animals? What do you think can be done to protect them?* Suggest that students graph the results for the whole class.

Vocabulary
ANIMAL CATEGORIES

Brainstorm a list of animals. Then help students use a chart like the one below to sort the list according to whether the animal is domestic, wild, or both. Then have students identify organizations that support the welfare of animals in each category. For example, local animal shelters usually care for house pets, while the SPCA cares for both domestic and wild animals.

	Domestic	Wild	Both
Animals	dog	peregrine falcon	horse
Organizations	local animal shelters	Audubon Society	SPCA

POINT-BY-POINT

HOW PEOPLE HELP THE PEREGRINE

4 The staff check the eggs' moisture levels. They turn the eggs and repair damaged shells.
▼

5 Scientists watch for signs of hatching. Sometimes they peep to encourage the chicks to hatch.
▼

BREAKING OUT

ach chick has a hard pointed knob on the ›p of its beak. This is called an *egg tooth.* ne chick pushes against the inside of the ell with its egg tooth and breaks the shell.

Ask: What is an egg tooth?

The first crack in the egg is called the *p.* When the pip appears, the egg is moved › a special hatching **chamber**. There the g will take 24 to 48 hours to hatch. During is time somebody watches it all the time. ›me chicks are too weak to break out of eir shells. Then the scientists are there to lp them.

Often two eggs begin to hatch at about e same time. Then they are put next to ch other. When a chick is ready to hatch, begins to **peep** inside its shell. The two icks can hear each other peep. This seems **encourage** them to move around and reak their shells. Sometimes when there is nly one egg, the scientists make peeping ›unds for the chick to hear.

Starting at the pip, the chick slowly rns, pressing its egg tooth against the shell. Soon the crack becomes a ring around the shell. Then the chick pushes its head against the top of the shell, and the shell pops open. After hatching, the egg tooth is no longer needed, and in a week or so it falls off.

Ask: Why do scientists put two chicks together?

Encourage elaboration: What happens if the chicks are too weak to break the shell?

BEFORE YOU MOVE ON...

1. **Summary** Tell a partner what the scientists do to take care of the eggs.
2. **Vocabulary** What words would you use to describe the work the scientists do in the laboratory? Does your partner agree or disagree?

e first crack in the egg is called e pip.

The chick breaks a ring around the entire shell.

Then the chick pushes its head against the top of shell, and the shell pops open.

amber room that is very small
eep make a weak, high-pitched noise
encourage help

REVIEW KEY VOCABULARY

3 Use Structural Clues to Meaning
Write the word endings *-tion*, *-ment* and *-ance* and ask students to find the key vocabulary words that have these endings. (pollution, environment, ignorance) Discuss the meaning of each word. Then ask: *What part of speech are these words?* (nouns) Explain that *-tion*, *-ment,* and *-ance* are noun endings. Have students list other nouns with these endings. (solution, contribution, government, contentment, tolerance, allowance)

CHECK COMPREHENSION

4 Answers to "Before You Move On"

1. **Summary** Scientists place the eggs in incubators to keep them warm and moist. They turn them several times a day. Sometimes they repair the eggs with glue.
2. **Vocabulary** Answers will vary. Possible word choices are: gentle, humane, caring, and important.

CLOSE AND ASSESS

Have students revisit the mind maps they created on page T291 and add new information prompted by reading this article.

COMMUNITY CONNECTION

Environmental Groups Ask students to use the Yellow Pages and the Internet to find out what animal support and environmental groups are active in their community. They can collect brochures and Web site information to share with the class. You might also arrange a field trip to visit one of these organizations or ask a representative to visit the class and speak with students about the work they do.

Grammar Minilesson

▶ ACTIVE AND PASSIVE VERBS

TEACH Read the caption for the middle photograph on page 301: *The chick breaks a ring around the entire shell.* Have students identify the subject and verb. Explain that the verb is active since the subject is doing the action. Then write:

A ring is broken around the shell
by the chick.

Identify the subject (*ring*) and the verb (*is broken*). Tell students that the verb is passive because the subject *ring* is not doing the action. Say: *The chick is still the one breaking the ring, but it is not the subject.* Point out the phrase *by the chick* and say: *Sometimes the person or animal doing the action is named following the word* ***by***. Erase the phrase and say: *But often the person or animal may not be named.* Explain that forms of the verb *be* (*am, are, is was, were, shall, will*) are used to form passive verbs. Read several sentences in the first column of page 300 and identify which have active and passive verbs.

PRACTICE Have students rewrite sentences from the selection to change the verb from passive to active.

READ PAGES 302–303

OBJECTIVES

Function: Read a Selection
Grammar: Active and Passive Verbs
Listening: Listen to a Selection
Reading and Learning Strategies: Set a Purpose for Reading; Ⓣ Use SQ3R
Comprehension: Summarize; Ⓣ Identify Details; Ⓣ Identify Cause and Effect; Make Inferences

SET PURPOSE

1 Read aloud the section titles on pages 302 and 303. Set the purpose for reading: *Find out how newborn chicks are cared for. Then learn how scientists prepare the baby birds to return to the wild.*

READ AND THINK

Tape 5A
CD 5 Track 1

2 **Strategy Focus: Use SQ3R** Involve students in reading pages 302–303 and adding to their SQ3R Charts.

See the **Multi-Level Strategies** on page T298 to tailor the reading experience to all proficiency levels.

Use visuals: Use the picture to help you describe a newly hatched chick.

A newly hatched chick eats a tiny piece of meat.

CARING FOR THE CHICKS

The newly hatched chick is wet and its down feathers are **matted** together. A cotton swab is used to clean the feathers. If necessary, **ointment** is put on the chick's navel to prevent **infection**. In the shell the chick gets **nutrients** from the **yolk** through its navel. Normally, by the time a chick hatches, the yolk has been totally **absorbed** and the navel has closed.

In the wild, a mother bird **broods** her chicks by sitting on top of them to keep them warm and dry. In the laboratory, the dry chick is placed with one or more others in a small container called a brooder. A heater keeps the chicks warm. The chick will rest in the brooder for eight to twelve hours. Then it will be ready for its first meal.

Ask: What is a brooder?

In the wild, the father peregrine hunts birds and brings them back to the nest. Then he and the mother peregrine tear off small bits of meat to feed each chick. The hungry chicks beg for food by peeping and opening their mouths wide.

Ask: What do peregrine chicks eat?

Bird meat is also used to feed chicks in the laboratory. First the meat is put through a meat grinder to break it into small pieces. The newly hatched chicks are then fed tiny pieces with tweezers. For somewhat older chicks the ground meat can be squeezed through a bag with a **nozzle**.

Define *tweezers*: tool us for handling small objec

matted pressed down
ointment medicine
infection disease caused by germs
nutrients food
yolk yellow part of an egg
absorbed taken in
broods uses her wings to cover
nozzle cap with a small opening

REACHING ALL STUDENTS

Language Development
EXPRESS INTENTIONS AND JUSTIFY

Discuss with students what ordinary people can do to help animals. Then help students state their intentions to take specific actions. Provide frames, such as:

I promise to ______. (exercise my dog regularly)

I will do this because ______. (he depends on me)

I cannot promise to______ (stop whale hunters) because ______. (I'm too young to go out on rescue missions)

Music Connection
SOARING COMPOSITIONS

Ask students to choose pieces of music that make them think of a peregrine falcon soaring across the sky. Have each student play his or her selection for the class and supply some background information. They can give the title of the piece, tell who composed it, and tell about the composer's life. If possible, have students tell why the piece was written or what the composer had in mind when writing it. Ask why the music reminds them of a peregrine falcon.

REPARING FOR FREEDOM

n though the peregrine chicks are cared by people, it is important that they ain wild. During the first week or so, chicks cannot see very well. Then it does matter if people feed them directly. But hey get older, their contact with people st be **limited**.

Young animals identify with the other mals they see during the first weeks of . This is called **imprinting**. Most young mals only see their parents in early life, they imprint on them.

Peregrines raised in the laboratory that be returned to the wild must be rinted on adult peregrines. One way to p them do this is to feed them with a peregrine-shaped puppet. The puppet fools the peregrine chicks and they behave as if it were a real bird. When a peregrine chick is three days to a week old, it is put into the nest of an adult bird that has been imprinted on people.

Clarify: If chicks imprint on people, they will not understand how to behave in the wild.

Unfortunately there are not enough adult peregrines to care for all the hatched chicks. Another more common bird, the prairie falcon, is very much like the peregrine, and it is often used as **a substitute** parent for very young peregrine chicks. During the **breeding season**, a female prairie falcon will care for **adopted peregrine chicks**. She will keep them warm and feed them as if they were her own. When the chicks are one to two weeks old, they are put into nests of peregrines which are not imprinted on people. Then, at the age of three weeks, the young peregrines are ready to go back to wild nests.

Ask: Why are prairie falcons used as substitute parents?

eregrine chick thinks this puppet is its parent.

ain stay
ted as little as possible
rinting a learning process that establishes havior pattern
bstitute a replacement
eding season time for making chicks
pted peregrine chicks chicks she has taken in

POINT-BY-POINT

HOW PEOPLE HELP THE PEREGRINE

6 Scientists clean the chicks, keep them warm, and feed them.

7 Scientists make sure the chicks imprint on adult birds.

BEFORE YOU MOVE ON...

1. **Summary** Use these words to retell how the chick hatches and how the scientists care for it: *egg tooth, pip, brooder.*
2. **Details/Inference** What are some things the scientists do to help the chicks after they hatch?
3. **Cause and Effect** Why do the scientists make sure the peregrine falcons do not imprint on people?

CHECK COMPREHENSION

3 Answers to "Before You Move On"

1. **Summary** Possible answers are: The baby chick uses its egg tooth to crack the egg. This first crack is called a "pip." Scientists put the baby chick in a brooder that keeps it warm.
2. **Details/Inference** Possible answers are: They keep chicks warm and feed them ground meat. They put pairs of baby chicks near each other.
3. **Cause and Effect** If they imprint on humans, they will not accept their natural parents in the wild.

CLOSE AND ASSESS

Ask pairs of students to draw a series of sketches showing how scientists care for the newly hatched peregrine chicks and prepare them for freedom.

Art Connection

MASKS AND PUPPETS

Invite students to make peregrine falcon masks or puppets. Demonstrate how to use papier maché to make a mask. Students may want to build their masks on a modeling clay form. Point out the picture on page 303 as an example of what a mitten-type puppet might look like. Students can use the masks and puppets to role-play parts of the article and then display the artwork on the classroom walls.

Grammar Minilesson

▶ ACTIVE AND PASSIVE VERBS

TEACH Read the caption for the photo on page 302. Ask students to identify the verb and subject. Elicit that the verb is active because the subject is doing the action. Then write the second sentence on page 302.

A cotton swab is used to clean the feathers.

Help students identify the verb and note that it is passive: *a verb is passive when the subject does not perform the action.* Explain that the person or thing doing the action may not be named.

Ask: *Who is using the cotton swab?* (a scientist) Then have students add this information to the sentence:

A cotton swab is used by the scientist to clean the feathers.

PRACTICE With students, continue reading sentences on pages 302–303, identifying active and passive verbs, and telling who does the action. Students can rewrite sentences to change verbs from active to passive and vice versa.

▶ **Practice Book** page 142

READ PAGES 304–305

OBJECTIVES

Function: Read a Selection
Listening: Listen to a Selection
Reading and Learning Strategies: Set a Purpose for Reading; Ⓣ Use SQ3R; Paraphrase; Relate to Personal Experience
Literary Analysis: Evaluate the Impact of Author's Point of View on Literature; Evaluate Literature

SET PURPOSE

1 Read aloud the section title on page 304. Set the purpose for reading: *Find out what happens to the baby birds after they are returned to the wild.*

READ AND THINK

Tape 5A
CD 5 Track 1

2 **Strategy Focus: Use SQ3R** Involve students in reading pages 304–305 of the selection. Remind them to use the SQ3R strategy.

See the **Multi-Level Strategies** on page T298 to tailor the reading experience to all proficiency levels.

IN THE WILD

Ask: How has the work of the scientists affected the survival of peregrine falcons

The chicks are put into a special wooden pack and taken to the nest **site**. There the mountain climber puts the pack on his back and climbs to the nest. He **removes** the plaster eggs and puts in the young chicks. Then he leaves as quickly as possible. He does not want to **disturb** the parent birds any more than necessary.

The parent birds soon return to the nest. Although they are surprised at first to find healthy chicks instead of eggs in their nest, the parents quickly accept their new babies. The hungry chicks beg for food, and the parents' natural response is to feed them. The chicks are finally on their way to growing up as wild peregrines.

The peregrine falcon is a beautiful bird, and it would be sad to let it become **extinct** simply through **ignorance** or **carelessness**.

Encourage elaboration: What might the falcons do if they return to find a person near the nest?

Many animals that once **roamed** the earth are now gone because people destroyed or polluted their environments. For the present, the peregrine falcon has been saved from extinction. Through the work of many people around the world, its numbers are increasing each year. If you ar lucky, maybe where you live, you can see one of these magnificent birds soaring high in the sky.

BEFORE YOU MOVE ON...

1. **Paraphrase** How do the scientists return the babies to the parent birds?
2. **Personal Experience** Talk to your partner about other animals that are also in danger of extinction.

ABOUT THE AUTHOR

Caroline Arnold, who lives with her husband in Los Angeles, California, has written over 100 books, most about natural science. She has been interested in birc and the environment for a long time. When discussin her research, she said, "Few experiences can match the thrill of seeing hawks and falcons up close and then watching them soar skyward after their release." Caroline Arnold has a web page on the Internet wher people can learn more about her, her books, and her thoughts about writing. Her home page address is: http://www.geocities.com/Athens/1264/

site location, place
removes takes away
disturb bother
carelessness not being careful
roamed walked around

REACHING ALL STUDENTS

Vocabulary

LOCATE WORD ORIGINS: ACRONYMS

Using DDT as an example, explain the concept of an acronym (a word formed from the initial letters or parts of a longer word or phrase). Say: *DDT is the acronym for* **d**ichloro**d**iphenyl**t**richloroethane. Introduce other acronyms and elicit their meanings (UN, CD-ROM). Point out that some acronyms are spoken letter-by-letter (YMCA), but others are pronounced as words (UNICEF). Help students brainstorm a list of acronyms they use at school or that are currently in the news.

A WORLD OF LANGUAGES

Word Order/Syntax The arrangement of words in a sentence differs across languages, but words always work together to cue meaning. In Asian languages, spoken tone also cues meaning. As an example, compare the placement of adjectives in English and some other languages.

The adjective comes before the noun: *the beautiful bird*	**The adjective comes after the noun:** *the bird beautiful*
Bengali, Cantonese, English, Estonian, Hindi, Japanese, Korean, Latvian, Mandarin, Sinhalese, Tagalog, Tamil	Albanian, Arabic, Burmese, Farsi (Persian), Fijian, Lao Malay, Spanish, Tahitian, Thai, Tongan, Vietnamese

POINT-BY-POINT

HOW PEOPLE HELP THE PEREGRINE

1. Scientists search for eggs affected by DDT.
2. Climbers take eggs from the nest. They replace them with plaster eggs.
3. They take the real eggs to the laboratory in an incubator.
4. The staff check the eggs' moisture levels. They turn the eggs and repair damaged shells.
5. Scientists watch for signs of hatching. Sometimes they peep to encourage the chicks to hatch.
6. Scientists clean the chicks, keep them warm, and feed them.
7. Scientists make sure the chicks imprint on adult birds, not humans.
8. Scientists return chicks to the wild.

ı August 20, 1999, the peregrine falcon was officially removed from the **endangered** ecies list. As of that day, there were at least 1,650 breeding pairs in the United States! though the banning of DDT made the peregrine's recovery possible, the hard work the scientists really did make a difference: their work was the main reason the numbers peregrines increased so quickly.

ecies plants and animals

CHECK COMPREHENSION

3 Answers to "Before You Move On"

1. **Paraphrase** A climber carries a chick to the nest, removes an artificial egg, and puts the chick in its place.
2. **Personal Experience** Comments will vary. Students may mention the black rhinoceros, the Siberian tiger, Grevy's zebra, and the right whale.

ABOUT THE AUTHOR

4 Evaluate Literature: Author's Point of View Read aloud or ask students to read About the Author. Point out the quotation that describes the thrill the author feels when she sees birds being released into the wild. Ask: *How do you think the author's point of view influences her writing?* Suggest that students visit Caroline Arnold's Web page and find out how many of her books reflect an interest in the environment and endangered species.

CLOSE AND ASSESS

Have each student write on an index card one thing that happens when scientists return the chicks to the wild. Partners exchange cards and write what comes before or after that step.

Learning Styles

STRATEGIES FOR CONSTRUCTING MEANING

Ask students to summarize the article using their preferred form of expression:

- **Visual Learners** Students make flow charts to show the steps in the process.
- **Auditory Learners** Students listen to the **Selection Tape/CD** and orally state the key steps in the process.
- **Kinesthetic Learners** Students use puppets or masks to act out the steps in the process.

Literary Analysis Minilesson

▶ EVALUATE LITERATURE: ACCURACY OF INFORMATION

TEACH Point out the caption on page 305 and note that someone using a source dated before 1999 might not know whether the peregrine falcon is still endangered. Remind students that it is important to check the date an article was written and conduct research to see if information is missing or out of date.

PRACTICE Ask students to use the library and the Internet to search for current science articles to evaluate how up-to-date the information in "Saving the Peregrine Falcon" is.

Web Sites

Web sites undergo frequent modifications, but here are two you may want to suggest to students:

www.peregrinefund.org

www.nbpc.co.uk

▶ **Practice Book** page 143

RESPOND

OBJECTIVES

SUM IT UP
Function: Write
Reading, Learning, and Critical Thinking Strategies: T Use SQ3R; T Draw Conclusions; T Summarize
Literary Analysis: Respond to Literature
Writing: Reflection Log

THINK IT OVER
Function: Engage in Discussion
Critical Thinking and Comprehension: T Summarize; Form Generalizations; Form Opinions; Make Judgments

EXPRESS YOURSELF
Function: Verify Information

CHECK YOUR UNDERSTANDING

1 **Sum It Up** Ask students to suggest possible endings for the sentence starters. As they discuss their conclusions, paraphrase statements to help all students understand.

▶ **Practice Book** page 144

2 **Think It Over** Possible answers are:

1. **Summary** Peregrines were in danger because DDT made their eggs weak. Scientists protected the eggs until the chicks hatched. Then they returned them to their parents.
2. **Generalization** Like the peregrines, many other endangered animals have become sick and weak because of chemicals in the environment.
3. **Making Decisions** You can join or make a donation to a conservation group and promote recycling at school.

3 **Express Yourself** Be sure students read aloud the information they use to verify their answers.

CLOSE AND ASSESS

Ask students to write a "Did You Know?" list of information about peregrine falcons to share with another class.

Respond to the Article
Check Your Understanding

SUM IT UP

Review the Article Use the "Point-By-Point" feature on page 305 to review the article and check the answers you found to the questions you had before reading.

Respond to Literature Use your questions and answers about the selection to make a reflection log.

Reflection Log

The answers to the important questions are ________	I was surprised to learn that ________
It's interesting that ________	I'd like to find out more about ________

Draw Conclusions Take a class poll on this question: Is it worth the time and money it takes to save an endangered animal? Tally the yes and no answers, and then discuss reasons. Complete the following paragraph to summarize the discussion.

> (number) members of our group think that it is worth it to save an endangered animal because (reason). (number) members of our group think that it is not worth it to save an endangered animal because (reason).

THINK IT OVER

Discuss and Write Talk about these questions with a partner. Write the answers.

1. **Summary** What did you learn about peregrine falcons and the effort to save them
2. **Generalization** How does the peregrine's situation apply to endangered animals in general?
3. **Making Decisions** How can you make a difference and help save endangered animal

EXPRESS YOURSELF ▶VERIFY INFORMATIO

Take turns with a partner and make a statemen based on information from the article. You can make a true statement, such as "DDT causes the birds to lay eggs with thin shells." Or, you can make a false statement, such as "Peregrines make their nests on the ground." Verify that your partner's statement is true or false. Read the text that proves your conclusions.

306 Unit 5 | Challenges

REACHING ALL STUDENTS

Multi-Level Strategies
SUM IT UP OPTIONS

BEGINNING Have students work as a group to review questions and answers on their SQ3R Chart for completeness. Then brainstorm entries for a group Reflection Log. Have students answer the conclusion question and write the numbers and reasons in the summary paragraph.

INTERMEDIATE Have pairs compare SQ3R Charts and add ideas from other pairs' charts. Next, ask them to complete Reflection Logs on their own, using the sentence starters on page 306 as a guide. Then they write and share their conclusions with each other.

ADVANCED Students discuss their SQ3R Charts as a group and then complete Reflection Logs on their own. Invite them to exchange and discuss logs. Have students write conclusions on their own and then exchange papers for peer critique.

ASSESSMENT
Selection Test 17 on page 83 of the Assessment Handbook tests students' mastery of the reading strategies and the vocabulary, comprehension, and language arts skills taught with this selection.

anguage Arts and Literature

GRAMMAR IN CONTEXT

SE THE PAST PERFECT TENSE

earn About the Past Perfect Tense Some ast actions are completed before another action the past. To tell about them, use the **past erfect tense**. It is formed in this way:

had + past participle

tudy these examples.

The babies were born in the laboratory because the researcher **had taken** the eggs from the falcons' nests.

The researcher **had cared** for the chicks until she released them into the wild.

eview Past Participles Add *-ed* to form the ast participle of most verbs. Memorize the past articiple forms for irregular verbs. See andbook pages 450–451 for a list.

ractice Write this paragraph. Add these verbs. ut the verbs in the past perfect tense.

eat	spray	poison

A few years ago, the peregrine falcon as almost extinct. Farmers in Central and outh America ____(1)____ their fields with DDT. his pesticide ____(2)____ the smaller birds hat peregrines like to eat. Once the lcons ____(3)____ the poisoned birds, the hells of their eggs became very thin.

WRITING

WRITE A THANK-YOU LETTER

Imagine that you are a peregrine falcon. Write a thank-you letter to a scientist who helped to save your chicks.

1. **Write Your Draft** Give specific details that show you know how the scientist helped your chicks.

Sample Letter

February 21, 2002

Dear Doctor Zayas,

I saw you take my eggs. You thought you tricked me, but I knew what you were doing. Thanks to you, my chicks are alive and well. Thank you again and again!

Sincerely,
P. Falcon

2. **Edit Your Letter** Did you use the words "thank you"? Have you included the date, a greeting, and a closing? Check your letter for correct spelling and punctuation.

3. **Deliver Your Letters** Take turns reading your letters aloud. Consider sending them to real scientists.

Review **punctuation marks** and **spelling** on Handbook pages 462–469.

RESPOND

OBJECTIVES

VERBS IN THE PAST PERFECT TENSE
Grammar: Ⓣ Past Perfect Tense Verbs

WRITE A THANK-YOU LETTER
Functions: Write; Express Gratitude
Writing: Letter

LANGUAGE ARTS AND LITERATURE

1 **Use the Past Perfect Tense** Answers to the Practice items are:

1. had sprayed
2. had poisoned
3. had eaten

▶ **Practice Book** page 145

2 **Write a Thank-You Letter** To provide support, suggest that students:

- review their SQ3R Charts and choose two or three specific details to mention in their letters
- write their letters using the first person "I"
- check to see that they used commas in the date, greeting, and closing

CLOSE AND ASSESS

Invite students to write a quiz question about the lesson.

Multi-Level Strategies

PRACTICE OPTIONS FOR PAST PERFECT TENSE

BEGINNING Give students additional examples based on classroom activities: *We had watched a video before we wrote our report.* Provide verbs and guide students in forming the past participle and creating a sentence with the past perfect tense of the verb. Complete the Practice with students.

INTERMEDIATE Have students work with a partner to complete the Practice items. Review and make needed revisions with students.

ADVANCED Have students work independently to complete the Practice, then use the past perfect tense in three new sentences about "Saving the Peregrine Falcon." Students can work with a partner for review and revision.

RESPOND

OBJECTIVES

GRAPH POPULATION CHANGES

Function: Give Information

Speaking: Interact with Peers

Learning Strategies, Critical Thinking, and Research Skills: Gather Information; Take Notes; Make Comparisons; Ⓣ Draw Conclusions

Representing: Graph

INVESTIGATE THE LEGISLATIVE PROCESS

Function: Give Information

Concepts and Vocabulary: Legislative Process—*bill, law, legislative branch, Senate, House of Representatives*

Learning Strategies, Critical Thinking, and Research Skills: Gather, Organize, and Synthesize Information; Take Notes

Representing: Flow Chart

CONTENT AREA CONNECTIONS

1 **Graph Population Changes** Use the graph in the student book to model how to interpret a bar graph.

▶ **Practice Book** page 146

2 **Investigate the Legislative Process** To prepare students to do the activity, introduce these terms:

- ***bill, law*:** Tell students that *bill* has several meanings. Point out that this lesson is about the legislative process. Help students find the correct definition in the dictionary. (a draft of a proposed law presented to a legislative body for approval) Have volunteers define *law*, then check the definition in the dictionary. (a rule established by authority, society, or custom)
- ***legislative branch, Senate, House of Representatives*:** Explain that the government's legislative branch, called the Congress, makes laws. It is made up of the Senate and the House of Representatives. Explain: *The Senate has 100 members, 2 from each state, elected for a 6-year term. The House of Representatives has 435 members; House elections are held every 2 years.*

Respond to the Article, continued

Content Area Connections

MATHEMATICS

REPRESENTING/SPEAKING

GRAPH POPULATION CHANGES

With a group, choose an endangered animal species, and research how its population has changed over time.

1 **Collect Data** Use wildlife magazines, encyclopedias, almanacs, and the Internet to find population statistics. Note why the population changed, too.

2 **Create a Graph** Use your data to make a bar graph that shows the population of the species over a period of time.

Graph

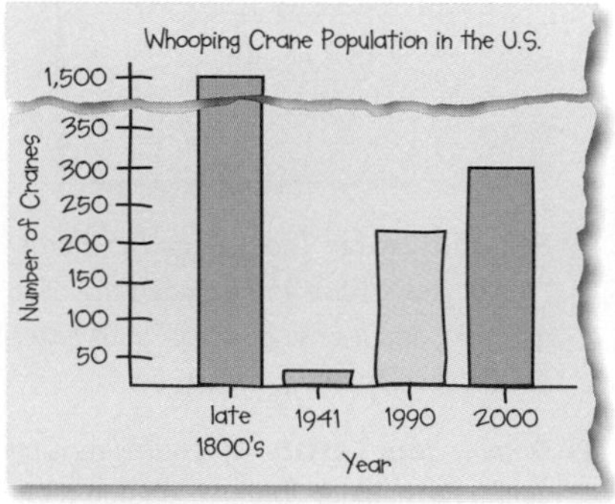

3 **Draw Conclusions and Report Your Findings** Present your graph as you share what you learned with the class.

SOCIAL STUDIES

WRITING/VIEWING

INVESTIGATE THE LEGISLATIVE PROCESS

The Endangered Species Act is a law that protects endangered animals. This law began as a bill. Make a flow chart to show how a bill becomes a law.

1 **Find Information** To find information:

- Use a social studies textbook.
- Call the office of a U.S. Senator or member of the House of Representatives.
- Contact an environmental group like the Sierra Club.

Take notes about each step of the process.

2 **Organize Your Information** Put each step on a different notecard. Put your cards in order and number them.

3 **Prepare Your Report** Use your notecards to make a flow chart that shows the steps a bill takes to become a law. Describe the process to a group.

Learn about **flow charts** on Handbook page 371.

REACHING ALL STUDENTS

Multi-Level Strategies

OPTIONS FOR INVESTIGATING THE LEGISLATIVE PROCESS

BEGINNING Display a social studies textbook flow chart showing how a bill becomes a law. Review the process, pausing to explain terms and paraphrase captions. Prompt students to copy the flow chart onto their poster.

INTERMEDIATE Ask pairs of students to use different sources to research information. Then have them share their findings with the group and decide how to build the flow chart for their poster. Students can take turns describing the steps in the legislative process to the class.

ADVANCED Encourage students to choose a specific environmental bill and trace its progress as it became a law. Suggest that they use magazine and newspaper articles and ask the librarian for help finding information. Students should make a flow chart to explain the process to the class.

TECHNOLOGY/MEDIA

SCIENCE

AKE AN INFORMATIONAL POSTER N AN ENDANGERED ANIMAL

/hy are animals endangered? With a group, esearch an endangered species and make an formational poster about it.

Choose a Species Decide which animal to research. Make a list of questions about it, for example: Why is it endangered? What is being done to protect it?

Gather Information and Take Notes Use the name of the species as a key word to search print and electronic sources. Start with these sites, but remember the Internet is always changing.

INTERNET

INFORMATION ON-LINE

Web Sites:
- **Endangered Species**
  - endangered.fws.gov
  - www.endangeredspecie.com

Download helpful images and take notes for your poster.

3 Make a Poster Write sentences that answer your research questions. Use pictures to illustrate the information. Then display your poster in the classroom or media center.

Sample Poster

WHALE REPORT

Why are Whales Endangered?
Whale hunters killed many whales for oil and other products through the 1800s and 1900s.

What is being done to protect them?
- The International Whaling Commission (IWC) told all countries to stop hunting whales from 1986 until further notice.
- In 1994, the IWC created the Southern Ocean Sanctuary as a protected place for whales.

For more about the **research process**, see Handbook pages 394–399. Learn to use the **Internet** on pages 392–393.

OBJECTIVES

INFORMATIONAL POSTER

Function: Give Information

Concepts and Vocabulary: Endangered Species—*ecology, ecosystem, food chain, habitat destruction, over-exploitation*

Learning Strategies and Research Skills: Gather, Organize, and Synthesize Information; Take Notes

Technology/Media: Use the Internet; Use a CD-ROM Encyclopedia

Representing: Poster

3 Make an Informational Poster To prepare students to do the activity, introduce the following terms:

- ***ecology, ecosystem, food chain*:** Define *ecology* as "the study of plants and animals and their environments." Use the example of an African tropical forest ecosystem as a community of plants and animals that depend on each other for survival. Give an example of a *food chain:* fruit > chimpanzee > leopard
- ***habitat destruction, over-exploitation*:** Using examples, explain *habitat destruction* (as African forests are cleared for agriculture, chimpanzees lose their food supply and can become endangered) and *over-exploitation* (the taking of extremely large numbers of leopards for their skins threatens the survival of the species).

▶ **Practice Book** page 147

CLOSE AND ASSESS

Ask students to choose an endangered species and answer this question on an index card: *What do you think should be done to protect this species?*

Research Skills

▶ USING A CD-ROM ENCYCLOPEDIA

TEACH Demonstrate how to use a CD-ROM encyclopedia.

Show how to use the search feature to find articles about a subject. For example, enter "ecology" in the search space and discuss the list of articles displayed. Some CD-ROM encyclopedias have a word search feature that lists all articles in which a certain word appears.

Then show students how to find pictures by looking for icons (or the words *Multimedia* or *Visuals*) that indicate an article has visuals.

PRACTICE Have pairs of students practice using a CD-ROM encyclopedia. They should:

- list all the articles with the word "endangered" in them
- skim an article relating to peregrine falcons
- locate a picture of a peregrine falcon

PREPARE TO READ

OBJECTIVES

THINK ABOUT WHAT YOU KNOW

Reading Strategies: Activate Prior Knowledge; Build Background; Use Text Structures (globes and maps)

LEARN KEY VOCABULARY Ⓣ

Vocabulary Strategy: Relate Words

LEARN ABOUT AUTHOR'S POINT OF VIEW AND PURPOSE

Reading Strategy: Identify Author's Point of View; Ⓣ Identify Author's Purpose

THINK ABOUT WHAT YOU KNOW

1 **Idea Exchange** Model an idea exchange: *I learned that the Everglades is protected because it is important to the people and animals in Florida. What did you learn?*

LEARN KEY VOCABULARY

2 **Relate Words** Divide the class into five groups and have each group make 4-squares for two words. Invite groups to share their work.

Use the Vocabulary Options in the **Multi-Level Strategies** to tailor the activity to proficiency levels.

▶ **Practice Book** page 148

LEARN ABOUT AUTHOR'S POINT OF VIEW/PURPOSE

3 **Model How to Identify Author's Point of View and Purpose** Define *point of view* and *purpose*. Model the steps with **Transparency 77**:

- As you read the passage, note facts and words that show how the author feels about the topic. Record the author's point of view.
- Use the question in the last box to determine and record the author's purpose.

CLOSE AND ASSESS

Ask students to tell a partner how to determine the author's point of view and purpose.

A Celebration of the Everglades

article by Ted Levin

poems by Frank Asch

Prepare to Read

THINK ABOUT WHAT YOU KNOW

Idea Exchange What do you know about the Florida Everglades? Scan pages 311–313. Tell a partner one thing you learned.

canal waterway built by people

dike wall of stone or earth that holds back water

extinction end of life for a whole category of plants or animals

levee wall of earth built along a river to prevent floods

marsh area of low, wet land with grasses

preserve keep safe, protect, keep the same from year to year

runoff rainfall that does not go into the ground but runs from higher to lower ground

temperate zone area between the Tropic of Cancer and the Arctic Circle or between the Tropic of Capricorn and the Antarctic Circle

tropics part of the earth's surface between the Tropic of Cancer and the Tropic of Capricorn

wetland wilderness low, wet land where people do not live

LEARN KEY VOCABULARY

Relate Words Study the new words and their definitions. Make a four-square chart for each word.

Word marsh	Picture 
Definition low, wet land with grasses	Sentence Birds make their nests in the marsh.

Students car paraphrase the definitio in the appropriate square of the diagrams. Students' sentences ar pictures will vary.

LEARN ABOUT AUTHOR'S POINT OF VIEW AND PURPOSE

An author's **point of view** is how the author feels about a subject. His or her reason for writing is the **purpose**. When you know the author's poin of view and purpose, you can better evaluate what you read.

READING STRATEGY

How to Identify Author's Point of View and Purpose

1. Take notes on the words or phrases that show how the author feels about a subject.
2. Ask yourself: Does the author want to tell me a story, explain something, or persuade me to do something?

As you read "A Celebration of the Everglades," look for clues to help yo determine the authors' purposes and points of view.

REACHING ALL STUDENTS

Multi-Level Strategies

VOCABULARY OPTIONS

BEGINNING Group students to read ***Rachel Carson*** or the Key Points Reading on **Master 78**. (See page T314.) Work with the vocabulary in those selections.

INTERMEDIATE Show pictures that illustrate the vocabulary words. Use a globe or map to show the location of the *temperate zone* and *tropics*.

ADVANCED Encourage students to write sentences using at least two key words in each sentence.

Transparency 77 / Master 77

POINT OF VIEW AND PURPOSE

Directions: Read the passage. Fill out the chart to help you identify the author's point of view and purpose in writing the passage.

The Endangered Alligator

The alligator was named an endangered species in the 1970s, and it is still not completely out of danger. Poachers break the laws against hunting alligators and kill them to get their skin. The poachers sell the skin to people who use it to make handbags, shoes, belts, and other items. Do we need these trinkets more than we need a whole species?

The alligator's habitat in the Everglades is also threatened by the building of dams, canals, and levees that drain the water from the alligators' homes. In order to save this magnificent reptile, protected areas like the Everglades National Park are needed. Support the preservation of the Everglades!

What are some facts? People have killed alligators for their skins. People are draining water from the alligators' habitat.	**What words show the author's feelings?** Do we need these trinkets...? Support the preservation of the Everglades!
What is the author's point of view? The author believes the alligator should be protected.	**What is the author's purpose?** The author wants to persuade me to help preserve the Everglades.

Transparency 77 Level B, Unit 5 | Challenges

REFERENCE POINT

verglades: The River of Life

any people once thought of e Florida Everglades as a ›eless swamp. In fact, it a rich and unique natural source important to e survival of the people, imals, and plants of orida. Today Everglades tional Park is a special ea protected by the U.S. vernment.

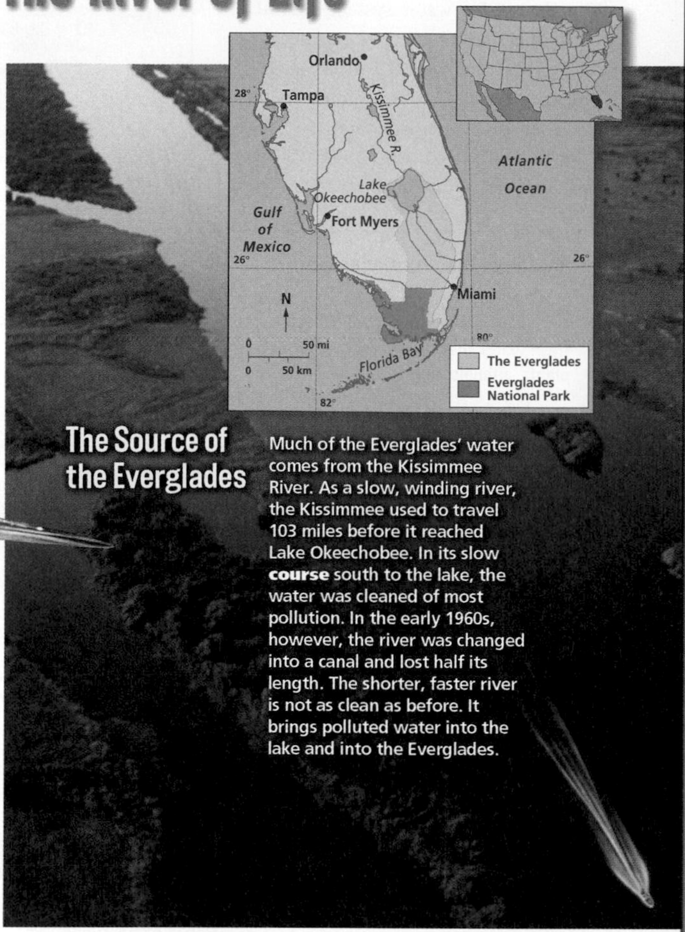

The Source of the Everglades

Much of the Everglades' water comes from the Kissimmee River. As a slow, winding river, the Kissimmee used to travel 103 miles before it reached Lake Okeechobee. In its slow **course** south to the lake, the water was cleaned of most pollution. In the early 1960s, however, the river was changed into a canal and lost half its length. The shorter, faster river is not as clean as before. It brings polluted water into the lake and into the Everglades.

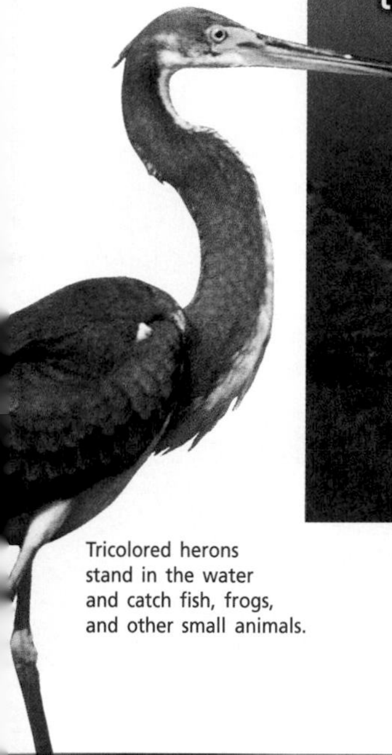

Tricolored herons stand in the water and catch fish, frogs, and other small animals.

course path

USE MAPS AND GLOBES

Latitude and Longitude Point out the vertical and horizontal lines on the map. Explain that the horizontal lines tell the *latitude*, or distance north or south from the equator. Point out the equator on a globe and track up to show the latitude lines just north and south of Lake Okeechobee.

Then explain that the vertical lines tell the *longitude*, or distance east or west of the prime meridian. Point out the prime meridian on a globe and track the longitude lines to show those that are just east and west of the lake.

Trace the square that the lines form and then show students how to locate Lake Okeechobee by using the latitude and longitude coordinates. (27°N latitude, 81°W longitude)

Have students work in pairs to find the Kissimmee River, Everglades National Park, and other Florida sites. Tell students to write down the name of each place and its coordinates. Have volunteers demonstrate finding other locations.

THE BASICS BOOKSHELF

- ***Rachel Carson: A Woman Who Loved Nature*** adapted from *Rachel Carson* by William Accorsi

Ever since Rachel Carson wrote *Silent Spring*, more people than ever before have begun to work to protect America's unique and various ecosystems, such as the Everglades. In this biography, simple text introduces basic vocabulary for plants and animals both on land and in the sea. Wildlife sketches and photographs of Rachel at various times in her life, increase access for beginning English learners.

For Lesson Plans: See the Teacher's Guide for ***The Basics Bookshelf***.

PREPARE TO READ

OBJECTIVES

Reading Strategy: Use Text Structures (diagrams)

USE TEXT STRUCTURES

Diagrams Define *diagram* as "a drawing that shows how parts of a process or a cycle relate to each other." Use the water cycle diagram at the top of page 312 to teach students how to read a diagram.

Use the Activity Options in the **Multi-Level Strategies** to teach all students about diagrams.

Then involve students in creating another diagram to show a cycle. Some examples to choose from are: phases of the moon, the change of seasons, and the life cycle of a frog.

Red annotations offer opportunities to clarify meaning and check for understanding. REFERENCE POINT

Why Is the Everglades Important?

The Everglades water system is **vital to** the plants and animals that live there. It is also needed for human life. The connection between the Kissimmee River, Lake Okeechobee, and the Everglades forms a great river of life that supports much of southern Florida.

The Everglades: Water for Life

Southern Florida depends upon rainfall for its fresh water. The Everglades is an important part of the water cycle that brings rain to southern Florida. Here is how the cycle works:

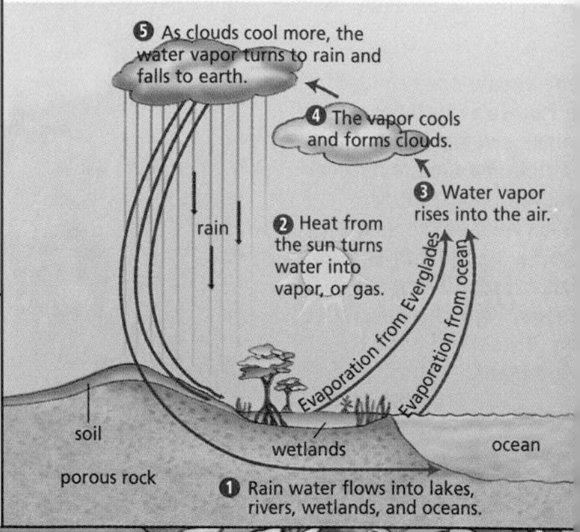

How Does the Everglades Work?

This diagram explains the importance of the Everglades to southern Florida. Without the fresh water that the Everglades provides, no plants, animals, or people could live there.

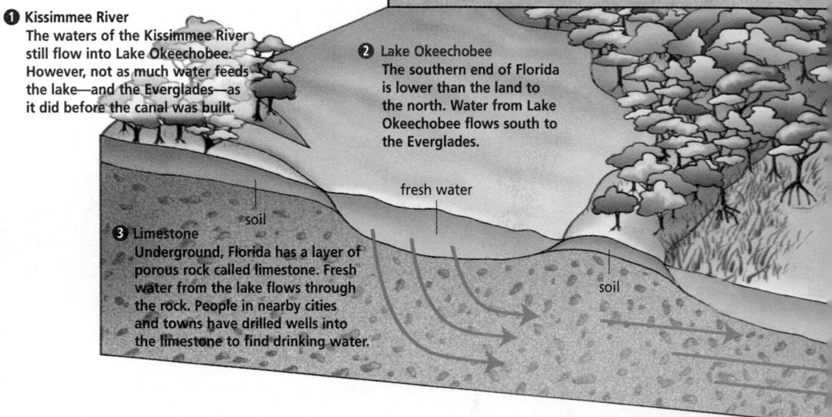

vital to needed in order to keep alive

Use visuals: Point out specific locations on the map and trace the water path in the diagram.

Florida panthers once lived throughout much of the southeastern United States. Today they are found only in southwestern Florida.

REACHING ALL STUDENTS

Vocabulary

PREPOSITIONS

Students will benefit from using prepositions to describe the bottom diagram on pages 312–313. Use gestures and sentences with prepositions to describe each step on the diagram: The water flows **from** the Kissimmee River **into** Lake Okeechobee. The water goes **through** the soil **into** the limestone.

Multi-Level Strategies

ACTIVITY OPTIONS FOR READING A DIAGRAM

BEGINNING Read aloud the title and the introduction to the water cycle diagram and ask: *What will you learn from this diagram?* Point out the numbered steps and ask students to locate the place to start reading the diagram. As you read aloud and paraphrase the steps of the cycle, ask students to locate and interpret other visual information in the diagram that helps clarify meaning. (arrows, illustrations)

INTERMEDIATE / **ADVANCED** Have students read the title and the introduction to the diagram. Elicit questions they think will be answered in the diagram. Ask students to trace the sequence of steps. Point out arrows and illustrations that can help students understand the process. Then invite students to work with a partner to read through and discuss the water cycle.

A Friend of the Everglades

Marjory Stoneman Douglas understood the importance of the Everglades to both people and wildlife. She began working to gain government protection of the Everglades in the 1920s.

Encourage elaboration: How is a water system similar to a blood system?

In her own words:

*Our most important resource and the most **imperiled** is water. It is the lifeblood on which the health of Florida's economy depends. In South Florida, protecting our water requires the destruction of the Kissimmee Canal so that water can flow down to Lake Okeechobee, which serves as nature's **filter** for the pollution from the marshlands now used for grazing and sugar growing. At all costs we must clean up the lake itself, which is now highly polluted.*

*All of our fresh water in South Florida comes from rainfall, and 80% of our rainfall comes from the **evaporation of the wet Everglades**.*

*We have the laws on the books to **prevent all this pollution**, and nothing has been done about it. We must prevent the unregulated dumping of dairy wastes into Lake Okeechobee. The best we can do is protect our great natural resources. This must be done or we will lose everything.*

Ask: Why does the writer believe we must clean up the lake?

—*Marjory Stoneman Douglas*, Florida Trend

Clarify: Water is one natural resource. What are some others?

mperiled in danger
ilter cleaner
vaporation of the wet Everglades water of the verglades changing into vapor
revent all this pollution keep all this pollution rom happening

USE TEXT STRUCTURES

Diagrams Direct students' attention to the diagram at the bottom of pages 312–313. Point out that pictures help you understand the text in the diagram. Using note 2 about Lake Okeechobee, trace along the illustration to show how the lower level of the land to the south results in water flowing down into the Everglades.

Invite students to discuss with a partner how other parts of the illustration clarify the notes. Ask each pair to share an observation with the class.

HOME CONNECTION

Living Spaces Have students interview a family member who has lived in a place other than the Everglades. Model questions such as: *What is the climate like? What kinds of plants/flowers grow there? Does the area have mountains, or is it flat? Is it near the ocean, or is it inland? What kinds of animals are native to the area?* Suggest that students tape record the interview and play the tape or summarize the interview for the class.

Science Connection

EVERGLADES CYCLE

Assign students the roles of water, Lake Okeechobee, the limestone rock, the Everglades, and the Gulf of Mexico. Encourage students to use prepositions correctly as they describe their roles. For example, a student representing water describes Step 1 on the diagram: *I start out in the Kissimmee River and flow into Lake Okeechobee.* Another says: *I'm Lake Okeechobee. Some of the freshwater flows into the limestone under my lake bed.*

READ THE SELECTION

OBJECTIVES

Function: Read a Selection
Listening: Listen to a Selection
Reading Strategies: Preview; Set a Purpose for Reading; Use Graphic Organizers (reflection log); Identify Author's Point of View; Ⓣ Identify Author's Purpose

INTRODUCE THE SELECTION

1. **Preview** Read aloud the title and the authors' names on page 314. Have students look through pages 314–321 to see photographs of the plants and animals they will read about. Then read the text on page 314 and explain the meaning of *sing the praises.*

A Celebration of the Everglades
from *Sawgrass Poems* by Frank Asch and Ted Levin

Theme Connection The photographs and poems explain challenges faced by the plants and animals in the Everglades.

Selection Summary and Awards The introduction on page 314 of the student book offers a summary. *Sawgrass Poems* won the John Burroughs Award for nature writing for children in 1996.

Background The word *Everglades* originated with the Old English word *glyde*, meaning a bright, shimmering place in a forest. Visitors to Everglades National Park can bike or walk on the raised wooden trails. Canoeists can use the Wilderness Waterway.

REACHING ALL STUDENTS

Transparency 78 / Master 78

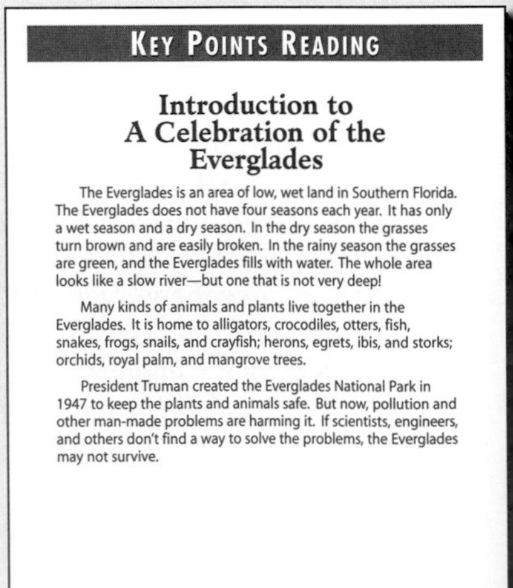

KEY POINTS READING

Introduction to A Celebration of the Everglades

The Everglades is an area of low, wet land in Southern Florida. The Everglades does not have four seasons each year. It has only a wet season and a dry season. In the dry season the grasses turn brown and are easily broken. In the rainy season the grasses are green, and the Everglades fills with water. The whole area looks like a slow river—but one that is not very deep!

Many kinds of animals and plants live together in the Everglades. It is home to alligators, crocodiles, otters, fish, snakes, frogs, snails, and crayfish; herons, egrets, ibis, and storks; orchids, royal palm, and mangrove trees.

President Truman created the Everglades National Park in 1947 to keep the plants and animals safe. But now, pollution and other man-made problems are harming it. If scientists, engineers, and others don't find a way to solve the problems, the Everglades may not survive.

Transparency 78 Level B, Unit 5 | Challenges © Hampton-Brown

ntroduction

ıe Everglades is a **wetland wilderness**, ɔrn in the sky and **sustained** by rain. It ıs no winter, summer, fall, or spring, like e rest of North America. Instead, like the **ropics**, the Everglades has two seasons—et and dry. During the dry season, from ovember to April, the seemingly **endless retches** of grassy **marshes** are brown ıd **brittle**, and the sky is blue, horizon to ɔrizon. During the wet season, from May to ctober, the landscape is green and lush and oks like a wide, **shallow**, slow-moving river.

Nowhere else in North America do plants ıd animals of both the **temperate zone** ıd the tropics **mingle**. Nowhere else in merica can you see manatees and crocodiles; one-hundred-foot-tall royal palms; or ouquets of orchids and colorful snails. In e dry season, alligators dig holes to stay et, and water-loving animals—otters, fish, ıakes, frogs, turtles, snails, crayfish—join em. Thousands of herons, egrets, ibis, ıd storks feast on the trapped fish, cover e **crowns of mangroves** like fresh snow, ıd decorate the Florida skies in one of merica's wild and wondrous **pageants**.

In 1947, Harry S. Truman dedicated the ɔ of south Florida as Everglades National ırk. It was the first national park in the world to be **preserved** for its unusual gathering of plants and animals rather than its spectacular scenery. Now, almost fifty years later, the Everglades has another unique distinction. It is the most endangered national park.

Ask: How is the Everglades different from the rest of the continent?

Alligator holding a softshell turtle in its mouth at Eco Pond in the Everglades.

Water is the very soul of the Everglades, but nearby man-made **dikes** and **levees interrupt its flow**. **Canals** drain water away and send it to the ocean. When water finally reaches the Everglades National Park, it often arrives at the wrong time of year, polluted by **runoff** from the farm fields.

Clarify: Water that runs off fields contains fertilizers and pesticides.

stained kept alive
ıdless stretches long distances
ittle dry and easily broken
allow not very deep
ıngle live together
crowns of mangroves top branches of mangrove trees
pageants shows
interrupt its flow stop the water from running

READ PAGE 315

SET PURPOSE

2 Point out the Introduction to pages 315–316. Set the purpose for reading the Introduction: *Read to find out why the authors presented these poems and photographs, and how they feel about the Everglades.*

READ AND THINK

Tape 5A CD 5 Track 2

3 Strategy Focus: Identify Author's Point of View and Purpose Have students complete the Reflection Log on **Master 79** as they read the Introduction.

Choose Reading Options in the **Multi-Level Strategies** to allow all students to participate.

The recording of the Introduction in "A Celebration of the Everglades" on the **Selection Tape/CD** offers an oral language model and the opportunity to build reading fluency.

Multi-Level Strategies

READING OPTIONS FOR LESSON 12

BEGINNING Distribute copies of **Master 78** to conduct a Key Points Reading of the Introduction. Work together to create sentences that tell the author's purpose.

INTERMEDIATE Read aloud the Introduction or play the **Selection Tape/CD**, pausing to clarify meaning. Fill in the information on **Transparency 79** as a group.

ADVANCED Have students read the Introduction with a partner, identifying words or phrases they don't know. Clarify meaning. Distribute copies of **Master 79** so partners can complete the Reflection Log. They can then share their information with another pair.

Transparency 79 / Master 79

REFLECTION LOG

A Celebration of the Everglades

What are some facts?	What words show the author's feelings?
The Everglades National Park was created in 1947. It is the most endangered national park. Canals drain the water away. The water is polluted by runoff from fields.	The landscape is green and lush. Nowhere else… …one of America's wild and wondrous pageants. Water is the very soul of the Everglades.
What is the author's point of view? The author cares deeply about the Everglades.	**What is the author's purpose?** The author wants me to care about the Everglades.

Transparency 79 Level B, Unit 5 | Challenges © Hampton-Brown

READ PAGE 316

OBJECTIVES

Comprehension: Ⓣ Identify Cause and Effect; Make Inferences

CHECK COMPREHENSION

4 Answers to "Before You Move On"

1. **Cause and Effect** Canals cause water to be drained away from the Everglades towards the ocean. When water does reach the Everglades, it often arrives at the wrong time of year and it is often polluted. Sometimes there is too much water, and sometimes there is not enough.
2. **Inference** The author wants to celebrate the Everglades because it is so unique. The author also probably wants to bring the Everglades to readers' attention because it is in danger of permanent damage.

CLOSE AND ASSESS

Invite students to share the interesting words and phrases they have recorded in their Reflection Logs.

Marjory Stoneman Douglas, in her book *The Everglades: River of Grass* (1947), called the Everglades a river. The Everglades is actually the largest freshwater marsh in North America, one hundred miles long and about fifty miles wide (at its widest). Before the central and northern Everglades were diked and dammed, a high count of nearly 265,000 wading birds nested in the mangroves in Everglades National Park. Now the number of wading birds has fallen to about 18,500.

—Ted Levin

Use text features and visuals: Read the caption and have students study the picture. **Ask:** What crops grow near the river?

Define *biologists, hydrologists, engineers,* and *politicians*: people who study living things, study water, design structures and systems, make laws.

Sometimes the park gets too much water. Sometimes it gets too little. Now, teams of biologists, hydrologists, engineers, and politicians have **pledged** to help **restore** the flow of water by removing some of the levees, plugging some of the canals, and cleaning the farmland runoff. No one knows if the Everglades, which has survived for five thousand years, will survive for fifty more.

These poems and photographs are a celebration of the Everglades. Frank and I want her to speak for herself. If, after sitting with these poems, you want to **immerse yourself in** the southern tip of Florida, we have succeeded. Long may she flow and her wild winds blow.

—Ted Levin

pledged promised
restore bring back
immerse yourself in learn much more about

BEFORE YOU MOVE ON...

1. **Cause and Effect** What changes have canals caused in the Everglades?
2. **Inference** Why does Ted Levin want to celebrate the Everglades?

REACHING ALL STUDENTS

INTERNET

MATHEMATICS CONNECTION

Have students use the Internet to find the average monthly rainfall for the Everglades and their own area. Students can then make graphs to show and compare the rainfall in the two locations. Use an on-line encyclopedia or the Internet. Web sites undergo frequent modification, but here are two you may want to suggest:

Web Sites

www.weatherlabs.com

orca.rsmas.miami.edu

CULTURAL PERSPECTIVES

World Cultures: Symbolic Animals
Show a picture of a bald eagle and explain that, in the United States, it symbolizes strength, courage, and independence. Then invite student pairs or small groups to investigate animals that are symbolic in other cultures. The Chinese calendar yields many examples of symbolic animals. Other examples are the lion in India and the toucan in Belize.

A Celebration of the Everglades
CONTINUED

Some Rivers

Some rivers rush to the sea.
They push and tumble and fall.
But the Everglades is a river
with no hurry in her at all.
Soaking the cypress
that grows so tall;
nursing a frog,
so quiet and small;
she flows but a mile
in the course of a day,
with plenty of time
to think on the way.
But how can she cope
with the acres of corn
and sorrowful cities that drain her?
With hunters and tourists and levees
that chain and stain and pain her?
Does the other half of her that's left
think only of the past?
Or does she think of her future
and how long it will last?
Some rivers rush to the sea.
They push and tumble and fall.
But the Everglades is a river
with no hurry in her at all.

—Frank Asch

Ask: How is the Everglades different from some other rivers?

Ask: Why does the poet refer to the river as "her" and "she"?

Soaking Covering with water
nursing protecting
flows travels
the course of a day one day's time
cope with handle, manage
drain her use up her water

BEFORE YOU MOVE ON...

1. **Mood or Tone** Describe the feeling that Frank Asch's poem "Some Rivers" creates.
2. **Inference** What does the poet mean by the phrase "the Everglades is a river with no hurry in her at all"?

READ PAGE 317

OBJECTIVES

Function: Listen Actively
Listening: Listen to a Poem
Reading Strategies: Identify Author's Point of View; Ⓣ Identify Author's Purpose
Comprehension: Make Inferences
Literary Analysis: Mood; Tone

SET PURPOSE

1 Explain to students that they will now listen to several poems about the Everglades. Set the purpose: *Listen for how the poet describes the Everglades.*

LISTEN AND READ

Tape 5A
CD 5 Track 2

2 **Strategy Focus: Identify Author's Point of View and Purpose** Play the **Selection Tape/CD** or read each poem aloud.

Choose Activity Options in the **Multi-Level Strategies** to allow all students to participate.

CHECK COMPREHENSION

3 **Answers to "Before You Move On"**

1. **Mood or Tone** The poem has a sad feeling because of the river's future.
2. **Inference** The poet may mean that the Everglades does not move swiftly the way some rivers do.

Multi-Level Strategies

ACTIVITY OPTIONS FOR LESSON 13

BEGINNING Select simpler stanzas and lines for use with these students, for example: the first four lines on page 317, the first and last stanzas of "Old Man Mangrove," and all of "Two Baby Snail Kites." Use the photographs and the red annotations to clarify meaning. Pause after reading for students to copy words or phrases from the poem that make the animals in the Everglades seem special.

INTERMEDIATE / **ADVANCED** Read all the poems, using the visuals to enhance the descriptions. Have students take notes in a chart:

Words That Make Me Like the Plants and Animals	Words That Make Me Worry About the Everglades
does she think of her future?	sorrowful cities hunters

READ PAGE 318–319

OBJECTIVES

Vocabulary Strategy: Locate and Use Definitions

Reading Strategies: Ⓣ Identify Author's Purpose

Comprehension: Make an Inference

Literary Analysis: Style; Repetition; Personification

REVIEW KEY VOCABULARY

4 Locate and Use Definitions

Materials: Index Cards

Assign Key Vocabulary words to pairs of students. Have them write each word on a card, then locate and copy the definition on the back. Collect the cards. Ask a student to choose a card and read the meaning aloud. Another student names the word and uses it to describe something from the selection.

Mangrove forests are found in quiet waters throughout the tropics worldwide. In the Everglades there are three species of mangroves that each live in water of different depths with different amounts of salt in it. Because they continually shed their nutrient-rich leaves, mangrove forests are among the most naturally productive areas in the world. The fallen leaves form a basic part of the food chain as they **decompose**.

—Ted Levin

Use text features and visuals: Read the caption and ask: How is a mangrove tree different from other trees?

Old Man Mangrov

Old Man Mangrove
lives by the sea.
He's a sailor, he's a farmer,
he's a rookery.

Ask: How do you think a tree can be like a sailor, a farmer, and a rookery?

All year long he
drops green leaves,
enriching the soil
for other trees.

Shrimp and lobster
spawn on his farms.
Thousands of birds
nest in his arms.

Ask: In what wa is the mangrov like the Everglad River?

Covered in oysters,
living on land,
he seems to creep
across the sand.

He moves at the pace
of a tired old snail,
till the tide comes in
and he sets sail.

—Frank Asch

decompose break down into tiny pie

rookery place where birds and other animals build nests

enriching adding food to

spawn lay eggs

pace speed

sets sail floats away as if on a boat

REACHING ALL STUDENTS

Cooperative Learning

FOR VOCABULARY: Words About the Everglades

Make a Word Web Group students according to language proficiency levels. Assign topics related to the Everglades, such as animals, plants, or threats to the environment. Have each group create a word web with their topic at the center. Give each group one large piece of paper. As the paper is passed from student to student, new words are added.

Explain the Word Webs Have students explain the placement of the words on their web. Combine the webs to make a wall-sized web about the Everglades.

Debrief the Content Direct students to share insights they gained from creating the word webs, for example: *What did you learn about the* manatee *and the* crocodile?

Debrief the Cooperative Process Have students evaluate how the activity helped them learn, for example: *How did sharing one piece of paper help you think of new words?*

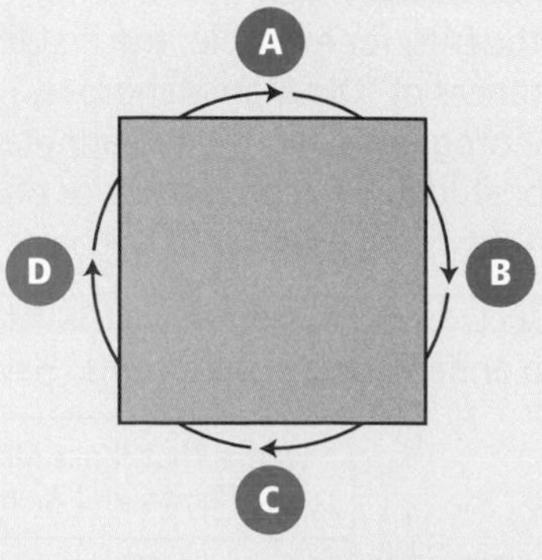

Cooperative Learning Structure: Team Word Webbing

A Celebration of the Everglades CONTINUED

Two Baby Snail Kites

Two baby snail kites
sitting in their nest,
hungry and endangered,
hoping for the best.

Pose choices: Does a snail kite have wings or a shell?

Apple snails for dinner.
Apple snails for lunch.
And every Sunday morning,
apple snails for brunch.

Two baby snail kites,
eyes still and steady,
waiting for a meal,
mouths wide and ready!

Apple snails for dinner.
Apple snails for lunch.
And every Sunday morning,
apple snails for brunch.

Ask: Who eats apple snails for dinner, lunch, and brunch?

"Hey Mom! Hey Dad!
How about some meat?"
"So sorry, little ones.
Snails is what we eat."

Apple snails for dinner.
Apple snails for lunch.
And every Sunday morning,
apple snails for brunch.

—Frank Asch

Snail kites are an endangered tropical member of the hawk family. Because snail kites feed mostly on apple snails that rise to the surface of the water to breathe, these kites are especially endangered by the draining of the Everglades. Anything that affects the well-being of the apple snail seriously affects the snail kite.

—Ted Levin

Read the caption and ask: Why is the snail kite endangered?

BEFORE YOU MOVE ON...

1. **Inference** What message does the poem about the mangrove tree tell readers?
2. **Author's Style** Identify two examples of personification in each poem.
3. **Author's Purpose** Why do you think the author wrote each of these poems? Do you think he was successful? Explain.

brunch a late morning meal that combines breakfast and lunch

still and steady looking straight ahead

CHECK COMPREHENSION

5 Answers to "Before You Move On"

1. **Inference** The tree is important to the soil and animals in the Everglades.
2. **Author's Style** Examples from "Old Man Mangrove" are *birds nest in his arms* and *he seems to creep.* Examples from "Two Baby Snail Kites" are *hoping for the best* and telling what the baby and parent birds "say" to each other.
3. **Author's Purpose** He wanted to make people care about the Everglades. Opinions will vary.

Language Development

ROLE-PLAY

Have students take the role of an Everglades creature and describe a typical day in its life. Encourage students to use vocabulary from the poems. Model sentences such as: *Hi, I'm a manatee. I live in the water and eat seaweed. One day a speedboat almost hit me. I didn't like that.*

Literary Analysis Minilesson

▶ REPETITION AND PERSONIFICATION

TEACH Draw attention to the title "Old Man Mangrove." Tell students that referring to a non-human object in human terms is called *personification.* Explain the root word *person* as a memory aid and illustrate with "birds nest in his arms."

Next read aloud the repeated lines in "Two Baby Snail Kites." Tell students that poets repeat words or phrases to emphasize key ideas. This is called *repetition.* Point out the root word *repeat* as a memory aid.

PRACTICE Have teams find more examples of personification and repetition.

Personification
use of *he*
"birds nest in his arms"
"he seems to creep"

Repetition
Man/Mangrove
"Apple snails for dinner"

▶ **Practice Book** page 149

READ PAGE 320–321

OBJECTIVES

Function: Listen Actively
Grammar: Present Perfect Tense Verbs; Ⓣ Past Perfect Tense Verbs
Listening: Listen to a Poem
Reading and Learning Strategies: Identify Author's Point of View; Ⓣ Identify Author's Purpose
Comprehension: Ⓣ Draw Conclusions
Literary Analysis: Ⓣ Metaphor; Evaluate Impact of Author's Background on Literature

CHECK COMPREHENSION

6 Answers to "Before You Move On"

1. **Metaphor** The poet thinks the manatee is like a goat or a cow because they all eat grasses.
2. **Conclusions** People can destroy or damage the plant and animal life in the Everglades, or they can help preserve it by limiting activities that cause damage.

Manatees are plant-eating water creatures distantly related to elephants. Like whales, these gentle, friendly mammals give birth in the water. Although manatees have no known enemies, they are frequently injured or killed by speeding powerboats.

—*Ted Levin*

Use text features and visuals: Read the caption and ask students to compare a manatee and a whale.

Hey You, Manatee!

You're no mermaid mama.
Yes, that's true!
But I can understand
how those ancient sailors
fell in love with you.
You whisker-nosed blubber blob!
You seaweed-munching sea slob!
You mossbacked moat goat,
slow-motion victim of speedboat!
Quietly munching
cow of the sea,
I confess—
I love you, manatee!

—*Frank Asch*

Define *moat*: a trench filled with water.

Ask: Why does the poet call the manatee the "cow of the sea"?

Ask: What endangers the manatee?

BEFORE YOU MOVE ON...

1. **Metaphor** How is a manatee like a goat or a cow to the poet?
2. **Conclusions** What conclusions can you form about how people make a difference in the Everglades?

slow-motion slow-moving
victim of something that gets hurt by
munching chewing
confess tell the truth

REACHING ALL STUDENTS

Social Studies Connection

NATIONAL PARKS

Explain that the U.S. National Park System is a network of over 357 sites, including 50 national parks, that are set aside by the national government in an effort to preserve and protect natural scenery, wildlife, and historic places. Have each pair or small group choose one national park and use an encyclopedia or other reference source to find out more about the park. They can create an illustrated class chart containing the features of the parks. Invite each pair or team to make an oral presentation to the class, telling why they chose the park, where it is located, and what its major features are.

Name of Park	Location	Features
Yellowstone	Wyoming	• geysers • Old Faithful • bubbling mud ponds
Yosemite	California	• Half Dome • Bridal Veil Falls • Yosemite Valley

ABOUT THE POET

ank Asch grew up close to ture. "I had a brook next to ere I lived ... and I could always nder around," he explains. His poems and books courage readers to take care of the earth. He els that the energy fueling his work comes from light, bright future—the future where the earth esn't get blown up or drown in its own pollution."

ABOUT THE PHOTOGRAPHER

Ted Levin has visited the Everglades many times and never ceases to be amazed by its beauty. His photographs and articles have appeared in many publications such as *National Geographic Traveler* and *Natural History*. Ted Levin lives with his wife, son, a baby weasel, and a bunny in Thetford, Vermont.

ABOUT THE POET AND PHOTOGRAPHER

7 Evaluate Literature: Author's and Photographer's Backgrounds
Read About the Poet and About the Photographer aloud. Point out that the poet and photographer both have a great love of nature and are very familiar with the Everglades. Ask: *How have Frank Asch's and Ted Levin's experiences with nature influenced their work?*

CLOSE AND ASSESS

Have students share the words and phrases they recorded as they listened to the poem.

Vocabulary

WETLAND WORDS

Write *Wetland Words* in the center of a web. Invite students to look through the selection to find all of the words that refer to wetlands, such as *swamp, slough,* and *bog.* Encourage students to write explanations that distinguish one term from another. Ask: *How is a bog different from a marsh?*

Grammar Minilesson

▶ VERBS IN PRESENT PERFECT AND PAST PERFECT TENSES

TEACH Reread the biography about Ted Levin and write this adaptation of the first sentence:

> I have visited the Everglades many times and never cease to be amazed by its beauty.

Underline *have visited* and review the formation of the present perfect tense: *To form the present perfect tense, use* has *or* have *plus a past participle.*

Then write:

> I had visited the Everglades many times before I saw a manatee.

Underline *had visited* and review the formation of the past perfect tense: *To form the past perfect tense, use* had *plus a past participle.*

PRACTICE Have students write variations of the example sentences to describe places they have visited:

> I have visited Muir Woods and never cease to be amazed by the size of the redwood trees. I had visited Muir Woods many times before I knew how unique the redwoods are.

▶ **Practice Book** page 150

RESPOND

OBJECTIVES

SUM IT UP

Function: Write

Reading and Learning Strategies: Use Graphic Organizers (chart)

Literary Analysis: Respond to Literature; Ⓣ Evaluate Literature

Writing: Literary Critique

THINK IT OVER

Function: Engage in Discussion

Critical Thinking and Comprehension: Ⓣ Summarize; Ⓣ Draw Conclusions; Make Comparisons; Make Judgments

EXPRESS YOURSELF

Function: Ⓣ Persuade

Listening and Speaking: Speech

CHECK YOUR UNDERSTANDING

1 Sum It Up Students' paragraphs will vary. Look to see if they included three reasons and used examples from the selection.

▶ **Practice Book** page 151

2 Think It Over Possible answers are:

1. **Summary/Conclusion** When one part of the system isn't healthy, it can't fulfill its function in the system. Damage to one part damages the whole.
2. **Comparisons** Douglas uses emotional, forceful words; Levin creates appealing visual images; Asch creates empathy by giving readers a view through the eyes of plants and animals.
3. **Judgments** If these ecosystems disappear, they will be gone forever.

3 Express Yourself Suggest that students choose three convincing arguments for their speeches and use strong action verbs.

CLOSE AND ASSESS

Ask students to summarize their feelings about the images in the poetry.

Respond to the Article and Poems

Check Your Understanding

SUM IT UP

Respond to Literature Complete your charts to show how the poems made you feel.

Words that Make Me Like Plants and Animals	Words that Make Me Worry About the Everglades
Old Man Mangrove mermaid mama	sorrowful cities hunters

Evaluate Literature The poet and the photographer created this selection to make you care about the Everglades. Study your charts and think about what you learned in the selection. Then write a paragraph to tell if the poet and the photographer achieved their purpose. Give three reasons to support your answer. Include examples from the article, poems, and photographs.

THINK IT OVER

Discuss and Write Talk about these questions with a partner. Write the answers.

1. **Summary/Conclusion** How do the plants, animals, and climate of the Everglades form a connected system? What happens to the whole system if one part of it is sick or damaged?
2. **Comparisons** Marjory Stoneman Douglas and the authors of "A Celebration of the Everglades" want to persuade you to save the Everglades. How do their persuasive techniques differ?
3. **Judgments** Why is it necessary to protect the Everglades?

EXPRESS YOURSELF ▶ PERSUADE

Give a three-minute speech to persuade your classmates to do something to help preserve the Everglades.

LANGUAGE ACQUISITION ASSESSMENT
See page 81 of the Assessment Handbook.

REACHING ALL STUDENTS

Multi-Level Strategies

SUM IT UP OPTIONS

BEGINNING Provide frames for students to use to compose a group paragraph:

We like *(name of poem)* very much.
The author's purpose is to ________.
He *(informed, persuaded, entertained)* us very well.

INTERMEDIATE Have students work with a partner. One partner can write the purpose statement and the other the statement about how well the author achieved his purpose. Then they work together to combine the two statements into one paragraph.

ADVANCED Have these students compose paragraphs on their own and then work with a partner to revise and improve their writing.

RESPOND

OBJECTIVES

METAPHOR
Critical Thinking: Make Comparisons
Literary Analysis: Ⓣ Metaphor
Writing: Metaphors

RHYMING POEM
Functions: Write
Literary Analysis: Rhyme Scheme; Rhythm
Writing: Rhyming Poem

ASSESSMENT
Selection Test 18 on page 85 of the Assessment Handbook tests students' mastery of the reading strategies and the vocabulary, comprehension, and language arts skills taught with this selection.

anguage Arts and Literature

LITERARY ANALYSIS

SE FIGURATIVE LANGUAGE: METAPHOR

earn About Metaphors A metaphor akes a comparison by saying one thing *is* nother thing.

The otter **is a clown.**
The cloud **was a giant pillow.**

letaphors paint pictures with words. They help eaders create images in their minds.

ind Metaphors Read the following lines from Old Man Mangrove." What are the metaphors? ow is the tree like these things?

> Old Man Mangrove
> lives by the sea.
> He's a sailor, he's a farmer,
> he's a rookery.

ractice Create metaphors about these plants nd animals in the Everglades.

crocodiles
turtles
orchids
palm trees

LITERARY ANALYSIS
WRITING

WRITE A RHYMING POEM

Learn About Rhyme Scheme The pattern of rhymes in a poem is called the **rhyme scheme**. You can use letters to label which lines have the same rhyme. In this stanza from "Two Baby Snail Kites," the last words in the second and fourth lines rhyme.

Two baby snail kites *a*
sitting in their nest, *b*
hungry and endangered, *c*
hoping for the best. *b*

The rhyme scheme for this poem is *abcb*.

Learn About Meter The beat of a poem is the **meter**. It makes the poem musical and fun to read aloud.

Read aloud the stanza from "Two Baby Snail Kites." Clap for each syllable, and notice the beats in each line.

Practice Now write a two-stanza rhyming poem. Develop a rhyme scheme and meter for it. You can use "Two Baby Snail Kites" and "Hey You, Manatee!" as models.

LANGUAGE ARTS AND LITERATURE

1 **Use Figurative Language: Metaphor** Give more examples of metaphors:

The river is a snail.
The sun is a sparkling diamond.
The sawgrass is a razor.

Emphasize that metaphors do not contain *like* or *as.*

▶ **Practice Book** page 152

2 **Write a Rhyming Poem** To provide writing prompts and support, you may want to do the following:

- Have students create a list of key nature words to use as topics.
- Provide a rhyming dictionary for students to use.
- Assist as necessary in marking the rhyme scheme and meter for students' poems.
- Read students' poems aloud to them and clap beats with them to clarify the meter and rhymes.

▶ **Practice Book** page 153

CLOSE AND ASSESS

Invite students to think, pair, and then share one new idea they learned in this lesson.

Multi-Level Strategies

PRACTICE OPTIONS FOR METAPHORS

BEGINNING Draw sketches to show the items being compared: *The sky is a blue blanket.* Then have students draw these concrete objects: pretty ballerina, brown rock, soggy sponge. Provide frame sentences with blanks where students can add words and pictures to create metaphors:

The egret is a ____. (pretty ballerina)
The turtle is a ____. (brown rock)
The ground in the rainy season is a ____. (soggy sponge)

INTERMEDIATE / **ADVANCED** Have students work in small groups to create their metaphors. First, they select an object to be the focus of the metaphor and write: *The river is* ____. Then they brainstorm objects for comparison. Finally, each student writes a metaphor for the object.

RESPOND

OBJECTIVES

PROPAGANDA IN THE MEDIA

Function: Give Information

Concepts and Vocabulary: Words About Propaganda—*bandwagon, testimonial*

Speaking: Oral Report

Learning Strategies and Research Skills: Gather Information; Use Graphic Organizers (chart); Use a Newspaper

Comprehension and Critical Thinking: Analyze and Evaluate Information; Identify Propaganda; Make Comparisons

Technology/Media: Select, Compare, and Evaluate Media

CONTENT AREA CONNECTIONS

1 Evaluate Propaganda in the Media
Prepare students by previewing content area vocabulary:

- ***bandwagon*:** Define *band* as "a group of people with a common purpose, such as a musical group" and *wagon* as "a four-wheeled vehicle used to carry goods." Explain that together they form a compound noun literally meaning "a wagon used to carry a band."

  Explain that the phrase is used informally to describe a group of people who get together and do the same thing. Ads that use a bandwagon technique appeal to a person's desire to be part of the group.

- ***testimonial*:** Write the root *test* and explain that it means "to witness or affirm." Teach that the meaning of the word *testimonial* is "a formal statement about the value of something." For example, if an ad tells you that a celebrity singer drinks milk, you might want to drink milk, too.

▶ **Practice Book** pages 154–155

Respond to the Article and Poems, continued

Language Arts and Content Area Connections

TECHNOLOGY/MEDIA

REPRESENTING/SPEAKING

EVALUATE PROPAGANDA IN THE MEDIA

People often use **propaganda** in the media to convince others to think or feel a certain way. Find and evaluate different examples of propaganda.

❶ **Learn About Propaganda** Here are two types of propaganda.

A **bandwagon** ad tries to convince you that everyone is doing something. The idea is that you should do it because everyone else is.

A **testimonial** ad uses a famous person to talk about an issue. Many people are influenced by the words of famous athletes and artists.

❷ **Collect and View Propaganda** Study several different kinds of propaganda in newspapers and magazines. If possible, you might record radio broadcasts and TV commercials, too.

❸ **Evaluate Techniques** Make a comparison chart. Identify the types of propaganda you have collected. Evaluate how effective each propaganda technique is. Use your chart to present your ads to the class.

Media	Technique	Effectiveness
magazine ad	testimonial by a famous actor	very effective, because people like and respect him

For tips on **viewing**, see Handbook page 403.

REACHING ALL STUDENTS

Research Skills

▶ USING A NEWSPAPER

TEACH Display editorials from local newspapers. Explain that editorials are written to persuade people to think a certain way about an issue of local or national interest. Tell students that an editorial is based on an opinion and contains facts that support the opinion.

Present a news story about a related topic. Explain that the purpose of a news story is to inform rather than persuade.

Point out factual statements in both examples and persuasive language in the editorial.

PRACTICE Have students work in pairs or groups of three to analyze an editorial. They should identify:

- the issue and the writer's opinion
- facts used to support the opinion
- persuasive language
- the action readers should take

Have them locate a related news story and compare it to the editorial.

SOCIAL STUDIES
REPRESENTING/SPEAKING

XPLORE GEOGRAPHY

lap the Climate Zones "A Celebration of the verglades" tells about the temperate zone and ne tropics. Find out about other climate zones nd show them on a map.

Research Climate Zones Earth has many climate zones including:

Desert	Tundra
Subtropical	Highland
Subarctic	Humid Continental

Use the Internet or an encyclopedia to learn where each climate zone is.

Prepare and Present Your Map Draw and label the climate zones on a world map. Use different colors to distinguish them. Highlight the Everglades section of Florida. Make a map key to tell what the colors mean. Then display your map in the classroom.

For tips on **representing**, see Handbook pages 404–405.

SCIENCE
REPRESENTING

MAKE A WILDLIFE REPORT

Research a plant or animal that is found in the Everglades. Report your findings to the class.

1. **Choose a Topic** Select a plant or animal from those listed on page 315.
2. **Research and Take Notes** Use an encyclopedia and other reference materials to learn about the habitat and life cycle of the plant or animal you chose. What is its place on the food chain? Take notes.
3. **Report to the Class** Choose from one of these ideas to present what you learned:
   - Write a report.
   - Make a poster.
   - Create a diorama with models of plants and animals.
   - Write a song or a rap.
   - Make a plant or animal puppet and have the puppet tell about its life.

OBJECTIVES

EXPLORE GEOGRAPHY

Function: Give Information

Concepts and Vocabulary: Words About Climate—*temperate, the tropics, desert, subtropical, subarctic, tundra, highland, humid, continental*

Learning Strategies and Research Skills: Use an Atlas and Globe; Gather Information

Representing: Map

WILDLIFE REPORT

Function: Give Information

Learning Strategies and Research Skills: Gather Information; Take Notes

Technology/Media: Evaluate and Select Media

Representing/Writing: Report

2 **Explore Geography** Prepare students by discussing the local climate and the climates in other areas where students may have lived. Then preview content area vocabulary:

- ***temperate, the tropics, desert, subtropical, subarctic, tundra, highland, humid, continental*:** Tell students these terms all refer to climate zones. Have students work in pairs to look up each word in a dictionary. Then provide pictures representing various kinds of climates, asking students to identify the vocabulary words that apply to each.

  Students should then work in small groups to create their own pictures to represent each of the words. Have groups share their pictures and determine the words represented by other groups' pictures.

3 **Make a Wildlife Report** Prepare students by making a class chart with the names of plants and animals that live in the Everglades.

CLOSE AND ASSESS

Invite students to share as many new ideas as they can which were gained from this lesson.

Research Skills

▶ USING AN ATLAS AND GLOBE

TEACH Display an atlas and a globe. Explain that both show countries and the Earth's physical features. Discuss different types of maps found in an atlas— physical, political, climatic. Show examples of each and model how to find information.

Point out the poles and the equator on the globe. Then contrast the details shown on a map in an atlas to the same area on the globe. Guide students in identifying advantages of each, such as in determining location and direction and tracing features that cross political boundaries.

PRACTICE Have students find a climate map in an atlas or an encyclopedia to use in the Geography activity above. Once they identify the areas in each zone, have them locate the areas on the globe.

▶ **Practice Book** page 156

INTRODUCE THEME 2

OBJECTIVES

Function: Engage in Discussion
Concepts and Vocabulary: Challenges—*intellectual, physical, social*
Viewing: Respond to a Photograph
Learning Strategies: Relate to Personal Experience; Use Graphic Organizers (chart)
Critical Thinking: Classify; Generate Ideas

TAP PRIOR KNOWLEDGE

1 **Think, Pair, Share About Personal Limits** Define: *limit, physical, intellectual,* and *social.* Ask: *What does it mean to have a physical limit?* Invite students to think of a time when they faced a physical limit and tell a partner about the experience. The partner then relates the experience to the class.

VIEW AND DISCUSS

2 **Classify Information** Read the caption as students view the photograph. Then ask students to look back at the WW II time line on pages 255–257. Review events and conditions of that era. Point out social limits with which Jesse Owens would have had to contend in Hitler's Germany. (racial prejudice) Ask: *What other limits did Jesse face?* (physical limits of the human body)

Read the quotation. Ask: *How was Jesse Owens able to "grapple for that extra ounce of guts"?* Have students chart the physical, intellectual, and social strengths that probably helped Jesse Owens push past his limits.

Jesse Owens was probably...

Physically	Intellectually	Socially
strong athletic	determined serious	confident active

Use the Discussion Prompts in the **Multi-Level Strategies** to involve all students in making the chart.

REACH BACK INSIDE YOURSELF AND GRAPPLE FOR THAT EXTRA OUNCE OF GUTS . . . .

—*Jesse Owens*

In 1936, Adolf Hitler attempted to use the Olympic Games in Berlin to establish the superiority of his race. African American athlete Jesse Owens pushed past the limits of racial prejudice to prove him wrong. This grandson of former slaves went on to win four gold medals at the Games. Jesse Owens showed the world that talent and determination, rather than race, distinguish one person from another.

REACHING ALL STUDENTS

Multi-Level Strategies

DISCUSSION PROMPTS

BEGINNING Provide a list of adjectives used to describe courageous people. (strong, brave, determined, proud, confident, hopeful, bold, fearless, courageous) Have students choose the adjectives that describe Jesse Owens. Add them to the chart.

INTERMEDIATE Have students work in a group to brainstorm adjectives for each column in the chart. Then ask them to use these adjectives to describe in complete sentences what they see or infer about Jesse Owens.

ADVANCED Ask students to discuss the kinds of challenges an African American athlete may have faced in the 1930s. Have students describe the kinds of traits that would help a person overcome these challenges. Prompt students to tell about other people they know who also have these characteristics.

otations offer strategies for
eginning students

THEME 2

Pushing Past the Limits

efine *limit*: a boundary,
thing that stops you.
est examples: Some jobs
re a college degree. If you
hard and graduate from
ge, you can push past limits
e jobs you can get.

- What are some limits people have in their lives? Give examples of physical, intellectual, and social skills that help people push past these limits.

Define *challenge*:
ething that requires
use of your efforts
talents.

- What are some challenges that people face alone? How do people face challenges together?
- Who are the people you admire most for pushing past a limit? Explain. **B Suggest examples:** Think about family members and people you know, as well as famous people such as scientists, inventors, artists, and leaders.

EME-RELATED BOOKS

na Unlimited
athleen Krull
na Rudolph could barely
as a child, but she overcame
ppling disease to become a
medalist at the Olympics.
INNING

Wings
by Jane Yolen
The Greek myth of Icarus, who learned the secret of flight.
INTERMEDIATE

NOVEL

Call It Courage
by Armstrong Sperry
Determined to conquer his fear of the sea, Mafatu goes to sea all alone, survives a frightening ordeal, and returns to his village a hero.
ADVANCED

DISCUSS THE GUIDING QUESTIONS

3 Set the Theme Some key points to develop during the discussion are:

- People face many limits every day: physical limits (not being able to run as fast as someone else), social (feeling unsure around new people or in new situations), and intellectual (not understanding how to do something).
- People must face some challenges on their own, but there are many that people can face together (studying for a test, working against racism). It is often less difficult to face a challenge when you meet it with others.
- We all know about famous people who have pushed past limits to accomplish great things. But we also admire friends and family members who have shown character and courage when facing a limit.

Form groups and use the **Multi-Level Strategies** so all students can participate.

CLOSE AND ASSESS

Have students draw pictures of people meeting new people, practicing an instrument, or batting a baseball. Have them label their pictures as representing physical, intellectual, or social skills.

Multi-Level Strategies

GROUPING GUIDELINES

BEGINNING Group students so you can define words and pose choices for responses. See suggestions in red on the facsimile for page 327.

INTERMEDIATE Have students work in small groups. Suggest that they use a dictionary or thesaurus to clarify unfamiliar words and phrases. Instruct them to select a recorder to write down key ideas that arise during the group discussion of the questions. The recorder then uses these notes to report about the group's discussion.

ADVANCED Invite students to read and discuss the questions with a partner. Have them agree on answers to each question and a list of people they admire. Then they report their results to the class.

THEME LIBRARY

■ ***Wings*** by Jane Yolen

Encourage students to read *Wings.* Explain that the story of Daedalus and Icarus has been told many times in many writing styles. Help students evaluate this version. Ask: *Why do you think the story has inspired so many writers? What important lessons about meeting challenges does this story teach? With which character did you identify most? Why? What do the illustrations add to the story?*

BUILD LANGUAGE AND VOCABULARY

OBJECTIVES

Function: Listen Actively; Ⓣ Elaborate
Concepts and Vocabulary: Survival Words
Patterns and Structures: Ⓣ Future Perfect Tense Verbs
Learning Strategy: Use Graphic Organizers (word web)
Critical Thinking: Make Predictions; Generate Ideas
Writing: Sentences

START WITH A COMMON EXPERIENCE

1 **View and Listen** Have students look carefully at the illustration and imagine how the boy must feel. Then play the excerpt from "Hatchet" on the **Language Tape/CD** or read aloud the script on page T414.

Tape 1B
CD 1 Track 7

2 **Model How to Elaborate** Say: *When you hear an exciting story like this, you might want to tell a friend about it. Your friend will appreciate the story more if you elaborate, or tell more about what happened.* Then model how to elaborate.

How to Elaborate

- Tell the big idea: *A tornado has left Brian with nothing—again.*
- Add details: *It is pitch dark; The winds have ripped down the trees; Brian's fire, shelter, tools, and bed are gone.*
- Tell more about Brian's thoughts and feelings: *Brian was back to square one, but with the hatchet, he could rebuild again.*

3 **Discuss the Quotation and Make Predictions** Have students speculate on what the quotation means and predict how Brian will go about rebuilding his life. Encourage students to base their ideas on what they learned about Brian from listening to the tape.

Use the Activity Options in the **Multi-Level Strategies** to involve all students in making predictions.

Build Language and Vocabulary

ELABORATE

Study the painting and listen to the tape. Then read the quotation. What do you think Brian has learned about challenges and survival?

I might be hit but I'm not done.
When the light comes, I'll start to rebuild.

—*Gary Paulsen, from* Hatchet

REACHING ALL STUDENTS

Multi-Level Strategies

ACTIVITY OPTIONS–ROLES FOR COOPERATIVE GROUPS

BEGINNING / **INTERMEDIATE** / **ADVANCED** Remind students that Brian had only a hatchet left after the storm. Then form heterogeneous groups and assign roles as follows:

▶ **Illustrator** ▶ **Recorder** ▶ **Reporter**

Have students make a storyboard to show how Brian rebuilds his life. Illustrators draw the scenes and sequence them. Recorders create captions. Reporters present the group's storyboard to the class.

AKE A WORD WEB

ake a large copy of the word web to put up in your classroom. Think of allenges that people face, and add them to the web. Bring in pictures that ustrate a challenge or show people who have met challenges and survived. dd them to the web, too.

UILD YOUR VOCABULARY

urvival Words These verbs are often used in talking about survival. Tell hat each one means. Use a dictionary to find the meanings of words you on't know.

im·pro·vise (im´ pru vīz) ***v.*** to make something from whatever is available.

Word Bank

Survival Words

choose
consider
discover
exceed
exert
improvise
learn
plan
prepare
risk
strive

SE LANGUAGE STRUCTURES ▶Future Perfect Tense Verbs

riting: Explain and Elaborate Write three sentences to tell what Brian ill have done if he makes it through the storm. Use verbs in the future erfect tense.

Examples:

Brian **will have considered** different ways to protect himself. He **will have chosen** the best way to survive. He **will have learned** that he can trust his own judgment.

Build Language and Vocabulary **329**

CONDUCT THE ACTIVITIES

4 Make a Word Web Invite students to bring in pictures or photos of challenges to add to the web.

5 Build Your Vocabulary: Survival Words Once students find the meanings of unknown words, encourage them to use the words in sentences.

6 Use Language Structures: Future Perfect Tense Verbs Present the skill, using the definition and examples on **Transparency 80**. Have students look at pages 450–451 of the Handbook to find past participles of irregular verbs. Then have students complete the paragraph in Try It!

Writing: Explain and Elaborate Conduct the activity at the bottom of page 329. Have students refer to the class word web for ideas.

Use the Writing Activity Options in the **Multi-Level Strategies** to adjust instruction.

▶ **Practice Book** page 157

CLOSE AND ASSESS

Have the class agree on how to complete this sentence using *discover* in the future perfect tense: *I _____ a new route home by nightfall.* Then have students make up a sentence using one of the other survival words in the future perfect tense.

Multi-Level Strategies

WRITING ACTIVITY OPTIONS

BEGINNING To help students elaborate on a topic, provide a frame for each sentence in the paragraph: *If he makes it through the storm, Brian will have _____. He also will have _____. Finally, Brian will have _____.* Students can use a different survival word in each sentence.

INTERMEDIATE Students can work in pairs to make up sentences using Brian as the subject and the survival words as the verbs. Encourage students to write their sentences using verbs in the future perfect tense.

ADVANCED Encourage students to write an ending to Brian's suspenseful tale of courage, using one of the storyboards created in Step 3 on page T328. Have them begin their narrative with this quotation: *I might be hit, but I'm not done. When the light comes, I'll start to rebuild.* Remind students to include in their narrative some verbs in the future perfect tense.

Transparency 80 / Master 80

Future Perfect Tense Verbs

A verb in the **future perfect tense** tells about an action that will be completed at a specific time in the future.

By the end of camp, I **will have learned** how to survive in the wilderness.

1. To form the future perfect tense, use the helping verb **will have** plus the past participle of the main verb.

   I also **will have made** many friends before the summer is over.

2. The past participle of a regular verb ends in **-ed**. Irregular verbs have special forms for the past participle.

Verb	Past	Past Participle
like	liked	liked
make	made	made
build	built	built
do	did	done

Try It!

Complete the paragraph with the future perfect tense of the verb.

By the end of summer camp, I __(do)__ many new things. I __(make)__ a fire on my own. I __(build)__ a shelter. I __(learn)__ to cook over a campfire.

Transparency 80 Level B, Unit 5 | Challenges

PREPARE TO READ

OBJECTIVES

THINK ABOUT WHAT YOU KNOW
Reading Strategy: Relate to Personal Experience

LEARN KEY VOCABULARY Ⓣ
Vocabulary Strategy: Locate and Use Definitions

LEARN TO RELATE CAUSES AND EFFECTS
Reading Strategy: Ⓣ Relate Causes and Effects

THINK ABOUT WHAT YOU KNOW

1 **Share Your Experiences** To extend, have students write paragraphs that tell about their partners' experiences.

LEARN KEY VOCABULARY

2 **Locate and Use Definitions** Read each word. Use one to model completing the chart.

Use Vocabulary Options in the **Multi-Level Strategies** to tailor the activity to proficiency levels.

▶ **Practice Book** page 158

LEARN TO RELATE CAUSES AND EFFECTS

3 **Model How to Relate Causes and Effects** Define *cause* and *effect*. Provide an example: *The streets are wet because it rained.* Explain that rain is the cause and wet streets are the effect. Model the steps with **Transparency 81**:

- Read the first two paragraphs. Pause to circle the signal word *because*.
- Write the Original Cause and the First Effect.
- Continue reading and noting other effects.

CLOSE AND ASSESS

Have students write one cause and one effect sentence about an event in their lives. Give an example: *Cause: I ate too much candy. Effect: I got a stomach ache.*

The Circuit
autobiography
by Francisco Jiménez

Prepare to Read

THINK ABOUT WHAT YOU KNOW

Share Your Experiences Did you ever make a big change in your lif
What was it? Why did you make the change? Tell a partner about it.

camp foreman person in charge of workers in a camp
crate box, container
enroll sign up
grape season time of the year when grapes are picked
labor camp place where workers live
migrant worker person who moves to find work
shack small, poorly built house, hut
vineyard field where grapes are grown
year-round job permanent job

Answers for students' guesses in the vocabulary activity will vary, but definitions should reflect the above annotations in red.

LEARN KEY VOCABULARY

Locate and Use Definitions Study the new words. Write each word
a chart and guess what it means. Use the Glossary to confirm its mean

Word	What I Think It Means	What It Really Means	✓
camp foreman	head person in a camp	person in charge of the workers in a camp	✓

LEARN TO RELATE CAUSES AND EFFECTS

The **cause** is the reason something happens. The **effect** is what happer
If you can relate causes and effects, you can understand how one actic
leads to another in a chain of events.

READING STRATEGY
How to Relate Causes and Effects

1. Look for words that signal a cause *(since, because)* and words that signal an effect *(so, as a result, therefore).*
2. Ask: What happened? Why did it happen?
3. Notice how one cause leads to another in a chain of events.

As you read "The Circuit," take notes about the causes and effects.

REACHING ALL STUDENTS

Multi-Level Strategies

VOCABULARY OPTIONS

BEGINNING Group students to read ***Crops*** or the Key Points Reading on **Master 82.** (See page T333.) Work with the vocabulary in those selections.

INTERMEDIATE Have students work in groups to generate possible meanings before consulting the glossary. Compare the predicted and actual meanings.

ADVANCED Have students complete the chart on their own, then compare their charts with a partner.

Transparency 81 / Master 81

HOW TO RELATE CAUSES AND EFFECTS

Directions: Read the passage. Then use information from the passage to fill out the Cause-and-Effect Chain.

Time to Move On

For two weeks, thick, dark clouds dumped torrents of rain along the coast. Rosa and her mother sat in the doorway of their small house and watched the rain turn the fields into muddy pools. Because of the rain, strawberries turned brown and soggy.

"The crop is ruined," said Mama. "You know what this means, Rosa."

Rosa sighed. "Yes, I know. Since there are no strawberries to pick, there is no work here. So we need to move on. Where do you think we should go?"

Mama stared out over the soggy fields, as if in a trance. Then she looked at Rosa and smiled.

"We will go to a place where there is sunshine, Rosa. There we will find berries that are bright and red and ready to pick. There will be plenty of jobs, so that is the place for us."

Cause-and-Effect Chain

Original Cause	First Effect	Second Effect	Third Effect
It rained every day for two weeks. →	The strawberry crop was ruined. →	There is no work. →	Rosa and her mother move to find work.

Transparency 81 Level B, Unit 5 | Challenges © Hampton-Brown

The Circuit

by Francisco Jiménez

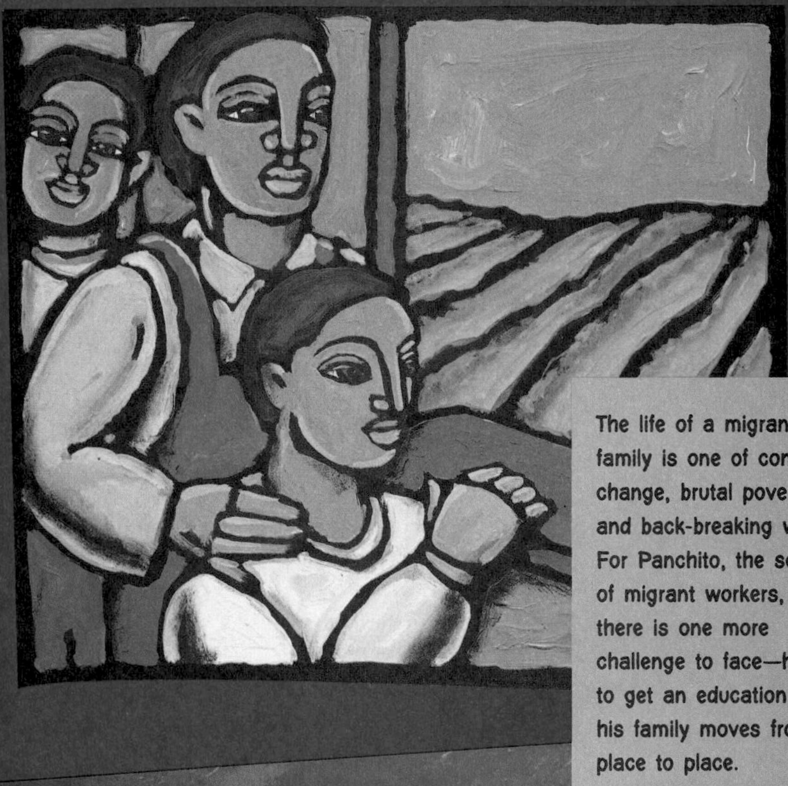

The life of a migrant family is one of constant change, brutal poverty, and back-breaking work. For Panchito, the son of migrant workers, there is one more challenge to face—how to get an education as his family moves from place to place.

331

READ THE SELECTION

OBJECTIVES

Reading Strategies: Preview; Predict
Literary Analysis: Autobiography

INTRODUCE THE SELECTION

4 **Preview and Predict** Read aloud the title, author's name, and introduction to the selection. Then have students view the illustration on page 331. Invite students to make predictions based on this information. Ask: *What do you think the life of this family is like? Why?* (Their life is probably very hard. They are poor and must move often.)

5 **Identify Genre: Autobiography** Point out the photograph of Francisco Jiménez on page 339 and explain that he wrote this selection about his own life. Explain that Panchito is a nickname for Francisco. Remind students that a true story about the author's own life is called an autobiography.

The Circuit
by Francisco Jiménez

Theme Connection This selection tells about the challenges faced by a young migrant worker and his family.

Selection Summary and Awards The introduction on page 331 of the student book offers a summary. "The Circuit" is from a book of the same title that won the Américas Award for Children's and Young Adult Literature, the Jane Addams Children's Book Honor Book Award, the Boston Globe/Horn Book Award for Fiction, and the California Library Association John and Patricia Beatty Award.

Background The migrant work force in the United States numbers over 2 million and is made up mostly of workers from Mexico and Central America.

THE BASICS BOOKSHELF

■ ***Crops*** by Fred Ignacio

Understanding a circuit of seasonal crops is made easy in this book that tells about the growth and harvesting of crops from farming regions within the United States. Simple text introduces basic vocabulary related to crops and farming, while colorful photos, charts, maps and graphs provide opportunities to discuss many facets of this industry.

For Lesson Plans: See the Teacher's Guide for ***The Basics Bookshelf***.

READ PAGES 332–333

OBJECTIVES

Function: Read a Selection
Listening: Listen to a Selection
Reading and Learning Strategies: Set a Purpose for Reading; Ⓣ Relate Causes and Effects; Use Graphic Organizers (cause/effect chain); Visualize

SET PURPOSE

1 Read aloud the introduction on page 332. Set the purpose for reading: *Read for details about Panchito's home and life.*

READ AND THINK

Tape 5B
CD 5 Track 3

2 **Strategy Focus: Relate Causes and Effects** As students read the selection, have them complete Cause-and-Effect Chains.

Choose Reading Options in the **Multi-Level Strategies** to tailor the reading to proficiency levels.

The recording of "The Circuit" on the **Selection Tape/CD** offers an oral language model and the opportunity to build reading fluency.

Red annotations offer opportunities to clarify meaning and check for understanding.

1

THE MOVE TO FRESNO

Panchito's family moves from place to place, following the crops. Once the strawberry season is over, they must move to Fresno to work in the vineyards.

Build background: American farmers depend on migrant workers to harvest their crops. To support their families, these workers must go wherever there are crops that need to be harvested.

At sunset we drove into a **labor camp** near Fresno. Since Papá did not speak English, Mamá asked the **camp foreman** if he needed any more workers. "We don't need no more," said the foreman, scratching his head. "Check with Sullivan down the road. Can't miss him. He lives in a big white house with a fence around it."

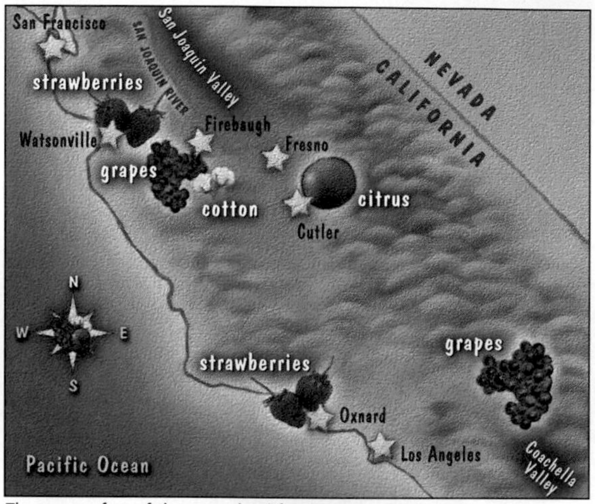

These are a few of the central California crops that **migrant workers** help to grow and harvest.

When we got there, Mamá walked up t the house. She went through a white gate, past a row of rose bushes, up the stairs to the house. She rang the doorbell. The porch light went on and a tall **husky** man came out. They **exchanged** a few words. After the man went in, Mamá **clasped her hands** and hurried back to the car. "We have work! Mr. Sullivan said we can stay there the whole season she said, **gasping** and pointing to an old garage near the **stables**.

The garage was worn out by the years. It had no windows. The walls, eaten by **termites**, **strained to support** the roof full of holes. The dirt floor, populated by earthworms, looked like a gray road map

That night, by the light of a **kerosene lamp**, we unpacked and cleaned our

Ask: How would you feel about the place where the family is going to live?

Pose choices: Is Mamá hap about finding work or abou staying in a garage?

husky heavy, large
exchanged spoke
clasped her hands put her hands together to show happiness
gasping breathing hard
stables building where horses are kept
termites insects that eat wood
strained to support were almost unable to hold up
kerosene lamp lamp that burns kerosene oil

REACHING ALL STUDENTS

Multi-Level Strategies

READING OPTIONS FOR LESSONS 4–5

BEGINNING Students should work with ***Crops*** while the class reads "The Circuit." Or distribute copies of **Master 82** to conduct a Key Points Reading of "The Circuit." Work together to identify at least one cause and two effects in each paragraph.

INTERMEDIATE Read the selection aloud or play the recording on the **Selection Tape/CD**, pausing to use the red annotations in the facsimile pages to clarify meaning. Have students work in small groups to identify causes and effects and record them in the Cause-and-Effect Chain on copies of **Master 83**.

ADVANCED Have students work with a partner to do a paired reading. Encourage them to use the monitoring strategies taught on pages 333, 334, 337, and 338. Partners can complete the Cause-and-Effect Chains on **Master 83** together.

ʼw home. Roberto swept away the loose ʼt, leaving the hard ground. Papá plugged e holes in the walls with old newspapers ɑd tin can tops. Mamá fed my little ʼothers and sister. Papá and Roberto then ʼought in the mattress and placed it on the ʼ corner of the garage. "Mamá, you and e little ones sleep on the mattress. ɔberto, Panchito, and I will sleep outside ɑder the trees," Papá said. **Ask:** What do you learn about the family from the way they organize their living space?

Early the next morning Mr. Sullivan ɑowed us where his crop was, and after ʼeakfast, Papá, Roberto, and I headed for e **vineyard** to pick. **Ask:** What kind of work will they do?

Around nine o'clock the temperature had sen to almost one hundred degrees. I was completely **soaked in sweat** and my mouth felt as if I had been chewing on a handkerchief. I walked over to the end of the row, picked up the jug of water we had brought, and began drinking. "Don't drink too much; you'll get sick," Roberto shouted. No sooner had he said that than I felt sick to my stomach. I dropped to my knees and let the jug roll off my hands. I remained motionless **with my eyes glued on** the hot sandy ground. All I could hear was the **drone** of insects. Slowly I began to recover. I poured water over my face and neck and watched the dirty water run down my arms to the ground. **Ask:** What made Panchito sick?

aked in sweat wet with perspiration
th my eyes glued on while staring at
one continuous sound

MONITOR YOUR READING

3 Visualize Read aloud the description of the family's new home on pages 332–333, beginning with *The garage was worn out by the years.* Ask students to form a mental picture of the garage based on the author's description.

Explain to students that visualizing the place where the family will live will help them understand and appreciate the feelings the writer is trying to convey.

Transparency 82 / Master 82

KEY POINTS READING

The Circuit

Panchito and his family move from place to place to find work. They find work in Fresno and move into their new home, an old garage. The garage is old and dirty. Mamá and the little ones sleep on a mattress. The others sleep outside under the trees. The next day, Panchito and his brother work in the vineyard with Papá.

When the grape season is over, Panchito goes to school. He is happy not to work in the fields. When Panchito arrives at school, he is very nervous. His teacher, Mr. Lema, is kind to Panchito. He gives Panchito extra help with his reading. Then Mr. Lema promises to teach Panchito how to play the trumpet. Panchito wants to tell Mamá and Papá this exciting news. But when he opens the door to the garage, he sees that his family has packed and is ready to move again.

Transparency 82 Level B, Unit 5 | Challenges © Hampton-Brown

Transparency 83 / Master 83

CAUSE-AND-EFFECT CHAIN

Directions: As you read each part of the selection, identify the causes and effects. Record these in the chain. Make predictions to show what might happen when the work in Fresno is over.

The Circuit

Original Cause	First Effect	Second Effect
Strawberry season is over.	The family moves to Fresno.	The family gets work picking grapes.
The grape season is over.	Panchito goes to school.	Panchito meets Mr. Lema and makes a new friend.
The work in Fresno is over.	Answers will vary.	Answers will vary.

Transparency 83 Level B, Unit 5 | Challenges © Hampton-Brown

READ PAGES 334–335

OBJECTIVES

Vocabulary Strategy: Use New Words in Context

Grammar: Ⓣ Past and Future Perfect Tense Verbs

Reading Strategy and Critical Thinking: Paraphrase

Comprehension: Identify Author's Point of View; Ⓣ Identify Cause and Effect; Form Opinions

MONITOR YOUR READING

4 **Paraphrase** Explain that paraphrasing helps you remember what you have read. Have students work with a partner to retell the events in the story up to this point. The partner who listens should point out any inaccuracies in the speaker's telling and should add any important details that the speaker omits. Then partners switch roles and retell the story again.

334 **Unit 5** | Challenges

REACHING ALL STUDENTS

Vocabulary
ROOTS AND PREFIXES

Point out the title of the selection and explain that a *circuit* is "a circular pathway." Ask: *Which part of* circuit *sounds like* circle? Then explain that *cir-* is a Latin prefix meaning "around" and that it is found in such words as *circle* and *circumstance.* Then introduce the Greek root *cycl-,* explaining that it means "circle" or "ring" and is found in such words as *cycle* and *bicycle.* Have students think of other words that include this root or prefix and write them in a chart.

Root	Meaning	Words
cycl-	circle ring	bicycle cycle
Prefix	**Meaning**	**Words**
cir-	around	circle circumstance

HOME CONNECTION

Family Goals Send home a copy of *High Point Newsletter 10* in the **Teacher's Resource Book.** In this home activity, students and their family members work together to set and meet a goal. Suggest possible challenges such as cleaning out a garage, helping a family member quit smoking, or going without TV for a week.

Clarify: Papá wants the boys to hide from the school bus because he knows the law says that school-aged children should be in school.

I still felt dizzy when we took a break to lunch. It was past two o'clock and we underneath a large walnut tree that was the side of the road. While we ate, Papá ed down the number of boxes we had ;ed. Roberto drew designs on the ground a stick. Suddenly I noticed Papá's face **n pale** as he looked down the road. re comes the school bus," whispered loudly **in alarm**. **tinctively**, Roberto and I and hid in the vineyards. did not want to get in ble for not going to school. neatly dressed boys about age got off. They carried ks under their arms. After crossed the street, the bus ve away. Roberto and I ne out from hiding and ed Papá. ***"Tienen que er cuidado,"*** he warned us.

After lunch we went back to work. sun **kept beating down**. The buzzing ects, the wet sweat, and the hot dry dust de the afternoon seem to last forever. ally the mountains around the valley **ched out and swallowed the sun**.

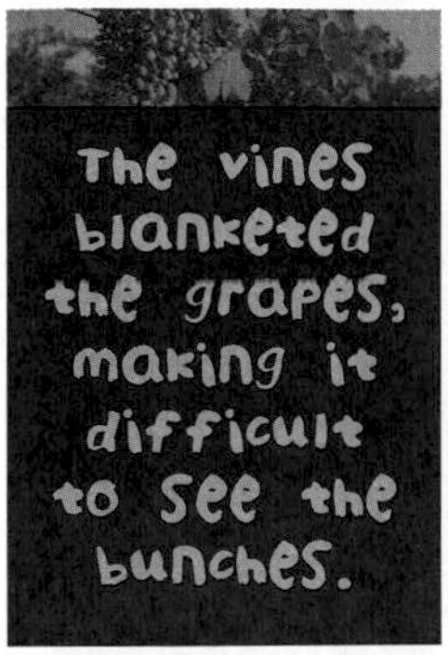

Ask: Why is it important for Papá to keep a careful record of what they have picked?

Within an hour it was too dark to continue picking. The vines blanketed the grapes, making it difficult to see the bunches. ***"Vámonos,"*** said Papá, signaling to us that it was time to quit work. Papá then took out a pencil and began to figure out how much we had earned our first day. He wrote down numbers, crossed some out, wrote down some more. ***"Quince,"*** he **murmured**.

When we arrived home, we took a cold shower underneath a water hose. We then sat down to eat dinner around some wooden **crates** that served as a table. Mamá had cooked a special meal for us. We had rice and tortillas with ***"carne con chile,"*** my favorite dish.

Encourage elaboration: Why doesn't Panchito take a shower in the house?

BEFORE YOU MOVE ON...

1. **Point of View** This story is autobiographical. Which character do you think represents the author?
2. **Cause and Effect** Why did Panchito and Roberto hide when Papá said the school bus was coming?
3. **Opinion** Do you think Panchito would rather have been in school than working in the vineyard? Explain your answer.

n pale lose its color
larm with fear and surprise
tinctively Without having to think
nen que tener cuidado You must be careful panish)
t beating down continued to shine ht and strong
reached out and swallowed the sun hid the setting sun
Vámonos Let's go (in Spanish)
Quince Fifteen (in Spanish)
murmured said softly
carne con chile meat with chili (in Spanish); a spicy meat stew

REVIEW KEY VOCABULARY

5 Use New Words in Context Have pairs create a scene to illustrate the meaning of as many key vocabulary words as they can. Have students label items in the scene. Invite the class to vote on the best scene. Post the pictures.

CHECK COMPREHENSION

6 Answers to "Before You Move On"

1. **Point of View** Panchito represents the author.
2. **Cause and Effect** The law says school-aged children should be in school every day.
3. **Opinion** Opinions will vary but should be supported by details from the story.

CLOSE AND ASSESS

Have groups share the information they have placed in their Cause-and-Effect Chains. Did they note first and second effects?

Language Development

GIVE INFORMATION

Explain that many kinds of work, like the crop work in this selection, are only available during certain seasons. Elicit other examples such as lifeguards working during the summer and ski instructors during the winter. Have students create a flyer or poster advertising for seasonal workers. Suggest that they include the following information in the advertisement: who (contact person), what (type of work), where (location), when (weeks or months of work available), why (pay rate), how (phone number, address).

Grammar Minilesson

▶ LINKING VERBS

TEACH Write this sentence:

By nine o'clock, the temperature had risen to almost 100 degrees.

Identify *had risen* as a verb in the past perfect tense that tells about an action that happened before another time in the past. Say: *Use the helping verb* had *and the past participle of the main verb to form the past perfect tense.* Write:

By nightfall, Panchito will have picked hundreds of grapes.

Identify *will have picked* as a verb in the future perfect tense to show an action that will be complete before a specific future time. Explain: *Use* will have *with the past participle of the main verb.*

PRACTICE Have students complete the sentences with the correct verb form.

1. At the end of the grape season, Panchito _____ in school. (enroll; past perfect)
2. By the end of the year, they _____ many different kinds of fruits. (pick; future perfect)

▶ **Practice Book** page 159

READ PAGES 336–337

OBJECTIVES

Function: Read a Selection
Listening: Listen to a Selection
Reading and Learning Strategies: Set a Purpose for Reading; Ⓣ Relate Causes and Effects; Use Graphic Organizers (cause/effect chain); Relate to Personal Experience
Literary Analysis: Theme

SET PURPOSE

1 Read aloud the introduction to pages 336–339. Set the purpose for reading: *Look for clues that tell you how Panchito feels about going to the new school.*

READ AND THINK

Tape 5B
CD 5 Track 3

2 **Strategy Focus: Relate Causes and Effects** Involve students in reading pages 336–339 of the selection. Encourage students to identify causes and effects in this part of the selection and to record them in their Cause-and-Effect Chains.

See the **Multi-Level Strategies** on T332 to tailor the reading to proficiency levels.

2

BACK TO SCHOOL

On Panchito's first day of school, his teacher offers to spend extra time to help him with his reading. Mr. Lema also offers to teach him to play the trumpet.

The next morning I could hardly move. My body **ached** all over. I **felt little control over** my arms and legs. This feeling went on every morning for days until my muscles finally got used to the work.

It was Monday, the first week of November. The **grape season** was over and I could now go to school. I woke up early that morning and lay in bed, looking at the stars and **savoring the thought** of not going to work and of starting school for the first time that year. Since I could not sleep, I decided to get up and join Papá and Roberto at breakfast. I sat at the table across from Roberto, but I kept my head down. I did not want to look up and face him. I knew he was sad. He was not going to school today. He was not going tomorrow, or next week, or next month. He would not go until the cotton season was over, and that was sometime in February. I rubbed my hands together and watched the dry, acid stained skin fall to the floor in little rolls.

Ask: How do you think Panchito felt about going to school?

Ask: Why didn't Panchito want to look at his brother?

When Papá and Roberto left for work, I felt **relief**. I walked to the top of a small **grade** next to the **shack** and watched the ***Carcachita*** disappear in the distance in a cloud of dust.

Two hours later, around eight o'clock, I stood by the side of the road waiting for school bus number twenty. When it arrived I climbed in. Everyone was busy either talking or yelling. I sat in an empty seat in the back.

When the bus stopped in front of the school, I felt very nervous. I looked out the bus window and saw boys and girls carrying books under their arms. I put my hands in my pant pockets and walked to the principal's office. When I entered I heard a woman's voice say: "May I help you? I was **startled**. I had not heard English for months. For a few seconds I remained speechless. I looked at the lady who waited for an answer. My first instinct was to answe her in Spanish, but I held back. Finally, after **struggling for** English words, I **managed**

ached hurt
felt little control over did not have enough strength to use
savoring the thought enjoying the idea
relief calm, less worry
grade hill
Carcachita car (in Spanish slang)
startled surprised
struggling for trying hard to think of
managed found a way

REACHING ALL STUDENTS

A WORLD OF LANGUAGES

Common Word Structures Students' knowledge of word structure in their native language can transfer and help them learn English. For example, the French, Czech, Estonian, Ukrainian, Korean, and Spanish languages all use endings attached to the base word. Although the English endings may be different, the concept of adding an ending will transfer. Vietnamese, Mandarin, Thai, and Indonesian do not use endings.

Common Endings Which Transfer

ENGLISH	SPANISH	FRENCH
-er (worker)	*-or* (trabajador)	*-eur* (travailleur)
-tion (education)	*-ción* (educación)	*-tion* (éducation)
-ous (nervous)	*-oso* (nervioso)	*-eux* (nerveux)

tell her that I wanted to **enroll**. After
swering many questions, I was led to
e classroom.

Mr. Lema, the teacher, greeted me and
signed me a desk. He then introduced me
the class. I was so nervous and scared at
at moment when **everyone's eyes were**
n me that I wished I were with Papá and
oberto picking cotton. After taking roll,
r. Lema gave the class the assignment for
e first hour. "The first thing we have to do
is morning is finish reading the story we
gan yesterday," he said **enthusiastically**.
e walked up to me, handed me an English
ook, and asked me to read. "We are on
ge 125," he said politely. When I heard this,
felt **my blood rush to my head**; I felt
zzy. "Would you like to read?" he asked **hesitantly**. I opened the book to page 125. My mouth was dry. My eyes began to water. I could not begin. "You can read later," Mr. Lema said **understandingly**.

Ask: What shows that the teacher was kind and understanding?

During recess I went into the rest room and opened my English book to page 125. I began to read in a low voice, pretending I was in class. There were many words I did not know. I closed the book and **headed** back to the classroom.

Mr. Lema was sitting at his desk correcting papers. When I entered he looked up at me and smiled. I felt better. I walked up to him and asked if he could help me with the new words. "Gladly," he said.

The rest of the month I spent my lunch hours working on English with Mr. Lema, my best friend at school.

eryone's eyes were on me everyone was
oking at me
thusiastically with great energy
blood rush to my head hot and embarrassed
hesitantly without being sure if I could
understandingly with knowledge of how I felt
headed started to go

MONITOR YOUR READING

3 Relate to Personal Experience Ask students to review the first paragraph on page 337 in which Panchito describes entering the classroom. Draw students' attention to the sentence that begins "I was so nervous. . . ." Ask students to think of times in their lives when they were nervous about entering a new situation or when they felt that everyone's eyes were on them. Point out that this is an example of a social limit. Ask students to write privately in their journals about this event. Then ask volunteers to give Panchito advice about how to cope with his situation.

COMMUNITY CONNECTION

Services for New Families Tell students that every community has services available to people who are new to the area, whether they are migrants, immigrants, or relocating for other reasons. Have students research the services available in their community for families new to the area. Encourage them to research resources to assist with the following issues: education, health, housing, childcare, employment.

Literary Analysis Minilesson

▶ THEME

TEACH Define *theme* as "a story's message about life or human nature." Explain that several pieces of literature might have related themes. Ask: *What is the theme we are studying?* (Pushing Past the Limits) *How is this theme related to life or human nature?* (Life is full of limits which people can push past.)

Invite students to find passages that show how "The Circuit" relates to this theme. Ask: *What is Panchito learning about life and limits?*

PRACTICE Invite students to create a theme map to show how the selections address the theme.

Pushing Past the Limits
The Circuit Panchito pushes past the limits of poverty to find work and get an education. Mother to Son __________
The Clever Wife __________

▶ **Practice Book** page 160

READ PAGES 338–339

OBJECTIVES

Reading Strategies: Paraphrase; Make Predictions
Comprehension: Ⓣ Draw Conclusions; Make an Inference
Literary Analysis: Respond to Literature

CHECK COMPREHENSION

4 Answers to "Before You Move On"

1. **Paraphrase** Panchito was nervous and afraid to speak.
2. **Evidence and Conclusion** Mr. Lema cared about Panchito. He helped him with his reading and offered to teach him to play the trumpet.
3. **Inference** He realized when he saw everything packed in boxes. He felt sad and discouraged.

MONITOR YOUR READING

5 Make Predictions Tell students the story ends like it began: the family is about to move on, since the work in Fresno has ended. In the last row of **Master 83** (see page T333), have students predict the effects caused by the end of work in Fresno.

One Friday during lunch hour Mr. Lema asked me to take a walk with him to the music room. "Do you like music?" he asked me as we entered the building. "Yes, I like ***corridos***," I answered. He then picked up a trumpet, blew on it, and handed it to me. The sound **gave me goose bumps**. I knew that sound. I had heard it in many *corridos*. "How would you like to learn how to play it?" he asked. He must have **read my face** because before I could answer, he added: "I'll teach you how to play it during our lunch hours." **Ask:** How does Panchito plan to spend his lunch hours from now on?

That day I could hardly wait to tell Pap and Mamá the great news. As I got off the bus, my little brothers and sister ran up to meet me. They were yelling and screaming. I thought they were happy to see me, but when I opened the door to our shack, I sav that everything we owned was neatly packe in cardboard boxes.

Ask: Why were his brothers and sisters yelling?

BEFORE YOU MOVE ON...

1. **Paraphrase** In your own words, tell what Panchito's first day back at school was like.
2. **Evidence and Conclusion** Did Mr. Lema care about Panchito? How do you know?
3. **Inference** When did Panchito realize that the family was about to move again? How did he feel?

corridos traditional songs, ballads (in Spanish)
gave me goosebumps caused little bumps to appear on my skin because it excited me
read my face known what I was thinking by looking at my face

REACHING ALL STUDENTS

Cooperative Learning

FOR LANGUAGE DEVELOPMENT: Elaborate

Explore Other Points of View Explain that since the selection is autobiographical, it tells mainly how Panchito feels. Say: *Now you will explore the feelings of others.*

Role-Play Interviews Have groups of four choose an event in the story. Three students role-play the mother, the father, and Roberto. The fourth member acts as an interviewer. Role-players decide how their characters might have felt at the time of the event and explain it to the interviewer.

After all characters have been interviewed, groups pick another event and take new roles until each student has played all roles.

Debrief the Content Ask: *What did you learn about the other characters' points of view from this activity?*

Debrief the Cooperative Process Have students evaluate the interviews. Ask: *Did you explain your characters' feelings clearly? Did the interviewer ask effective questions? Explain.*

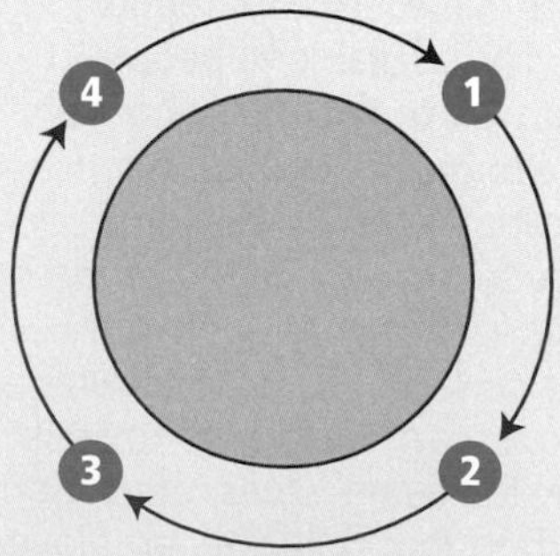

Cooperative Learning Structure: Roundtable

Epilogue

Define *professor*: college teacher

Not long after this **episode**, I returned Mexico. A few months later, I got the apers I needed to live in the United States. y brother and I moved to Santa Clara, alifornia. We both got **year-round jobs** janitors. This job allowed me to settle in ne place and complete my education.

I always loved learning. I studied ard and did very well. I **earned several scholarships to** Santa Clara University and a Woodrow Scholarship to Columbia University.

After I finished school, I became a professor of Spanish Language and Latin American Literature at Santa Clara University.

In 1999, I began writing the **sequel** to *The Circuit*, though I never learned to play the trumpet.

—*Francisco Jiménez*, January 2000

Pose choices: Which of these did Panchito become: a trumpet player, a migrant worker, a college professor, a janitor, a writer?

isode event, time in my life

rned several scholarships to won ards of money in order to attend

quel next part

About the Author

Francisco Jiménez had a purpose in mind when he wrote about his experiences as the child of a migrant family. It was to fill the need for understanding about the hardships endured by migrant families in the United States. Francisco Jiménez overcame obstacles and met a personal challenge to achieve his goals. He became a successful educator and an award-winning writer of such books as *The Circuit* and *La Mariposa*, which is also about the migrant experience.

ABOUT THE AUTHOR

6 Evaluate Literature: Author's Background: Read the Epilogue and About the Author and ask: *Do you think Panchito's experiences in this selection portray the life of the migrant farm worker? Why do the experiences seem so real?* As students discuss, remind them that Panchito is the same person as the author, Francisco Jiménez. Ask: *What limits did Panchito push past?* (poverty, disrupted education) *What choices did he make that caused his success?* (got a job, finished his education, studied hard, earned scholarships) *What were the effects of his getting an education?* (He became a professor and a writer.)

CLOSE AND ASSESS

Have students add information from Panchito's story to the unit mind map.

Vocabulary

IDIOMS

Remind students that idioms are expressions that do not mean the same thing as the individual words in the expression. Point out idioms from the selection such as *lump in my throat* and *can't miss him.* Have students record these idioms and their definitions in charts in their class or individual dictionaries. Encourage them to add to their charts as they come across new ones.

Literary Analysis Minilesson

▶ RESPOND TO LITERATURE

TEACH Define response as "a reaction." Explain that each person responds to a piece of literature in his or her own unique way.

Explain that a person's response to a selection can be based on many things, including the person's point of view, past experiences, background, opinions, and feelings.

Reinforce the idea that there is no one correct response to a piece of literature and that each person's response is valid.

PRACTICE Have students write a sentence or two giving their response to "The Circuit" on an index card. Provide a model:

> I admire Panchito's parents because they worked hard like my parents did.

Collect the index cards and share the varied responses to reaffirm the wide range of valid responses to a text.

▶ **Practice Book** page 161

RESPOND

OBJECTIVES

SUM IT UP

Function: Retell a Story; Engage in Discussion

Reading Strategies and Critical Thinking: Ⓣ Relate Causes and Effects; Use Graphic Organizers (cause/effect chain); Make Comparisons

THINK IT OVER

Function: Engage in Discussion

Critical Thinking and Comprehension: Identify Author's Point of View; Make Predictions; Ⓣ Draw Conclusions

EXPRESS YOURSELF

Function: Clarify; Ⓣ Elaborate

Speaking and Listening: Oral Presentation

CHECK YOUR UNDERSTANDING

1 **Sum It Up** Students should use the chains they developed while reading the selection. For the last chain, invite students to predict effects of the cause. Then conduct the comparison activity.

▶ **Practice Book** page 162

2 **Think It Over** Possible answers are:

1. **Author's Point of View** Panchito may not like moving, and he tries to learn as much as he can when he's in school.
2. **Prediction** Panchito might be nervous, but he may feel more confident because of his experience with Mr. Lema.
3. **Conclusions** Answers will vary but may include that through any kind of hard work, people become more prepared to meet the next challenge.

3 **Express Yourself** Students should conclude by explaining the effects these persons had on their lives.

CLOSE AND ASSESS

Ask students to explain what they learned about causes and effects in this lesson.

Respond to the Autobiography

Check Your Understanding

SUM IT UP

Relate Causes and Effects to Retell a Story Show what happened when each season ended. Then use your Cause-and-Effect Chains to retell the story to a partner.

Cause-and-Effect Chains

Original Cause	First Effect	Second Effect
The strawberry season ended.		

Original Cause	First Effect	Second Effect
The grape season ended.		

Compare Life Stories In "Twins" you read about deaf twins who have overcome a number of challenges. How are they and Panchito alike? How are they different? Compare their families, their feelings, and the changes they go through. Discuss your ideas in a group.

THINK IT OVER

Discuss and Write Talk about these questions with a partner. Write the answers.

1. **Author's Point of View** What does Panchito think about having to move from place to place?
2. **Prediction** How do you think Panchito will feel the next time he has to start over in a new school?
3. **Conclusions** How did Panchito's hard work a[s] a migrant worker prepare him for the challenges of getting a college education?

EXPRESS YOURSELF

▶CLARIFY AND ELABORATE

Think about the ways in which Mr. Lema helpe[d] Panchito. Then tell about a teacher, coach, or other adult who has been important to you. Give examples that show how this person has helped you.

✔ **LANGUAGE ACQUISITION ASSESSMENT See page 82 of the Assessment Handbook.**

REACHING ALL STUDENTS

Multi-Level Strategies

SUM IT UP OPTIONS

BEGINNING Ask yes/no questions or pose choices. *Did both Panchito and the twins like to go to school? Who was deaf? Did both the twins and Panchito go to college? Did Panchito or one of the twins become a professor?* Write students' answers to form a comparison paragraph.

INTERMEDIATE Have students brainstorm everything they know about the twins and Panchito, and then work with a partner to make statements about each detail, for example: *The twins pushed past the limits of deafness. Panchito pushed past the limits of changing schools frequently.*

ADVANCED After having the group brainstorm details about the lives of Panchito and the twins, encourage them to write comparison statements on their own.

ASSESSMENT
Selection Test 19 on page 87 of the Assessment Handbook tests students' mastery of the reading strategies and the vocabulary, comprehension, and language arts skills taught with this selection.

ɔnguage Arts and Literature

GRAMMAR IN CONTEXT

SE THE FUTURE PERFECT TENSE

ɛarn About the Future Perfect Tense Some tions will start and be completed at a specific me in the future. To tell about these actions, ɛe the **future perfect tense.** It is formed in is way:

will have + past participle

ɹudy these examples.

By sunset, the workers **will have filled** many boxes with strawberries.

ɛe sunset will take place in the future. Filling ɛe boxes will also happen in the future, but at a ɛecific time—before the sunset.

ɬake Up Sentences Complete these sentences ith a verb in the future perfect tense.

By lunchtime, I ________ .

When school ends, you ________ .

ɹactice Write the paragraph. Use the verb in ɜrentheses in the future perfect tense.

By the time his family moves on, Panchito (learn) many new English words. He (start) music lessons. Before spring, however, the family (move) to a new place. When he is grown up, Panchito (live) in many different places.

WRITING

USE LOGICAL ORDER IN WRITING

Learn About Logical Order When authors present information, they often use a **logical order**. "The Circuit" follows a circle—it starts and ends with the family moving. Some other examples of logical order are:

- A news article gives the most important information first.
- A description of a place may start at the front and move to the back, or it may describe details in a left-to-right direction.
- A persuasive letter often begins with the reason for writing it, followed by supporting ideas and details.

Choose a Writing Form Choose one of these ways to rewrite the story of Panchito's life in another logical order. Then share your writing with a group.

- Write a news story about Panchito's graduation from college.
- Describe a scene from the story, such as Panchito's home, the vineyard, or the school.
- Write a persuasive letter that suggests ways to improve life for migrant farm workers.

Multi-Level Strategies

WRITING OPTIONS FOR LOGICAL ORDER

BEGINNING Select an illustration showing a scene from the story, such as the classroom on page 337. Start by asking students to identify the items shown in the picture. Provide a list of prepositions such as *next to, above, across from,* and *to the left*. Then work with students to write a detailed description of the scene, moving from left-to-right or front to back.

INTERMEDIATE / **ADVANCED** Distribute copies of a newspaper article and an editorial. Have students analyze and discuss how those models show logical order. Help students create outlines showing how the writers arranged the information. Then have students write in a similar order. Partners can trade papers and edit each others' work.

RESPOND

OBJECTIVES

FUTURE PERFECT TENSE
Grammar: Ⓣ Future Perfect Tense Verbs

LOGICAL ORDER IN WRITING
Function: Write; Give Information; Describe; Ⓣ Persuade
Writing: Newspaper Article, Description, or Persuasive Letter

LANGUAGE ARTS AND LITERATURE

1 Use the Future Perfect Tense Possible sentences in "Make Up Sentences" are:

1. By lunchtime, I will have read two stories.
2. When school ends, you will have learned about the future perfect tense.

Answers to the Practice items are:
- will have learned
- will have started
- will have moved
- will have lived

▶ **Practice Book** page 163

2 Use Logical Order in Writing Once students have completed their writing, remind them to review what they have written to check for logical order. Point out that an objective person (a person who did not write the piece) can often spot problems more easily. Invite students to give and get the benefit of an "objective eye" by exchanging their writing with a partner for review.

▶ **Practice Book** pages 164–165

CLOSE AND ASSESS

Have students work in heterogeneous groups to create sentences telling what they learned in this lesson. Groups should share their sentences with the class.

RESPOND

OBJECTIVES

EXPLORE GEOGRAPHY

Function: Give Information

Concepts and Vocabulary: Word Families—*migrant, migrate, migration, migratory*

Learning Strategy and Research Skills: Gather and Organize Information; Use Maps

Representing: Circuit Map

STUDY THE "SALAD BOWL TO THE WORLD"

Function: Give Information

Learning Strategy and Research Skills: Gather and Organize Information; Take Notes

Technology/Media: Use the Internet

Representing: Profile Map

CONTENT AREA CONNECTIONS

1. **Explore Geography** Teach this content area vocabulary:
   - ***migrant, migrate, migration, migratory*:** Display the words. Write *migr–* and explain that it means "move." Have students find definitions and parts of speech for the words in a dictionary. Have students use each word in sentence.
2. **Study the "Salad Bowl to the World"** Explain that the Central Valley of California is called "Salad Bowl to the World" because a large percentage of the world's salad vegetables grow there. Students can write target questions on cards, then add the answers as they research.

CLOSE AND ASSESS

Ask students to share what they learned in this lesson.

Respond to the Autobiography, continued

Content Area Connections

SOCIAL STUDIES

EXPLORE GEOGRAPHY

Make a Circuit Map Migrant workers like Panchito and his family follow crops from place to place. They move with the harvest and the needs of the growers. Use atlases, maps, and the Internet to find the answers to these questions:

- What crops are grown in the southwestern United States?
- Where are the major areas in which these crops are grown?
- How long is the growing season of each crop? When is each crop harvested?

Use the answers to these questions to make a "circuit map." Show the circular route a typical family might take as they follow the crops thoughout the year.

Harvesters pick lettuce in California.

TECHNOLOGY/MEDIA

SOCIAL STUDIES

STUDY THE "SALAD BOWL TO THE WORLD

With a group, make a profile map of one of th counties in the California Central Valley, the "salad bowl to the world."

1. **Gather Information and Take Notes** Loc up the names of the Central Valley counties and choose one to research. Use its name as key word to find out about the number of crops grown there, where the crops are shipped, and other facts. Try these Web sites to get started. Take notes and download interesting photos.

INTERNET

INFORMATION ON-LINE

Web Sites:

- **Information about the Central Valley**
  - www.californiacv.com
- **Information about California Farms**
  - www.cfbf.com

2. **Make a Profile Map** Draw a map of the county you choose. Write captions that list interesting facts that you found. Include pictures of the crops grown there.

Learn to use the **Internet** on Handbook pages 392–393.

REACHING ALL STUDENTS

Research Skills

▶ USING MAPS: LONGITUDE AND LATITUDE

TEACH Display a globe or world map. Elicit recall of the lesson on T311. Remind students that latitude lines are parallel to the equator; the distance between them is given along the side of a map. Those above the equator indicate degrees north of the equator, to 90° north at the North Pole. Those below show degrees south.

Point out the prime meridian and the International Date Line as the reference points for longitude. Locations east of the meridian to the Date Line show degrees east; lines to the west show degrees west. Longitude spacing is given at the top of the map.

Model locating your state and writing the location, for example: 45°N 68°W.

PRACTICE Have partners locate places where specific crops are grown and mark the locations with a map flag labeled with the longitude and latitude.

▶ **Practice Book** page 166

lother
to Son

poem
by Langston Hughes

Prepare to Read Poetry

THINK ABOUT WHAT YOU KNOW

Share Parents' Sayings What kinds of things do your parents say to you again and again? Share these sayings with a group and explain why your parents think they are important.

rd flat piece of wood

stal very high quality
s that people value for its
ıty

ding flat area at the
of a number of steps

inter small, thin, sharp
e of wood

ir set of steps that goes
ı one level or floor to the
t

k small, sharp nail

LEARN KEY VOCABULARY

Relate Words Study the new words and their definitions. Make a Venn diagram to show how a crystal stair and a wooden stair are alike and different.

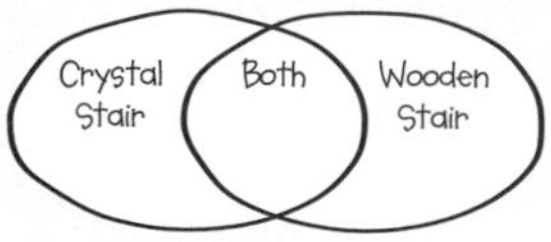

LEARN TO INTERPRET METAPHORS

A **metaphor** makes a comparison. Poets use metaphors to paint a picture with words.

READING STRATEGY

How to Interpret Metaphors

1. Ask yourself: What two things does the poet compare?
2. Form a picture in your mind of the metaphor. What does the comparison mean?
3. Restate the comparison in your own words.

As you read "Mother to Son," visualize the metaphor the poet uses.

Multi-Level Strategies

VOCABULARY OPTIONS

BEGINNING Direct students to the picture in the Glossary of *crystal* (page 480). Read aloud the sample sentences for *crystal, board,* and *stair* from the Glossary.

INTERMEDIATE Have students work in pairs to complete the Venn diagram activity.

ADVANCED Students should complete the activity on their own, then compare their diagrams with a partner.

Transparency 84 / Master 84

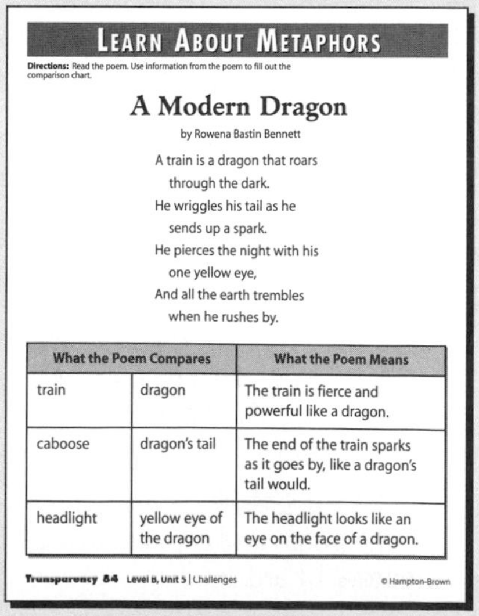

LEARN ABOUT METAPHORS

Directions: Read the poem. Use information from the poem to fill out the comparison chart.

A Modern Dragon

by Rowena Bastin Bennett

A train is a dragon that roars
through the dark.
He wriggles his tail as he
sends up a spark.
He pierces the night with his
one yellow eye,
And all the earth trembles
when he rushes by.

What the Poem Compares		What the Poem Means
train	dragon	The train is fierce and powerful like a dragon.
caboose	dragon's tail	The end of the train sparks as it goes by, like a dragon's tail would.
headlight	yellow eye of the dragon	The headlight looks like an eye on the face of a dragon.

Transparency 84 Level B, Unit 5 | Challenges © Hampton-Brown

PREPARE TO READ

OBJECTIVES

THINK ABOUT WHAT YOU KNOW

Reading Strategy: Relate to Personal Experience

LEARN KEY VOCABULARY Ⓣ

Vocabulary Strategy: Relate Words

LEARN TO INTERPRET METAPHORS

Literary Analysis: Ⓣ Metaphor

THINK ABOUT WHAT YOU KNOW

1 Share Parents' Sayings Provide examples: *It pays to tell the truth. It takes hard work to succeed.* Have students discuss their parents' sayings and find common messages among them.

LEARN KEY VOCABULARY

2 Relate Words Read each word and clarify meanings. Conduct the Venn diagram activity.

Use Vocabulary Options in the **Multi-Level Strategies** to tailor the activity to proficiency levels.

▶ **Practice Book** page 167

LEARN TO INTERPRET METAPHORS

3 Model How to Interpret Metaphors Define *metaphor* as "an expression that shows similarity between two different things." Demonstrate with **Transparency 84**:

- Read the title and the poem aloud. Read the first two lines of the poem again. Ask: *What two things is the poet comparing?* Record *train* and *dragon* in the chart and elicit what the comparison means.
- Say: *Once you see what the poet is comparing, you understand other ways the comparison is made. What other dragon parts are mentioned?* (tail, eye) *What are these compared to?* Add these metaphors to the chart.

CLOSE AND ASSESS

Ask students to create a metaphor for life. Provide a frame, such as: *Life for me is a ______.*

READ PAGE 344

OBJECTIVES

Function: Read a Poem
Vocabulary Strategy: Interpret Figurative Language (metaphor)
Listening: Listen to a Poem
Literary Analysis: Ⓣ Metaphor

SET PURPOSE

1 Read aloud the title and give students a moment to look at the photo. Set the purpose for listening to the poem: *As you listen, think about what the mother is saying to her son and what she really means.*

LISTEN AND READ

Tape 5B
CD 5 Track 4

2 **Strategy Focus: Interpret Metaphors** Play "Mother to Son" on the **Selection Tape/CD** or read the poem aloud for all students to hear the entire poem. Then play or reread the poem, pausing after every few lines to visualize and discuss the metaphors.

Choose Activity Options in the **Multi-Level Strategies** to involve all students in the activity.

Mother to Son

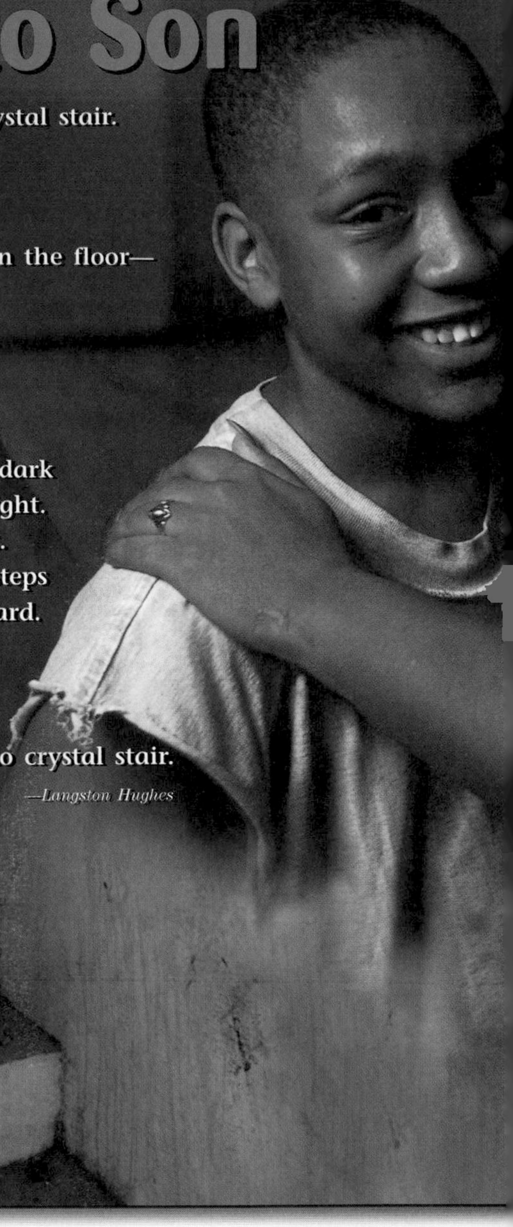

Well, son, I'll tell you:
Life for me ain't been no crystal stair.
It's had tacks in it,
And splinters,
And boards torn up,
And places with no carpet on the floor—
Bare.
But all the time
I'se been a-climbin' on,
And reachin' landin's,
And turnin' corners,
And sometimes goin' in the dark
Where there ain't been no light.
So, boy, don't you turn back.
Don't you set down on the steps
'Cause you finds it kinder hard.
Don't you fall now—
For I'se still goin', honey,
I'se still climbin',
And life for me ain't been no crystal stair.

—Langston Hughes

ain't been no hasn't been a
I'se I have
a-climbin' climbing
kinder kind of, sort of

REACHING ALL STUDENTS

Language Development

ADJUST COMMUNICATION TO THE OCCASION

Point out that the mother in this poem speaks informally because she is talking to her son, someone she is very close to and loves. Generate a discussion about the settings and occasions for using formal and informal speech.

Formal	Informal
talking to the Principal	at a party
giving a speech	at lunch with friends

Multi-Level Strategies

ACTIVITY OPTIONS FOR UNDERSTANDING METAPHORS

BEGINNING Ask yes/no questions and pose choices to help students interpret metaphors. Say: *Does a crystal stair or splinters mean an easy life? Is it easier to find your way in the dark or in the light?* Provide a frame for stating the overall metaphor of the poem: This mother's life has been _____, not like a crystal stair.

INTERMEDIATE Help students restate each metaphor by asking such questions as: *What do the tacks, splinters, torn-up boards, and bare floor mean?* (hard times) *What does the mother say about giving up?* (Don't sit down or turn back.)

ADVANCED Invite students to identify all the metaphors they can find in the poem and explain how each one relates to the overall metaphor of the mother's hard life.

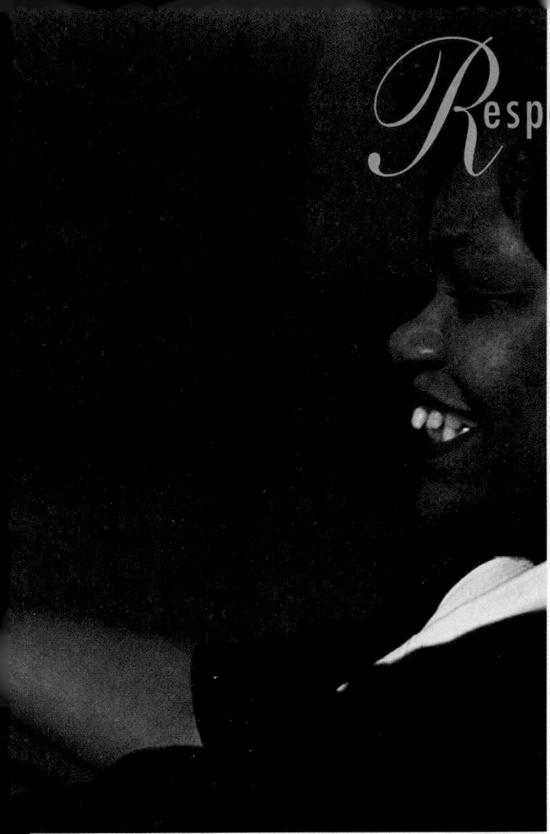

Respond to the Poem

THINK IT OVER

Discuss Talk about these questions with a partner.

1. **Comparisons** What other metaphors could be used to describe life's journey?
2. **Personal Experience** What advice about life would you give to someone who is younger than you?

EXPRESS YOURSELF

▶ JUSTIFY

What experiences or situations could cause the mother in the poem to have this talk with her son? Take the role of the mother and justify her position. Explain why she feels her son needs her advice.

ABOUT THE POET

Langston Hughes earned his place as one of America's greatest poets by writing about the trials, hopes, and triumphs of ordinary black people. Langston Hughes was born at the beginning of the 20th Century, a time when African Americans had very few civil rights. He survived the Great Depression and lived to see the beginning of the civil rights movement. In one of his essays, "The Negro Artist and the Racial Mountain," he wrote, "We build our temples for tomorrow, as strong as we know how, and we stand on top of the mountain, free within ourselves." Langston Hughes died in 1967.

Language Development

EXPRESS FEELINGS AND OPINIONS

Have students work in small groups to write a poem entitled "Son to Mother." Tell students they may use one of the scenarios they came up with for the Express Yourself activity. Remind them to write from the son's point of view. Encourage groups to share their poems.

RESPOND

OBJECTIVES

THINK IT OVER

Function: Engage in Discussion

Critical Thinking and Comprehension: Make Comparisons; Relate to Personal Experience

EXPRESS YOURSELF

Function: Justify

Speaking and Listening: Role-Play

ABOUT THE POET

Literary Analysis: Evaluate Impact of Author's Background on Meaning

THINK IT OVER

3 Possible answers are:

1. **Comparisons** Students may suggest a road or a trip. Ask them to explain their choices.
2. **Personal Experience** Answers will vary. Encourage elaboration.

EXPRESS YOURSELF

4 **Justify** As a class, brainstorm the kinds of situations that could lead a mother to give this advice. Students should select one situation and plan what they will say in their performances.

ABOUT THE POET

5 **Evaluate Literature: Author's Background** Have students read About the Poet. Point out the hardships Langston Hughes faced as an African American at the beginning of the 20th century. Ask: *How do you think these difficulties led him to write this poem? What evidence of his life do you see in the poem?*

CLOSE AND ASSESS

Have students choose a line from the poem that is significant to them. Ask: *Which line did you choose? Why?*

PREPARE TO READ

OBJECTIVES

THINK ABOUT WHAT YOU KNOW
Reading Strategy:
Activate Prior Knowledge

LEARN KEY VOCABULARY Ⓣ
Vocabulary Strategy:
Relate Words

LEARN TO SUMMARIZE
Reading Strategy: ⓉSummarize

THINK ABOUT WHAT YOU KNOW

1 **Quickwrite** Have students tell about folk tales from their home culture. Then ask them to think about qualities and elements common to all folk tales. Have students quickwrite their ideas in a journal and then share what they have written with the class.

LEARN KEY VOCABULARY

2 **Relate Words** Have students read each vocabulary word and its definition. Clarify meanings. Then conduct the ranking activity.

Use the Vocabulary Options in the **Multi-Level Strategies** to tailor the activity to proficiency levels.

▶ **Practice Book** page 168

LEARN TO SUMMARIZE

3 **Model How to Summarize** Define *summary*. Demonstrate the steps in the box with **Transparency 85**:

- Read the passage. Pause to collect and list the details.
- Check the most important details.
- Work with the group to write the summary statement.

CLOSE AND ASSESS

Ask students to agree on why it is helpful to summarize after each section they read. (When you summarize, you are sure you have understood the overall idea before moving on to the next section.)

The Clever Wife Prepare to Read

folk tale from
ancient China
retold by Carol Kendall
and Yao-wen Li

THINK ABOUT WHAT YOU KNOW

Quickwrite Think about folk tales you know. What kinds of challenges usually appear in folk tales? Write a few sentences about them in your journal and share your ideas with the class.

appalling arrogance strong and shocking pride

boastful speaking with too much pride, bragging

braggart person who brags or praises himself or herself too much

capability ability to do something well

cleverness intelligence

conceited too proud of oneself

incomparable wisdom knowledge without equal or beyond compare

matchless wit clever and powerful mind that has no equal

remarkably proud unusually pleased or satisfied

swollen head feeling of being better than others

unusually clever more intelligent and creative than most people

LEARN KEY VOCABULARY

Relate Words Study the new words and their definitions. Then put the words in order from the highest degree to the lowest.

Diagram

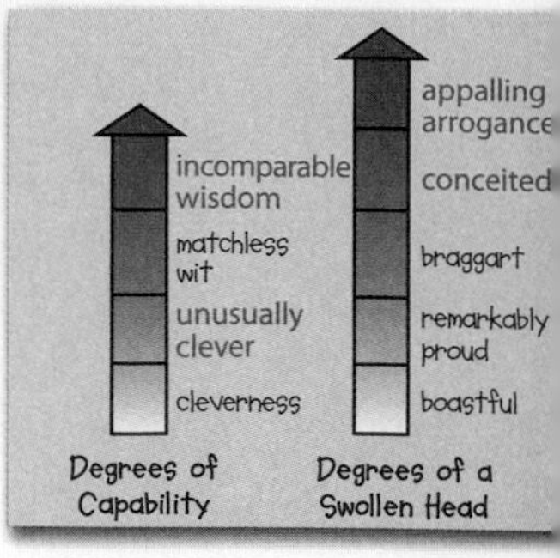

LEARN TO SUMMARIZE

A **summary** tells the most important ideas in a story and helps you remember what you read.

READING STRATEGY

How to Summarize

1. Make a list of important details in each section of the story.
2. Read through your list and put a check next to the most important details.
3. Write a summary statement that uses these important details and tells the main idea of the section.

As you read "The Clever Wife," collect important details for each section and write a summary statement.

REACHING ALL STUDENTS

Multi-Level Strategies

VOCABULARY OPTIONS

BEGINNING Group students to read ***Sunny and Moonshine*** or the Key Points Reading on **Master 86**. (See page T349.) Work with the vocabulary in those selections.

INTERMEDIATE Work with students to decide where to place each vocabulary word.

ADVANCED Students can rank the words on their own and then compare their answers with those of a partner. Have partners discuss answers that don't match.

Transparency 85 / Master 85

HOW TO SUMMARIZE

The Legendary Origin of Vietnam

Lac Long Quan, the great dragon king, and Au co, the beautiful fairy queen, fell deeply in love. They married and soon the lovely Au co gave birth to one hundred fine sons.

In time, the fairy queen took fifty of the strong, handsome sons. They returned to the mountains. They became the mountain and hill tribes of Vietnam. Their skill was in hunting and upland farming.

The mighty dragon took the other fifty sons to the sea. These sons became the fine fishermen and the lowland farmers.

Then Lac Long Quan called the first born son to himself. He gave him the title of Hung Vuong. Hung Vuong was the founder of the first great Hung Vuong dynasty that lasted from 2879 to 258 BCE.

Important Details

☐ **1.** Lac Long Quan and Au co fall in love.

☑ **2.** They marry, and have 100 sons.

☑ **3.** Au co takes 50 sons to become hunters and farmers.

☑ **4.** The mighty dragon takes 50 sons to become fishermen and farmers.

☑ **5.** The first born son founds the first dynasty.

Summary Statement Lac Long Quan and Au co marry and have 100 sons who become the hunters, fishermen, and farmers of Vietnam. The first born founds the first dynasty.

Transparency 85 Level B, Unit 5 | Challenges

The Clever Wife

an ancient Chinese folk tale retold by
Carol Kendall and Yao-wen Li

Fu-hsing is a simple but wealthy man, thanks to his wife's cleverness. When his pride in her is mistaken for a swollen head about himself, however, the district magistrate promises to punish Fu-hsing. Once again, Fu-hsing's wife must use her wits to help her husband face this challenge.

347

READ THE SELECTION

OBJECTIVES

Reading Strategies: Preview; Predict
Literary Analysis: Folk Tale

INTRODUCE THE SELECTION

4 **Preview and Predict** Read the title, author's name, and introduction to the folk tale. Lead a discussion about the illustration. Ask students to guess the identity of the passenger. Next, have students page through the story, looking at the pictures. Students can then make predictions about the story based on information gathered from the illustrations.

5 **Identify Genre: Folk Tale** Tell students that this is an ancient, well-known story that has been passed down from one generation to the next among people in China. Explain that this kind of story is called a folk tale.

The Clever Wife
an ancient Chinese folk tale retold by
Carol Kendall and Yao-wen Li

Theme Connection In this Chinese folk tale, a wife uses her cleverness to help her husband meet a seemingly impossible challenge.

Selection Summary and Awards The introduction on page 347 of the student book offers a summary of the selection. This selection appeared in *Sweet and Sour: Tales from China.* The book won the Parents' Choice Award in 1982 and was named a Newbery Honor Book in 1960.

THE BASICS BOOKSHELF

- ***Sunny and Moonshine: A Love Story***
  by Shirleyann Costigan

Moonshine is in love with Sunny, but seems forever separated from him by time and space. How will they ever get together? The simple text in this modern *pourquoi* tale about the eclipse of the sun introduces the names of the planets and other celestial bodies. Illustrations about the solar system and a solar eclipse give beginning English learners access to the facts behind the fiction.

For Lesson Plans: See the Teacher's Guide for ***The Basics Bookshelf***.

READ PAGES 348–349

OBJECTIVES

Function: Read a Selection
Listening: Listen to a Selection
Reading and Learning Strategies: Set a Purpose for Reading; Use Graphic Organizers (summary chart); Ⓣ Summarize
Comprehension: Identify Character's Motive; Make Judgments
Literary Analysis: Plot (conflict)

SET PURPOSE

1 Read aloud the introduction to pages 348–349. Set the purpose for reading: *Read to understand what Fu-hsing wrote and why his words made the magistrate angry.*

READ AND THINK

Tape 5B
CD 5 Track 5

2 **Strategy Focus: Summarize** Have students collect details in each part and use them to write a summary statement.

Choose Reading Options in the **Multi-Level Strategies** to tailor the reading to proficiency levels.

The recording of "The Clever Wife" on the **Selection Tape/CD** offers an oral language model and the opportunity to build reading fluency.

Red annotations offer opportunities to clarify meaning and check for understanding.

1

FU-HSING PRAISES HIS WIFE

Fu-hsing writes words in praise of his clever wife. A magistrate thinks the words are about Fu-hsing himself and wants to punish him.

Build background: There are many Chinese tales about human character traits. In this Chinese folk tale, a man's pride in his wife's cleverness gets him into trouble.

A very long time ago there lived in a far corner of China, in Sinkiang, a good and simple man named Fu-hsing, who had an **unusually clever** wife. All the day long he would run to her with questions about thus-and-such, or about such-and-thus. No matter how difficult the problem he took to her, she always thought of a solution. Thanks to her extreme intelligence, the house of Fu-hsing enjoyed success and good **fortune**. **Ask:** How did Fu-hsing's wife help him?

Fu-hsing was **remarkably proud** of his wife and often spoke of her as his "**Incomparable Wisdom**," his "**Matchless Wit**," or his "Dearest **Capability**." He only wished that all who passed his house could know it was her **cleverness** that had brought him such good fortune. For months he puzzled his head over a **suitabl** **way of declaring his gratitude**. He at las created **a couplet** that **delicately conveye** his feeling. He wrote the lines on twin **scrolls** and **posted** them on the gate befor his house:

> A Matchless Wit like Fu-hsing's
> Does with ease a million things.

All who passed the house saw the scro Those who knew Fu-hsing thought he was true and honest husband to praise his wife in this way. **Ask:** What did his neighb think of Fu-hsing's sign?

Use visuals: Have students identify cultural details in the pictures. (clothing, hairstyles, architecture, lettering)

fortune luck
suitable way of declaring his gratitude way to thank her that matched all the good she had done for him
a couplet two rhyming lines of poetry
delicately conveyed used the perfect words to show
scrolls rolls of paper for writing
posted put, hung

REACHING ALL STUDENTS

CULTURAL PERSPECTIVES

Home Culture: Showing Gratitude Explain that different cultures have different ways of expressing gratitude. Point out that Fu-hsing showed his gratitude by creating a couplet, or two-line poem, for his wife. In other cultures people may show gratitude by making a public statement or by giving a card, flowers, or a gift. Ask students to make a brief presentation to the class, describing or showing how gratitude is expressed in their home culture.

Multi-Level Strategies

READING OPTIONS FOR LESSONS 12–14

BEGINNING Students should work with ***Sunny and Moonshine*** while the class reads "The Clever Wife." Or distribute copies of **Master 86** to conduct a Key Points Reading of "The Clever Wife." Work together to create a sentence that summarizes each part.

INTERMEDIATE Read the folk tale aloud or play the recording on the **Selection Tape/CD**, pausing to use the red annotations on the facsimile pages to clarify meaning. Record the important details on **Transparency 87** as a group. Work with the group to agree on a summary statement.

ADVANCED Have students read the selection on their own, identifying words or phrases they don't know. Clarify meanings. Distribute copies of **Master 87** so that students can complete the Summary Chart independently. Have students discuss their summary statements with a partner.

One day, however, the **district**
agistrate happened to pass that way.
reading the scrolls, he **drew** his mouth
wn and his eyebrows together in a terrible
wn. "What a **boastful**, **conceited** fellow
es there!" he thought. "What **appalling**
rogance! Such boastfulness should not
unpunished!"

When he returned to his quarters,
ordered Fu-hsing to appear before him.
is frightened Fu-hsing so much that he
uld hardly tell his wife of it. ". . . can't
derstand . . . **I'm law-abiding** . . . good
izen . . . pay taxes without cheating. . . ."
pulled at his hair, dropping strings of it
the floor. "My dear Capability, what did
lo to bring this upon myself?"

Ask: Why is Fu-hsing so upset?

His wife laid a calming hand on his before he could tear out the last of his thinning hair. "It must be," she said, after a moment's thought, "that the scrolls on the gate gave the wrong **impression**. Really, it is not worth worrying about! Go see the magistrate and have no fear. If you run into difficulty, we can talk it over when you return."

Ask: What will happen when he sees the magistrate?

BEFORE YOU MOVE ON...

1. **Character's Motive** Why did Fu-hsing post the scrolls on his gate?
2. **Conflict** What problem did the scrolls create? How could it have been prevented?
3. **Judgment** Compare how Fu-hsing and his wife each reacted to the magistrate's order. Who would be better at pushing past limits? Why?

strict magistrate person who carries
t the law in the town
ew pulled
I'm law-abiding I follow all laws
impression idea

CHECK COMPREHENSION

3 Answers to "Before You Move On"

1. **Character's Motive** He wanted all who passed his house to know about his wife's cleverness.
2. **Conflict** When the magistrate saw the scrolls, he thought Fu-hsing was talking about himself. The magistrate wanted to punish him for being boastful. This could have been prevented if Fu-hsing had made it clear that the "Matchless Wit" referred to his wife.
3. **Judgment** Fu-hsing was filled with panic and worry. His wife was calm and collected. She would probably be better at meeting a challenge because it is easier to push past limits with a calm and positive outlook.

CLOSE AND ASSESS

Have students share their summary statements for pages 348–349. Check for focus: Do the sentences note what Fu-hsing did and how the magistrate reacted?

Transparency 86 / Master 86

KEY POINTS READING

The Clever Wife

Fu-hsing and his clever wife live in China. Fu-hsing has good fortune because of his wife's cleverness. He writes a couplet about her cleverness and hangs it outside his house. The magistrate sees the poem and is angry. He thinks Fu-hsing is boastful. He orders Fu-hsing to come before him.

The magistrate gives him three tasks to prove his cleverness. He tells him to do three things: weave a cloth as long as a road, make as much tea as there is water in the ocean, and raise a pig as big as a mountain. Fu-hsing is worried, but his wife tells him what to do.

Fu-hsing goes back to the magistrate and gives him a ruler, a bowl, and a scale. He asks the magistrate to do three things: measure the road with the ruler so he will know how long to make the cloth, measure the ocean's water with the bowl so he will know how much tea he must make, and weigh the mountain with the scale so he will know how big a pig he must raise. The magistrate is surprised at Fu-hsing's cleverness. He lets him go without punishment.

Transparency 86 Level B, Unit 5 | Challenges © Hampton-Brown

Transparency 87 / Master 87

SUMMARY CHART

Directions: For each part, write the important details in the top box and the summary in the bottom box.

The Clever Wife

1 Fu-hsing Praises His Wife	2 Fu-hsing Faces a Challenge	3 The Clever Wife Meets the Challenge
Details:	Details:	Details:
Summary Statement:	Summary Statement:	Summary Statement:

Transparency 87 Level B, Unit 5 | Challenges © Hampton-Brown

Vocabulary

FIGURATIVE LANGUAGE: METAPHORS

Write: *The magistrate thought that Fu-hsing was a windbag.* Tell students that this comparison is an example of a metaphor. Remind them of the metaphors they studied in the poem "Mother to Son." Then brainstorm other metaphors for people's behavior or personality traits (such as *stuffed shirt, wallflower, sunshine,* and *anchor*). Have students make a list of the terms and use them in sentences that show meaning through context.

READ PAGES 350–351

OBJECTIVES

Function: Read a Selection
Listening: Listen to a Selection
Reading and Learning Strategies: Set a Purpose for Reading; Use Graphic Organizers (summary chart); Ⓣ Summarize; Make Predictions
Comprehension: Make Comparisons; Identify Character's Motive
Literary Analysis: Onomatopoeia

SET PURPOSE

1 Read aloud the introduction to pages 350–351. Set the purpose for reading: *As you read, note the three tasks the magistrate gives Fu-hsing and Fu-hsing's reaction to the tasks.*

READ AND THINK

Tape 5B
CD 5 Track 5

2 **Strategy Focus: Summarize** Involve students in reading pages 350–351 of the selection.

See the **Multi-Level Strategies** on page T348 to tailor the reading experience to proficiency levels.

2

FU-HSING FACES A CHALLENGE

The magistrate tells Fu-hsing to perform three impossible tasks or he will be punished. Fu-hsing asks his wife to help him.

Much relieved, Fu-hsing soon was standing before the magistrate. By now his eyebrows were crossing each other. He stared frowning from behind **an immense** table. His arms were folded into his sleeves.

"So!" he exclaimed "This is the **braggart** who posts scrolls on his gate to boast of his extraordinary **cleverness**." He **leant** forward to **glare** into Fu-hsing's face. His terrible eyebrows **bristled** like angry hedgehogs. "You think you can do anything at all, do you! No matter how difficult? Very well!"

Loosing his arms from his sleeves, he **struck** an angry fist on the table. "I have three small **tasks** for you to perform. At once! For a fellow of your remarkable talents, they should provide no difficulty. No difficulty whatsoever.

"First, then," and *pound* went the fist, "you shall make a cloth as long as a road. Second," *pound, pound,* "you shall make as much tea as there is water in the ocean. Third," *pound, pound, pound,* "you shall raise a pig as big as a mountain."

Role-play: Have students act out this scene.

With an awful smile, the magistrate opened his fist to wave a long finger unde poor Fu-hsing's nose. "Of course, if you do not complete these tasks for me one, two, three, you will soon learn how this court deals with a **swollen head!**"

Wretched and **anxious**, Fu-hsing **hastened** home to his wife and told her about the three impossible tasks.

His wife threw back her head and laughed. "Foolish husband," she said. "The hardest problems are those with the simplest answers!"

Fu-hsing continued to **wring his hands** "But what shall I do? I know that you can accomplish anything, but this is **beyond all reason. . . .**"

Madame Fu-hsing's smile stopped him. "It is really quite simple. Rest well tonight. Tomorrow you must go back to the magistrate. You will present to him three quite ordinary tools which I shall make rea for you. I will give you certain words to tal along with these tools. You must say them to the magistrate just as I tell them to you."

Encourage elaboration: What does his wife's answer tell you about her?

an immense a huge, a very large
leant leaned
glare stare deeply
bristled became stiff
struck pounded
tasks jobs
Wretched Very unhappy, Miserable
anxious worried
hastened hurried
wring his hands squeeze and twist his hands together
beyond all reason too much for anyone to be able to do

350 Unit 5 | Challenges

REACHING ALL STUDENTS

INTERNET

ART CONNECTION

Encourage students to visit museum Web sites to take a virtual tour of Chinese art. Suggest they draw a sketch of their favorite piece, gather information about it, and make a presentation to the class. Web sites undergo frequent modifications, but here are two you might suggest:

Web Sites

The Metropolitan Museum of Art:
www.metmuseum.org./collection

The Hong Kong Museum of Art:
www.lcsd.gov.hk/CE/Museum/Arts

Vocabulary

CONTEXT CLUES

Have students use context clues to discover the meanings of unfamiliar terms in the story. Point out such terms as: *puzzled his head, frown, appear before, remarkable,* and *respectfully.* Elicit prior knowledge of context clues. Model how to use different types of clues (such as logic, paraphrasing, synonyms, and contrasting) to discover meanings. Have pairs choose one term and use context clues to find the term's meaning. They should then share their findings and describe the method they used.

BEFORE YOU MOVE ON...

1. **Comparison** Compare the person Fu-hsing was with the person the magistrate believed him to be.
2. **Character's Motive** Why did the magistrate give Fu-hsing impossible tasks to perform?
3. **Prediction** Do you think Fu-hsing's wife will succeed in helping her husband? What clues does the author give?

CHECK COMPREHENSION

3 Answers to "Before You Move On"

1. **Comparison** Fu-hsing was a simple and easily frightened man, but the magistrate thought he was boastful and conceited.
2. **Character's Motive** The magistrate wanted to humble Fu-hsing and show him that he was not as clever as the magistrate.
3. **Prediction** Fu-hsing's wife is clever and will probably be able to help her husband. The author says she smiled and laughed to show that she was not at all worried about the tasks.

CLOSE AND ASSESS

Have students share their summary statements for pages 350–351. Check for focus: Do the sentences note the three tasks the magistrate gave to Fu-hsing? Do they mention Fu-hsing's reaction and the reaction of his wife?

Language Development

DRAMATIZE

Have students dramatize descriptions in the story that show what a character is feeling. Point out descriptive phrases in the selection, such as: *Fu-hsing continued to wring his hands; His wife threw back her head and laughed; [the magistrate] drew his mouth down and his eyebrows together in a terrible frown.* Ask students to act out a passage of their choice, then have the class guess what feeling is being dramatized.

Literary Analysis Minilesson

▶ ONOMATOPOEIA

TEACH Draw attention to the paragraph on page 350 that begins *"First, then," and* pound *went the fist, "you shall make a cloth as long as a road."* Call on a student to read the paragraph aloud and to pound on the desk each time he or she reads the word *pound.* Point out to students that the word *pound* resembles the real sound to which it refers and is called onomatopoeia. Illustrate the concept with *hiss* and *buzz.* Call on students to think of other examples of onomatopoeia.

PRACTICE Provide pairs of students with one of the following words:

beep	bong	chirp
click	cuckoo	crunch
honk	ping	quack
splash	thump	clang

Have them write a sentence using the word. Call on them to share their sentences with the class.

▶ **Practice Book** page 169

READ PAGES 352–353

OBJECTIVES

Function: Read a Selection

Listening: Listen to a Selection

Reading and Learning Strategies: Set a Purpose for Reading; Ⓣ Summarize; Use Graphic Organizers (summary chart); Relate to Personal Experience

Comprehension: Make Comparisons

Literary Analysis: Respond to Literature; Characterization (protagonist and minor characters)

SET PURPOSE

1 Read aloud the introduction to pages 352–353. Set the purpose for reading: *Read to find out how Fu-hsing's clever wife helps him meet the magistrate's challenge.*

READ AND THINK

Tape 5B

CD 5 Track 5

2 **Strategy Focus: Summarize** Involve students in reading pages 352–353 of the selection.

See the **Multi-Level Strategies** on page T348 to tailor the reading experience to proficiency levels.

3

THE CLEVER WIFE MEETS THE CHALLENG

Fu-hsing follows his wife's plan and asks for more information about the three tasks. The magistrate cannot answer and lets Fu-hsing go without punishment.

Ask: What tools did Fu-hsing's wife give him?

Fu-hsing listened carefully to his wife's instructions. The next morning, carrying a ruler, a large measuring bowl, and a balancing scale, he stood in front of the magistrate once again.

When he started speaking, the magistrate's eyebrows were **as tightly knotted** as before. But when Fu-hsing laid the three tools down, his brows lifted up and up until they became flying birds of **astonishment**.

"This morning, as I was setting out to do the tasks you gave me," Fu-hsing began, "I realized that I needed **further instruction** from you before I could finish. Therefore, your Honor, I have brought these three tools to help you. I must respectfully ask you, first, to measure the road with this ruler so that I know the length of the cloth I must make. Second, measure the ocean's water with this bowl so that I know how much tea I must make. Third, weigh the mountain

Ask: Was it possible to answer Fu-hsing's questions? Why or why not?

with this balance so that I know how big a pig I must raise."

Fu-hsing **bowed** deeply. "Just as soon as you have made the measurements, your Honor, I shall be pleased to finish the tasks

The magistrate was so surprised by the **cunning** solution that he allowed Fu-hsing to go without punishment, and never bothered him again. Truly, the magistrate believed Fu-hsing's Matchless Wit could do a million things.

Ask: Who does the magistrate think is the Matchless Wit?

BEFORE YOU MOVE ON...

1. **Comparison** How were the three things Fu-hsing asked the magistrate to do similar to the three tasks the magistrate had asked him to do?
2. **Personal Experience** Give an example of a time when someone helped you or you helped someone push past a limit. Briefly explain what happened.

as tightly knotted showing as much anger
astonishment surprise
further instruction more directions
bowed leaned forward at the waist
cunning very clever

REACHING ALL STUDENTS

Social Studies Connection

MAPS

Display a topographical map. Point out that this type of map could have helped answer some of the questions Fu-hsing posed to the magistrate. Explain that topographical maps give information about features of the Earth's surface, such as the elevation of mountains and the depth of oceans. Have students use the map to answer such questions as: *What is the highest mountain in Asia? In Australia? Where is the deepest part of the Atlantic Ocean? The Pacific?*

Mathematics Connection

ESTIMATION AND MEASUREMENT

Materials: ruler, bucket, cup, scale.

Tell students that the magistrate could have used estimation to give rough answers to Fu-hsing's questions. Have students work in groups to: use a ruler to measure off 2 feet of the hallway, then estimate its length; pour two cups of water into a bucket and estimate how many more cups it would take to fill the bucket; weigh one pair of shoes and estimate how much all the shoes in the classroom would weigh. Have groups share their estimates.

ABOUT THE AUTHOR

Carol Kendall was pleased with her first children's book, *The Other Side of the Tunnel*, but she dreamed of doing better. "I ached to write a book with meaning, a book that readers would take to their hearts and remember always." In time, she accomplished this goal and became famous for her fantasy novels. Carol Kendall is also proud of her collection of Asian folk tales. One of the books in this collection is *Sweet and Sour Tales*, which she and illustrator **Yao-wen Li** translated from Chinese into English. It includes the story of "The Clever Wife."

CHECK COMPREHENSION

3 Answers to "Before You Move On"

1. **Comparison** Fu-hsing asked the magistrate to take impossible measurements, just as the magistrate had ordered Fu-hsing to produce impossible amounts of things.
2. **Personal Experience** Answers will vary. Make sure students explain how someone pushed past a limit.

ABOUT THE AUTHOR

4 Respond to Literature Read aloud or have students read About the Author. Point out that it is important to the author to write books that will be meaningful to the reader. Ask: *Do you think this tale is meaningful? How? What message do you see in the tale? Is this an important message for you personally? Why?*

CLOSE AND ASSESS

Have students share their summary sentences for pages 352–353. Check for focus: Do the sentences explain how Fu-hsing's wife helped him meet the challenge?

HOME CONNECTION

Discover Clever Relatives Discuss with students how, in most families, there is at least one person who is considered "the clever one." Tell students they will interview family members to learn about "clever" relatives. Together, brainstorm interview questions. Have students interview family members, then report the results to the class.

Literary Analysis Minilesson

▶ **CHARACTERIZATION: PROTAGONIST AND MINOR CHARACTERS**

TEACH Have students identify the characters in "The Clever Wife." Explain that the main character, called the protagonist, has the most to gain or lose by the resolution of the plot. The others are minor characters. Help students complete this chart.

Character	Gains or Loses
Fu-hsing	
Wife	
Magistrate	

PRACTICE Have students analyze the information in the chart and complete these sentences:

_____ has the most to gain or lose.
_____ is the protagonist.
_____ has less to gain or lose
_____ is a minor character.
_____ has less to gain or lose.
_____ is a minor character.

They should determine the protagonist (Fu-hsing) and the minor characters (the wife, the magistrate).

▶ **Practice Book** page 170

RESPOND

OBJECTIVES

SUM IT UP

Function: Write

Reading and Learning Strategies: Ⓣ Summarize; Use Graphic Organizers (summary chart); Relate Main Ideas and Details

Writing: Summary

THINK IT OVER

Function: Engage in Discussion

Critical Thinking and Comprehension: Ⓣ Identify Author's Purpose; Make Judgments; Make Comparisons

EXPRESS YOURSELF

Function: Ⓣ Persuade

Speaking and Listening: Role-Play

CHECK YOUR UNDERSTANDING

1 **Sum It Up** Sample summary is: Fu-hsing writes a couplet to praise his clever wife and hangs it outside their house. A magistrate misunderstands the couplet and wants to punish Fu-hsing for bragging. He gives Fu-hsing three impossible tasks. Fu-hsing's wife cleverly meets the challenge by outsmarting the magistrate.

▶ **Practice Book** page 171

2 **Think It Over** Possible answers are:

1. **Author's Purpose** The tale has timeless themes.
2. **Judgment** Students may say he was wrong to brag because it caused so much trouble.
3. **Comparisons** Students should support their answers with evidence from the stories.

3 **Express Yourself** Prompt the use of new vocabulary, convincing arguments, and persuasive language.

CLOSE AND ASSESS

Ask students to tell which character in the tale is their favorite and why.

Respond to the Folk Tale

Check Your Understanding

SUM IT UP

Summarize Each Section Use the important details to complete a summary statement for each section of the folk tale.

1 Fu-hsing Praises His Wife	2 Fu-hsing Faces a Challenge	3 The Clever Wife Meets the Challenge
Details	Details	Details
Summary Statement	Summary Statement	Summary Statement

Summarize the Selection Put your summary statements together to create a summary for the entire folk tale. Share your work with a group.

THINK IT OVER

Discuss and Write Talk about these question with a partner. Write the answers.

1. **Authors' Purpose** Folk tales are told for ma years before they are written down. Why do you think the authors chose to write down this folk tale?
2. **Judgment** Was Fu-hsing right to brag about his wife so much? Explain your answer.
3. **Comparisons** How did Fu-hsing in "The Clever Wife" and Panchito in "The Circuit" overcome obstacles? What can you learn from each of them?

EXPRESS YOURSELF ▶PERSUADE

If you were Fu-hsing, how would you convince the magistrate that you are not a braggart? Fir a partner to play the role of the magistrate an deny that you are bragging about yourself.

REACHING ALL STUDENTS

Multi-Level Strategies

SUM IT UP OPTIONS

BEGINNING Have students draw pictures to go with the Key Points Reading of "The Clever Wife" on **Master 86**. (See page T349.) Pool the pictures and have students sequence them. Cut a copy of **Master 86** into sentence strips and use them to label the pictures. Help students read the text to summarize the story.

INTERMEDIATE Invite students to work in pairs to review the details and summary statements recorded in the Summary Chart on **Transparency 87** during the reading. (See page T349.) Have pairs discuss and revise the sentences, then write their final summaries in their notebooks.

ADVANCED Have partners compare and discuss their Summary Charts. Challenge them to condense the summaries to one or two sentences to share with the class.

ASSESSMENT
Selection Test 20 on page 89 of the Assessment Handbook tests students' mastery of the reading strategies and the vocabulary, comprehension, and language arts skills taught with this selection

anguage Arts and Literature

LITERARY ANALYSIS

VALUATE HOW SETTING AFFECTS HARACTERS

earn About Setting Where and when a story kes place is the **setting**. The setting has an pact on the way the characters think and act. The Clever Wife" takes place in China during e Han Dynasty (206 BCE–220 CE) at a time when e class system lets the magistrates rule the eople. Fu-hsing's problems seem more portant and believable because of the time d place where the story occurs.

ractice Study this chart about China during e Han Dynasty. Complete the chart to tell how e setting affects the actions of the characters "The Clever Wife."

Setting: The Clever Wife

Elements in the Setting	Effects on the Characters
The government encourages intelligent and educated thinking.	Fu-hsing wanted others to know about his wife's cleverness.
The magistrate could punish people by killing them.	Fu-hsing is very frightened when the magistrate calls him.
Any family member could be punished for the actions of another family member.	Fu-hsing is afraid that both he and his wife will be punished for his actions.

SPEAKING/LISTENING

SING YOUR PRAISES

Create a Rhyme Put your classmates' names in a box. Each person can draw out a name and write a two-line rhyme praising that person. Students can sing or say the rhymes.

Sample Rhyme

Jennifer is so very kind,
Her friends are always on her mind.

WRITING

WRITE A REVIEW OF A STORY

One way to tell others about a story is to write about it. Write a review of "The Clever Wife."

- In the first paragraph, tell the title, authors, and main idea. Summarize important events.
- In the second paragraph, tell how you feel about the story and why.
- In the third paragraph, tell the most important idea you learned from the story.

You may want to publish your review in a class newspaper.

Develop your skill in the **writer's craft**. See Handbook pages 414–423.

Multi-Level Strategies

SETTING ACTIVITY—ROLES FOR COOPERATIVE GROUPS

BEGINNING / **INTERMEDIATE** / **ADVANCED** Have students work in three heterogeneous groups. Assign roles as follows:

- **Tracker**
- **Chartmaker**
- **Scribe**

Assign one element of the setting to each group. Allow time for the group to collect information from the story that shows the effects of the elements on the actions of the characters. Challenge the groups to find as many effects as they can. Encourage them to imagine or predict other possible effects not given in the story.

Have Beginning students take the roles of Trackers and flag the locations of information in the selection. Intermediates are the Chartmakers and complete the chart. Have Advanced students act as Scribes to write explanations of the chart entries and present them to the class.

RESPOND

OBJECTIVES

SETTING AND CHARACTERS
Function: Engage in Discussion
Learning Strategy: Use Graphic Organizers (chart)
Literary Analysis: Setting; Characters

SING YOUR PRAISES
Function: Write
Speaking: Recite
Literary Analysis: Rhyme
Writing: Poem

WRITE A REVIEW OF A STORY
Function: Write
Literary Analysis: Ⓣ Evaluate Literature
Writing: Story Review

LANGUAGE ARTS AND LITERATURE

1 **Evaluate How Setting Affects Characters** Encourage students to discuss how a different setting would affect this tale.

▶ **Practice Book** page 172

2 **Sing Your Praises** Suggest that students begin by thinking of and writing words that describe the classmate. Then have them think of words that rhyme with these descriptive words.

3 **Write a Review of a Story** Have students exchange their reviews with a partner. Partners should point out at least one thing they like in the review and one thing they would suggest changing.

▶ **Practice Book** page 173

CLOSE AND ASSESS

Ask students to return to the mind map they started on page 291 and add ideas about meeting challenges and solving problems.

BUILD WRITING SKILLS

OBJECTIVES

Function: Engage in Discussion; Listen Actively

Reading Strategy and Critical Thinking: Use Text Structures (logical order); Analyze and Evaluate Information

Listening: Listen Critically

Literary Analysis and Writing: T Persuasive (speech)

INTRODUCE WRITING THAT PERSUADES

1 **Discuss Persuasive Writing** Read the introduction and ask students to describe times when they might use persuasive language.

2 **Study the Professional Model** Read the excerpt and ask students how they know it is an example of persuasive writing. (Writer takes a position—*we must protect our natural resources*—and gives arguments to support it.) Ask for examples of strong words. *(most important, most imperiled, destruction, must be done)*

3 **Explore Text Structure** Explain that persuasive writing is most effective when arguments are presented in logical order. Use the Diagrams of Logical Order to model this.

Use the Options for Studying Text Structure in the **Multi-Level Strategies** to adjust instruction.

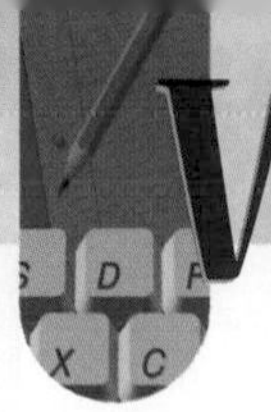

Writing That Persuades

Persuasive writing states an opinion and tries to convince readers to agree with it. Persuasive writing can be printed, or it can be delivered as a speech.

PERSUASIVE LANGUAGE IN PROFESSIONAL WRITING

"A Celebration of the Everglades" includes a persuasive speech by Marjory Stoneman Douglas. In it, she uses facts and strong words to state the problem and make her position clear.

***from* Marjory Stoneman Douglas's speech**

> Our most important resource and the most imperiled is water. It is the lifeblood on which the health of Florida's economy depends. In South Florida, protecting our water requires the destruction of the Kissimmee Canal so that water can flow down to Lake Okeechobee, which serves as nature's filter for the pollution from the marshlands . . . .
>
> The best we can do is protect our great natural resources. This must be done or we will lose everything.

LOGICAL ORDER IN PERSUASIVE WRITING

A persuasive speech is more effective when the arguments are delivered in a logical order. For example, a speaker might present an opinion, propose an action, and then tell why the action is important. Or, a speaker might state a position and then give the arguments in order from the least important to the most important.

Diagrams of Logical Order

Opinion Our most important resource is water. → **Position** Protecting our water requires the destruction of the Kissimmee Canal. → **Argument** Water needs to flow naturally to Lake Okeechobee in order to filter out pollution.

Your Position

Strong Argument
↓
Stronger Argument
↓
Strongest Argument

REACHING ALL STUDENTS

Transparency 88 / Master 88

DIAGRAM OF LOGICAL ORDER

Opinion
↓
Position
↓
Argument

Transparency 88 Level B, Unit 5 | Challenges © Hampton-Brown

Multi-Level Strategies

OPTIONS FOR STUDYING TEXT STRUCTURE

BEGINNING Using **Transparency 88**, work with students to develop an opinion, a position, and supporting arguments. You might explore a school dress code, consequences for certain behavior at school, or other school issues. As students draw, dictate, or pantomime their opinions and arguments, record the ideas in simple phrases on the transparency. Then use the diagram on page 356 to present the logical order of opinion, position, and argument in Marjory Stoneman Douglas's speech.

INTERMEDIATE / ADVANCED Work through the Diagrams of Logical Order for Marjory Stoneman Douglas's speech. Then distribute **Master 88** and ask students to complete it or create a diagram like the second one on page 356 for a school-related issue they care about. Encourage volunteers to share the ideas on their diagrams and use them as more examples to explore with the class.

DENT WRITING MODEL

ragraph Essay

tudents Should Not Fight!

y Jacob Tang

We need a No Play-Fighting Rule on our school grounds. The ay things are now, it's all right for kids to play-fight outside—as ong as they don't have weapons and aren't trying to hurt each ther. We must stop play-fighting though, and I'll give you some ood reasons why.

For one thing, play-fighting can look like real fighting. Little ids at the day school across the street see the big kids fighting ll the time. They might think it's all right to fight. It's not just ttle kids who think so. People walking by our grounds think that he kids are really fighting and that our school is not a safe lace to be.

Another reason is that play-fighting can lead to real fighting. ometimes two kids start off play-fighting, and then one of them its the other too hard by mistake. The other one hits back. uddenly, it's a real fight! This happened three times last month. ight kids were involved. Two of the kids had gotten into real ghts before. This happens because students' attitudes get worse fter they have a real fight. Next time they play-fight, they are neaner.

Play-fighting is especially bad because other people can get njured when kids pretend to fight. Just last week, a girl was urt when two boys who were play-fighting knocked into her. he fell and had to have five stitches. Accidents like this have appened before and will happen again.

In conclusion, play-fighting on our school grounds needs to be topped. Tell the principal that you want a No Play-Fighting Rule t our school. If we all speak up, we may be able to change the ules. At least we will have tried!

INTRODUCTION
Jacob **presents the issue** and states his position.

BODY
In the body, Jacob **presents his arguments in a logical order.** He starts with his least important argument and ends with the one he thinks is most important.

He includes **facts or examples** to support his opinions.

CONCLUSION
The last paragraph **sums up his position.** Jacob uses **persuasive words** to get his readers to take action.

STUDY A STUDENT WRITING MODEL

4 Listen for Logical Order Have students take notes on copies of **Master 88** as you read the Student Model aloud. Go over their notes together to identify the writer's position, arguments, and facts or examples.

5 Analyze and Evaluate a Persuasive Speech Display **Transparency 89** and lead students in studying the features of a persuasive speech. Students should then evaluate the Student Model against the rubric on the transparency.

Use the Roles for Cooperative Groups in the **Multi-Level Strategies** to involve all students.

CLOSE AND ASSESS

Have the **Recorder** from each group share conclusions from **Master 89.** Students can compare conclusions across groups, adding any information they may not have included.

Multi-Level Strategies

ROLES FOR COOPERATIVE GROUPS

BEGINNING / **INTERMEDIATE** / **ADVANCED** Have students of varying proficiencies work in groups of three to compare the model to the rubric on **Master 89.** Assign these roles:

▶ **Researcher** ▶ **Reader** ▶ **Recorder**

Before groups begin, work through the title and the first feature, pointing out the sample answer. Then prompt groups to read through the rest of the features and complete the master. The **Researcher** scans the model for examples of each feature; the **Reader** chooses and reads aloud phrases for that feature; and the **Recorder** checks the box and takes notes on the chart for future reporting to the whole group.

Transparency 89 / Master 89

FEATURES OF PERSUASIVE WRITING

Directions: Read "Students Should Not Fight!" and compare it to the features of a persuasive speech. Check the box if "Students Should Not Fight!" shows the feature. Then give an example.

A Persuasive Speech... Students Should Not Fight!

states an **opinion** or a **position.**	☑ "We need a No Play-Fighting Rule on our school grounds."
presents **strong arguments** in a **logical order.**	☑ **argument 1:** Play-fighting can look like real fighting. **argument 2:** Play-fighting can lead to real fighting. **argument 3:** People can get injured when kids pretend to fight.
has **facts** or **examples** and other **important details.**	☑ This happened three times last month. Just last week a girl fell and had to have five stitches.
includes **transition words.**	☑ For one thing, Another reason, In conclusion
uses **persuasive words** to get people to take action.	☑ Play-fighting needs to be stopped; Tell the principal that you want a No Play-Fighting Rule

Transparency 89 Level D, Unit 5 | Challenges © Hampton-Brown

BUILD WRITING SKILLS

OBJECTIVES

PREWRITE

Function: Write

Learning Strategies and Critical Thinking: Plan; Generate Ideas; Interact with Peers; Sequence Arguments; Organize Ideas; Self-Assess

Representing: Chart

Writing: Ⓣ Writing Process

PRESENT THE WRITING PROCESS AND PROMPT

Read the prompt together. Then leaf through pages 358–362 to review the stages in the Writing Process.

For more about the Writing Process, refer students to pages 408–413 in the Handbook.

PREWRITE

Before students begin their prewriting, preview the steps with the group and discuss the sample FATP chart.

Use the Prewriting Support in the **Multi-Level Strategies** to tailor this stage to proficiency levels.

CLOSE AND ASSESS

Have students work with a partner to answer the questions in Reflect and Evaluate.

The Writing Process

WRITING PROMPT

Choose an issue you feel strongly about. Write an essay to use for a speech that will persuade others at your school to agree with your position. Include three good arguments with strong evidence.

PREWRITE

❶ **Choose Your Issue** Think about issues at your school, in your neighborhood, or among your friends. Make a chart.

What's the issue?	What's my position?	Will this issue interest others?
Should kids be allowed to use school computers for personal use?	Yes – as long as it's not during class time.	Yes, if they are interested in going on-line.
Should the City Council include a couple of students as advisors?	Yes – it's the best way for kids to have a voice in city issues.	Yes. Everyone argues about this at school.
Is there too much violence in video games for kids?	No – kids know the difference between real and make-believe violence.	Yes – except most kids agree with me already. They don't need persuading.

❷ **Unlock the Writing Prompt** Before you begin writing, fill out an FATP chart to help guide your writing.

❸ **Collect Your Arguments and Evidence** Make two lists of arguments: one in favor of your position and one against your position. This will help you see the issue from both sides. Circle the strongest three arguments in favor of your position. Gather evidence that supports these arguments.

❹ **Get Organized** You might use a diagram like the one on page 356 to decide on an order for presenting your arguments.

FATP Chart

HOW TO UNLOCK A PRO[MPT]

Form: *speech*

Audience: *people at school*

Topic: *student advisors on the City Council*

Purpose: *to persuade students to send letters to the council supporting the idea of student advisors*

Reflect and Evalua[te]

- Does this issue really matter to you? It's easie[r to] persuade others when y[ou] believe in your topic!
- Have you looked at both sides of the issue? If you know why people might disagree with you, you c[an] make your arguments stronger.

REACHING ALL STUDENTS

Multi-Level Strategies

PREWRITING SUPPORT

BEGINNING Suggest school or community issues and prompt students to role-play situations to show their opinions about these issues. Record their ideas in simple phrases. Have students choose an issue and work with them to complete FATP charts. To plan their writing, students can write and draw each argument that supports their opinion on an index card.

INTERMEDIATE Partners can brainstorm ideas and fill out FATP charts. Check the charts to ensure that students choose opinions they can support. Help them organize their arguments on **Master 88** (see page T356) or create a diagram similar to that on the right on page 356.

ADVANCED Have students consider both sides of their issues and gather points of view from classmates or family. To organize the arguments, they can use **Master 88** (see page T356) or one like the second diagram on page 356.

FT

› your **FATP** chart handy to remind you why you are writing. Focus on ng down your ideas, not on correcting your grammar.

Vrite an Introduction Make your position clear.

Present and Support Your Arguments Use your chart and lists to lraft the body of your essay. For each argument, present important evidence that supports your position. Connect your arguments with good transitions.

Writer's Craft: Important Details and Transitions

Replace unimportant details with important information to strengthen your argument.

Just OK	Better
The City Council needs student representation. There have never been students on the council. Having student advisors would offer a new view of things.	The City Council needs student representation. Students have a unique point of view that is currently not represented on the council. Having student advisors would provide a new perspective.

Use transition words like *in addition* and repeat a key word or phrase like *student advisors* to connect your paragraphs.

Just OK	Better
We need to keep other students aware of and interested in city issues. It is important to keep all of our youth involved in our community.	In addition, student advisors would keep other students aware of and interested in city issues. It is important to keep all of our youth involved in our community.

Vrite a Conclusion Sum up your position. Remind your audience of your position, and be specific about the action you want them to take.

Writer's Craft: Effective Conclusions

Be clear and concise.

In conclusion, let me say that the City Council needs student advisors. Please join me in writing to all the council members. Urge them to vote YES for student advisors.

Reflect and Evaluate

- Read the draft of your essay. Will it hold—and keep—your audience's attention?
- Have you made your position clear in both your introduction and conclusion?

OBJECTIVES

DRAFT

Function: Ⓣ Persuade; Write

Learning Strategies and Critical Thinking: Generate Ideas; Self-Assess

Writer's Craft: Ⓣ Important Details and Transitions; Effective Conclusions

Writing: Ⓣ Writing Process

DRAFT

Before students begin their drafts, discuss the Writer's Craft models:

- In **Step 2**, ask volunteers to explain why the second model in each set is "Better."
- In **Step 3**, encourage volunteers to tell why the sample concluding paragraph is an effective way to end a persuasive speech.

Use the Drafting Support in the **Multi-Level Strategies** to tailor this stage to proficiency levels.

For more about the Writer's Craft, refer students to pages 414–423 in the Handbook.

CLOSE AND ASSESS

Have small groups discuss the questions in Reflect and Evaluate while you work with those who may need more support in assessing their drafts.

Multi-Level Strategies

DRAFTING SUPPORT

BEGINNING Guide students in writing their opinion and position in an introductory paragraph. Then work with them to sequence their index cards from strong argument to strongest argument. You can provide sentence starters such as: *One reason is* _____*; Another reason is* _____*; The best reason is* _____; or, have students describe their arguments so you can restate the ideas in simple phrases or sentences. Help students draft a strong conclusion.

INTERMEDIATE / **ADVANCED** Have partners apply the Writer's Craft skill as they revise the examples on **Master 90**. Then encourage students to use important details and transition words as they draft arguments to support their opinion.

Transparency 90 / Master 90

IMPORTANT DETAILS/TRANSITIONS

Directions: Read each writing tip and the example that is "Just OK." Change the example to make it "Better."

Writing Tips	Just OK	Better
Replace unimportant details with important information.	Play-fighting can look like real fighting. Lots of people walk on the sidewalk by the school. People might think our school is not a safe place to be.	Play–fighting can look like real fighting. People who see the play–fighting think that kids are really fighting each other. They think our school is not a safe place to be.
	Play-fighting can lead to real fighting. Two kids can play-fight. Then it can become a real fight.	Play-fighting can lead to real fighting. One kid might hit hard and the other kid will hit back. Then it can become a real fight.
Use transition words and repeat key words to connect paragraphs.	When kids fight, they can really hurt each other. Kids who just get in the way can get hurt.	When kids fight, they can really hurt each other. In addition, kids who get in the way of a fight by accident can get hurt.

Transparency 90 Level B, Unit 5 | Challenges

BUILD WRITING SKILLS

OBJECTIVES

REVISE

Function: Write; Engage in Discussion

Learning Strategies and Critical Thinking: Generate Ideas; Review; Clarify; Interact with Peers; Self-Assess

Listening and Speaking: Peer-Conferencing

Writing: Ⓣ Writing Process

REVISE

First have students reread their drafts. They should turn the entries on their FATP charts into questions to answer as they assess their work. For example: *Does my speech persuade students to send letters to the City Council?*

Next, model how to evaluate someone else's writing in a peer conference and how to give specific feedback to improve a draft. Also model how a writer makes revisions. Students can then conduct the peer conferences and revise their drafts.

Use the Peer Conference Support in the **Multi-Level Strategies** to model how to evaluate and revise writing.

CLOSE AND ASSESS

Have peers discuss the questions in Reflect and Evaluate.

Writing That Persuades, continued

REVISE

1. **Reread the Draft of Your Essay** Does it go with your **FATP**? Is your position clear? Have you included three persuasive arguments to support your position?

2. **Conduct a Peer Conference** Read your draft to a partner or to a small group. Speak clearly and don't rush. Ask your audience to answer these questions:
   - Did I include transition words to make my arguments easy to follow?
   - Did I include important details that you needed to know?
   - Was I persuasive?

3. **Mark Your Changes** Look over your notes and decide how you want to change your writing.

Reflect and Evalu

- Did your peer's commen help you improve your draft?
- Does your revised essay a better job of persuadi than your draft did?

REACHING ALL STUDENTS

Transparency 91 / Master 91

REVISING

Red annotations show changes related to the sample questions. Revisions should vary to reflect questions students propose.

Play-fighting is [^ especially] bad because other people can get injured when kids pretend to fight. Just last week, a girl was hurt when two boys who were play-fighting knocked into her. [^ She fell and had to have five stitches.] [^ In conclusion,] Play-fighting on our school grounds needs to be stopped.

Revising Marks

^	Add.
↺	Move to here.
↖	Replace with this.
⤼	Take out.

Give Feedback in a Peer Conference

1. Tell how the writing can be more persuasive.
   - I think that you could be more convincing about how bad it is.
   - I think that Students' comments will vary.
2. Tell what information could be added to support an argument.
   - Perhaps you could add details about what happened when the girl got hurt.
   - Perhaps you could Students' comments will vary.
3. Point out a need for transition words and other connecting phrases.
   - You might add transition words to connect this paragraph to the one before it.
   - You might Students' comments will vary.

Transparency 91 Level B, Unit 5 | Challenges © Hampton-Brown

Multi-Level Strategies

PEER CONFERENCE SUPPORT

BEGINNING Display **Transparency 91** and read the paragraph. To help students understand the concepts, show or sketch how play-fighting can hurt other kids. Then model how to evaluate the writing, using the sentence starters shown. Call on volunteers to provide other comments using the sentence starters. Then model how to revise the paragraph, based on the comments.

INTERMEDIATE / **ADVANCED** Display **Transparency 91**. Read the paragraph and have students identify parts that can be more persuasive or specific. Model with the sample comments and then have students suggest comments of their own. Call on volunteers to suggest revisions to the paragraph, based on the comments.

:AMMAR IN CONTEXT

:FECT TENSES

tense of a verb shows when an action happens. The perfect verb tenses formed with *has, have,* or *had* and the past participle of the main verb.

City Council

orm the **past participle** of regular verbs by adding **-ed**.

Examples: help help**ed** support support**ed**

regular verbs have special forms for the past participle:

Present	Past	Past Participle
is	was	been
know	knew	known
run	ran	run

se the **present perfect tense** to talk about an action that began in the past nd may still be going on. You can also use the present perfect tense when you ren't sure of the exact time of the past action.

Examples: I **have supported** our City Council for a long time.
The City Council **has talked** about the issues many times.

Helping Verbs for Present Perfect Tense

I have	we have
you have	you have
he has / she has / it has	they have

se the **past perfect tense** to talk about an action that was completed efore another action in the past.

Example: I **had supported** the Council even before last month's great decision.

se the **future perfect tense** to talk about an action that will be completed t a specific time in the future.

Example: By the end of this year, I **will have supported** the Council for three years.

:tice Complete each sentence. Write the verb in the tense shown.

	Tense	Sentence
	past perfect	1. City Council members _________ to add student advisors, but then they changed their minds.
	present perfect	2. Some members _________ that students are really not interested in city government.
ort	future perfect	3. At the end of this month, I _________ this issue for four years!
w	past perfect	4. I _________ for years that the council would be slow to act.

OBJECTIVES

GRAMMAR IN CONTEXT
Grammar: Ⓣ Perfect Tenses

GRAMMAR IN CONTEXT

1 Teach Perfect Tenses Work with students to read the definition and the rules regarding the formation of perfect tenses. Then study the examples.

2 Write Sentences Provide the following sentence starters and ask students to complete each one: *We have talked _____, We had talked _____, We will have talked _____.* Discuss different situations or sets of circumstances in which each perfect tense would be used. Then conduct the cooperative learning activity below.

3 Answers to Practice Items

1. had planned
2. have stated
3. will have supported
4. had known

CLOSE AND ASSESS

Have partners choose an action verb and write sentences using that verb in the present perfect, past perfect, and future perfect tenses.

Cooperative Learning

FOR LANGUAGE DEVELOPMENT: Perfect Tenses

Materials: index cards; writing paper

Formulate Perfect Tense Verbs Display the helping verbs from page 361. Divide students into groups of four and have them number off. Give each group a main verb written on an index card. Have the 1s write sentences using the present perfect tense of the verb, the 2s the past perfect tense, and the 3s the future perfect tense. The 4s can be facilitators and help group members as necessary.

Debrief the Skill Call on different numbers to share a sentence and identify the verb tense. Ask: *Why does using the correct verb tense in a sentence matter?*

Debrief the Cooperative Process Have students reflect on their own participation: *How did listening to the sentences your group formed help you understand how to use perfect tense verbs?*

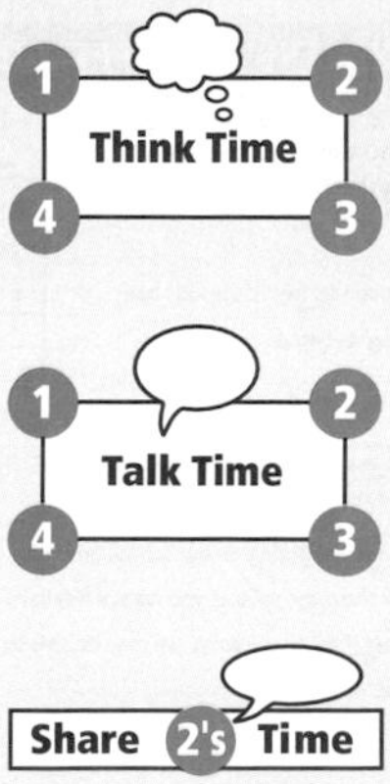

Cooperative Learning Structure: Numbered Heads

BUILD WRITING SKILLS

OBJECTIVES

EDIT AND PROOFREAD

Learning Strategies and Critical Thinking: Review; Clarify; Self-Assess

Writing: Ⓣ Writing Process

PUBLISH

Learning Strategies and Critical Thinking: Interact with Peers; Self-Assess; Make Decisions

Speaking: Deliver a Speech

Technology and Media: Record on a Computer

Writing: Ⓣ Writing Process

EDIT AND PROOFREAD

Before students edit and proof their own writing, use **Transparency 92** to model the process.

PUBLISH

Ask volunteers to share publishing ideas or have students choose from those suggested on page 362.

Use the Editing and Publishing Support in the **Multi-Level Strategies** to meet the varying needs of students.

CLOSE AND ASSESS

Have groups discuss the questions in Reflect and Evaluate. Monitor how students complete the checklist.

✓ LANGUAGE ACQUISITION ASSESSMENT
See page 82 of the Assessment Handbook.

✓ WRITING ASSESSMENT
Use the Writing Rubric on page 91 of the Assessment Handbook to evaluate this writing assignment.

Writing That Persuades, continued

EDIT AND PROOFREAD

1. **Check for Mistakes** Look through your essay and correct any mistakes in capitalization, punctuation, and spelling. Remember you will be using your essay to give a speech, and a sloppy paper is hard to read aloud! If you need help editing, use Handbook page 412.
2. **Check Your Sentences** Make sure your verb tenses are correct.
3. **Make a Final Copy** Make all the corrections you marked. For your final copy, leave an extra space between each line. This will make it easier for you to find your place when you give your essay as a speech.

PUBLISH

Now it's time to deliver your essay as a speech.

- Practice reading your speech aloud in front of a mirror. Are you looking up occasionally as you talk? Do you look interested in what you're saying?
- Then practice in front of other people. Can they understand what you are saying? Do you sound persuasive?

- If you have a computer with a microphone, record yourself reading your speech. Be your own critic. Do you sound persuasive? If so, send the sound file to a friend. Ask for feedback.

Key In TO Technology

You can record yourself on the computer, but experiment with first. Record yourself holding the microphone at different distances from your mouth. Try different tones—quiet, louder, friendly, serious. Play them back. Choose one that sounds best.

Reflect and Evalua

- Does your speech sound persuasive? Does it
  - ☑ have strong argument organized in an effective order?
  - ☑ focus on the importar details that listeners need to know?
  - ☑ include transition wor to help listeners follow your arguments?
  - ☑ use persuasive words get people to take action?
- Which was easier for you writing your essay or giving it as a speech?
- Are you pleased with how your speech turned out? What is the best thing about it?

REACHING ALL STUDENTS

Transparency 92 / Master 92

EDITING AND PROOFREADING

Directions: Read each sentence. Check for errors in capitalization, spelling, and punctuation. Use the Proofreading Marks to correct the mistakes.

1. Another reason is that play-fighting can lead to re(a)l fighting.
2. Eight kids were involved two of the kids had gotten into real fights before.
3. Next time they play-fight they ar(e) meaner.

Proofreading Marks

^	Add.
^,	Add a comma.
⊙	Add a period.
≡	Capitalize.
/	Make lowercase.
⌒	Take out.
¶	Indent.

Directions: Read the paragraph. Check for errors in capitalization, spelling, and punctuation. Check whether perfect tense verbs are used correctly. Use the Proofreading Marks to correct the mistakes.

In conclusion play-fighting on our school grounds needs to be stopped. Tell the princip~~le~~(al) that you want a No Play-Fighting Rule at our school if we all speak up, we may be able to change the rules. At least we ~~had~~ (will have) tried!

Transparency 92 Level B, Unit 5 | Challenges © Hampton-Brown

Multi-Level Strategies

EDITING AND PUBLISHING SUPPORT

BEGINNING Model finding and correcting errors in the top section of **Transparency 92**. After marking the edits, have students write out the corrected sentences. For publishing, encourage students to practice reading their speeches aloud to you or a small group, and then to the larger group.

INTERMEDIATE Guide students in finding and correcting the errors in the paragraph at the bottom of **Transparency 92**. For publishing, encourage students to practice reading their speeches in front of a mirror before reading to the class or another group.

ADVANCED Distribute copies of **Master 92** and have students work on the activities individually or with partners. Students may wish to deliver their speeches at a school event like an assembly or club meeting.

Overcoming Obstacles

UNIT 5

ASSESSMENT
The Unit 5 Test on page 93 of the Assessment Handbook measures students' progress in reading, language arts, literary study, and writing. Additional forms in the Assessment Handbook allow for:
- **Self Assessment on page 92**
- **Peer Assessment on page 101**
- **Portfolio Evaluation on page 103**

Look Back at the Unit

Make a Literary Report Card In this unit, you read selections about overcoming obstacles.

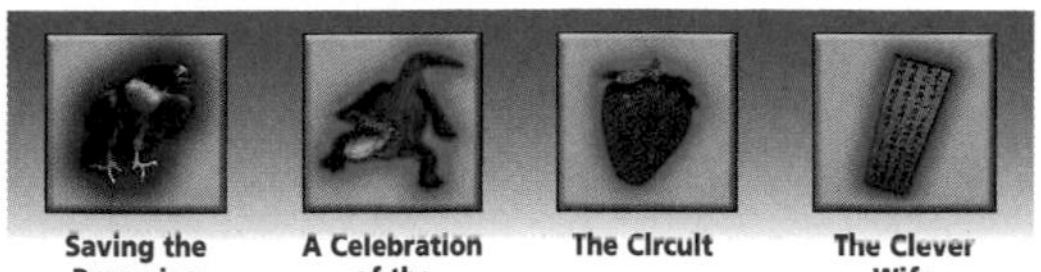

Write the title of each selection on an index card. Give an "A" to the selection that best describes a challenge. Then grade the other selections. On the back of each card, summarize the challenge and justify the way you graded the selection.

Show What You Know

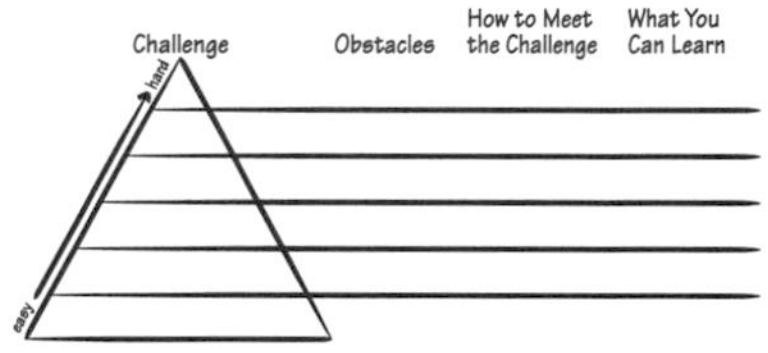

Sum It All Up Expand and organize your ideas on this mind map. Share your ideas about meeting challenges with a partner.

Reflect and Evaluate
Write about obstacles in your life:
- Describe a challenge from your past. Tell how you met it.
- Describe an obstacle that is still in your way. Tell how you will overcome it. .

Add this writing to your portfolio, along with the work from the unit that shows what you learned.

Make Connections

To Your Community Study articles in a newspaper, a magazine, or on the Internet. Look for stories about people who are overcoming obstacles. Plan a current events day to talk about these people. Then use the stories to create a bulletin board to inspire other students.

DEBRIEF UNIT 5

OBJECTIVES

Function: Engage in Discussion; Express Opinions

Learning Strategies and Critical Thinking: Interact with Peers; Generate Ideas; Make Judgments; Summarize; Self-Assess; Evaluate Information; Form Opinions; Use Graphic Organizers (mind map)

Literary Analysis: Respond to Literature; Compare and Evaluate Literature

EXPLORE "OVERCOMING OBSTACLES"

1. **Look Back at the Unit** Help students establish criteria for rating the selections, for example: *places me in the action.* Then begin the Cooperative Learning Activity.
2. **Show What You Know** Urge students to include work in their portfolios that reflects what they learned about overcoming obstacles.
3. **Make Connections** Encourage students to choose an individual as their personal hero or silent mentor.

CLOSE AND ASSESS

Have students tell you the most important thing they learned in the unit.

Cooperative Learning
FOR CRITICAL THINKING:
Form Opinions

Make a Literary Report Card After establishing criteria, allow time to review and rate the selections. Then have students form groups of four.

Discussing Selections After brief group discussion, ask a question that can be answered for each selection: *What obstacles were overcome? What can you learn from this story?* Each student gives a different answer to every question.

Debrief the Content Ask students what they learned from the unit and the group discussion. Model a response: *I learned that good writing can make me feel the joy of overcoming an obstacle.*

Debrief the Cooperative Process Ask students to evaluate their participation in the roundtable discussion. Ask: *Were you comfortable discussing your ideas with the group?*

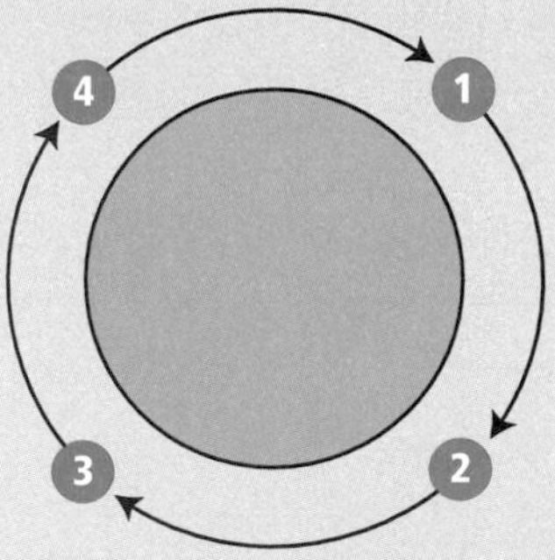

Cooperative Learning Structure: Roundtable

High Point Handbook

This Handbook is especially designed for English learners. Students can use the Handbook independently as a resource for learning as they participate in the language arts and content area activities that follow each literature selection. You may also want to use appropriate sections to teach or reinforce skills and strategies developed in the program.

HIGH POINT
Handbook

PART 1 Language and Learning

PART 2 Writing

PART 3 Grammar, Usage, Mechanics, and Spelling

Handbook: Language and Learning

Strategies for Learning Language

These strategies can help you learn to use and understand the English language.

1 Listen actively and try out language.

WHAT TO DO	EXAMPLES
Repeat what you hear.	You hear: "Way to go, Joe! Fantastic catch!" You say: "Way to go, Joe! Fantastic catch!" 
Recite songs and poems.	When the Ground Shakes When the ground shakes along the street, There's something happening beneath your feet. Earth layers are shifting, Slipping, Sliding, Bumping together. Shock waves are rising! "When the ground shakes along the street,..."
Listen to others and use their language.	You hear: "When did you know that something was missing?" You say: "I knew that something was missing when I got to class."
Add chunks of language to your speech.	You hear: "You can send the invitation by e-mail or snail mail." You think: Snails move very slowly, and e-mail is much faster than regular mail. Snail mail must be regular mail. You say: I'll send it by snail mail. There's plenty of time, and I have the invitation all written out on special paper.
Rehearse ways of speaking that match the social situation.	Formal: "Hello, Ms. Taylor. How are you?" "Fine, thank you. And how are you today?" Informal: "Hey, Paco. How's it going?" "Okay. And you?"

page 366

WHAT TO DO	EXAMPLES
Use the language you learn in one subject area in other subject areas and outside of school.	You read this in Social Studies: After almost two centuries of struggle, the Voting Rights Act of 1965 guaranteed all U.S. citizens the right to vote. You write this in your reading journal: *I wonder if The Secret of Gumbo Grove has something to do with voting rights. It'll be interesting to see what Raisin Stackhouse uncovers in the cemetery!* At home, you might say: "Mom, did you vote? You're guaranteed the right to vote."
Explore different ways of saying things.	All of these mean the same thing: My teacher helps me push my thinking. My teacher makes me think before I make up my mind. My teacher helps me stretch my mind to see different viewpoints. Before I make a decision, my teacher suggests I role-play different choices in my mind.

2 Ask for help and feedback.

WHAT TO DO	EXAMPLES
Interrupt politely.	"Excuse me. Please explain what the word 'habitat' means." Other options: "Pardon me, but could you say that again?" "Could you help me? I don't understand the phrase 'how precious life is.'"
Ask questions about how to use language.	"Did I say that right?" "Did I use that word in the right way?" "Which is correct, 'bringed' or 'brought'?"
Use your native language or English to ask for clarification.	You say: "Wait! Could you go over that point again, a little more slowly, please?" Other options: "Does 'have a heart' mean to be kind?" "Is 'enormous' another way to say 'big'?"

page 367

Strategies for Learning Language, continued

3 Use nonverbal clues.

WHAT TO DO	EXAMPLES
Use gestures and mime to get across an idea.	"I will hold up five fingers to show that I need five more minutes." 
Look for nonverbal clues.	"María wants me to go to the Subhumans' concert, but I think their music is awful—and downright insulting." "I'm not sure what she said about the Subhumans' music, but I can tell she doesn't like it. Just look at her!" 
Compare nonverbal and verbal clues.	"Let's give him a hand." "Everyone is clapping. 'Give him a hand' must mean to clap for him."

4 Verify how language works.

WHAT TO DO	EXAMPLES
Test hypotheses about language.	You try out what you learned: I can add *-ation* to the verb *observe* to get the noun *observation*. So maybe I can make a noun by adding *-ation* to all verbs that end in *-e*. Let's see. *Prepare* and *preparation*. Yes, that works! *Preserve* and *preservation*. That works, too. *Compare* and *comparation*. That doesn't sound right. I'd better see what the dictionary says... Now I see — it's *comparison*.

page 368

4 Verify how language works, continued

WHAT TO DO	EXAMPLES
Use spell-checkers, glossaries, and dictionaries.	You just finished your draft of a story, so you think: "Now I'll run the spell-check to see what words I need to fix."
Analyze the situation to determine the appropriate language to use.	Formal: "Thank you, Mr. Giacometti, for helping me enter the science fair." Informal: "Mom, thanks for getting the jars for my science fair exhibit." "Hey, Roberto, that was cool of you to help me set up."

5 Monitor and evaluate your learning.

WHAT TO DO	EXAMPLES
Assess your own language development.	"Did I use the right words? Was it correct to use 'they' when I talked about my grandparents?" "Were my words all in the correct order?" "Was I polite?"
Keep notes about what you've learned. Use your notes to practice using English.	How to Ask Questions • I can turn a statement around to make it a question: It is a nice day. Is it a nice day? • I can put the question at the end of a statement: It is a nice day, isn't it? • If I want more than a "yes" or "no" answer, I should use "who," "what," "where," "when," "how," or "why" at the beginning of my question: What will the weather be like today?

page 369

Handbook: Language and Learning

Graphic Organizers

You can use graphic organizers to highlight important points in your reading, to organize your ideas before writing, or to represent information for your readers.

CLUSTERS

Clusters help you connect information. You can use a cluster to show

▶ **How Words or Ideas are Related**

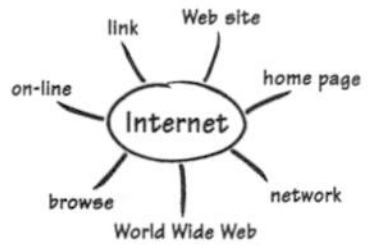

▶ **Details of an Event**

CHARTS

Charts have rows, columns, and labels to display information. Use a chart to

▶ **Picture Data**

Music Preferences Among Eighth Graders

Rap/Hip-hop	22
Rhythm & Blues	12
Swing	10
Rock	27
Reggae	13

▶ **Relate Ideas**

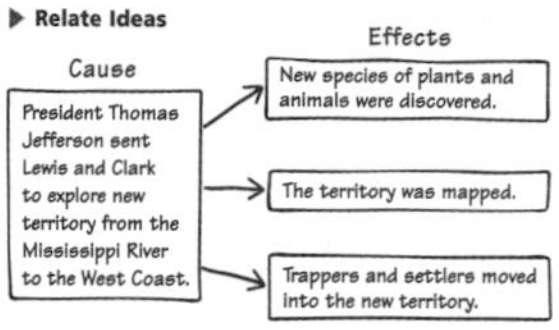

▶ **Compare and Contrast**

Stringed Instruments

Instrument	Number of Strings	How to Play	Relative Size
banjo	4, 5, or 6	pluck or strum	medium
cello	4	use bow	large
double bass	4	use bow or pluck	largest
guitar	6 or 12	pluck or strum	medium
violin	4	use bow	smallest

370 Handbook: Language and Learning

page 370

▶ **Record Observations**

Location:	Tide pools, Seaside Beach 11/15/00 10:45 a.m.
Sights:	Starfish, sea anemones, seaweed, barnacles
Sounds:	Seagulls calling, waves splashing against rocks
Smells:	Tangy salt air, seaweed
Textures:	Grainy sand, rough rocks, slimy seaweed
Comments:	The tide was out. We walked on the rocks and looked in the tidepools. Some waves splashed into the tidepools, so the living things in the pools were always wet.

▶ **Show the Steps in a Process**

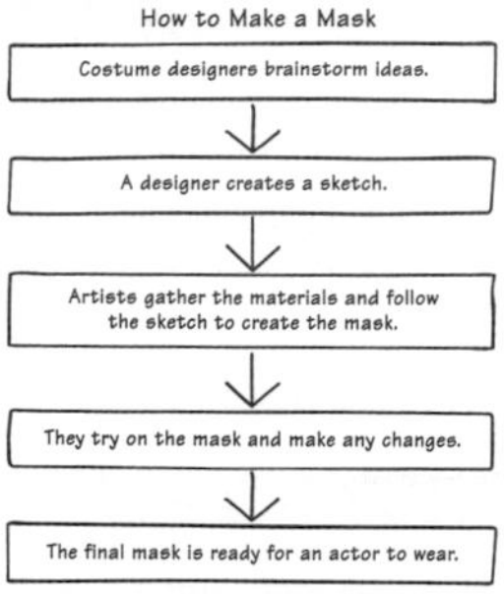

▶ **Show What You Know, What You Want to Learn, and What You Learned**

Topic: The Revolutionary War

What I Know	What I Want to Learn	What I Learned
The war was between England and the American colonies.	When was it? What started it?	**Fill in this column after you read.**
The colonies won and formed the United States.	How did the colonies defeat such a powerful country?	

▶ **Show Organization or Classification**

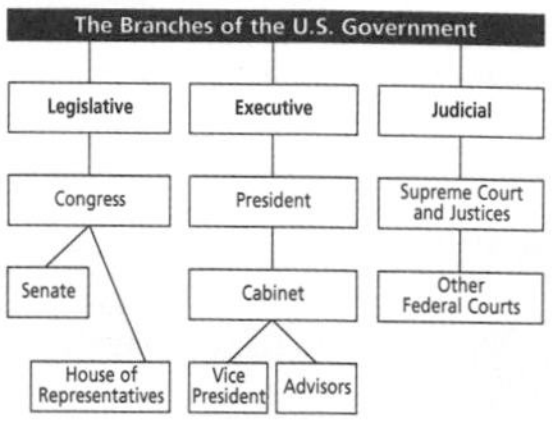

Graphic Organizers 371

page 371

Graphic Organizers, continued

GRAPHS

Graphs use words, numbers, lines, and other shapes to picture data. A graph can show

▶ **Parts of a Whole**

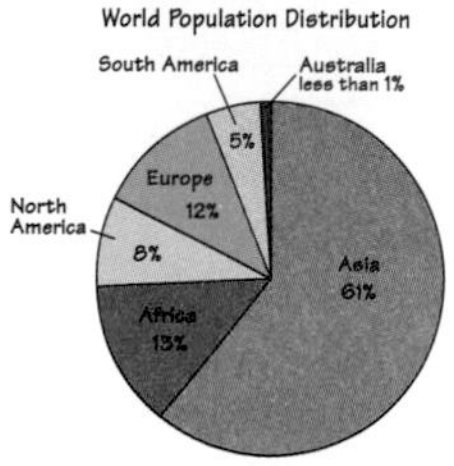

▶ **Comparisons**

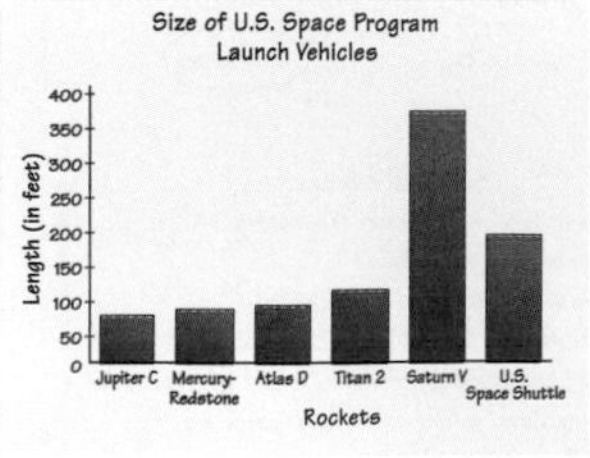

▶ **How Something Changes Over Time**

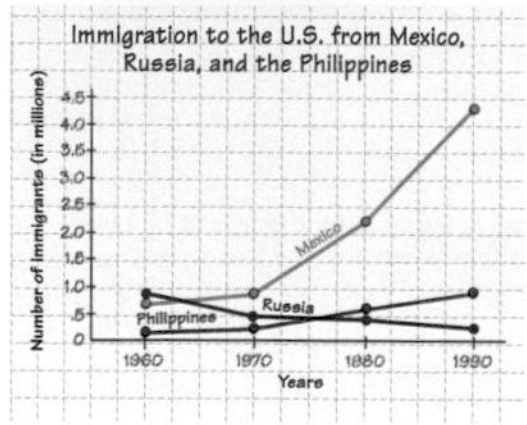

372 Handbook: Language and Learning

page 372

DIAGRAMS

Diagrams combine drawings and text to show where things are, how something works, or when something happens. Use a diagram to

▶ **Show When Events Happen**

▶ **Show Parts of Something**

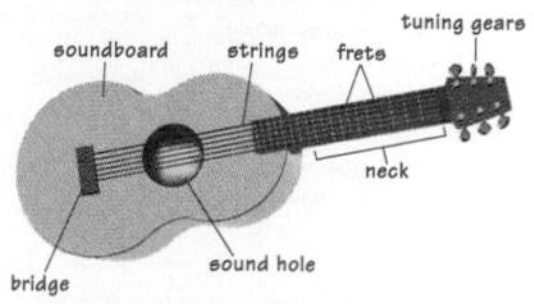

▶ **Explore the Meaning of Words**

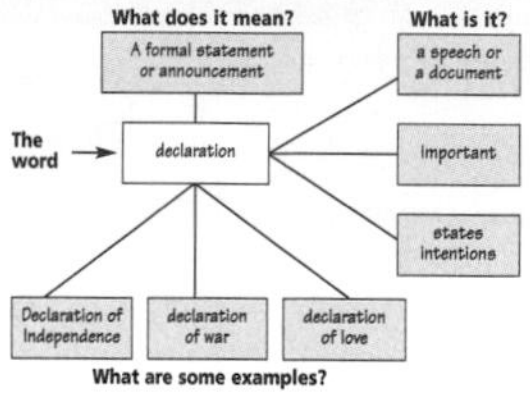

▶ **Show a Process that Repeats**

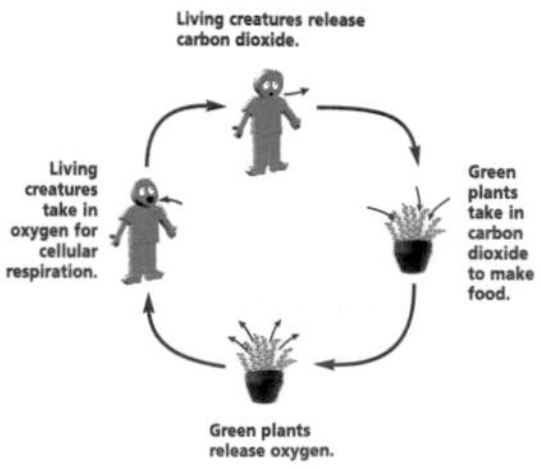

Graphic Organizers 373

page 373

Handbook: Language and Learning

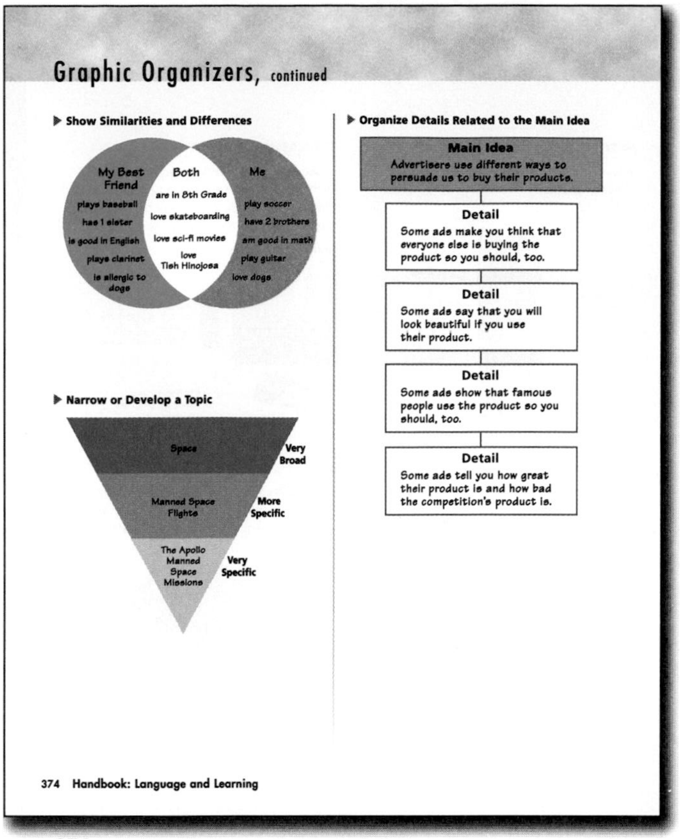

Graphic Organizers, continued

▶ **Show Similarities and Differences**

▶ **Narrow or Develop a Topic**

▶ **Organize Details Related to the Main Idea**

Main Idea
Advertisers use different ways to persuade us to buy their products.

Detail
Some ads make you think that everyone else is buying the product so you should, too.

Detail
Some ads say that you will look beautiful if you use their product.

Detail
Some ads show that famous people use the product so you should, too.

Detail
Some ads tell you how great their product is and how bad the competition's product is.

374 Handbook: Language and Learning

page 374

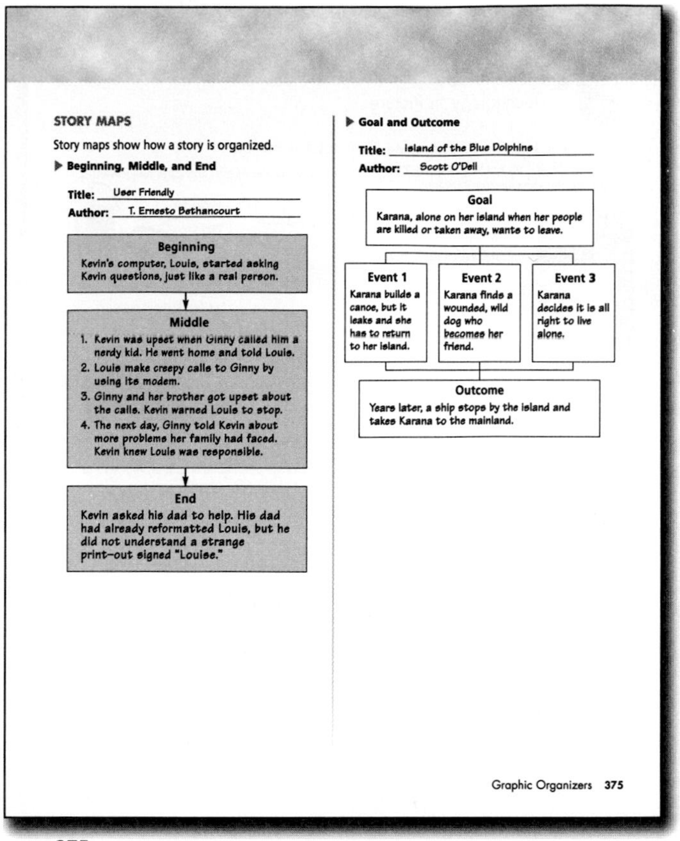

STORY MAPS

Story maps show how a story is organized.

▶ **Beginning, Middle, and End**

Title: User Friendly
Author: T. Ernesto Bethancourt

Beginning
Kevin's computer, Louis, started asking Kevin questions, just like a real person.

Middle
1. Kevin was upset when Ginny called him a nerdy kid. He went home and told Louis.
2. Louis make creepy calls to Ginny by using its modem.
3. Ginny and her brother got upset about the calls. Kevin warned Louis to stop.
4. The next day, Ginny told Kevin about more problems her family had faced. Kevin knew Louis was responsible.

End
Kevin asked his dad to help. His dad had already reformatted Louis, but he did not understand a strange print-out signed "Louise."

▶ **Goal and Outcome**

Title: Island of the Blue Dolphins
Author: Scott O'Dell

Goal
Karana, alone on her island when her people are killed or taken away, wants to leave.

Event 1
Karana builds a canoe, but it leaks and she has to return to her island.

Event 2
Karana finds a wounded, wild dog who becomes her friend.

Event 3
Karana decides it is all right to live alone.

Outcome
Years later, a ship stops by the island and takes Karana to the mainland.

Graphic Organizers 375

page 375

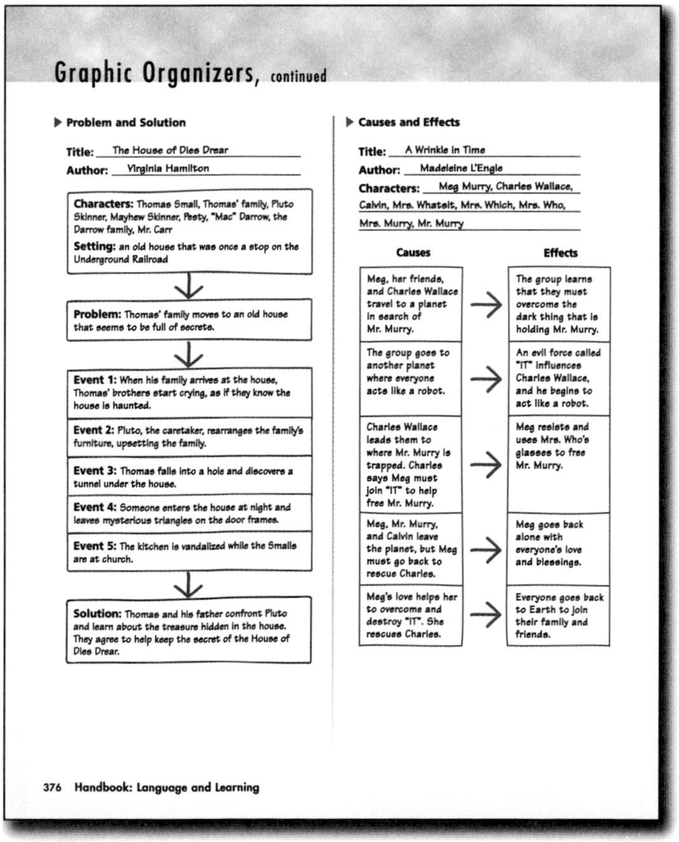

Graphic Organizers, continued

▶ **Problem and Solution**

Title: The House of Dies Drear
Author: Virginia Hamilton

Characters: Thomas Small, Thomas' family, Pluto Skinner, Mayhew Skinner, Pesty, "Mac" Darrow, the Darrow family, Mr. Carr
Setting: an old house that was once a stop on the Underground Railroad

Problem: Thomas' family moves to an old house that seems to be full of secrets.

Event 1: When his family arrives at the house, Thomas' brothers start crying, as if they know the house is haunted.

Event 2: Pluto, the caretaker, rearranges the family's furniture, upsetting the family.

Event 3: Thomas falls into a hole and discovers a tunnel under the house.

Event 4: Someone enters the house at night and leaves mysterious triangles on the door frames.

Event 5: The kitchen is vandalized while the Smalls are at church.

Solution: Thomas and his father confront Pluto and learn about the treasure hidden in the house. They agree to help keep the secret of the House of Dies Drear.

▶ **Causes and Effects**

Title: A Wrinkle in Time
Author: Madeleine L'Engle
Characters: Meg Murry, Charles Wallace, Calvin, Mrs. Whatsit, Mrs. Which, Mrs. Who, Mrs. Murry, Mr. Murry

Causes		Effects
Meg, her friends, and Charles Wallace travel to a planet in search of Mr. Murry.	→	The group learns that they must overcome the dark thing that is holding Mr. Murry.
The group goes to another planet where everyone acts like a robot.	→	An evil force called "IT" influences Charles Wallace, and he begins to act like a robot.
Charles Wallace leads them to where Mr. Murry is trapped. Charles says Meg must join "IT" to help free Mr. Murry.	→	Meg resists and uses Mrs. Who's glasses to free Mr. Murry.
Meg, Mr. Murry, and Calvin leave the planet, but Meg must go back to rescue Charles.	→	Meg goes back alone with everyone's love and blessings.
Meg's love helps her to overcome and destroy "IT". She rescues Charles.	→	Everyone goes back to Earth to join their family and friends.

376 Handbook: Language and Learning

page 376

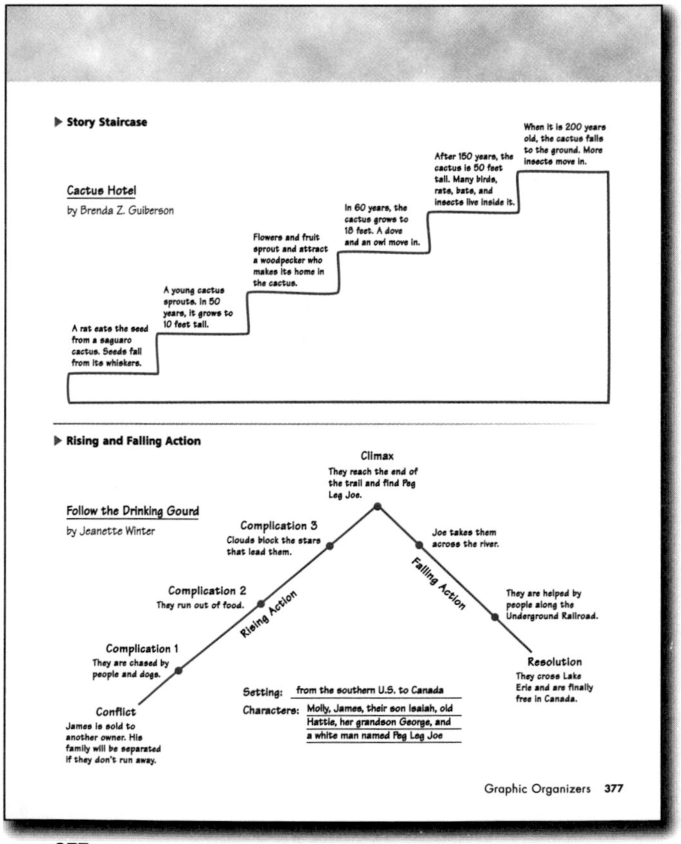

▶ **Story Staircase**

Cactus Hotel
by Brenda Z. Guiberson

▶ **Rising and Falling Action**

Follow the Drinking Gourd
by Jeanette Winter

Setting: from the southern U.S. to Canada
Characters: Molly, James, their son Isaiah, old Hattie, her grandson George, and a white man named Peg Leg Joe

Graphic Organizers 377

page 377

Handbook: Language and Learning

Technology and Media
Technology in Pictures

Technology is used every day in schools, offices, and homes. This section will help you recognize and use machines and electronic tools.

CALCULATOR

A **calculator** helps you do math. Use these keys when you:

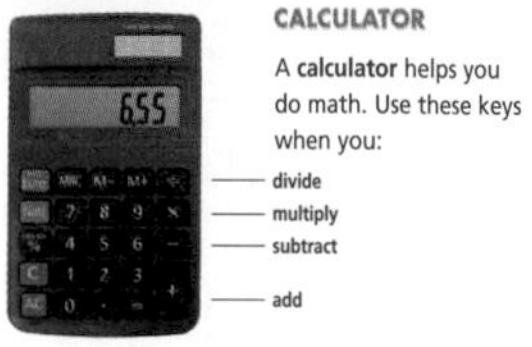

COMPACT DISC PLAYER

A **compact disc (CD) player** plays compact discs with music or other sounds.

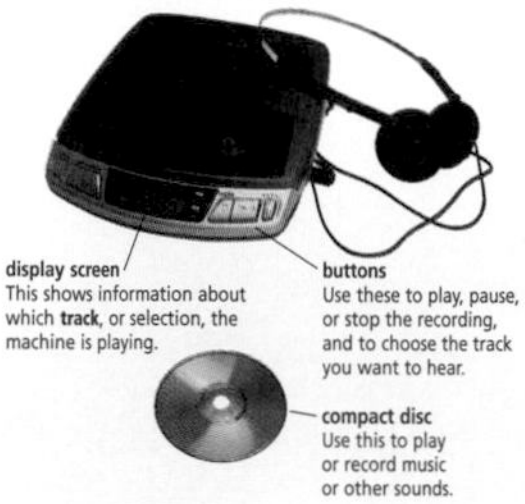

CASSETTE PLAYERS

A **cassette player** records and plays audiocassettes.

FAX MACHINE

A **fax machine** uses phone lines to send or receive a copy of pages with pictures or words.

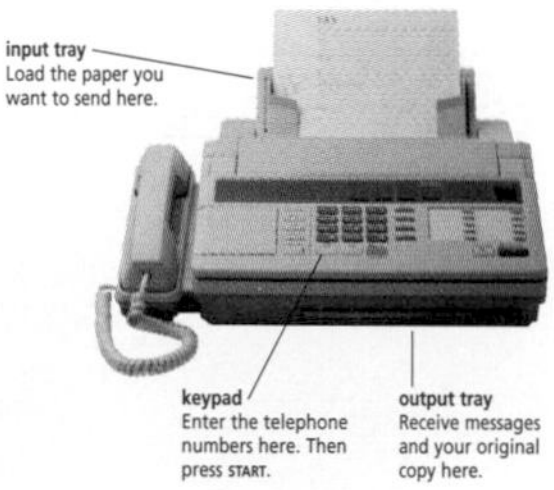

page 378

WIRELESS TELEPHONE

A **wireless telephone** lets you talk to people wherever you are.

CAMCORDER

A **camcorder** is a hand-held video camera. It records pictures and sounds on videotape. You can watch the videotape on a television.

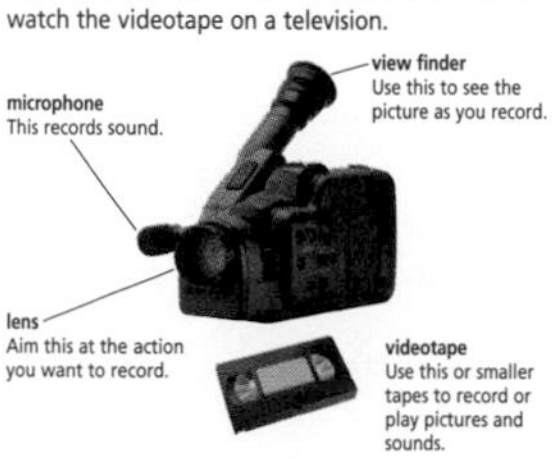

VIDEOCASSETTE RECORDER

A **videocassette recorder (VCR)** records and plays videotapes through a television. You can record television programs or watch videos that you make, buy, rent, or check out from the library.

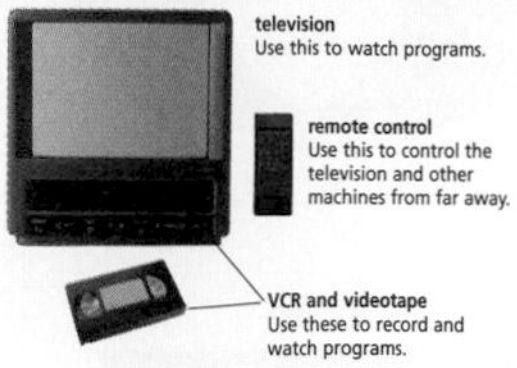

DIGITAL VIDEODISC PLAYER

A **digital videodisc (DVD) player** plays discs that have very clear pictures and sounds. You can watch movies by connecting a DVD player to a television or a computer.

page 379

Technology and Media, continued
Technology in Pictures, continued

THE COMPUTER

A **computer** is an electronic tool that helps you create, save, and use information.

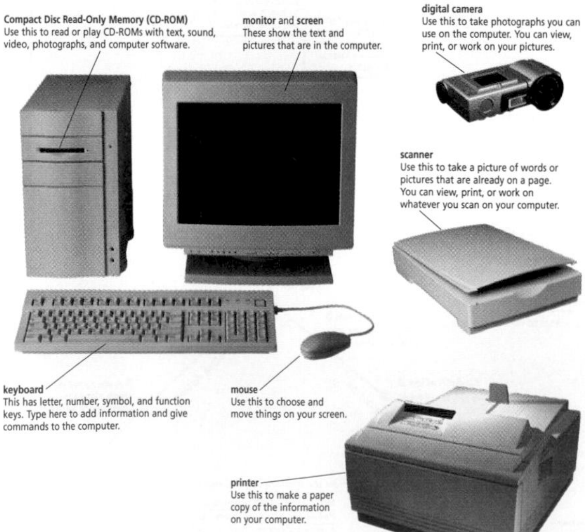

page 380

THE COMPUTER KEYBOARD

Use the **keys** on the **keyboard** to write, do math, or give the computer commands. Keyboards may look different, but they all have keys like these:

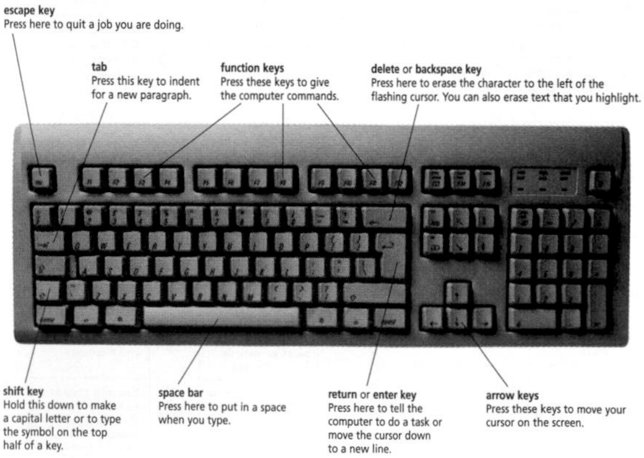

page 381

Handbook: Language and Learning

Technology and Media, continued

How to Send E-mail

E-mail is electronic mail that can be sent on-line from one computer to another. Anyone who has an e-mail address can send and receive messages. E-mail can travel around the classroom or around the world.

You can use e-mail to:

- write messages to one or more friends at a time
- send computer files
- save money on postage and telephone calls
- send and receive messages almost instantly

To send an e-mail message:

1. Open the e-mail program.
2. Open a new message.
3. Enter this information:
   - Type the recipient's e-mail address in the "To" box.
   - Type a short title for your e-mail in the "Subject" box.
   - Type your message.
4. Send your message.

Each e-mail program is different. Here is one example of a "mailbox":

E-mail Mailbox

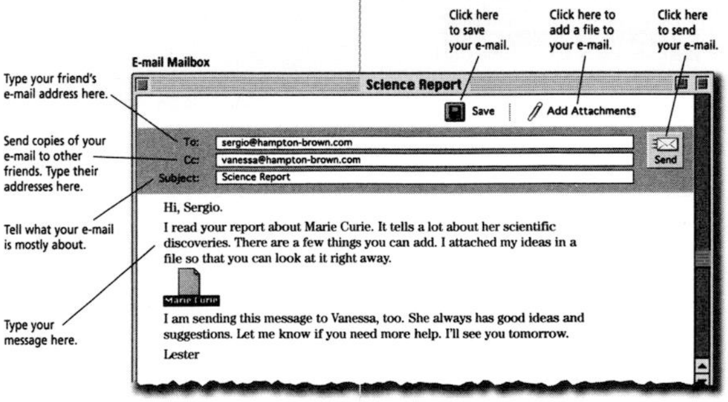

page 382

How to Use a Word-Processing Program

A **computer program** is a set of directions that tells a computer what to do. A **word-processing program** helps you create and store written work. You can use it to:

- store ideas, outlines, plans, and papers
- write drafts of your work
- revise, edit, and proofread your writing
- format and publish your work
- make written work look neat and organized.

There are many kinds of word-processing programs. There are also different ways to use the computer to make each job easier. This section of the Handbook will give you some ideas. Ask your teacher or classmates for other ways they have found to use your school's word-processing program.

Working on the computer

My First Day in an American School

by Marco Quezada

My first day of school in the United States was very scary because I didn't speak English. I didn't know how I was going to talk to people. I didn't have any friends. I tried to understand the teacher, but I couldn't. I felt like a chair.

Suddenly, a very loud bell rang. The teacher opened the door, and all the kids jumped up and rushed out the door.

Why was everyone leaving? In Haiti, we stayed in the same classroom all day. I followed the class, and we went into a new room. A stranger gave me a book and some papers. I was really puzzled. Fortunately, the man spoke some Creole and explained that he was my science teacher.

Finally, I understood. In America, there are special teachers for science, music, and gym. Students also move to new classrooms. At first, it was very confusing, but now I like having different teachers for my subjects.

page 383

Technology and Media, continued

How to Use a Word-Processing Program, continued

GET STARTED

1 How to Set Up a File Before you start to write, make a file—a place to keep your work. Follow these steps:

1. Click **File** to see the **File Menu**. A **menu** gives you a list of choices.

File Menu and New

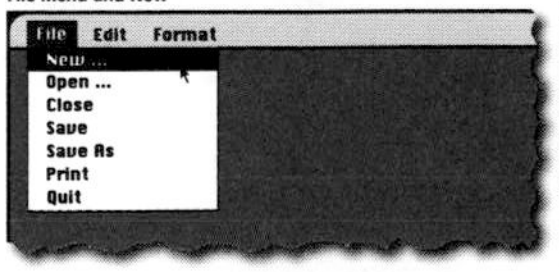

2. Click **New** to create a new document. A blank page will appear.

New Document

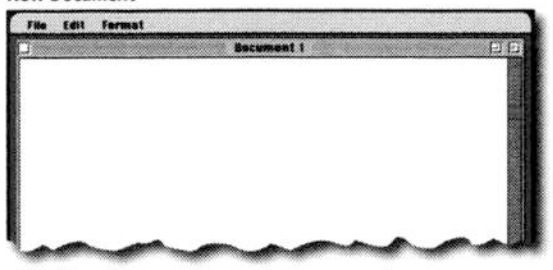

To save your new file in a folder, click **Save As** on the **File Menu.**

File Menu and New

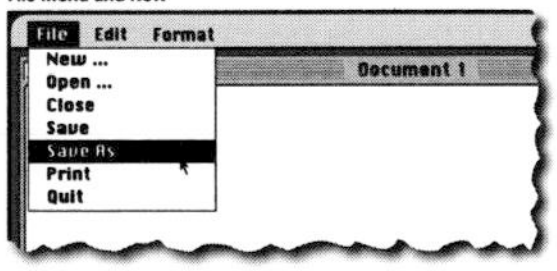

A **dialogue box** will appear to ask for information.

1. Type a short name for your file.
2. Make sure that the file name and folder are correct. If you don't have a folder for your work, ask your teacher for help to start one.
3. Click **Save** to save your file.

Save Dialogue Box

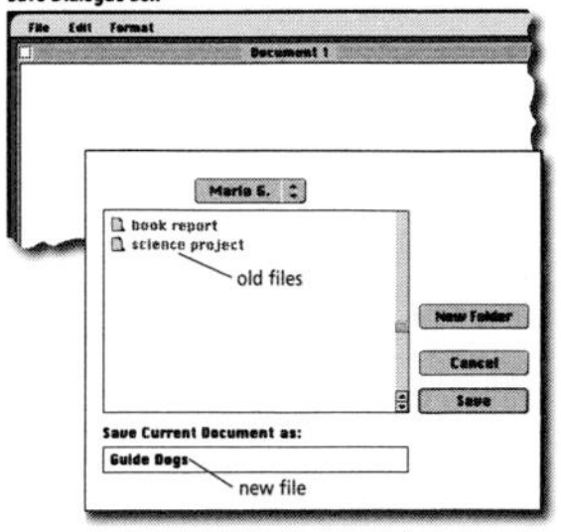

page 384

CREATE DOCUMENTS

1 How to Type a Document Now you are ready to type. Your work will appear in front of a flashing cursor. The **cursor** shows where you are working on the page.

Cursor

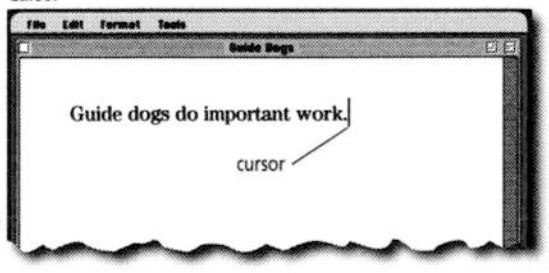

As you type, the **indicator box** shows where you are in the document. You can use the **scroll bar** to move up and down in your file.

- Click and hold the **up arrow** to move toward the top of the screen.
- Click and hold the **down arrow** to move toward the bottom of the screen.

Scrolling

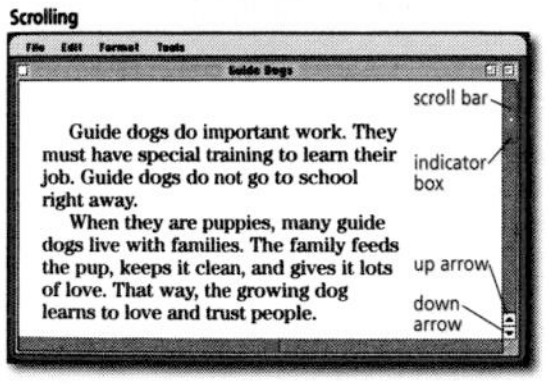

2 How to Save Your Work Remember to save your work as you write. If you do not save, you may lose the work you have done on your file. Remember:

✔ Save your work every 10 minutes!
✔ Save before you leave your computer.
✔ Save before you **Print.**
✔ Save before you **Quit.**
✔ Save, save, save!

To save your work, click **Save** in the **File Menu.**

Save

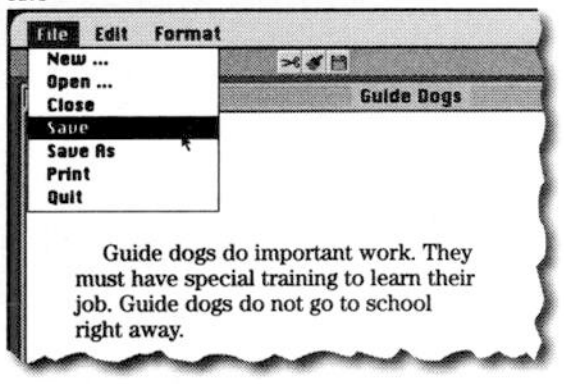

Or, click the **save icon** on the **toolbar.**

Toolbar Icons

page 385

Handbook: Language and Learning

Technology and Media, continued

How to Use a Word-Processing Program, continued

MAKE CHANGES TO YOUR WORK

❶ **How to Add Words** It is easy to add words to your work.

1. Use your mouse to move the cursor to the place where you want to add words.
2. Click the mouse once. The cursor will start to flash.

Add Words (before)

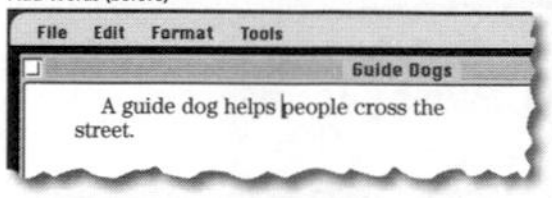

3. Type the new words.

Add Words (after)

❷ **How to Delete Words** When you **delete**, you take words out. Before you delete, you need to highlight the words you want to remove.

1. To remove one word, put the cursor on the word. Click the mouse twice.

Delete Words (before)

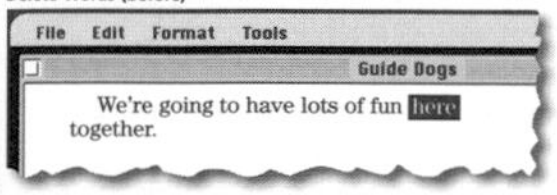

2. You can also **click and drag** to highlight and remove words.
   - Click and hold the mouse and slide it over all the words you want to take out. The words will be highlighted.

Delete Words (after)

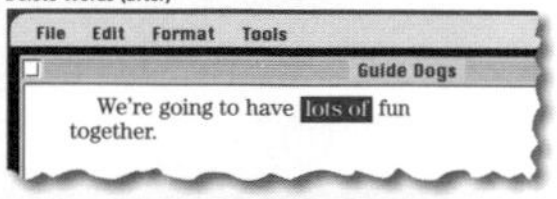

   - After the words are highlighted, press the **delete key**. The words will disappear from the screen.

Delete Words (after)

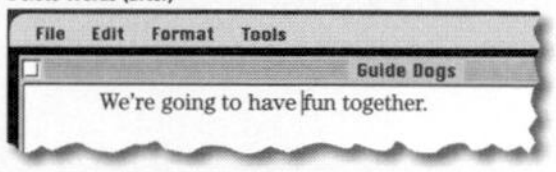

page 386

❸ **How to Cut and Paste** You can **cut and paste** to move sentences or paragraphs to a different place in your paper.

When you **cut** text, the computer takes out the highlighted words. The words are not deleted. They are stored in the computer's memory to be placed somewhere new.

To cut text, click **Cut** from the **Edit Menu**.

Cut (before)

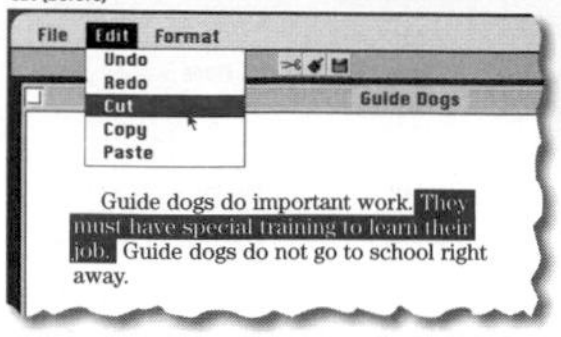

Or, click the **cut icon** on the **toolbar**.

Toolbar Icons

Your text will look like this:

Cut (after)

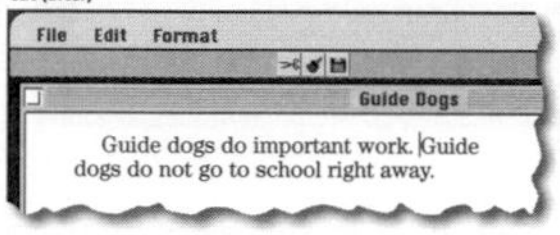

When you **paste** text, the cut words are placed at the flashing cursor. To paste text, move the cursor to where you want the text and click **Paste** from the **Edit Menu**.

Paste (before)

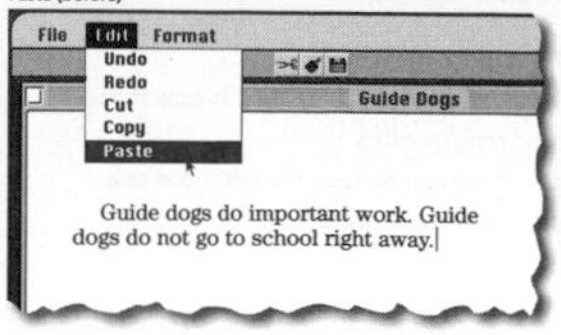

Or, click the **paste icon** on the **toolbar**.

Toolbar Icons

Your text will look like this:

Paste (after)

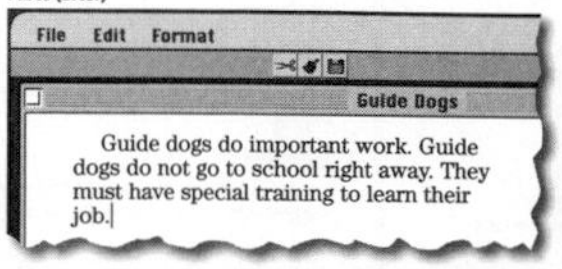

page 387

Technology and Media, continued

How to Use a Word-Processing Program, continued

❹ **How to Check Your Spelling** Most word-processing programs have tools to check your spelling. Follow these steps:

1. Open the **Tools Menu** and choose **Spelling**. The computer will show you a highlighted word from your text.
2. Choose the correct spelling from the list of suggestions. If the word is not listed, check a dictionary.

Spell Check

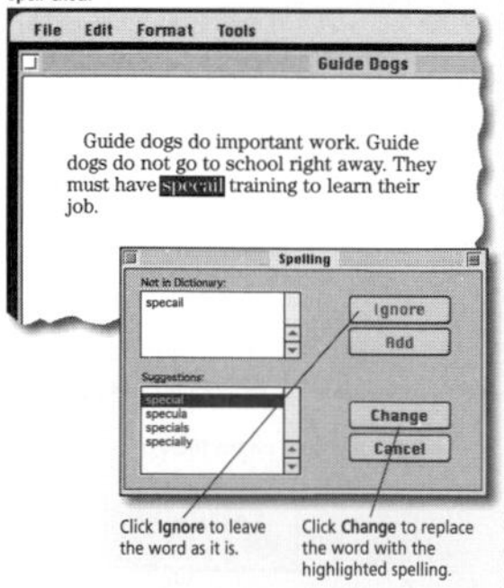

❺ **How to Find Synonyms** Use the computer's thesaurus to find synonyms for words you use.

1. Highlight the word you want to change. Then open the **Tools Menu** and choose **Thesaurus**.
2. Some words have different meanings. Choose the correct one from the list of Meanings.
3. Look at the list of synonyms for that meaning. Highlight the word you want.

Thesaurus

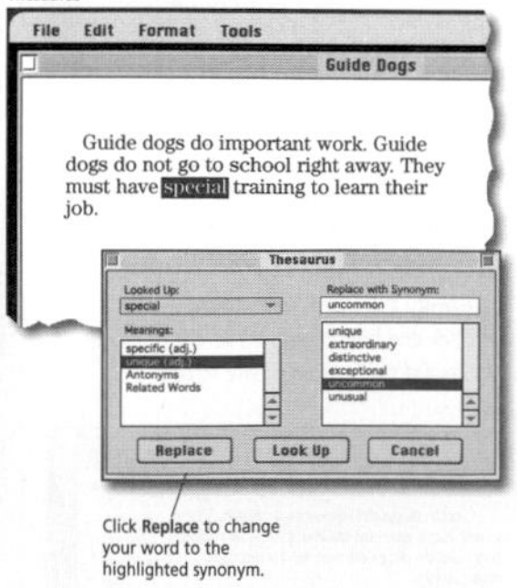

page 388

FORMAT YOUR PAPER

When you **format** your work, you make it look neat and organized. Here are some ways to format, or arrange, your paper.

❶ **How to Change the Font, Style, and Size** A **font** is a unique style for the letters and numbers that you type. Follow these steps:

- Highlight the section you want to change.
- Open the **Format Menu** and choose **Font**, or click the font, style, and size icons on your toolbar.

- Choose the font, word style, and word size you want for your text. Then click **OK**. You can choose from many fonts. For class work, choose a font that is clear and easy to read. If you are writing to friends, you can choose more fun styles! Here are some examples:

Fonts

good for reports	good for essays
good for a friendly letter	great for your journal

Styles

normal	*italic*
bold	<u>underlined</u>

Sizes

12	14	16	18

❷ **How to Change Text Alignment** When you set **text alignment**, you choose how words will line up on the page. You may want to put a title in the center of the page, or put your name in the right-hand corner. Follow these steps:

- Highlight the text you want to align.
- Click the icon that shows where you want the text placed. For example:

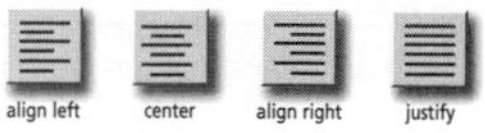

❸ **How to Set Spacing** You can choose the **spacing**—how much space comes between each line you type. Follow these steps:

- Open the **Edit Menu** and choose **Select All**.
- Click the correct spacing icon:

Ask your teacher or your friends for more ideas about how to format your work. Soon, your work will have a new style that is unique and attractive.

page 389

Handbook: Language and Learning

Technology and Media, continued

How to Create a Multimedia Presentation

A **multimedia presentation** uses technology to present ideas. Your audience can read, see, and hear your work.

LEARN ABOUT MEDIA

There are many ways to share information. Choose media that fit your purpose. Here are some possibilities:

▶ **Visuals**

- Use a computer to create slides of important points, outlines, or quotations.
- Scan tables or diagrams to show information.

▶ **Photographs**

- Scan photographs.
- Download pictures from the Internet.
- Use pictures from a CD-ROM.

▶ **Video and Animation**

- Use videos from the news.
- Create animation to show how something changes.
- Make a videotape of yourself or others.

▶ **Sounds**

- Play music on a cassette, CD, or CD-ROM.
- Make a recording of yourself or others.
- Download sound files from the Internet.

page 390

MAKE A MULTIMEDIA PRESENTATION

Follow these steps to give your own multimedia presentation.

1. **Plan** Think about how you can present your ideas creatively.
   - Put your ideas into a logical order.
   - Ask yourself: What pictures, videos, and sounds will help the class understand my ideas? What technology can I use?
   - Use a **graphic organizer** to put the steps of your presentation in order. Here is one example:

Flow Chart

Show title slide: Democracy in Ancient Greece.
↓
Talk about Greek city-states.
↓
Show slide of map of ancient Greece on the computer.
↓
Play 2-minute video of Greek elections.

2. **Practice** Rehearse your presentation until you are comfortable with your speech and the technology you will use.
   - Practice in front of your family and friends. Ask them for ideas and suggestions.
   - Unexpected things can happen when you work with technology. Before your presentation, test your equipment to be sure it works.
3. **Present** Remember that your goal is to give an effective presentation.
   - Speak slowly and clearly.
   - Give your audience time to understand the ideas you are sharing.
   - Have fun!

page 391

Technology and Media, continued

How to Use the Internet

The **Internet** is an international network, or connection, of computers that share information with one another. The **World Wide Web** allows you to find, read, go through, and organize information. The Internet is like a giant library, and the World Wide Web is everything in the library including the books, the librarian, and the computer catalog.

The Internet is a fast way to get the most current information about your topic! You'll find resources like encyclopedias and dictionaries on the Internet and amazing pictures, movies, and sounds.

WHAT YOU WILL NEED

To use the Internet, you need a computer with software that allows you to access it. You'll also need a modem connected to a telephone line.

HOW TO GET STARTED

You can search the Internet in many different ways. Ask your teacher how to access the Internet from your school. Usually you can just double click on the **icon**, or picture, to get access to the Internet and you're on your way!

HOW TO DO THE RESEARCH

Once the search page comes up, you can begin the research process. Just follow these steps.

1. **Type in Your Subject** Enter your key words in the search box and then click on the Search button. You'll always see a toolbar at the top of the screen. Click on the **icons** to do things like print the page.

Try different ways to type in your subject. You'll get different results!

- If you type in **Mars**, you'll see all the sites that have the word *Mars* in them. This may give you too many categories and sites to look through!
- If you type in **"Mars exploration,"** you'll see all the sites with the exact phrase, or group of words, *Mars exploration*.
- If you type in **Mars+exploration**, you'll see all the sites with the words *Mars* and *exploration* in them.

page 392

2. **Read the Search Results** All underlined, colored words are links, or connections, to other sites. They help you get from page to page quickly.
   - If you want to go directly to a Web page, click on a site.
   - Click on a category to see more options for information related to your topic.
   - Read the descriptions of the sites to save time.

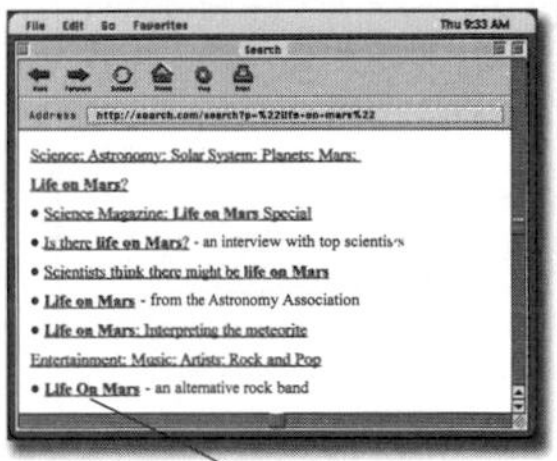

This site could be very interesting, but it probably won't help with your report.

3. **Select a Site and Read** You might want to pick a new site or start a new search. If so, click on the **Back** arrow to go back a page to the search results. If you want to go to another Web page, click on a link.

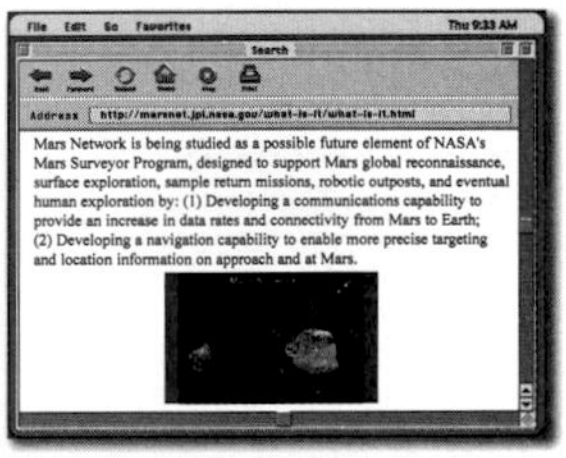

4. **Locate More Resources** If you already know the **URL (Uniform Resource Locator)**, or address, of a Web site, you can type it in the address box at the top of the screen.

   Remember that information on Web sites changes frequently. Sometimes Web pages are not kept up. If you can't access one Web site, try another one.

page 393

Handbook: Language and Learning

The Research Process

When you research, you look up information about a topic. You can use the information you find to write a story, article, book, or research report.

1 CHOOSE A TOPIC

Think of something you want to learn more about and something that interests you. That will be your research **topic**. Pick a topic that is not too general. A specific, or smaller, topic is easier to research and to write about. It is also more interesting to read about in a report. Look at these topics:

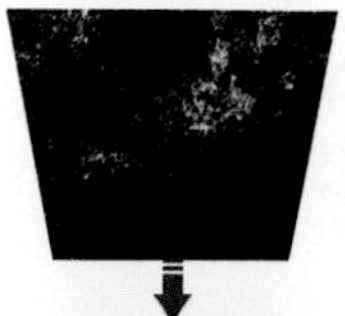

Outer Space
This is a big topic! There are a lot of things in outer space: stars, suns, planets, moons, and black holes. That would be too much to research or write about in one report.

Planets
This topic is better, but it's still too big. There are nine planets in our solar system! You could do a report on the planet Mars. But what is it you want to know about Mars?

Life on Mars
The topic "Life on Mars" is more specific than "Mars." Finding out if Mars has water, plants, animals, or Martians could be VERY interesting!

2 DECIDE WHAT TO LOOK UP

What do you want to know about your topic? Write down some questions. Look at the most important words in your questions. Those are **key words** you can look up when you start your research.

Is there life on Mars?
Is there water or oxygen on Mars?
Can people, plants, or animals live on the surface of Mars?
Have space missions studied Mars?
Did anyone find proof of Martian life forms?

3 LOCATE RESOURCES

Now that you know what to look up, you can go to different **resources** to find information about your topic. Resources can be people, such as librarians, teachers, and family members. Resources can also be books, magazines, newspapers, videos, or the Internet. You can find resources all around you.

Whatever your topic is, try exploring the library first. There you'll discover a world of information!

page 394

4 GATHER INFORMATION

When you gather information, you find the best resources for your topic. You look up your key words to find facts about your topic. Then you take notes.

How to Find Information Quickly Use alphabetical order to look up words in a list. In many resources, the words, titles, and subjects are listed in **alphabetical order**.

Look at these words. They are in order by the **first** letter of each word.

asteroid
moon
planet
sun

If the word you are looking up has the same first letter as other words in the list, look at the **second** letters.

Mars
Mercury
mission
moon

If the word you are looking up has the same first and second letters as others in the list, look at the **third** letters.

magnetic
map
Mars
mass

Skim and scan the text to decide if it is useful. When you **skim** and **scan**, you look at text quickly to see if it has the information you need. If it does, you can take the time to read it more carefully. If it doesn't, go on to another source.

To skim:

- Read the title to see if the article is useful for your topic.
- Read the **beginning sentences** and **headings** to find out more about an article's topic.
- Skim the ending. It often sums up all the ideas in the article.

To scan:

Look for **key words** or **details** in dark type or italics. If you find key words that go with your topic, you'll probably want to read the article.

PLANETS, STARS, AND SPACE TRAVEL

LOOKING FOR LIFE ELSEWHERE IN THE UNIVERSE

For years scientists have been trying to discover if there is life on other planets in our solar system or life elsewhere in the universe. Some scientists have been looking for evidence based on what is necessary for life on Earth—basics like water and proper temperature.

WHAT SCIENTISTS HAVE LEARNED SO FAR

Mars and Jupiter. In 1996, two teams of scientists examined two meteorites that may have come from **Mars** and found evidence that some form of life may have existed on Mars billions of years ago. In 1997, in photographs of Europa, a moon of **Jupiter**, scientists saw areas with icy ridges and areas without ice. It seemed that underneath the ice there might be water—one of the essentials of life.

New Planets. In 1996, astronomers believed they found several new planets traveling around stars very far away (many light-years away) from our sun. Scientists do not think life exists on these planets, because they are so close to their sun that they would be too hot. But scientists are hoping to find other stars with planets around them that might support life.

AND THE SEARCH CONTINUES

NASA (the National Aeronautics and Space Administration) has a program to look for life on Mars. Ten spacecraft are to be sent to Mars over the next ten years. Some will fly around Mars taking pictures, while others will land on Mars to study the soil and rocks and look for living things. The first two, *Mars Pathfinder* and *Mars Global Surveyor*, launched in 1996, were scheduled to reach Mars in 1997.

Another program that searches for life on other worlds is called **SETI**. SETI (an acronym for Search for Extraterrestrial Intelligence) uses powerful radio telescopes to look for life elsewhere in the universe.

Question: Is there life elsewhere in the universe? **Answer:** No one knows yet.

page 395

The Research Process, continued

4 GATHER INFORMATION, continued

How to Take Notes Write down important words, phrases, and ideas while you are reading and researching. These notes will help you remember **details**. They'll also help you remember the **source**. The source is where you got the information.

Set up your notecards in the following way so you can easily put your information in order when you write.

1. Include your research question.
2. Write down the source so you can remember where you found your facts.
   - For a book, list the title, author, and page number.
   - For a magazine or newspaper article, list the name, date, volume, and issue number of your source. Also, write the title of the article in quotation marks.
3. List the details and facts in your own words. Use quotation marks for exact words you copy from a source.

Notecard for a Book

Is there life on Mars?
Mars by Seymour Simon, page 27
—Viking spacecraft supposed to find out if there's life
—some think experiments showed there isn't
—others believe experiments were the wrong kind; maybe scientists looked in wrong places

Notecard for a Magazine or Newspaper

Is there life on Mars?
Time for Kids, Sept. 13, 1996
Vol. 2, No. 1 "Next Stop: Mars"
—maybe—Mars has some features like Earth. "It has volcanoes and giant canyons."
—hard to prove, but maybe space missions like Pathfinder can find something

page 396

5 ORGANIZE INFORMATION

Make an Outline An outline can help you organize your report. Follow these steps to turn your notes into an outline.

1. Put all the notecards with the same research question together.
2. Turn your notes into an outline.
   - First, turn your question into a main idea. Each main idea follows a Roman numeral.

     I. Life on Mars

   - Next, find details that go with the main idea. Add them to your outline. Each detail follows a capital letter. Each related detail follows a number.

     I. Life on Mars
     A. How Mars is like Earth
     1. Volcanoes
     2. Giant canyons

3. Write a **title** for your outline. The title tells what your outline is all about. You can use it again when you write your report.

Sample Outline

Mars: Is Anyone Up There?
I. Life on Mars
A. How Mars is like Earth
1. Volcanoes
2. Giant canyons
B. Fact-finding missions
1. Viking
2. Pathfinder
II. Signs of life on Mars
A. Studied by David McKay's team
B. Meteorite
1. Might contain bacteria fossils
2. Found in Antarctica
3. Probably from Mars
III. Continued search for life on Mars
A. Look underground
B. More study
1. Mission planned for near future
2. Gases in atmosphere
3. What rocks are made of

page 397

Handbook: Language and Learning

The Research Process, continued

6 WRITE A RESEARCH REPORT

Now use your outline to write a **research report**. Turn the main ideas and details from your outline into sentences and paragraphs.

Write the Title and Introduction Copy the title from your outline and write an interesting introduction to tell what your report is mostly about.

Outline

Mars: Is Anyone Up There?

Title and Introduction

Mars: Is Anyone Up There?

You've probably seen some pretty creepy outer space creatures in movies and on TV. Do they really look like that? Are there really living beings up there?

Write the Body Use your main ideas to write a topic sentence for each paragraph. Then use your details and related details to write sentences about the main idea.

Outline

I. Life on Mars
  A. How Mars is like Earth
    1. Volcanoes
    2. Giant canyons

Topic Sentence and Details

People have always wondered if there is life on other planets, especially Mars. Because Mars is similar to Earth, with features like volcanoes and giant canyons, it seems possible that there is life on Mars. There are lots of missions to Mars, like the spacecrafts Viking and Pathfinder, so it seems like we might find out soon!

Write a Conclusion Write a sentence for each main idea in the last paragraph of your report.

Outline

I. Life on Mars

II. Signs of life on Mars

III. Continued search for life on Mars

Conclusion

Basically, no one knows if there is or isn't life on Mars. It is possible that life does or did exist there. Spacecrafts that go to Mars in the future will give us more proof. Hopefully, the mystery will be solved soon for all of us!

page 398

A good research report gives facts about a topic in an organized and interesting way.

Mars: Is Anyone Up There?

You've probably seen some pretty creepy outer space creatures in movies and TV. Do they really look like that? Are there really living beings up there?

People have always wondered if there is life on other planets, especially Mars. Because Mars is similar to Earth, with features like volcanoes and giant canyons, it seems possible that there is life on Mars. There are lots of missions to Mars, like the spacecrafts Viking and Pathfinder, so it seems like we might find out soon!

David McKay and his team of scientists discovered possible signs of ancient Martian life. They think they found bacteria fossils in a meteorite that crashed into Antarctica thousands of years ago. They believe the meteorite is from Mars because it has the same chemicals in it as the Martian atmosphere. They think the fossils, which are a lot smaller than the width of a human hair, were alive on Mars from 3 to 4 billion years ago. At that time, there was water on the planet. Since the fossils were deep in the center of the meteorite, McKay's team feels that the fossils were definitely from Mars and not from Earth.

No one has seen a live Martian, but some scientists feel that we need to keep looking. Since no one has found water on the surface of Mars, maybe Martians live underground where there is water. A mission to look for Martian life and bring soil samples back to Earth is planned for the near future. Until then, scientists will continue to study the other aspects of Mars like the gases in its atmosphere and what its rocks are made of.

Basically, no one knows if there is or isn't life on Mars. It is possible that life does or did exist there. Spacecrafts that go to Mars in the future will give us more proof. Hopefully, the mystery will be solved soon for all of us!

INTRODUCTION
The **title** and **introduction** tell what your report is about. They get your reader interested.

BODY
The **body** of the report presents the facts you found. Each paragraph begins with a **topic sentence** that tells one main idea from your outline. The other sentences give **details** and **related details**.

CONCLUSION
The **conclusion** is a summary of the most important information about your topic.

page 399

Speaking and Listening

You talk, or speak, to others every day. That's how you express your ideas. You also listen to others to learn about new ideas.

HOW TO BE A GOOD LISTENER

Good listeners listen carefully to what others say.

How to Be a Good Listener

- Pay attention. Open your eyes and ears. Look at the speaker as you listen. That way you'll "hear" more.
- Be quiet while the speaker is talking.
- Don't interrupt unless you need the speaker to talk louder.
- Save your questions until the speaker is finished.

HOW TO PARTICIPATE IN A DISCUSSION

Sometimes you will discuss ideas as a class, in a group, or with a partner. You may also have a conference with a teacher or a peer to talk about your writing. Discussions are good ways to find information, check your understanding, and share ideas.

How to Participate in a Discussion

- Use good listening skills.
- Give each speaker a chance to make a statement. Wait until someone has finished speaking before you respond.
- Make positive comments about the ideas of others. Respect everyone's ideas and feelings.
- Think about the topic. Offer ideas about only that topic and not something else.
- Ask questions if you need more information.

HOW TO LISTEN CRITICALLY

There are many reasons to listen carefully. You can find out how to do something or learn more about a topic. You can also use what you hear to help you decide how you think and feel. As you listen:

- Think about what you are hearing. Try to relate what you hear to what you already know.
- Listen for key words and important details. Take notes to help you remember the ideas.

  Example:
  ecosystem: things in nature and how they work together

- Ask yourself: What is the speaker's purpose? Does the speaker want to inform or entertain the audience? Does the speaker want to persuade me to do something?
- Pay attention to the speaker's tone of voice, gestures, and expressions. What do they tell you about how the speaker feels about the topic?
- Think about who is speaking. Is the speaker an expert on the topic?
- Summarize what the speaker says in your own mind. Do you agree or disagree? What new information did you learn?

page 400

HOW TO GIVE AN ORAL PRESENTATION

What would you like to share with others? Choose an interesting topic. Then decide if you want to make a speech, give a report, recite a poem, or give a performance to share your ideas. Follow these steps to prepare your presentation.

1 Plan Your Presentation Think about your audience. What ideas do you want to share? What is the best way to present your ideas?

- Organize your information. You might use a graphic organizer to show the details and the order in which you'll present ideas.

  Example:
  I. Ecosystem
    A. Is like a community
    B. Includes all living things in nature
  II. Food Chain
    A. Is different in different places
    B. Has a sequence
      1. Microorganisms in soil
      2. Plants grow
      3. Animals eat plants

- Think of a way to grab the audience's attention and introduce your topic. You might use a quote, make a startling statement, or ask a question.
- Write your main points on notecards. Use them as you speak to help you remember what to say.

  Beginning of food chain
  —microorganisms in the soil create food for plants
  —plants grow

- Use visuals and technology to support your ideas. Organize them to match your notes.

Food Chain Poster

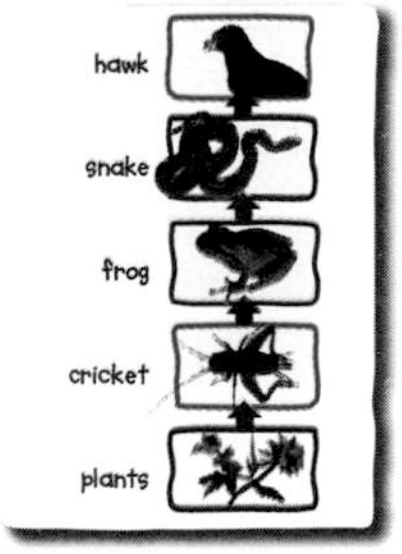

- Use your notecards, visuals, and technology to practice your presentation in front of a mirror or your family. Videotaping or tape recording your presentation may give you ideas about how to improve.

page 401

Handbook: Language and Learning

Speaking and Listening, continued

2 Choose Appropriate Language and Tone Are you speaking to your friends, to young kids, or to adults you don't know? Think about your topic, audience, and purpose to help you decide how to give your presentation.

To give a persuasive speech:
- Use a strong, clear tone of voice. Change your tone to emphasize important points.
- Use formal language to present the facts. Use persuasive words to give opinions.

To tell a story:
- Use informal language to make the characters seem real. Change your voice to show when a new character is speaking.
- Use facial expressions, gestures, and other movements to show the characters' feelings and actions.

To give a formal report:
- Use formal language to present the facts and information.
- Speak slowly and clearly so everyone can understand the information.
- Present the information in a logical order.
- Use examples and visuals that support your main points.

Use formal language to give a report.

3 Give Your Presentation Now you can stand up and be heard! As you present your ideas:
- Stand up straight.
- Make eye contact with the audience.
- Speak slowly and clearly in a loud voice so everyone can hear you.
- Use expressions and movements that go with the information you are presenting.
- Point to or hold up any visuals so your audience can follow along.
- Try to stay calm and relaxed.
- Thank the audience when you're done. Ask for questions when you are finished.

page 402

Viewing and Representing

You can get information from the things you see, or view. You can also use visuals to help you communicate and represent your ideas.

HOW TO EVALUATE WHAT YOU SEE

There are many things to view—photographs, videos, television commercials, graphs and charts, Web sites, and people who use gestures and movements to send messages without words. Here's how to evaluate what you see. Try out the process with the visual below.

1 View and Look for Details Take a minute or two to study the visual. Ask yourself:
- Who or what does the image show? Are there other details that tell when, where, why, or how?
- How does the visual make me feel? Do I enjoy looking at it? Does it scare me, make me laugh, or give me a good feeling?
- Do I like the colors? How does the size or shape of the visual affect me?

Persistent Sea No. 2, by O. Louis Guglielmi, oil on canvas.

2 Think About the Purpose and the Message What you see can influence the way you feel about a topic. Ask yourself:
- What message does the visual convey?
- Why did the artist create the visual? Does it make me want to do something? Does it give me new information?
- Does the visual represent the complete picture of the topic, or was it chosen to control my understanding of it?

3 Look for Stereotypes A stereotype is a general opinion that doesn't consider individual differences. It's like saying that because one dog is mean, all dogs are mean. Try to identify any stereotypes in the visual.

page 403

Viewing and Representing, continued

HOW TO REPRESENT YOUR IDEAS

There are many resources that can help you make your point more clearly. Choose media that match your purpose and your topic. Strong visual images will make a strong impression.

A beautiful **illustration** can add creativity and make a story come alive.

Illustration

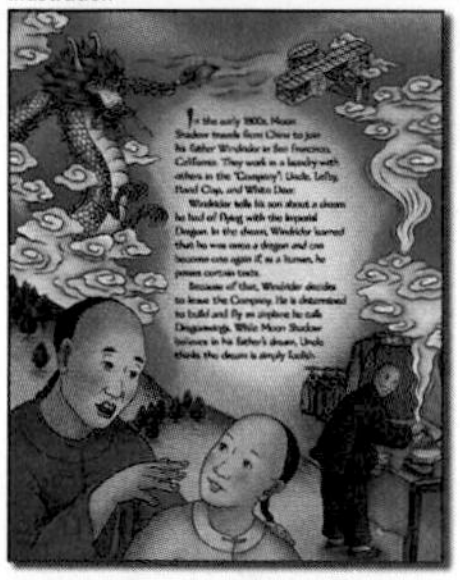

A **flow chart** can show steps in a process.

Flow Chart

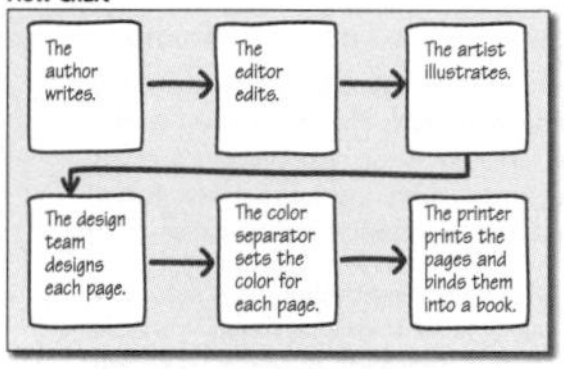

A **chart** or a **graph** can show comparisons. Look for more graphic organizers on pages 370–377.

Chart

Number of Endangered Species in the United States

Classification	Number of Species
Mammals	61
Birds	75
Reptiles	14
Fishes	69
Insects	28

Graph

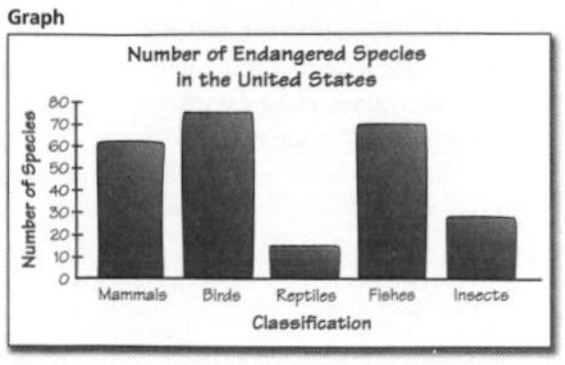

page 404

HOW TO MATCH MEDIA TO YOUR MESSAGE

Choose the best media to help you get your point across. It will help you get your audience's attention. Take a look at the different media you can use on Handbook pages 378–381. Here are a few examples.

1 To Entertain Include props, illustrations of the setting, or slides for a backdrop. Create a film strip, animation, or a video.

2 To Inform Include maps and charts to support your topic. You might make a time line to show chronological events or use a transparency to display information on an overhead projector.

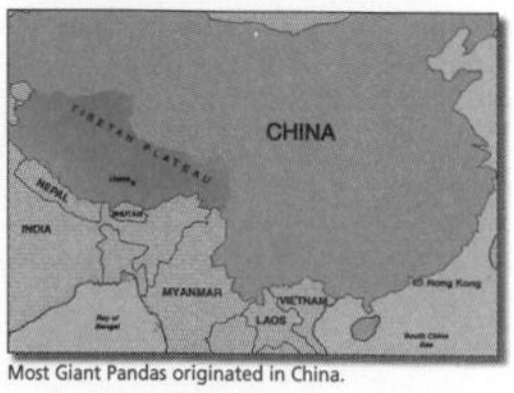

Most Giant Pandas originated in China.

3 To Persuade Show images that will change people's opinions. You might use slides or photographs that appeal to people's emotions.

Fewer than 1,000 pandas live in the wild.

page 405

Strategies for Taking Tests

These strategies will help you learn how to take tests and show what you know.

MULTIPLE-CHOICE TEST

For a multiple-choice test, you will mark the best answer from a list of choices.

1. **Read the Directions Carefully** The test directions tell you what you need to do. Words like *best, always, only, all,* and *never* will help you find the correct answer. There may be more than one correct answer, but only one is the "best" answer.

> **Directions: Read each question. Circle the best answer.**
> 4. Which type of transportation causes the least air pollution?
> A a bus (C) a bike
> B a car D a motorcycle

2. **Mark Your Answers** You may need to fill in a bubble on an answer sheet, circle an answer, or write your answer on a separate sheet of paper. When you use an answer sheet, be sure to match the item number on the test to the item number on the answer sheet.

> **Read the sentence. Mark the answer that gives the best meaning for the underlined word.**
> (5) People can recycle to help save the Earth.
> F use products over again
> G go backwards on a bicycle
> H throw away all their trash
> J keep trash in a special place
>
> 4. Ⓐ Ⓑ Ⓒ Ⓓ
> (5) ● Ⓖ Ⓗ Ⓙ

3. **Plan Your Time** Skip over any hard questions. Don't spend too much time on one question. If you have time, you can go back to it later.

4. **Read Items Again** If you are not sure about an answer, read the item again. Think about all the answer choices. Which one seems best?

TRUE-FALSE TEST

In a true-false test, you will decide if a statement is true or false.

1. **Read Carefully** If *any* part of the statement is false, the answer is false. If you're still not sure after reading an item, make your best guess!

2. **Look for Key Words** Watch for words like *never, always, all,* and *no.* Statements with those words are often false.

> _false_ 1. Businesses never monitor the dirty air from their factories.

406 Handbook: Language and Learning

page 406

SHORT-ANSWER TEST

Often a test item will ask for a short answer. Look for key words like *who* or *what* that tell you the information to include in the answer.

> 12. What do farmers put on their crops to kill insects? _pesticides_

ESSAY TEST

For an essay test, you will need to write one or more paragraphs to answer a question.

1. **Study the Item and Key Words** Read the question at least two times. Look for key words that tell you exactly what to do. You might see prompts like these on an essay test:
   - Compare the rainforest and the tundra.
   - Summarize how the transcontinental railroad influenced western expansion.
   - Describe the main events that led to the Civil War.

2. **Plan Your Answer** Think about the key words and the topic. Write facts or details you know in a web, chart, or another graphic organizer. Add numbers or make an outline to show how you will organize your writing.

3. **Write the Essay** Use the words in the prompt to help you write an introduction. Then use your notes and details to write your essay.
   - Write a topic sentence for each paragraph.
   - Include all the important details.
   - Sum up your essay with a concluding sentence.
   - Before you turn in your essay, read it over. Be sure that you have written about what was described in the prompt.

Prompt

> 1. Explain three ways that people can reduce air pollution.

Sample Answer

> People can reduce air pollution in three main ways. One way is to carpool. If people share rides, they can reduce the amount of car exhaust. A second way is to walk or ride a bicycle for short trips. That doesn't cause any air pollution! Finally, people can encourage businesses to stop the air pollution caused by their factories. If we do these things today, we'll have cleaner air in the future!

Strategies for Taking Tests 407

page 407

Handbook: Writing

The Writing Process

Writing is one of the best ways to express yourself. The steps in the Writing Process will help you say what you want to say clearly, correctly, and in your own unique way.

PREWRITE

Prewriting is what you do before you write. During this step, you collect ideas, choose a topic, make a plan, gather details, and organize your ideas.

1. **Collect Ideas** Writing ideas are everywhere! Think about recent events or things you've read or seen. You can brainstorm more writing ideas with your classmates, friends, and family. Collect your ideas in a computer file, a notebook, or a journal. Then when you're ready to write, check your idea collections.

2. **Choose a Topic** Sometimes you have a lot of ideas you want to write about. Other times, your teacher may give you a **writing prompt**, or a writing assignment. You will still need to decide exactly what to write about. Make a list of possible writing ideas. Then circle the one that is the most important or interesting to you. That idea will be your **topic**.

> I could write about...
> a concert my friends and I went to
> when my grandparents arrived in the U.S.
> why we need more school dances
> why the eagle is a popular symbol

3. **Plan Your Writing** An FATP chart can help you organize your thoughts and focus on the details that you'll need for your writing.

FATP Chart

HOW TO UNLOCK A PROMPT
Form: personal narrative
Audience: my teacher and classmates
Topic: when my grandparents arrived in the U.S.
Purpose: to describe a personal experience

Here are the ways an **FATP** chart can help you:

- The **form** tells you the type of writing. Study examples of the form to help you decide how to craft your writing.
- If you know your **audience**, you can choose the appropriate style and tone. For example, if you are writing for your friends, you can use friendly, informal language.
- A specific **topic** will help you collect only those details you need.
- The **purpose** is why you are writing. Your purpose can be to describe, to inform or explain, to persuade, or to express personal thoughts or feelings.

For more about writing for a specific audience or purpose, see pages 414–415.

page 408

4. **Gather Details** To write about a personal experience, you can just list the things you remember about an event. For other kinds of writing, you may need to talk about your topic with others or do research to gather information.

There are many ways to show the details you've gathered. You can

- make charts, lists, or webs
- draw and label pictures
- take notes on notecards
- make a story map
- use a gathering grid to write down answers to your questions

Gathering Grid

Topic: Vietnam	Get to Know Vietnam (book)	Internet
What is the population?		
What fuels the economy?		

Show your details in a way that works best for you and for your topic.

5. **Get Organized** Review your details and plan an interesting way to write about your topic. Put the details in the best order for your writing.
   - Sometimes you can organize the details as you write them down.
   - Other times, you can use numbers to order events in time sequence or to order the details from most to least important.
   - You could also make an outline to show main ideas and supporting details.

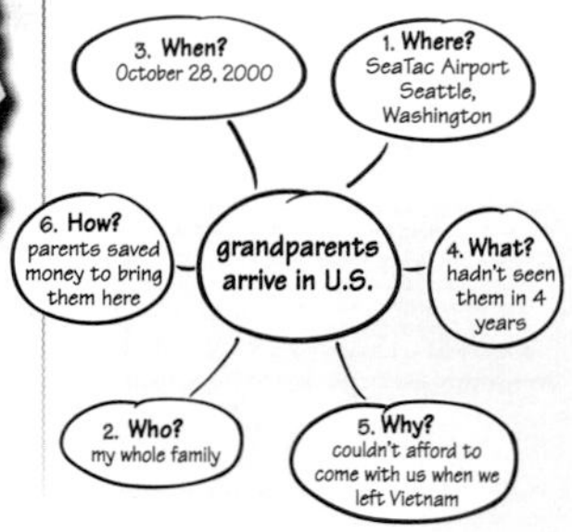

page 409

The Writing Process, continued

DRAFT

Now you are ready to start writing. At this stage, don't worry about making mistakes—just get your ideas down on paper! Turn your details into sentences and paragraphs. As you are writing, you'll probably think of new ideas. Add those to your draft.

Trang Bui's Draft

> My family stood by the windows and watched the plane land at SeaTac Airport in Seattle on October 28, 2000. We were so excited to see the plane. The people started coming through the door. We lined up so we could see. I had to lift my little sister up so she could see.
>
> Suddenly everyone was hugging and crying. "I see them," my mother cried. My little sister tried to hide. My sister didn't know my grandparents. She was feeling shy.

Write your ideas in a first draft.

REVISE

A first draft can always be improved. When you revise a draft, you make changes to it.

1. **Read Your Draft** As you read your draft, ask yourself questions about the most important ideas. Make sure your ideas are clear, complete, and presented in the best way.

Revision Checklist

- ☑ Did I follow the plan on my FATP chart? Is the language appropriate for the writing form and audience? Did I stick to the topic?
- ☑ Is my writing interesting? Did I use different kinds of sentences? Did I vary the sentence beginnings?
- ☑ Does my writing have a beginning, a middle, and an ending?
- ☑ Are my details organized in the best way? Should I change the order of any details?
- ☑ Did I include details to make my ideas clear? Should I add or cut any details?
- ☑ Did I use the best words to say what I mean? Did I avoid using the same words over and over again?

page 410

2. **Discuss Your Writing with Others** Arrange a time to meet with your teacher to talk about your writing. Ask for suggestions for what you can do to improve it. Make any changes your teacher suggests, and then meet again to see how you are doing.

You might also have a **peer conference** with your classmates. Their comments can help you identify things that you might not notice yourself.

Guidelines for Peer Conferences

When you're the writer:

1. Tell your purpose for writing. Then read your writing aloud, or give copies to the group.
2. Ask for help on specific points:
   - Should I add any details about . . . ?
   - Does the ending make sense?
   - Did I leave anything out?
3. Listen carefully to suggestions and take notes. Use the comments that you think will improve your writing.

When you're the reader:

1. Read the writing twice, or listen once and read it once. Make notes as you read. If you don't understand something, ask questions.
2. Look for the strongest parts of the writing. Why do they work? Tell the writer:
   - I like the way you . . .
   - One part you described well was . . .
   - You caught my interest when you wrote . . .
3. Make specific suggestions. Tell how the writer can improve the details, sentences, or organization.

3. **Mark Your Changes** What changes do you want to make to your draft? Use the Revising Marks or special features in your computer's word-processing program to show the changes.

Trang Bui's Revisions

> My family stood by the big, glass windows and watched the plane land at SeaTac Airport in Seattle on October 28, 2000. We were so excited! ~~to see the plane.~~ When the passengers ~~The people~~ started coming through the door, we lined up so we could see. I had to lift my little sister up so she could look over the heads of the people in front ~~see~~.
>
> Suddenly everyone was hugging and crying. "I see them," my mother cried. My little sister tried to hide because she ~~My sister~~ didn't know my grandparents and ~~She~~ was feeling shy.

Revising Marks

^	Add.
↰	Move to here.
⌃—	Replace with this.
⤳	Take out.

page 411

Handbook: Writing

The Writing Process, continued

EDIT AND PROOFREAD

After you revise your draft for content, it's time to check it for mistakes.

1. **Check Your Sentences** When you edit, check that your sentences are clear, complete, and correct. Ask yourself:
   - Does each sentence have a subject and a predicate?
   - Did I break up run-on sentences?
   - Are there any short sentences that I can combine into longer sentences?
2. **Check for Mistakes** Proofread to find and correct errors in capitalization, punctuation, grammar, and spelling. Look especially for:
   - capital letters, end marks, apostrophes, and quotation marks
   - subject-verb agreement
   - use of pronouns
   - misspelled words.
3. **Mark Your Corrections** Use the Proofreading Marks to show your corrections or make the corrections when you find them in your document on the computer.
4. **Make a Final Copy** Rewrite your work and make the corrections you marked. If you are using a computer, print your corrected copy. For more ideas about formatting your paper, see page 389.

Trang Bui's Proofread Draft

¶ When we left vietnam, my grandparents had to stay behind. "We are too old to go someplace new, my grandfather said. My grandmother cooked ~~a special~~ an incredible dinner for us before we left, but ~~he~~ she could not eat. We didnt know how long it would be before we would see each other again.

Proofreading Marks	
^	Add.
^	Add a comma.
⊙	Add a period.
≡	Capitalize.
/	Make lowercase.
⌒	Take out.
¶	Indent.

page 412

PUBLISH

Now that you have corrected your work, share it with others! Here are just a few ideas for publishing your writing.

- E-mail it to a friend or family member.
- Make a home video of you reading it.
- Put it on a poster, add pictures, and display it in your classroom.
- Send it to your favorite magazine for publication.

The Best Day of My Life
by Trang Bui

My family stood by the big, glass windows and watched the plane land at SeaTac Airport in Seattle on October 28, 2000. We were so excited! When the passengers started coming through the door, we lined up so we could see. I had to lift my little sister up so she could look over the heads of the people in front.

"I see them," my mother cried. Suddenly everyone was hugging and crying. My little sister tried to hide because she didn't know my grandparents and was feeling shy.

When we left Vietnam, my grandparents had to stay behind. "We are too old to go someplace new," my grandfather said. My grandmother cooked an incredible dinner for us before we left, but she could not eat. We didn't know how long it would be before we would see each other again.

My family came to Seattle to start a new life. My parents worked in the donut shop and sent some of the money they earned each month to my grandparents. It took four long years, but my grandparents finally arrived, and we're all together again.

EVALUATE YOUR WRITING

Save examples of your writing. Date them and collect them in a **portfolio**. Look through your portfolio from time to time to see how you are doing as a writer.

1. **Organize Your Portfolio** Try putting all your writing in order by date. Or, make special sections for works written for the same purpose or same audience. You might also group your writing by form—stories, research reports, or poems, for example.
2. **Survey the Work in Your Portfolio** Each time you add new work to your portfolio, ask yourself:
   - How does this writing compare to other work I've done?
   - Am I getting better in certain areas? What are they?
   - Are there things that I didn't do as well this time? Why?
3. **Think About How You Write** As you look over your writing, think about the words you like to use, the kinds of sentences you write, and what you like to write about. All of those things together are your writing style. That is what makes you a super writer with a style all your own!

I write with Style!

page 413

The Writer's Craft

Good writers are always working on their writing. You can use the ideas in this section to make your writing the best it can be.

HOW TO WRITE FOR A SPECIFIC PURPOSE

Good writers change how and what they write to fit their main purpose. The **purpose** is why you are writing.

PURPOSE	EXAMPLES	
To describe	You could write a description with lots of descriptive details to help your reader "see" what you are describing. My guitar is awesome. The body is a metallic black, and the new strings shine like silver.	For a poem, use colorful verbs to describe what something does. Sounds of A Guitar Strum, strum the silver strings, And sweet notes fill the air.
To inform or to explain	You might give directions to explain how to do something. To play the guitar, hold the neck with your left hand. Then curl your fingers over the frets. Use your right hand to strum or pick the strings over the sound hole.	Or, you could write a paragraph to give your readers important facts about a topic. An electric guitar has a solid body and six strings. The points under the strings change the vibrations into electronic signals. The signals are magnified by an amplifier and sent to loudspeakers where they are converted into sounds.
To persuade	In an advertisement, you can use persuasive words and phrases to convince someone to buy something. Electric Guitars Is excellent sound quality what you want? Then come on over to Guitar World. We've got the best brands at the best prices!  Guitar World 101 Main Street 555-8931	In an editorial, give your opinion and use persuasive words to change the way things are. I think the school board should vote to keep our music program. I love music, and so do many of my friends. As a matter of fact, we try to finish our homework just so we can get to music class.

page 414

PURPOSE	EXAMPLES
To express your thoughts and feelings	Write a journal entry to tell about your personal thoughts and feelings. June 10, 2001 I just saw the Top Dogs in concert. I wish I could play like their lead guitarist!
To entertain	You could write a joke to make your readers laugh. What did the old guitar say to the new one? "Don't fret. I'll carry the tune for you!"
To learn	It helps to write things down when you are learning about a topic. That way you can see what you already know—and what you don't know. Listening to music can help you relax. Now I want to know how it affects your brain and your body.

HOW TO WRITE FOR A SPECIFIC AUDIENCE

Who will read what you write? Your **audience**. Knowing your audience will help you decide what words to use and what kinds of details to include.

AUDIENCE	EXAMPLES
Adults and people you don't know	Use formal language and details to help them understand what they might not know. I did very well at my guitar lesson today. I learned how to press the tips of my fingers on top of the strings to play different notes.
Your friends	Use informal language because they'll probably understand exactly what you mean. My guitar lesson was great. Now I can jam with any band!
People younger than you	Use simple language so they'll understand. My guitar lesson was fun. Now I can play a song.

page 415

Handbook: Writing

The Writer's Craft, continued

HOW TO CHOOSE THE RIGHT WORDS

To help your readers really see what you are writing about, use just the right words.

1 Use Specific Nouns Choose nouns that say exactly what you mean.

Just OK	Much Better
The boat went across the water.	The sailboat sped across the lake.

2 Use Colorful Verbs Choose verbs that give the best picture of the action.

Just OK	Much Better
The wave came up on the beach.	The wave crashed on the beach.

3 Add Sensory Words Use words that tell what you see, hear, smell, taste, and touch to help your readers imagine they are there!

Just OK

> Mark sat on the beach by the water. He pushed the sand around. The sun shone down on his skin.

Much Better

> Mark sat on the beach by the crashing waves. He sifted the soft, white sand through his fingers. The hot sun beat down on his parched skin, and he could almost taste the salty air.

4 Use Words with Just the Right Meaning Some words seem similar in meaning but may give readers a different feeling.

Negative Connotation: skinny
Positive Connotation: slim, slender

5 Use Figurative Language Figurative language can help your readers "see" ordinary things in new ways.

- Try using a **simile** with *like* or *as* to make comparisons.

> The man dove like a dolphin into the waves.

- Use a **metaphor** to tell what something is like, without using the words *like* or *as*:

> The man was a playful dolphin.

- Use **personification** to give human qualities to a non-human thing:

> Seagulls laughed overhead.

- You might want to use **hyperbole,** or an exaggeration, to add humor to your writing.

> The squawking gulls could be heard around the world.

page 416

HOW TO IMPROVE YOUR SENTENCES

1 Combine Sentences Try different ways to combine a lot of short sentences into one longer sentence.

Just OK

> I pushed off on my snowboard.
> I sped down the hill.
> I headed toward the clubhouse.

Much Better

> I pushed off on my snowboard and sped down the hill toward the clubhouse.

> I pushed off on my snowboard, sped down the hill, and headed toward the clubhouse.

2 Break Up Sentences If a sentence runs on too long, it becomes hard to follow. Break up run-on sentences to make your meaning clear.

Just OK

> The first time I went snowboarding, it was hard to get off the chairlift and I kept falling, but as I watched other snowboarders, I realized that most of them fell, too, then I didn't feel so bad.

Much Better

> The first time I went snowboarding, it was hard to get off the chairlift. I kept falling. As I watched other snowboarders, I realized that most of them fell, too. Then I didn't feel so bad.

3 Start Sentences in Different Ways Make your writing more interesting by varying the way your sentences begin. That way your readers won't get bored.

Just OK

> **Darcy** went snowboarding for the first time last winter. **Darcy** started out just fine. **Darcy** tried to make a turn, but lost her balance and fell into a snowbank. **Darcy** laughed at herself, brushed off the snow, and got right back on her feet. **Darcy** fell several more times, but finally made it down the hill!

Much Better

> **Last winter,** Darcy went snowboarding for the first time. **She** started out just fine. **When she tried to make a turn,** she lost her balance and fell into a snowbank. **Laughing at herself,** Darcy brushed off the snow and got right back on her feet. **After several more falls,** Darcy finally made it down the hill!

page 417

The Writer's Craft, continued

WHAT IS A PARAGRAPH?

A **paragraph** is a group of sentences that all tell about the same idea. The **topic sentence** tells the main idea of the paragraph. The other sentences give **supporting details.** The supporting details tell more about the main idea.

Sometimes a topic sentence that states the main idea comes at the beginning of a paragraph.

> **The Pike Place Market in Seattle is a great place to spend an afternoon.** At the market, you can shop for fresh fruits, vegetables, and flowers. You can watch the fishsellers toss fish across the aisles to one another. If you're hungry, you can find just about any kind of food in the many cafes and food stands.

Sometimes a topic sentence that states the main idea comes at the end of a paragraph.

> At the market, you can shop for fresh fruits, vegetables, and flowers. You can watch the fishsellers toss fish across the aisles to each other. If you're hungry, you can find just about any kind of food in the many cafes and food stands. **The Pike Place Market in Seattle is a great place to spend an afternoon.**

HOW TO ORGANIZE PARAGRAPHS

There are many ways to organize your paragraphs.

1 Sequence Paragraphs Some paragraphs are organized by sequence. **Time order words** tell when things happen.

> One day I went fishing with Dad. **First** we rowed to the middle of the lake. **After** we put slimy worms on our hooks, we tossed our lines overboard. **Then** we waited forever for the fish to bite! We **finally** caught one fish. When Dad goes fishing again, I'm staying home!

2 Comparison Paragraphs Some paragraphs tell how things are alike and different. **Comparison words** signal the similarities and differences.

> **Like** human beings, whales are mammals. **Both** produce milk and give birth to live young. **Unlike** most mammals, **however,** whales store oxygen longer. This allows them to take fewer breaths and stay underwater longer.

3 Paragraphs in Space Order For a description, try using **space order** to tell what you see in order—left to right, near to far, or top to bottom. **Direction words and phrases** tell where things are.

> An octopus looks strange. Its head and body look like one big bulb. **Radiating from** the bulb are eight tentacles. Each tentacle has two rows of suckers **along the underside.** It uses the suckers to grip rocks and find food.

page 418

4 Cause-and-Effect Paragraphs In this kind of paragraph, the topic sentence tells the **cause,** or why something happens. Detail sentences tell the **effects,** or what happens as a result.

> Ricky was floating on his surfboard. Suddenly, he spotted a large, dark object swimming toward him. "Could it be a shark?" he thought. His heart pounded. He paddled frantically toward the beach. Looking back, he saw a huge log bobbing among the waves!

5 Paragraphs in Logical Order The order in which you present your ideas can vary with your topic. You may want to present ideas in order from general to specific or from most important to least important.

> If we over-fish the ocean, there will not be enough fish left to reproduce. Although there would be food at first, there would not be enough to feed people later. Several important fish species could go extinct. Other fish that depend on those fish for food would also suffer.

6 Opinion Paragraphs In an opinion paragraph, give your opinion about something. State your opinion in the **topic sentence.** Give the reasons for your opinion in the detail sentences.

> **I think the octopus is a fascinating sea creature.** It defends itself so well! An octopus turns colors to match its surroundings so predators can't see it. It ejects an inky cloud when it senses danger. It also has a soft body that fits into small hiding places. Don't you think the octopus is fascinating, too?

7 Persuasive Paragraphs A persuasive paragraph, begins with a **thesis statement** that gives your opinion or tells the main idea. Facts, reasons, and statistics that support your opinion are the **supporting arguments.**

> **The Eastern North Pacific gray whale should be put back on the endangered species list.** It was removed from the list in 1994 because its population stabilized. However, of the three large populations of gray whales, one is extinct and another is endangered. Gray whales stay close to the shore, and can become entangled in fishing nets. Their breeding grounds in Baja, California, are threatened by the expansion of salt-extraction plants. We should act now to save the Eastern North Pacific gray whale.

page 419

Handbook: Writing

The Writer's Craft, continued

HOW TO PUT PARAGRAPHS TOGETHER

If you write more than two paragraphs, organize your writing into three parts: the **introduction**, the **body**, and the **conclusion**.

1 Write a Strong Introduction Name the topic and grab your readers' interest.

- **Ask a question.**

  What's so hot about smoking?

- **Express an emotion or an opinion.**

  Smoking isn't just bad—it can kill you!

- **Describe an action or event.**

  Smoking is one of the biggest killers in the U.S.

- **Make a startling statement, or give an interesting or unusual fact.**

  Cigarettes contain more than fifteen harmful chemicals.

2 Develop the Topic in the Body Present your supporting details. Organize the paragraphs so they work together in the best order to support your main idea or thesis statement.

3 Write a Conclusion Express an emotion or include a thoughtful idea.

The easiest way to break a bad habit like smoking is never to start it in the first place!

HOW TO MAKE YOUR WRITING FLOW

1 Use Transition Words Words or phrases that help connect paragraphs are transition words. They will help your readers follow your ideas.

Examples:

As a result	Also	Even though
As soon as	In addition	However
Finally	Like	On the other hand
Then	Plus	Yet

2 Use the Same Point of View If you are expressing how you feel about something, tell about *your* feelings, not someone else's. If you are writing about a character or another person, use details that show how that person thinks or feels.

I think that smoking is an awful habit. If someone offers ~~my friend~~ me a cigarette, ~~he~~ I always ~~says~~ say, "No way."

3 Use the Same Verb Tenses Keep your verbs all in the same tense so your readers won't get confused about when things happen.

When someone offers me a cigarette, though, I always say, "No way." That's because I ~~knew~~ know how bad it ~~was~~ is for my lungs.

page 420

5-Paragraph Persuasive Essay

Smoking: A Bad Habit to Start

What's so hot about smoking? Nothing! I think that some kids start smoking because it makes them feel like they are grown up. Other kids just want to be part of the "in" crowd. When someone offers me a cigarette, though, I always say "No way." That's because I know how bad it is for my **lungs**.

Did you know that your **lungs** take nearly 26,000 breaths a day? They need clean air and oxygen to expand and contract the way they should. All the chemicals in cigarette smoke cause emphysema. This disease destroys the tiny air sacs in your lungs where oxygen and carbon dioxide are exchanged.

As soon as emphysema starts, it damages your **lungs**. Eventually every breath becomes a struggle. Wouldn't it be smart, then, to protect your lungs like you do other parts of your body?

Plus, if you decide to smoke, you are affecting other people's lungs as well as your own. About 3,000 non-smokers die every year from second-hand smoke. Young children are especially at risk because their lungs are just developing. Do you really want to harm someone else just to be "cool"?

Sooner or later someone is going to offer you a cigarette. Before you decide, take a deep breath of clean, fresh air. Think about how good you feel now. Then play it safe. Don't smoke!

INTRODUCTION
The introduction grabs the readers' interest and states the writer's opinion.

BODY
The body includes details, facts, and arguments to support the writer's opinion.

This writer connected paragraphs by **repeating a word or phrase** and by using **transition words**.

All the sentences go together to show this writer's point of view about the topic. The verbs the writer uses are all in the present tense.

CONCLUSION
In the last paragraph, the writer tries to convince the readers to take action.

page 421

The Writer's Craft, continued

HOW TO MAKE YOUR WRITING BETTER

The words that you choose, the way that you put them together, and the ideas that you present make your writing unique. Try these techniques.

1 Show, Don't Tell You can just tell your readers about an event or a person. To give your readers the best picture, though, show them exactly what you mean!

This tells:

Kevin hated eating in the cafeteria. He was new at school and didn't know anyone. So he sat in a corner by himself. Then one day, a girl in his math class asked him to sit at her table. After that, Kevin felt much more comfortable.

This shows:

"I can't wait to finish my lunch and get out of here," thought Kevin. "I don't know anyone, anyway."

Then one day, Kevin heard a cheery voice from behind him. "Hey, do you want to sit with us?" the girl asked. It was Roberta from his math class.

"Sure," said Kevin, grinning. "How's it going?" he asked Roberta.

2 Elaborate *Elaborate* means "Tell me more!" Try these ways to add information to your writing.

- **Tell what came before or after.**

  Without Elaboration

  The ball dropped into the basket.

  With Elaboration

  After rolling around on the rim, the ball finally dropped into the basket.

- **Add sensory details to clearly show what something is like.**

  Without Details

  Their player made an attempt for the basket. The entire crowd watched as the ball arched across the court and sank into the net without touching the rim.

  With Details

  Their tallest player made an attempt for the basket. The entire crowd watched silently as the orange ball arched high across the court and sank into the net without touching the skinny metal rim.

page 422

- **Add examples, facts, and other details.**

  Without Details

  The fans cheered.

  With Details

  The excited fans jumped up out of their seats, clapped their hands, and stomped their feet.

- **Add quotations or dialogue.**

  Without Dialogue

  The fans shouted.

  With Dialogue

  "Go, Rangers, go! You can do it!" the fans shouted.

3 Develop Your Own Writing Style and Voice As a writer, you have your own voice, or personality. That's because your writing will show the kinds of words you like, what ideas are important to you, and how you feel about things. To keep your writing interesting and exciting, let your readers "see" who you are.

Just OK

I dribbled the ball through the zone. I made a shot for the basket. The ball rolled for a while on the basket rim, then fell in. I made the final shot to win the game.

Much Better

My heart was pounding. I dribbled the ball through the zone and took my best shot. I just stood there with my arms still raised up in the air. Would the ball ever stop rolling on the rim? When it finally dropped into the basket, I couldn't believe it! It was awesome! That basket put us ahead to win the game by one point!

page 423

Handbook: Grammar, Usage, Mechanics, Spelling

Sentences

A sentence is a group of words that expresses a complete thought.
Every sentence has a subject and a predicate.
Every sentence begins with a capital letter.

SENTENCE TYPES	EXAMPLES
A **declarative sentence** tells something. It ends with a period.	The football game was on Friday. The coach made an important announcement.
An **interrogative sentence** asks a question. It ends with a question mark.	Can you tell me the news?

Kinds of Questions

Questions That Ask for a "Yes" or "No" Answer	Answers
Is it about the team?	Yes.
Did the team win the game?	Yes.
Has the coach ever made an announcement like this before?	No.
Are the players sad?	No.
Were the fans surprised?	Yes.
Tag Questions	
You will tell me the news, **won't you**?	Yes, I will. OR No, I won't.
You didn't forget it, **did you**?	Yes, I did. OR No, I didn't.
Questions That Ask for Specific Information	
Who heard the announcement?	The team and the fans heard the announcement.
What did the coach say?	He said the team will play in a special game.
Where will the team play this game?	In Hawaii.
When did the coach find out?	Right before the game.
Why was our team chosen?	Our team was chosen because we won a lot of games.
How many games has the team won this year?	All ten of them.
Which coach made the announcement?	The tall one.

page 424

SENTENCE TYPES, continued	EXAMPLES
An **exclamatory sentence** shows surprise or strong emotion. It ends with an exclamation mark.	That's fantastic news! I can't believe it!
An **imperative sentence** gives a command. It usually begins with a verb. It often ends with a period.	Give the team my congratulations.
If an imperative sentence shows strong emotion, it ends with an exclamation mark.	Don't keep any more secrets from me ever again!

NEGATIVE SENTENCES	EXAMPLES
A **negative sentence** uses a **negative word** to say "no."	The game in Hawaii was **not** boring! **Nobody** in our town missed it on TV. Our team **never** played better.
Use only one negative word in a sentence.	The other team could not do ~~nothing~~ anything right. They never scored ~~no~~ any points.

Negative Words

never	no one
no	not
nobody	nothing
none	nowhere

CONDITIONAL SENTENCES	EXAMPLES
Some sentences tell how one thing depends on another. These sentences often use verbs like can, will, could, would, or might.	**If** our team returns on Saturday, **then** we will have a party. **Unless** it rains, we can have the party on the football field. Or, we could have a dance in the gym **if** the coach lets us.

page 425

Sentences, continued

COMPLETE SENTENCES	EXAMPLES
A **complete sentence** has a **subject** and a **predicate**. A complete sentence expresses a complete thought.	**Many people** **visit our National Parks**.
A **fragment** is not a sentence. It is not a complete thought. You can add information to a fragment to turn it into a complete sentence.	**Fragment:** a fun vacation **Complete sentences:** You can have a fun vacation. Will we have a fun vacation at the park? Go to a national park and have a fun vacation.

Grand Canyon National Park, Arizona

SUBJECTS	EXAMPLES
To find the subject in a sentence, ask yourself: Whom or what is the sentence about?	
The **complete subject** includes all the words that tell about the subject.	**My favorite parks** are in the West. **People from all over the world** visit them.
The **simple subject** is the most important word in the complete subject.	My favorite **parks** are in the West. **People** from all over the world visit them.
A **compound subject** has two or more simple subjects joined by **and** or **or**.	**Yosemite** and **Yellowstone** are the most interesting to me. Either **spring** or **fall** is a good time to visit these parks.
Sometimes the subject is a **pronoun**. Be sure to include the pronoun in the sentence.	The map shows the campsites. **They** are by the river.
But: When you give a command, you do not have to include the subject. The subject **you** is understood in an imperative sentence.	Follow the rules of the park. Don't disturb the animals. Never throw trash in the streams.

Subject Pronouns

Singular	Plural
I	we
you	you
he, she, it	they

page 426

PREDICATES	EXAMPLES
The predicate of a sentence tells what the subject is, has, or does.	
The **complete predicate** includes all the words in the predicate.	Yosemite **is a beautiful park**. It **has huge waterfalls**. People **hike to the waterfalls**.
The **simple predicate** is the **verb**. It is the most important word in the predicate.	Yosemite **is** a beautiful park. It **has** huge waterfalls. People **hike** to the waterfalls.
A **compound predicate** has two or more verbs joined by **and** or **or**.	At Yosemite, some people **fish** and **swim**. My family **hiked** to the river or **stayed** in the cabin. I **have gone** to Yosemite often and **have enjoyed** every visit.

Waterfall in Yosemite National Park

SUBJECT-VERB AGREEMENT	EXAMPLES
The verb must always agree with the subject of the sentence.	
A **singular subject** names one person or thing. Use a **singular verb** with a singular subject.	Another popular **park** **is** the Grand Canyon. **It** **has** a powerful river.
A **plural subject** tells about more than one person or thing. Use a **plural verb** with a plural subject.	The **cliffs** **are** beautiful. **We** **were amazed** by their colors.

Singular and Plural Verbs

Singular	Plural
The park **is** big.	The parks **are** big.
The park **was** beautiful.	The parks **were** beautiful.
The park **has** campsites.	The parks **have** campsites.
The park **does** not **open** until spring.	The parks **do** not **open** until spring.

page 427

Handbook: Grammar, Usage, Mechanics, Spelling

Sentences, continued

SUBJECT-VERB AGREEMENT, continued	EXAMPLES
Study the chart to see how **action verbs** agree with their subjects. When you tell about one other person or thing, use an action verb that ends in **s**.	**More Singular and Plural Verbs** Singular / Plural I **hike** in the park. / We **hike** in the park. You **hike** in the park. / You **hike** in the park. He **hikes** in the park. / They **hike** in the park. She **hikes** in the park. The dog **hikes** in the park. / The dogs **hike** in the park.
The **subject** and **verb** must agree, even when other words come between them.	The **hikers** in the park **are looking** for animals. A **snake** with lots of stripes **lives** in this area.
If the simple subjects in a **compound subject** are connected by **and**, use a plural verb.	A **mule and** a **guide are** available for a trip down the canyon.
Sometimes the simple subjects in a **compound subject** are connected by **or**. Look at the last simple subject. If it is singular, use a **singular verb**. If it is plural, use a **plural verb**.	These **rafts or** this **boat is** the best way to go down the river. This **raft or** these **boats are** the best way to go down the river.
The **subject** and **verb** must agree even if the subject comes after the verb.	There **are** other amazing **parks** in Arizona. Here **is** a **list** of them.
In some questions, look for the **subject** between the **helping and main verbs**. The helping verb must agree with the subject.	**Has** your **friend visited** the parks? **Have** your **friends visited** the parks?

Mule riders in the Grand Canyon

page 428

PHRASES	EXAMPLES
A **phrase** is a group of related words that does not have a subject and a predicate. A **phrase** can be part of a complete sentence.	**during the gold rush** **before the discovery of gold** Many people came to California **during the gold rush**. **Before the discovery of gold**, about 15,000 people lived there.

CLAUSES	EXAMPLES
A **clause** is a group of words that has a **subject** and a **verb**. Some clauses are complete sentences. Some clauses are not.	The **population** of California **increased** to about 100,000 by 1849. because **miners came** to California
An **independent clause** expresses a complete thought and can stand alone as a sentence. A **dependent clause** does not express a complete thought. It is not a sentence.	The miners were called "forty-niners." because so many arrived in 1849
A **dependent clause** can be combined with an **independent clause** to form a sentence.	The miners were called "forty-niners" (independent clause) because so many arrived in 1849. (dependent clause) When they found gold, (dependent clause) the miners got rich. (independent clause)

Prospectors panned for gold in rivers and streams.

Words That Can Signal a Dependent Clause

Cause Words	Time Words		Words that Express Conditions	Relative Pronouns	
because	after	whenever	although	that	who
since	as	while	as long as	which	whom
	before	until	if		whose
	when		unless		

page 429

Sentences, continued

SIMPLE SENTENCES	EXAMPLES
A **simple sentence** is one independent clause. It has a **subject** and a **predicate**.	**The miners needed goods and services.**

COMPOUND SENTENCES	EXAMPLES
When you join two independent clauses, you make a **compound sentence**. Use a **coordinating conjunction** to join the clauses.	Some people opened food markets. The miners bought food. **Some people opened food markets, and the miners bought food.** Other people opened stores. It was still hard to get supplies. **Other people opened stores, but it was still hard to get supplies.**
Put a **comma** before the conjunction or use a **semi-colon** and no conjunction.	The miners used gold to buy things, and the shopkeepers ended up with the gold. The miners used gold to buy things; the shopkeepers ended up with the gold.

Coordinating Conjunctions

and	nor
but	or
for	yet

COMPLEX SENTENCES	EXAMPLES
To make a **complex sentence**, join an independent clause with one or more dependent clauses. If the dependent clause comes first, put a **comma** after it.	Many writers visited the camps (independent clause) where the miners worked. (dependent clause) While they were there, (dependent clause) the writers wrote stories about the miners. (independent clause)

COMPOUND-COMPLEX SENTENCES	EXAMPLES
You can make a **compound-complex sentence** by joining two or more independent clauses and a dependent clause.	Many miners never became rich, (independent clause) but they decided to settle in the West (independent clause) because they found other jobs in California. (dependent clause)

page 430

Parts of Speech

All the words in the English language can be categorized into eight groups. These groups are the eight parts of speech. Words are grouped into the parts of speech by the way they are used in a sentence.

THE EIGHT PARTS OF SPEECH	EXAMPLES
A **noun** names a person, place, thing, or idea.	**Samantha** lives in **Minnesota**. She skates on the **ice** every **day** to build her **skill**.
A **pronoun** takes the place of a noun.	**She** practices a dance routine for a show.
An **adjective** describes a noun or a pronoun.	She is a **powerful** skater. She is **graceful**, too.
A **verb** can tell what the subject of a sentence does or has. A **verb** can also link a word in the predicate to the subject.	Samantha **twists**, **turns**, and **jumps**. She **has** talent! Like many skaters, Samantha **is** a competitor. But, unlike most skaters, Samantha **is** deaf.
An **adverb** describes a verb, an adjective, or another adverb.	The music plays **loudly**, but she cannot hear it. Still, Samantha has become a **very** good skater. How can she perform **so** well?
A **preposition** shows how two things or ideas are related. It introduces a prepositional phrase.	A skating coach helps Samantha skate **on** the ice. He gives her signals as she moves **around** the rink. **During** the show, the people **in** the stands cheer **for** the skater.
A **conjunction** connects words or groups of words.	Samantha can't hear the people cheer, **but** she sees their smiles. Samantha smiles **and** waves back to the crowd.
An **interjection** expresses strong feeling.	Some people shout, **"Hooray!"** Others say, **"Wow!** What a talented skater!"

page 431

Handbook: Grammar, Usage, Mechanics, Spelling

Nouns

A noun names a person, place, thing, or idea.
There are many different kinds of nouns.

COMMON AND PROPER NOUNS	EXAMPLES
A **common noun** names any person, place, thing, or idea.	A **teenager** sat by the **ocean** and read a **book**. It was about **ecology**.
A **proper noun** names one particular person, place, thing, or idea. The important words in a proper noun start with a capital letter.	**Daniel** sat by the **Atlantic Ocean** and read ***Save the Manatee.***

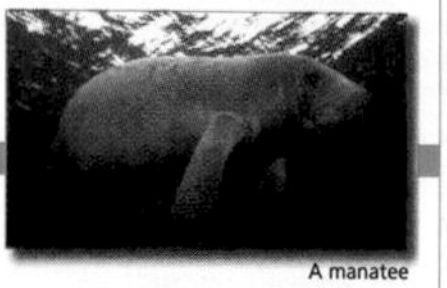
A manatee

COMPOUND NOUNS	EXAMPLES
A **compound noun** is two or more words that express one idea. A compound noun can be: • two words • two words joined into one word • a hyphenated word	Some people call manatees **sea cows**. Manatees live in shallow waters where there is plenty of **sunlight**. In his book, Daniel saw a picture of a manatee baby and a **grown-up**.

COLLECTIVE NOUNS	EXAMPLES
A **collective noun** names a group of people, animals, places, or things.	Daniel took pictures of manatees on a trip to Florida with his **family**.
A collective noun can be the **subject** of a sentence. It usually needs a **singular verb** because the group is seen as one unit.	Our **class** **hopes** to see the pictures Daniel took. His **club** **has** already **seen** them.

Some Collective Nouns

Groups of People	Groups of Animals	Groups of Places	Groups of Things
band	flock	Hawaiian Islands	mail
class	herd		money
family	litter	United States	set
team	pack		trash

page 432

SINGULAR AND PLURAL NOUNS	EXAMPLES				
	The singular form of a count noun names one thing. The plural form names more than one thing.				
Count nouns are nouns that you can count. Follow these rules to make a count noun plural:					
• Add **-s** to most count nouns.	desk desk**s**	book book**s**	teacher teacher**s**	apple apple**s**	line line**s**
• If the noun ends in **x**, **ch**, **sh**, **s**, or **z**, add **-es**.	box box**es**	lunch lunch**es**	dish dish**es**	glass glass**es**	waltz waltz**es**
• For nouns that end in a consonant plus **y**, change the **y** to **i** and add **-es**.	story stor**ies**	sky sk**ies**	city cit**ies**	penny penn**ies**	army arm**ies**
• For nouns that end in a vowel plus **y**, just add **-s**.	boy boy**s**	toy toy**s**	day day**s**	monkey monkey**s**	valley valley**s**
• For most nouns that end in **f** or **fe**, change the **f** to **v** and add **-es**. For some nouns that end in **f**, just add **-s**.	leaf lea**ves**	knife kni**ves**	half hal**ves**	roof roof**s**	chief chief**s**
• If the noun ends in a vowel plus **o**, add **-s**. For some nouns that end in a consonant plus **o**, add **-s**. For others, add **-es**.	radio radio**s**	kangaroo kangaroo**s**	banjo banjo**s**	potato potato**es**	tomato tomato**es**
• A few count nouns have irregular plural forms.	child **children**	foot **feet**	person **people**	man **men**	woman **women**
• For a few count nouns, the singular and plural forms are the same.	deer **deer**	fish **fish**	salmon **salmon**	sheep **sheep**	trout **trout**

page 433

Nouns, continued

SINGULAR AND PLURAL NOUNS	EXAMPLES
Noncount nouns are nouns that you cannot count. A noncount noun does not have a plural form.	My favorite museum has **furniture** and **art**. Sometimes I wonder how much **money** each item is worth.

Types of Noncount Nouns

					Examples
Activities and Sports					
baseball	camping	dancing	fishing		I love to play **soccer**.
golf	singing	soccer	swimming		
Category Nouns					
clothing	equipment	furniture	hardware	jewelry	My **equipment** is in the car.
machinery	mail	money	time	weather	
Food					
bread	cereal	cheese	corn	flour	I'll drink some **water** on my way to the game.
lettuce	meat	milk	rice	salt	
soup	sugar	tea	water		
You can count some food items by using a measurement word like **cup**, **slice**, **glass**, or **head** plus the word **of**. To show the plural form, just make the measurement word plural.					I'll drink **two glasses of water** on my way to the game.
Ideas and Feelings					
democracy	enthusiasm	freedom	fun	health	I'll also listen to the radio for **information** about the weather.
honesty	information	knowledge	luck	work	
Materials					
air	fuel	gasoline	gold		The radio says the **air** is heavy. What does that mean?
metal	paper	water	wood		
Weather					
fog	hail	heat	ice	lightning	Uh-oh! First came the **lightning** and the **thunder**. I want **sunshine** for my next soccer game!
rain	smog	snow	sunshine	thunder	

Some words have more than one meaning. Add **-s** for the plural only if the noun means something you can count.	Throw me those **baseballs**. I want to learn to play **baseball**.

page 434

ARTICLES	EXAMPLES
An **article** is a word that helps identify a noun. An article often comes before a count noun.	After **the** game, we found **a** coat and **an** umbrella on **the** field.
Use **a** or **an** before **nouns** that are not specific. Use **the** before **nouns** that are specific.	**A boy** walked around the field. **The coach's son** walked around the field.
Use **a** before a word that starts with a consonant sound.	**a b**all **a g**ate **a p**layer **a** one-way street (o is pronounced like w) **a c**ap **a k**ick **a n**et **a u**niform (u is pronounced like y)
Use **an** before a word that starts with a vowel sound.	**a**: an **a**nt, an **a**pron, an **a**mount, an **a**rtist **e**: an **e**lbow, an **e**el, an **e**lection **i**: an **i**nch, an **i**dea **o**: an **o**live, an **o**cean, an **o**wl, an **o**range **u**: an **u**mbrella **silent h**: an **h**our
Do not use **a** or **an** before a noncount noun.	The soccer ball was made of ~~a~~ leather.
Do not use **the** before the name of: • a city or state • most countries • a language • a day, a month, or most holidays • a sport or activity • most businesses • a person.	Our next game will be in **Dallas**. Games in **Texas** are always exciting. We will play a team from **Mexico**. People will be cheering in **Spanish** and **English**. The game will take place on **Monday**. Is that in **February**? Yes, on **President's Day**. That will be a good day to play **soccer**. The fans will have hot dogs to eat from **Sal's Market**. You may even see **Sal** himself.

page 435

Handbook: Grammar, Usage, Mechanics, Spelling

Nouns, continued

POSSESSIVE NOUNS	EXAMPLES
A **possessive noun** is the name of an owner. All possessive nouns include an **apostrophe**.	Several bands performed in our **town's** parade. Everyone liked the **musicians'** costumes.
Follow these rules to make a noun possessive:	
• If there is one owner, add **'s** to the owner's name.	Some kids played the trumpet. One **boy's** trumpet was very loud. **Marsha's** baton went high in the air.
But: If the owner's name ends in **s**, you can add **'s** or just the apostrophe. Either is correct.	**Louis's** hat fell off. **Louis'** hat fell off.
• A noun that names two or more owners is plural and often ends in **s**. If so, just add **'**.	The **girls'** section sang loud songs. I could barely hear my **brothers'** tubas.
But: If the plural noun that names the owners does not end in **s**, add **'s**.	The **men's** cooking club marched with the band. The **children's** band rode on tricycles.

CONCRETE AND ABSTRACT NOUNS	EXAMPLES
A **concrete noun** names something you can see, touch, hear, smell, or taste.	The **band** will be in the **parade** that goes down **Main Street**.
An **abstract noun** names something you can think about but cannot see, touch, hear, smell, or taste.	The parade will add to the **spirit** of the **day**.

A parade

page 436

Pronouns

A pronoun takes the place of a noun or refers to a noun.

NOUN AND PRONOUN AGREEMENT	EXAMPLES
When nouns and pronouns agree, they both tell about the same person, place, or thing.	
The noun is the **antecedent**, and the **pronoun** refers to it.	**Janet and Scott** talk to a counselor. **They** learn about careers. (antecedent: Janet and Scott; pronoun: They)
A **pronoun** must agree in number with the noun it refers to. **Singular pronouns** refer to one person. **Plural pronouns** refer to more than one person.	The counselor has an office at school. ~~They meets~~ He meets there with students.
Use **she, her,** and **hers** to tell about females. Use **he, him,** and **his** to tell about males.	Janet is interested in animals. ~~He~~ She wants to know what veterinarians do. Scott wants the counselor to tell ~~her~~ him about careers in photography.

Some Singular and Plural Pronouns

Singular Pronouns	Plural Pronouns
I, me, my, mine	we, us, our, ours
you, your, yours	you, your, yours
he, him, his she, her, hers it, its	they, them, their, theirs

page 437

Pronouns, continued

PERSON OF PRONOUNS	EXAMPLES
Use a **first-person pronoun** to talk about yourself.	**I** may want to be a photographer some day. At **our** house **we** take pictures of **my** family all the time.
Use a **second-person pronoun** to identify the person you are talking to.	Scott, do **you** have a photograph of **your** grandparents? Did **you** use this camera to take the picture?
Use a **third-person pronoun** to identify the person or thing you are talking about.	Scott got a new video camera for **his** birthday. Mother gave **it** to Scott. **She** thinks **he** will be a movie director someday.

USES OF PRONOUNS	EXAMPLES
Use a **subject pronoun** as the **subject** of a sentence.	**Janet** likes animals. **She** works at a pet shop.
The pronoun **it** can be used as a **subject** to refer to a noun.	Janet lives near the **shop**. **It** is on First Street.
But: The pronoun **it** can be the **subject** without referring to a specific noun.	**It** is interesting to work in the shop. **It** is fun to play with the animals. **It** is important to take care of them, too.
Sometimes you talk about a person twice in a sentence. Use a **reflexive pronoun** to refer to the **subject**.	**Janet** taught **herself** about the life cycle of parrots. The **shop owners themselves** learned some things from Janet.

Subject Pronouns

Singular	Plural
I	we
you	you
he, she, it	they

Subject and Reflexive Pronouns

Singular		Plural	
I	myself	we	ourselves
you	yourself	you	yourselves
he she it	himself herself itself	they	themselves

page 438

USES OF PRONOUNS, continued	EXAMPLES
You can use an **object pronoun** after an **action verb**.	The parrots get hungry at 5 o'clock. Janet **feeds them** every day.
You can also use an **object pronoun** after a **preposition**.	The parrots squawk **at her** to say "thank you."
A **possessive pronoun** tells who or what owns something.	
A **possessive pronoun** can refer to the name of an owner. It is sometimes called a **possessive adjective**.	**Janet's** posters are about pet care. **Her** posters show what dogs need.
A **possessive pronoun** can take the place of a **person's name and what the person owns**.	Which one is **Janet's poster**? The big one is **hers**.

Object Pronouns

Singular	Plural
me	us
you	you
him, her, it	them

Possessive Pronouns

Use these pronouns to refer to the name of an owner. These pronouns always come before a noun and act as adjectives.		Use these pronouns to replace a person's name and what the person owns. These pronouns are always used alone.	
Singular	Plural	Singular	Plural
my	our	mine	ours
your	your	yours	yours
his, her, its	their	his, hers, its	theirs

DEMONSTRATIVE PRONOUNS	EXAMPLES
A **demonstrative pronoun** points out a specific noun without naming it.	Look at the puppies. **That** is a cute puppy. **Those** are sleeping.

Demonstrative Pronouns

	Singular	Plural
Nearby	this	these
Far Away	that	those

page 439

Handbook: Grammar, Usage, Mechanics, Spelling

Pronouns, continued

INDEFINITE PRONOUNS	EXAMPLES
When you are not talking about a specific person or thing, use an **indefinite pronoun**.	**Everybody** loves to visit the pet shop. **Something** is happening in the pet shop today.

Some Indefinite Pronouns

These **indefinite pronouns** are always singular and need a **singular verb**.

				Examples
another	each	everything	nothing	
anybody	either	neither	somebody	**Someone is photographing** the dogs.
anyone	everybody	nobody	someone	**Nobody knows** why.
anything	everyone	no one	something	

These **indefinite pronouns** are always plural and need a **plural verb**.

both few many several

Several of the dogs **are eating**.
Both of the puppies **have** bones.

These **indefinite pronouns** can be either singular or plural.

all any most none some

Look at the phrase that follows the pronoun. If the noun in the phrase is plural, use a **plural verb**. If not, use a **singular verb**.

All of the dogs **are barking**.
All of their food **is gone**.

RELATIVE PRONOUNS	EXAMPLES
A **relative pronoun** introduces a **relative clause**. It connects, or relates, the clause to a word in the sentence.	**Some Relative Pronouns**: who, whose, that, whom, which
Use **who**, **whom**, or **whose** for people.	The man **who photographed the dogs** is a writer.
Use **which** for things.	His book, **which** I have read, shows all kinds of dogs.
Use **that** for people or things.	The writer **that** created the book is famous. The photo **that** I like best in his book was taken in the pet shop.

440 Handbook: Grammar, Usage, Mechanics, Spelling

page 440

Adjectives

An adjective describes, or modifies, a noun or pronoun. It can tell what kind, which one, how many, or how much.

DESCRIPTIVE ADJECTIVES	EXAMPLES
An **adjective** can tell what something is like.	Where can you find **brown** rabbits and **white** egrets?
It can tell the color, size, or shape. It can describe a feeling.	A swamp has **large** and **small** animals like these. The egret has **round** eyes and a **pointed** beak. I feel **happy** when I spend a day in the swamp.
An adjective can tell how something sounds, feels, looks, tastes, or smells.	I like the **noisy** birds. The egrets are **beautiful**.

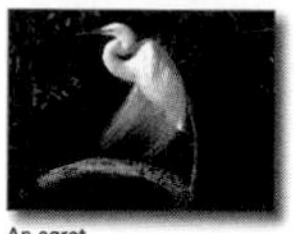
An egret

Adjectives That Appeal to the Senses

Hearing	Touch	Sight	Taste	Smell
crunchy	hard	beautiful	bitter	fishy
noisy	rough	dark	salty	fragrant
quiet	smooth	huge	sour	fresh
soft	wet	shiny	sweet	rotten

Usually, an **adjective** comes before the noun it describes.	An **old alligator** hides in the **dark mud**.
But: A **predicate adjective** appears in the predicate and still describes the noun or pronoun in the **subject**.	The **alligator** is **powerful**. **It** is **dangerous**, too.
Sometimes two or more **adjectives** come before a **noun**. Use a comma (**,**) between the adjectives if they both describe the noun.	Alligators walk on **short, strong** legs.
An **adjective** is never plural, even if the **noun** it describes is plural.	Many **hungry birds** look for food near the water. Their **eyes** are **good**, but they don't see the alligator. Soon the **tasty birds** are the alligator's dinner!

An alligator

Pronouns/Adjectives 441

page 441

Adjectives, continued

DEMONSTRATIVE ADJECTIVES	EXAMPLES
A **demonstrative adjective** points out the noun that follows it. It answers the question "Which one?"	**These** otters are by my boat. **That** otter over there belongs to one of them.

Demonstrative Adjectives

	Singular	Plural
Nearby	this	these
Far Away	that	those

NUMBER WORDS	EXAMPLES
Number words are often used as **adjectives**.	Today in the swamp I saw **one** snake, **two** alligators, and **six** turtles.
Sometimes the number word tells the **order** that things are in.	The **first** day I saw many kinds of birds. The **second** day I saw a lot of alligators. What will I see on the **third** day?

INDEFINITE ADJECTIVES	EXAMPLES
Use an **indefinite adjective** when you are not sure of the exact number.	I didn't see **much** wildlife on the third day. All I saw were **a few** frogs.
Some indefinite adjectives tell **how many** things there are. Use these adjectives before nouns you can count. Some indefinite adjectives tell **how much** there is of something. Use these adjectives before nouns you cannot count.	**Some Indefinite Adjectives** (see below)
In a negative sentence, use **any** instead of **some**.	I saw some turtles, too. However, I didn't see ~~some~~ any insects.

Some Indefinite Adjectives

To Tell How Many	To Tell How Much
many insects	**much** sunshine
a few insects	**a little** sunshine
some insects	**some** sunshine
several insects	**not much** sunshine
no insects	**no** sunshine

PROPER ADJECTIVES	EXAMPLES
A **proper adjective** is formed from a proper noun. It always begins with a capital letter.	There are many swamps in America. The **American** alligator is found in the southeastern United States.

442 Handbook: Grammar, Usage, Mechanics, Spelling

page 442

ADJECTIVES THAT COMPARE	EXAMPLES
	Adjectives can help you show how things are alike or different.
Use a **comparative adjective** to show how **two** things are alike or different. Add **-er** to most adjectives. Also use **than**.	Deserts may be small or large. The Sechura Desert in South America is **smaller than** the Sahara Desert in Africa.
Use **more. . .than** if the adjective has three or more syllables.	Is the Sechura Desert **more interesting than** the Sahara Desert?
You can use either **-er** or **more** to make a comparison with some two-syllable adjectives. **Be sure not to use both.**	Most desert animals are ~~more~~ livelier at night than during the day. / Desert flowers are ~~more~~ prettier than swamp grasses.
Use a **superlative adjective** to compare **three or more** things. Add **-est** to most adjectives. Use **the** before the adjective.	The Sahara Desert is **the largest** desert in the world. The Libyan Desert has **the** world's **highest** record temperature.
Use **the most** with the adjective if it has three or more syllables.	Both habitats have some of **the most interesting** animals in the world.
Some **adjectives** have **special forms** for comparing things: good, better, best; bad, worse, worst; some, more, most; little, less, least	Today's weather in the desert is **bad**. Tomorrow's weather will be **worse**. Next week's weather is expected to be **the worst** of the summer.
Use **less** or **the least** to compare things you cannot count.	Deserts have **less** rainfall than swamps. Deserts have **the least** rainfall of any habitat.
Use **fewer** or **the fewest** to compare things you can count.	Some deserts have **fewer** days of rain than others. Which desert had **the fewest** number of visitors last year?

Sahara Desert

Adjectives 443

page 443

Handbook: Grammar, Usage, Mechanics, Spelling

Verbs

Every sentence is divided into two parts: a subject and a predicate. The verb is the key word in the predicate. A verb tells what a subject does or links words in a sentence.

ACTION VERBS	EXAMPLES
An **action verb** tells what the subject does. Most verbs are action verbs.	The dancers **leap** across the stage. The spotlight **shines** on the lead dancers. Each dancer **twirls** around and around.
Some **action verbs** tell about an action that you cannot see.	The audience **enjoys** the lively music.

Ballet dancer

LINKING VERBS	EXAMPLES
A **linking verb** connects, or links, the subject of a sentence to a word in the predicate.	The dancers **look** powerful.
The word in the predicate can describe the subject.	Their costumes **are** colorful.
Or, the word in the predicate can be another way to name the subject.	These dancers **are** ballerinas.

Linking Verbs

Forms of the Verb be

am	was
is	were
are	

Other Linking Verbs

appear	seem	become
feel	smell	taste
look		

HELPING VERBS	EXAMPLES
Some verbs are made up of more than one word. The last word is called the **main verb**. It shows the action. The verb that comes before is the **helping verb**.	Ballet dancers **are regarded** as athletes and storytellers. They **can jump** high into the air. They **might leap** several feet across the stage. They **are building** up muscle strength.

page 444

HELPING VERBS, continued	EXAMPLES
The **helping verb** agrees with the subject.	The dancers **have practiced** for hours. The exercise **has made** them strong.
The word not always comes between the **helping verb** and the main verb.	The dancers **do** not **tell** a story in the usual way.
Other adverbs can come between a **helping verb** and the **main verb**, or appear in other places in the sentence.	They **will** never **use** their voices to tell a story. The story **is** always **told** through their graceful movements. Often slow movements **will show** an emotion like sadness. Happiness **is shown** best by quick, springy movements.
In questions, the subject comes between the **helping verb** and the **main verb**.	**Have** you **seen** a performance? **Does** your family **enjoy** ballet?

Helping Verbs

Forms of the Verb be
am — was
is — were
are

Forms of the Verb do
do — did
does

Forms of the Verb have
have — had
has

Other Helping Verbs

To express ability:
I **can** dance.
I **could** do the jump.

To express possibility:
I **may** dance tonight.
I **might** dance tonight.
Perhaps I **could** do the dance.

To express a need or want:
I **must** dance more often.
I **would** like to dance more often.

To express an intent:
I **will** dance more often.

To express something you ought to do:
I **should** practice more often.
I **ought** to practice more often.

page 445

Verbs, continued

TRANSITIVE VERBS	EXAMPLES	
Action verbs can be transitive or intransitive. A **transitive verb** needs an **object** to complete its meaning. The object receives the action of the verb.	**Not complete:** Many cities **use** **Not complete:** Fireworks **make** **Not complete:** They also **provide**	**Complete:** Many cities **use fireworks**. **Complete:** Fireworks **make noise**. **Complete:** They also **provide** a good **celebration**.
The object can be a **direct object**. A direct object answers one of these questions: • Whom? • What?	The noise **surprises** the **audience**. The people in the audience **cover** their **ears**.	

INTRANSITIVE VERBS	EXAMPLES
An **intransitive verb** does not need an object to complete its meaning.	**Complete:** The people in our neighborhood **cheer**. They **shout**. They **laugh**.
An **intransitive verb** may end the sentence, or it may be followed by other words that tell how, where, or when. These additional words are not objects since they do not receive the action of the verb.	The fireworks **glow** brightly. Then slowly, they **disappear** in the sky. The show **ends** by midnight.

Fireworks

page 446

The tense of a verb shows when an action happens.

PRESENT TENSE VERBS	EXAMPLES
The **present tense** of a verb tells about an action that is happening now.	My mom **looks** at her charts. She **checks** her computer screen.
The **present tense** of a verb can also tell about an action that happens regularly or all the time.	My mom **works** for the local TV station. She **is** a weather forecaster. She **reports** the weather every night at 5 p.m.
The **present progressive** form of a verb tells about an action as it is happening. It uses the helping verb **am**, **is**, or **are** and a main verb. The main verb ends in **-ing**.	Right now, she **is getting** ready for the show. "I can't believe it!" she says. "I **am looking** at the biggest storm of the century!" "**Are** those high winds **traveling** toward the coast?" asks her boss.

PAST TENSE VERBS	EXAMPLES
The **past tense** of a verb tells about an action that happened earlier, or in the past.	Yesterday, my mom **warned** everyone about the hurricane. The storm **moved** over the ocean toward land. We **did** not **know** exactly when it would hit.
The past tense form of a **regular verb** ends with **-ed**. See page 469 for spelling rules.	The shop owners in our town **covered** their windows with wood. We **closed** our shutters and **stayed** inside.
Irregular verbs have **special forms** to show the past tense. See the chart on pages 450–451.	The storm **hit** land. The sky **grew** very dark. It **began** to rain.

Some Irregular Verbs

Present Tense	Past Tense
begin	began
do	did
grow	grew
hit	hit

page 447

Handbook: Grammar, Usage, Mechanics, Spelling

Verbs, continued

PAST TENSE VERBS, continued	EXAMPLES
The past progressive form of a verb tells about an action that was happening over a period of time in the past. It uses the helping verb **was** or **were** and a main verb. The main verb ends in **-ing**.	The wind was blowing at high speeds. Our shutters were really shaking during the storm. Were the trees falling down?

FUTURE TENSE VERBS	EXAMPLES
The future tense of a verb tells about an action that will happen later, or in the future. To show future tense, use:	
• the helping verb **will** plus a main verb.	After the storm, everyone will come out of their houses. They will inspect the damage.
• the phrase **am going to**, **is going to**, or **are going to** plus a verb.	I am going to take the tree branches out of my yard. The city is not going to clean every street. We are all going to help each other. Are you going to help?
The future progressive form of a verb tells about an action that will be happening during a period of time in the future. It uses the helping verbs **will be** plus a main verb. The main verb ends in **-ing**.	The weather forecasters will be checking radar screens for other storms. I will be living away from the shore as soon as possible!

Wind damage from Hurricane Floyd, 1999

page 448

PERFECT TENSE VERBS	EXAMPLES

Verbs in the perfect tenses use the helping verbs *has, have,* or *had* and a form of the main verb that is called the *past participle.*

For **regular verbs**, the past tense and the past participle end in **-ed**.

Regular Verb	like	I like the Internet.
Past Tense	liked	I liked the Internet.
Past Participle	liked	I have always liked the Internet.

Irregular verbs have special forms for the past tense and past participle. See pages 450–451.

Irregular Verb	know	I know a lot about the Internet.
Past Tense	knew	I knew very little about the Internet last year.
Past Participle	known	I have known about the Internet for a long time.

Use the present perfect tense when you want to tell about: • an action that began in the past and may still be going on. • an action that happened in the past, but you aren't sure of the exact time.	The public has used the Internet since the mid-1980s. This year, we have gone to many different Web sites. The information on the Internet has not been hard to find. Have you found some interesting Web sites?
The past perfect tense tells about an action that was completed before some other action in the past.	Before the Web was developed, people had done their research in the library. Librarians had helped people find information long before the invention of computers.
The future perfect tense tells about an action that will be completed at a specific time in the future.	By 2010, researchers will have started using a new Internet. By the end of next year, 100,000 people will have visited our Web site.
Verbs in the perfect tenses can describe ongoing action.	Our school librarian has been using the Internet for a long time. She had been helping us learn the Internet until last year. By graduation, we will have been using the Internet a lot.

page 449

Verbs, continued

FORMS OF IRREGULAR VERBS

Irregular Verb	Past Tense	Past Participle	Irregular Verb	Past Tense	Past Participle
be: am, is	was	been	eat	ate	eaten
are	were	been	fall	fell	fallen
beat	beat	beaten	feed	fed	fed
become	became	become	feel	felt	felt
begin	began	begun	fight	fought	fought
bend	bent	bent	find	found	found
bind	bound	bound	fly	flew	flown
bite	bit	bitten	forget	forgot	forgotten
blow	blew	blown	freeze	froze	frozen
break	broke	broken	get	got	got, gotten
bring	brought	brought	give	gave	given
build	built	built	go	went	gone
burst	burst	burst	grow	grew	grown
buy	bought	bought	have	had	had
catch	caught	caught	hear	heard	heard
choose	chose	chosen	hide	hid	hidden
come	came	come	hit	hit	hit
cost	cost	cost	hold	held	held
creep	crept	crept	hurt	hurt	hurt
cut	cut	cut	keep	kept	kept
dig	dug	dug	know	knew	known
do	did	done	lay	laid	laid
draw	drew	drawn	lead	led	led
dream	dreamed, dreamt	dreamed, dreamt	leave	left	left
drink	drank	drunk	lend	lent	lent
drive	drove	driven	let	let	let

page 450

FORMS OF IRREGULAR VERBS, continued

Irregular Verb	Past Tense	Past Participle	Irregular Verb	Past Tense	Past Participle
lie	lay	lain	sink	sank	sunk
light	lit	lit	sit	sat	sat
lose	lost	lost	sleep	slept	slept
make	made	made	slide	slid	slid
mean	meant	meant	speak	spoke	spoken
meet	met	met	spend	spent	spent
pay	paid	paid	stand	stood	stood
prove	proved	proved, proven	steal	stole	stolen
put	put	put	stick	stuck	stuck
quit	quit	quit	sting	stung	stung
read	read	read	strike	struck	struck
ride	rode	ridden	swear	swore	sworn
ring	rang	rung	swim	swam	swum
rise	rose	risen	swing	swung	swung
run	ran	run	take	took	taken
say	said	said	teach	taught	taught
see	saw	seen	tear	tore	torn
seek	sought	sought	tell	told	told
sell	sold	sold	think	thought	thought
send	sent	sent	throw	threw	thrown
set	set	set	understand	understood	understood
shake	shook	shaken	wake	woke, waked	woken, waked
show	showed	shown	wear	wore	worn
shrink	shrank	shrunk	weep	wept	wept
shut	shut	shut	win	won	won
sing	sang	sung	write	wrote	written

page 451

Handbook: Grammar, Usage, Mechanics, Spelling

Verbs, continued

TWO-WORD VERBS	EXAMPLES
A **two-word verb** is a verb followed by a preposition. The meaning of the two-word verb is different from the meaning of the verb by itself.	I like to **call** you, but you never answer me. The coach **calls off** the game because of the rain. The workers **call for** higher pay.

Some Two-Word Verbs

Verb	Meaning	Example
break	to split into pieces	I didn't **break** the window with the ball.
break down	to stop working	Did the car **break down** again?
break up	to end	The party will **break up** before midnight.
	to come apart	The ice on the lake will **break up** in the spring.
bring	to carry something with you	**Bring** your book to class.
bring up	to suggest	She **brings up** good ideas at every meeting.
	to raise children	**Bring up** your children to be good citizens.
check	to make sure you are right	We can **check** our answers at the back of the book.
check in	to stay in touch with someone	I **check in** with my mom at work.
check up	to see if everything is okay	The nurse **checks up** on the patient every hour.
check off	to mark off a list	Look at your list and **check off** the girls' names.
check out	to look at something carefully	Hey, Marisa, **check out** my new bike!
fill	to put as much as possible into a container or space	**Fill** the pail with water.
fill in	to color or shade in a space	Please **fill in** the circle.
fill out	to complete	Marcos **fills out** a form to order a book.
get	to go after something	I'll **get** some milk at the store.
	to receive	I often **get** letters from my pen pal.
get ahead	to go beyond what is expected of you	She worked hard to **get ahead** in math class.
get along	to be on good terms with	Do you **get along** with your sister?
get out	to leave	Let's **get out** of the kitchen.
get over	to feel better	I hope you'll **get over** the flu soon.
get through	to finish	I can **get through** this book tonight.

page 452

TWO-WORD VERBS, continued

Some Two-Word Verbs

Verb	Meaning	Example
give	to hand something to someone	We **give** presents to the new baby.
give out	to stop working	If she runs ten miles, her energy will **give out**.
give up	to quit	I'm going to **give up** eating candy.
go	to move from place to place	Did you **go** to the mall on Saturday?
go on	to continue	Why do the boys **go on** playing after the bell rings?
go out	to go someplace special	Let's **go out** to lunch on Saturday.
look	to see or watch	Don't **look** directly at the sun.
look forward	to be excited about something that will happen	My brothers **look forward** to summer vacation.
look over	to review	She always **looks over** her answers before she gives the teacher her test.
look up	to hunt for and find	We **look up** information on the Internet.
pick	to choose	I'd **pick** Lin for class president.
pick on	to bother or tease	My older brothers always **pick on** me.
pick up	to go faster	Business **picks up** in the summer.
	to gather or collect	**Pick up** your clothes!
run	to move quickly on foot	Juan will **run** in a marathon.
run into	to see someone you know unexpectedly	Did you **run into** Chris at the store?
run out	to suddenly have nothing left	The cafeteria always **runs out** of nachos.
stand	to be in a straight up-and-down position	I have to **stand** in line to buy tickets.
stand for	to represent	A heart **stands for** love.
stand out	to be easier to see	You'll really **stand out** with that orange cap.
turn	to change direction	We **turn** right at the next corner.
turn up	to appear	Clean your closet and your belt will **turn up**.
	to raise the volume	Please **turn up** the radio.
turn in	to go to bed	On school nights I **turn in** at 9:30.
	to give back	You didn't **turn in** the homework yesterday.
turn off	to make something stop	Please **turn off** the radio.

page 453

Verbs, continued

ACTIVE AND PASSIVE VERBS	EXAMPLES
A verb is **active** if the **subject** is doing the action.	In this sentence, the subject—Mr. Ingram—does the selling: **Mr. Ingram sold** hamburgers for a nickel in 1921.
A verb is **passive** if the **subject** is not doing the action.	In this sentence, Mr. Ingram still does the selling, but he is not the subject. He is named after the word **by**. **Hamburgers were sold** by Mr. Ingram for a nickel in 1921. Sometimes the person or thing doing the action may not be named. **Hamburgers were sold** for a nickel in 1921.

VERBALS	EXAMPLES
A verbal is a word made from a verb but used as another part of speech.	
An **infinitive** is a verb form that begins with **to**. It can be used as a noun, an adjective, or an adverb.	Mr. Ingram liked **to cook**. (noun) When you go to the hamburger stand, Mr. Ingram is the man **to see**. (adjective) Mr. Ingram cooks **to have** fun. (adverb)
A **gerund** is a verb form that ends in **-ing**. It is used as a noun. It can be the subject of a sentence, the object of a verb, or the object of a preposition.	**Cooking** was Mr. Ingram's best talent. (subject) Mr. Ingram enjoys **cooking**. (object of the verb) Mr. Ingram was very talented at **cooking**. (object of the preposition)
A **participle** is a verb form that is used as an adjective. It ends in **-ing** or **-ed**.	His **sizzling** hamburgers smelled good. He made them from **flattened** meatballs.
A **participle** can start a **phrase**. Be sure to place the phrase next to the noun it describes.	**Standing by the grill**, Mr. Ingram cooked the hamburgers. *Not:* Mr. Ingram cooked the hamburgers, **standing by the grill**.

page 454

Adverbs

An adverb tells more about a verb, an adjective, or another adverb.

USE OF ADVERBS	EXAMPLES
An **adverb** can tell about a **verb**. It can come before or after the verb.	Our team **always wins** our basketball games. The whole team **plays well**.
An **adverb** can make an **adjective** or another **adverb** stronger.	Gina is **really good** at basketball. She plays **extremely well**.

TYPES OF ADVERBS	EXAMPLES
Adverbs answer one of the following questions: • How? • Where? • When? • How much? or How often?	Gina **carefully** aims the ball. She tosses the ball **high**, but it misses the basket. She will try again **later**. She **usually** scores.

ADVERBS THAT COMPARE	EXAMPLES
Some **adverbs** compare actions. Add **-er** to compare two actions. Add **-est** to compare three or more actions.	Gina runs **fast**. Gina runs **faster** than her guard. Gina runs **the fastest** of all the players.
If the **adverb** ends in **-ly**, use **more** or **less** to compare two actions. Use **the most** or **the least** to compare three or more actions.	Gina aims **more carefully** than Jen. Jen aims **less carefully** than Gina. Gina aims **the most carefully** of all the players on her team. Jen aims **the least carefully** of all.
Be careful not to use an adjective when you need an adverb. Never use an adverb after a **linking verb**.	Everyone plays ~~fair~~ fairly. My teacher **is** ~~fairly~~.

page 455

Handbook: Grammar, Usage, Mechanics, Spelling

Prepositions

A preposition comes at the beginning of a prepositional phrase. Prepositional phrases add details to sentences.

USES OF PREPOSITIONS	EXAMPLES
Some **prepositions** show location.	The Chávez Community Center is **by my house**. The pool is **behind the building**.
Some **prepositions** show time.	The Youth Club's party will start **after lunch**.
Some **prepositions** show direction.	Go **through the building** and **around the fountain** to get to the pool. The snack bar is **down the hall**.
Some **prepositions** have multiple uses.	We'll make new friends **at the party**. Meet me **at my house**. Come **at noon**.
PREPOSITIONAL PHRASES	**EXAMPLES**
A **prepositional phrase** starts with a **preposition** and ends with a noun or a pronoun. It includes all the words in between. The noun or pronoun is the **object of the preposition**.	I made a new friend **at the party**. Next week I'm going to the movies **with her**.

Some Prepositions

Location		Time	Direction	Other Prepositions	
above	near	after	across	about	for
behind	next to	before	around	against	from
below	off	during	down	along	of
beside	on	till	into	among	to
between	out	until	out of	as	with
by	outside		through	at	without
in	over		toward	except	
inside	under		up		

page 456

Conjunctions and Interjections

A conjunction connects words or groups of words. An interjection expresses strong feeling.

CONJUNCTIONS	EXAMPLES
A **coordinating conjunction** connects words, phrases, or clauses.	The zoos in San Diego **and** Atlanta have giant pandas. In China, giant pandas can be found in the wild **or** in panda reserves. Pandas will eat other animals, **but** mostly they eat bamboo.
Correlative conjunctions are used in pairs. The pair connects phrases or words.	In the past, pandas lived **not only** in central China **but also** in southern China and Vietnam. Now **both** the giant panda **and** the red panda are rare. **Either** a survey of wild pandas **or** protection of their habitat could help save the pandas.

Coordinating Conjunctions

Conjunctions	Uses
and	To connect two ideas that are alike
but, yet	To show a difference between two ideas
nor	To put two negative ideas together
or	To show a choice between two ideas
so, for	To show how one idea follows another

Some Correlative Conjunctions

both . . . and
either . . . or
neither . . . nor
not only . . . but also
whether . . . or

page 457

Conjunctions and Interjections, continued

CONJUNCTIONS, continued	EXAMPLES
A **subordinating conjunction** introduces a **dependent clause** in a complex sentence. It connects the **dependent clause** to the main clause.	Pandas can't find enough bamboo to eat **because their habitat is being destroyed**. **If all the bamboo is wiped out**, the pandas will die.
A **conjunctive adverb** joins two independent clauses. Use a semicolon before the conjunction and a comma after it.	Pandas do not easily digest plants**; therefore,** they need to eat large amounts of bamboo. China has set aside bamboo-rich reserves for pandas**; however,** these reserves have not always supplied enough food for the pandas.
INTERJECTIONS	**EXAMPLES**
An **interjection** is a word or phrase that shows strong feeling. An exclamation mark follows an interjection that stands alone.	**Help!** **Ouch!** **Oops!** **Oh boy!** **Oh my!** **Wow!**
An interjection used in a sentence can be followed by a comma or an exclamation mark.	**Oh**, it's a baby panda! **Hooray!** The baby panda has survived!

Some Subordinating Conjunctions

after	before	till
although	if	until
as	in order that	when
as if	since	where
as long as	so that	while
because	though	

Some Conjunctive Adverbs

besides	meanwhile	then
consequently	moreover	therefore
however	nevertheless	thus

page 458

Capital Letters

A reader can tell that a word is special in some way if it begins with a capital letter.

PROPER NOUNS	EXAMPLES
	A common noun names any person, place, thing, or idea. A proper noun names one particular person, place, thing, or idea.
All the important words in a **proper noun** start with a capital letter.	Person: captain — **C**aptain **M**eriwether **L**ewis Place: land — **L**ouisiana **T**erritory Thing: team — **C**orps of **D**iscovery Idea: destiny — **M**anifest **D**estiny
Proper nouns include: • names of people and their titles	Laura Roberts Captain Meriwether Lewis ***But:*** *Do not capitalize a title if it is used without a name:* The captain's co-leader on the expedition was William Clark.
• abbreviations of titles	**Mr.** Ramos **Mrs.** Ramos **Dr.** Schuyler **Ms.** Nguyen
• words like ***Mom*** and ***Dad*** when they are used as names	"**Mom**, can you tell me more about the expedition?" said Laura. ***But:*** *Do not capitalize names if they follow a word like* my. I ask my **mom** lots of questions.
• organizations	United Nations Science Club Wildlife Society Lodi City Council
• names of languages, subject areas, and religions	Spanish Vietnamese Mathematics Social Studies Buddhism Christianity

Abbreviations of Titles

Capt. for the captain of a boat or in the armed forces
Pres. for the president of a country, a company, a club, or an organization
Sen. for a member of the U.S. Senate
Rep. for a member of the U.S. House of Representatives

page 459

Handbook: Grammar, Usage, Mechanics, Spelling

Capital Letters, continued

PROPER NOUNS, continued	EXAMPLES
• names of geographic places	**Cities and States** Dallas, Texas Miami, Florida St. Louis, Missouri **Countries** Iran Ecuador Cambodia **Continents** Asia South America Africa **Streets and Roads** King Boulevard Main Avenue First Street **Landforms** Rocky Mountains Sahara Desert Grand Canyon **Public Spaces** Hemisfair Plaza Central Park Muir Camp **Bodies of Water** Yellowstone River Pacific Ocean Great Salt Lake Gulf of Mexico **Buildings, Ships, and Monuments** Empire State Building *Titanic* Statue of Liberty **Planets and Heavenly Bodies** Earth Jupiter Milky Way
• abbreviations of geographic places	**Words Used in Addresses** Avenue Ave. Boulevard Blvd. Court Ct. Drive Dr. East E. Highway Hwy. Lane Ln. North N. Place Pl. Road Rd. South S. Square Sq. Street St. West W.

Abbreviations for State Names in Mailing Addresses

Alabama	AL	Hawaii	HI	Massachusetts	MA	New Mexico	NM	South Dakota	SD
Alaska	AK	Idaho	ID	Michigan	MI	New York	NY	Tennessee	TN
Arizona	AZ	Illinois	IL	Minnesota	MN	North Carolina	NC	Texas	TX
Arkansas	AR	Indiana	IN	Mississippi	MS	North Dakota	ND	Utah	UT
California	CA	Iowa	IA	Missouri	MO	Ohio	OH	Vermont	VT
Colorado	CO	Kansas	KS	Montana	MT	Oklahoma	OK	Virginia	VA
Connecticut	CT	Kentucky	KY	Nebraska	NE	Oregon	OR	Washington	WA
Delaware	DE	Louisiana	LA	Nevada	NV	Pennsylvania	PA	West Virginia	WV
Florida	FL	Maine	ME	New Hampshire	NH	Rhode Island	RI	Wisconsin	WI
Georgia	GA	Maryland	MD	New Jersey	NJ	South Carolina	SC	Wyoming	WY

• months, days, special days and holidays	January February March April May June July August September October November December Sunday Monday Tuesday Wednesday Thursday Friday Saturday New Year's Day Mother's Day Thanksgiving Hanukkah Kwanzaa

page 460

PROPER ADJECTIVES	EXAMPLES
A **proper adjective** is formed from a **proper noun**. Capitalize proper adjectives.	Napoleon Bonaparte was from **Europe**. He was a **European** leader in the 1800s. Napoleon ruled the country of **France**. He was the **French** emperor.

IN LETTERS	EXAMPLES
Capitalize the first word used in the **greeting** or in the **closing** of a letter. Street, city, and state names in the address, as well as their abbreviations, are also capitalized.	Dear Kim, I wish you could explore the Academy of Natural Sciences with me. I've learned so much about the flora and fauna that Lewis and Clark found. The museum even has some of the original samples! I'll tell you about it when I get home. See you soon. Your friend, Jamal Kim Messina 10250 W. Fourth St. Las Vegas, NV 89015

IN TITLES AND QUOTATIONS	EXAMPLES
Capitalize the **first word** in a **direct quotation**.	Clark said, "**There is great joy in camp.**" "**We are in view of the ocean,**" he said "**It's the Pacific Ocean,**" he added. "**We are finally here.**"
All important words in a **title** begin with a capital letter. Short words like *a, an, the, in, at, of,* and *for* are not capitalized unless they are the first or last word in the title.	**book:** *The Longest Journey* **poem:** "Leaves of Grass" **magazine:** *Flora and Fauna of Arizona* **newspaper:** *The Denver Post* **song:** "The Star-Spangled Banner" **game:** Exploration! **TV series:** "Bonanza" **movie:** *The Lion King*

page 461

Punctuation Marks

Punctuation marks make words and sentences easier to understand.

PERIOD	EXAMPLES
Use a **period**: • at the end of a statement or a polite command	Georgia read the paper to her mom. Tell me if there are any interesting articles.
• after an abbreviation	There's a new restaurant on Stone St. near our house. It opens at 10 a.m. today. ***But:*** *Do not use a period in an acronym:* National Aeronautics and Space Administration **NASA** *Do not use a period in the abbreviation of a state name written in a mailing address:* Massachusetts **MA** Illinois **IL** Texas **TX** California **CA** Florida **FL** Virginia **VA**
• after an initial	The owner is J.J. Malone.
• to separate dollars and cents. The period is the decimal point.	The article says lunch today costs only $1.50.
• in an Internet address. The period is called a dot.	The restaurant has a Web site at www.jjmalone.org.

QUESTION MARK	EXAMPLES
Use a **question mark**: • at the end of a question	What kind of food do they serve?
• after a question that comes at the end of a statement	The food is good, isn't it? ***But:*** *Use a period after an indirect question. In an indirect question, you tell about a question you asked.* I asked how good the food could be for only $1.50.

page 462

EXCLAMATION MARK	EXAMPLES
Use an **exclamation mark**: • after an interjection	Wow!
• at the end of a sentence to show that you feel strongly about something	One-fifty is a really good price!

COMMA	EXAMPLES
Use a **comma**: • to separate three or more items in a series	Articles about the school, a big sale, and a new movie were also in the newspaper. The school will buy a new bus, 10 computers, and books for the library.
• when you write a number with four or more digits	There was $500,000 in the school budget.
• before the **coordinating conjunction** in a compound sentence. See page 457 for a list of coordinating conjunctions.	The school could buy books, **or** it could buy a sound system. All the teachers discussed it, **and** they decided books were more important.
• to set off a short word or phrase at the beginning of a sentence	Good, we really need some new books.
• to set off words that interrupt a sentence	Books about geography, for example, would be great additions to the library.
• before a question at the end of a statement	We need books on that topic, don't we?
• to set off the name of a person someone is talking to	Georgia, does the article say why the school is buying a new bus? Just a minute, Mom, let me look.
• between two or more adjectives that tell about the same noun	The old, rusty school bus is broken.

page 463

Handbook: Grammar, Usage, Mechanics, Spelling

COMMA, continued	EXAMPLES
Use a **comma**: • before and after an appositive phrase. An **appositive phrase** renames the noun or pronoun before it.	Mr. Ivanovich, **the bus driver,** says the bus will cost too much to fix.
• after a long **introductory phrase**	**In the last few months,** the bus had to be fixed six times.
• after an **introductory clause**	**Because the bus is old,** it keeps breaking down.
• before someone's exact words	Mr. Ivanovich said, "It is time for a new bus!"
• after someone's exact words if the sentence continues	"I agree," said the principal.
• before and after a **clause** if the clause is not necessary for understanding the sentence	At the end of the article, **where computers are discussed,** there is a letter by a student.
Use a **comma** in these places in a letter: • between the city and the state • between the date and the year • after the greeting • after the closing	144 North Ave. Milpas, AK July 3, 2002 Dear Mr. Okada, I really like computers and am glad that we have them at school, but ours are out-of-date. As principal, can you ask the school board to buy us new ones for next year? Sincerely, Patrick Green

page 464

SEMICOLON	EXAMPLES
Use a **semicolon**: • to separate two simple sentences used together without a conjunction	Some movies advertised in this paper look interesting; others don't.
• before a conjunctive adverb that joins two simple sentences. Use a **comma** after the adverb. See page 458 for a list of conjunctive adverbs.	I'd like to go to the movies today; however, my favorite store is having a sale.
• to separate a group of words in a series if the words in the series already have commas	It is selling warm, fluffy coats; green, red, and orange mittens; and summer shorts!

APOSTROPHE	EXAMPLES
Use an **apostrophe** when you write a **possessive noun**. • If there is one owner, add **'s** to the owner's name.	The **newspaper's** ads for yard sales are interesting, too. ***But:*** *If the owner's name ends in s, you can add **'s** or just the apostrophe. Either is correct.* **Mrs. Ramos's** chair is for sale. **Mrs. Ramos'** chair is for sale.
• If there is more than one owner, add **'** after the **s**.	The **Martins'** dog had puppies, and I want to buy one. ***But:*** *If the plural noun that names the owners does not end in s, add **'s**.* The **Children's** Choir is holding a yard sale.
Use an **apostrophe** to replace the letters left out in a **contraction**. • In contractions with a verb and **not**, the word **not** is usually shortened to **n't**.	could not → couldn't — I **couldn't** go to the yard sale. ***Exceptions:*** cannot → can't; will not → won't; I am not → I'm not
• In many other contractions, the verb is shortened.	I would → I'd — **I'd** like to see the vase you bought.

page 465

QUOTATION MARKS	EXAMPLES
Use **quotation marks** to show: • a speaker's exact words	"Listen to this!" Georgia said.
• the exact words quoted from a book or other printed material	The announcement in the paper was "The world-famous writer Josie Ramón will be at Milpas Library Friday night."
• the title of a song, poem, or short story	Her poem "Speaking" is famous.
• the title of a magazine article or newspaper article	It appeared in the magazine article "How to Talk to Your Teen."
• the title of a chapter from a book	On Friday night she'll be reading "Getting Along," a chapter from her new book.
• words used in a special way	We will be "all ears" at the reading.
Always put **periods** and **commas** inside quotation marks.	"She is such a great writer," Georgia said. " I'd love to meet her."

COLON	EXAMPLES
Use a **colon**: • after the greeting in a business letter • to separate hours and minutes • to start a list	356 Oak St. Milpas, AK Sept. 24, 2002 Features Editor *Milpas Post* 78 Main St. Milpas, AK Dear Sir or Madam: Please place this announcement in the calendar section of your paper. Friday at 7:15 p.m., the writer Josie Ramón will be speaking at Milpas Library. When people come, they should bring: 1. Questions for Ms. Ramón. 2. Money to purchase her new book. 3. A cushion to sit on! Thank you. Sincerely, Hector Quintana

page 466

DASH	EXAMPLES
Use a **dash** to: • show a break in an idea or the tone in a sentence	It's so helpful to read the paper—I really like the ads—to find out what is happening in town.
• emphasize a word, a series of words, a phrase, or a clause	There's so much information here—restaurant openings, store sales, news stories about people in our town.

PARENTHESES	EXAMPLES
Use **parentheses** around extra information in a sentence.	This news story (written by my mom) is very interesting!

HYPHEN	EXAMPLES
Use a **hyphen** to: • connect words in a number and in a fraction	The news story reported on a survey of **seventy-five** people. **One-third** of them wasted water everyday.
• join some words to make a compound word	A **15-year-old** boy and his **great-grandmother** have started an awareness campaign.
• connect a letter to a word	They have sent **e-mail** messages to everyone they know. They also designed a **T-shirt** for their campaign.
• divide words at the end of a line. Always divide the word between two syllables.	Please join us in our aware- ness campaign.

ITALICS AND UNDERLINES	EXAMPLES
When you are using a computer, use **italics** for the names of: • magazines and newspapers • books • plays, movies, musicals, music albums, and TV series	I just read an article about a good book in the ***Milpas Post***. The name of the book is ***My Hopes and Dreams***. The article said the new movie ***All About Jack*** is based on this book.
When you write by hand, use an **underline** to indicate italics.	The Milpas Post gave that new movie, All About Jack, a great review.

page 467

Handbook: Grammar, Usage, Mechanics, Spelling

Spelling

Follow these rules and your spelling will get better and better.

HOW TO BE A BETTER SPELLER

Spelling Tips

1. To learn a new word:
   - Study the word and look up its meaning.
   - Say the word out loud. Listen as you repeat it again.
   - Picture how the word looks.
   - Spell the word out loud several times.
   - Write the word five or ten times for practice. Try to use the word often in a sentence until you are sure you know its spelling.
2. Learn the following spelling rules.
3. Use a dictionary to check your spelling.
4. Keep a notebook of words that are hard for you to spell.

Q + U	EXAMPLES
Always put a **u** after a **q**.	The **qu**ick but **qu**iet **qu**arterback asked **qu**antities of **qu**estions. ***Exceptions:*** Iraq Iraqi

IE, EI	EXAMPLES
Use **i** before **e** except after **c**.	The f**ie**rce rec**ei**ver was always ready to catch the ball. ***Exceptions:*** • **ei**ther, h**ei**ght, th**ei**r, w**ei**rd, s**ei**ze • w**ei**gh, n**ei**ghbor (and other words where **ei** has the long **a** sound)

PLURALS	EXAMPLES
To form the plural of a noun that ends in **x**, **ch**, **sh**, **s**, or **z**, add **-es**. For most other nouns, just add **-s**.	Their team was called the Fox**es**. Their players made great catch**es** in the end zone.

page 468

Y TO I	EXAMPLES
If a word ends in a consonant plus **y**, change the **y** to **i** before you add **-es**, **-ed**, **-er**, or **-est**.	The coach was the happ**iest** when his players tr**ied** their best.
For words that end in a **vowel** plus **y**, just add **-s** or **-ed**.	For five day**s** before the game, the team stay**ed** at practice an extra 30 minutes.
If you add **-ing** to a verb that ends in **-y**, do not change the **y** to **i**.	The players learned a lot from study**ing** videos of their games.

-ED, -ING, -ER, -EST	EXAMPLES
When a word ends in silent **e**, drop the **e** before you add **-ed**, **-ing**, **-er**, or **-est**.	The players notic**ed** what they did wrong. Lat**er**, they talked about their mistakes.
When a one-syllable word ends in one vowel and one consonant, double the final consonant before you add an ending.	Then they pla**nned** some new plays for the game. They got set for their **biggest** challenge.

PREFIXES AND SUFFIXES	EXAMPLES
Add a **prefix** to the beginning of a root word. Do not change the spelling of the **root word**.	They **replayed** the video often. The team never got **discouraged**.
When you add a consonant **suffix**, do not change the spelling of the **root word**.	We had a **lovely** day for the game. ***Exception:*** happy happiness
For most **root words** that end in silent **e**, drop the **e** before adding a vowel **suffix**.	Our quarterback won the Most **Valuable** Player award for the game.

Some Prefixes and Suffixes

Prefixes

anti-	in-	pre-
bi-	im-	re-
dis-	inter-	sub-
extra-	mis-	un-

Suffixes Beginning with a Consonant

-ful	-ly	-ness
-less	-ment	-tion

Suffixes Beginning with a Vowel

-able	-ent	-ish
-al	-er	-ive
-ant	-ible	-ous

page 469

Glossary of Literary Terms

Glossary of Literary Terms

Action/Reaction Action/reaction is the connection between one action or event and another that occurs as a result.
See *also* **Characterization**

Advertisement An advertisement is a public notice of something that is for sale. It generally uses persuasive techniques.
See *also* **Persuasion**

Alliteration Alliteration is the repetition of the same or similar consonant sounds at the beginning of words. An example from "Human Family" is

> I've sailed upon the seven seas
> and stopped in every land

See *also* **Assonance; Consonance**

Article An article is a short piece of nonfiction writing on a specific topic. Articles usually appear in newspapers and magazines.
Examples: **"Twins," "Saving the Peregrine Falcon"**

Assonance Assonance is the repetition of the same or similar vowel sounds between different consonants in words that are close together. An example is the recurring long *e* sound in this line from "Old Man Mangrove":

> All year long he
> Drops green leaves

See *also* **Alliteration; Consonance**

Autobiography An autobiography is the story of a person's life written by that person.
Example: **"The Circuit"**

Biographical Fiction Biographical fiction is a story that tells the facts of a real person's life and includes fictional details as well. It may be written from the point of view of a real or an imaginary character; the conversations are usually invented.

Biography A biography is the story of a person's life written by another person.
Example: **"Anne Frank," "Teammates"**

Cause and Effect Cause and effect is the relationship between two events. The one that happens first, the cause, brings about the effect that follows. This sentence from "The Great Migration" is an example of cause and effect:

> Many northern workers were angry
> because they had to compete with
> migrants for housing and jobs.

Chant A chant is a type of poetry that is meant to be read aloud. It has a strong beat and musical language.

Character A person, animal, or imaginary creature in a story is called a character.
See *also* **Characterization; Character Traits**

Characterization Characterization is the way a writer creates and develops a character. Writers use a variety of ways to bring a character to life: through descriptions of the character's appearance, thoughts, feelings, and actions; through the character's words; through the words or thoughts of other characters.
See *also* **Character Traits; Motive; Point of View**

page 470

Character Sketch A character sketch is a short, vivid description of a person.
See *also* **Characterization; Character Traits**

Character Traits Character traits are the special qualities of personality that writers give their characters.
See *also* **Character; Characterization**

Climax The climax of a story or play is the turning point or most important event. At the climax, the resolution of the story is in sight. For example, in "The Mother Who Lost Her Daughter," the climax occurs when Zeus tells Hades that he must return Persephone to her mother for part of the year.
See *also* **Plot**

Complication Complication is part of the plot. It includes the events in a story that make it difficult for characters to solve problems.
See *also* **Conflict and Resolution; Plot; Rising Action and Falling Action**

Compressed Language Compressed language is the use of only a few words to convey a great deal of meaning. Poets often use compressed language.

Conflict and Resolution Conflict and resolution are parts of the plot of a story. Conflict describes the problem a character has, and resolution tells how or if the problem is solved.
See *also* **Plot**

Consonance Consonance is the repetition of the final consonant sound preceded by different vowels. An example of consonance is *clip clop.*
See *also* **Alliteration; Assonance**

Description A description is writing that tells about a person, place, or thing. It often uses images that appeal to the five senses: sight, sound, touch, smell, and taste. An example from "Amir" is

> When I saw the garden for the first time, so green among the dark brick buildings, I thought back to my parents' Persian rug. It showed climbing vines, rivers and waterfalls, grapes, flower beds, singing birds, everything a desert dweller might want. The garden's green was as soothing to the eye as the deep blue of that rug.

Dialogue Dialogue is what characters say to one another. Writers use dialogue to develop characters, move the plot forward, and add interest. In most writing, dialogue is set off by quotation marks; in play scripts, however, dialogue appears without quotation marks.

Diary A diary is a book written by a person about his or her own life as it is happening. It is made up of entries that are written shortly after the events occur. The writer of a diary often expresses feelings and opinions about what has happened.
Example: **"The Diary of a Young Girl"**

Essay An essay is a short piece of nonfiction writing that deals with a single subject. Its purpose may be to inform, to entertain, or to persuade.
Example: **"Talking Walls"**

Exaggeration Exaggeration is saying that something is bigger or more important than it actually is.
See *also* **Hyperbole**

page 471

Glossary of Literary Terms, continued

Fable A fable is a short story that teaches a lesson about life. Many fables have animals instead of humans as characters. Fables often state the lesson they are teaching at the end.

Family History A family history is a record that includes important information about your ancestors and the people now in your family. It tells how family members are related and describes important events such as births, weddings, and deaths.
Example: **"The Keeping Quilt"**

Fantasy Fantasy is writing that includes unreal or magical characters and events. Fairy tales, science fiction, and fables are examples of fantasy.
See *also* **Science Fiction**

Fiction Fiction is writing that is made up by the writer. The events and characters may be based in part on reality, as in biographical, historical, or realistic fiction; or they may be made up entirely. Fiction includes novels and short stories.
Examples: **"Amir," "A House of My Own"**

Figurative Language Figurative language is the use of words or phrases to express something different than their usual meanings. Writers use figurative language to say things in vivid and imaginative ways, but what they say is not really true. Hyperbole, imagery, metaphor, personification, and simile are examples of figurative language.
See *also* **Hyperbole; Imagery; Metaphor; Personification; Simile**

Flashback A flashback is an interruption in the action of a story to tell about something that happened earlier. It is often used to give the reader background information about a character or situation.

Folk Tale A folk tale is a very old and simple story that has been passed down through the years. Most folk tales were told for generations before they were written down.
Example: **"The Clever Wife"**

Foreshadowing Foreshadowing is a hint that an author gives about an event that will happen later in a story.

Free Verse Free verse is poetry with lines that do not have regular rhyme and regular rhythm. Free verse often sounds like ordinary speech.
Examples: **"Chrysalis Diary," "Mother to Son"**
See *also* **Poetry; Rhyme; Rhythm**

Genre Genre is a kind or type of literature. The four main genres are fiction, nonfiction, poetry, and drama.

Goal and Outcome Goal and outcome are the parts of the plot that tell what a character's ambition is and whether he or she attains it.
See *also* **Plot**

Historical Fiction Historical fiction is a story based on events that actually happened or people who actually lived. It may be written from the point of view of a real or an imaginary character, and it usually includes invented dialogue.
Example: **"Ginger for the Heart"**

How-to Article A how-to article is a short piece of writing that gives step-by-step directions for making or doing something.
Example: **"Starting a Community Garden"**

page 472

Hyperbole Hyperbole is extreme exaggeration for the purpose of emphasis or humor. The line "Check out this twenty-foot trout" from "Big Eaters" is an example of hyperbole.
See *also* **Exaggeration**

Imagery Imagery is the use of words and phrases that create mental pictures in readers' minds. It helps readers imagine how things look, sound, taste, smell, and feel. Because it appeals to the five senses, it is sometimes called sensory language.
See *also* **Figurative Language**

Interview An interview is a meeting between two people in which one person asks questions of the other one.
Example: **"An Interview with Poet Gary Soto," from "The Power of Poetry"**

Journal A journal is a personal record. It may include accounts of events, stories, poems, sketches, thoughts, essays, interesting information one has collected, or just about anything the journal writer wishes to include. It is similar to a diary.

Legend A legend is a traditional story about a famous person or event. The subject of a legend can be a real or a make-believe person. Legends often contain elements of fantasy and usually exaggerate the subject's personal qualities or accomplishments.

Letter A letter is a message written and sent from one person to another. Letters can be personal and private, or public, as a letter to the editor of a newspaper is.

Metaphor A metaphor is a kind of figurative language that compares two unlike things by saying that one thing is the other thing. An example from "The Clever Wife" is

> . . . the magistrate's eyebrows . . .
> became flying birds of astonishment.

See *also* **Figurative Language; Simile**

Meter Meter is a pattern of stressed and unstressed syllables in poetry.
See *also* **Rhythm**

Mood and Tone Mood is the overall feeling that a piece of writing gives to the reader. For example, the mood in the poem "Big Eaters" is playful. Tone is the author's attitude toward what he or she wrote. The tone of "Big Eaters" is mildly annoyed.

Motive A motive is the reason a character has for his or her thoughts, feelings, actions, or words. For example, in "The Clever Goatherd," Manuel tells his story because he wants to marry the king's daughter.
See *also* **Characterization**

Myth A myth is a very old story that explains something about the world. Myths often involve gods, goddesses, and other superhuman characters.
Example: **"The Mother Who Lost Her Daughter"**

Narrative Poetry Narrative poetry is poetry that tells a story. It has characters, a setting, and a plot; it may include elements of poetry such as rhythm and rhyme.
See *also* **Poetry**

page 473

Glossary of Literary Terms

Glossary of Literary Terms, continued

Nonfiction Nonfiction is writing that tells about real people, real places, and real events.

Examples: **"Teammates," "The Great Migration," "The Big Blast"**

Onomatopoeia Onomatopoeia is the use of words that imitate the sounds associated with the things they describe. *Buzz*, for the sound of a bee; *hiss*, for the sound of a snake; and *gurgle*, for the sound of a stream are examples of onomatopoeia.

Pantomime Pantomime is communication through the use of gestures, body movements, and facial expressions, rather than through speech.

Personification In personification, animals, things, or ideas are described as having human characteristics. An example from "The Circuit" is

> Finally the mountains around the valley reached out and swallowed the sun.

Persuasion Persuasion is an attempt to affect the feelings, beliefs, and actions of others. Persuasion is used in advertisements, editorials, sermons, and political speeches. In "The Mother Who Lost Her Daughter," Demeter persuades Zeus to help her get back Persephone.

Photo-Essay A photo-essay is a short nonfiction piece that includes photographs and captions. The photographs are as important as the words in giving information to the reader.

Play A play is a story written to be performed by actors on a stage. In most plays, a story is told through the words and actions of actors in the roles of different characters.

Example: **"The Mother Who Lost Her Daughter"**

Plot Plot is the series of events that makes up a story, play, or narrative poem. Plot is usually divided into four parts: problem or conflict, complication, climax, and resolution.

See also **Climax; Complication; Conflict and Resolution; Problem and Solution; Rising Action and Falling Action**

Poetry Poetry is a kind of writing that expresses ideas in few words. Poets often choose words and phrases that appeal to our senses. Many poems are arranged in sections called stanzas and use rhythm and rhyme.

Examples: **"Some Rivers,"** from **"A Celebration of the Everglades," "We're All in the Telephone Book"**

See also **Imagery; Rhyme; Rhythm; Stanza**

Point of View Point of view is the particular view from which a story is told. In a story told from the first-person point of view, the narrator is a character in the story who uses words such as *I*, *me*, and *we*. A story told from the third-person point of view is told by a narrator outside the story who uses words such as *he*, *she*, and *they*.

Example of first-person point of view: **"The Diary of a Young Girl"**

Example of third-person point of view: **"Anne Frank"**

page 474

Problem and Solution Problems and solutions are parts of the plot of a story. Problems are described at the beginning of a story. Solutions are described at the end.

See also **Plot**

Realistic Fiction Realistic fiction is literature about imaginary characters who really could exist and imaginary events that could actually happen.

Example: **"Amir"**

Repetition Repetition is the repeating of words or phrases to create an effect. An example from the poem "Two Baby Snail Kites" is

> Apple snails for dinner.
> Apple snails for lunch.
> And every Sunday morning,
> apple snails for brunch.

See also **Rhythm**

Report A report is a short piece of nonfiction writing on a particular topic. It is different from an essay in that it usually includes only facts and does not express opinions.

Rhyme Rhyme is the repetition of sounds at the ends of words. Rhyme helps create rhythm and adds a musical quality to the poetry.

Examples in **"Old Man Mangrove"** and **"Two Baby Snail Kites,"** from **"A Celebration of the Everglades"**

Rhyme Scheme Rhyme scheme is the pattern of rhyme in a poem.

See also **Rhyme**

Rhythm Rhythm is a musical quality resulting from the repetition of stressed and unstressed syllables in poetry. Rhythm is also created by the repetition of words, phrases, and sentences.

Rising Action and Falling Action Rising action and falling action are parts of the plot. Actions or events that lead to the climax are the rising action. The actions or events that follow the climax are the falling action.

See also **Climax; Complication; Conflict and Resolution; Plot**

Science Fiction Science fiction is a story based on real or imaginary scientific discoveries. It often takes place in the future.

Example: **"Fat Men from Space"**

See also **Historical Fiction; Realistic Fiction**

Self-portrait A self-portrait is a description that a person writes or tells about himself or herself.

Examples in **"Beyond the Color Lines"**

Sensory Language *See* **Imagery**

Setting The setting is the time and the place in which the events of a story occur. The setting of "Amir," for example, is Cleveland, Ohio, in the present day.

Short Story A short story is a short fiction piece that has a single problem and a simple plot.

Simile A simile is a comparison between two unlike things that uses the words *like*, *as*, or *than*. Similes are one kind of figurative language. An example from "The Circuit" is

> The dirt floor...looked like a road map.

Stanza A stanza is a group of lines that form a unit in a poem. A stanza in a poem is similar to a paragraph in prose writing. Stanzas are separated by spaces.

Examples in **"Old Man Mangrove,"** from **"A Celebration of the Everglades"**

page 475

Glossary of Literary Terms, continued

Story A story is a piece of fiction writing that has characters, a setting, and a plot.

Style Style is a particular way of writing. It is developed through choice of words, tone, sentence length, and use of imagery and dialogue.

See also **Word Choice**

Suspense Suspense is a feeling of curiosity, tension, or excitement in the reader. Suspense makes the reader want to find out what is going to happen next. In "Fat Men From Space," for example, there is a feeling of suspense when William gets the news bulletins of the invasion by the spacemen.

Theme A theme is the main idea in a work of literature. It is often a message that can be expressed very simply. The theme of "Human Family," for example, is that no matter how much people differ, they are basically alike.

Tone *See* **Mood and Tone**

Word Choice Word choice is the kind of language an author uses. Word choice is one of the elements that contribute to style.

See also **Style**

page 476

Glossary of Key Vocabulary

Glossary of Key Vocabulary

Many words have more than one meaning. The definitions in this glossary are for the words as they are introduced in the selections in this book.

Pronunciation Key

Symbols for Consonant Sounds

b	box	p	pan
ch	chick	r	ring
d	dog	s	bus
f	fish	sh	fish
g	girl	t	hat
h	hat	th	Earth
j	jar	th	father
k	cake	v	vase
ks	box	w	window
kw	queen	wh	whale
l	bell	y	yarn
m	mouse	z	zipper
n	pan	zh	treasure
ng	ring		

Symbols for Short Vowel Sounds

a	hat
e	bell
i	chick
o	box
u	bus

Symbols for Long Vowel Sounds

ā	cake
ē	key
ī	bike
ō	goat
yū	mule

Symbols for R-controlled Sounds

ar	barn
air	chair
ear	ear
īr	fire
or	corn
ur	girl

Symbols for Variant Vowel Sounds

ah	father
aw	ball
oi	boy
ow	mouse
oo	book
ü	fruit

Miscellaneous Symbols

shun	fraction
chun	question
zhun	division

Parts of an Entry

The entry shows how the word is spelled and how it is broken into syllables.

The pronunciation shows you how to say the word.

part of speech
n. for noun
v. for verb
adj. for adjective
adv. for adverb

be•gin (bi-**gin**) *v.* to start or do the first part *When will we **begin** to practice the play?*
Past tense: **began** *I **began** to learn my part last week.*

The definition gives the meaning of the word.

The sample sentence uses the word in a way that shows its meaning.

Sometimes there is additional information about the word.

page 477

A

a•buse (u-**byūs**) *n.* mean words or treatment *Many people work to prevent **abuse** of animals.*

ad•just (u-**just**) *v.* to get used to *It takes time to **adjust** to living in a new place.*

ad•vanced (ad-**vanst**) *adj.* up-to-date; the most recent *We are lucky to have the most **advanced** computers at our school.*

ad•ver•si•ty (ad-**vur**-su-tē) *n.* hard times; difficult situation *Facing and overcoming **adversity** made her a stronger person.*

ag•i•tat•ed (**aj**-u-tā-tid) *adj.* nervous; upset; worried *We became **agitated** by the news that a storm was coming.*

a•like (u-**līk**) *adj.* like one another *My sister and I look **alike**.*

an•nex (**an**-eks) *n.* a part added to a building *We are building an **annex** to our garage.*

appalling arrogance strong and shocking pride *He had few friends because of his **appalling arrogance**.*

a•pron (**ā**-prun) *n.* piece of clothing worn over a person's other clothes to protect them *When Mom cooks, she always wears an **apron**.*

at•ten•tion (u-**ten**-shun) *n.* care and thoughtfulness *The teacher asked us to give our full **attention** to the speaker.*

av•a•lanche (**av**-u-lanch) *n.* a sudden falling of snow or rock down a mountain *The hikers ran from the path of the **avalanche**.*

B

ba•bush•ka (bu-**büsh**-ku) *n.* a scarf worn over the head and tied under the chin *Her grandmother often wore a colorful **babushka**.*

bear fruit to produce ripe fruit in time for harvest *We hope our new apple tree will **bear fruit** this fall.*

be•long•ing (bi-**long**-ing) *n.* a comfortable feeling of being in the right place *She had no sense of **belonging** when she visited the country for the first time.*

ben•e•fit (**ben**-u-fit) *n.* a good result or reward for doing something *An enjoyable trip is a **benefit** of careful planning.*

board (bord) *n.* a flat piece of wood *He used a **board** to fix the fence.*

boast•ful (**bōst**-ful) *adj.* speaking with too much pride; bragging *She was **boastful** in talking about how many contests she had won.*

both•er (**both**-ur) *v.* to make an effort *I didn't **bother** to find out if Inez was home before I went to her house.*

bou•quet (bō-**kā**) *n.* a bunch of flowers *The child gave the princess a beautiful **bouquet**.*

bouquet

brag•gart (**brag**-urt) *n.* a person who brags or praises himself or herself too much *No one wants to be around a **braggart** for very long.*

bride (brīd) *n.* a woman about to be married or just married *The **bride** wore a beautiful long white dress.*

C

call-up notice a message from the Nazi police that ordered a person to be at a certain place at a certain time *They were frightened when they received the **call-up notice**.*

camp foreman the person in charge of workers in a camp *The **camp foreman** hires the workers.*

ca•nal (ku-**nal**) *n.* a waterway built by people *The **canal** carries water from the river to the fields of growing crops.*

ca•pa•bil•i•ty (kā-pu-**bil**-u-tē) *n.* the ability to do something well *He has the **capability** to become a good teacher.*

cap•ture (**kap**-chur) *v.* to take or catch by force *They used a trap to **capture** the skunk.*

cat•er•pil•lar (**kat**-ur-pil-ur) *n.* the worm-like stage in the life cycle of a butterfly or moth *A **caterpillar** is sometimes furry and colorful.*

page 478

cav•i•ty (**kav**-u-tē) *n.* a hole in a tooth *The dentist filled the **cavity** with a special hard material.*

cease (sēs) *v.* to stop *She asked me to **cease** the noise so she could talk on the phone.*

cel•e•brate (**sel**-u-brāt) *v.* to have special activities in honor of an event *We will **celebrate** my birthday with a visit to the zoo.*

cer•e•mo•ny (**sair**-u-mō-nē) *n.* a formal event *They wore their best clothes for the wedding **ceremony**.*

chal•lenge (**chal**-unj) *v.* to disagree with; take a stand against *He decided to **challenge** the rule about who could enter the contest.*

change (chānj) *n.* something different *Sunshine is a nice **change** after the rain.*

chron•i•cle (**kron**-u-kul) *n.* a record of events in the order in which they happened; history *He kept a **chronicle** of his trip across Africa.*

chrys•a•lis (**kris**-u-lis) *n.* the stage in the life of some insects when they are enclosed in a hard shell *A caterpillar changes into a **chrysalis**, and a **chrysalis** changes into a butterfly.*

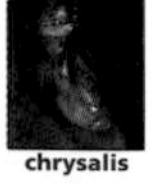
chrysalis

clev•er•ness (**klev**-ur-nis) *n.* intelligence *Her parents and teachers were amazed at the child's **cleverness**.*

col•o•niz•er (**kol**-u-nīz-ur) *n.* a plant or animal that moves to a new place to live *The tiny plant was a **colonizer** that did well in its new surroundings.*

com•bat (kom-**bat**) *v.* to fight against ***Combat** waste—recycle newspapers, cans, and glass!*

com•mon (**kom**-un) *adj.* ordinary *Our dog is not a special kind, he's just a **common** dog.*

com•mu•ni•ca•tion (ku-myū-nu-**kā**-shun) *n.* the sending and receiving of messages *Sign language is a means of **communication** for deaf people.*

com•mu•ni•ty (ku-**myū**-nu-tē) *n.* a group of people who live in the same neighborhood *We got to know everyone in our little **community** very quickly.*

com•pete (kum-**pēt**) *v.* to try to win a contest or game *My sister will **compete** in the spelling bee contest.*

con•ceit•ed (kun-**sē**-tid) *adj.* too proud of oneself *After she won the speech contest, she became very **conceited**.*

con•cen•trate (**kon**-sun-trāt) *v.* to focus on or think about only one thing *It's hard to **concentrate** on homework when the TV is on.*

concentration camp a place where prisoners of war are held *She lived to tell the story of her years in the **concentration camp**.*

con•di•tion (kun-**dish**-un) *n.* health or physical state *People who play sports must keep in good **condition**.*

con•duc•tor (kun-**duk**-tur) *n.* a leader or guide on a trip *The **conductor** led the group through the unfamiliar city.*

con•fi•dent (**kon**-fu-dunt) *adj.* feeling sure of yourself; believing in yourself *George was **confident** that he would pass the test.*

con•ti•nu•i•ty (kon-tu-**nü**-u-tē) *n.* going on or continuing in the same way *The **continuity** of their lives was interrupted by the war.*

con•ver•sa•tion (kon-vur-**sā**-shun) *n.* a friendly talk between two or more people *We had a long **conversation** on the telephone.*

crafts•man•ship (**krafts**-mun-ship) *n.* the skill or ability to do special work *The beautiful chair he made is an example of fine **craftsmanship**.*

crate (krāt) *n.* a box; container *Each **crate** was packed with oranges.*

cra•ter (**krā**-tur) *n.* a bowl-shaped hole at the top of a volcano *The scientists looked down into the volcano's **crater**.*

page 479

Glossary of Key Vocabulary

cre•a•tiv•i•ty (krē-ā-ti-vu-tē) *n.* the ability to think of new ideas and to express them *Her art showed great* ***creativity****.*

cru•el (krü-ul) *adj.* mean *It was* ***cruel*** *to tease Carla about her funny old shoes.*

crys•tal (kris-tul) *n.* very high quality glass that people value for its beauty *She has a collection of beautiful pieces of old* ***crystal****.*

crystal

cul•ture (kul-chur) *n.* arts, beliefs, customs, and traditions *I want to learn more about Japanese* ***culture****.*

cus•tom (kus-tum) *n.* a way of acting that is special to a nation or culture *In some countries it is the* ***custom*** *to bow when you meet someone.*

D

damp (damp) *adj.* slightly wet; moist *The house was cold and* ***damp*** *in winter.*

dan•gle (dang-gul) *v.* to hang down loosely *We watched the spider* ***dangle*** *from its thread.*

debt (det) *n.* money that is owed to another person *He saved his money to pay his* ***debt****.*

de•ci•sion (di-sizh-un) *n.* a choice *She could not make a* ***decision*** *about which job to take.*

declare war on to tell a country of plans to fight against it *Many people did not think the U.S. would* ***declare war on*** *Germany in 1941.*

de•light (di-līt) *v.* to make very happy *The trip to the zoo will* ***delight*** *the children.*

den•tist (den-tist) *n.* a doctor who cleans and repairs teeth *Your* ***dentist*** *will teach you how to take care of your teeth.*

de•ter•mined (di-tur-mund) *adj.* having one's mind set on doing something *Robert was* ***determined*** *to finish his work before dark.*

di•ar•y (dī-ur-ē) *n.* a notebook in which private thoughts are written *She wrote in her* ***diary*** *each night and kept it in a secret place.*

dike (dīk) *n.* a wall of stone or earth that holds back water *The* ***dike*** *protected the town from flooding.*

discriminate against to harm or treat differently from others because of color, race, age, or religion *When we* ***discriminate against*** *others, we are being unfair to them.*

dis•solve (di-zolv) *v.* to disappear; vanish *Mountains* ***dissolve*** *in the distance when we drive away from them.*

dome (dōm) *n.* a large round top *The building was covered by a* ***dome****.*

dream (drēm) *n.* a strong hope; an important goal *Her* ***dream*** *was to become a great actress.*

dull (dul) *adj.* not shiny *Coins become* ***dull*** *very quickly when many people handle them.*

E

earth•quake (urth-kwāk) *n.* a sudden movement of the earth *The* ***earthquake*** *damaged houses and bridges throughout a large area.*

ef•fect (u-fekt) *n.* result *The* ***effect*** *of the heavy rains was a dangerous flood.*

el•der (el-dur) *n.* an older person or leader *The village* ***elder*** *told the children stories and taught them old songs and dances.*

en•dan•gered (en-dān-jurd) *adj.* in danger of dying out or disappearing forever *For many years, the list of* ***endangered*** *animals grew very quickly.*

en•gaged (en-gājd) *adj.* promised in marriage *The* ***engaged*** *woman wore a large diamond ring.*

en•roll (en-rōl) *v.* to sign up *She will* ***enroll*** *at the middle school this year.*

en•vi•ron•ment (en-vī-run-munt) *n.* the air, land, and water that people, plants, and animals need to live *Each of us can do things to protect the* ***environment****.*

ep•i•dem•ic (ep-i-dem-ik) *n.* a sickness or disease that affects most of the people in a place *Our school was closed during the flu* ***epidemic****.*

page 480

e•rup•tion (i-rup-shun) *n.* a sudden, violent release of something *An* ***eruption*** *of ashes and lava poured out of the volcano.*

es•cape (e-skāp) *v.* to break loose or get free *They planned to* ***escape*** *by climbing over the high fence.*

ex•cel (ek-sel) *v.* to do something extremely well and better than others *The children in his family all* ***excel*** *in music.*

ex•cuse (ek-skyūs) *n.* a reason given for doing something *He used the hot day as an* ***excuse*** *for taking a nap.*

ex•haust•ed (eg-zaw-stid) *adj.* very tired *Sonia was* ***exhausted*** *after working all day in the garden.*

ex•o•dus (ek-su-dus) *n.* the move of a very large number of people from an area *There has been a recent* ***exodus*** *from the farm to the city.*

ex•pe•ri•ence (ek-spear-ē-uns) *n.* something that happens to a person *Meeting a bear in the woods is a frightening* ***experience****.*

ex•tinct (ek-stingkt) *adj.* not living anymore; gone forever *Dinosaurs are* ***extinct****.*

ex•tinc•tion (ek-stingk-shun) *n.* the end of life for a whole category of plants or animals *The blue whale was once hunted nearly to* ***extinction****.*

ex•traor•di•nar•y (ek-stror-du-nair-ē) *adj.* very unusual; special *He had an* ***extraordinary*** *ability to speak and write three languages well.*

F

fas•ten (fas-un) *v.* to attach; join; connect *When you get into a car, you should* ***fasten*** *your seat belt.*

feast (fēst) *n.* a large meal served for a special event *Mother spent hours preparing the Thanksgiving* ***feast****.*

fee (fē) *n.* money paid to do something *There was no* ***fee*** *for using the library.*

fill•ing (fil-ing) *n.* metal or other material used to fill a cavity *The new* ***filling*** *made my tooth feel much better.*

flat (flat) *n.* an apartment *Our* ***flat*** *has six rooms.*

flow (flō) *n.* a stream; steady movement *The* ***flow*** *of water ran across the sidewalk for hours.*

force (fors) **1.** *n.* power; energy *The* ***force*** *of the wind blew down trees.* **2.** *v.* to make something move *He tried to* ***force*** *open the door.*

free•dom (frē-dum) *n.* the state of not being under the control of another person *The American colonists won* ***freedom*** *from England.*

G

gar•ment (gar-munt) *n.* a piece of clothing *His favorite* ***garment*** *was an old jacket.*

ginger root the part of ginger, a spice plant, that grows underground ***Ginger root*** *adds an interesting flavor to foods.*

gloom•y (glü-mē) *adj.* sad; not cheerful *The rainy day made Kim feel* ***gloomy****.*

gold field a place where gold is found *People rushed to the* ***gold field*** *in hopes of becoming rich.*

grain (grān) *n.* the seed of wheat or other cereal grasses *The* ***grain*** *was used to make flour.*

gran•ar•y (gran-ur-ē) *n.* a place where grain is stored *After a good harvest, the* ***granary*** *will be full.*

granary

grape season the time of year when grapes are picked *Many workers are needed during* ***grape season****.*

page 481

H

har•vest (har-vist) *v.* to gather crops when they are ripe *Farmers use special machines to* ***harvest*** *their crops.*

harvest

harvest festival a celebration that takes place when harvest is over *Farmers and their families eat, dance, and play games at a* ***harvest festival****.*

hearing-impaired unable to hear or hear well *Teachers for* ***hearing-impaired*** *people learn special ways to help their students.*

his•tor•y (his-tur-ē) *n.* the story of a country and its people *We are studying the* ***history*** *of the United States.*

hos•til•i•ty (ho-stil-u-tē) *n.* hateful actions; mean thoughts *Their* ***hostility*** *toward us was plain to see by looking at their faces.*

hu•mil•i•a•tion (hyü-mil-ē-ā-shun) *n.* a feeling of shame or embarrassment *Her* ***humiliation*** *at being rudely scolded caused her to cry.*

hus•band (huz-bund) *n.* a man who is married *They have been* ***husband*** *and wife for ten years.*

I

ig•no•rance (ig-nur-uns) *n.* not having education or knowledge about something *He was not able to answer the question because of his* ***ignorance*** *on the subject.*

i•mag•ine (i-maj-un) *v.* to see something in your mind *Although I have never seen the place, I can* ***imagine*** *what it looks like.*

im•pres•sion (im-presh-un) *n.* idea *The painting gave me an* ***impression*** *of the sea.*

incomparable wisdom knowledge without equal or beyond compare *With her* ***incomparable wisdom****, she made the best decision possible.*

in•de•pen•dent (in-di-pen-dunt) *adj.* able to do things alone or without help *Learning to be* ***independent*** *is an important part of growing up.*

in•for•ma•tion (in-fur-mā-shun) *n.* facts *He collected all the* ***information*** *he could about teeth.*

in•spired (in-spīrd) *adj.* filled with ideas; encouraged to create *The* ***inspired*** *musicians wrote several new songs.*

in•ter•est•ed (in-tris-tid) *adj.* caring *An* ***interested*** *listener pays attention to the person who is speaking.*

in•ter•fere (in-tur-fear) *v.* to get in the way; block *It makes me angry when you* ***interfere*** *with the way I do things.*

in•tim•i•date (in-tim-u-dāt) *v.* to frighten *She tried to* ***intimidate*** *him by saying she would hit him if he didn't do what she wanted.*

in•vad•er (in-vā-dur) *n.* a person who enters a country by force to attack it or to steal *He watched a movie about an* ***invader*** *from space.*

in•va•sion (in-vā-zhun) *n.* the act of entering a country by force *The* ***invasion*** *of Poland by German troops began without warning.*

in•ven•tive (in-ven-tiv) *adj.* able to think of new ideas; creative *His* ***inventive*** *mind was full of plans for decorating his room.*

J

jour•ney (jur-nē) *n.* a trip *The* ***journey*** *across the ocean took almost a week by boat.*

K

ker•nel (kur-nul) *n.* a seed of corn or wheat *A* ***kernel*** *of corn was caught between his teeth.*

king•dom (king-dum) *n.* a country controlled by a king or queen *Children's stories often take place in a make-believe* ***kingdom****.*

L

labor camp a place where workers live *The employer cleaned up the* ***labor camp*** *before the workers arrived.*

land•ing (lan-ding) *n.* a flat area at the top of a number of steps *While climbing the stairs, she stopped to rest at the* ***landing****.*

page 482

land•lord (land-lord) *n.* a person who owns a building and takes money from others who live in it *Our* ***landlord*** *keeps our building in good repair.*

launch (lonch) *v.* to send into the air by force *The United States will* ***launch*** *a rocket into space this week.*

laun•dro•mat (lawn-dru-mat) *n.* a place of business with self-service washing machines and dryers *We take our dirty clothes to the* ***laundromat*** *every Saturday.*

la•va (lah-vu) *n.* hot melted rock that comes out of a volcano *The* ***lava*** *covered everything in its path as it flowed down the mountain.*

law (law) *n.* a rule made by the government that controls what people can and cannot do *Our town has a* ***law*** *to stop people from making a lot of noise.*

leg•a•cy (leg-u-sē) *n.* a thing or idea handed down from the past *His* ***legacy*** *to future generations was his belief in the importance of education.*

lev•ee (lev-ē) *n.* a wall of earth built along a river to prevent floods *They sat on the* ***levee*** *and watched the boats on the river.*

levee

lo•cal (lō-kul) *adj.* close to where you live, work, or go to school *We shop at the* ***local*** *markets and stores because they are convenient.*

lot (lot) *n.* a small piece of land *The empty* ***lot*** *was used as a playground by the neighborhood children.*

M

mag•ma (mag-mu) *n.* hot melted rock below the earth's surface *When* ***magma*** *reaches the earth's surface, it becomes lava.*

marsh (marsh) *n.* an area of low, wet land with grasses *A* ***marsh*** *may have fresh water or it may have salt water.*

matchless wit a clever and powerful mind that has no equal *Her* ***matchless wit*** *made everyone eager to talk with her.*

mat•ter (mat-ur) *v.* to be important *Nothing seems to* ***matter*** *when you are feeling bad.*

me•men•to (mu-men-tō) *n.* a reminder of the past; souvenir *The photograph was a* ***memento*** *of her vacation at the beach.*

me•mo•ri•al (mu-mor-ē-ul) *n.* something that keeps alive the memory of a person or event *The statue was a* ***memorial*** *to the great poet.*

mem•or•y (mem-ur-ē) **1.** *n.* the ability to remember *His* ***memory*** *is very good.* **2.** *n.* something remembered from the past *My* ***memory*** *of my fifth birthday is still very clear.*

mer•chant (mur-chunt) *n.* a person who sells things to make money *The* ***merchant*** *sold clothing for men, women, and children.*

migrant worker a person who moves from place to place to find work *The* ***migrant worker*** *stayed only a few weeks at each job.*

mi•gra•tion (mī-grā-shun) *n.* the move from one place to another by a group of people *The opening of new factories caused a* ***migration*** *of workers to the city.*

min•er (mī-nur) *n.* a worker who digs in the earth for minerals *The* ***miner*** *found gold in the mountain and became very rich.*

mon•u•ment (mon-yu-munt) *n.* something built to last a long time that honors a person or an event *The statue is a* ***monument*** *to the soldiers who fought in the war.*

mo•tive (mō-tiv) *n.* a reason for doing something *Her* ***motive*** *for phoning was to let her family know that she was all right.*

mur•al (myur-ul) *n.* a large picture painted on a wall or other large surface *Many people helped paint the* ***mural*** *on the bank building.*

page 483

Glossary of Key Vocabulary

N

net•work (**net**-wurk) *n.* a group of people or things that work together as one *He belongs to a **network** that helps deliver supplies in times of disaster.*

new•com•er (**nü**-kum-ur) *n.* a person who has recently come to an area *The class made the **newcomer** feel welcome.*

night•dress (**nīt**-dres) *n.* a loose garment worn in bed *Her old **nightdress** was soft and comfortable.*

O

ob•vi•ous (**ob**-vē-us) *adj.* clear *The thunder and lightning were **obvious** signs that a storm was coming.*

op•por•tu•ni•ty (op-ur-**tü**-nu-tē) *n.* a chance to do something *She was happy for the **opportunity** to earn some money of her own.*

or•di•nar•y (**ord**-un-air-ē) *adj.* not special; regular *We live in an **ordinary** neighborhood with ordinary neighbors.*

own (ōn) *v.* to have; possess *We do not **own** any pets but our friends let us play with the dog they **own**.*

own•er (**ō**-nur) *n.* the person to whom something belongs *Keith is the proud **owner** of a brand-new skateboard.*

P

pal•ace (**pal**-is) *n.* the home of a king or queen *The **palace** was built of beautiful stone and had more than 100 rooms.*

per•e•grine (**pair**-u-grin) *n.* a falcon; a hunting bird with a dark head, gray and white feathers, and a hooked bill ***Peregrine** falcons hunt and kill other birds for food.*

peregrine

per•mis•sion (pur-**mish**-un) *n.* approval to do something *We had **permission** from the farmer to walk across his land.*

pe•ti•tion (pu-**tish**-un) *n.* a form asking for change *Many people signed the **petition** for a new city park.*

plan•ta•tion (plan-**tā**-shun) *n.* a large farm with many workers *Crops from the **plantation** could feed many families.*

pol•lu•tion (pu-**lü**-shun) *n.* chemicals, dirt, smoke, and garbage that make the air, water, and soil unclean and unsafe ***Pollution** can harm or kill many living things.*

population shift a change in the number of people living in a certain area *The **population shift** lowered the number of farm families and increased the number of city families.*

por•tray (por-**trā**) *v.* to make a picture of *The pictures **portray** life as it was long ago.*

pow•er (**pow**-ur) *n.* the ability to make people do what you want *People can use their **power** to help others or hurt others.*

pre•oc•cu•pied (prē-**ok**-yu-pīd) *adj.* thinking about something else; lost in thought *She was so **preoccupied** that she didn't hear the knock on the door.*

pre•serve (pri-**zurv**) *v.* to keep safe; protect; keep the same from year to year *It will take a lot of work and money to **preserve** the old house.*

pres•sure (**presh**-ur) *n.* the energy used to press one thing against another *The **pressure** of the water caused the dam to break.*

pris•on•er (**priz**-u-nur) *n.* a person who is held in a place and not allowed to leave *The **prisoner** was kept in jail for three days.*

priv•i•lege (**priv**-u-lij) *n.* something special you get to do *It was a **privilege** for me to take dancing lessons.*

pro•vide (pru-**vīd**) *v.* to give or supply *My parents **provide** the money for my music lessons.*

page 484

Q

quilt (kwilt) *n.* a cover for a bed made of small pieces of cloth sewn together *Each piece of cloth in the **quilt** brought back a different memory.*

quilt

R

racial prejudice a dislike of people because of their race ***Racial prejudice** divides communities.*

re•al (**rē**-ul) *adj.* true; not imagined ***Real** stories are often more exciting than ones that are made up.*

re•ceive (ri-**sēv**) *v.* to get *I expect to **receive** a letter from my sister today.*

rec•og•nize (**rek**-ug-nīz) *v.* to know someone when you see him or her again *I will easily **recognize** her when I see her again.*

remarkably proud unusually pleased or satisfied *He was **remarkably proud** of himself for winning first place in the contest.*

rent (rent) *n.* money paid to live in an apartment or house that another person owns *We pay the **rent** for our house on the first day of every month.*

re•pair (ri-**pair**) *v.* to fix *She tried to **repair** the broken bowl so she could use it again.*

re•place (ri-**plās**) *v.* to put one thing in place of another *Mother couldn't find a new plate to **replace** the broken one.*

rep•re•sent (rep-ri-**zent**) *v.* to be an example or model of something *Some people think that cowboys **represent** the real West.*

re•shape (rē-**shāp**) *v.* to change into a new form *Can you **reshape** this ring so that it will fit my finger?*

re•spect (ri-**spekt**) *v.* to feel or show a high opinion of *We have great **respect** for our grandparents.*

re•ward (ri-**word**) *n.* money or a prize given for something a person does *He received a **reward** for finding and returning the bracelet.*

right (rīt) *n.* something that is allowed by law *Every adult citizen has the **right** to vote.*

rou•tine (rü-**tēn**) *n.* something that is done the same way all of the time *Part of my daily **routine** is to eat a good breakfast.*

runaway slave a person who tries to get away from someone who owns him or her *The **runaway slave** found freedom in the North.*

run•off (**run**-awf) *n.* rainfall that does not go into the ground, but runs from higher to lower ground *The **runoff** collected in the pools.*

S

se•cure (si-**kyur**) *adj.* safe; without worry or fear *She feels **secure** in the house when the doors are locked.*

seg•re•ga•tion (seg-ru-**gā**-shun) *n.* the separation of one group of people from another *Most people today believe that **segregation** is wrong.*

ser•i•ous (**sear**-ē-us) *adj.* thoughtful *He is a **serious** person and doesn't laugh very much.*

shack (shak) *n.* a small, poorly built house; hut *They hoped to move out of the **shack** into a better house.*

shed (shed) *v.* to lose by natural process *Some snakes **shed** their skins six times a year.* Past tense: **shed** *All the trees **shed** their leaves last month.*

shiv•er (**shiv**-ur) *v.* to shake with cold, fear, or excitement *The thought of walking home alone in the dark made him **shiver**.*

shock (shok) *n.* a great and sudden surprise *It was a **shock** to hear about his accident.*

short•age (**shor**-tij) *n.* too small a number or amount *There was a **shortage** of food and water after the flood.*

shrivel up to become dry and smaller in size *The crops began to **shrivel up** because there had been no rain for weeks.*

page 485

slav•er•y (**slā**-vur-ē) *n.* the custom or practice of owning slaves *In the United States, **slavery** ended more than one hundred years ago.*

space•man (**spās**-man) *n.* a man who comes from another planet *The **spaceman** arrived on Earth from Mars.* Plural: **spacemen** *The **spacemen** wore silver helmets.*

space•men (**spās**-men) the plural of **spaceman**

splin•ter (**splin**-tur) *n.* a small, thin, sharp piece of wood *A **splinter** in your finger can be quite painful.*

sprout (sprowt) *v.* to begin to grow *Certain seeds **sprout** very quickly.*

stair (stair) *n.* a set of steps that goes from one level or floor to the next *The **stair** went from the basement to the roof.*

sta•tion (**stā**-shun) *n.* a place that sends out radio signals *The **station** gives weather and traffic reports every hour.*

stay tuned stay on the same radio station *The announcer said, "**Stay tuned** for more news after these messages."*

steer (stear) *v.* to direct; guide *Can you **steer** me toward the library?*

sto•ry•tell•er (**stor**-ē-tel-ur) *n.* a person who tells stories *My little sister thinks grandma is the best **storyteller** at the library.*

stunned (stund) *adj.* greatly surprised *She was **stunned** to find the house on fire.*

sur•vive (sur-**vīv**) *v.* to live through a dangerous time or event *They were lucky to **survive** the terrible flood.*

sur•vi•vor (sur-**vī**-vur) *n.* an animal or plant that lives through a dangerous event *The pilot was the only **survivor** of the plane crash.*

swollen head a feeling of being better than others *He went around with a **swollen head** because he was the only student who got an A on the test.*

T

ta•ble•cloth (**tā**-bul-klawth) *n.* a cloth for covering a table, used especially at meals *Grandma always uses a special **tablecloth** for holiday meals.*

tack (tak) *n.* a small, sharp nail *He used a **tack** to hold the photo on the bulletin board.*

tai•lor (**tā**-lur) *n.* a person who makes and mends clothes to earn money *The **tailor** could easily fix the tear in her dress.*

temperate zone the area between the Tropic of Cancer and the Arctic Circle or between the Tropic of Capricorn and the Antarctic Circle *There are four distinct seasons in the countries of each **temperate zone**.*

tem•po•rar•y (**tem**-pu-rair-ē) *adj.* not permanent; for a limited time *My **temporary** summer job will end when school begins.*

threat (thret) *n.* words that tell of future harm *They made a **threat** to punish me if I didn't do my work.*

thrive (thrīv) *v.* to grow; do well *Plants **thrive** when they have water and light.*

tow•er (**tow**-ur) *n.* a tall and narrow structure or building *They could see for miles from the top of the **tower**.*

tower

trade (trād) *v.* to give one thing and take another in its place *Will you **trade** your apple for my orange?*

tra•di•tion (tru-**dish**-un) *n.* a way of acting that is passed from one generation to the next *Spending all our holidays together is a **tradition** in my family.*

trib•ute (**trib**-yūt) *n.* something given to show thanks or respect *The many flowers she received were a **tribute** to her wonderful performance.*

tri•umph (**trī**-umf) *n.* success; victory *We held a parade in honor of our team's **triumph**.*

page 486

trop•ics (**trop**-iks) *n.* the part of the earth's surface lying between the Tropic of Cancer and the Tropic of Capricorn *It is quite warm all year long in the **tropics**.*

U

un•a•like (un-u-**līk**) *adj.* different *He and his brother are **unalike** in most ways.*

un•der•world (**un**-dur-wurld) *n.* to ancient Greeks, the underground home for the dead *The hero of the mythical story traveled to the **underworld** to find his dead father.*

unusually clever more intelligent and creative than most people *He is **unusually clever** in the way he writes and says things.*

V

van•ish (**van**-ish) *v.* to disappear; fade *Clouds **vanish** quickly after a storm.*

va•ri•e•ty (vu-**rī**-u-tē) *n.* a number of different kinds *The **variety** in meals makes eating more interesting.*

vil•lage (**vil**-ij) *n.* a community that is smaller than a town *Anna knows everyone in her **village**.*

vil•lag•er (**vil**-i-jur) *n.* a person who lives in a village *The **villager** had a small garden and kept chickens.*

vine•yard (**vin**-yurd) *n.* a field where grapes are grown *Almost a hundred workers harvested grapes in the large **vineyard**.*

W

wash•room (**wosh**-rüm) *n.* a bathroom or a small room with a sink *We always like to know where the **washroom** is when we visit new places.*

wedding huppa a cloth supported on poles that a couple stands under when being married *The bride and groom said their vows under the **wedding huppa**.*

wetland wilderness low, wet land where people do not live *The **wetland wilderness** is now a national park.*

wetland wilderness

with•er (**with**-ur) *v.* to become dry *Plants **wither** when they don't get enough water.*

Y

year-round job a permanent job *He found a **year-round job** in his favorite city.*

page 487

Staff Development

Meeting the Multi-Level Challenge

English learners entering middle school come from a variety of backgrounds. Some bring a solid educational foundation from their native country. In their home language, they have developed academic skills that are on a par with their native English-speaking peers. Some of these students may be literate in languages such as Arabic, Russian, Chinese, or in other non-Roman alphabet scripts. Even with the challenge of a new written code to crack, these students already bring many of the skills and experiences that will help them succeed in a structured academic setting. They will be able to build on their academic foundation and draw upon an established repertoire of learning strategies as they approach the challenge of learning English and new academic content in English.

High Point offers standards-based instruction with specialized strategies for English learners.

Other English learners come with a patchwork of academic and life experiences. War, epidemics, natural disasters, or economic conditions may have caused students and their families to relocate within their home country or in other countries even before arriving in the U.S. School attendance may have been sporadic, with acquisition of skills and content more random than systematic. Such students may also be affected by the emotional aftermath of violence or trauma. Limited academic experiences and the lack of formal literacy skills create special challenges for these students and their teachers. However, the depth of their life experiences can also enrich learning for both peers and teachers.

Between these ends of the spectrum are English learners with every possible constellation of academic and life experiences. The goal of ***High Point*** is to ensure that each of these students succeeds in becoming a fluent speaker of English and moves into the academic mainstream at a level comparable to fluent English-speaking peers. How is it possible to meet this range of diverse needs?

One key part of the solution is to use standards-based instruction as the medium for learning English. The language arts, mathematics, science, and social studies content of ***High Point*** is aligned to national and state curriculum standards, ensuring that students gain important experience with key grade-level concepts, vocabulary, and themes as they progress towards fluency in English.

Another key part of ensuring success for all English learners is to tailor the instruction to students' stages of language acquisition. Language acquisition is a process that moves learners through predictable stages of language development on the path toward native-like fluency. However, the way individuals progress through these stages varies widely depending on many factors, including academic background, life experiences, learning styles, and other aspects of individual development. Progress along the pathway toward fluency is not always signalled by forward movement alone. Rather, a student who shows a growth spurt in acquiring new vocabulary, for example, may exhibit less control in using it grammatically. Such spurts and lags in language development are highly individual, and are a normal part of the language acquisition process. For this reason, it is important to identify where each student stands on the language acquisition continuum, and to then use the instructional strategies and techniques that will be most effective in creating continuing language growth and development.

High Point offers differentiated instruction for students across the stages of language acquisition. These differentiated instructional strategies and techniques are embedded throughout the **Teacher's Guide** (see the Multi-Level Strategies features), and are summarized on page T398 to help you target individual students with the most effective language development strategies for their stages of English acquisition.

The Stages of Language Acquisition

High Point *incorporates instructional strategies and techniques to help English learners move through the stages of language development.*

STAGES AND BEHAVIORS	TEACHING STRATEGIES
BEGINNING **Students with limited formal schooling:** • have a language acquisition profile that is similar to Early Beginning students • need lots of age-appropriate oral-to-print and emergent literacy experiences • understand new concepts best when they are previewed in their home language **Early Beginning students:** • need to gain familiarity with the sounds, rhythm, and patterns of English • understand simple messages presented with contextual support (gestures, role-play, etc.) • respond non-verbally by pointing, gesturing, nodding, or drawing • begin to respond with yes/no or one- or two-word answers • read simple language that has already been experienced orally • write labels, patterned sentences, one- or two-word responses **Advanced Beginning students:** • understand "chunks" or gist of language, and the gist of group reading by relying on picture clues, titles, and summaries • repeat and recite memorable language; use routine expressions independently • respond with phrases, fragments, and simple subject/verb-based structures • respond to literature with structured support • read familiar, patterned text; read Language Experience texts • write patterned text, short captions; complete simple cloze sentences	**BEGINNING** **Students with limited formal schooling benefit when teachers:** • implement an intensive individualized or small-group emergent literacy program • include them in group activities by using strategies for Beginning students • pair students with a "buddy" with the same home language **Beginning students benefit when teachers:** • provide abundant opportunities for active listening, utilizing props, visuals, and real objects • avoid forcing students to speak before they are ready • model memorable language with songs, raps, and poems • pair or group students with more proficient learners • activate prior knowledge, build background, and use visuals before reading activities • ask yes/no, either/or, and Who? What? Where? questions; have students complete sentences with one- or two-word responses • expose students to a variety of understandable texts • have students label/manipulate pictures and real objects • provide writing frames and models
INTERMEDIATE **Early Intermediate students:** • understand more details in spoken English • respond using longer phrases or sentences with increasing grammatical accuracy • respond using newly-acquired receptive vocabulary to form messages in English • read material independently following oral previews or experiences with print • respond to literature by explaining, describing, comparing, and retelling • write from models for a variety of purposes **Advanced Intermediate students:** • participate more fully in discussions, including those with academic content • understand and respond with increasing levels of accuracy and correctness • respond with connected discourse, using more extensive vocabulary • respond with higher-order language (persuade, evaluate, etc.) • read and comprehend a wider range of narrative genre and content texts • read, write, and discuss content-area concepts in greater depth • write connected narrative and expository texts	**INTERMEDIATE** **Intermediate students benefit when teachers:** • have students describe personal experiences, objects, etc. • structure group discussion • structure research projects and guide use of reference material for research • provide opportunities to create oral and written narratives • focus on communication in meaningful contexts where students express themselves in speech and print for a wide range of purposes and audiences • ask open-ended questions; model, expand, restate, and enrich student language • use graphic organizers or storyboards for retelling or role-plays • provide content-area texts, trade books, newspapers, magazines, etc., to promote conceptual development • respond genuinely to student writing and hold conferences that highlight student strengths and progress
ADVANCED **Early Advanced students:** • understand non-literal, idiomatic, everyday, and academic language • respond with connected discourse, extensive vocabulary, and decreasing grammatical errors • read a wider range of narrative and expository texts with increasing comprehension, including self-selected material • write using more standard forms with increased depth and breadth of topics and purposes and more creative and analytical writing **Advanced/Transitioning students:** • respond using varied grammatical structures and vocabulary comparable to native English speakers of the same age • read and write a range of grade-level texts in a variety of subjects • use a repertoire of language-learning strategies to self-monitor, correct, and further develop English language skills	**ADVANCED** **Advanced students benefit when teachers:** • structure group discussion • guide use of reference material for research • facilitate more advanced literature studies • provide for meaningful writing experiences in a variety of modes and forms (fiction, research, penpals, etc.) • publish student-authored stories, newsletters, bulletins, etc. • encourage drama, art, music, and other forms of creative expression to represent meaning and increase students' sense of aesthetics • continue on-going language development through integrated language arts and content-area activities

Good Teaching Practices for English Learners

*The **High Point** Teacher's Editions incorporate these instructional strategies to address the varying needs of English learners and to maximize growth in language and concept development.*

SET STUDENTS UP FOR SUCCESS!

In ***High Point*** students acquire English as they learn key grade-level curriculum. To allow students to maximize language learning while processing complex and abstract ideas, each unit begins in a way that sets students up for success:

- **Hands-On Experiences** Each unit is launched with a quick experiential activity that makes the theme of the unit concrete and explicit. For example, in a Community unit, individual students view a visual and list elements that they observe, then repeat the process with a group. This illustrates the powerful dynamics of a community, and the benefits and challenges of working together.
- **Unit Mind Map** As students debrief the Unit Launch activity, they begin to generate key vocabulary that is recycled and developed as the unit progresses. The Unit Mind Map provides an open-ended structure for collecting unit vocabulary, empowering students to take ownership of their learning while providing a structure to facilitate the processing of higher-order vocabulary.
- **Guiding Questions** Each unit explores two related themes. Guiding questions introduced at the outset of each theme establish some of the key ideas to explore through literature, language arts, and content activities. These questions give students an overview of the exploration they are about to undertake and serve as touchstones while the unit progresses. This process helps make learning objectives—and their mastery—visible to students, further empowering them as learners.

The ***High Point*** program is structured so that key ideas, vocabulary, and content are reviewed, revisited, and expanded at various points within and across courses. This spiraling helps students connect new learning to familiar material and provides an expanding contextual base to help students assimilate new language and concepts with increasing facility.

BUILD BACKGROUND AND ACTIVATE PRIOR KNOWLEDGE

All English learners—even those with limited or no formal schooling—have enough life experience and knowledge to acquire the complex concepts appropriate for middle school students. However, many students do not have a strong enough command of English to rely on spoken or written language alone to grasp new concepts. Here are two crucial strategies that build context for new concepts:

- **Activate Prior Knowledge** Before you introduce new concepts, review familiar, related concepts that help build context. When you invite students to share their experiences, it helps build a common knowledge base. For newly-arrived students, a quick preview in the home language is often the most effective way to ensure that students grasp a complex new concept. If you cannot provide this support, enlist the help of students, volunteers, or bilingual instructional assistants.
- **Build Background** When students have no prior experience with new concepts, common experiential activities, such as the Unit Launch experiences, will help build the concepts and vocabulary that allow students to grasp complex new concepts.

MAKE IT MEANINGFUL!

Imagine listening to a radio newscast in an unfamiliar language. How much do you think you would really comprehend? Help your students get as much meaning as possible from the language they experience:

- **Use Visuals** A picture is worth a thousand words—in any language! In addition to the visuals included in ***High Point***, you may wish to begin a picture file with images from magazines, Internet downloads, and content-area books. Although you may not consider yourself artistic, you'll be pleasantly surprised to see how much a simple sketch on the chalkboard can convey to your students! Real objects that students can hold and manipulate also help anchor new vocabulary and concepts in memory.
- **Use Graphic Organizers** Graphic organizers are concrete visuals that help students see the relationship between words and ideas. (See "Graphic Organizers" on pages T366–T367 for a variety of formats.) Quick sketches added to graphic organizers enhance the comprehensibility of these visuals for Beginners.
- **Body Language** Get creative with facial expressions, gestures, pantomime, and role-plays and see how much information you can convey!

- **Restate, Repeat, Reduce Speed** Once you become aware of these simple modifications, you can make your language more comprehensible and build new vocabulary. Incorporate familiar vocabulary and structures into your speech. After using a familiar word, pause and restate using a new expression. This paraphrasing helps link the meaning of new vocabulary to familiar terms. You should also be aware of the length, speed, and complexity of your speech, and modify it to fit your students' needs.

ENCOURAGE INTERACTION

When students learn through an interactive approach, lessons become more memorable and meaningful. Vocabulary and language patterns become anchored in memory, especially for kinesthetic learners.

- **Cooperative Learning** Cooperative learning activities provide a structure that allows students with varying levels of proficiency to participate meaningfully in group projects. These projects offer authentic communication for a wide range of meaningful purposes—from dealing with the logistics of choosing roles, to identifying resources and gathering information, to presenting findings. (See "Cooperative Learning Strategies" on pages T402–T403 for detailed descriptions.)
- **Interactive Writing** Dialogue journals provide a low-risk context for written student/teacher or peer exchanges. (See "Using Journals and Logs" on page T401 for details on journals, including dialogue journals.)

In an interactive approach, lessons are more memorable and meaningful.

CREATE MIXED GROUPINGS

If your class includes students at various levels of English proficiency, use heterogeneous groupings to turn this challenge to your advantage. When students at differing proficiency levels work together, they all must stretch their communication skills in order to accomplish their goals. This also builds a positive, cooperative learning environment.

LOOK AT LEARNING STRATEGIES

When students understand the strategies that help build language, they are empowered to support their own learning process.

- **Build Metacognitive Awareness** Be sure to familiarize students with the "Strategies for Learning Language" in the Handbook (see page T365). Encourage students to identify and share strategies they use successfully.
- **Reflect in Writing** Reflection logs or journals, learning logs, and peer- or self-evaluation all provide excellent opportunities for students to focus on the role of learning strategies in language development. (See "Using Journals and Logs" on page T401 for details.)
- **Capitalize on Cognates** Students' home languages can provide helpful information for building context and meaning. As you preview literature, encourage students to look for home-language cognates, and to see how much they already know! (See "English–Spanish Cognates" on pages T404–T405 for a list of some cognates in the literature selections.)

SEND LEARNING HOME

The *High Point Newsletters* (available in seven languages; see the **Teacher's Resource Book**) allow you to extend learning into students' homes, where families can participate in exploring unit themes in their home language.

CONNECT TO CULTURE

High Point reflects a wide range of cultural traditions. Extend this inclusive approach in your classroom by welcoming students' contributions about the cultural traditions they know best. When students respect each others' linguistic and cultural backgrounds, they will all feel more secure as they learn the language and culture of the United States. A comfortable, non-threatening classroom environment helps all learners achieve at optimum levels.

Using Journals and Logs

*Activities in **High Point** promote the use of journals and logs—essential tools for English learners.*

Self-expression is essential not only to second-language fluency, but also to the development of critical thinking. Journals and logs are, therefore, essential tools in the ESL classroom. There are many different forms and structures for these writing exercises. Some are impersonal and highly structured to promote a specific kind of thinking; others are free-form and more personal to promote fluency. Some include interactions with the teacher and/or peers; others are primarily for personal use.

Journals and logs enhance language instruction because they:

- engage students in non-threatening development of ideas and language
- provide records of students' thoughts, organization of ideas, language concepts, and reflections
- inspire students to see themselves as writers who set personal goals and self-monitor progress
- provide data for assessment of language development
- serve as a warehouse of ideas for future writing

TYPES OF JOURNALS AND LOGS

Dialogue Journal

Purpose: To focus the student's attention on targeted skills and provide modeling of conventions of English through a written conversation between a student and teacher or peers.

How to Use: Set up pages in two columns.

- Assign free writing or focus attention on a particular idea.
- Invite students to write in one column.
- Respond or invite peer response to the student's writing in the other.
- Use as a Reading Journal to discuss specific selections or as a free-form dialogue about topics of student interest.

Reflection Log or Journal

Purpose: To support development of specific critical thinking skills and to record information for use in follow-up activities.

How to Use: Set a focus for reflection such as identifying main ideas, defining an issue, developing solutions, or applying ideas to personal life.

- Ask students to record their reflections.
- Use as one-time exercises or invite students to continue adding thoughts to their journals as they study a complex topic.

Double- or Multiple-Entry Journal

Purpose: To structure responses for specific kinds of critical thinking.

How to Use: Set up pages in two columns.

- Ask students to title the columns for specific text features or information such as cause and effect, problem and solution, quotation and paraphrase, or literal meaning and interpretation.
- Invite students to respond with entries in each column.
- Expand the number of columns to focus on more than two aspects such as character/plot/setting or word/context/hypothesis/verification.

Learning Log

Purpose: To elicit prior knowledge about a topic, provide a framework for new learning, and intrinsically motivate students toward further study.

How to Use: Set up three columns on a page.

- Have students brainstorm what they already know about a topic in one column.
- Invite students to record questions they hope to answer during study in the second column.
- Encourage students to record answers to their questions during and following study of the topic in the third column.
- Encourage students to record new questions for further research.

Note-Taking Log

Purpose: To promote note-taking efficiency and language fluency and to support recall of information and vocabulary for future assignments.

How to Use: Assign a topic, language structure, or thinking focus for the activity.

- Invite students to take notes about the assigned focus.
- Expand to create a double-entry journal with one column for taking notes from the text and the other for recording the thoughts, questions, and reflections on the text.

Response Journal

Purpose: To provide a low-risk environment for self-expression through written personal responses to literature.

How to Use: Focus attention on a particular aspect of reading about a topic.

- Invite students to record personal thoughts.
- Encourage students to use entries to support evaluation of literature or other critical thinking activities.

Cooperative Learning Strategies

***High Point's** cooperative learning activities involve students of varying language proficiencies in content-rich activities.*

STRUCTURE & GRAPHIC	DESCRIPTION	BENEFITS & PURPOSES
ROLES FOR COOPERATIVE GROUPS 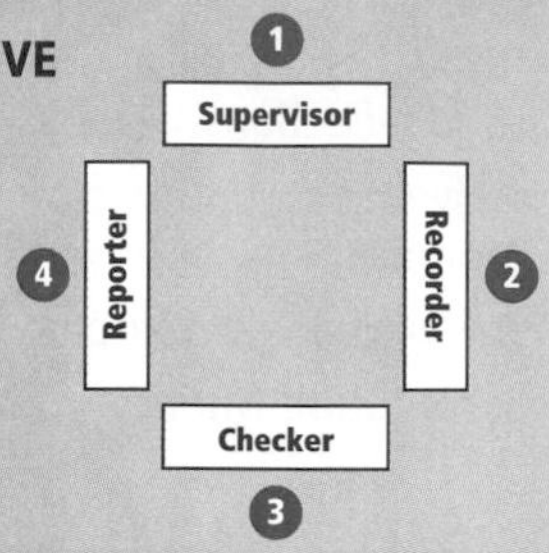	• Form groups according to the number of topics or aspects to be studied. • Assign roles, such as: Facilitator, Reporter Researcher, Materials Monitor Illustrator, Scribe (recorder) • Assign task or project. • Allow time for project completion. • Have groups present their projects.	• When used with heterogeneous groups, roles can be assigned based on language abilities. • Roles can be assigned according to skills or strengths of individuals or to stretch students' skills and abilities. • Assigning roles teaches cooperation and coordination skills. • Assigning roles enhances organizational skills of the group toward task completion.
CORNERS 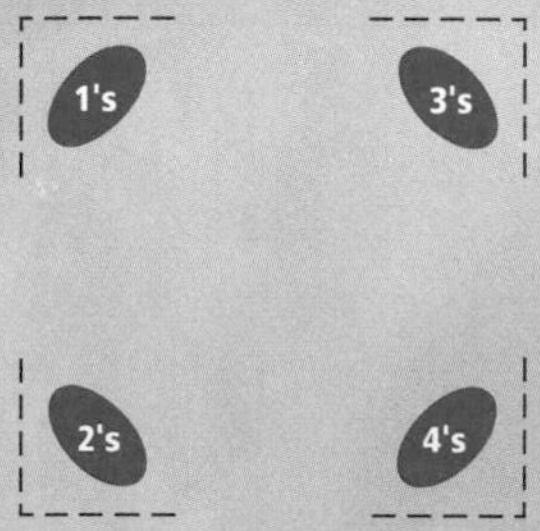	• Corners of the classroom are designated for focused discussion of four aspects of a topic. • Students individually think and write about the topic for a short time. • Students group into the corner of their choice and discuss the topic. • At least one student from each corner shares about the corner discussion.	• By "voting" with their feet, students literally take a position about a topic. • Focused discussion develops deeper thought about a topic. • Students experience many valid points of view about a topic.
FISHBOWL 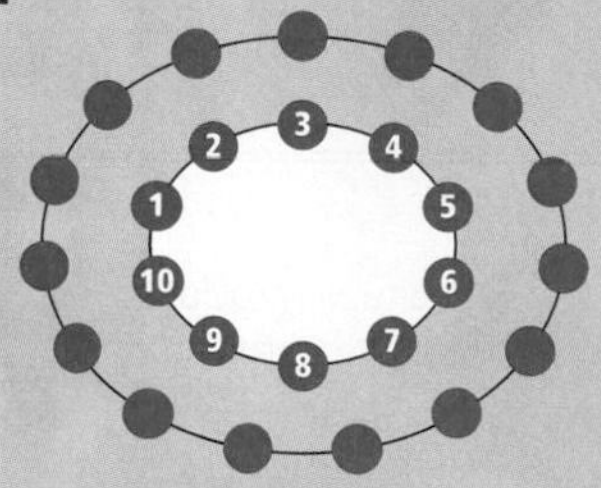	• One-half of the class sits in a close circle, facing inward; the other half of the class sits in a larger circle around them. • Students on the inside discuss a topic while those outside listen for new information and/or evaluate the discussion according to pre-established criteria. • Groups reverse positions.	• Focused listening enhances knowledge acquisition and listening skills. • Peer evaluation supports development of specific discussion skills. • Identification of criteria for evaluation promotes self-monitoring.
INSIDE-OUTSIDE CIRCLE 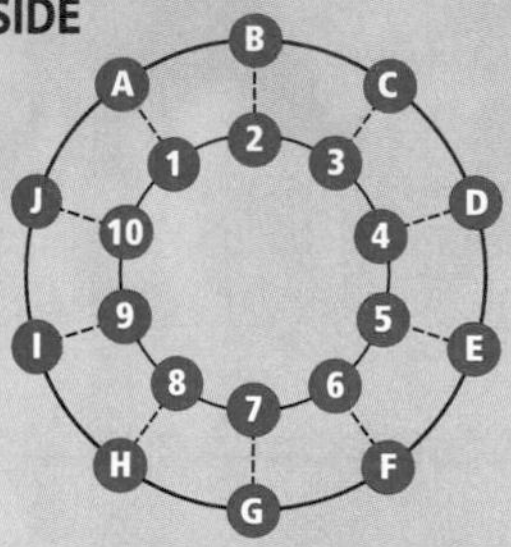	• Students stand in concentric circles facing each other. • Students in the outside circle ask questions; those inside answer. • On a signal, students rotate to create new partnerships. • On another signal, students trade inside/outside roles.	• Talking one-on-one with a variety of partners gives risk-free practice in speaking skills. • Interactions can be structured to focus on specific speaking skills. • Students practice both speaking and active listening.
JIGSAW 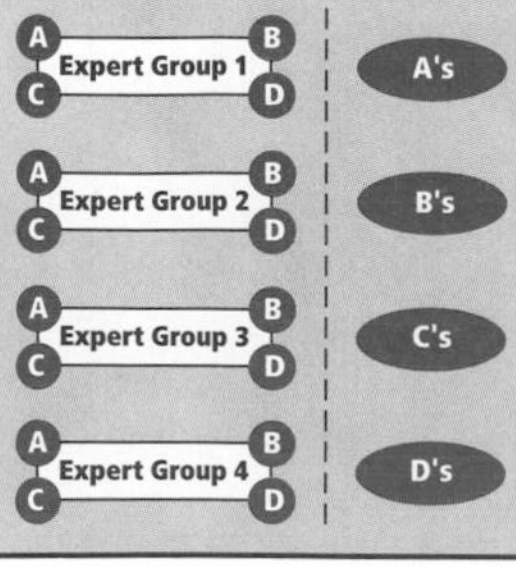	• Group students evenly into "expert" groups. • Expert groups study one topic or aspect of a topic in depth. • Regroup students so that each new group has at least one member from each expert group. • Experts report on their study. Other students learn from the experts.	• Becoming an expert provides in-depth understanding in one aspect of study. • Learning from peers provides breadth of understanding of over-arching concepts.

STRUCTURE & GRAPHIC	DESCRIPTION	BENEFITS & PURPOSES
NUMBERED HEADS 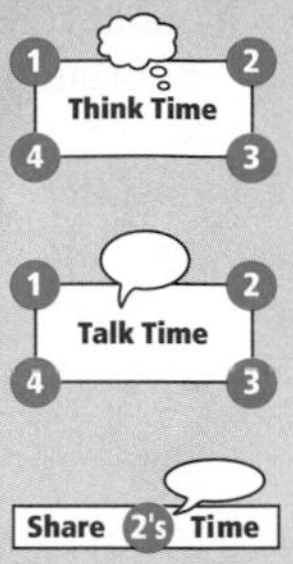	• Students number off within each group. • Teacher prompts or gives a directive. • Students think individually about the topic. • Groups discuss the topic so that any member of the group can report for the group. • Teacher calls a number and the student from each group with that number reports for the group.	• Group discussion of topics provides each student with language and concept understanding. • Random recitation provides an opportunity for evaluation of both individual and group progress.
ROUNDTABLE 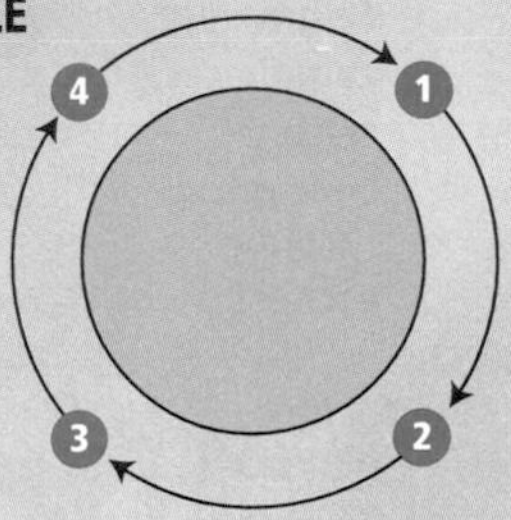	• Seat students around a table in groups of four. • Teacher asks a question with many possible answers. • Each student around the table answers the question a different way.	• Encouraging elaboration creates appreciation for diversity of opinion and thought. • Eliciting multiple answers enhances language fluency.
TEAM WORD WEBBING 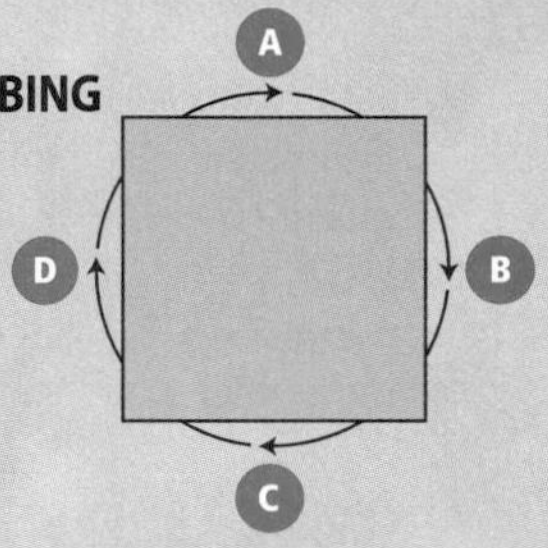	• Provide each team with a single large piece of paper. Give each student a different colored marker. • Teacher assigns a topic for a word web. • Each student adds to the part of the web nearest to him/her. • On a signal, students rotate the paper and each student adds to the nearest part again.	• Individual input to a group product ensures participation by all students. • Shifting points of view support both broad and in-depth understanding of concepts.
THINK, PAIR, SHARE 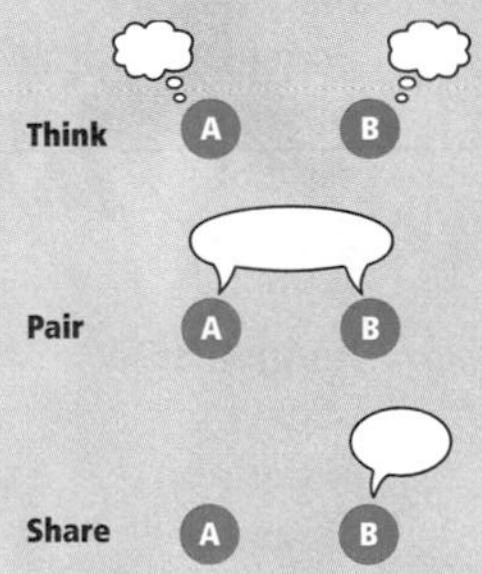	• Students think about a topic suggested by the teacher. • Pairs discuss the topic. • Students individually share information with the class.	• The opportunity for self-talk during individual think time allows the student to formulate thoughts before speaking. • Discussion with a partner reduces performance anxiety and enhances understanding.
THREE-STEP INTERVIEW 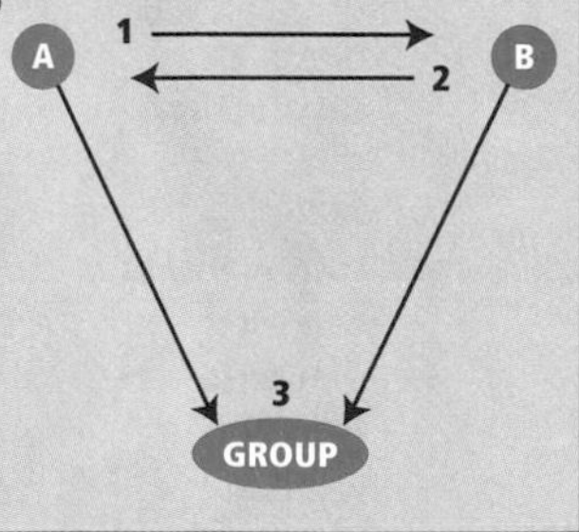	• Students form pairs. • Student A interviews student B about a topic. • Partners reverse roles. • Student A shares with the class information from student B; then B shares information from student A.	• Interviewing supports language acquisition by providing scripts for expression. • Responding provides opportunities for structured self-expression.

English–Spanish Cognates

When you call attention to these cognates, Spanish speakers will see how many English words they already know!

UNIT 1: COMMUNICATION

The Power of Poetry

hamburgers	hamburguesas
giraffe	jirafa
animals	animales
April	abril
August	agosto
memory	memoria
inventive	inventivo
creativity	creatividad
routine	rutina
concentrate	concentrar
study	estudio
literature	literatura
lines	líneas
attention	atención
person	persona
rhyme	rima
verse	verso
motives	motivos
criminals	criminales
recognize	reconocer
identify	identificar

Talking Walls

Diego Rivera's Murals

paint	pintar
pages	páginas
murals	murales
glorious	glorioso
history	historia
babies	bebés
tremendous	tremendo
energy	energía
revive	revivir
art	arte
form	forma
represent	representar
economy	economía
industry	industria
technology	tecnología

The Vietnam Veterans Memorial

Veterans	veteranos
names	nombres
monument	monumento
architect	arquitecto
result	resultado
extend	extender

False Cognates:

letters: *not* letras, *but* cartas

support: *not* soportar, *but* apoyar

Pablo Neruda's Gate

poet	poeta
military	militar
government	gobierno
secretly	secretamente
poems	poemas
surprised	sorprendido
published	publicado
favorite	favorito
admirers	admiradores
continue	continuar
visit	visitar

Tales Across Time

The Farmer's Tale

proclamation	proclamación
palace	palacio
insist	insistir
throne	trono
plantation	plantación
grain	grano
repeating	repitiendo
fortune	fortuna

The Clever Goatherd

invent	inventar
palace	palacio
announce	anunciar
guards	guardias
continue	continuar

Fat Men from Space

dentist	dentista
electricity	electricidad
galaxy	galaxia
imagining	imaginando
volume	volumen
rhythmical	rítmico
music	música
language	lenguaje
directions	direcciones
conversations	conversaciones
remote	remotas
navigation	navegación
atmosphere	atmósfera
affiliated stations	estaciones afiliadas
indicate	indicar
hamburgers	hamburguesas
panic	pánico
residents	residentes
fruits	frutas
vegetables	vegetales

UNIT 2: BELONGING

The Keeping Quilt

Anna	Ana
boots	botas
wagon	vagón
flowers	flores
day	día
Russia	Rusia
school	escuela
English	inglés
air	aire
border	borde
soup	sopa
tradition	tradición
use	usar
salt	sal
linen	lino
promise	promesa
celebrate	celebrar
George	Jorge
Mary Ellen	María Elena
fruit	fruta
Amazon	amazona
jungle	jungla

Human Family

serious	serios
comedy	comedia
variety	variedad
delight	deleitar
obvious	obvio

Beyond the Color Lines

Janell

Creator	Creador
customs	costumbres
ceremonies	ceremonias
reservation	reservación

Jenny

clarinet	clarinete
composer	compositor
collection	colección
mysteries	misterios
privileges	privilegios
accent	acento
personality	personalidad
respect	respetar
interesting	interesante

Christian

liturgy	liturgia
immigrant	inmigrante
politically	políticamente
energies	energías
similarities	similitudes

Teammates

prejudice	prejuicio
automobiles	automóviles
tanks	tanques
heroes	héroes
hotels	hoteles
restaurants	restaurantes
famous	famoso
compete	competir
intimidate	intimidar
excuse	excusa
humiliations	humillaciones
difficulties	dificultades
abuse	abuso
hostility	hostilidad
circulate	circular
petition	petición
provoke	provocar

Amir

India	India
appreciate	apreciar
community	comunidad
cauliflower	coliflor
route	ruta
concentration camp	campo de concentración
orchestra violinist	violinista de orquesta
arrest	arresto
admired	admirado

False Cognate:

fabric: *not* fábrica, *but* tela

Starting a Community Garden

interested	interesado
guardian	guardián
lot	lote
permission	permiso
individual	individuo

UNIT 3: DREAMS AND DECISIONS

Ginger for the Heart

fragrant	fragante
symbol	símbolo
devotion	devoción
solid	sólidos
harmonies	harmonías
miners	mineros
extinguish	extinguir
epidemic	epidemia
buttons	botones
firm	firme
banquet	banquete
satisfaction	satisfacción

Twins

communicate	comunicar
trimester	trimestre
diagnose	diagnosticar
establish	establecer
regularly	regularmente
independent	independiente
impact	impacto
exist	existir

The Great Migration

history	historia
migration	emigración
exodus	éxodo
industrial	industriales
movement	movimiento
conflict	conflicto
triumph	triunfo
adversity	adversidad
justice	justicia
dignity	dignidad
agents	agentes
ignored	ignorado
professionals	profesionales
doctors	doctores
patients and clients	pacientes y clientes
vote	votar

Follow the Drinking Gourd

escape	escapar
sympathizers	simpatizantes
secret	secreto
captured	capturados
conductor	conductora
directions	direcciones
fugitives	fugitivos

A House of My Own

spirit	espíritu
lottery	lotería
car	carro
ordinary	ordinarias
pass	pasar
temporary	temporal
tulips	tulipanes
concrete	concreto
porch	porche

UNIT 4: CONTINUITY AND CHANGE

The Mother Who Lost Her Daughter

Greece	Grecia
myths	mitos
chorus	coro
obey	obedecer
throne	trono
petals	pétalos
preserve	preservar
plant	plantar

Chrysalis Diary

chrysalis	crisálida
future	futuro
cataclysm	cataclismo
multitudes	multitudes
chronicle	crónica
import	importancia
diary	diario
dissolving	disolviendo
fragrant	fragante
distance	distancia

The Big Blast

volcano	volcán
eruption	erupción
avalanche	avalancha
register	registrar
pressure	presión
liquid	líquido
violently	violentamente
geologists	geólogos
blocks	bloques
valley	valle
column	columna
crater	cráter
predictions	predicciones
protect	proteger

Anne Frank

generations	generaciones
discriminate	discriminar
possessions	posesiones
annex	anexo
entrance	entrada
office	oficina
members	miembros
dentist	dentista
frustration	frustración
pages	páginas
bicycle	bicicleta
discover	descubrir
materials	materiales
detailed	detallado
devoted	devota
special	especial
imaginary	imaginario
publish	publicar
copy	copiar
paper	papel
prisoners	prisioneros
Poland	Polonia
conditions	condiciones
terrible	terrible
infirmary	enfermería
survive	sobrevivir
popular	popular
museum	museo
inspiration	inspiración

False Cognate:
support: *not* soportar, *but* apoyar

The Diary of a Young Girl

diary	diario
balcony	balcón
agitated	agitada
visions	visiones
visiting	visitando
suspense	suspenso
silence	silencio
apparently	aparentemente
disappeared	desaparecieron
exhausted	exhausta
refrigerator	refrigerador
suffocating	sofocando
creature	criatura
note	nota
impression	impresión
destination	destino

False Cognates:
present: *not* presente, *but* regalo
library: *not* librería, *but* biblioteca

UNIT 5: CHALLENGES

Saving the Peregrine Falcon

scientists	científicos
differences	diferencias
admired	admirado
ability	habilidad
produce	producir
Central America	América Central
insects	insectos
calcium	calcio
nature	naturaleza
combat	combatir
laboratory	laboratorio
mountain	montaña
incubator	incubadora
evaporate	evaporar
air	aire
prevent	prevenir
repair	reparar
contact	contacto
identify	identificar
animals	animales
adult	adulto
substitute	substituto
ignorance	ignorancia
destroy	destruir
numbers	números

False Cognate:
parents: *not* parientes, *but* padres

A Celebration of the Everglades

vast	vasto
mysterious	misterioso
extinction	extinción
poet	poeta
photographer	fotógrafo
tropics	trópicos
horizon	horizonte
zone	zona
crocodiles	cocodrilos
orchids	orquídeas
dedicate	dedicar
preserved	preservado
unique	único
biologists	biólogos
engineers	ingenieros
restore	restaurar

The Circuit

constant	constante
education	educación
rose	rosa
stables	establos
kerosene	queroseno
lamp	lámpara
instinctively	instintivamente
control	control
muscles	músculos
acid	ácido
nervous	nervioso
instinct	instinto
trumpet	trompeta
professor	profesor

False Cognates:
introduced: *not* introdujo, *but* presentó
pretending: *not* pretendiendo, *but* imaginando

The Clever Wife

solution	solución
gratitude	gratitud
honest	honesto
arrogance	arrogancia
impossible	imposible
respectfully	respetuosamente

High Point Scope and Sequence

Language Development and Communication

LEVELS	THE BASICS	A	B	C
SOCIAL AND ACADEMIC LANGUAGE FUNCTIONS				
Listen actively	●	●	●	●
Repeat spoken language	●			
Express social courtesies	●	●		
Ask and answer questions	●	●	●	
Use the telephone	●	●		
Conduct a transaction	●	●		
Demonstrate non-verbal communication	●	●	●	●
Adjust communication to the occasion or audience (formal/informal)		●	●	●
Express likes and dislikes	●	●	●	●
Express feelings, needs, opinions, intentions	●	●	●	●
Give and carry out commands	●	●	●	
Describe people, places, things, events	●	●	●	●
Listen to a preview of a selection	●	●		
Listen to a selection	●	●	●	●
Recite	●	●	●	●
Read a selection	●	●	●	●
Give/Follow directions	●	●	●	●
Role-play	●	●	●	●
Dramatize	●	●	●	●
Ask for/Give information	●	●	●	●
Make comparisons	●	●	●	●
Engage in discussion	●	●	●	●
Persuade		●	●	●
Retell a story	●	●	●	●
Tell an original story		●	●	●
Define and explain		●	●	●
Clarify		●	●	●
Verify or confirm information		●	●	●
Justify		●	●	●
Elaborate		●	●	●
Negotiate		●	●	●
Write	●	●	●	●
LANGUAGE PATTERNS AND STRUCTURES				
Statements	●	●		
Statements with *There is/are/was/were* and *Here is/are/was/were*	●	●		
Statements with infinitives	●	●		
Questions/Exclamations/Commands	●	●	●	
Negative sentences	●	●	●	
Complete sentences		●	●	●
Compound sentences		●	●	●
Complex sentences		●	●	●
Relative clauses			●	●
Compound-complex sentences				●
Conditional sentences			●	●
Pronouns and pronoun agreement	●	●	●	●

LEVELS	THE BASICS	A	B	C
LANGUAGE PATTERNS AND STRUCTURES, continued				
Demonstrative pronouns	●	●		
Indefinite pronouns			●	●
Adjectives	●	●	●	●
Adjectives that compare		●	●	●
Modals (*can, could, would, might, must,* etc.)	●	●	●	●
Present tense verbs	●	●	●	●
Past tense verbs	●	●	●	●
Future tense verbs	●	●	●	●
Present perfect tense verbs		●	●	●
Past perfect tense verbs			●	●
Future perfect tense verbs			●	●
Progressive forms of verbs	●	●	●	●
Two-word verbs		●	●	●
Active/passive voice			●	●
Gerunds			●	●
Contractions	●	●	●	
Adverbs	●	●	●	
Adverbs that compare		●	●	●
Prepositions	●	●	●	

Concepts and Vocabulary

LEVELS	THE BASICS	A	B	C
EVERYDAY CONCEPTS AND VOCABULARY				
Greetings and other social courtesies	●	●		
Personal information (name, address, etc.)	●	●		
Categories: Clothing, Food, School, etc.	●	●		
ACADEMIC CONCEPTS AND VOCABULARY				
In Language Arts and Literature	●	●	●	●
In Science, Social Studies, Mathematics	●	●	●	●
In Fine Arts: Music, Art, Drama		●	●	●
VOCABULARY STRATEGIES				
Relate words	●	●	●	●
Structural clues	●	●	●	●
Compound words	●	●		
Prefixes and suffixes	●	●	●	●
Latin and Greek roots			●	●
Context clues	●	●	●	●
Multiple-meaning words	●	●	●	●
Idioms	●	●	●	●
Figurative language			●	●
Analogies			●	●
Denotation and connotation			●	●
Locate and use definitions		●	●	●
Locate word origins			●	●

Reading

LEVELS	THE BASICS	A	B	C
LEARNING TO READ				
Use concepts of print (directionality, etc.)	•			
Recognize high-frequency words	•	•		
Develop phonemic awareness	•			
Associate sounds and symbols	•			
Blend sounds to decode words	•			
Recognize word families	•	•	•	•
Use word patterns to decode words	•			
Use letter patterns to decode words	•			
Identify root words and inflectional endings	•	•	•	
Identify root words and affixes	•	•	•	•
Recognize Greek and Latin roots			•	•
Divide words into syllables	•			
Identify syllable types	•			
Read multisyllabic words	•	•	•	•
Build reading fluency	•	•	•	•
READING STRATEGIES				
Pre-Reading Strategies	•	•	•	•
Activate prior knowledge/Relate to personal experience	•	•	•	•
Preview	•	•	•	•
Build background	•	•	•	•
Predict	•	•	•	•
Set a purpose for reading	•	•	•	•
Relate reading rate to purpose		•	•	•
Skim		•	•	•
Scan			•	•
Use graphic organizers to prepare for reading	•	•	•	•
Self-Monitoring Strategies	•	•	•	•
Ask questions	•	•	•	•
Clarify	•	•	•	•
Visualize	•	•	•	•
Paraphrase	•	•	•	•
Use visuals	•	•	•	•
Relate to personal knowledge or experience	•	•	•	•
Compare selection to other texts with similar theme, genres, or text structures	•	•	•	•
Make, confirm, and revise predictions	•	•	•	•
Adjust purposes for reading		•	•	•
Confirm word meaning	•	•	•	•
Use punctuation clues	•	•		
Use signal words	•	•		
Corrective Strategies	•	•	•	•
Reread	•	•	•	•
Read on	•	•	•	•
Search for new clues		•	•	•
Adjust reading rate	•	•	•	•
Reduce the amount of text read at one time		•	•	•
Use reference aids (glossary, dictionary, etc.)		•	•	•

LEVELS	THE BASICS	A	B	C
READING STRATEGIES, continued				
Comprehension Strategies ***(See also Comprehension)***	•	•	•	•
Review	•	•	•	•
Connect new information to known	•	•	•	•
Use text structures	•	•	•	•
Use text and graphic features	•	•	•	•
Use graphic organizers to relate ideas	•	•	•	•
Retell	•	•	•	•
Use SQ3R			•	•
Summarize	•	•	•	•
COMPREHENSION				
Follow directions	•	•	•	•
Identify details	•	•	•	•
Classify	•	•	•	•
Identify character's traits, feelings, point of view, motive	•	•	•	•
Identify sequence	•	•	•	•
Identify steps in a process	•	•	•	•
Identify or relate cause and effect	•	•	•	•
Identify or relate main idea and details	•	•	•	•
Identify or relate problem and solution	•	•	•	•
Identify or relate goal and outcome	•	•	•	•
Make comparisons	•	•	•	•
Make an inference	•	•	•	•
Draw conclusions	•	•	•	•
Summarize	•	•	•	•
Form generalizations			•	•
Identify author's purpose		•	•	•
Identify author's biases and point of view		•	•	•
Identify author's assumptions and beliefs			•	•
Analyze story elements	•	•	•	•
Analyze information	•	•	•	•
Distinguish between facts and opinions	•	•	•	•
Recognize missing information				•
Identify fallacies of logic				•
Identify multiple levels of meaning			•	•
Distinguish between fantasy and reality	•	•	•	•
Distinguish between relevant and irrelevant information			•	•
Distinguish between important and unimportant information		•	•	•
Distinguish between apparent message and hidden agenda			•	•
Form opinions	•	•	•	•
Make judgments or decisions	•	•	•	•
Support judgments	•	•	•	•
Identify propaganda		•	•	•
Evaluate information		•	•	•
Synthesize information			•	•
Recognize how personal background and viewpoint influence interpretation of a selection		•	•	•

Literary Analysis and Appreciation

LEVELS	THE BASICS	A	B	C
RECOGNIZE GENRES				
Article	•	•	•	•
Autobiography		•	•	•
Biographical fiction			•	•
Biography	•	•	•	•
Character Sketch		•	•	•
Description	•	•	•	•
Diary/Journal	•	•	•	•
Documentary				•
Drama		•	•	•
Essay	•	•	•	•
Fable		•	•	•
Family portrait/Self-portrait		•	•	
Fantasy		•	•	•
Fiction	•	•	•	•
Folk tale/Legend	•	•	•	•
Historical account	•			•
Historical fiction	•	•	•	•
How-to article	•	•	•	•
Interview	•	•	•	•
Memoir/Personal narrative	•	•	•	•
Myth	•	•	•	•
Nonfiction	•	•	•	•
News article/Newscast	•	•	•	•
Persuasive essay		•	•	•
Photo or art essay	•	•	•	•
Play		•	•	•
Poetry	•	•	•	•
Rhymed verse	•	•	•	•
Free verse	•	•	•	•
Proverb/Saying		•	•	•
Quotation		•	•	•
Realistic fiction	•	•	•	•
Report	•	•	•	•
Science article	•	•	•	•
Science fiction		•	•	•
Song/Chant	•	•	•	•
Speech			•	•
Short Story			•	•
Tall tale	•	•		
RECOGNIZE LITERARY DEVICES				
Alliteration		•	•	•
Allusion				•
Analogy				•
Assonance and consonance			•	•
Characterization	•	•	•	•
Compressed language				•
Description		•	•	•

LEVELS	THE BASICS	A	B	C
RECOGNIZE LITERARY DEVICES, continued				
Dialect				•
Dialogue		•	•	•
Figurative language		•	•	•
Hyperbole/Exaggeration		•	•	•
Imagery/Sensory language		•	•	•
Simile		•	•	•
Metaphor		•	•	•
Personification			•	•
Irony				•
Mood and tone		•	•	•
Narrator's Point of view		•	•	•
Onomatopoeia			•	•
Plot development	•	•	•	•
Goal and outcome or Problem and solution	•	•	•	•
Conflict/Complications/Climax/Resolution		•	•	•
Rising and falling action			•	•
Flashback			•	•
Foreshadowing			•	•
Suspense				•
Repetition		•	•	•
Rhyme	•	•	•	•
Rhyme scheme			•	•
Rhythm/meter		•	•	•
Setting	•	•	•	•
Style		•	•	•
Symbolism			•	•
Theme		•	•	•
Word choice		•	•	•
RESPOND TO LITERATURE				
Interpret literature	•	•	•	•
Apply literature to personal life	•	•	•	•
Identify questions of personal importance and answer them through literature	•	•	•	•
Develop personal preferences in reading	•	•	•	•
Recognize how literature expands and enriches personal viewpoints and experiences	•	•	•	•
Recognize that literature may elicit a variety of valid responses	•	•	•	•
EVALUATE LITERATURE				
Evaluate the impact of literary devices, medium, or genre on meaning or quality		•	•	•
Evaluate the impact of the author's background, qualifications, biases, or point of view on meaning		•	•	•
Evaluate the impact of culture, time period, customs, or outlooks on meaning		•	•	•
Evaluate the literary quality of a selection		•	•	•
Compare literature on a variety of points (theme, genre, point of view, etc.)		•	•	•
Recognize the defining characteristics of classical literature (timelessness, universality of themes, etc.)			•	•

Cognitive Academic Skills

LEVELS	THE BASICS	A	B	C
LEARNING STRATEGIES				
Strategies for Language Learning	•	•	•	•
Listen to and imitate others	•	•	•	•
Recite songs and poems	•	•	•	•
Use gestures and mime to get across an idea	•	•	•	•
Explore alternate ways of saying things	•	•	•	•
Test hypotheses about language	•	•	•	•
Ask for help, feedback, and clarification	•	•	•	•
Use visuals to construct meaning	•	•	•	•
Compare nonverbal and verbal cues	•	•	•	•
Compare and contrast elements of language and identify patterns in language	•	•	•	•
Incorporate language "chunks"	•	•	•	•
Use reference aids to verify language/spelling		•	•	•
Practice new language (repeating, etc.)	•	•	•	•
Analyze situations to determine appropriate language use (formal/informal)		•	•	•
Self-monitor language use and self-assess	•	•	•	•
Strategies for Reading *See page T331*	•	•	•	•
Strategies for Listening, Speaking, Viewing, Representing, Writing	•	•	•	•
Activate prior knowledge	•	•	•	•
Relate to personal knowledge or experience	•	•	•	•
Predict	•	•	•	•
Ask questions	•	•	•	•
Clarify		•	•	•
Visualize		•	•	•
Paraphrase		•	•	•
Connect new information to known	•	•	•	•
Review		•	•	•
Make comparisons	•	•	•	•
Use graphic organizers	•	•	•	•
Interact with peers	•	•	•	•
Plan and set goals	•	•	•	•
Brainstorm	•	•	•	•
Generate and organize ideas	•	•	•	•
Gather information	•	•	•	•
Make observations	•	•	•	•
Take notes	•	•	•	•
Outline		•	•	•
Summarize	•	•	•	•
Self-monitor and self-assess	•	•	•	•
STRATEGIES FOR TAKING TESTS				
Read directions carefully		•	•	•
Plan time for each item/section		•	•	•
Clarify vocabulary in passages/questions		•	•	•
Use typographic clues to meaning		•	•	•
Reread passages to clarify information		•	•	•
Note test format and select appropriate strategies		•	•	•
Mark answers and check for legibility		•	•	•

LEVELS	THE BASICS	A	B	C
CRITICAL THINKING				
Classify	•	•	•	•
Relate events in a sequence	•	•	•	•
Relate steps in a process	•	•	•	•
Relate cause and effect	•	•	•	•
Relate main ideas and details	•	•	•	•
Relate problem and solution	•	•	•	•
Relate goal and outcome	•	•	•	•
Formulate questions	•	•	•	•
Formulate hypotheses			•	•
Clarify information		•	•	•
Make comparisons	•	•	•	•
Make inferences	•	•	•	•
Draw conclusions	•	•	•	•
Summarize	•	•	•	•
Form generalizations			•	•
Analyze information	•	•	•	•
Form opinions	•	•	•	•
Make judgments or decisions	•	•	•	•
Evaluate information		•	•	•
Synthesize information			•	•
Generate ideas	•	•	•	•
Solve problems	•	•	•	•
RESEARCH SKILLS				
Use the research process	•	•	•	•
Locate resources (library, computerized card catalog, *Reader's Guide*, etc.)	•	•	•	•
Gather information	•	•	•	•
Use alphabetical order		•		
Survey/Skim and scan/Look up key words		•	•	•
Use print resources	•	•	•	•
almanac			•	•
atlas, globe	•	•	•	•
books	•	•	•	•
dictionary		•	•	•
thesaurus			•	•
encyclopedia			•	•
magazines and newspapers		•	•	•
Use electronic resources: CD-ROM, electronic encyclopedia, the Internet		•	•	•
Use audio-visual resources	•	•	•	•
Use graphic aids (charts, time line, etc.)	•	•	•	•
Conduct observations, surveys, experiments, and interviews	•	•	•	•
Take notes	•	•	•	•
Organize and synthesize information from multiple sources		•	•	•
Generate new research questions			•	•
Write a research report		•	•	•
Cite sources			•	•

Listening, Speaking, Viewing, and Representing

LEVELS	THE BASICS	A	B	C
LISTENING AND SPEAKING				
Listen actively	•	•	•	•
Listen for information	•	•	•	•
Listen critically to determine purpose and message		•	•	•
Listen to a poem or song	•	•	•	•
Listen to a selection	•	•	•	•
Listen and speak effectively in a discussion	•	•	•	•
Listen and speak effectively in a peer conference		•	•	•
Listen and speak effectively to work with a partner or on a team	•	•	•	•
Speak at an appropriate rate and volume		•	•	•
Make eye contact		•	•	•
Use language and tone appropriate to the audience, purpose, and occasion		•	•	•
Give and follow directions or commands	•	•	•	•
Express feelings, needs, ideas, and opinions	•	•	•	•
Describe	•	•	•	•
Ask and answer questions	•	•	•	•
Conduct an interview	•	•	•	•
Recite	•	•	•	•
Read aloud	•	•	•	•
Role-play or dramatize	•	•	•	•
Retell a story	•	•	•	•
Tell a story		•	•	•
Inform or explain	•	•	•	•
Give an oral report		•	•	•
Give a speech		•	•	•
Persuade		•	•	•
Participate in a debate		•	•	•
Demonstrate non-verbal communication	•	•	•	•
REPRESENTING IDEAS AND INFORMATION				
Create graphic organizers	•	•	•	•
Create illustrations or photographs	•	•	•	•
Create posters and other visual displays	•	•	•	•
Create a map	•	•	•	•
Create a multimedia presentation		•	•	•
VIEWING				
Respond to a visual image	•	•	•	•
Interpret a visual image	•	•	•	•
Identify visual symbols	•	•	•	•
View critically to determine purpose and message		•	•	•
Recognize various types of mass media		•	•	•
Compare and evaluate media		•	•	•

Writing

LEVELS	THE BASICS	A	B	C
HANDWRITING				
Letter formation and spacing	•			
Left-to-right directionality	•			
WRITING PURPOSES, MODES, AND FORMS				
Write for a variety of purposes and audiences	•	•	•	•
Choose the mode and form of writing that works best for the topic, audience, and purpose		•	•	•
Write in a variety of modes	•	•	•	•
Narrative	•	•	•	•
Expository	•	•	•	•
Descriptive	•	•	•	•
Expressive	•	•	•	•
Persuasive		•	•	•
Write in a variety of forms	•	•	•	•
Biography	•	•	•	•
Character sketch		•	•	•
Critique		•	•	•
Description	•	•	•	•
Diary/Journal entry	•		•	•
E-mail/ Internet page		•	•	•
Essay		•	•	•
Fact sheet	•	•	•	•
Letter	•	•	•	•
Magazine/News article/Newscast		•	•	•
Myth			•	
Paragraph	•	•	•	•
Personal narrative/ Self-portrait/ Memoir	•	•	•	•
Persuasive essay		•	•	•
Play				•
Poem/Rhyme/Song	•	•	•	•
Poster	•	•	•	•
Quickwrite		•	•	•
Report	•	•	•	•
Sentences	•	•	•	•
Speech		•	•	•
Story		•	•	•
Summary		•	•	•
WRITING PROCESS				
Prewriting	•	•	•	•
Analyze published and student models		•	•	•
Brainstorm and collect ideas	•	•	•	•
Choose a topic	•	•	•	•
Plan writing with an FATP Chart (**F**orm, **A**udience, **T**opic, **P**urpose)		•	•	•
Organize ideas	•	•	•	•

Writing, continued

LEVELS	THE BASICS	A	B	C
WRITING PROCESS, continued				
Drafting	●	●	●	●
Write to communicate ideas	●	●	●	●
Use writing techniques appropriate to the purpose, audience, and form		●	●	●
Use appropriate organizing structures	●	●	●	●
logical order	●	●	●	●
sequential order	●	●	●	●
spatial order		●	●	●
to make comparisons	●	●	●	●
to show causes and effects		●	●	●
to show goals and outcomes	●	●	●	●
to show problems and solutions	●	●	●	●
to show thesis and supporting arguments		●	●	●
Revising	●	●	●	●
Evaluate the draft	●	●	●	●
Participate in peer-conferencing		●	●	●
Add, elaborate, delete, combine, and rearrange the text to improve the draft	●	●	●	●
Editing and Proofreading	●	●	●	●
Check the revised copy for correct conventions of written English and make corrections	●	●	●	●
Use reference materials (dictionary, etc.)		●	●	●
Publishing	●	●	●	●
Create the final version of the work and prepare it for publication, using visuals or multimedia to complement or extend meaning	●	●	●	●
Reflect and Evaluate		●	●	●
Use rubrics to evaluate the work		●	●	●
Use evaluations to set goals as a writer		●	●	●
WRITER'S CRAFT				
Introductions that catch the reader's interest		●	●	●
Effective conclusions		●	●	●
Word choice: colorful, specific, precise words; vocabulary appropriate for the audience, etc.	●	●	●	●
Effective sentences		●	●	●
Combine sentences		●	●	●
Break up run-on sentences		●	●	●
Sentence variety		●	●	●
Effective paragraphs	●	●	●	●
Topic sentence and supporting details	●	●	●	●
Transition words			●	●
Consistent verb tense and point of view			●	●
Show, don't tell		●	●	●
Include important or interesting information		●	●	●
Exclude unnecessary details		●	●	●
Elaborate		●	●	●
Use visual and organizational aids	●	●	●	●
Develop a personal voice or style			●	●
Constantly evaluate the writing		●	●	●
Keep a writing portfolio	●	●	●	●

Grammar, Usage, Mechanics, Spelling

LEVELS	THE BASICS	A	B	C
SENTENCES				
Sentence types	●	●	●	●
Negative sentences	●	●	●	●
Conditional sentences			●	●
Sentence structures	●	●	●	●
Phrases		●	●	●
Clauses		●	●	●
Simple sentences	●	●	●	●
Compound sentences		●	●	●
Complex sentences		●	●	●
Compound-complex sentences				●
Properly placed clauses and modifiers			●	●
Subjects and predicates		●	●	●
Complete subject		●	●	●
Simple subject		●	●	●
Understood subject (*you*)		●	●	●
It as the subject (*It* is raining)		●	●	●
Compound subject			●	●
Complete predicate		●	●	●
Simple predicate (verb)		●	●	●
Compound predicate			●	●
Complete sentences/Fragments		●	●	●
Subject–verb agreement	●	●	●	●
PARTS OF SPEECH				
Nouns	●	●	●	●
Common and proper	●	●	●	●
Count and noncount	●	●	●	●
Plurals	●	●	●	●
Possessive	●	●	●	●
Articles		●	●	●
Pronouns	●	●	●	●
Subject	●	●	●	●
Object	●	●	●	●
Possessive	●	●	●	●
Reflexive		●	●	●
Indefinite		●	●	●
Demonstrative	●	●	●	●
Relative			●	●
Adjectives	●	●	●	●
Adjectives that compare		●	●	●
Verbs	●	●	●	●
Action	●	●	●	●
Linking	●	●	●	●
Modals (*can, could, would, might, must,* etc.)	●	●	●	●
Helping	●	●	●	●
Transitive and intransitive verbs			●	●

Grammar, Usage, Mechanics, Spelling, continued

LEVELS	THE BASICS	A	B	C
PARTS OF SPEECH, continued				
Verb tenses	•	•	•	•
Present tense	•	•	•	
Habitual present tense	•	•	•	•
Past tense (regular and irregular)	•	•	•	•
Future tense	•	•	•	•
Present perfect tense		•	•	•
Past perfect tense			•	•
Future perfect tense			•	•
Progressive forms of verbs	•	•	•	•
Two-word verbs		•	•	•
Active/passive verbs			•	•
Gerunds				•
Participial phrases				•
Contractions		•	•	•
Adverbs	•	•	•	•
Adverbs that compare		•	•	•
Prepositions and prepositional phrases	•	•	•	•
Conjunctions		•	•	•
Interjections		•	•	•
CAPITALIZATION				
First word of a sentence	•	•		
Pronoun *I*	•	•		
Proper nouns	•	•	•	•
Abbreviations of proper nouns	•	•	•	•
Proper adjectives	•	•	•	•
In letters		•	•	•
In titles		•	•	•
In direct quotations		•	•	•
PUNCTUATION				
Period	•	•	•	•
Question mark	•	•	•	•
Exclamation mark	•	•	•	•
Comma		•	•	•
Apostrophe	•	•	•	•
Quotation marks		•	•	•
Colon			•	•
Semicolon			•	•
Dash			•	•
Hyphen			•	•
Italics			•	•
Underline			•	•
Parentheses			•	•
SPELLING				
Use spelling strategies	•	•	•	•
Memorize reliable rules	•	•	•	•

Technology/Media

LEVELS	THE BASICS	A	B	C
TECHNOLOGICAL LITERACY				
Identify forms, purposes and functions of technology		•	•	•
Operate a computer		•	•	•
Operate audio and visual recording devices		•	•	•
USING TECHNOLOGY				
Use e-mail		•	•	•
Use audio, video, and electronic media to generate ideas, gather information, conduct interviews, etc., during the writing process	•	•	•	•
Use word-processing software		•	•	•
Use desktop publishing or multiple media to publish work		•	•	•
Use the Internet and other technology to locate resources		•	•	•
Evaluate quality and reliability of information from electronic resources		•	•	•
Make databases and spreadsheets			•	•
MEDIA STUDY AND MULTIMEDIA PRESENTATIONS				
Evaluate and select media for presentations (based on message, purpose, audience)		•	•	•
Design and create multimedia presentations		•	•	•
Compare print, visual, and electronic media			•	•
Explain how the use of different media affects the message			•	•

Cultural Perspectives

LEVELS	THE BASICS	A	B	C
MULTICULTURAL AWARENESS AND APPRECIATION				
Connect personal experiences and ideas with those of others	•	•	•	•
Compare oral traditions, folk tales, and literature across regions and cultures	•	•	•	•
Read and conduct research to increase knowledge of many cultures		•	•	•
Understand that language and literature are the primary means by which culture is transmitted			•	•
Recognize universal themes that cross cultures		•	•	•
Appreciate the diversity of cultures and generations	•	•	•	•
Appreciate and share aspects of the home, U.S., and world culture	•	•	•	•
History	•	•	•	•
Language	•	•	•	•
Folklore and literature	•	•	•	•
Symbols	•	•	•	•
Holidays, customs, and traditions	•	•	•	•
Political systems and government	•	•	•	•
Media		•	•	•

Audio Scripts for Building Language and Vocabulary

The Studio page T13

Narrator: *Look at the picture on page 12. Listen to what a group of students say about it.*
Kim: Hey—Felicia, Roberto—come take a look at this great painting!
Roberto: Wow! Neat!
Felicia: Well. . . .Do your really like it, Kim? It looks kind of odd to me.
Kim: Yes, I do like it. What's so odd about it?
Felicia: Do you see those little things that look like eyes? I think they're weird. I like the colors, though.
Roberto: Do you think gray's a good color? It seems pretty dull to me.
Kim: What about the red and yellow? They make the painting exciting.
Felicia: I think the whole thing is confusing. What is it supposed to be, anyway?
Roberto: It's called "The Studio." A studio is where an artist paints. Do you think the figure with the three eyes is the artist?
Felicia: I don't have a clue what it is, or what the whole thing's about.
Kim: I don't think it has to be about anything. Maybe it's just supposed to be whatever you think it is.

The Rooster and the Jewel page T144

Narrator: *Look at the pictures on page 144 as you listen to the Vietnamese tale, "The Rooster and the Jewel."*
Voice: The Rooster and the Jewel: A Vietnamese tale

There was a rooster who became separated from his flock. He was hungry. He was weak. The rooster pecked here and there around the countryside for any food he could find. He pecked under logs. He pecked under leaves. He pecked around rocks. He pecked through pebbles.

Suddenly the rooster paused. He stared at a stone on the ground. This stone was different from the other stones. This stone was very shiny.

The rooster walked around the stone. He looked at it from one side. He looked at it from another side. Then he said, "Humans would call you a jewel. They would fight to the death for you. But to me, you are worth less than a kernel of corn." And the starving rooster stepped over the beautiful jewel and continued pecking.

Pollution Control page T294

Narrator: *Look at the photos on page 294 in your book. Now, listen to this persuasive message about protecting the ocean environment.*
Voice: I'm here today to talk to you about a problem that is of great concern to me. That problem is the pollution of our seas and oceans.

It is no exaggeration to say that people have produced more toxic wastes in the last 50 years than they had produced in the previous several hundred years. No matter how we try to get rid of our waste, most of it ends up in the ocean. Pollution has fouled many parts of our oceans and killed off many kinds of plants and animals that live there. If we want to save our oceans, we cannot continue to use them as all-purpose dumps. It is clear that the situation will only become worse unless we do something about it. We need to pass laws to control pollution, and we cannot do this without your help. I urge you to join the fight by repeating the words of famous oceanographer and environmentalist Jacques Cousteau. Cousteau had worked in his profession for only a short time when he realized the need for speedy action. He said, "The time has come when speaking is not enough, applauding is not enough. We have to act." I urge you, every time you have an opportunity, make your opinions known by physical presence. Do it!"

HATCHET page T328

Narrator: *Study the painting on page 328. Then listen to this excerpt from* Hatchet *by Gary Paulsen*

Voice 1: Thirteen-year-old Brian Robeson started out by air to visit his father in Canada. When the pilot died, Brian took on the frightening task of landing the plane by himself. That was only the first of a series of difficulties he had to overcome. He was left lost and alone in the wilderness with only a hatchet. He had to struggle to find food, shelter, water, and other things that had always been provided for him. One of the most difficult times Brian faced was the night of the terrible storm.

Voice 2: The tornado tore one more time at the shore on the opposite side of the lake—Brian could hear trees being ripped down—and then it was done, gone as rapidly as it had come. It left nothing, nothing but Brian in the pitch dark. He could find nothing of where his fire had been, not a spark, nothing of his shelter, tools, or bed, even the body of the foolbird was gone. I am back to nothing he thought, trying to find things in the dark—back to where I was when I crashed. Hurt, in the dark, just the same.

As if to emphasize his thoughts the mosquitoes—with the fire gone and protective smoke no longer saving him—came back in thick, nostril-clogging swarms. All that was left was the hatchet at his belt. Still there. But now it began to rain and in the downpour he would never find anything dry enough to get a fire going, and at last he pulled his battered body back in under the overhang, where his bed had been, and wrapped his arms around his ribs.

Sleep didn't come, couldn't come with the insects ripping at him, so he lay the rest of the night, slapping mosquitoes and chewing with his mind on the day. This morning he had been fat—well, almost fat—and happy, sure of everything, with good weapons and food and the sun in his face and things looking good for the future, and inside of one day, just one day, he had been run over by a moose and a tornado, had lost everything and was back to square one. Just like that.

A flip of some giant coin and he was the loser.

But there is a difference now, he thought—there really is a difference. I might be hit but I'm not done. When the light comes I'll start to rebuild. I still have the hatchet and that's all I had in the first place.

Index

Program Features and Resources

Reading and Learning Strategies, Critical Thinking, and Comprehension

Language and Vocabulary

Index, continued

Literary Concepts

Listening and Speaking

Viewing

Representing

Writing

Index, continued

Writing, continued

Grammar, Usage, Mechanics, and Spelling

Technology and Media

Research Skills

Index, continued

Instructional Strategies

Acknowledgments, continued

The Bodley Head: (non-U.S. rights) "The Clever Wife" from *Sweet and Sour: Tales From China* by Carol Kendall and Yao-wen Li. Published by The Bodley Head.

Carolrhoda Books, Inc.: Excerpt from *Saving the Peregrine Falcon* by Caroline Arnold. Photos by Richard R. Hewett. Copyright © 1985 by Caroline Arnold. Published by Carolrhoda Books, Inc., Minneapolis, MN. Used by permission of the publisher. All rights reserved.

Chappell & Co., Inc.: "The House I Live In." Words and music by Lewis Allan and Earl Robinson. Copyright © 1942 (renewed) Chappell & Co., Inc. (ASCAP). All rights reserved. Used by permission.

Jewell Reinhart Coburn: "Legendary Origin of Vietnam" and "Rooster and the Jewel" from *Beyond the East Wind*, an award winning collection of Vietnamese folktales by Jewell Reinhart Coburn, Ph.D.

Dell Publishing, a division of Random House, Inc.: "Neshmayda and Suzette Aguayo" from *The Book of Twins* by Debra and Lisa Ganz, with Alex Tresniowsky. Photographs by Bill Ballenberg. Copyright © 1998 by Byron Preiss Visual Publications, Inc. and Dreammaker, Inc. Photographs copyright © 1998 by Bill Ballenberg. Used by permission of Dell Publishing, a division of Random House, Inc.

Doubleday, a division of Random House, Inc.: "Diary entry for July 8, 1942" from *The Diary Of A Young Girl—The Definitive Edition* by Anne Frank. Otto H. Frank & Mirjam Pressler, editors. Translated by Susan Massotty, translation copyright © 1995 by Doubleday, a division of Bantam Doubleday Dell Publishing Group, Inc. Used by permission of Doubleday, a division of Random House, Inc.

Florida Trend: "An Ominous Cloud Over The Everglades" by Marjory Stoneman Douglas. Copyright © 1988 *Florida Trend Magazine*.

Victoria Forrester: "In Music Meeting" from *Song and Dance* by Victoria Forrester.

Groundwood Books/Douglas & McIntyre: "Ginger for the Heart" from *Tales from Gold Mountain*. Text copyright © 1989 by Paul Yee. Illustrations copyright © 1989 by Simon Ng. First published in Canada by Groundwood Books/Douglas & McIntyre. Reprinted by permission of the publisher.

Harcourt, Inc.: Selected excerpts from *Teammates* by Peter Golenbock. Text copyright © 1990 by Golenbock Communications, Inc. Illustrations copyright © 1990 by Paul Bacon. Selections from *Sawgrass Poems: A View Of The Everglades* by Frank Asch. Text copyright © 1996 by Frank Asch, Introduction and Notes copyright © 1996 by Ted Levin, photographs copyright © 1996. Reprinted by permission of Harcourt, Inc.

HarperCollins Publishers: *Amir* by Paul Fleischman. Text copyright © 1997 by Paul Fleischman. "Starting a Community Garden" from *City Green* by DyAnne DiSalvo-Ryan. *The Great Migration* by Jacob Lawrence. Copyright © 1993 by The Museum of Modern Art, New York, and The Phillips Collection. "Chrysalis Diary" from *Joyful Noise: Poems for Two Voices* by Paul Fleischman. Text copyright © 1988 by Paul Fleischman. "The Mother Who Lost Her Daughter" from *The Robber Baby: Stories from the Greek Myths* by Anne Rockwell. Copyright © 1994 by Anne Rockwell. All used by permission of HarperCollins Publishers.

HarperCollins Publishers, Inc. William Morrow: "Open Letter to a Young Negro" by Jesse Owens, from *Blackthink* by Jesse Owens and Paul G. Neimark. Copyright © 1970 by Jesse Owens and Paul G. Neimark. Reprinted by permission of HarperCollins Publishers, Inc. William Morrow.

Holiday House, Inc.: "Janell" and "Jenny" from *Under Our Skin: Kids Talk About Race* by Debbie Holsclaw Birdseye. Text copyright © 1997 by Debbie Holsclaw Birdseye and Tom Birdseye. Photographs copyright © 1997 by Robert Crum. All rights reserved. Used by permission of Holiday House, Inc.

Henry Holt and Company, LLC: *Anne Frank* by Yona Zeldis McDonough. Text copyright © 1991, 1997 by Yona Zeldis McDonough. Reprinted by permission of Henry Holt and Company, LLC.

Houghton Mifflin Co.: (U.S. rights) "The Clever Wife" from *Sweet and Sour: Tales From China* by Carol Kendall and Yao-wen Li. Copyright © 1978 by Carol Kendall and Yao-wen Li. Reprinted by permission of Clarion Books/Houghton Mifflin Co. All rights reserved.

Alfred A. Knopf, a division of Random House, Inc.: "We're All in the Telephone Book" and "Mother to Son" from *Collected Poems* by Langston Hughes. Copyright © 1994 by the Estate of Langston Hughes. Excerpt from *Follow the Drinking Gourd* by Jeanette Winter. Copyright © 1988 by Jeanette Winter. All reprinted by permission of Alfred A. Knopf, a division of Random House, Inc.

David Krieger: From "Captain Cousteau's Legacy: Rising to Our Full Stature as Human Beings" by David Krieger, at Nuclear Age Peace Foundation website: www.wagepeace.org.

John Malone: "Bath" from *Poetry Playground* Course Materials by John Malone. Copyright © 1999 by John Malone. All rights reserved. Used by permission.

NASA/JPL/Caltech: "Mars Network." Courtesy of NASA/JPL/Caltech.

New Moon Publishing: "The Storyteller" by Dawn Lippert. Reprinted, with permission, from *New Moon ®: The Magazine For Girls And Their Dreams*, copyright New Moon Publishing, Duluth, MN.

Daniel Pinkwater: *Fat Men From Space* by Daniel Pinkwater. **Random House:** "Human Family" from *I Shall Not be Moved* by Maya Angelou. Copyright © 1990 by Maya Angelou. Reprinted by permission of Random House, Inc.

Scholastic: "Questions and Answers About Poetry" adapted from *A Fire in My Hands, a Book of Poems* by Gary Soto. Copyright © 1990 by Scholastic Inc. Reprinted by permission.

Simon & Schuster: "Christian Tico" from *Quilted Landscape: Conversations With Young Immigrants* by Yale Strom. Copyright © 1996 Yale Strom. *The Keeping Quilt* by Patricia Polacco. Copyright © 1988 Patricia Polacco. *Volcano: The Eruption and Healing of Mount St. Helens* by Patricia Lauber. Copyright © 1986 Patricia Lauber. Selected excerpts from *Hatchet* by Gary Paulsen. Copyright © 1987 Gary Paulsen. All reprinted with the permission of Simon & Schuster Books for Young Readers, an imprint of Simon & Schuster Children's Publishing Division.

Gary Soto: "Big Eaters," "Letter to a Father Working in Tulare, California," and "What They Don't Tell You About Cereal." Text copyright © 1999 by Gary Soto. Used with permission of the Author and BookStop Literary Agency.

Tilbury House Publishers: Untitled segment from "Diego Rivera" and "Vietnam Veterans Memorial" from *Talking Walls* by Margy Burns Knight. Copyright © 1992, Tilbury House, Publishers. Untitled segment from "Pablo Neruda" from *Talking Walls: The Stories Continue* by Margy Burns Knight © 1996, Tilbury House, Publishers.

University of New Mexico Press: Selected excerpts from *The Circuit* by Francisco Jiménez. Copyright © 1997 by Francisco Jiménez. Reprinted with permission from University of New Mexico Press.

World Almanac Group: "Looking for Life Elsewhere in the Universe" from *World Almanac for Kids*. Reprinted with permission from *The World Almanac for Kids 1998*. Copyright © 1997 World Almanac Education Group. All rights reserved.

Photographs:

AFF/AFS/Amsterdam: ppT273, T274, T277 (Auguste van Pels, Peter van Pels, Hermann van Pels, Otto Frank, James Kleiman, © AFF/AFS/Amsterdam), ppT273, T274, T277 (script from diary, Anne with neighbor, Miep Gies, © AFF/AFS/Amsterdam).

Angie Aguayo: ppT161-T163 (twins photos, © Angie Aguayo).

AP/Wide World Photos: ppT104, T113 (detail), pT105 (baseball players, © AP/Wide World Photos), pT106 (Ted Williams, © AP/Wide World Photos), pT107 (Robinson, © AP/Wide World Photos), pT112 (Major League, © AP/Wide World Photos), pT326 (Jesse Owens, © AP/Wide World Photos), pT273 (Anne with Hannah Goslar, © AP/ Wide World Photos).

Archive Photos: pT105 (stadium, © Henry Hammond/Archive Photos), pT109 (Pee Wee Reese, © Archive Photos), pT111 (Jackie Robinson, © New York Times Co./Archive Photos), pT111 (Crosley Field, © APA/Archive Photos), pT111 (Pee Wee Reese, © Sporting News/Archive Photos), pT259 (German soldier with warning sign, © Popperfoto/Archive Photos), pp T258, T259, T260, T265, T266, T270, T275, T276 (Anne Frank family photos, © Anne Frank Fonds, Basel/Anne Frank House Amsterdam/Archive Photos), ppT256, T257 (arrested Jews, Jews enroute to camps, © Archive Photos), pT345, © Janet Sommer/Archive Photos).

Art Resource: p18 (telescope, Scala/Art Resource, NY), ppT292, T293 (*Endangered Species*, Andy Warhol silkscreen, frog inset, © 2000 Andy Warhol Foundation for the Visual Arts, ARS, New York/Art Resource, NY).

Banco de México Diego Rivera & Frida Kahlo Museums Trust: pT26 (The Mechanization of the Country, © 2000 Banco de México Diego Rivera & Frida Kahlo Museums Trust and Schalkwijk/Art Resource, NY).

Cascada Expediciones: pT31 (fence, © Luis Hernan Herreros Infante/Cascada Expediciones).

CMCD: pT36 (books, gramophone, telephone, television, telephone cords, power cords, clock and computer: CMCD, type block: Glenn Mitsui, Chinese text and English text: Steve Cole), pT37 (power cords and type block: CMCD).

CORBIS: (All © CORBIS) p18 (Jules Verne), pT27 (Rivera), pT28 (Lin), pT29 (Vietnam Memorial), pT30 (Neruda), pT106 (Paige), pT110 (Reese/Robinson), pT137 (family), pT290 (mountain background), pT291 (Mt. Everest), ppT250-T251 (flag), ppT250, T251 (soldiers at Normandy), pT213 (crescent moon), ppT254, T258, 271, 278 (inset), p256 (German aircraft, German at Pearl Harbor), pT257 (soldiers on coast of Normandy), pT261 (movable bookcase), pT277 (Miep Gies), pT282 (earthquake), pT287 (Toussaint), pT311 (Kissimmee River), pT327 (race), pT342 (harvesters), pT344-T345 (stairs), pT386 (giving a speech), pT429 (gold miner), pT448 (storm damage), pT478 (astronaut), pT480 (disabled athlete), pT485 (satellite).

Cordon Art B.V.-Baarn-Holland: pT214 "Sky and Water I" by M.C. Escher © 2000. All rights reserved.

Corel: (All © Corel) p18 (Mayan ruin), pT216 (column), pT313 (crane), pT313 (Everglades at sunset), pT432 (manatee), pT441 (alligator), pT441 (egret), pT443 (Sahara Desert), pT444 (ballet dancer), pT446 (fireworks).

Digital Stock: pT36 (Earth), pT482 (launch).

Digital Vision Ltd.: (All © Digital Vision) pT24, T32 (detail), pT25 (Talking Walls), pT394 (galaxy).

Janjaap Dekker: ppT14, T15, T17, T19, T22 (detail, © Janjaap Dekker).

M.C. Escher: ppT214-T215 (*Sky and Water 1*, M.C. Escher, woodcut, 1938).

FPG International, LLC: ppT168-T169 (graduates: VCG).

Feldman & Associates, Inc.: ppT142-T143 (Family Group by Henry Moore).

Francine Seders Gallery: pT174 (Jacob with family, © Courtesy of Jacob Lawrence and Francine Seders Gallery).

Liz Garza Williams: pp4–5 (children, background), p8 (girl)

Henry Holt: p13, pT72 ("Liberty" by Robert Silvers, reprinted with permission of the publisher, © Robert Silvers), ppT261, T271, T278 (hiding place, close-up of apartment, full view of apartment).

Holiday House, Inc.: pT91 (girls), ppT92-T95 ("Beyond the Color Lines," © 1997 by Robert Crum. All rights reserved. Used from *Under Our Skin: Kids Talk About Race* by permission of Holiday House, Inc.).

Houghton Mifflin Co.: p3, pT5, pT140b, pT140 (inset, illustration from *The Mysteries of Harris Burdick* © 1984 by Chris

Acknowledgments, continued

Van Allsburg. Reprinted by permission of Houghton Mifflin Co. All rights reserved.).

The Image Works, Inc.: ppT261, T271, T278 (hiding place, close-up of apartment, full view of apartment).

Index Stock: ppT1, T380 (football players)

Jim Jennings: pT305 (peregrine falcon, © Jim Jennings).

Kirkendahl Spring Photography: pT246 (bicyclists at Mount St. Helens Volcanic Monument, © Kirkendahl Spring/Kirkendahl Spring Photography).

Liaison Agency Inc.: p3, pT7, ppT290a–T290b, pT290, pT363 (ice climbers: Gamma Liaison, Wald Beth), pT255 (Hitler, © Hulton Getty/Liaison Agency), pT257 (release of surviving Jews, © Hulton Getty/Liaison Agency).

Ted Levin: ppT315, T316, T318, T319, T320, T321, T322 (alligator with turtle, corn crop, mangrove forest, young snail kites, manatees, Everglades at sunset, Frank Asch, detail, © Ted Levin).

Paul McDonough: pT265 (Anne Frank at public hall, © Paul McDonough).

Miami Herald Publishing Co.: pT313 (Marjory Stoneham Douglas, © Courtesy of Miami Herald Publishing Co.).

Lee Missbach: ppT190-T201 (Esperanza, © Leah Missbach).

Henry Moore Foundation: ppT142-T143 (detail) Reproduced by permission.

Museum of Jewish Heritage, New York: pT255 (Star of David, © Gift of Sidi Herzberg, Museum of Jewish Heritage, New York).

The Museum of Modern Art, New York, and the Phillips Collection: pT12 (The Studio. Paris [winter 1927-28; dated 1928]. Oil on canvas, 59" x 7' 7" [149.9 x 231.2 cm] © The Museum of Modern Art, New York. Gift of Walter P. Chrysler, Jr. Photograph © 2000 The Museum of Modern Art, New York. ARS, New York), ppT172, T181 (detail), pT173 (cover), pT176 (busy train), pT177 (damaged crops, walking), pT178 (transportation, segregation), pT179 (steel mills, landscape), pT180 (schools) (All photos copyright © 1993 by The Museum of Modern Art, New York, and the Phillips Collection. Used by permission of HarperCollins Publishers.).

NASA: p19 (chimp), pT212 (moon: NASA).

National Baseball Hall of Fame Library & Archive: pT108 (Brooklyn Dodgers, © National Baseball Hall of Fame Library & Archive, Cooperstown, N.Y.).

National Museum of American Art: pT170 (Pioneers of the West, © National Museum of American Art, Washington DC/Art Resource, NY).

Nova Development Corporation: (All © Nova Development Corporation) pT268 (posters), pT309 (whale).

Odyssey: pT27 (Wall Painting, © Robert Frerck/Odyssey/Chicago).

PhotoDisc: p3, pT6, ppT212a–T212b, pT212 (moon), p11 (gymnast), p19 (astronaut), p19 (Earth), p22, T126 (hawk, snake, frog, grasshopper, plants), ppT140a–T140b, pT141 (compass), pT168 (clouds), ppT271, T274, T277 (frame), pT294 (environmentalist), ppT296, T297, T306 (falcon detail, Peregrine Falcon), pT376 (calculator), pT376 (cassette), pT376 (fax), pT376 (microphone), pT377 (cell phone), pT377 (video tape), pT377 (camcorder), pT378 (printer), pT378 (computer), pT378 (microphone), pT379 (TV), pT379 (keyboard), pT383 (teacher & student), pT390 (ram, tiger, koala), pT390 (TV), pT402 (student report), pT405 (panda), pT410 (writing), pT427 (waterfall in Yosemite), pT487 (wilderness).

PhotoEdit: ppT6, T212, T289 (moon), pT66 (student discussion, © Michael Newman), pT68 (Luca Benini, © Michael Newman), pT97 (soccer, © David Young Wolff), pT100 (nuts background, © PhotoLink), pT128 (kids planting tree, © Rhoda Sidney) pT129 (people with wheelbarrow: Skjold, kids digging holes, © Deborah Davis), pT210 (Cousin Hector, © PhotoDisc), pT286 (peer conference, © Michael Newman), pT360 (students in classroom, © Michael Newman), p T379 (boy with basketball, © Michael Newman).

Photo Link: pT331 (soil background: Kent Knudson/PhotoLink).

PictureQuest: pT137 (cricket, © David Simson/Stock, Boston/Picture Quest), pT362 (students, © Nubar Alexanian/ Stock, Boston Inc./PictureQuest), pT431 (skater, Caroline Wood/Allstock/Picture Quest), pT436 (town parade, Tim Ribar/Stock South/PictureQuest), pT479 (coach, © Picture Quest), pT484 (prisoner, © Sovfoto/Eastfoto/Picture Quest).

Rain City Productions: pT240 (volcano, © Gary Rosenquist/ Rain City Productions), pT282 (volcano opens, side of mountain, rock shatters, © GaryRosenquist/Rain City Productions).

Richard R. Hewitt Photography: ppT299, T300, T301, T302, T303 (rock climber, gluing peregrine egg, first crack in egg, full ring of egg broken, shell pops open, new chick, chick with puppet, © Richard R. Hewitt/Richard R. Hewitt Photography).

Scholastic Press, a division of Scholastic Inc.: p3, pT3, ppT8a–T8b, pT8 "Joy" from *Voices of the Heart* by Ed Young. Copyright © 1997 by Ed Young. Reprinted by permission.

Siede Preis: p13, pT73 (flag, Siede Preis).

Simon & Schuster Children's Publishing Division: pT10 (Israeli Stamp reprinted with the permission of Simon & Schuster Books for Young Readers, an imprint of Simon & Schuster Children's Publishing Division from *The Space Between Our Footsteps* by Naomi Shihab Nye. Copyright © 1998 by Naomi Shihab Nye.), ppT76, T84 (detail), pT77-T83, pT132 ("The Keeping Quilt," Reprinted with permission.), ppT90, T98 (detail), pT91 (boy), pT96 (boy on subway, Reprinted with permission of Simon & Schuster Children's Publishing Division from *Quilted Landscape* by Yale Strom, © 1996 Yale Strom.).

Sony: (All courtesy of Sony Electronics) pT376 (boombox), pT376 (Discman), pT376 (headphones/Walkman), pT377 (DVD player).

The Stock Market: p6 (books and cap), ppT100-T101 (the Golden Gate Bridge, © 98 Richard Berenholtz).

Stone: COVER (Monument Valley, AZ © Stone Images/David Muench), p7, p10, T2 (Pyramid of Cheffren, Giza, Egypt © Stone Images/Michel Setboun; Gateway Arch, St. Louis, MO © Stone Images/Donovan Reese; Monument Valley, AZ © Stone Images/David Muench; Central Bank of China, Hong Kong © Stone Images/Michel Setboun), pT38 (Native American drawings, © David Hiser), pT87 (detail), ppT88-89 (© Jon Bradley), pT216 (tourists, © Rich Frishman), ppT236, T238, T241, T243, T245 (detail, volcano blast, © Ralph Perry), pT294 (sea turtle, seal inset, © Schrichte), pT310 (Everglades detail, © David Job), pT311 (tricolor heron, © Art Wolfe), ppT311, T314 (Everglade aerial view, © David Job), ppT344-T345 (mother/son, © Kevin Horan), ppT354-T355 (kid with basketball, © Jon Riley), pT428 (tourists on mules, © Tom Bean).

Tom Stack & Associates: pT312 (Florida panther, © Victoria Hurst/Tom Stack & Associates).

U.S. Geological Survey: pT242 (volcano, © Tom Casadevall/ U.S. Geological Survey), ppT241, T243 (mudflow, © Lyn Topinka/ U.S. Geological Survey), ppT244, T245 (Mount St. Helens before eruption/after eruptions, © Harry Glicken/U.S. Geological Survey).

USDA Forest Service: pT243 (boulders, © Jim Hughes/USDA Forest Service).

USHMM Photo Archives: pT264, (Entrance gate to Auschwitz concentration camp, © Instytut Pamieci, Narodoweij/Institute of National Memory).

Author Photos:

pT21 (Gary Soto, © Janjaap Dekker); pT31 (Margy Burns Knight); pT46 (Dawn and Margaret Lippert); pT58 (Daniel Manus Pinkwater, © 1999 Kathy McLaughlin); pT83 (Patricia Polacco); pT89B (Maya Angelou, Courtesy of Lordly & Dame, Inc.); pT112 (Peter Golenbock); ppT123, T234 (Paul Fleischman, © Becky Mojica); pT154 (Paul Yee); pT164 (Debbie and Lisa Ganz, © 1998 by Bill Ballenberg); pT180 (Jacob Lawrence, © Spike Mafford); pT200 (Sandra Cisneros, copyright © Diana Solis); pT227 (Anne Rockwell, © Lizzy Rockwell); pT246 (Patricia Lauber); pT265 (Yona Zeldis McDonough); pT304 (Caroline Arnold); pT321 (Ted Levin, © Ted Levin); pT321 (Frank Asch, © Ted Levin); pT339 (Francisco Jiménez, © University of New Mexico Press); pT353 (Carol Kendall, © Ruth Berman).

Illustrations:

Michelle Angers: ppT15-19 (The Power of Poetry, © Michelle Angers); **Jean Cassels:** pT298 (The Peregrine Falcon, © Jean Cassels/Portfolio Solutions LLC); **Centre Georges Pompidou:** p3, p12, pT4, pT70b, ppT70-71 (detail), pT139 (*Rhythm, Joie de Vivre*, Robert Delauney, © L & M SERVICES B.V. Amsterdam 200315/Photo Phillippe Migeat/Centre Georges Pompidou); **Chi Chung:** pT149 (Gold Rush Map); **David Diaz:** ppT330-T338, T340 (detail); **Leonid Gore:** pT328 (painting; story of Brian, © Leonid Gore/HK Portfolio); **Merilee Heyer:** ppT146, T155 (detail), ppT147-T154 (Ginger for the Heart), p26, pT204 (Character Map drawings); **Mary King/Sheryl Beranbaum:** pT102 (In Music Meeting, © Mary King/Sheryl Beranbaum Rep.); **Kathleen Kinkopf:** pp14-17, p20, ppT116, T124 (detail), pp15–16, ppT116-T123 (Amir) ppT127, T130 (detail), ppT128-T129 (Community Garden); **The Mapping Specialist Limited:** ppT27, T29, T31, T311 (Map, map inset, © The Mapping Specialists Limited), pT237 (globe/map, © The Mapping Specialist Ltd.); **Sandra McMahon Medical Art:** ppT237, T242 (diagram/mudflow, © Sandra McMahon/Sandra McMahon Medical Art), ppT312, T313 (Everglades/water for life, © Sandra McMahon/Sandra McMahon Medical Art); **Mike Reed:** pT144 (rooster art, © Mike Reed/HK Portfolio); **Bill Scott:** ppT231, T235 (details), ppT232-T234 (Chrysalis Diary, © Bill Scott/Nachreiner Boie Art Factory Ltd.); **Francine Seders Gallery:** pT175 (self portrait, © Courtesy Jacob Lawrence and Francine Seders Gallery); **Kat Thacker**: ppT40-T47 (Tales Across Time, © Kat Thacker/Iremli Holmberg Rep.), pT219 (The Origin of Myths), ppT218, T228 (details), ppT220-T227 (The Mother Who Lost Her Daughter); **Jean and Mou-sien Tseng:** ppT346, T354 (details), ppT347-T353 (The Clever Wife, © Jean and Mou-sien Tseng); **Martin Walz:** pT188 (Underground RR Map, © Martin Walz).

The High Point Development Team

Hampton-Brown extends special thanks to the following individuals and companies who contributed so much to the creation of this series.

Editorial: Susan Blackaby, Janine Boylan, Bonnie Brook, Shirleyann Costigan, Mary Cutler, Phyllis Edwards, Ramiro Ferrey, Cris Phillips-Georg, Fredrick Ignacio, Barbara Linde, Dawn Liseth, Daphne Liu, Sherry Long, Jacalyn Mahler, Marlyn Mangus, S. Michele McFadden, Debbi Neel, Wilma Ramírez, Michael Ryall, Sarita Chávez Silverman, Sharon Ursino, Andreya Valabek, Alison Wells, Virginia Yeater, Lynn Yokoe, Brown Publishing Network, Ink, Inc., and Learning Design Associates, Inc.

Design and Production: Lisa Baehr, Marcia Bateman Walker, Andrea Carter, Darius Detwiler, Jeri Gibson, Lauren Grace, Debbie Saxton, Curtis Spitler, Alicia Sternberg, Jennifer Summers, Debbie Wright Swisher, Margaret Tisdale, Andrea Erin Thompson, Donna Turner, Alex von Dallwitz, JR Walker, Teri Wilson, Adpartner, Art Stopper, Bill Smith Studios, Chaos Factory & Associates, Ray Godfrey, Hooten Design, Proof Positive/Farrowlyne Associates, and Rose Sheifer.

Permissions: Barbara Mathewson